RUINS OF THE JESUITS' CHURCH AND COLLEGE.

p. 34

# WHAT I SAW

ON THE WEST COAST OF

# SOUTH AND NORTH AMERICA,

AND AT THE

# HAWAIIAN ISLANDS.

BY

H. WILLIS BAXLEY, M. D.

NEW YORK:
D. APPLETON & COMPANY,
443 & 445 BROADWAY.
1865.

*TO MY SONS*

CLAUDE AND HENRY WILLIS,

THIS VOLUME IS DEDICATED BY THEIR

FATHER.

# PREFACE.

The Author, as *Special Commissioner of the United States*, visited in the years 1860, 1861, and 1862, *parts of the West Coast of America, and the Hawaiian Islands.* When not occupied by the duties of his commission, he availed of wayside opportunities of observation, and of otherwise obtaining information of these countries. In the intervals of professional engagements since his return, this, and incidental reflections, have been thrown together, and are embraced in this volume. Among other things noted are the doings of certain religionists. This has been done with the freedom and candor demanded by the importance of the subject.

> "I speak not of men's creeds—they rest between
> Man and his Maker—but of things allowed,
> Averr'd and known—and daily, hourly seen."

The old Hawaiian paganism, which once protected from punishment those guilty of the greatest crimes who sought the inviolable "Pahonua," ceased to give immunity to wrong. Surely Christianity, which has followed it, should afford no refuge to false disciples, who "are hearers and not doers of the Word." The religion of Revelation is best served by the exposure and condemnation of such, wherever found, and whatever their profession of faith. "Faith without works, like the body without the spirit, is dead," says an Apostle of Christ.

BALTIMORE, *March*, 1865.

# CONTENTS.

## CHAPTER VIII.



## CHAPTER IX.



## CHAPTER X.



## CHAPTER XI.



## CHAPTER XII.



## CHAPTER XIII.



## CHAPTER XIV.

## CHAPTER XV.



## CHAPTER XVI.



## CHAPTER XVII.



## CHAPTER XVIII.



## CHAPTER XIX.



## CHAPTER XX.



## CHAPTER XXI.

## CHAPTER XXII.



## CHAPTER XXIII.



## CHAPTER XXIV.



## CHAPTER XXV.



## CHAPTER XXVI.



## CHAPTER XXVII.



## CHAPTER XXVIII.

## CHAPTER XXIX.



## CHAPTER XXX.



## CHAPTER XXXI.



## CHAPTER XXXII.



## CHAPTER XXXIII.



## CHAPTER XXXIV.



## CHAPTER XXXV.

## CHAPTER XXXVI.



## CHAPTER XXXVII.



## CHAPTER XXXVIII.



## CHAPTER XXXIX.



## CHAPTER XL.

# WEST COAST

OF

# SOUTH AND NORTH AMERICA, ETC.

---

## CHAPTER I.

### VOYAGE FROM NEW YORK TO ASPINWALL.

One who has adorned English literature with the fadeless coloring of rare genius, has said, in answer to the question—

"But why then publish? There are no rewards
Of fame or profit, when the world grows weary.
I ask in turn—why do you play at cards?
Why drink? why read?—To make some hour less dreary.
It occupies me to turn back regards
On what I've seen or pondered, sad or cheery:
And what I write I cast upon the stream,
To swim or sink—I have had at least my dream."

In the contemplation of the ocean that lies before me, and through which for weary days we shall cleave a pathless way, it is wise to seek the means "to make the hours less dreary." And another inducement for noting the incidents and thoughts of travel, is found in the entertainment, and possibly profit, that may thereby be afforded to friends whose hearts will welcome all that comes from the wanderer. For their pleasure, then, as well as for my own pastime, I find myself imitating earlier efforts in chirography, when uniformity was a stranger to manuscript, and straight lines and curved made a merit of changing places. A pitching, rolling, and tremulous steamship, is not the most desirable writing academy, however appropriate for extemporaneous gymnastics, feats of which are constantly being performed by those who have not yet "got on their sea legs," for the amusement of others who have heretofore been mustered into service. The "Northern Light," under full head of steam, bound from New York to Aspinwall, illustrates the absurdity of striving for preëminence in either art, when subjected to a discipline destructive of physical equilibrium.

The "hauling out" of a vessel bound on a long voyage, freighted with a full cargo of passengers, is a scene of deep interest to those united by a sympathy proceeding from a like destiny. And when fairly under way, there are presented phases of character and conduct amusing to look on, when the new tenants take proprietary possession of state-room and berth, and, going to housekeeping in a small way, begin to arrange their own and investigate their neighbor's affairs. Here, as elsewhere on the voyage of life, impatience, jealousy, envy, and discontent, characterize the many; while happily for the amiably constituted, a spice of pleasantry and contentment distinguish the few. Fortunately for those who cherish the graces of a gentle and joyful spirit, there is a pacificator on ship-board that never fails in due time to avenge the wrongs inflicted on them by ill-nature. With the upheaving swell beneath, and the saucy waves rudely boxing the intruding craft, *sea-sickness* soon merges dissatisfaction in indifference to all things, and the troubles of the spirit are forgotten in those of the stomach. Thanks to this discipline of nature, by the time the penalty of human frailty is fully paid, a general humility prevails; anger subsides, arrogance becomes quite accommodating, and all are ready to enter into any commutation of damages for outraged dignity. It is fortunate for commanders that there is such a panacea for the malevolent distempers of those "who go down to the great deep in ships."

I shall spare you the description of specialities of suffering, where nearly all of several hundred passengers seemed as if they had been indulging in bumpers of antimonial wine, and that, too, often without regard to the recognized code of politeness. Even the "old salt" who paced the deck, swab in hand, giving practical lessons in good manners, did not withhold his commentary on the sad delinquency of those who ashore arrogated a superior refinement.

Exempted myself from such ills, it was pleasant to have attention diverted to other scenes. The deep blue ocean, when fairly off soundings, is of wondrous beauty, and this color is especially the characteristic of the Gulf Stream. Whether this be owing to greater depth, or to motion, density, or more active chemical properties, is a question for learned and experienced nautical philosophers to solve. As mere amateurs, we were sufficiently interested in seeking the line where the darker waters of the Stream, we are told, from its higher level overflow laterally its ocean water banks, and mingle with the common water of the sea. And crossing its nearly a hundred miles of width, rocked by saucy waves, the offspring of atmospherical disturbances so likely to ensue from the tropical caloric embosomed in the giant flood, that rolls eternally onward to meet in antagonism the icy currents of the north, ample time was afforded to contemplate the grandeur, and reflect on the phenomena of the ocean-river, which, more than the greatest of earth, carries benefactions wherever it flows. A vast vitalizing stream of creation, equalizing extremes of temperature which otherwise would consume with fervid heat the fairest portion of the world, and bind in fetters of ice regions, which through its agency yield rich tribute to rejoicing millions; feeding the winds with warm vapors, to fall in refreshing rain on the thirsty land; facilitating navigation and commerce; and guarding nature from the terrible consequences of aqueous stagnation; while it contributes to the genial movements of the air so necessary to the healthful economy of our planet. The west of Europe, in contemplating its exemption from polar frost, should not forget its obligation to this grand "hot water apparatus" of Nature. Without it, Victoria's carriage of state might degenerate into a Kamschatka dog-sledge, the "Emerald Isle" lose its jewelled appellation, and ice palaces adorn the Seine for the fêtes of Napoleon. And who can say that future generations may not be indebted to the Gulf

Stream for an "overland route" between Europe and America, when the deposits of boulder, rock, and earth, brought by myriads of icebergs from the far north, and unloaded by the resistless agency of the heated current which meets these freighted carriers on the Grand Banks of Newfoundland, shall have accumulated until these shoals, emerging from the sea, shall assert their prerogative to terrestrial distinction?

Many a gem of literature lies hidden by modest merit in the fugitive corner of a portfolio. The following apostrophe to the Gulf Stream, by a young Baltimore poetess, should not be allowed to rest in its place of concealment:

"Pulse of the Ocean's bounding heart,
Wild throbbing through the deep.
Bursting the calmer tides apart
With an impetuous sweep,
Where have thy waves their place of rest?
Where do thy warm tides flow?
Vein of the ocean's heaving breast,
Bearing the tropic's glow!

Far down below the solemn deep,
Like ancient funeral pyre,
The ling'ring ashes scatter'd sleep
Of old volcanic fire;
But all their gleaming heat and light
Have perish'd long ago—
Save Him who guides thy torrent's might,
Thy mysteries none may know.

Hast thou a buried treasure hid,
Of gold and gleaming pearls,
Where island gems are set amid
Thy wavelet's silv'ry curls?
And dost thou pour thy crystal foam
Along Columbia's strand,
To girdle in the patriots' home,
The freeman's favor'd land?

Still flowing ever through the deep,
Thou mark'st thine onward way
By restless waves that never sleep,
When other tides delay;

Bearing the warmth of southern clime
  Upon thy surges free,
Sweeping afar in power sublime,
  Wild current of the sea!

Like to a strong, resistless will,
  Deep in the earnest soul,
That through all change, and trial, still
  Speeds to the conqueror's goal;
Cleaving its way through threat'ning storm,
  Breasting the battle's strife,
Then spreading waves of passion warm
  O'er calmer seas of life!"

There's the dinner gong! Shall I sentimentalize or gormandize? The calls of grosser humanity make themselves heard at times above refined persuasives. I am mortal; good-bye.

The beauty of a crimson dawn at sea induced an early "turn out" this morning. A hard blow last night caused a rollicking sea, which looked, indeed, decidedly "blue." And well it might, for the waves had been at their noisy revels through the small hours, and the roar of their mirth, and wild chorus of their music, told of a merry time in their boundless starlit banquet hall. But a tranquil atmosphere brought smooth water, inviting invalids on deck, who seemed to think, despite their late despair, that they still had a chance of treading *terra firma* in the future, and hence essayed to walk; a feat awkwardly and amusingly performed, for reeling and lateral motions preponderated over progressive, and the varying angles and incidents of inclination and declination, were many degrees from a desirable perpendicular. However, perseverance afforded a good performance of a "Comedy of Errors."

Among the results of this release of the "cabin'd, crib'd, confin'd," was the renewed function of the vocal organism, a piece of the human mechanism of no use during sea-sickness. But when convalescence is established, Babel, I am sure, did not put forth a greater confusion of tongues than are uttered on the decks of a California steamer crowded to repletion. All nations are represented on board the "Northern Light," and by the time there were compounded the varied tones and semi-tones of the *English*, its masculine, feminine, and *neuter* (I speak of its tones), its sharp, its shrill, its mellow; its high, its low; its sonorous, its nasal; its oral, its guttural; its grave, its gay; its fast, its slow; its tearful, its joyful; its sobbing, its cachinatory; and so on *ad libitum*—by the time these vocal modifications were commingled with extravagances of emphasis, varied articulation, and diverse pronunciation, with other "high falutin" et ceteras of style, into which illiterate Americans, with a due admixture of the extreme Yankee, and of the foreign cross, male and female, are capable of twisting, distorting, contracting, expanding, and otherwise *doing* the English language; and the compound was blended with an approximative variety of *German* and *Irish*, and a slight sprinkling of *French*, *Spanish*, and other tongues, the possessors of which catching the spirit of trans-Atlantic transcendentalism of style seemed resolved not to be outdone, and therefore clamored more vociferously, screamed louder, and gesticulated more furiously, setting conventionalities of social law, as well as the laws of sound, at defiance; I say, by the time these vocal phenomena were commingled there was produced, as chemists call it, a *resultant* (I will not say a *mean* resultant for fear of being misapprehended) that out-babbled Babel.

And as if this wordy war were not sufficiently discordant, music, too, as it was libellously termed, was brought to aid in the desecration of surrounding sublimity; and a villanous accordeon and execrable guitar, more villanously and execrably thumbed, and attuned to human tones alike their own, made day hideous, and drowned the solemn requiem the ocean was chanting around.

"Land, ho!" was cried this morning—five days from New York. It was the island of Mariguana, one of the easternmost of the Bahamas. We steered through the Pass of the same name between it and Crooked Island. Large quantities of seaweed betokened our approach to land, cheering us as it did Columbus, whose dejected mariners it encouraged to hold on their way until they at last reached San Salvador, one of the same group somewhat to the west of our present southerly course; thus the ocean drift was made to point the way to the Western World.

Running along the west shore of Inagua, during the afternoon the intensity of tropical heat was realized, the easterly breeze which had previously refreshed us being shut off by that island. It is one of the Bahama salt factories, and produces little else. It presents a sterile look, and is of no value to any but an aggressive nation like the British, who own it, and to whom in war it serves as a port of shelter and supply, and from which assaults may be advantageously made on enemies. American commerce, large and increasing with unprecedented growth, is everywhere overlooked by these marine watch-towers, and especially do these "lookouts" command the hundreds of millions of productions flowing in a continuous stream from the cotton States, and from the fertile basin of the northern continent by the Mississippi River.

A dilapidated village on the southwest end of Inagua, with a few schooners at the wharf, showed but little commerce; and a nominal light-house near by, which is said never to cheer the mariner with a welcome ray in darkness and storm, evinces a neglect or parsimony not common with the British Government. The Mariguana Pass is much used, and marine interests call for a light on the important headland overlooking it. A due southerly course brought us next off Maysi Point, the west end of Cuba; and steering still south, we steamed through the Windward Passage, Santo Domingo lying to the east, and faintly seen in the distance. The remembrance of the bloody passages in its history, when, in the negro insurrection of 1791, the demon of relentless savagery and ruin, under the standard of a white infant impaled on a stake, in two months laid waste with fire and sword more than a thousand sugar, coffee, and cotton estates; massacring two thousand persons of all ages, and both sexes; sawing some asunder, crucifying and chopping others in pieces, perpetrating atrocities more horrible than death on wives and daughters, whose eyes were scooped out in revelry of brutality; and when children, "untimely ripp'd from their mother's womb," were thrown as food to hogs; was not calculated to inspire a wish to draw nearer to that ill-fated island, once the home of refinement, and a rich garden of tropical production; now the domain of semi-barbarity, and throughout the greater part an uncultivated waste.

From thirty to forty miles further on our route the little guano island, Navasa, was seen. Its value as such was discovered a few years since by a Baltimore mariner—Captain Cooper—who took possession, and proceeded to ship the fertilizing deposit. The Haytiens attempted to displace him, but being unable to show title to the island, the United States maintained their citizen's right of discovery and settlement.

We are steering southwest across the Caribbean Sea for Aspinwall—Jamaica invisible to the west. Happily we shall pass on its windward side; its airs are not burthened with the perfumes of Ceylon. A dimpled sea and pleasant east wind, are the agreeable attendants of the present; and the spirits and appetites of passengers are responsive. Not to speak of the steerage, it may be said that the more pretentious passengers, the upper-ten of the cabin, are wonderfully characterized by quantitative propensity, while the omnivorous nature of man is illustrated by them still more strikingly. The tables, formerly almost untenanted, are now crowded with the disciples of sensualism. The art of gastronomy is clearly in the ascendant. Fish, flesh, fowl, familiar with ice alternated with tropical heat, and hence passing into that abnormal condition known by pathologists as *ramolissement;* vegetables in season and out of season, the hebdomedal occupants of the ship's hold, some, doubtless, the forestallers residuum, withered, wilted, and decaying; clams from Squam Beach, and Shrewsbury oysters, which had long ceased to mourn their lost sea-homes, and had passed into that state of dissolution indicative of speedily being no longer "tenants at will;" pickles, pastry, puddings, and pecans, duly decorated with those dernier resorts of the dinner table, almonds, raisins, and filberts, which generally prove alike first in the order of morbid causation, and first in that of retroversive result; all these in varied style devised to deceive the inexperienced and unwary, simple and complex, underdone and overdone, and not done at all, with the liquid accompaniments of champagne-cider and cider-champagne, brandy and Bordeaux, pale-ale, porter, and pop, are "pitched into," and pitched into themselves by old and young, with a voracity and perseverance indicative of a probable short allowance on the morrow, if Aspinwall should not then be reached.

It should not excite surprise that passengers who are guilty of such indiscretions, with that, commonly superadded, lingering long and sometimes sleeping on deck during a greater part of the night in the tropics, should have dangerous illness to ensue; especially, when in disembarking, often homesick and dispirited, they indulge in the excessive use of unaccustomed fruits, and become enfeebled by the intensity of the land heat. The observance of customary habits, when these are conformable to temperance, and the avoidance of unseasonable exposure, fatigue, and that undue excitement which results in indirect debility, will contribute much to prevent the ill effects of the numerous agencies of mischief ever in activity in tropical regions. And attention to these rules, before and during a voyage, will prevent or aid the recovery from sea-sickness; relief from which may also to some extent be had by occupying the waist of the ship, especially at the commencement of a voyage, this part not being subjected to extremes of motion like the bow and stern. Attention should also be given to reading, and even to writing, if practicable, to avoid looking at the pitching and rolling of the vessel, more palpably indicated when measured by surrounding objects. It is sufficiently distressing to realize these motions when sitting on deck, without magnifying through the eye their effects on the brain, and through it aggravating also these on the stomach. Mental occupation will preclude, too, to some extent, apprehensions of evil, which cannot but aggravate the reality that must come sooner or later to nearly all. The maintenance of a quiet position by reclining is comforting, and cannot be avoided in severe cases. But the voyager must accustom himself to the ship's motion at last, and the sooner he essays to do this in the open air, and by moderate approaches, the earlier will he secure comfort and acquire the privilege of personal locomotion. Violent cases of gastric irritation and vomiting may require a resort to anodynes or sedatives. Among the most valuable and safe of the latter, is ice. The ship's surgeon should be consulted in the use of others. If none be on board, a person's customary dose of laudanum, morphia, chlorodine, or prussic acid, may be resorted to; and good brandy will be found a useful stimulant. Even in sickness, ice cannot be had on board this steamer, except at extra charge. This should not be in the dog days, considering the immense and cheap supply in New York, and the high passenger fare on this route.

I would not incur the charge of captiousness, and shall avoid reference to sundry inconveniences and discomforts to which passengers are subjected on the New York end of the California Line, beyond the control of the commanders of steamers, and only to be remedied by the proprietor. But a custom of universal reprobation should not pass without remark; I refer to a charge on this steamer of ten cents per pound on all baggage exceeding fifty pounds weight. It is sufficiently extortionate to be subject to the highest steamship fare known to any greatly travelled route, without the addition of this unjust, and as it often happens, grievous charge. The reason assigned for it is, to prevent transportation of merchandise. If this be so, it would be a sufficient protection against imposition to subject a passenger's legitimate baggage—his wearing apparel—in all cases of suspicion, to inspection. But who can be expected to travel thousands of miles on a continuous route, consuming several weeks of time, in hot weather and cold, wet and dry, with but fifty pounds of baggage, including the weight of the trunk? That alone, even empty, will sometimes "kick the beam" of such restriction, certainly if an overcoat be strapped on the top. It looks like the inauguration of rates of charge according to personal weight and measure. If this shall follow—and who can gauge the conscience that recognizes no rule of action but the gratification of avarice—it will be well for travellers to apply practically their juvenile lessons in subtraction and reduction. This indirect mode of levying on the necessities of the travelling community, is alike oppressive to those of restricted means, and insulting to the rich, both of whom would respect a manly frankness, but despise while they are indignant at indirection and injustice. The many-hued and changeful dolphin, the type of unreliability, with unsatiated greediness follows its prey, the helpless flying-fish, until bounding from the water to escape its powerful foe, the little victim encounters a new enemy in the swooping sea-gull, and both pursue it alternately in sea and air to the death. Men have their similitudes in nature. He will not be envied by the just and noble, who finds his resemblance in the voracious dolphin, or in the mean and ungenerous sea-hawk.

The lofty headlands of the Province of Porto Bello, in the Republic of New Granada, are in sight. The lifting up, or flitting by of clouds in the distance, revealing hills and valleys beneath or beyond, clad in verdure and constantly developing some new and lovely combination of light and shade, is so fair to look on, so refreshing to the water-wearied eye, so typical of the brief and changeful visions of happiness sometimes coming to us in dreams, when the darker curtain of care is drawn aside, and the liberated imagination looks out on the beautiful scenes of its own creation, that I must cheat you of these moments, and regale the eye and cheer the spirit with these exquisite dissolving views of nature. Such they seem; for, as we flit past them, so rapid is the change of the picture, that ere we can say "look, look, how beautiful!—'tis gone."

Aspinwall was reached in a little over eight days from New York—distance two thousand miles—and too late to make the railroad connection with Panama; hence we must stay all night in this miserable abortion of a town, which is destitute of comfortable accommodations, but affords an undoubted chance of our imbibing a sufficient quantity of malarious poison to produce yellow fever, a malignant type of which has been prevailing here for some weeks. The voyage was formerly made in less time, and could be now in perfect safety, and with great economy of time to travellers, but for the parsimony of the monopolist of this end of the California steamer route.

Aspinwall cannot be surpassed for filth, nuisance, and noxious effluvia. The houses—mostly shanties of deal boards—are built on piles in the midst of a marsh, with the railroad similarly supported, and filled between the cross-ties with earth brought from a distance, forming the main street, a few alleys crossing these at right angles, being nothing but bog pathways, with logs or planks to keep the pedestrian from premature interment, or submersion. The water-lots (there are no yards) are covered with green, offensive, and poisonous scum, oozing up between the flooring of the lower stories; and every where, in and around, the premises are surcharged with animal and vegetable matter, in all stages of putrefaction and decomposition. With the exception of the employés of the Panama Railroad Company, the inhabitants are of the inferior races, from the Jamaica negro through all grades of cross and hue, up to the Chiriqui Indian; and having the filthiest and vilest habits, knowing no restraints of appetite or passion, is it surprising that this seething cauldron of physical abomination and moral degradation is a pest-house of the Isthmus? Many of a population of seven hundred to eight hundred are now down with malarious fever, of the fatal types Chagres and yellow. It is dangerous for a native of the North to tarry at Aspinwall in summer; and the natives are by no means exempt from these climate diseases, owing to their uncleanliness, debauchery, general vices, and consequent impairment of vital energies. A physician of the town informed me that "more than half of the population *changed hands* every year." I did not inquire into whose hands they had gone; the specimens left removed any doubt.

## CHAPTER II.

### RAILROAD TRIP ACROSS THE ISTHMUS OF PANAMA.

From Aspinwall to Panama the trip is made by railroad forty-seven miles long; the time varies from three to four hours. This road, commenced in 1850, had its conception in the remarkable forecast of the trade and travel destined to demand facilities of travel between the two great oceans, and was commenced and prosecuted to completion under circumstances of peril, privation, and difficulty, unparalleled in the annals of similar improvements, and constituting it an imperishable monument of the skill, enterprise, and energy of Messrs. George M. Totten and John C. Trautwine, engineers; and in the finality of its construction, and subsequent management, of the administrative ability of David Hoadley, Esq., the present President. In the building of this great national highway, laborers were gathered from the various countries to be benefited by it; and especially did thousands of Irish, Germans, and Coolies suffer, sicken, and die, in their efforts to bring into closer commercial relations distant countries of the globe. Such, indeed, was the terrible mortality attendant on the employment of unacclimated foreigners, that it was, after much and sad experience, found necessary to employ the natives of neighboring provinces and of Jamaica, with whose labor the road was finally completed in 1855.

Leaving Aspinwall on the east side of Navy Bay, the road soon crosses the narrow channel that separates the marshy island of Manzanilla, on which the town is built, from the mainland. Rounding the head of the bay the road then stretches across the peninsula between it and Chagres River, occasionally following the windings of the stream, while at other times it makes the chord of its curves, and reaching Barbacoas, twenty-five miles from Aspinwall, crosses by a magnificent wrought-iron bridge, six hundred and twenty-five feet in length, from the right to the left bank of the Chagres, along which it runs to the mouth of the Obispo River, thirty-one miles from the Atlantic terminus. The river scenery is picturesque, and pleasing to look upon, considering that we were journeying in a few hours over a distance that formerly required several days to make by boating. The Chagres has made itself memorable in the annals of death. Every mile of its turbid and sluggish stream can tell sad tales of suffering and dissolution produced by its poisonous waters, and the no less fatal malaria resulting from rank luxuriance and rapid decay of vegetation along its banks.

Abundant rain, uninterrupted heat, and a virgin soil, give an unsurpassed richness of coloring to nature's foliage and flowers in the valley of the Chagres. Crimson, purple, orange, blue, pink, and white, flit across the eye in such continued and rapid succession, as to seem an ever-varying and endless kaleidoscope; and green throws in and around its sombre and its brilliant shades, to heighten the general charm. So emulous of continuous life is this region, that it conceals the proofs of death and decay; clothing the sapless trunk of the giant cedro and other trees, branchless and toppling to their fall, with parasitic vines; twining their fibrils and clustering leaves around, and even at times weaving for their heads coronets of flowers that cheat the gaze. The representative tree of all sketches and engravings of tropical scenery, is seen along the line of the route in great variety and luxuriance; and no one can contemplate the uses to which it is put by the natives, from the posts of their rude huts, and its thatch roof of broad leaves, to their food, beverage, and domestic utensils, without considering the *palm* as great a blessing, as it is a beauty, in this tropical region. The superstitious native may be excused for believing the soil favored of heaven, which produces so great a boon; and especially when thereto is added the spontaneous bread-fruit, plantain, yam, banana, pine-apple, orange, mango, papaya, alligator-pear. Nor would it be a libel on his simplicity of character and credulity to suppose, that he regarded as an unquestioned proof of that favor, the growth here of that "Flor del Espiritu Santo"—the flower of the Holy Ghost; its graceful blossom, of alabaster whiteness and delicious perfume, enclosing the image of a dove, perfectly proportioned, subdued, and meek, the emblem of innocence and celestial purity.

But few of the richly-feathered tropical birds are seen by the passenger as he speeds his way along the railroad; perhaps, because of the noisy and startling encroachment upon their domain. Parrots, black and yellow turpiales, and a few scarlet breasted toucans with huge bills, having a less body of a bird attached to them, embraced the only ornithological specimens observed.

It was a great relief to have this beautiful nature without, to attract attention from that less pleasing within. "Black spirits and white," with brown, yellow, and copper, had possession of the cars, and mingled their interminable shadings as if envious of nature's surrounding varieties. And the representatives of these closely-approximative tints, free and familiar as their near relationship of mongrelism authorized, ignorant or reckless of the comities of life, were, both men and women, busily puffing the vilest weed known to the vegetable kingdom, raising clouds of smoky stench to offend eyes, nose, and lungs; accompanied by such extravagant gesticulations, and vociferous jargon of spurious Spanish, as revived the scene of the weird witches.

Seated before me in one of the cars of the accommodation train were two negroes, with their arms tied behind them by strong ropes, and near them four others unpinioned, but all under military guard. I took them for convicts, but was informed by the conductor that they were impressed soldiers; part of a contingent called for by the Executive of New Granada, to meet the exigencies of an existing revolution. The two guards were of like color, uniformed with extraordinary simplicity, a striped cotton shirt and pants hiding so much of their natural ebony as a paucity of material would allow; while belt, bayonet, and rusty musket, which might probably have been the original of the comprehensive description, "without stock, lock, or barrel," made up the formidable accoutrements of the imposing warriors, under the command of an officer a shade lighter in complexion, and of more pretentious costume, for he was both capped and shod. This system of military impressment to supply the wants of the army, I was informed, was the frequent and favorite one of the authorities; certainly it is an inconsistent example of *free* negroism of one of the young Republics, whose universal *liberty and equality* are much boasted of. If an undesirable element of Central American population in other respects, the negro seems here to be considered at least fit "food for gunpowder."

At the several "way-stations" along the line of the road native villages are seen, the huts of which are built mostly of bamboo, with steep pitched palm-leaf thatched roof. Sometimes four posts support the roof, the space below being unenclosed, while a notched upright post in the middle serves the purpose of a ladder or rude stairway to ascend to the garret above, the dormitory of the whole family. At some of these stations variegated women presented themselves with the fruits of the country for sale. They wore heavily-flounced thin muslin dresses, hanging slatternly off the shoulder, and close to the unshapely person; not uncommonly with a child astride the hip and clinging to the mother's neck, while she had both hands and head supporting baskets. Most of the inhabitants, however, not engaged in traffic with the "señors" and "señoras," presented a near approach to nudity; a simple cotton skirt (crinoline is a myth) hung from the hip of the women, and with men pants similarly supported, being the almost universal costume, except where nature, always with children, repudiated even the artificiality of a palm leaf. But whatever the style, material, use, or freedom from dress, two customs were always observed, the wearing of plaid kerchiefs or straw hats by the women, and the retention of a filthy and knotty apology of a beard by the men. A razor would be regarded as a sign of modern civilization, and a barber's pole a harbinger of cleanliness and decency, along this highway of nations. Hurrying along the winding way, thinking of our own disturbing and dangerous doctrine of "squatter sovereignty," exemplified, too, by the pseudo-Spaniard and half-breed, the Indian and African, who occupy and hold as much land as seems to them good, without let or hindrance—and who, from attach-

BASALTIC CLIFF. p. 29

ing no value to what cost them nothing, are correspondingly lazy and negligent of cultivation, merely living as benificiaries of a bountiful nature, we finally reached the "summit," two hundred and fifty-eight feet above the Atlantic level, and thence descending rapidly a grade of sixty feet to the mile, the surrounding scenery becoming bolder and more picturesque than that already passed, we came to a singular basaltic cliff, the huge crystals of which were scattered round, disjointed, broken, and jagged, proofs of the utilitarian spirit which has cast down and crushed its massive columns; the pillars of earth's great architecture, perhaps, in ages past, but degraded now to the baser use of ballasting a railroad. Mountain peaks here become striking features in the scenery, and the little babbling brook of Rio Grande leads the way hence to the valley of Paraiso; beyond which is seen, lifting its bold brow above the Pacific Ocean, the proud Mount Ancon, which, long before the generations of man, looked haughtily and unabashed upon the great sea that humbly washes its graceful foot, on which now sits the historic city of Panama. We approached this through a fine undulating country, showing better cultivation, adorned with groves of cocoanut and palm trees, through which were revealed, near at hand, the quaint tiled roofs, dilapidated fortifications, and pearl shell towers of the cathedral. Landed at the depot my companions of voyage proceeded forthwith aboard of the California steamer awaiting them in the bay, while I sought the omnibus, and soon found myself trundled over narrow streets familiar with ancient paving stones, and dumped out, without pity for person or purse, at the entrance of the "Aspinwall Hotel" of Panama.

# CHAPTER III.

## THE CITY OF PANAMA, AND ENVIRONS.

The city of Panama, the capital of the State of the same name, one of eight confederated States forming the Republic of New Granada, has been for ten years the focus of California emigration from the United States and Europe, directing it to the golden North; as formerly the tide of adventure sought its sunny strand, ere sweeping on to found new colonies in the South, as well as North Pacific, to levy the jewelled tribute which Spanish avarice extorted of the simple and unsuspecting natives. It has been so long the subject of history, so often the theme of the traveller, and even of daily journalism, that if my story of it be stale, it will be excused because the dish is so common that the spice of novelty can no longer be found to season it.

This city is built on a small rocky peninsula, by some considered of volcanic origin, water-washed on three sides, stretching eastward into the Bay of Panama, from the Pacific shore of the Isthmus of the same name; in latitude 8° 56′ N. and longitude 79° 31′ W. It stands on the foot of a somewhat elongated hill of five hundred and forty feet height called "Cerro Ancon," which commands the town and defences, and being unfortified, would be quickly occupied by an observing enemy. The city proper, embracing the parish of San Felipe, confined strictly to the tongue of land before spoken of, covers about ninety or one hundred acres, and consists of two and three-story houses, of dingy and antiquated appearance, built of stone, mixed occasionally with bricks, stuccoed; roofed with large heavy concavo-convex tiles, so arranged as to present an undulating appearance, and of such great weight as to demand supporting rafters of unusual size and strength. The heat, moisture, and innumerable insects of the climate, some of them *borers*, very destructible to all timber except pitch-pine, would soon destroy shingles. Slate and metal are objectionable, because of expense and the heat of the climate. The roof projects over rude and ricketty balconies, which overhang narrow sidewalks, thus protecting pedestrians from sun and rain. Windows are rare; in their stead wide double doors are seen, opening both below on the street, and above on the balconies, affording free ventilation when open, but when closed during heavy rains, suffocation might be threatened were it not for small sigmoid, lozenge, or star-shaped holes in the walls, which serve as ventilators to the rooms. Most of the houses are furnished, also, with niches in front for porous jars, in which water is kept pleasantly cool by constant evaporation. The luxury of Northern ice is only to be had at considerable cost. In the better class of houses the rooms are large; and the ceilings, which are merely the rough boarding and rafters of the floor of the room above, except in the few instances of plank lining, are high, thus securing airiness. Chimneys are unknown to Panama house architecture; cooking is done on stone tables in the kitchen or little court-yard, when this latter is found, but generally in a primitive way in the highway or byway according to necessity. The streets run north and south, east and west, corresponding to the sides of the nearly quadrilateral peninsula on which the town is built; they are paved with cobble stone, and vary in width from fifteen to thirty feet, including the sidewalks, which are from three to four feet wide, mostly of flat stone. The proximity of the houses on many of the streets affords a ready means of gossiping; while from opposite balconies, prying into the domestic affairs of neighbors may be indulged in, by the envious, jealous, and mischievously inclined. Clumsy flower boxes, monkeys, and parrots, are the usual occupants of the balconies, for yards, either for floral culture, or for the accommodation of the latter Panamanian necessities, are rarely seen; and hence, also, children who contrive to escape from domestic thraldom, generally display their naked charms in the street, a custom which gives to Panama a peculiar claim upon the attention of the young artist as a school for the study of unadorned nature. The lower floors of nearly all the houses are occupied for business purposes, families preferring the upper for residences; not merely because of more airiness, but being less liable to intrusion, they are better adapted to the careless and indolent habits of the natives, to whom a hammock, cigar, nothing to do, and I might say of many of them almost "nothing to wear," appear the *ne plus ultra* of human happiness.

Several small unoccupied pieces of ground are called plazas, one of these near the centre of the city being considered *the* plaza; and this from its unattractive and unadorned old field appearance, would be entitled to no more distinction than the others, but that on its west side stands the cathedral, an antiquated grave looking stone edifice, two hundred and twenty by one hundred and fifty feet in size, with two weather-beaten stucco towers studded with pearl-oyster shells, boastful of bells for every modification of ceremonial and prayer; to which they are constantly devoted from the gray dawn to twilight eve, in giving formulary utterance; while the personal devotee is going through the pantomimic formulary within. The interior is only imposing for size, the general architectural design is defective, the details unharmonious, and the decorations in wretched taste, exemplifying the rudest provincialism. On the south side of the plaza is the *Cabildo*, for municipal purposes, a long two story whitewashed stone building, with a plain, unpretending double colonnade supporting arches in front, above and below. A government house in another part of the town might be mistaken for common military barracks, if not told that therein were assembled at stated periods the supreme officers of the State.

Churches are numerous. Besides the Cathedral there are La Merced, San Francisco, Santo Domingo, San Felipe, Monjas, San José, Santa Ana, San Miguel, and Malambo—chapel of Jesus, all, of course, Roman Catholic; and nearly all, although presenting a decaying appearance, are still used as places of religious worship. Perhaps the church of Santo Domingo is the only one that may be regarded as irrecoverably dilapidated,

RUINS OF THE CHURCH OF SANTO DOMINGO. p. 33

although the effort to preserve its memory as a sanctuary is still made by a couple of old devotees, who occupy a rude building adjacent to it as a chapel; where they alone repeat their daily prayers, perhaps with more sincerity than the tinsel clad clergy of grander temples. When gazing on the remains of this edifice, now fast crumbling before the silent touches of time, its lofty walls, noble columns and pilasters, and superb arches, standing like mournful monuments of departed grandeur; with luxuriant nature draping with eternal verdure these mementoes of the past, hanging her graceful festoons from cornice and capitol, and crowning keystones with chaplets of shrubbery; whilst grasses richer than tapestry decorate the walls, and their green mantle carpets the earthen floor; while I stood and gazed on these, and recalled the time when the deep peal of the organ reverberated within, and the solemn chant awakened the religious sentiment and holy zeal of the Spanish cavalier, to extend the dominion of the Cross, I did not wonder that the remnant of the once powerful people who worshipped here, seen in the aged pair who still linger under the shadow of this formerly magnificent temple, should partake the holy sentiment, and cling to the memory of the glorious past. The poet of another land may have mourned over such a memorial when he sang

"Here once the glad Te Deum flung abroad
To heaven the music of its matchless song;
Here once the Miserere wailed to God,
Joy echoing sweet, and sorrow sobbing long.

But silent now, through ages dim and drear,
In their old consecration standing dumb,
The holy walls rise sad to heaven, and hear
Through the long gloom those deeper voices come—

Voices that know nor gladness nor lament—
That thrill with no desire, nor conflict ken,
The breeze, and billow, in one long Amen,
To all God's will and all His ways consent,

Here once the prayers were more than words could tell,
Impatient wishes that besieged the sky;
Nor was there doubt of any miracle
Save that life's longings and its hopes could die.

But now subdued by tedious toils and cares,
    Desire falls faint—hope falters on the strain;
And Time and Nature with a deep Amen,
    Fill up the breaks and echoes of old prayers.

Amen! Amen! No warmer voice of praise
    The ruined walls, the silent soul, may find;
But oh, thou solemn sea, and mournful wind,
    Take up the burden of our elder days!

Amen! Our hearts are hushed, we frame again
    No other gospel of fresh hopes in store,
But weary of all tempests, join the strain,
    That beats in grave accord on this stern shore.
        Amen! Amen! Amen!"

A short distance west of Santo Domingo are the more extensive ruins of the church and college of the Jesuits, the foundations of which were laid in 1739; and they were built on so grand and costly a scale, that they were not completed in 1773 when that order was suppressed, and being expelled from Spanish America the structures were never finished. Decay is written on every part of these once proud proofs of the wealth and power, as well as of the religious zeal and pomp, of their priestly founders; trees, shrubbery, and weeds, are the sole tenants of halls, once designed for the nobler culture of the sciences; roots and branches, like resistless levers, are overthrowing columned corridor and massive arch; and the best preserved part, the still unshattered walls of the church, no longer resounding with choral voices, is now, in obedience to the promptings of a degenerate race, desecrated by being used as a cock-pit, where Panameños of all complexions assemble, frequently presided over by a parish-priest, to wrangle over the brutal national amusement which is the disgrace of their humanity. Strolling among these perishing relics of the past on a balmy tropical night, it seemed to me as if the pale moonbeams crept more gently through the thick foliage that fanned the falling ruins as it waved in the soft sea breeze, and fell sadly on prostrate column and cornice, as if to touch with a last radiance their departing grandeur.

Of the seven convents once inhabited by friars and nuns, six are now in ruins, the property by law having reverted to the State; and one only is occupied, by four nuns, situated near the "Puerta de las Monjas"—gate of the female monks; which is surmounted by a crumbling sentry-box, once probably of awful import to the challenged intruder, but now disregarded by the men-o'-war's boats' crews who generally land at this point. This property will also pass into the hands of the State on the extinguishment of the order, the lingering remnant of which still offer their faint orisons in the verdure covered cloisters; where vegetable nature presents a striking picture of undying vigor, in contrast to the waning mortality within. This reversion to the State will probably occur ere long, for the order is not likely to recuperate by voluntary enlistment, the grace of celibacy not being much coveted—the bridal being preferred to the religious veil by the languishing Panameñas.

The southeast corner of the peninsula on which the town stands, projects about five hundred feet in the same direction; and upon this is built the rampart, consisting of a strong casemated wall upon a solid rock foundation apparently of lava and shell, from twenty-five to thirty feet high to the top of the parapet, and an equal width, forming a fine esplanade, now used as a public "paseo" for promenading, and which from the casemate caves situated beneath is called by the natives "Bovedas." Two or three circular watch-towers are still standing on projecting bastions, but like the wall they are gradually bowing to time and tempest; and another century will not have passed, ere the ceaseless assaults of the sea, from whose rocky foundations was obtained the material of which wall and towers were in part built, will have claimed its own. The casemates are now used as vile and filthy apologies for prisons; the convicts being promiscuously thrown together and unemployed, of course are engaged in concocting mischief, and the adepts in instructing the uninitiated in crime. An arsenal and barracks are also parts of the dilapidated fortification, all of them defectively built, dirty, and disorderly. These emptied themselves as I promenaded the *paseo*, of a miscellaneous battalion on parade, of divers hues, ebony and mahogany predominating. They were neither uniform in complexion nor costume. Some were jacketed, others coated, shirt-sleeved, or bare-armed; some wore shoes, the feet of others rejoiced in the vindication of their naked rights; some wore caps, some wool slouches, and others slouched wool; but all boasted of a yellow belt with bayonet, and an old musket that looked as if it might have long lain in some speculator's locker, until it found a market in revolutionary New Granada at two dollars and fifty cents "*per barrel*," yielding at that a handsome profit. They were a wretched and forlorn looking set of warriors as they appeared on parade. Dejection was written on their faces, and timidity and apprehension characterized their awkward attempts at drill. In one thing these victims of military despotism were alike; with all of them the lower half of the face was covered, or sprinkled, according to the fertility of the soil, with dirty wool, of a texture conforming to the departure from the genuine negro standard. The retention of this grisly appendage, formidable in filth, is a privilege of degeneracy. The semi-barbarous are prone to imitate the more vulgar practices of a higher civilization, especially when they conform to natural indolence or love of the ferocious. On the ramparts facing the sea, a single cannon on a broken carriage is all that remains of the formidable battery that bade defiance to the bold buccaneers, who longed to seize the golden deposits of which Panama was the custodian. The mongrel descendants of the stern old conquerors, who once fearlessly looked out on threatening fleets, are now so destitute of armament as to be unable to interchange a national salute with foreign men-o'-war entering the harbor.

Around the whole of the city, thus far described, is a strong stone wall both land and seaward, erected when modern Panama was founded in the year 1670, in its present site, by special order of the king of Spain, to protect this depot of colonial treasures from the marauders who had plundered and burnt the first city of Panama, founded in 1519, about four miles northeast of the present location. A wide ditch, the almost obliterated remains of which only are now visible, also protected the city on the land side; and two gates on the land, and two on the sea side, afforded communication with the city; the former have been destroyed, the position of one of them only being recognized by a street through a dilapidated part of the wall, and the ruins of arch and drawbridge, with general rubbish filling the moat.

Just outside of the site of this western gateway—"Puerta del tierra"—is the considerable faubourg of Santa Ana, mostly of frame houses, a precinct of abominations repugnant to sight, hearing, and smell. And just beyond this on each side of the long street leading to the country, are cane huts, sometimes of open wicker work, at others bedaubed with mud, with high pitched grass thatched roofs, looking rather like cattle shelters of an inferior American farm, than abodes of human beings. These form the suburbs of San Miguel and Caledonia, and are occupied by wretched negroes and hybrids, whose habits are assimilated to those of the brutes—donkeys, dogs, and hogs—which are seen to be a joint tenantry. Here nakedness stalks abroad in shameless indifference to notice; laziness and squalid poverty, inseparably united, assert undisputed dominion, and but for the kindly offices of the carrion crow, accumulated filth would breed a pestilence. Such are the disgusting precincts through which the foreign resident must pass, when, seeking relaxation from the toil of the day, he drives at evening along the only highway leading from the city.

The population of Panama is ten thousand, of whom about six thousand live within the wall, and four thousand outside. Intelligent foreigners of long residence represent, that not five hundred of the entire population of ten thousand are of the pure white race—the boasted "Blanco Puro," the rest are mongrels of every cross of the European, African, Chinaman, and Indian. The experiment of practical amalgamation is here being fully tested, and self-boastful philanthropists may here learn results of applied theories, without putting to shame a profession of superior intelligence, and deteriorating inherited exaltation of race. Panama, once the proud mistress of the Pacific, the seat of Spanish power, civilization, and refinement, on the Isthmus, and the dictator of colonial destiny; the grand entrepot of South American and Mexican commerce and affluence, where accumulated silver and gold were estimated by the ton, and precious stones vied with the stars in beauty and brilliancy; this gem of the coronet of Spain, by a people's disregard of the distinctions of nature's ordinances, by their submission to the rule of unbridled passion, rather than to the laws of Him who made every "creature after its kind, and saw that it was good," has descended to a more degraded condition than the aboriginal Indian race from whom the country was wrested.

In the degenerate ownership of the present day, decay and ruin seem written on all around; walls and fortresses, whose cost of many millions led to a monarch's inquiry if "they were being built of silver or gold," are rapidly disappearing, no hand being raised for their preservation. Churches, whose spires shone with pearls, and whose altars were decorated with the jewels of false gods, are now crumbling in a common dust with the idol temples from which they were taken by fraud or force; showing the error of that assumption, which inculcates the better adaptation of a religion of ceremonial to ignorance and debasement—the impotency of such merely, with the enlightened and reasoning, not being denied. The imposing grandeur of art may awaken the sensibilities to emotion of all, but divine truth alone can impress these with the enduring precepts fitting man for his sphere of usefulness and progress here, and exaltation hereafter. It is an unworthy pretence of religion that reposes upon no greater glory than the glitter of earthly things and unintelligible forms, while the longings of the immortal spirit are disregarded, and the soul is left free to riot in error, licentiousness, and vice, ignorant or unmindful of the pure precepts of truth, righteousness, love, mercy, and charity, whose observance is the measure of happiness in life, and of peace in death.

No greater proof of the degeneracy and debasement of this country can be mentioned, than the abstraction by the government of the revenue for collegiate instruction, and its appropriation to other purposes. Even primary education cannot be had in Panama, beyond the reading and writing taught by four decrepid nuns, shut out from the world, knowing nothing of its wants, ignorant of progress and improvements, and who, to become competent teachers, would have to return to the world and learn anew themselves. The very few young men who aspire to literary and scientific attainments seek them in Europe or the United States; and the still fewer young ladies, who, like their common mother, desire to pluck the "fruit of the tree of knowledge," must at great cost employ private teachers to show them how—a dangerous experiment oftentimes, for the knowledge "of good" and the knowledge "of evil" are so apt to become confounded under the tuition of a modern Apollo, that many a young Hebe learns that there is a serpent's sting in the arts of her teacher, only when she has realized the earliest sorrow of Eden.

The American traveller destined for the west coast of America, on arriving at Panama, must amiably lay aside home habits and conform himself to customs as he finds them. He cannot reasonably expect to change the usages of the countries he proposes to visit, and therefore must change his own. This ready adaptation will invite freedom of communication, a desirable means of information to a stranger; and although he may be required to breakfast at ten, and dine at five to seven, going supperless to bed, he will soon find nature under physiological laws accommodatingly inclined; and even if he be required to live, as he assuredly will, in an atmosphere of tobacco smoke, he may philosophically yield to its soporific influence, and become unconscious of actual annoyance in dreams of bliss. Servant he must be to himself where all are on an equality, and where the negro, having been restored to his original privilege of indolence, would rather suffer want than perform a servile office, or labor in any form. As to the ceaseless pounding of bell-metal, giving clamorous expression to religious fervor, which would thus arrest the attention of heaven and commend itself to divine approval, forgetful that the unuttered prayer of the truly penitent pierceth beyond the din of the self-righteous, one need not consider this a reflection on his less demonstrative notions of what is right and acceptable, but rather let the "sounding brass and tinkling cymbal" remind him of the "charity" that "endureth all things and hopeth all things," and thus while it teaches him to *bear*, it will serve also to encourage his *hope* of the future. For recollecting as he will the "*fire* worshippers" of his own country who once gloried in the grandeur of the wild element, and their achievements in staying its career, the echo even of whose discordant clamor is lost in the scarcely heard pulsations of the great agent which has revolutionized the system of protection against the terrible destroyer, he will be led to think that this senseless clatter may also cease, with other usages of an ignorant and bigoted people, under the plastic touch which has linked two oceans in commercial union across this isthmus, and is now slowly and imperceptibly moulding its destinies.

The *tout ensemble* of Panama and its surroundings, exquisitely beautiful as these are, when, in the case of the former, "distance lends enchantment to the view," should be seen from some adjacent eminence. All Americans who visit Panama are indebted to A. B. Corwine, Esq., United States Consul, and his accomplished lady, for hospitalities and attentions. For these I cannot be sufficiently grateful. Accompanied by Mr. and Mrs. C., we left the city by the Cruces road, and at the distance of a mile and a half, alighting at a now unoccupied country seat of a former British Consul, we walked along one of several winding paths, pleasantly shaded, up a gradual ascent, which terminated in a summit known as "Cerro de los Buccaneros;" on which, for the accommodation of the weary, is found a tasteful rustic arbor. Clad in luxuriant vegetation of rich and varying green, rarely is so beautiful a spot seen even in the tropics; nor was I surprised to learn that its former owner, for whom the social life of Panama could have no attractions, yet lingered many years in the balmy air of its shadowy groves. The queen of the Adriatic, on whose waveless canals he now floats, knows not the abounding loveliness of this retreat.

"In Venice Tasso's echoes are no more,
And silent rows the songless gondolier;
Her palaces are crumbling to the shore,
And music meets not always now the ear;
Those days are gone—but beauty still *is here.*
States fall, arts fade—*but Nature doth not die.*"

In this tropical paradise gracefully the palm waves its plumed leaf in the southern breeze, to fan the golden pine-apples nestling beneath in their green couches that border the shaded paths, and peep forth to breathe their fragrance, and tell the intruder how happily life may pass in this sweet solitude. Here also hang the clustering plantain and banana, while the gay orange and blushing mango give their brighter tints to enliven the graver hues of the luscious granadilla, nespero, and mamei de cartajena.

Tradition says, that from this hill of the Buccaneers, the notorious English freebooter, Sir Henry Morgan, on his way from the mouth of the Chagres River across the Isthmus, first gazed on the spires of old Panama, when, in 1669, he executed his long-meditated and deliberately-prepared foray in the British Island of Jamaica, against a Spanish possession. Our national cousins pretend a holy horror of *fillibustering*—a word of modern coinage implying a practice, as they profess, of modern origin, and which in its application to aggression and intermeddling, they and others have contrived, with persisting effrontery, to fasten on Americans as a special national propensity. Thus they would divert attention from like deeds of their past history, and acts of the present, dignified by grandiloquent diplomacy as "balance of power," "release of commerce from the shackles of selfish exclusiveness," "protection of Christians from infidel intolerance," "cause of the oppressed," "natural rights of man," "necessities of civilization," and so on *ad nauseam*. The authentic narratives of events which have transpired on this coast, have recorded enduringly the international outrages of Sir Henry Morgan and Sir Francis Drake; and to these might be added the violations of neutrality of Lord Cochrane, to show how shallow is the artifice that would for selfish and ungenerous purposes, assail the character of another and kindred nation. While the British tattoo boastfully encircles the earth with its continuous echo, telling a tale of astounding aggression and annexation; and France, just freed from the intermeddling of combined Europe, has appropriated to herself Algeria, Tahiti, and Savoy, and is now recalling her forces from China and Syria, to instruct Mexico in the duties of good government, or to establish her "natural boundary" of the Rhine; with such examples of *fillibustering* before them, Americans may smile at a foreign diplomacy so ignoble, and a popular jealousy so unworthy as that which would stigmatize as the special offence of others, acts signally illustrative of their own history.

From the summit of Cerro de los Buccaneros we gazed upon the scene below and beyond, with different emotions from those which the titled fillibuster, Morgan, may be supposed to have experienced; when, intent on plunder, the devoted city, the depository of countless treasures, lay revealed before him. Away to the west and north rolled verdure clad hills of exquisite outline; while loftier heights, faintly seen in the distance, showed where the snowy Cordillera of the Southern Continent was extending its lower spurs, like the taper fingers of a polished arm, to receive the hard grasp of its rocky neighbors of the north. Valleys of virgin soil lay about their feet, mantled in fadeless green, reposing in unbroken silence, save by the shrill whistle and rumbling clamor of the locomotive, as hastening along the iron way which winds among these solitudes, it awakens their sleeping echoes, and teaches them the exultant notes of progress and civilization. Off to the east four or five miles, close down on the sea-shore, was seen the lone tower which marks the spot where all that remains of proud Panama of old lies buried. A sad memorial of vanity and departed grandeur, it stands, like many others, deserted, neglected, and forgotten, without a hand to renew its mournful graces but that of nature, which, year by year, hangs garlands about its shattered summit, twines a green mantle around its body as if to shelter it from sunshine and storm, and wraps its foot with clustering and imperishable verdure. To the southwest rises the bold "Cerro Ancon," with the long line of quaint huts at its eastern base, picturesque in the distance, however repulsive when near, extending to the city, seen further on stretching into the beautiful bay, with its towers and turrets reflecting the setting sun, and its buttressed wall looking darkly upon the ocean whose waves break ceaselessly at its base, flinging at times their snowy spray even on its frowning battlements. And still further beyond, reposing tranquilly as if on the bosom of the sea, are seen the islands of Taboga, Taboguilla, Flamenco, Perico, Islando, and Calebra, forming a beautiful archipelago of ocean gems. The first named, about nine miles from the city, is cultivated in fruits and vegetables for the Panama market, and having upon it the extensive machine shops of the British Pacific Steam Navigation Company; and the last

TOWER OF SAN JEROME AT OLD PANAMA. p. 42

four, two miles off, belong to the American Pacific Mail Steamship Company, on one of which the shops of this company are erected. The steamers of these two lines lie near their respective islands, the American having an advantage for convenience of loading and discharging in the proximity of its anchorage to the city.

Surpassingly beautiful as was the picture on which we gazed, the delight of its contemplation was heightened by the proofs of commercial enterprise seen in the distance. There floated the American and British ensigns, side by side, the guarantee of improvement in man's destiny, and amelioration of human condition. We beheld the proofs of American enterprise, energy, and capital, spanning the neck of land so long a barrier in the path of commerce, linking together its great highways, and speeding its progress to the North Pacific, and to Central America, by the establishment of lines of splendid steamers. And so, too, was seen the illustration of British enterprise in the unsurpassed steamships forming an uninterrupted communication with the extreme South Pacific, and collateral branches of this great line to intermediate ports; both nations standing ready with men-o'-war on each ocean to guard the great avenue of trade across the isthmus for the benefit of the world. Such are some of the triumphs of peace—such the results of generous emulation and cordial coöperation. May we not hope that these will always prevail over contracted envy and unworthy antagonism?

It would give no pleasure for me to write, or you to read, a detail of manners and customs moulded in all things by selfishness and sensuality. If the people of this country are capable of responding to the purifying influences of a rational and spiritual religion, and to the elevating power of education—a problem which contrariety of opinion leaves of doubtful solution—these are not here to exercise their benign control; and hence indolence is the negative evil, while licentiousness, gambling, brutal amusements, disregard of domestic obligations and the decencies of life, stand forth conspicuous and positive vices. I speak of the larger part of the population. The smaller fraction, less than one-twentieth, of Caucasian blood, whose misfortune it is to mingle its pure stream with this Dead Sea of social being, true to its inheritance, is found here as elsewhere to assert its prerogative of superiority in mind and morals—in education, in virtue, and in the refinements of domestic and social life.

The unchanging heat of this intertropical climate produces great enervation, particularly during the wet season and prevalence of sultry southern airs, from May to December; and inducing disinclination to exercise, it thus impairs physical resources, and produces general deterioration, made very manifest when corresponding races are compared with the standards of temperate latitudes. A smaller and wasted frame characterizes both men and animals, a fact noticed by the least observing tourist. Acute disease is not, however, so prevalent in Panama as generally believed in the United States, and in Europe. Open directly to the sea, exposed to an unchanging north wind in the dry, and an uninterrupted south breeze in the wet season; and built on a rock foundation with an unbroken reef on three sides, swept by a tide of from nineteen to twenty-two feet height twice every day; there are no miasmata in its immediate vicinity capable of producing the much-dreaded "Panama fever," so much spoken of in other countries. Great injustice has been done this city in the belief elsewhere of the origin of that fatal disease here. The town of Chagres, on the Atlantic side of the Isthmus, and its deadly river of the same name, with the imprudences and exposures to rain and sun incident to travel on it, and after leaving its malarious bed in crossing the intervening region, without necessary comforts or a change of clothing when drenched, caused frequent and malignant fevers before the completion of the railroad; and the victims having reached Panama just before, or immediately after the development of the disease, to suffer and often to die here, this city was made by common rumor to bear an undeserved odium. My own observations, and facts derived from those correctly informed, lead me to the conclusion that Panama is safer than Aspinwall for travellers detained on the Isthmus—an event of common occurrence with Americans going to and returning from the west coast of South America; for the Royal West India Company is interested in preventing a connection of the British Pacific Steam Navigation Company's steamships with the New York line, by which connection passengers could often be conveyed to and from Europe through the United States, in less time than by the Royal West India Company's line to Southampton. Thus is public convenience made subservient to private interest. But Americans have no right to complain of this selfishness as a special sin of a foreign company, for who in a more censurable degree than the monopolizer of the New York and Aspinwall line of steamers illustrates the wickedness of intense selfishness, and disregard of public comfort, convenience, and safety?

## CHAPTER IV.

### VOYAGE FROM PANAMA TO PORT PAITA, AND TO CALLAO.

A GUEST on board the United States man-o'-war "Lancaster," with Flag Officer Montgomery in command of the Pacific Squadron, and Captain Rudd of the flag ship, as my hosts, and the accomplished officers of the ward room as occasional companions, what more could be desired to secure a delightful voyage from Panama to Callao but propitious elements?

To a landsman a first-class man-o'-war, when its decks are trod for the first time, seems something of a mystery; and like most mysteries creates a sense of awe, to be overcome only by the exercise of the American's inalienable right to question. I hope my shipmates forgave earnest efforts to get rid of a disagreeable ignorance; certainly my exertions appeared to receive the commendation of the old quartermaster, who pronounced me a "tolerable swab" ere the end of our voyage.

The "Lancaster" is considered as superb a specimen of naval architecture as can be boasted of by any country; of two thousand three hundred and sixty tons, length two hundred and seventy, and breadth of beam forty-six feet, full rigged and with steam power, her full armament twenty-eight guns, her present complement twenty-two; twenty guns on the main deck carrying nine-inch shells, and two pivot guns on the spar deck weighing, with carriage, twenty-five thousand pounds each, carrying eleven-inch shells weighing each one hundred and forty-two pounds, or solid shot of one hundred and eighty-two pounds weight, with an effective range of two and a half miles. Her complement of men is four hundred and six, and yet her size, arrangement, and discipline are such, that one is not sensible of the presence of one-fourth of that number. Her engine, of beautiful construction and finish, has a power of eleven hundred horses, and gives a speed of eleven knots an hour if her full consumption of thirty-five tons of coal per day be used, without carrying sail, which with a good breeze would of course greatly increase her speed. Her double-bladed propeller, weighing eight tons, can be triced up so as not to impede her motion when under sail alone. The "Lancaster" is supposed to have no superior afloat, in effective force, or as a steamer and sailer.

If the direct and manly policy which has characterized the past history of our country be followed by future administrations of the Government, in its adjustment of international difficulties; if justice, candor, boldness, and resolute purpose, should be the attributes of diplomacy in its negotiations with ministerial tortuosity, delay, and frivolous pretext; if the patriotic declarations of Jefferson and Webster, that "an American deck is American soil," and that "the flag covers all who are under its folds," are still to be the proud boasts of American statesmen; if freedom from search is to continue hereafter as heretofore the American principle of maritime law and justice; and if British cruisers are not to be permitted to play the part of high constables of the ocean over American commerce; then is it necessary that the United States should show a preparation to maintain their rights by sending abroad such defenders as the "Lancaster," always a more convincing argument with unwarrantable assumption, falsehood, and chicanery, than wordy discussion, however ingenious and earnest.

But it may become necessary not to stop at the achievement of even such a hitherto unsurpassed triumph in ship building as that of the "Lancaster," for the proposal to clad vessels of war in iron has indeed revolutionized the whole system of naval warfare, and placed the formidable fleets of the past at the mercy of smaller and apparently insignificant ships cased in impenetrable armor. The experiments of "La Gloire" and "The Warrior," which have been made, enabled the French and English to test the feasibility and effectiveness of the proposition, their capacity of resistance, aggression, and sea-worthiness. Being successful, others desiring to maintain national power have been prompt to remodel their navies.

As formidable as is the merely passive display of this ship, it is not until she is seen awakened into warlike life and activity, that her tremendous power and capability of destruction can be realized. Early this morning the drum beat to quarters, and instantly, as if a foe were bearing down upon us, every man of the crew of four hundred was at his post, but a few moments being required to bring into effective condition for attack or defence every engine of death of this terrible machine. The manning of her prodigious batteries on the main deck; the activity, energy, and order of the men; their precision, promptness, and regularity of movement of the guns; the coöperation of each one with another, and the noiseless harmony of all, no word being spoken but that of command; the ease and rapidity with which the ponderous Dahlgrens of the spar deck, of twenty-five thousand pounds weight, were handled, loaded, turned, elevated, depressed, aimed, discharged, and the effects at two and a half miles distance of the bursting shell, upheaving the placid sea and showering the iron fragments far and wide upon its dark bosom; the manning of bulwarks by boarders with gleaming blade, pike, and battle-axe, a living wall of terror, supported by the stern and disciplined marines, in peace the sailor's jest, in battle his truest defenders; the rapid, yet steady and cool passage of ammunition from the ship's hold, as if the ascending buckets were holding the streams of life instead of the agents of death; the startling cry of "fire," the signal bell, the attachments to the engine, the instantly flashing torrents ascending to the topmost spars; these counterfeits of war bursting unlooked for on the sight, and passing in less time than I have taken to describe them, with a rapidity and order the result alone of extraordinary drill and discipline, carried conviction of the perfection of command and general training on board the "Lancaster," and warranted the belief that from past experience of naval warfare, no just estimate can be formed of the dreadful carnage, perhaps to mutual and total destruction, to result from future encounters of ships of war armed with the present terrible engines of destruction, and directed by the perfect skill and discipline which now characterize the service.

Do not suppose from this "pride, pomp, and circumstance

of glorious war," that my shipmates do not recognize the obligations of peace, and that there is no prayer uttered that all may live under its dominion. In your city this Sabbath day, with its many churches lifting their lofty spires and swelling domes to the skies, and frescoed ceilings and arches reverberating the diapason of the pealing organ and the solemn eloquence of the chant, or echoing the words of Divine truth; however impressive these, and however elegantly attired, graceful, and responsive the congregations that throng their cushioned pews and carpeted aisles, there is not a more reverential and attentive assemblage than that coming together for religious worship on the gun-deck of this ship; one more sincerely imbued with the spirit that comes of a conviction of the existence of a Supreme Being, and our moral obligation to strive to conform our lives to His standard of truth and righteousness. With the vaulted heavens above and the boundless ocean around us, all felt in His august presence alike humble; officers and men came together, unmindful of the distinction of worldly rank, conscious of a common brotherhood of dependence, to offer up their united gratitude for preservation from the wrath of the tempest, and their one prayer for a continuance of the protection of His sheltering arm. Truly did they know, as with one voice they declared it, "The sea is His and He made it, and His hands prepared the dry land;" and never was the Psalmist's apostrophe more impressively uttered than when it came from the lips of these brave, honest, and earnest sailors, who stood surrounded by the tremendous engines of battle, and "bruised arms," with which they were familiar, "O, come, let us worship and fall down, and kneel before the Lord our Maker! For the Lord is a great God, and a great King above all gods"! And appropriate was the prayer of those bound on a mission of liberty and civilization, the protectors of their country's example of constitutional government to other nations, "Oh! God, who art the Author of peace, and Lover of concord, in knowledge of whom standeth our eternal life, whose service is perfect freedom, defend us thy humble servants in all assaults of our adversaries; that we surely trusting in Thy defence, may not fear the power of any adversaries."

Such a scene of sincere devotion as that aboard the "Lancaster" to-day, was calculated to confirm confidence in the increasing power and influence of our country, which cannot fail to be established by the continued observance, hereafter as in the past, of the Christian precept, "deal justly, and love mercy." It called to mind the illustrative anecdote told of the great queen of a kindred nation—great because she practices the rules of duty and virtue inculcated by Divine authority—who, when presented with costly gems by a foreign prince, was asked in return to tell him the secret of England's greatness and glory. "Say to your prince," she replied to the ambassador, handing him at the same time a copy of the Bible, and in the spirit of faith and love which that book teaches, "say to your prince, that this is the secret of England's greatness."

After a day of heavy rain yesterday we are now steaming along leisurely under a clear sky, the thermometer at delicious 80°, and a pleasant breeze dead ahead prohibiting the use of a foot of canvas.

Do you remember the pretty tale of the "Arabian Nights," in which it is related that a beautiful princess by the name of Mary—most Marys are beautiful, you know—received from her grandmother, who was an enchantress, when dying, *a bead* having many faces to it, on each of which was engraven the figure of some object, the rubbing of which immediately secured the possession of the real object itself? The first use to which the princess put the talismanic bead was to obtain possession of a magic couch capable of transporting its occupants instantly, and without danger, to any desired part of the world, and to perpetrate the very common indiscretion of making off with a husband. But the most shameful part of the transaction—one which appears unhappily to have served as a precedent even down to modern times—was that Mary ran off *with another woman's* husband; for it appears by the veracious history referred to, that Aladdin Abushamat, the Mohammedan whom she inveigled, was already married to a sweet little lute player named Zobeide. Aladdin having some compunctions of conscience, or a lingering attachment for Zobeide, did not like to abandon her altogether, and persuaded his new bride to take her along; so the amiable and forgiving Zobeide mounted the charmed couch with the runaways, and off they flew together, insensible to fear, forgetful of danger, and unconscious of weariness, to a valley, where, we are told, contentment and happiness made the winged hours pass unheeded. Whether their abode was fixed in the vicinity of our own scandalized Salt Lake, and whether they were the original colonists of the Mormon settlement there located, strangely in conformity with the policy of American statesmanship, and the moral sentiment of self-righteous religionists who "strain at a knat and swallow a camel," is not stated in the narrative.

In seeking an illustration of present realities, I do not fear a misunderstanding of my meaning, or an impeachment of having been carried off by even a Princess; for *my* Mary being along, somebody would have to go off the enchanted couch with the certainty of a rapid descent and a hard fall. But it is natural in these moments of welcome relief from the wearing and wasting excitements of the busy world, to recall the recollections of early years and their delights; and what visions of bliss and brightness should the strange and pleasing novelties by which I am surrounded, so naturally revive, as those which fed the young fancy, and gave to maturer manhood many of the gilded frames in which were set the pictures of real life? Like the happy heiress of the enchanted bead, I too feel as if I had suddenly come into possession of a talisman having power to lift me above earthly things, and bear me unharmed, and insensibly to myself, to distant regions. During the day, through the delicate attentions of my courteous hosts, I partake in their spacious cabin of the comforts, elegancies, and social refinements of a charmed life. At night, "I lay me down and sleep in peace," without even the shadow of fear to darken my dreams, for I know that a sleepless eye, experience, and skill, keep the watch, and that a tried and veteran hand holds the helm.

We are going at moderate speed along the west coast of South America between Point Galena and Cape Francisco, the latter being thirty-nine miles north of the Equator, and forming the S. W. boundary of a deep concavity scooped out of this continent, called by the old Spaniards "La Mar Tranquilla"—the Tranquil Sea, or Region of Calms, of English charts. We shall cross the equator in a few hours—just one year to day since this ship crossed it in her northward voyage after doubling the Horn. This coincidence, however, is not so remarkable as that which attended Napoleon's passage to his prison at St. Helena, when his crossing the line gave neither latitude, longitude, nor declination. Such an extraordinary fact might well attend an event having no parallel in history; an act without honor, bravery, or mercy; a monstrous example of injustice, cruelty, and fear; a nation's imprisonment for life, on an ocean bound rock, of a man who had confidingly surrendered himself to those he deemed magnanimous enemies, as a prisoner of war—entitled to the immunities of such in the eyes of Christendom and civilization; and the more so in the estimation of the truly noble, because of his sublime genius, wonderful achievements, and grand conceptions of human progress! The deed must ever remain a dark spot on the escutcheon of Great Britain; and if it were not sufficiently blackened by the self reproach of suicide, an everlasting stain also on the memory of her prime minister "Carotid artery cutting Castlereagh."

The great superiority of steamships of war over sailing vessels, is strikingly exemplified in this voyage to Callao. Despite calms, or the still greater impediment of head winds, which have thus far attended us, the Lancaster is progressing steadily and speedily toward the accomplishment of an object, the prompt execution of which is considered of great importance to the national interests. Had the St. Mary's, now lying at Panama, a fine ship of her class but without auxiliary steam power, been despatched to Callao, she would have been baffled or been beating about for many weeks, or have been under the necessity of stretching far out to westward beyond the direct course, and then standing south of her destination for favorable winds to bring up to her port, have consumed nearly two months in doing what with steam may be accomplished in eight to ten days. The British Admiralty have ceased to regard sailing vessels as reliable in war, or as efficient instruments of peace. The innovation of iron armor protection renders them still less deserving of consideration. And the French, by extraordinary energy, perseverance, great foresight, and liberal expenditure, have command at this time of a steam navy rapidly assuming the impenetrable feature, but little if any less formidable than that of Great Britain. The command of the ocean must certainly be surrendered, in the event of war, to that nation which has the largest steam marine and steel clad navy. So far from it being economical to keep in commission sailing vessels to avoid the cost of steamships, it really presents the paradox of *an expensive piece of saving;* for apart from their certain loss in a fight, and greater danger in many conditions of weather and position, the embargoes laid upon them in harbor by stress of weather, adverse winds, and tides; the loss of time incident thereto, and the great expense attendant on this inactivity; the wasteful consumption of time, too, in beating for thousands of miles to and fro, or the standing off and on for immense distances to reach a port of destination not one-fourth as far in a direct line, and which could be run under steam at a cost of fuel far less than the aggregate of seamen's wages who have been kept uselessly drifting or beating about; must satisfy the rational mind that steam as an auxiliary element is essential to naval efficiency, and that those who avail of this certain motive power, must hold supremacy over the slower and less enterprising members of the family of nations.

Yesterday the thermometer showed 76°—it was the last day of summer to us; in the evening we crossed the equator, and now we are in the last winter month of the Southern hemisphere. The transition is imperceptible in all respects—geographical extremes compromise their differences on a line of mutual agreement without violent result; and in this set an example of wisdom to more impracticable humanity. A bright and balmy atmosphere, and smooth sea, are around us. The coast is but seven or eight miles distant; Monte Christo in the back ground about fifteen miles inland, and fifteen hundred feet high, standing forth the prominent object of the ever-changing panorama. Cape San Lorenzo, a few miles ahead, is seen jutting out into the ocean with bold and weather-beaten brow, guarded by two prominent and rocky islets looking defiantly on the waves that break at their feet, one of them bearing a close resemblance to a well-proportioned light house. Experienced mariners inform me that, besides being incomplete, the old Spanish charts of this coast are often found inaccurate; and the English charts, although in the general more reliable, are in some instances copied from the Spanish with their errors uncorrected. Since the independence of these South American countries, their governments have been so much occupied in the business of political organization, their pecuniary resources have been so limited or so shamefully misapplied, and they have been so perpetually subject to the disturbing influences of revolution, that no attention whatever has been bestowed on the surveys necessary to secure detailed and accurate knowledge, needful for safe navigation and for the desirable development of the great resources of New Granada and Ecuador, along which we are coasting. If the leading commercial nations of the world, Great Britain, France, and the United States, would unite for the purpose; or either would explore with small steamers, and competent surveying parties, this long line of sea coast, minutely examining its bays, harbors, shoals, reefs, rocks, soundings, tides, currents, and prevailing winds, and publish corrected charts, great advantage would result to them, and all others interested in the safe navigation of this part of the Pacific.

In doubling Cape San Lorenzo a pretty little village is seen on a cove indenting the coast just south of the cape. Groves of cocoanut trees embower the picturesque cottages, and the inhabitants appear to be dragging nets along shore. They seem to be fishermen, and we have named the town Piscatoria. It is not designated on the charts. About fifteen miles S. S. W. of Cape Lorenzo, Plata Island is seen, so called by the Spaniards from their belief that Sir Francis Drake, who, nearly three centuries ago, captured off Cape San Francisco a Spanish treasure ship, divided his plunder at this island. It is about three miles long, presents a high bluff along its eastern face, except where receding it forms a small harbor, the only landing visible. Sterility seems to hold dominion over it, and man does not appear disposed to dispute its right.

The life of the Devonshire skipper, Sir Francis Drake, as told by the historian Motley, was a remarkable one; after coasting as such, he says, "in narrower seas, his spirit took a bolder flight, and ventured on a voyage with the old English slave trader John Hawkins, whose exertions in that then considered honorable and useful avocation had been *rewarded by Queen Elizabeth with her special favor*, and with a coat of arms, the *crest whereof was a negro's head, proper, chained*." Such was an instance of England's agency, under the rule of the "good and great Queen Bess," in entailing upon America a social condition, which she is striving to regulate alike consistently with humanity, and with her own safety; but for the existence of which, she is strangely considered deserving of harsh denunciation by the admirers of that right royal woman, and the descendants of that great race who laid the foundation of England's old renown and present commercial grandeur. Soon after this, Drake, "the terrible Sea-King, ploughed his memorable furrow round the earth," carrying dismay and destruction into the Spanish commerce of distant regions, and returning to England, as is asserted, with treasure enough to enable Queen Elizabeth "to maintain a war with the Spanish King for seven years," besides enriching the private speculators who had embarked in his bold enterprise of striking terror into the Spanish possessions all over the earth. It was during this voyage that he made the capture above referred to, and secured and assorted the treasure at Plata Island.

We did not "cross the line" until the night of yesterday; consequently Neptune, engaged in taking his nap, did not come aboard to assert his ancient prerogatives. This morning, however, he presented himself in *propria persona*, and announced that although he had on a former occasion been aboard of this craft with his royal family, and administered the ceremony of initiation to all trespassers on his dominion, yet he was duly informed by his detectives that she had since taken aboard one who had never paid tribute to his sovereignty. But that inasmuch as he was aware through diplomatic channels that I was a special commissioner on behalf of a nation in whose nautical deeds he gloried, who had covered his seas with matchless triumphs, enriched them with the wealth of commerce, and spread upon their bosom the blessings of civilization and knowledge throughout the world; and as he knew that my mission was designed to promote the comfort and welfare of the brave and hardy mariners who acknowledged his rule, and were entitled to his protection; therefore, not doubting my homage, and in deference to the obligations of international courtesy, he would exempt me from the customary ceremonial, and merely require the payment of a trifling tribute in *pro forma* recognition of his maritime rights. I was an attentive, and as you will suppose, a deeply interested listener to this address—for I had heard of the terrible ordeal and humiliation of the victims of this awful rite—and when the conclusion was reached, and my self-possession was recovered, I acknowledged a sincere and deferential appreciation of Neptune's august consideration of my country and its representative; and complying with the required recognition of his rights, expressed, in diplomatic phrase, the very high gratification felt at the favorable opinion entertained by his marine majesty of the objects of my Government, which, in its zeal to prove its distinguished consideration of his friendship, had never rested in its progress, until traversing a continent it was able to plant its foot on the Rocky Mountains, and stretching its arms to the Atlantic and the Pacific could exclaim, we may not encroach on thy imperial domain, but thus let us stand in mutual relation and support, inseparable in manifestations of greatness, grandeur, and power.

Yesterday my narrative of an audience was interrupted by an intimation from the "orderly" that I was wanted on deck. On obeying the summons and looking out, I saw something "very like a whale"—but whether it had some apprehension of a harpoon, or a shell, or was too modest to be gazed at by the strange leviathan steaming alongside, I know not—taking a hurried glance and a "spout," it disappeared in the depths below. Shortly afterwards a school of black-fish came along, a species of porpoise, resembling it in general appearance and habits, and like it a breathing, or *blowing* animal. In the latter particular, too, it bears a resemblance to certain terrestrial creatures known as "blowers" and "hangers on," not only in *spouting* propensity, but also in *ubiquity* and *tenacity;* for look in whichever direction we would for miles around, there they were apparently innumerable, sporting their *self-conceits*, following us for hours, and holding on with a persistence that finally became wearisome and disgusting.

The black-fish is larger than the porpoise, being from fifteen to eighteen feet long. It yields an abundance of oil of an inferior quality to that of the whale, and therefore not sought so long as a sufficiency of the latter can be had. But when whalers have nearly completed their cruise, without having secured a full cargo of the better quality, they frequently fill up with black-fish oil rather than protract their voyage.

When my narrative of Neptune's visit was interrupted yesterday by the "orderly's" summons, I was about to say that when he was taking leave, his countenance assumed a threatening aspect indicative of a serious flare up. In explanation of this it must be said that we have aboard the "Lancaster" the Fleet Surgeon of the Pacific Squadron, and eminently qualified he is for his responsible office by varied attainments, skill, and experience. The doctor, like many of his prescriptions, is a compound of many and miscellaneous materials. I cannot quote the trite figure of speech, and say that he is "neither fish, flesh, nor fowl," for his substantial dimensions give an unqualified contradiction to the metaphor, all of these having entered as component parts, and liberally too, into his massive frame. Nor can he be considered unlike "any thing in the heavens above, or the earth beneath, or in the waters under the earth," for although he does not present the special characteristics of any one thing of either of these divisions of the universe, yet there is that about him so diverse in constitution and physical organization, so complex in mental and moral nature, so bountiful in resource, and sharing so largely in the properties, attributes, phenomena, and capacities of what pertains to air, earth, and sea, that the similitude may be correct in a compound if not in an elementary sense. The storehouses of land, ocean, and atmosphere, have been ransacked by him for knowledge and amusement; and besides his generalities of resources, it may be added that he is specially qualified to hold the helm of state, or the helm of a ship. He can navigate the Bay of Panama or any other, with the same skill as the "Sick-Bay" aboard ship, in which many skippers go to the bottom. And woe to the officer of the deck, who, when the doctor is near, shall "miss stays," or "haul on a wrong tack." With the first officer and Jimmy Ducks, the hospital steward, and the loblolly-boy, he is both oracle and idol; and when he is on deck, and under full headway of talk, a visitor is as likely to take him for the commodore as for the fleet-surgeon. Every one consults him; all quote him; the officers have faith in and respect him; the men adore and swear by him. His state-room, six by seven feet, the size likely to be demanded for his earthly grave, if unhappily he should die ashore, contains a greater variety, and more things in number and bulk of the curious, convenient, comfortable, comprehensive, and compendious, than were ever before crowded and condensed into any corresponding compartment. I will not attempt their enumeration, for, never a proficient in arithmetic, in this effort it would be sure to fail me. Nor will I essay to name them, for my *language* would certainly prove a *dead* one before I could get half through the catalogue.

Some days since, the doctor, in the prosecution of his untiring investigations, determined to summon witnesses from the vasty deep, and for that purpose attached one of his mechanical contrivances to the stern rail of the ship. This machine is a compound of a massive trout reel and a watchman's rattle. There is no necessity to watch the baited hook attached to it by a line and trailing in the ship's wake, for any thing seizing it and drawing on the line sounds its own death-knell. Scarcely had the doctor "cast his bread upon the waters," when a courser of the sea, on some mission of his imperial master, indiscreetly laid hold of the tempting morsel, and thus sounded the alarm, which resulted in his being wound in by ratchet and spindle, and hauled aboard. It was this irreverent act of the doctor that excited the ire of Neptune on his recent equatorial visit to the ship. Looking sternly for awhile at his old disciple, who had grown gray as the mariner's friend, whose home was on the wave, and whose resting-place ere long will probably be beneath it, the "short passing anger" soon faded away, and shaking his venerable locks, he spoke rather in pity than in passion, somewhat after this wise: "My ancient friend—I will not offend thy republican ears by saying *subject*, however absurd thy notions of popular capacity and right, and disastrous hitherto the experiments of self-government—I know thy proclivity for sounding the depths of all things, and that thou canst not restrain thy frailty for diving into the dangerous abyss of knowledge; and therefore I forgive thy injury and detention of my messenger—doubtless undesignedly caused. But thou must be more careful in future when thou heavest thy lead, and see that there is not attached thereto any of those barbs fashioned from that hellish harpoon, which has become the terror of my noblest creatures, and which I am resolved to prevent the barbarous use of, even if I must let loose a typhoon every week and sink all the accursed Yankee whalers afloat on my domain." He then bowed, "not like a dancing-master at the head of his drill'd nymphs, but like a gentleman," courteously, yet with dignity, and disappeared. This considerate caution seemed to have but little effect in restraining the doctor's researches; for on a subsequent visit to the ward-room to condole with him on the unfortunate result of his late investigations in natural history, I found him getting his "tattler" ready for another marine foray. And he rather irreverently intimated that Neptune had been "sold" in supposing that he had been "heaving the log;" he was not thinking of taking "deep sea soundings," but *was deep* in a conspiracy of getting "other fish to fry." Wherever the winds may blow, the billows bear this noble representative of the medical profession, may he, as now, rejoice the hearts and guard the health of his shipmates, continuing happy in the conscious possession of their confidence and affection!

We had head winds in crossing the mouth of the Gulf of Guayaquil, one hundred and twenty miles wide from its northern point, St. Helena, to its southern, Cape Blanco; the latter a high and bold headland, sloping gradually toward the sea—its whiteness giving its name. The doubling of Cape Blanco is so often difficult of accomplishment, the winds being baffling and the sea rough, that mariners consider it the Cape Horn of the west coast. Roughness and difficult navigation are, however, characteristics of the whole coast southward as far as Farina Point, the north cape of Paita Bay, including Talara Point midway. The coast between Cape Blanco and Farina Point is cliffy and bare, presenting a picture of barrenness and desolation. It trends nearly due north and south, being the most westwardly projecting part of the Pacific shore of the southern continent of America. Hence, however smooth the sea may be along other parts of the coast, here considerable roughness is apt to be encountered. And such was our experience, for head wind and swell continued to increase from the time we made Cape Blanco; and when nearing Farina Point—the shore being but a mile distant, for we hugged it pretty close here—they became so violent as to make it necessary to send down all top-hamper, furl every thing left standing, and stow away wind sails and all other loose canvas ordinarily untouched. Farina Point is a dark, frowning, rugged, rocky bluff, eighty or ninety feet high, shelving abruptly down to a reef extending half a mile to the westward, from which the breakers send up a fierce and ceaseless warning. Our ship rolled and pitched in a manner to disturb the gastric equanimity of all but veteran seamen, and making physical equilibrium a stranger to novices, except when, after sundry evolutions, marchings, countermarchings, gyrations, circumgyrations, side-steps, lock-steps, and no steps at all, they finally "came to" in a horizontal position. Having myself practically abjured allegiance to land, and passed equatorial muster, the only effect of this morning's commotion was, by a few feats of gymnastics, to give zest to life, and whet a sea-appetite for breakfast. We doubled the Point in from seven to ten fathoms of water, and are now steaming toward Port Paita with a smoother sea; the mountains of Amatapa, a spur of the Andes, looming up on our left, from three thousand to four thousand feet high, trending from the northeast to the southwest, and although thirty miles from the coast, they are seen at all points from Cape Blanco to Port Paita.

Our whole course yesterday off the Gulf of Guayaquil was across a famous fishing ground, on which whales have been taken in great numbers. Many were seen by us, some coming quite near. One monster, apparently nearly a hundred feet in length, rose a few yards from the ship, spouted two columns of water shaming the streams of a steam fire-engine, and then hastily disappeared, perhaps to announce the coming of an intruder in Peruvian waters.

The town of *Paita*, incorrectly spelt Payta on most maps published in the United States, and having its affluent Spanish pronunciation of vowels superseded to North American ears by the New England whaler impoverishment *Pay-tay*—is the most northern seaport of Peru on the Pacific Ocean. It is in south latitude 5° 5′, and west longitude 81° 15′, and has a population, according to the estimate of the United States Vice Consul, of twenty-five hundred, which is probably more correct than Findlay's statement of five thousand. The harbor is very accessible and has a fine depth of water; our ship is anchored in nine fathoms, half a mile from shore. The appearance of Paita is not prepossessing. The houses are clustered closely on the beach at the foot of a sand bluff about one hundred and fifty feet high, without a tree or blade of grass to relieve the unbroken barrenness around. A substantial mole receives passengers on landing, and on this they pass a short distance to the custom house, an iron structure prepared in England for erection on its arrival here a few years since. It is a two-story building, sixty feet square, surrounded by a neat iron balcony, and is surmounted by a cupola, from the staff of which floats the Peruvian flag. Behind the custom house is the public store, of the same material. All other houses are built in the rudest manner and of indifferent materials; usually of rough timber frames, filled in with clumsy sun-dried bricks—adobes, of all shapes and sizes; or of Guayaquil reeds, whole or split, daubed with mud. A few houses of the *élite*, and the front of the cathedral, have, in addition to the mud, a rough cast of lime stucco, or are whitened with a wash made from the shell strata seen seaming the sand cliff back of the town. High pitched roofs are made of stout reed rafters, thatched nine or ten inches thick with flag leaves. Chimneys and windows are curiosities, the door admitting air, light, dust, and denizens, in common. The streets are narrow, irregular, unpaved; and when you are informed that the bluff in the rear of the town is the commencement of a sandy plain or *tablaza*, of thirty to forty miles in extent, down the coast, and into the adjacent province of Piura, of which Paita is the seaport—a desert on which rain rarely falls, and dews never—you may imagine the depths and drifts of sand blown from the neighboring hills, through which the pedestrian must wade; and the quantity of dust he must inhale when stirred by the breeze. The burial service, "dust thou art and unto dust thou shalt return," seemed about to be illustrated in the midst of life, as, sight-seeing, we threaded the byways—highways, there were none. Eyes, nose, ears, and lungs were the recipients of bountiful contributions of this plastic element of creation; nor was it at all surprising to us after a day's wandering about Paita, to find that the natives had already taken the complexion of the earth to which they must finally return. It seemed a foreshadowing of fate, and may serve the same purpose as the death's head and marrow bones exhibited in their churches, to remind the people of mortality. And yet this assiduity on the part of a painstaking priesthood to cherish a conviction of what we are and what we must become, does not appear required by any indifference of the municipal authorities to "keep it before the people." Strolling about, I came to the cemetery at the foot of the bluff, inclosed by a close reed fence daubed with the inevitable mud. Its surface was level, of sand, with pieces of board stuck sparsely in spots, to mark the resting-places of the dead. Epitaphs were unseen; grave-mounds there were none, and monumental marble the sacred place probably had never known. The rude blast had revealed the secrets of the grave, in many instances disinterring skeletons, parts of which were lying scattered about, strangers now to their life-long companions. The scantiest covering and meanest memorial were denied to these sad remains of mortality. Happily for England, even her country church-yards have known no such neglect; if so, the elegy of the poet would not have touchingly told of "the rude forefathers of the hamlet":

"Yet e'en these bones from insult to protect
Some frail memorial still erected nigh,
With uncouth rhymes and shapeless sculpture deck'd,
Implores the passing tribute of a sigh.

"Their name, their years, spelt by th' unletter'd Muse,
The place of fame and elegy supply;
And many a holy text around she strews,
That teach the rustic moralist to die.

"For who, to dumb Forgetfulness a prey,
This pleasing, anxious being ere resign'd;
Left the warm precincts of the cheerful day,
Nor cast one longing, lingering look behind?"

In the middle of the cemetery is a pyramid of bleached skulls—I counted more than a hundred on its exterior—gathered, no doubt, from the scattered testimonials of this Golgotha, interspersed with various other specimens of human osteology, to give the structure form and compactness. Surmounting it is a wooden crucifix eight or ten feet high, the whole forming a monument of Paita piety, refinement, and sentiment; not likely, despite the novelty of the design, to be copied by Anglo-American taste and sensibility.

Paita is a considerable resort of whalers for repairing and refitting after a long cruise; and for the transshipment of oil to home ports when it is desired to continue fishing. The last quarterly return shows the large amount of two hundred and thirty thousand dollars in value of oil brought into this port. Paita is also the outlet of the increasing productions of the interior of the northern part of Peru, among the most valuable of which are orchilla weed, cacao, and cotton. Many bales of the latter were seen on the mole, awaiting the arrival of the regular British steamer for transportation: most of it is shipped to Mexico, but some of it finds its way to European markets. It is spoken of here as being next in quality to the North American Sea Island cotton. The soil and climate are said to be well adapted to its cultivation; but I found it difficult to procure satisfactory information in Paita, in regard either to the mode of cultivation, extent of production, effective labor, or procurement of supply; the evident purpose being, on the part of those interested, as I was informed by the United States Vice Consul, to keep all the information relating to it as far as possible a secret. This is the more readily done because of the intervening desert between Paita and the cotton-growing region establishing a partial non-intercourse with inquisitive foreigners. This absence of reliable information is the more to be regretted by manufacturing nations in particular, and by the people generally of the world, interested in a comfortable, convenient, and cheap material of clothing, because of domestic disturbances threatening to destroy temporarily, if not permanently, the chief source of supply. For five years, from 1856 to 1860, inclusive, Great Britain, the greatest manufacturing country, received from her own great empire of India, and therefore likely to obtain its entire exportation of cotton, an average of but 192,005,878 pounds; whilst from the United States, a country exporting largely to other nations, as well as reserving for home consumption, she received an average of 869,126,742 pounds; the last year of the series, 1860, the quantity reaching 1,115,890,608 pounds, being five times the import from India during the same year.

Orchilla weed, referred to above as one of the chief exports of Paita, is a product of all the northern part of Peru. It has a parasitic rather than an independent vegetable existence; is stripped or picked from trees both large and dwarfed, and is sent in large quantities to Europe, where it is used for its valuable property as a dye.

In consequence of immediately surrounding barrenness, fresh provisions are brought to Paita from a great distance, and therefore command at all times a high price. Wood and water are among the great wants of the place; they are brought from the interior, twenty-five or thirty miles, on donkeys, and sold, the former at two reals—a quarter of a dollar—per "*cargo*" of twenty-four sticks of algaroba, the size of an arm; the latter at three to four reals for twenty gallons. The natives may get enough water to drink, but it is *palpably* too costly for cleanliness.

Game-cocks appear to be the favorite and best cared-for denizens of Paita: trimmed to the top of the fashion, sleek and saucy, quite conscious of their importance, and that without them no *soi-disant* Spaniard could exist, they were found everywhere, the "observed of all observers," enjoying all privileges, except that of full locomotion, for they were tethered alike to rum-shop, custom house, private residence, and cathedral; the last named having two tied to its portal. Is this intended to signify the church's greater *devotion*—to the cock-pit? or its custom of *crowing* its own praises? or to remind modern disciples of their predecessor St. Peter's denial of his Master before the cock crew, and the duty of striving against a like human faithlessness? Certainly priests and people are equally addicted to the ignoble pastime of cock-fighting, and the former is said to show himself often the more accomplished gaffsman, and more skilful handler of his bird. Apart from this national amusement—and excepting the very few of a better class who are engaged in business pursuits—most of the natives, palpably of mixed Spanish, Indian, and Negro blood, appeared to be squatting on dirt floors eating melons, swinging indolently in hammocks, or celebrating a church festival by dancing and low buffoonery in the streets in fantastic dresses.

Paita being but a few degrees from the equator, it might be supposed that its climate is uncomfortably warm. But so far from this being the fact, the thermometrical range this September day has been from 60° to 70°. Residents inform me that it is seldom warmer, and that they sleep under blankets the entire year. Dr. Davine, an Italian physician, who has been engaged in the practice of his profession in Paita for several years, says that in consequence of the coolness of the climate and the quantity of dust in the atmosphere, a residence here is unfavorable to the health of persons predisposed to pulmonary diseases, and that such affections once in existence are always aggravated by continuance in the climate.

Fourteen leagues inland across the sandy plain is the city of *Piura*, the principal town of the province of the same name. Although often represented as having been the first Spanish settlement in South America, it is said by accurate historians not to be the same founded by Pizarro in 1531, shortly after landing at Tumbez. That settlement stood on the plain of Targasola, a short distance from the present town, and it was subsequently abandoned in consequence of the insalubrity of the site. The climate of the present city of Piura is equally warm, and so dry that it is said if a piece of paper remain on the ground all night, so perfectly dry will it be found next morning that it will admit of writing on equally well with one protected by a portfolio. This uniform temperature and dryness of the air, it is thought, adapt this climate admirably to the treatment of syphilitic diseases; and many persons from other parts of South America, laboring under various and obstinate forms of this affection, resort to Piura for greater certainty of cure. I am assured by an intelligent physician of this neighborhood, that the syphilitic opprobria of other districts of country are often speedily removed at this place. It is believed, however, and not without reason, that the water drank at Piura contributes much to the reëstablishment of health. In their course the streams often flow over extensive beds of sarsaparilla and fallen guaiacum trees, thus becoming strongly imbued with the virtues of these valuable medicinal agents. At certain seasons the waters are so low that the strength of the infusion is greatly increased, thus materially adding to their remedial virtues. This fact, and the uniform dry climate, may reasonably account for the many remarkable cures said to be effected at Piura.

Bidding adieu to Paita, we hove our anchor of six thousand one hundred pounds weight as easily as if it had been a fish-hook, and "catted and fish'd" it in five minutes to the shrill fife's rendering of Old Dan Tucker, to which three hundred seamen in double file marked time, exhibiting a showy nautical manœuvre, as they hauled on "cat and fish tackle fall." Speedily under way, a few minutes sufficed to bring us to Point Paita, the southern projection of land bounding the port, which, differing from the sandy bluff nearer the town, presents here a steep, irregular rocky cliff, pierced so as to form an arch of fifty feet span, through which the breakers rolled and dashed, indicating that ere long it must bow to the ceaseless war old ocean wages against this exposed part of the coast.

In rounding this Point, and for many miles north and south, a fine view is had of the "Silla or Saddle of Paita," a cluster of peaks joined at their bases, situated some distance within the Point, and stretching southerly. The top of the ridge is undulating, and aided by an accommodating imagination it may as appropriately be likened to a saddle as to any thing else.

Fairly at sea again on our southerly course, several coasting traders were seen, sometimes called *bastas*, oftener *balsas;* they are rather a raft of logs than a hull, are made of basta wood as light as cork, and have but a single sail to propel them. They are a frail-looking craft to live at sea, but are said to ride breakers in landing when boats would be swamped.

Off the mouth of Sechura Bay yesterday, the sea was rough —wind dead ahead and cool—60°. Passed Aguja Point, the southern limit of the bay, at night, steering south-southeast so as to pass outside of the Lobos Islands, to the west of the southernmost of which we are steaming moderately along this morning. We have been out of sight of land nearly ever since losing yesterday that admirable landmark "The Saddle." Consequently we had an unbroken view of the moon rising from her ocean bath last night, and burnishing the sea with a flood of light surpassing in brilliancy and beauty the moonlit water-scenes of the northern hemisphere. The stars trembled in their cold, clear, silvery garment, and the southern cross hung out its undimmed banner as if it delighted to share in the adornment of the placid heavens. It was a beautiful effulgence on which I once gazed with a now translated one, that polished the bosom of Champlain with subdued radiance as it sported its dimples in the breeze. How like her pure and joyful life! And how truly the transcendent splendors of the scene which last night was spread illimitably around us, pictured the sublimity and the eternity of her celestial existence! Owing to the unvaried clearness of the sky at and in the vicinity of Paita, there being no mists, dews, or fogs, the heavenly bodies are more distinctly seen there than perhaps in any other part of the world; and hence the sailor's simile, "as bright as the moon at Paita." This fact has not been overlooked by astronomers; and it is hoped that at some future day—when the Peruvians shall no longer be the victims of political agitation; when they learn that national good consists rather in cultivating knowledge, encouraging industry, and promoting morality, than in countenancing and becoming the agents of constant revolutions instigated by factionists, demagogues, and corrupt officials; and when they become convinced that permanent government, subject only to the restrictions of constitutional provisions duly administered, is essential to national prosperity—they will see their duty in contributing to the means of progress and knowledge, by erecting and endowing an astronomical observatory in the neighborhood of Paita.

This morning the men were beat to quarters for general inspection by the commanding officer, according to the naval regulations requiring it on the first Sunday of every month. After which, officers and men were mustered on the spar deck to hear read by the executive officer of the ship, the Articles of War, a duty also observed monthly; so that all, understanding the requirements of the service, and the penalties of neglect or violation, may be prepared faithfully to obey, or submissively to suffer. The Portuguese Hymn, then performed by the band, announced Divine service, when all but those on duty repaired to the main deck, there to listen to the *Articles of God's Law*, and to hear proclaimed the more terrible and enduring punishment that shall attend *their* violation. And there to acknowledge also, as all did in sincerity and truth, for the proofs were around and about, that "The Lord is in His holy temple;" to recognize the justice of the exalted precept, "Righteousness exalteth a nation, but sin is a reproach to any people;" and to pray that the "Eternal God, who alone spreadest out the heavens and rulest the raging of the sea; who has compassed the waters with bounds, until day and night come to an end, would be pleased to receive into His almighty and gracious protection the persons of the ship on which we serve; that we may be preserved from the dangers of the sea, and from the violence of the enemy; that we may be a safeguard unto the United States of America, and a security for such as pass on the seas upon their lawful occasion; that the inhabitants of our land may in peace and quietness serve Thee our God; and that we may return in safety to enjoy the blessings of the land, with the fruits of our labor, and with a thankful remembrance of Thy mercies." And believing with the Psalmist that it is "a good thing to sing praises unto God—a joyful and a pleasant thing to be thankful," the sound of "lute and harp" went out over the broad bosom of His own waters with vocal thanks and praise, for that "His mercy is greater than the heavens, His truth reaching even unto the clouds!"

For more than a day numerous birds have accompanied us resembling domestic pigeons; and for that reason, and because they are "native to the manor" of Cape Horn, called

Cape-pigeons. They attach themselves to vessels doubling that Cape and follow them to warmer latitudes, when they return with any ship they may fall in with going toward their favorite cruising ground—the tempest-beaten shore of Terra del Fuego. They leave for a time their inhospitable home for the refuse thrown overboard by the ship's steward. They are web-footed, and very light, from the great quantity of plumage compared with the size of their bodies; and sitting on the water to eat their food, they ride the waves with the grace of swans. Time often hangs heavy on the sailor's hands, and he resorts to fishing and fowling for amusement. The albatross is caught with baited hook, and the Cape-pigeon and smaller birds by becoming entangled in a cotton thread floating at one end loose in the current of air astern caused by the steamer's headway.

Jack, as all sailors are generically called, is in the estimation of "all the world" a queer animal. And he reciprocates the questionable compliment by a very unquestionable notion that "all the world"—among whom he does not desire to be classed, but prefers to compose that choice and anomalous part thereof referred to by an eminent functionary under the title of "the rest of mankind"—are not deserving through any merit, either active or passive, of the salvation of being caught by the foretop when sinking to perdition. Voracious as sharks, in his opinion landsmen will steer a fellow awry, and then plunder him when caught sailing on a wrong tack ashore. And as to knowledge, of which they boast so loudly, they are fools indeed, in his opinion, who are ignorant of the difference between a jibstay and a ratlin, or, as in the case of a former Secretary of the Navy, who is said "not to have known a boatswain from a commodore."

A stroll about the ship affords an opportunity to observe sailors' habits, and take lessons in nautical discipline, that might prove useful in other pursuits. At one time Jack is found busy washing decks—giving them daily a cleanliness and polish surpassing the parlor floors of fashion; at another skilfully manœuvring immense batteries and handling them with a celerity and precision and with a general perfection of ordnance drill that would justify the conclusion that he had never been familiar with the use of a "squilgee" and a "swab."

One moment he may be seen lying listlessly on the deck, or engaged in reading, writing on his ditty-box to the "girl he left behind him," or playing a game of chess or draughts on a checker-cloth spread on the deck; and the next instant all motion, energy, and activity, when suddenly summoned to lower a boat and ply the flashing oar, to save a shipmate fallen overboard and struggling for life amid the boiling billows. One hour swinging in his hammock in deep sleep, and then quickly leaping to his feet at the shrill piping of the boatswain, and mounting with alacrity the giddy mast, swinging to and fro in the reeling heavens, unseen from the deck below, conversant alone with the storm-cloud above, the tempest around, and the dark wave that lifts its crest in challenge to the surging spar to which he clings, as faithfully performing his duty as if the eye of authority was upon him, and the voice of command could reach his ear. Again, washing his garments as if trained in a laundry, and speedily joining in the infantry drill with the precision of a veteran marine. One moment patching a shirt, pea-jacket, and his stern-breeching, or improving that nether garment—spoiled by a lubberly tailor—by giving it a shape in consonance with nautical taste; and the next, executing the flying-artillery tactics with brass pieces on the main deck, in a manner to outbrag Captain Bragg of Buena Vista renown. Jack *is* "an institution" *sui generis;* and whether taken at handling a helm or a scrubbing-brush, a Dahlgren or a derrick, cutlass or a cathead, a game of all-fours, fight, or fun, chess, checkers, foot-ball, or leap-frog, he is hard to beat. Such is the opinion of one who has seen standard specimens of the creature aboard the "Lancaster."

The Andes are in sight, a hundred miles distant, lifting their snowy summits above the clouds! How impressive the scene! The most magnificent chain of mountains and the grandest ocean on our globe, confronting each other in mutual wonder, and mutually proclaiming "So far shalt thou go and no farther"!

As we are nearing Callao, the autocrat of the quarter-deck, considering it unseamanlike to enter port with rigging awry, ordered up the top-hamper sent down a few days since to present less surface to a stiff head wind, and in an hour the ship looked as trig as if a spar or a stay, a brace or a becket, a truck or a tackle had not been disturbed. No belle just from her toilet, rigged for the promenade, ever looked more a-taunt-o than the "Lancaster," with her head-gear tossed jantily aloft and strolling skyward, as if making coquettish incursions into the clouds.

We steamed along leisurely during last night, our captain feeling his way cautiously on approaching our port of destination in the dark, and anchored in the Bay of Callao at eight this morning, a mile from shore, in seven fathoms.

## CHAPTER V.

### HARBOR AND CITY OF CALLAO.

The harbor of Callao, in latitude 12° S., is about six miles in length and breadth, with ample depth of water, and entirely protected—no safer harbor being found. The city of Callao, and a prolonged beach, bound the harbor on the east; the island of San Lorenzo, four and a half miles long and one mile wide, rugged, barren, and from one thousand to twelve hundred feet high, stands on the west, with the small island of El Fronton and the Palminos rocks to the southwest, serving the purposes of superb breakwaters in these directions; on the south is a long, low, sandy peninsula—Callao Point—extending westwardly toward San Lorenzo, but leaving a strait called the *Boqueron* between its extreme point and that island; and on the north the harbor is open to the sea, this being the principal entrance to the port. The Boqueron, the southerly entrance, is about two miles wide; and although there is depth of water enough in its rather narrow channel for vessels of largest draught, and it is sometimes used by sailing vessels with a favorable wind, its navigation by such is not deemed safe, as there is not sufficient room for beating, and a strong current—always found—may carry a ship ashore. Hence marine insurance is made subject to avoiding the passage of the Boqueron. Steamers from and to the south use this channel in safety, and avoid the loss of time consequent on doubling San Lorenzo. In this harbor one hundred and fifty vessels are now riding at anchor. Among those flying the United States flag are three men-o'-war, the "Lancaster," "Wyoming," and "Narraganset," all carrying auxiliary steam power, and mounting metal enough to batter down Callao and its defences, and take the Peruvian frigate "Apurimac," lying alongside, by way of reprisal for the seizure by the Peruvians of two American merchantmen. The controversy growing out of this act drags its vexatious length along, and is likely to hang fire indefinitely, false-hearted diplomacy and insolence of office being submitted to rather than risk the possible inconvenience that might result from a peremptory demand for redress of grievances. At this moment the "Lancaster" is absurdly pretending international courtesy and friendship not felt, by belching forth a salute, causing the sea to tremble. It is truly a magnificent cannonade, making the tall Andes to clap their hands in joy:

> "The glee
> Of the loud hills shakes with its mountain mirth,
> As if they did rejoice o'er a young earthquake's birth."

Callao has a capacious mole for landing merchandise, and a smaller one for landing passengers in smooth water within that used for cargo. A sentinel stands at the head of the stairway. When we went ashore a large number of loafers of the darker tints, both sexes, and all degrees of impoverishment, were seen lounging about. Despite this, however, there was an appearance of business activity near the pier: *fleteros*, keeping their boats in perpetual motion, seeking employment; and *cargadores*, carrying their burdens, bags, boxes, and bundles to the railroad depot near by, and to which passengers were hurrying for the next train to Lima. A large quantity of miscellaneous merchandise was seen in a picket-fenced custom-house storage lot, designed for articles under temporary official restriction; no building being necessary for the protection of such from rain, where none ever falls to damage goods.

Callao is cursed by a hotel. May those who come here be saved by friends from expiating their sins in such a purgatory! The population is twenty-five thousand, mostly of the mixed breeds, who from the frequent occurrence of earthquakes, and the destruction of life as well as property that has attended them, are not inclined to indulge extravagant fancies in building large and costly houses. It is considered safer to have them of but one story, and of the lightest and most yielding materials, that they may yield and accommodate themselves to shocks generally without being prostrated. The high, slender walls of burnt brick of our northern cities would soon be shaken to pieces here. Most of the houses are small and low, consisting of a light scantling frame about twelve feet high, resting usually on timbers lying on the ground—there being no cellar. The interspaces of the frame are latticed or lathed with cane, split reed, or cornstalks, plastered with mud, in which chaff or horse dung is made to answer the purpose of hair in mortar. Sometimes this rough coating is yellow or whitewashed. A large door and iron-grated window, often unglazed, with unplaned plank floor, one or two mud-daubed cane partitions, and a roof of thatch, or board, covered, when desired to protect the inmates from the sun's rays, with a considerable thickness of dried mud as a non-conductor, complete the edifice, which, however suitable and lasting it may prove here, would be left untenanted in the bleak and variable north, where well-grounded apprehensions would be entertained of its being blown or washed away by a specimen equinoctial storm of that region.

The better class of houses—embracing but few—and especially those built for storage of merchandise, have a stronger foundation, usually of stone sunk several feet in the earth, on which is erected a frame of timber filled in with large sun-dried bricks—adobes—which are used in preference to fire-burnt brick, because cheaper, and also less apt to become cracked and overthrown by earthquakes. This wall, one story high and two feet thick, is plastered with mud. On it is built a second story, called *the alto*, of lighter materials, usually split reeds, and slender framework, slightly rough coated as before described. This attention to flexible and elastic materials is considered indispensable in the construction of the higher story, inasmuch as its greater distance from the centre of motion makes it more liable to sway to and fro in terrestrial undulations. With a very thick wall of porous substance to break the force of shocks, for the first story, and for the second, light and flexible building materials, falling houses from earthquakes are not as frequent as when the Spaniards first settled this country. The altos are usually furnished with balconies of lattice or venetian, and sometimes close woodwork with curtained windows, which look tasteful, airy, and convenient for the bright black eyes that peer from them on the outer world in mischievous security; but they would not suit the utilitarian architecture and incendiarism of our large cities. Even the best built of these houses could not withstand the severities of a northern climate, although well adapted to the moderate temperature and absence of rain of this. Heavy rains, and severe and quickly alternating frost and thaw, would speedily disintegrate them. The flat roofs of the better houses, formed of rafters, rough boards, and covered in most cases thickly with dried mud, are paved in some few others with brick. Two or three dormer-window looking skylights, always presenting a large funnel-like mouth toward the south, like the expanded upper part of a windsail, stand on the roof for the purpose of ventilating and lighting the rooms below, when, as is often the case, there are no side windows. This ventilator is called a *teatina*, and was the invention of the San Cayetano order of friars, for the purpose of catching the south wind invariably blowing here, and directing it below: it has shutters within, which may be closed or opened by cords suspended within reach. To a North American eye it has a clumsy and awkward appearance. The style and structure of the houses are certainly unattractive, and housewifery is equally untidy. Negligence, disorder, and dirt prevail, whether from want of servants, where most persons in Callao look like such, or from indifference and laziness, I know not; but certainly brooms, brushes, and dusters are at a discount. If such household implements be dutiable, the impost cannot be *ad valorem*, for that would involve a defeat of revenue where *value* is not recognized. It is probably owing in part to the want of use of these insect exterminators, that a traveller landing at this commercial gate of Peru, must become familiar with fleas, and submit to terrestrial torture. My constant experience is a pungent reminder of early professional duties—of minor surgical operations, phlebotomy and acupuncturation. It may be safely assumed that Peru is remarkable for insect "industrial exhibitions," and the señoras and señoritas will testify that crinoline is the great amphitheatre in which these are held. My first night here subjected me to the onslaught of a legion of fleas that preoccupied the bed, and revelled in a sanguinary saturnalia through the dark hours; some of them even ambushing themselves in shirt, drawers, and socks, to assail their victim mercilessly the next day.

The streets of Callao rarely exceed fifteen or twenty feet in width, and are paved with cobble stone, with narrow sidewalks of slab. A few of the streets in the neighborhood of the fortress are wider. A promenade—the Alameda—at the north end of a principal street, is well laid off, and when finished will be a handsome improvement. At one end of it a singular mound is seen, four or five hundred feet in diameter at its base, and gradually rising to a height of thirty feet. It is composed entirely of shingly deposit, oval-shaped, somewhat flattened, smooth, polished, unmixed with either sand or earth, and merely with the dust of human bones. From the great number of these in every stage of disintegration, it may be supposed that it was probably used by the Indians for burial purposes, and is one of the many *huacas* found in this vicinity, unless, indeed, it was the place of interment of the defenders of the castle during the long siege, when famine and pestilence did what the patriot army of Peru was unable by direct assault to accomplish—reduce a stronghold defended by an equally indomitable Castilian courage and tenacity. This shingle furnishes an inexhaustible supply of excellent paving material. It may have been rolled up by the sea, which perhaps formed an eddy here, in its ebb and flow, at some remote period, when the land had not its present relative elevation.

In regard to this subject of the comparative height of the land, my observations forbid the adoption of Dr. Darwin's opinion, that the western coast of this continent is gradually rising and encroaching on the sea, or the opposite view of other geologists, as being invariably applicable to the question at issue. For although shells of the conchyliæ, native to this sea-coast, have been found at an elevation of eighty to one hundred feet on the island of San Lorenzo, thus showing a lifting of the land, yet it is well known that the *Camotal*, now an extensive shallow between the main land and a part of the above-named island, was, since the discovery of Peru, so high above water as to have been extensively cultivated, and produced large quantities of *camotes*—sweet potatoes—whence the name of the shallow. And further, the small islands of Santo Domingo, Farallones, and Pachacamac, about seven leagues south of Callao—on the last named of which were, in 1842, ruins that may have had some connection with the great temple in that neighborhood—*formed part of the continent as promontories*, and were separated by the earthquake of 1586, the former peninsular connection now being beneath the sea. So that, while there are proofs of rising in some places, and of sinking of the land at other parts of the continent, it is most reasonable to suppose that these results, contingent on earthquakes, have been attended by varying phenomena.

The shingle of the mound before described is similar to that of which the coast barricade is formed, which has been washed up by the sea to the height, in many places, of twenty to twenty-five feet, serving the purpose of a natural breakwater to prevent inundations—to which parts of Callao would be liable at high water but for this defence.

The streets of this city are badly lighted with oil lamps. There are capitalists here who would gladly introduce gas, but the comprehensive charter of a Lima company, obtained by a system of bribery unhappily not confined to Peru, is construed into an exclusive right to illuminate the whole country. Thus the barbarians outside of the capital will probably be restricted to the means of making darkness visible, until it may suit Limenian monopolists to engage in the enterprise.

But if not well lighted, Callao may at least claim a numerous and noisy night-watch. Throughout the dark hours the cry of the *serenos* may be heard, as, pacing their beats, they, often with considerable pretension to musical execution, announce the hour and condition of the weather—"Ave Maria purissima! Viva Peru! Las dies handado y sereno!" which may be rather freely rendered, for the sake of measure, thus:

Holy Virgin! may Peru e'er be seen!
The hour is ten—the evening is serene.

A different condition of weather causes the watchman to vary his cry, but that seldom happens.

The churches are all Roman Catholic, and are destitute of architectural merit. The largest of them is now undergoing repair of extensive damage from a recent earthquake, the severest known here for nearly a century, and which destroyed many houses, and caused a general smashing of crockery and glass. *Chorillos*, the fashionable resort for sea-bathing, about seven miles south of Callao, it is said suffered still more; among other consequences of the shock there having been one which has given rise to a nice question of law. A house and lot were moved by the earthquake and deposited on adjacent premises. Who owns the house and lot?—a question threatening to occupy the legal mind of Peru, and pass through the courts of First Instance, Superior, and Supreme.

The most imposing structure about Callao is the old Royal Fortress—*Real Felipe*—built from 1770 to 1775, and costing the Spanish Government thirty millions of dollars; a sum so large that the king is said to have ordered, in bitter irony, a telescope to be carried to the top of his palace in Madrid that he might look at the fortification on which that enormous treasure for the period had been expended. A suspicion may have lurked under this imperial joke, partaken of under like circumstances in later times, and in governments self-boastful of purer popular element. The fortress, covering about fifteen acres of ground, is quadranguler, has very thick walls and parapet about twenty feet high, is surrounded by a wide and deep moat, and has two projecting towers of great strength at the seaward angles—the *Torreon de la Patria* and the *Torreoñ de la San Fernando.* Outside of the enclosure of the chief fortress and several hundred yards to the west of it is the smaller tower *de la Santa Rosa.* It has been stated that this royal fortress formerly mounted four hundred pieces of cannon. My conductor through it says that the number never was so great. Many of the pieces, however, were of very large calibre, and most of them were of brass. There are but forty-eight now remaining; nearly all those formerly on the fortification having been sold by a president of this republic; who, having mainly through the command of this formidable place, elevated himself to the first office of the government, and knowing from personal experience the advantage that would be given by the position to a rival who might be its commandant, determined to dismantle it and thus destroy a nursery of sedition. It was one of the last royalist defences that surrendered to the South American revolutionists in their war for independence. Many of the wealthy and faithful adherents of the Spanish crown withdrew into this stronghold during the reverses of the mother country; and not until they had stood an eighteen months' siege, suffered great privations, and had their number reduced by starvation and death from many thousands to but two hundred survivors, did they surrender; and then on terms of honorable capitulation.

The court-yards of this fortress have of late years been used for other than military purposes. Here are the custom house offices, and warehouses for the public storage of merchandise. Within its walls is found also the *Casas Matas*, a prison, than which no country has one more dismal, dirty, undisciplined, and pestiferous. It consists of three subterranean apartments, each about eighty by forty feet in extent, apparently former bomb-proofs of the fortress, with light and air admitted by one only small grated side window communicating with a vertical funnel descending from the surface of the earth above, thus effectually precluding communication with outsiders. No bedding is provided for the prisoners, and no food by the prison government. Instead of the latter, two reals—nominally twelve and a half cents each—are allowed per day to a prisoner, to purchase subsistence from victuallers who are permitted to cook and sell provisions in the prison yard. Free intercourse is allowed among those confined within, old criminals instructing novices; and there is no labor required of them inside, and only occasional "wheel barrow" work at any time on the streets and roads. There are now one hundred and fifty persons in the prison; the accused awaiting trial and the condemned undergoing punishment being indiscriminately thrown together; the certainly guilty and the possibly innocent faring alike in all things. A more odious prison system, and disgraceful den of moral and physical abomination, cannot be conceived of than this; and in the opinion of every just and rational traveller it is a reproach to the Peruvian Government.

In another part of the fortress are barracks for the accommodation of two thousand army recruits, who are here taught the drill—this being one of the chief schools of practice. They are all cholo mongrels and negroes—are armed with Minié muskets, are well uniformed, have rude bunks for sleeping, and an abundance of coarse rations. The President—Castilla—is said to take good care of those who fight *for him*. In answer to an inquiry of an officer—How long do your men serve? he said, "As long as the government wants them." To another question—Do they enlist voluntarily? he replied, "They are taken when wanted wherever they may be found and whatever they may be about, and made to serve—no questions being heeded and no answers given." The rope's end was applied to several delinquents, showing the discipline in vogue. This is a South American *Republic!* And ours of the north is affirmed to be its model!

A free hospital, that of Guadalupe, is established here for natives: foreigners are admitted on paying a per diem of four reals. It has one hundred and fifty beds, nearly all occupied. Sick paupers, soldiers, seamen, convicts—white, black, and cholo—men and boys—room together. Women have separate wards.

A favorite dance of parts of this coast is called *Zama Cueca*. It consists in two persons—male and female—standing opposite to each other, and at the sound of music making a few steps backward and forward, elegantly or otherwise according to the grace or clumsiness of the dancer, and then passing each other, turning in the act so as again to face, at the same time waving a handkerchief each over the head of the other alternately. Sometimes in the advance and retreat the parties whip at each other coquettishly, at the same time that the body is thrown into lascivious attitudes. The music of a guitar, or some ruder instrument, accompanies the dance, and also the voice of the musician in a monotonous improvising chant.

Strolling along the street last night with a friend, our attention was attracted to a large door of one of the humbler dwellings thrown wide open, and showing the front room of the house to be occupied by twenty-five or thirty men and women sitting along the sides of the room, while at its farther end facing the door was what appeared to be a rude altar consisting of a covered table, crucifix, candles, pictures of the Holy Family, and gilt paper cuttings, above which was an open coffin standing on end containing the corpse of a child a year or two old, dressed in the habiliments of death. A bandage round its body prevented it from falling forward, its hands were crossed on its breast, and a wreath of flowers was on its head, fresh, bright, and beautiful, in mockery of the half-open dimmed eyes, sunken cheeks, and marble hue and coldness of mortality below, contrasted with them. We stood looking on a strange national custom—a mark of respect here, not an act of rudeness as it would have been considered in some other countries; and shortly after, in token of the inmates' appreciation of our kindly interest in the early fate of the little innocent thus publicly exhibited, a bottle of *pisco*, and a *copeta* resembling a cordial glass, were handed out to us, that we might join the friends in honoring the memory of the departed. We moved our hats and touched the copeta to our lips. In the mean time a guitar was tuned by one of the men, who then passed it to a woman of olive complexion and long raven hair hanging dishevelled over well-turned shoulders, who we presumed to be the mother of the deceased child; and who, after striking a few plaintive notes, glided into a monotonous air, two of the company rising simultaneously and dancing in the manner of the country the Zama Cueca. The musician also gave vent to her feelings in a recitative lament, plaintively sung, touchingly describing the interesting traits of the lost one, the failure of their efforts to save its sweet life, and the resignation of its friends in view of its happier destiny. When the dance ceased, the cordial beverage of the country—pisco—was passed round, all of the company partaking; and again we were invited to join them. After this the dance was resumed by other couples to the same monotonous note and sad song, while other guests of both sexes smoked cigarettes, conversed freely, and some of them mirthfully. We left the party thus engaged, my friend, who was familiar with the usages of the country, informing me that in this manner the night would be spent, and also that they believed that their chances of eternal happiness would be increased by this presence of an angel in the little corpse they were thus singularly honoring.

The next night we witnessed the funeral of the deceased. This consisted of a procession of the friends walking in double-file after the pall-bearers, each person carrying a lantern; in this latter particular the ceremony resembling the ancient *rope* torchlight procession which gave origin to the term funeral. Hurried movement and boisterous conversation detracted from the otherwise impressive effect of the illuminated scene and solemn occasion. On arriving at the cemetery situated at Bella Vista, a long iron rod like a provision merchant's trier, was thrust into the gravel and sand to a depth of two or three feet, to ascertain if any previous interment had taken place at that spot, no stone or head-board being there to designate the resting-place of the dead. After trials in several places success finally crowned the efforts of the inspector, and no impediment being encountered, one of the pall-bearers dug a hole, in which the *angelita* was deposited and hastily covered. A last drink of the funereal pisco was taken over the grave in memory of the departed and to refresh the weary watchers, who then in procession returned home in gleesome mood; believing no doubt that they had performed the rites of sepulture in a becoming manner. Among the common people this is the usual mode of interment of a child, after a suitable celebration of its death by song and sentiment, pirouette and pisco. And fond as they are of children, and convinced of their purity and happy destiny, rather than omit honoring the event of their translation, and, appropriating to themselves the highest influence of their goodness, they will even *borrow* an angelita from an unfortunate neighbor too poor to defray the expense of a celebration, and, removing it to their own house, distinguish the occasion by a considerable outlay of money and a general "good time." It is said that these celebrations are always characterized by mingled sadness, cheerfulness, personal respect, and good will; never by the wrangling, violence, and brutality which so frequently attend the Irish wake.

Last Sunday the singular spectacle was witnessed of an ecclesiastical dignitary recently appointed Archbishop of Lima, received at Callao *with military honors.* He was on his way from Arequipa, of which he was formerly bishop, to take possession of the metropolitan see, and landed here under a salute of artillery; a rabble crowd, black, white, and undistinguishable, pressing forward apparently seeking the martyrdom of being crushed to death, or trampled under foot, in striving for the privilege of kissing his most reverend hand, extended for the purpose as he hastened by with an indifference or contempt befitting such servility. In Lima a grand parade attended his reception; the clergy dressed in fantastic canonicals, and many thousands of the populace, particularly black and mulatto women, repairing to the railroad station to welcome him with burning incense, and to strew his way with flowers as he passed along making the sign of the cross, while the deluded people exclaimed, " Gracios a Dios, ya mi taitita me echo la bendicion " —Thanks be to God, my father has at last bestowed on me his benediction. The examples of personal degradation seen on this occasion showed that these people have made no step forward in the true dignity of human nature since they shook off the Spanish yoke. When the simple sacrifice of a lowly spirit to God is all that is demanded for His service by divine law, enlightened conviction and pure religious sentiment could not fail to be offended by the *public lavation* of the archbishop at the cathedral to remove his *bodily impurities*, ere consecration by being robed in bedizened vestments transferred on silver waiters by episcopal hands, which alone were fitted for the mysteries of the sacred toilet. And surely neither good taste nor good sense could approve of a street parade for three days by priests and people, for the purpose of propitiating the favor of the Almighty against a recurrence of the earthquake of October, 1746; the absurdity of the parade being heightened by the superstitious multitude conveying in procession to every church in the city a painting of " Señor de los Milagros," which is said to have been miraculously saved on that occasion, when the church to which it belonged was destroyed—God, as is here believed, having interposed in behalf of this valued specimen of the fine arts, although He declined to do so in favor of the church dedicated to His service. Following this sainted picture were thousands of people, who addressed it their prayers, sought its blessings, and enveloped it in clouds of incense from a hundred censers, swung, it cannot be said with truth, by the *fair* hands of women, for most of them were *dingy;* while many had the hue of darkness typical of their minds.

I am told, but shall not be here to see, that according to annual custom there will soon be a similar celebration in Callao, on which occasion an effigy called "Señor del Mar," duly dressed and decorated, will be carried in religious procession to all the churches, and then to the sea-shore, for the purpose of conciliating the "vasty deep," and obtaining absolution from the punishment once before incurred for sin, when a great wave washed away this town. The event was a sad one—earth and sea appearing to have conspired to destroy those of the Spanish race whose crimes and cruelties, in their dominion in this country, dimmed the lustre of their discoveries.

You of the north realize a "firm-set earth," but here its heavings and vibrations are terribly demonstrative. Proofs are perpetually repeated in the south to show that the solid earth can "melt, thaw, and resolve itself;" that its crust has been broken up by subterranean forces, and its dissolved materials, carrying with them the tenants of lower levels, have risen to unwonted heights; while other parts have sunk, burying their inhabitants beneath the ruins of cities, leaving desolation and the dirge of the retiring wave where but a few moments before were the pomp of the festival and the exultant peal of the Te Deum.

On the night of October 28, 1746, while the feasts of two of the Apostles were being celebrated, St. Simon and St. Judas —the latter a model of many political disciples of modern times in bribery if not in suicide—a series of earthquakes commenced, during the one hundred and twelve days' continuance, of which four hundred and thirty shocks occurred, shaking the foundations of earth, and threatening total destruction to the cities throughout this portion of South America. *Three minutes* of that time sufficed to destroy Lima almost entirely; and

Callao, in the same brief period, was utterly overwhelmed, for what the earthquake did not throw down and dash to pieces, an ocean wave, leaping its accustomed barriers, and sweeping over the devoted city, totally destroyed, entombing in the sepulchres of their demolished houses and churches, nearly five thousand persons. But two hundred of the population of this chief seaport of Peru escaped death, a few of whom were on a bastion of the fortress of strength sufficient to resist the shock, and the remainder were washed on the island of San Lorenzo. In wandering over the plain where Callao formerly stood, nearer to the southern shore and to the extremity of the peninsula called Callao Point than the present city, the ruins were still seen; mouldering brick and bone mingling their dust, and blown hither and thither, the sport of the idle wind, telling of the emptiness of earthly splendor, and the uncertainty and brevity of life; while this remnant of mortality—perhaps of beauty and of power—serves also an inglorious use of the builder, furnishing, indeed, the chief material of mud plaster.

> "Oh that the earth, which kept the world in awe,
> Should patch a wall to expel the winter's flaw!"

Parts of a few nearly-buried arches are still visible. Into one of the best preserved of these I descended, and found a large number of human bones, which, with the substantial masonry of the arch, justifies the opinion that this was probably a part of the substructure of the cathedral, a portion of a vault, perhaps, in which deceased prelates and others of the clergy had been buried, according to Catholic usage. But a careful examination of these relics revealed so many bones of women and younger persons, as to lead to the conclusion that as the first shock of the earthquake was felt at the hour at which the religious ceremonial of the feast referred to was in progress, probably many of the worshippers, young and old, descended to the vaults of the church, as well from confidence in them as places of security from the unusual strength of the foundation, as from their sanctity, which superstition would be apt to clothe with protective power. But although sheltered from the falling building, they could not escape the ocean deluge which instantly followed the shock of the earthquake, and they thus perished by drowning.

It is said by some travellers that a part of the ruins of old Callao may be seen on a calm and bright day, at the bottom of "Mar Brava"—rough sea—south of Callao promontory. Others deny that these are visible at that place, and with more reason, for not only do the few remaining ruins clearly indicate the location of the former town, but if any part of old Callao had been situated at the spot where ruins are supposed by the fanciful to be submerged, they certainly could not have remained there to this time, because, constructed chiefly of reed, adobe, and mud, the materials of the houses would have been speedily washed away by this very rough arm of the ocean, beating constantly and wildly under the pressure of an unchanging south wind on the stony barricade erected by itself along the shore. Even if hard brick walls had been there overthrown, these would have been rounded by incessant water action and attrition, and thrown upon the beach; but none such are found among the wide-spread gravel and boulders, to tell like the latter a tale of origin and action—whence they came and how they reached the shore. Ere long Cowper's description of man's perishable vanities will apply to old Callao:

> "We build with what we deem eternal rock:
> A distant age asks where the fabric stood;
> And in the dust sifted and searched in vain
> The undiscoverable secret sleeps."

It is not without uncomfortable apprehension that one strolls over this vast charnel-house, and surveys the testimonials of an instantaneous and fearful sacrifice to offended right and justice. For who can doubt that punishment was the desert of the Spaniards, who, in their subjugation of the ancient Peruvians, shamelessly violated these, and indulged in the grossest atrocities? And yet with witnesses of evil and proofs of error around them, the people of this land continue to cling to the chief idol which has hitherto led and still directs them in dark and devious ways. So, too, they continue to be rocked by terrestrial convulsion, the type of those which so often cause their political and social systems to tremble, and which will never become firmly and happily established until religious inculcations and observances more in consonance with the principles and precepts of the Christianity of the Bible shall guide them.

## CHAPTER VI.

### CALLAO AND LIMA RAILROAD.—CITY OF LIMA.

Formerly the journey from Callao to Lima, although a distance of scarcely seven miles, was both disagreeable and dangerous; for if travellers were not suffocated with dust, they were almost certain to be robbed or murdered by highwaymen, who then infested the route, and, in bold defiance or with the connivance of government, levied contributions on them. Now, the greater comfort and safety of a railroad are enjoyed, and passengers are conveyed to the capital in thirty or forty minutes, at a half-dollar fare, exclusive of baggage, which, if the bulk of a trunk, costs as much more. The road has but a single track, with an ascending grade, from the coast to Lima—seven miles—of four hundred and ninety-eight feet. Twelve trains run each way daily, yielding, at the lowest estimate, five hundred dollars per day net profit. The road belongs to Señor Candamo, the wealthiest citizen of Peru, who owns two-thirds of the stock, and an English capitalist, who owns the remaining third, except one share belonging to another person, who has refused $20,000 offered for it by Señor Candamo. He has a fancy to pry into the mystery of management and receipts, commonly an enigma to stockholders. The above-mentioned profit does not include the freight on merchandise, which is not as large as might be expected between the principal seaport and the capital, for the reason that the owners of the railroad have been intimidated by threats of negro and cholo *arrieros* and *carreteros*, and they have sought to conciliate these dangerous enemies by restricting the carriage of merchandise, allowing the most of it to find its way by mule caravans and the clumsy old-fashioned carts of the country, seen by the railroad passengers, trudging and trundled on the Lima turnpike, running parallel nearly the entire length, at from one to two miles an hour, knee deep and hub deep in ruts, and enveloped in clouds of dust.

The fields and meadows on each side of the railway are enclosed by low adobe walls; the soil is a dark rich-looking loam, and the vegetation near to Lima looks exceedingly luxuriant, especially where the thickly-clustered tropical fruit trees are seen growing.

About a mile and a half from Callao the road passes the village of Bellavista, formerly the fashionable country residence of the wealthy inhabitants, and near to which is the only Protestant cemetery in Peru. A commodious hospital for foreign seamen is located at this place; also a naval foundry; and it was here that the Chileans, in their last war with Peru, erected the batteries for bombarding the fortress of Callao, which soon after was surrendered. Near Bellavista may be seen a rude wooden cross planted on a mound, to mark the spot, as tradition says, to which a Spanish frigate was carried and wrecked by the sea, which finished the work of destruction nearly completed by the earthquake in 1746. Farther on another cross indicates the spot to which the wave ascended the inclined plane toward the mountains.

Nearer Lima the remains of old canals used for irrigation are seen, and also the once celebrated Alameda, with its central drive and lateral promenades, bordered by shade trees, and having turn-outs and stone benches for the wayworn and lounger. This avenue was designed by its founder, the Viceroy Higgins, to be completed the entire distance to Callao, in the same style of convenience and adornment seen near Lima; but his death arrested the progress of the work, and the railroad is now likely to convert it into a dilapidated monument of the past.

The railroad enters the city abruptly at its southwest quarter, and the passenger finds himself without the usual suburban approach suddenly in close contact with mud walls and compactly built mud houses, demanding a strict observance of a "notice" once seen in an American railroad car, "don't put your head or *feet* out the window." On reaching the station, the traveller, on extricating himself from the motley crowd, among whom he has taken the chances of suffocation from cigar smoke, if the windows should be closed, and from the dust of a rainless region, if they should be open, will find cholos as eager to take his baggage as those nuisances of American railroads and steamboats, called porters, and that is saying enough to convince him of the propriety of watching his valuables. Two dollars per trunk, and five for a hack to the hotel, are the penalties of being a foreigner, unless Spanish enough can be mustered to strike a bargain beforehand.

My observations must be *posted* without keeping a *day-book.* The moments thus bestowed are those only incidentally falling by the wayside of necessary official engagements. Hence, if note of time were made, the proof of how rapidly it is passing would prove annoying without adding to the interest of what I have to say. So that there shall be no occasion to mourn over the wasted moments of the present, nor to lament the collective sum of the past and future, we should be content.

Lima, the capital of Peru, was founded by Don Francisco Pizarro, in January, 1534, on the day celebrated by the Roman Church as the Epiphany, or feast of the worshipping of the kings or magi of the east, and hence called by him *La Ciudad de los Reyes*, the city of the kings. Pizarro being desirous of planting a city on the sea-coast, sent officers to select a suitable site; and the Bay of Callao affording a safe harbor and other commercial facilities, as well as being sufficiently central in view of territorial acquisition, they followed the river Rimac, which empties into the northern part of the bay, and finding that it flowed through a fertile valley on the slope of the western foot hills of the Andes, and furnished a bountiful supply of pure water, they recommended the southern bank of that stream, two leagues from the coast, as a suitable site, on which Pizarro accordingly ordered the city to be built.

The present name of the capital, Lima, is derived from and is considered a softened corruption of Rimac, the Indian name of the river. The valley, we are told by Stevenson, an English traveller of great intelligence, was called by the aborigines *Rimac Malca*, the place of witches, it being the custom among them to banish to this valley persons accused of witchcraft. But Prescott ("History of the Conquest of Peru") states that the word Rimac signifies in the Quichua tongue, "*one who speaks*, from a celebrated shrine situated there, and much resorted to by Indians for the oracles delivered by its idol." I cannot venture to decide the point of difference between these authors. But it may be said in this connection, that Mr. Prescott is in error in stating that "the capital was somewhat less than two leagues from its (the river's) mouth, which expanded into a commodious haven for the commerce that the eye of the founder saw would one day float on its waters." The distance is *not* less than two leagues from the mouth of the river to the city, nor does the Rimac expand and form any part of the harbor whatever: it is insignificant for such a purpose; a fishing-boat can scarcely navigate the shallows at its mouth; while the truly "commodious haven for the commerce" that centres here is on a scale of extent and depth becoming an arm of the ocean it really is, with islands and promontories as natural breakwaters against the heavy swells and fierce winds which sometimes endanger shipping on other parts of this coast. It would be as just to regard the Gulf of Mexico as the "expanded mouth" of the Mississippi River, as the Bay of Callao that of the Rimac.

Although Lima is but 12° 2′ south of the equator, the temperature is not excessive, and is so equable as not to vary more than 25° throughout the year; 60° of Fahrenheit being the lowest, and 85° the highest indicated by the thermometer during several years, as shown by the carefully kept record of Sr. Pas Soldan, a resident of the capital, as distinguished for his scientific attainments as for his enlightened patriotism. Thus March is shown to have been the hottest, and July the coldest month of this part of the southern hemisphere. A corresponding equable temperature prevails in Callao. An examination of the meteorological registers of the United States men-o'-war "Wyoming" and "Narraganset," the detention of which in the harbor of Callao in the year 1860, embraced a joint period of eight months, from June to January inclusive, showed that the minimum temperature was but 59° (in August), and the maximum 78°, a variation of but 19°. And Mr. Decourcy, of Callao, informed me that a diary kept by him for ten years reported but 10° variation for any one year, marked by a thermometer hung in a non-conducting mud mansion, and exposed neither to reflected rays of the sun nor to currents of air, the lowest degree having been 62°, and the highest 72°. An extraordinary uniformity, perhaps unsurpassed in any part of the world.

In attempting to account for the equable climate of Lima and its vicinity, we must seek the probable explanation, first, in the influence of the neighboring snow-capped mountains, and the unvarying southerly breeze, in modifying a solar heat which in a corresponding latitude of the northern hemisphere is almost insupportable; and secondly, in the scarcely varying temperature of the vast ocean which washes these shores, and with which the same wind comes freighted to moderate the cold of winter. Doubtless the absence of rain may also account in part for the fact that no sudden transitions of temperature are known here. Dews, amounting at times to heavy mists, fall at night, dampening the atmosphere often for several hours after sunrise. These yield the required moisture for the luxuriant vegetation of the valley, but they are detrimental to health, and counteract the otherwise beneficial influence of this equable climate over pulmonary diseases.

The streets of Lima, in its central districts, run corresponding to the points of the compass, crossing at right angles; those of the suburbs are without regularity. Their width varies from twenty to thirty feet, and they are paved with hard rubble stone, having sidewalks from three to four feet wide, of flat stone, singularly enough imported from England, labor being too costly, or the natives too lazy to quarry granite found in inexhaustible beds a few miles east of the city.

The river Rimac, running from east to west, divides the city into two parts. One, the larger portion, embracing four-fifths of the city, is situated south of the river; and enclosed as it is by an adobe wall twelve feet high, with gates and bastions now in process of dilapidation, which touches the southern bank of the Rimac, by its extreme ends east and west, it presents a semicircular shape, the length being about two miles and its width but little over one. The other and smaller part is the irregular shaped suburb of San Lazaro, forming the remaining one-fifth of the city, and situated on the north side of the river, being united to the larger part by a substantial stone bridge, five hundred feet long, resting on six heavy piers, and which has withstood uninjured the destructive earthquakes that have visited the capital.

Lima has a general declivity from southeast to northwest, and those streets which run from east to west, and some few running from south to north, have in the middle canals, about two feet wide, walled, and arched in places to allow of vehicles crossing to opposite sides of the street, but open above throughout the intervening extent. These canals are called *acequias*, and through them run streams of water introduced by natural flow from the Rimac, the declivity allowing an uninterrupted passage, the river heading about fifty miles east among the mountains, and having a rapid fall the whole distance from its source to the sea.

Probably these acequias were originally intended to convey through the city pure water for domestic use, cleanliness, and general hygiene. But they are now the depositories of all sorts of garbage and filth; and by the disregard of municipal regulations forbidding such use except after midnight, they have become, without reference to time, the substitutes of water-closets, the latter rarely being found, the night-bucket forming the usual intermedium, and the direct use of the acequia a not uncommon custom in the less respectably inhabited parts of the city. These aqueducts, indeed, have degenerated into public cesspools, revolting to decency, repugnant to comfort, and detrimental to health; distributing the foul contents and poisonous malaria wherever a stream meanders; and if perchance this, from obstruction, should cease to flow, there results an abiding and intolerable offensiveness. The acequias are the favorite resorts of that most obnoxious of the feathered family, turkey buzzards, the municipal scavengers and privileged proprietors not merely of these pestiferous premises, but also of the arcade and house-tops, and the church towers, from which they complacently survey their domain below, and swoop down to their repast whenever the uprising stench of a deposit announces the spread of another foul banquet. That malignant yellow fever, with such a source of pestilence in its midst, should have prevailed in this city a few years since, is not surprising, although in this mild climate and with ordinary attention to public hygiene, and domestic and personal cleanliness, that disease could never have originated here, nor spread if imported. It is unpleasant to refer to these things, but it is only by considering their habits and municipal regulations, that the condition of a people can be determined.

The houses of Lima, like those of Callao, are of a structure demanded by its climate and liability to earthquakes. The latter requires that they should be built of unusually massive and strong walls, capable of resisting shocks, or of yielding and elastic materials, adapting themselves to terrestrial movement, and recovering their original condition. As the former mode of building would be too costly for ordinary dwelling-houses, it is used only for churches, prisons, and the most expensive edifices, and even for these only in the lower story; the upper, when such exists, having the lighter materials of ordinary dwellings. Dwellings are of two classes, according to the rank and wealth of their proprietors. The common kind are of very simple construction, usually one story in height, built on a line with the street, or in long rows at right angles with it, and communicating therewith by a court or *cul-de-sac.* A scantling frame is first put up, the interspaces of which are filled with split Guayaquil cane, or with the wild cane of Peru, *cana brava*, these either being passed through holes bored in the timbers above and below, and arranged parallel and near to each other, or interlaced obliquely, according to the fancy of the builder. Upon both sides of this framework a plaster is spread, consisting of mud mixed with cut straw or chaff. Partitions are made of split cane and mud plaster, separating one or more apartments. Chimneys in such houses are dispensed with, the mildness of the climate rendering artificial heat unnecessary for personal comfort, and the yard, when such is found, being the primitive kitchen of the common people. A door, and a window, often without glass, and grated with iron bars, together with roof of thatched flags, or plank covered with mud several inches thick, complete the building. Two stories and several apartments are sometimes found, built of like materials, floored, and generally more commodious and comfortable.

The residence of a wealthy inhabitant occupies the four sides of a square open court, or *patio*, as it is called, the approach to which is by a well-secured gateway large enough to admit a carriage, and usually guarded by a porter. The court is tastefully paved with small rubble stone, or with the bleached vertebræ, or other small bones of animals, arranged so as to form ornamental figures. The house, one or two stories high, has galleries facing the court, the *alto*, when it exists, being protected by a projecting roof, and having a stairway leading to its gallery, which gives access to the upper rooms, all of which open on the gallery. The alto in front is provided, also, with a latticed or glass window balcony above the gateway, something like a bay-window overlooking the street, which serves the very important purpose of ladies' observatory. The principal material of these houses is usually sun-dried bricks, adobes, for the lower story, the wall of which is very thick, though sometimes the entire building even of this class is framework and cane, the stucco of the inside being not so coarse as that in common use. Wall paper hides the defects of the interior plastering, and partitions are made of board covered with papered canvas. In Lima, as in Callao, the mud roof is preferred as the best non-conductor of heat in warm weather, but plank and cement roofs are also used. The invariably flat roof is often furnished with a *mirador*—a look-out. Occasionally a first-class residence is seen tolerably well frescoed, and neatly, conveniently, and even luxuriously arranged and furnished. They certainly have an advantage over North American city residences, in that they have no steep, narrow, and endless stairways to climb. The wealthy light their mansions with gas, and a very few have, also, water introduced into their houses; but both are used at an exorbitant charge: for gas, nine dollars per one thousand cubic feet; for water, fifty dollars per annum for a single flow. The streets are well lighted by gas. If there be stabling on the premises, it occupies a small court behind the dwelling, and is accessible only through the front gateway and patio. Cellars are not dug. Earth so near the lower floor would be detrimental to health, but that it is always dry in this rainless climate. Necessary out-buildings, common among the lower classes of North Americans, are not found in Lima, and a modern water-closet is unknown, from which there result great discomfort, injury to health, and public as well as private indecency. A stranger, accustomed to the observances of a higher civilization, in passing along thoroughfares of this capital, cannot avoid offence to his delicacy; and a municipal regulation tolerates the weekly call at houses by an incorporated French company, in the broad face of day, for revolting contributions that have failed to find their way into the filthy acequias, and are perpetually passing by drayloads through crowded business streets, to the disgust of foreigners and the annoyance of well-bred citizens.

The many cracked, inclined, warped, and twisted houses seen in Lima, attest the force by which they have been tried; and show the discretion of the people in sacrificing appearance to security, and in seeking the best means of guarding against the effects of that power which heaves the granite foundations of the earth, lifts and sunders its crust, and moves even the ocean to its will. North American thin walls of brittle materials, ambitious of height and often measuring the ambition of vulgar owners, would crumble into fragments under the might of a Peruvian earthquake, involving all, property and people, in destruction. But secure against ordinary danger by architectural ingenuity, and having the accessible patio to escape to in the event of threatened demolition of his house, the patriotic Limeño would rather take the risk of the earth's ague paroxysm than not to make a sensation in the world. He seems to have pleasure in knowing that his country can get up a phenomenon that cannot be equalled elsewhere.

Hotels! What shall be said of them? Send a live Yankee down here, with plenipotentiary powers to take Maury's Hotel Français, Morin's Hotel, Hotel de la Bola de Oro, Hotel de l'Europe, and Hotel l'Universo, and put them together; let him turn them inside out, expel the fleas, drive out the billiard and rochambor tables and their devotees from the best and most public apartments, and get rid of the worthless cholo apologies for servants; let him bring clean table and bed linen, and not forget a lot of Irish chambermaids and a cargo of well-trained waiters of the genuine sable standard; let him have full authority to do all things in general and every thing in particular as he may decide to be according to the last New York model; and above all, let him bring with his characteristic shrewdness, intelligence, energy, activity, and go-ahead-ativeness, that ethical element so hard for hotel keepers to compass, to wit: conscience enough to charge but twice the worth of a thing, and there would then be one house of refuge for the way-worn traveller such as Lima has not seen, and is not likely to possess by any other process. It would be a waste of words to describe the present hotels of this capital. What do you think of a hotel in which, if you are not a billiard player, you must either go to your chamber or into the street? Without parlor, reading room, or reception room, for a weary guest to sit in; without a servant to wait on you except at table, or a bell to ring for one even if he could be had. Indeed, the possession of a house bell is the singular exception to the rule. The American Minister's residence has one, and it serves to remind his wandering countrymen of the conveniences of home. Indeed, bell-metal appears to have been all used in the manufacture of church bells, and it may be that the natives have come to the sage conclusion that they make noise enough for the whole city. It may be safely assumed that if Paradise is to be won by perpetual peals from tower and tinklings at the altar, surely the people of Lima have a cheery prospect ahead, for the former cease only to call the faithful to the house of prayer, that the latter may remind them when there of their duties as worshippers; and so a continuous religious ceremonial, in which bell-metal performs a chief part, is in progress from morning until night.

A few words more about hotels—for even among evils there is a choice. If, then, fate should direct your steps to this city of filth, festivals, and fleas—and the rest of Christendom can produce none such as the last mentioned for numbers, magnitude, and ferocity, and it is doubtful if Mohammedan Turkey can—seek Maury's Hotel Français; there, and there only, you may stand a chance of not compromising your character for chastity, and of retiring to your chamber without a *tapada* insisting on accompanying you to cheer the loneliness of night. But as you will be charged for every thing that you get, and many that you do not get, from the *portero's* fee when you enter the front gate, to his unconscionable exaction when you pass out; for the modicum of candle which lights you to bed, to that which should light you when you have to go in the dark; and many things unnecessary to specify now, but which *will be* specified in the bill of whoever shall go there, it may be useful to assist you in the settlement of your account by giving some information about Peruvian currency. As strangers are expected to pay liberally for the benefits and pleasures of travel, it is not to be presumed that they will have any use for lesser values, nevertheless they may be named.

SILVER COIN.

| | | | |
|---|---|---|---|
| Cuartillo, ($\frac{1}{4}$ Real.) | equal to | $3\frac{1}{8}$ | cents. |
| Medio, ($\frac{1}{2}$ Real.) | " | $6\frac{1}{4}$ | " |
| Real, | " | $12\frac{1}{2}$ | " |
| Peceta, | " | 25 | " |
| Peso, | " | 1 | dollar. |

GOLD COIN.

| | | | |
|---|---|---|---|
| Cuartillo de oro, | equal to | $1\frac{1}{16}$ | dollars. |
| Escudo, | " | $2\frac{1}{8}$ | " |
| Doblon, | " | $4\frac{1}{4}$ | " |
| Media onza, | " | $8\frac{1}{2}$ | " |
| Onza, | " | 17 | " |

There is no Peruvian money being coined at this time; and the little of former dates in circulation is rapidly disappearing before the more debased Bolivian currency. Small change is scarce, and dealers substitute it by halving reals for medios, and these latter they cut again for cuartillos. The paper issue unhappily sometimes known in our own country in violation of its organic law—the Constitution—which gives the Government only the power "to *coin* money and regulate the value thereof;" which prohibits the emission of "bills of credit," and makes nothing "but gold and silver coin a tender in payment of debts;"

the unlawful representative of value, which, on each recurring mercantile crisis causing a suspension of specie payments, favors rogues and defrauds the honest, has no existence in Peru. Arbitrary and absolute as is this Government's disregard of constitutional provisions, yet it has not ventured on such an extreme of usurpation as to trample under foot the legal standards of value, and to substitute an illusive invention of financial craft for the precious metals. It recognizes the truth that international commerce demands, and will have, *actuality* of value; and whatever its other tyranny, it has stopped short of the oppression which would enforce the circulation among its own people of that which itself will not receive in payment of imposts, and which it could not become a purchaser with in a foreign market. In the matter of currency, at least, this Government has set an example of justice and consistency to some others of loftier pretension, however faulty in fulfilment.

The scarcity of small change does not appear to restrain the national propensity for gambling, shown by the almost daily drawing of lotteries adapted to the means of the poorer people, who would rather go without food than lose the *chance* of getting a prize by staking their real or medio. The streets swarm with lottery ticket venders, crying at the top of their voices the tempting prizes—"Mil pecos! para mañana." "Mil pecos! para luego." "Quarto mil pecos! para lunes." These venders are the pests of the streets. No one is free from their importunities. They are like the newsboys of large American cities; you cannot turn round without running against one. In the restaurant, the hotel, the market, even at the church door, one is buttonholed and ceaselessly screamed at—"Mil pecos! para mañana." Great as the national vice of gambling has always been, it is said to be actually increasing. Nor is it likely to diminish among the lower classes while those in high official stations and of great social influence, encourage, as they do, the practice by public example, staking thousands on the turn of a card, even in the presence of their wives and children. If General Castilla is the chief gambler as well as the chief magistrate of Peru, losing sixty thousand dollars a night and drawing his draft as President on an English Banking House for its payment next morning, what is to be expected but that his supporters will become his imitators in official fraud as well as in the base habit of seeking another's fortune at the cost of possible impoverishment of his family? And what can be hoped for in a claim for indemnity for national outrage against such an Executive but prevarication, quibbling, and delay, which have characterized his conduct in the negotiation now about to be closed by our national self-respect?

Those who spend their small earnings, and what they can beg or borrow, in the licensed street-gambling of lotteries, are of the lower classes of the populace. But as the classification of society here differs from any of which you have personal knowledge, it is proper to say in what it consists. And premising that it rests rather on the comparative superiority of blood—the natural distinction of race—than upon any adventitious circumstances, it may be sufficient to say that the aboriginal race was the Indian; and that subsequently there came into this country the Spaniard, then the Negro, and recently the Chinaman, to enable one to come to tolerably correct conclusions as to results, when it is added that the proposal of North American miscegenation has in South America been practically applied. To wit:

The White and Indian have given to Peru the *mestizo*.

White and Negro, the *mulatto*.

White and Chinese, the *chino-blanco*.

Indian and Chinese, the *chino-cholo*.

Negro and Chinese, the *zambo-chino*.

Indian and Negro, the *chino*.

White and mulatto, the *cuarteron*.

White and mestiza, the *creole*—so called here, but altogether different from the creole of the Southern States of North America.

Indian and mulatto, the *chino-oscuro*.

Indian and mestiza, the *mestizo-claro*.

Negro and mulatto, the *zambo-negro*.

Negro and mestiza, the *mulatto-oscuro*.

With these data, and knowing that the created distinctions of the primary races have been shamelessly disregarded by man, and that the baser passions have subverted reason, sentiment, and sympathy, the many modifications of admixture and relative proportions of blood may be surmised, which characterize a population presenting a greater variety of tints, of physical and mental endowments, than can be found probably elsewhere in the world. The definitive terms Spaniard, Cholo, Zambo, Negro, are generally heard, to signify the White, Indian, Mixed, and Black, but it is becoming customary to designate all except the anthropological antipodes—Caucasian and Negro—as *cholos;* and thus the originally mild, inoffensive, industrious, and provident Indian people, will probably soon have to father all the physical and moral debasement resulting from this indiscriminate crossing of original races and this corrupted progeny; all the feebleness, vicious organization, and defective vitality of the mongrel element proceeding from violations of the laws of creation; producing, too, perpetual conflicts, both in social and political life, until those laws shall be vindicated, as they inevitably will be, and the outrages inflicted upon nature as well as upon the original Indian race, shall be repaired by the extinction of all title to perpetuity on the part of the numerically weak, and the aboriginal element still dominant on this part of the continent shall be restored to the condition it held at the time of the Spanish conquest. And this event will be hastened by the late act of the Peruvian Government emancipating the negro slaves, who have consequently become, according to the testimony of observing and intelligent citizens, a curse to the country and to themselves—robbers, assassins, drunkards, and general disturbers of the public peace. Idle and debased, they are passing through a transition of barbarism to extinction, a final event contemplated with satisfaction by all who are interested in the social elevation, political stability, and general prosperity of Peru.

Another evil resulting from the legislative abolition of judicious and responsible control over so large, and when freed from disciplinary restraints so disturbing an element of society, and from the withdrawal of this labor from industrial pursuits, especially of rural districts, is the importation of Chinese Coolies to supply the wants of agriculture. Thus, instead of a system of servitude, in which it was the interest of the planter to cherish and protect, from physical and moral evils, the laborer, whose life and well-being were the measure of his own prosperity, one has been introduced attended with unprecedented cruelties. In fact, the importation of Coolies has taken the place of the African slave trade, with an aggravation of the sufferings of the "middle passage," as shown by the startling proportion of deaths on the voyage, and the frightful picture of emaciation and disease on landing in Peru. And when sold into temporary slavery, which has been glossed to dazzle dupes with the term "free apprenticeship," it is to learn that the more work can be forced from him during his term of service, and the scantier his food and clothing, the larger will be the employer's profits—there being actually no motive of interest in husbanding the Coolie's resources of health and life beyond the limit of the bond. Hence the treatment he receives on the hacienda, which is his territorial prison during the term of service which consumes the prime of his years, is characterized by great inhumanity. The task-masters of Coolies are negroes or mulattoes, whose natural insensibility and proclivity to cruelty fit them for drivers; and who, it is the general opinion here, seem to consider that if the Coolie succumbs to the severity of discipline, and becomes enfeebled or diseased, it is better by additional severity to rid the hacienda of him altogether—giving him the choice solely of death, or seeking the cold charity of strangers. Hence the frequent meeting of impoverished and emaciated Chinamen on the streets of Lima; and the pitiful spectacle presented by the poor wretches in the pest-house of the *Refugio.*

The Limeñians of pure Spanish descent, and especially the women, are quick in detecting any shade of the innumerable adulterations of blood, however slight the deterioration; and priding themselves upon their nobler race and their freedom from taint, they may be excused the very common weakness of announcing the discovery of another's misfortune. The white skin is the badge of superiority universally recognized, notwithstanding the pronunciamentos of *equality* by aspiring military chieftains, to conciliate the brutal blacks and mongrels, who have thus become *the ready instruments of revolutions and the agents in a de facto political enslavement of the nation.* In countries boasting of constitutional government, there has yet been no such utter disregard of law and personal rights, no such bold and unblushing executive encroachment on the prerogatives of coördinate branches of the Government, both legislative and judicial, as in Peru. By Presidential command, the army, armed police, and battalions of negro cargadores and aquadores, march to the polls on days of election, and excluding all by threat and violence who differ with those exercising official power, fulfil the prearranged programme of the Executive. The halls of national legislation have been closed by Castilla's order, and fixed bayonets gleaming in the black hands of a *republican* tyrant's tools have prevented the exit of deputies, until, under threat, they have revoked decrees passed in conformity with constitutional right, and offensive alone to his despotic will. Elections in distant parts of the State have been annulled by the President when his favorites and partisans were not returned; judgments in international questions have been rendered in courts in obedience to his instructions, and have afterwards been quoted in diplomatic discussions as judicial decisions demanding his official recognition and fulfilment; and wars have been declared, and decrees of imprisonment and banishment violative of personal rights, proclaimed and enforced against citizens obnoxious to his suspicion and jealousy, proving the actual Government an absolute despotism rather than a constitutional republic. Events transpiring here, from day to day, may well suggest the inquiry, What have Peruvians gained by casting off the monarchical yoke of Spain, unless it be the privilege of *voluntary submission to a Presidential yoke not less galling, and going to destruction in their own way?*

Near the centre of the city is the public square, dignified by the name *Plaza Mayor.* The great square embraces about four acres. It is neither enclosed, paved, nor adorned, except by a monumental fountain, consisting of a column supporting a figure of Fame spouting water from its trumpet, which falls with that issuing from other parts of the column and its ornamental appendages into a capacious basin, whence it is taken by *aquadors*—water-carriers. For its transportation two kegs are placed endwise in hoops, attached to a pack-saddle on the back of a donkey. The aquador, armed with a formidable prop-stick for supporting one keg when he removes the other, and which is freely used for beating his little beast also, mounts behind the load, his feet often trailing on the ground, and thus he traverses the city furnishing the indispensable element at about a real the load. Several other fountains, of less pretensions, all supplied, as is the principal one, by water from the river Rimac, through pipes, are located in other parts of the city.

The patient and much-abused donkey is the chief agent in the general carrying trade of the city; whether it be milk, bread, fruit, meat, grass, charcoal, wood, adobes, earth, reed, or other useful and ornamental articles requiring transportation, the indispensable donkey and his pannier are brought into requisition. And it is interesting to observe with what intelligence and safety he performs his task; large caravans, with but one driver, threading the narrow, and at times nearly obstructed streets, in single file, and with an obedience and precision deserving of more considerate and merciful treatment than they usually receive from their brutal negro task-masters; who seem to have been relieved in Peru from compulsory labor only to become the more cruel in their inflictions upon animals but little less intelligent, and far more useful and amenable to authority, than themselves.

On the north, south, and west sides of the plaza, are arcades in front of the houses, covering the sidewalks, which are here wider than elsewhere, and handsomely paved with marble tiles. These arcades, columned and arched toward the plaza, form sheltered promenades for the fashionables, who resort here as well for pleasure and sight-seeing as to make purchases at the fancy and other shops that border the arcades, and brilliantly illuminate them at night with their show-window gas-lights. On the north side of the plaza, behind the shops, is a court-yard, with a portal guarded by armed soldiers, and over which floats the national flag. Around this space are the buildings for the accommodation of the criminal court, the office of the

Intendente, and the former Viceroy's palace, now the official residence of the President of Peru, but unoccupied by General Castilla, who continues to reside in his private mansion in another part of the city. The whole block on the north side of the plaza is called Palace Square, but it has neither grandeur nor extent to justify the name. The archbishop's palace has a slight claim to consideration as such. All others called palaces are built of common materials, and are unimposing, squatty, and dirty-looking edifices. On the west side of the plaza there is found nothing worthy of mention. Nor is the south side remarkable for aught except, about the middle of it, the entrance to *el callejon de petateros*—mat-maker's alley—the site of Pizarro's palace; where, on the 26th June, 1541, he was, after an extraordinary career as a discoverer and a conqueror, and the acquisition of an influence and power only second to those of his sovereign, assassinated by a band of eighteen or twenty conspirators; who, as unfortunate followers of Almagro, the former companion in arms of the conqueror, but subsequently basely murdered by his brother Hernando Pizarro, had followed their young chieftain, Diego, the son of Almagro, to his compulsory confinement in Lima. And being disappointed in long-expected redress of their grievances, and indignant at the ridicule, scorn, and contumely heaped upon them by the officials and companions of Pizarro, finally determined, by a bold assault, to rid Peru of one they considered a tyrant, and thus release themselves and friends from intolerable oppression. As is the case with most desperate enterprises, daringly prosecuted by fearless spirits acting in concert, well knowing that certain death will be the penalty of failure, this proved entirely successful. Inured to danger, confident in his prowess, accustomed to triumph, Pizarro disregarded the warnings of a confidential attendant against the "men of Chile," as Almagro's followers were derisively called, and thus allowed himself to be attacked at disadvantage in his own house. He perished, however, as became a Castilian, and one of the greatest warriors of that warlike age, having first offered up several of his enemies on the altar of his sacrifice. So easily is the passive multitude controlled by the active and resolute few, that the scorned and derided men of Chile of an hour before, became, instantly on their successful revolt becoming known throughout the capital, the recognized dictators of Peru; and the body of the man who had just ceased to breathe, and on whose breath when living had hung the destinies of the State, and the fortune or fate of each of its citizens, was hastily wrapped in its bloody shroud, and stealthily buried by the dim light of a few tapers in an obscure corner of the cathedral vault, unhonored in his passage to the tomb by the pageant which had so often garnished his path of triumph, and unattended, save by a few domestics, and by one the spirit of charity designates his wife—although the impartial historian throws a doubt over the relation, but not on the fact, by saying "he was never married." Since then, on the erection of the present cathedral, his remains were removed for the second time from their resting-place, and with pomp and ceremony deemed appropriate to a just consideration of his eminent services to his country, they were deposited in the vault of the metropolitan church. Here they are said to be exhibited for a trifling gratuity by the sacristan. Certainly the mummied remains of human bodies are seen in stone niches of the cathedral vaults; but I do not believe common rumor—commonly a liar—which designates one of these as the body of Pizarro, any more than I believe in a reproductive power of the holy cross, or of Pizarro's shirt; which last, if you will consider the remark a truth and not a paradox, it may be said you can *buy* a piece of, if you wish to be "*sold*." Most visitors are represented to have carried away a piece of this miraculous garment, but there it is, the same snuff-colored mystery, in a tolerable state of integrity yet. A few years since an English speculator, emulous of Barnum's sensational enterprise, surreptitiously cut off and bore away the mummy's hands; and there are those in Lima, who, deterred by a belief in the sacrilege from descending into the vault, yet state that the vital forces were temporarily renewed in the offended limbs until the hands were reproduced. But the act of regeneration has only happened in the fancy of the credulous; the extremities are seen, but in the mutilated condition referred to, and the old sacristan has been too honest to strengthen the delusion *by attaching other hands.* Nor did he say any thing to me to encourage the impression that this is Pizarro's body. He states, that some years since several bodies without inscriptions were disinterred. This one of them he considers the remains of a former well-known prelate. If it be true, as we are historically informed, that Pizarro "was tall in stature and well proportioned," then certainly the body spoken of is not his, for it is not over a medium height, and but for the block underneath would be decidedly flat-chested. What, perhaps, is more correct than many of the stories about this body, is, that not long ago an old pair of shoes, mouldy, pliable, and represented as having belonged to the great conqueror, were sold to an antiquarian at a high cost. Their value was seriously depreciated on a subsequent critical examination, by the discovery on them of the nearly obliterated stamp of a Lynn manufactory. Italy is not alone in the readiness with which she imposes on the credulous. If paintings of the old masters can be produced to order, so can the shoes and shirts of discoverers and conquerors. Pizarro was slain in 1541, and buried hastily, without embalming. His remains were twice removed and reinterred, the last time in 1607—sixty-six years after the first burial. How much of them was probably found at that time? The historian Prescott says, "his *bones* were removed to the new Cathedral." And yet sensationists who, with Hudibras, "can see what is not to be seen," point out a tolerably well-preserved *body* as that of Pizarro!

On the east side of the plaza stands the cathedral referred to above, and the archiepiscopal palace. The base on which the cathedral stands is ten feet above the level of the plaza, embracing a spacious paved area enclosed by an iron balustrade, giving the building a suitable elevation to exhibit its great size to advantage, this being not less than one hundred and seventy feet front by four hundred depth. The walls and the pillars within are massive and strong, of stone, burnt brick, and adobes, with coarse stucco. But although the size of the building is imposing the architectural design is not so, an inharmonious assemblage of orders, and a rude composite with an undue proportion of crude fancies, giving an *ensemble* at variance with rule and good taste. Two towers surmounting the front façade, contain fine peals of bells, two of these of unusual size, having an exquisitely rich tone; their vibrations, especially in the still hour of midnight, floating on the air in lingering melody and prolonged cadence, as if the heavens gave back the sweet notes in token of acceptance. The white, slate, red, and yellow wash, on the exterior of the church, detract much from the effect which would otherwise be produced by its massive proportions. The sombre hue of age, and this is now measured by centuries, would be much more imposing than the glare of a vulgar wall-coloring. The interior has thirty-two immense square columns, supporting arches, mostly gothic. The floor is paved with brick, much worn from long use. The roof is of narrow plank, arched, and covered outside with a thin coat of plaster. Having been thrice thrown down by earthquakes, that now described was built and has been found best suited to resist shocks. The embellishments are on a scale of considerable grandeur, and would be effective but for the quantity of tinsel obtruded everywhere, not only on the high altar and choir, near the middle of the church, but from the twelve or fourteen altars, or rather distinct chapels, which occupy the large spaces between the heavy pilasters against the walls, corresponding to the columns supporting the roof. The side altars are rich, and the high altar is truly magnificent; but it is to be regretted that the effect of its grandeur is destroyed by the intervention of the choir between it and the main entrance, especially when its beautiful columns, capitals, cornices, and mouldings, its statuary, gold-wrought custodium, embossed silver altar table, immense silver candelabra, and innumerable decorations of precious woods and marble, as well as of metals, are gleaming in the radiance of a thousand wax candles, as in the ceremonial of grand festivals. Among the heavy and elaborately-carved oak chairs appropriated to high functionaries, one is pointed out which is said to have been used by Pizarro, when, weary with war, satiated with the blood of innocent victims to his lust of power and plunder, and perhaps realizing the vanity and vexation of life, he sought to conciliate divine clemency by a public show of sanctity. It was not because of the proffered "honor" by the sacristan that it was availed of to rest; but for the reason that the immense area of the church, although thronged at times with worshippers, is so nearly destitute of the means of seating them, that it would have been unwise to refuse an opportunity that might not again have been presented in this large edifice to relieve my fatigue.

Another church, that of San Augustin, is much visited by strangers. It is large, and its interior architectural and other embellishments are thought by the citizens to excel those of the cathedral. This cannot be doubted, if glare and glitter are regarded as the essentials of beauty, for from entrance to altar, from floor to ceiling and dome, there was a rarely-equalled display of gilt and gaudiness, in the celebration last night of the eve of the feast of the nativity of the blessed Virgin Mary. Crimson tapestry covered the large columns and draped the walls. Many colored muslins, blue and buff, scarlet and green, and lighter tissues of as gay tints, forming banners and looped pennants, sparkling with spangles, and shining also with silver paper figures, foliated, radiated, stellated, and twisted into every imaginable form and device, were festooned from column to column, and hung in endless profusion from arches and altars; of which latter there were, besides the grand altar, twelve others along the side walls. All these were loaded, too, with other glittering decorations, so that the eye burned with the intensity of reflected light wheresoever it gazed. All glared with gilt and plated vases and candelabra, and a hundred images of the virgin and of angels, clad in embroidered silks, satins, lawns, bedizened muslins, and laces, wreathed with artificial flowers, and holding in their hands bouquets of the same sorry imitations. To all this gay attire of religionism was added statues and paintings of Christ and the Mother, and of saints innumerable, in every fashion of dress and of gaudy coloring; the meek countenance and holy character of the latter being burlesqued sometimes by the dress of a *bloomer*, with indelicately-abbreviated skirts; at others by an extravagant amplitude of modern crinoline. Variegated lamps, too, radiated their rainbow hues, as if in rivalry of civic fêtes; while really rich chandeliers of glass, and candelabra of glass, of silver, and as is said, and it really seemed, of gold, holding a thousand wax candles, reflected the flashing rays, until the church seemed a blaze of light. This brilliant illumination recalled the descriptions of the ancient Peruvian temples of the Sun, whose golden mirrors gathered the beams of the great luminary, to dazzle the vision of its sincere and simple-minded worshippers.

It might reasonably be expected that the effect of such a spectacle, aided by the impressive chanting of a hundred richly-robed prelates and priests, seconded by a powerful choir with Sconcia and Cecchi to lead, would be deeply impressive upon the compact assemblage of devout women, who kneeled or sat immovable for two hours on the floor, spread only by their small woollen rugs, usually borne by themselves or servants to church for that purpose. As to the men, they were deemed the lucky few who secured a remote standing corner, even at the cost of a coat from the descending showers of melted wax from flaring candles. Would it be uncharitable to suppose that they were excluded from the body of the church because of their idolatry? Most of them seemed to be worshippers of the modern Marys, whose flashing eyes served to increase the brilliancy of the scene.

The religious services above spoken of were repeated on the succeeding day at the church of San Augustin, the feast of the nativity of the Blessed Virgin being observed as one of the most holy of the Roman church. Secular business was suspended, and all the churches were open and filled with the faithful. The occasion afforded an opportunity to see in public the famed, and somewhat fabulous beauty of Lima. So extravagant have been the pictures drawn by travellers of the personal attractions of Limeñas, that one may be excused for having allowed his attention to be withdrawn from the spiritual to the temporal, from the Virgin Mother of the past to the virgin daughters of the present—from Bethlehem to beauty. But candor will not permit my joining the general acclaim to their transcendent charms. The Limeña of pure Castilian descent, uncontaminated by inferior blood, it is true, is sometimes found a model of symmetry and grace; with regular features, clear complexion, arched dark eyebrows, a profusion of black hair, small hands and feet, and a flashing black eye, but little less dangerous than the tender blue that less frequently sheds its mild ray from out the constellation of dazzling neighbors. But the departures from this standard are many, even among those of untainted Spanish lineage, and innumerable among others of impure blood and degraded caste. It is probable that if those who formerly testified to a universal Limeña loveliness, could see the women in later fashions of dress, they would conclude that the *saya-y-manto*, the mysterious garment then worn, did much to shape their opinions. The interest felt in that unique dress may justify a description of it.

The name is composed of two substantive words, as the dress consists of two essential parts. The *saya* is a skirt hanging in apparently quilted folds from the waist nearly to the ground. In consequence of this quilting it is drawn in, or narrowed about the knees, so as to give an appearance of want of freedom in the use of the limbs, which, however, is more apparent than real, because of the elasticity of the skirt. The material of the saya is usually black silk. The *manto*, made of a lighter material than silk, but also black, is attached to the saya at the waist behind and at its sides, whence it is brought up over the shoulders and head, concealing one arm entirely, which is folded up to hold the opposite sides of the manto together across the breast, and revealing only a part of the other arm, and the hand, which is raised for the purpose of drawing it over the face, leaving but one eye exposed. A well-turned arm and small hand, with taper fingers, adorned with brilliants, not more dazzling than the flashing eye, near which they loiter in coquettish mischief, show to great advantage in such a costume, and very naturally lead to the conclusion that all the unseen is in beautiful harmony. A gay colored shawl, usually crimson, is worn under the manto, and over the shoulders, covering the bust and falling in front, aiding by the bright reflection in beautifying the revealed arm and hand, always left exposed when the wearer is of pure Caucasian descent. Owing to the awkward appearance given to the figure by the contraction of the saya at the knee, and which gave to it also the name *saya ajustada*—drawn in—the Limeñas improved the style by opening out the skirt, letting it drop free and unconfined, and giving an air of greater ease and grace to the person, this being called in contradistinction *saya despliegada.* And thus it was worn until a few years since, convenient to the wearer for all artful purposes, and bewitching to the beholder—the chirimoya of dress—its captivating mysteries not to be described by language any more than the nectared sweets of that elysian fruit.

A few years since European fashions, under the skilful leadership of a few cunning beauties, began to make inroads upon the previously irresistible saya, which had placed the least favored in personal charms, provided she had but a bright eye, and understood the art of using it, on the same vantage ground with the loveliest. As in most important questions that have agitated the world, a compromise was the result, and the *saya-y-manto* is now supplanted by a large shawl, usually black, which the wearer throws over her head; and when it pleases her to be concealed, it is drawn over the face from each side in such manner as to hide all but one eye, one end of the shawl being thrown carelessly over the shoulder after the manner of a Spanish cavalier's cloak. A Limeña is said to be *tapadad*, and she is called a *tapada*, when thus covered. The shawl thus worn answers all the purposes of concealment afforded by the manto, but is by no means as becoming. Indeed, so clumsy is it unless of very fine and flexible material, and adroitly managed, and so troublesome to the wearer, that the prettier women, unembarrassed by the necessities of intrigue, are outwitting their less comely cotemporaries, and with ready pretexts appear in public adorned as of old in the rich and courtly Spanish veil, and some of them even in that artful invention of modern millinery, the cunning little bonnet. It is refreshing to see this irresistible device of Parisian civilization, on the form, fit, color, and embellishment of which hang the hopes and happiness of nearly half of the Caucasian race; and when, here in Lima, where it has not yet fully established its empire, it happens occasionally nearly to touch one's cheek as it flits by on the narrow footway, it brings thoughts of rosebuds and sweetness, pleasant thoughts and tender emotions.

So far then as relates to the once celebrated Limeña costume, the *saya-y-manto*, it may be written a thing of the past, preserved as a relic of the wardrobe, or donned by pretty señoras occasionally to prove to curious strangers how fascinating those might become even if a little mystery were necessary to awaken the imagination to charms, in their own cases too real to need artificial aids. And its successor, the less elegant tapada, which has nothing but its adaptation to deeds of darkness to recommend it, is travelling along the same road; ere long its decline and fall will be written too—fashion has so decreed. But woe to those who, not made of porcelain clay, fall into the trap set for them by charms that seek the light. The raising of Mokanna's veil brought not more certainly horror to his sworn priestess, than the removal of the tapada sometimes brings disappointment and disgust to the worshipper of fancied beauty; for it is said that liaisons unwittingly indulged in with *mestizas* and *negras* in the favoring shades of night, aiding the deception of white-gloved arms and whitened eyelids, have resulted in a *denouement* recalling the Prophet of Khorassen's fearful apostrophe:

> "Here—judge if hell, with all its power to damn,
> Can add one curse to the foul thing I am."

However unlucky those whose misfortune it will be to stand revealed in repulsive feature, and doubtful or undoubted complexion, the sooner this masking costume, a lingering badge of immorality, is driven from Limenian society the better for its reputation. Whatever sufficient considerations led to its adoption—and its admirers and apologists have been ingenious in suggesting many—whether modesty, protection from weather, diffidence, reserve, convenience in dispensing unseen and unknown the charities of life, it must be conceded that its perversion to disreputable purposes, the facility with which it can be and has been used for intrigue, and for the avoidance of detection when exposure would invite just condemnation, make it desirable that the revolution in dress already begun should not be arrested. The sooner it is completed the better for the character of the really virtuous, who have unhappily borne an unjust odium from the follies of the indiscreet, and the sins of their frailer sisters. The beneficial influence such change would exercise in reforming actual immorality cannot be doubted.

A description of the seventy churches, parish and conventual, of Lima, would be tedious and uninteresting. They resemble each other in general appearance and structure externally and internally, varying in size, some of them being insignificantly small, while others although large are without grandeur, and arrest the attention merely by being overloaded with tasteless and unharmonious decorations. The mention of a few may be excused. The church of San Pedro, more than two hundred years old, is next in size and nearly as large as the cathedral; but time and frequent earthquakes have so damaged and disfigured it, as to render an outlay sufficient to restore its original strength and style beyond the straitened means of those who administer its trusts. And indeed the appropriation of so large a sum for purposes of pomp and vanity, would be of doubtful propriety even if possessed, when the wants of the crowd of beggars surrounding its portal, and petitioning the nearly as impoverished looking devotees passing in and out, is considered. The halt, the blind, the poor, might well invoke curses rather than blessings upon those who, indifferent to their suffering and destitution, should divert the gifts of divine beneficence and the means of charity to purposes of empty show, and a splendor that would shame the pretences of those who profess to obey and teach the precepts of Christ, and yet would witness the afflicted pauper kneel day by day unrelieved at the door of His sanctuary.

The church of Nuestra Señora de la Merced, also large and elaborately ornamented, is in a better state of preservation than San Pedro. It belongs to an order of priesthood considered one of the richest in South America at this time. Our Lady of Mercy is the patroness of the army of Peru, by whom her bedizened effigy is escorted with great military parade on all occasions observed in her honor.

The church, monastery, and college of San Francisco, with their gardens, cover a space of from twenty to twenty-five acres. The church still retains much of the splendor for which it was formerly distinguished; but this order of priesthood has lost its former sources of wealth, and the monastic buildings are rapidly going to ruin. The porch, pillars, cornices, mouldings, panelled roof, statuary, hangings, altar, and general ornaments, with the steeples and fine bells of the church, show that this part of the once celebrated establishment still possesses a strong hold upon the religious sentiment and reverence of the people. The *chapel del milagro* also retains the traces of tasteful embellishment, a remaining few of the finest collection of paintings of the old masters ever owned in America by a religious institution —but nearly all purloined, sold, or perishing from neglect—and the vestiges of a high altar, Madonna's niche, elaborate carvings, and general architectural decorations, showing that these must have originated in extraordinary religious zeal, or love of magnificence, and a high appreciation of the fine arts, and great affluence. The Madonna, once sacredly cherished in this chapel, formerly stood over the entrance to the church; and it is related of it and believed by these superstitious people, that on the occurrence of a severe shock of an earthquake in 1630, the figure turned round facing the altar and lifted up its hands in a supplicating manner, thus preserving the city from destruction. For this miraculous intercession the Madonna received, by a special ecclesiastical decree approved by popular sentiment, the addition to her holy title of *del milagro.*

The convent of San Francisco was founded in 1657, and completed at a cost of twelve millions of francs. In its present ruins the evidences are seen of former magnificence and opulence, dilapidated cloisters, untenanted studios, deserted banquet halls, corridors that no longer resound with the footstep of monastic power, and arches that do not now echo the revelry of licentiousness, defaced frescoes of the good saint's life, falling arbors, uprooted gardens, walks neglected, grass-grown and nurseries of weeds, and broken fountains which have long since ceased to cool the air with their refreshing waters, mark the retribution which has overtaken the luxury, dissoluteness, and debauchery of which it was the undoubted and shameless seat, and which disgraced their profession of faith when its five hundred resident monks stripped the miserable natives of natural rights as well as of their silver and gold, and robbed their temples of jewelled idols to recast for the enrichment and celebration of their own scarcely more rational rites, and to coin into the purchase money of sensual indulgences and a profligacy that dishonored the memory of their excellent and benevolent founder. But the penalty of sin and wickedness was finally paid, and there lingers but a miserable remnant of this once powerful order. These are the occupants of cloistered cells, damp and dreary, now shown to the visiting stranger in proof of their self-sacrificing devotion to the cause of religion; with little else to cheer their loneliness but a wooden crucifix, and a human skull whose speechless eloquence reminds us "to this complexion we must come at last," an ox-hide bed and a blanket, brown bread, and cruse of water. May penance and prayer procure them a happier destiny than the present! The hand of military despotism which they upheld and strengthened, and which so long oppressed the feeble and once happy natives of the soil, at length has been stretched forth to seize and appropriate the property purchased and adorned by their ill-gotten wealth; and the cholo soldiers of the *nominal* President but *actual Dictator* Castilla, the mongrel descendants of the ancient Peruvians, are now seen revelling in the refectories, drilling in the arcades, and hanging their burnished arms against the pillars and altars of this convent.

An Irish gentleman—a Catholic—temporarily domiciliated in the convent, gave me much information about church matters; and if at times my remarks upon these seem severe, the facts on which they are based must certainly be regarded as coming in his case from love of truth rather than from sectarian prejudice. He showed me through the buildings and grounds, pointed out the proofs of earthquake power, in shattered walls, demolished cornices, and crumbling corridors, and directed attention to a dome of elaborately-carved woodwork of surpassing elegance, and to some fine paintings still remaining of the many which formerly adorned the walls of the monastery. The few paintings left have been removed from different parts of the establishment to the "Retreat" by the present worthy Superior, for better preservation, and protection from the hands of clerical spoilsmen, who, in many instances, taking advantage of secular demand for valuable works of art, were discovered to have sold numerous masterpieces belonging to the monastery, for the means of gratifying their lusts, indulging the vanities of mistresses, and providing for the necessities of their children!

My cicerone was a religious formalist of the strictest school, and not only a zealous defender of the faith but also of the somewhat celebrated women of the famed capital of Peru, who he considered shamefully slandered not merely by common rumor, but also by the tales of more responsible travellers. As we were sauntering along a panelled corridor and vestry, admiring a Rubens, and as some assert, a Murillo, my new-made acquaintance indulged—as I thought rather fiercely—in denouncing the libels on Limeña virtue; when, stopping suddenly before an image of the Virgin, he devoutly made the sign of the cross, knelt, and muttered doubtless an appropriate prayer. Then rising, and while still *vis-à-vis* with the Holy Mother, he shocked me by the abrupt, and considering the presence especially profane remark, that "those who circulate such vile charges against the women of Lima are a pack of damned liars and scoundrels." A candid chronicler should not withhold this opinion, but give Limeñas the benefit of it. Doubtless my Hibernian friend was sincere; certainly he was much incensed at the imputation; I know not why, for he did not intimate that he had been subjected to any suspicion of demonstrative investigations. But uttered as was his emphatic denunciation in the presence of his professed patroness, may it not be supposed that he designed thereby to commend himself to her special protection, in confidence that his irreverence would be overlooked in the appreciation of the chivalric zeal that dictated a defence of her maligned sex—as daughters of earth, deserving heavenly care? A change of public opinion on this delicate subject it must be conceded, however, will be more likely to follow good deeds than a lavish expenditure of quixotism; and the abolition of the *saya-y-manto* and *tapada*, when thoroughly accomplished by the persistent efforts as well as prayers of those whose acts need no disguise, will effect much to this end.

One other church is regarded with so much superstitious

reverence as to be entitled to brief notice, and then I shall speak of institutions in which will be found more practical charity and benevolence; and therefore they are to be regarded as the truly religious in an honest Christian sense.

The church of Santo Domingo is said to be the oldest in the city. It has the appearance of great antiquity, and enjoys the distinction, as well as the danger, of having the tallest steeple in Lima; a preëminence certainly not to be envied in view of its liability to be toppled over—if not a sacrifice to fireworks—by that no respecter of persons and things so apt on this continent to shake down the monuments of man's vanity. The general architecture and decorations of this church, like those of the other religious edifices, are in profusion, and also, in the main, in bad taste. But in addition to the several altars in the common and tawdry style, there is one, the altar of our Lady of the Rosary, which looks as if its various parts were of massive silver; pedestals, columns, capitals, cornices—chased, embossed, and fluted—present a superb display of the precious metal. No altar in Lima can compare with this in effective and actual richness, although excelled by some others in massive proportions. The niche for the figure of my Lady of the Rosary is of exquisite material and workmanship; and her dresses, numerous as the days of the year, and gorgeous in brocade, lace, and embroidery, can challenge the wardrobe of the vainest of earth's temporal queens in variety and richness. The rosary of the saint is formed of pearls of largest size linked by diamonds, emeralds, rubies, and other precious stones, which, with her finger and ear-rings, are valued at hundreds of thousands of dollars.

This church being the custodiary of the properties of this jewelled Saint Rosario, the wealthiest of the calendar, and who still continues to have large accessions made to her estates by the bequests of the dying who desire her holy intercession for forgiveness of sins, has a large surplus beyond the support of her great state, and thus can maintain a great number of holy fathers. These minister luxuriously to their own, as well as to the necessities of the saint, who, although dead and buried, and therefore it should rationally be supposed having no temporal wants, is yet by her devotees considered specially deserving of posthumous honors because of her life of extraordinary purity amid unusual temptations of poverty; her obscure place of interment having been indicated by the miraculous growth on her grave of a rose-bush in token of the divine purpose to have perpetuated the memory of her virtues. The age of pious frauds has not passed, happily for the holy fathers of Santo Domingo.

On the annual celebration of the feast of the rosary, besides a brilliant illumination within the church, from silver lamps, candelabra, and chandeliers, the display of gaudy hangings of crimson velvet, embroidered muslin, and silk, and an atmosphere of perfume from scented vapors, costly drugs, and spices, to intoxicate the senses of the votary, the exterior is in full feather with flags, fireworks, and variegated lamps, with a clatter of bells beaten through an unending gamut of discord. It is the *ne plus ultra* of inflammable display, noise, and nonsense of Lima religionism. It resembles a New York Independence day in riot, combustion and explosion, disorder and disgrace to municipal government. The deluded victims of ignorance, priestcraft, and superstition here, seem to think that heaven can be most effectually startled into a recognition of their wants and vows, by letting loose all the explosives of human invention—rockets, fire-crackers, torpedoes, roman-candles, flaming-circles, spit devils, and fiery serpents—by the cargo; and by a din and uproar unparalleled save by the wild tumult of modern American rowdyism and partisan pyrotechnics, which have disgracefully superseded orderly political meetings and enlightened discussion.

## CHAPTER VII.

DESCRIPTION OF LIMA CONTINUED—BENEVOLENT INSTITUTIONS—SCHOOL OF MEDICINE—PUBLIC PROMENADES—AMPHITHEATRE AND NATIONAL AMUSEMENTS—MONUMENTS—CHAMBER OF DEPUTIES—SENATE CHAMBER—FORMER TRIBUNAL OF THE INQUISITION—RELIGIOUS INTOLERANCE—PERUVIAN ARMY—SENATORS AND DEPUTIES—ADMINISTRATION OF JUSTICE—EDUCATION.

Most of the important and really benevolent institutions of Lima, are under the control of one special board of directors. Many years since a philanthropic citizen bequeathed a considerable property for charitable purposes, and named the managers of the trust. The property thus donated for public charities has been added to from time to time by others, some of whom have given money, a part of them bestowing real estate, the annual revenue from all of which amounts to $250,000; and it was said to me by an intelligent citizen of Lima, that but for neglect and pilfering, it would have amounted by this time to nearly twice that sum. The Peruvian Government, regardless of the illegality of the act, abolished a few years ago the board of managers appointed under the bequest, and nominated one of directors in its stead, consisting of eighteen citizens, authorized to fill their own vacancies, thus perpetuating their official control, and with power to appropriate the large income derived from investments, in such manner as to them should seem best for the promotion of the objects originally designed. This board is subdivided into executive committees, for the better supervision of the several institutions, and they have a duly appointed corps of "administrators"—employés—consisting of major domos, physicians, surgeons, pharmaceutists, nurses, who are in all cases sisters of charity, porters, and servants, a total number of two hundred and forty-two, who are distributed among, and perform the duties demanded for the care of the following institutions supported by this munificent trust:

1. The Hospital of San Andres, for men, consisting of a large central room surmounted by a dome; from this room radiate several long and commodious wards with high ceilings. Each ward has light admitted from above, there being no side windows for the accommodation of impertinent curiosity, or to endanger patients by draughts of air, atmospheric purity being secured by suitable ventilators above and below. The floor is of highly-polished asphaltum—easily cleansed. Neat iron bedsteads have superseded here, as they should in every hospital, the more cumbrous and less durable bug-breeders of wood, and bedding is abundant and clean. Closets, bath rooms, and an ample supply of hot and cold water, and all accessories needful for the comfort of the sick, and the convenience of the convalescent, are provided. Each bed is numbered, and has suspended at its head in brief, the daily medical record of the occupant's condition. A permanent dressing-table in the surgical ward has numerous drawers, supplied with necessary dressings and instruments to meet sudden emergencies; charpie, rollers, cushions, sponges, plasters, ointments, can be had at a moment's notice, and without the delay often realized in similar establishments at home for such articles to be brought. The operating room is spacious and well lighted, and the attendance of internes upon the visiting surgeon, the quiet and orderly manner of performing their respective duties, each having his specially assigned office, and no one interfering with that of his colleague; the personal presence, also, of the nurse to give information if sought, and to make, herself, a note of the prescribed diet, as the chief interne does a record of the progress of the case, and the assistant that of the medical prescription; the presence, too, of a servant with water and napkin for the surgeon-in-chief, so that each patient shall be examined with unsoiled hands; and numerous other evidences of order, decorum, foresight, promptitude, cleanliness, and discipline, are entitled to commendation, and make San Andres a model worthy of North American imitation. The larger wards are occupied by charity patients, and these are certainly more comfortably provided for than any simi-

lar class of patients my various official positions have brought under my notice. There are smaller and less crowded wards for patients not on the charity list, at a moderate per diem; and neat, well-furnished private rooms, for the better class of pay-patients, at a charge of one and a half to two dollars per day. These rooms, having all the comforts and conveniences of a private residence, with faithful and experienced attendants, are much sought by invalid strangers in Lima.

I have not seen anywhere a dispensary at all comparable with that of San Andres. It has three large-sized apartments for preparing, compounding, and dispensing medicines; and for completeness, arrangement, and decoration, of cases, shelves, and shop furniture in great variety, and for numbers, quantity, and quality of medicines, it may be confidently said, that the *botica* of San Andres Hospital is not surpassed by the showy apothecary shops of the chief cities of the United States. Although admitted—by special courtesy to a stranger—to the private apartments of the Sisters of Charity, a sense of propriety forbids a reference to the arrangements of their seclusion, further than to say that these are remarkable for the perfection of order, neatness, yet appropriate plainness, characteristic of these good Samaritans everywhere. The sisterhood having charge of this hospital, and of several others in Lima, came from France a few years since on this special mission of benevolence. The Superior, bearing the appropriate name Angelica, and who illustrates her title by her good deeds, is a lady distinguished alike by her accomplishments, exalted character, disinterested charity, and administrative ability. In the Crimean war, like Florence Nightingale, now an historical character, enjoying in life the rare happiness of witnessing the effulgence shed by a self-sacrificing devotion to good on the destiny of mankind, she, too, proved an angel of mercy to the suffering, the distressed, and the dying. Answering the appeal of humanity again, she has come to this distant land to serve those who need her kindly aid and admonition, as well as the influence of her holy example; and none but a bigot would fail to honor her noble character and generous deeds, and wish for her a present happiness, flowing from consciousness of good done here, and a realization of more glorious reward hereafter.

It may be added, that the mode of cooking by steam is well adapted to the wants of this large establishment, and that the arrangement and economy of the cuisine are as perfect as the other departments of the hospital, among which is an extensive and well-regulated laundry.

The Hospital of San Andres has five hundred and fifty beds, and there are at this time in its wards three hundred and nineteen patients. The following are the most prevalent diseases: Dysentery, diarrhœa, rheumatism, fevers of various kinds—particularly intermittent—pleurisy, pneumonia, pulmonary consumption, and venereal, the last being especially the pestilence of the place.

I am indebted to Dr. Ornellas, a Portuguese physician of great eminence, and surgeon-in-chief of San Andres Hospital, for politely conducting me through this and similar institutions, as well as through a fine botanic garden attached to the hospital, and for much information on medical and other subjects relating to this country.

2. The Hospital of Santa Ana, for women, is another of the munificently endowed charities under the direction of the *Beneficentia.* It is similar in general plan, extent, construction, and administration, to San Andres, and therefore need not be described. It is subject to the same rules of admission, and is governed by similar regulations. More than three hundred beds are provided for patients, and there are at this time two hundred laboring under the same diseases found in San Andres.

3. A Lunatic Asylum is also provided by the same beneficent administration, having now one hundred insane inmates treated according to the present rational system, adopted first in France, and now pursued in all enlightened countries. The building is constructed with reference to the improved treatment, and a moderate space is provided for the out-of-door exercises, amusements, and occupations, which make a part of it. It is the only institution of the kind yet established in the three most northern republics of the west coast of South America, New Granada and Ecuador having nothing but prisons for the confinement of lunatics, merely for security. These are, in fact, *moral pest houses* for creating and confirming insanity. Such have been the favorable results of the rational system of treat-

ment in Lima that the countries named send many of this class of unfortunates here; and when their friends are unable to recompense the institution, the Beneficentia has been governed by an enlarged philanthropy and received them without remuneration. Pay patients are charged as in American asylums, according to the accommodations required.

4. Another of the excellent institutions of Lima is a Maternity, or lying-in hospital, in which midwives are practically taught the duties pertaining to that department of medical practice. An obstetric college annexed to the Maternity, under the direction of La Señora Benita Paulina Fossel, has a collection of preparations illustrating every branch of instruction in midwifery, with instruments, manikins, natural objects, and monstrosities. There are, also, a professor of the anatomical structures relating specially to this branch of science, a professor of the physiology of the same, and a professor of the theory and practice of obstetrics, with female internes and externes in attendance.

5. The Beneficentia has also founded orphan asylums for boys and girls, in which they are instructed until fitted by age and education to be placed under other care to be taught some useful occupation. An appendage to this is a foundling hospital for abandoned children, conducted similarly to those of France, and thought by some excellent citizens to diminish the frequency of infanticide. Besides these various institutions, the Beneficentia has purchased, enclosed, laid out, and adorned a cemetery for public use, called—

6. The Pantheon, from the building which is its chief ornament, and which is situated just within the main entrance. It is situated outside of the city wall, beyond which it is reached by an unpaved road covered nearly knee deep with dust. The Pantheon occupies a space of probably ten or twelve acres. It is without shrubbery or trees within the main enclosure, except along the principal avenue; the foreground being also sparsely planted with flowers. But with such a soil, climate, and dews, flowers should be perennial, clothing the tombs in a perpetual garb of beauty, and breathing forth their fragrance a sweet offering to the memories of the departed. The cemetery is sur-

rounded by a high, mud-colored adobe wall, except a small space in front embraced within a plain iron railing. The mode of sepulture is above ground, in cells or niches of brickwork, arranged in tiers three or four feet deep, each cell receiving an adult body placed in it horizontally. When the cells are entirely closed, a block of them presents the appearance of a massive wall seven or eight feet high and as many thick. Sometimes the blocks of cells are arranged on the three sides of a square, so as to enclose an open court on which they face, and from which they are reached for burial purposes. Each court is called a department, and is designated by the name of a saint. When wanted for use, the cell is opened by removing the bricks which temporarily close it; and when the body has been laid within, generally but not invariably coffined, the mouth of the cell is again closed by a marble slab, suitably inscribed, not to be removed again if the cell has been purchased for *permanent* occupation by the payment of one hundred dollars; otherwise, if *leased* for the usual term of two years, by the payment of ten dollars it will be opened after the lapse of that time, the remains removed to a deep pit in the centre of the cemetery, the common receptacle of all such, and the cell *re*-leased to some other tenant. If burial be sought as a charity, it is given in that "tomb of all the Capulets." There are now but six monuments indicating *subterranean* interment. Four of these are directly within the main entrance, between it and the Pantheon, and were erected probably by an act of Government, in memory of the Peruvian Marshals Gamarra, Nicochea, La Mar, and General Salazar. They are tasteful, appropriate, and well executed, relieving somewhat the stern sameness of the scene; and it is surprising that the beauty of the sculptured marble does not tempt wealthy survivors to place over their departed similar memorials of affection, honorable alike to the living and to the dead. The Pantheon proper—the edifice—designed for ornament rather than for use, is a chaste structure of about fifty feet height, and proportionate diameter. The dome, light and graceful, is supported by eight interior columns, within the circle of which, upon a suitable pedestal, is a group of three beautifully sculptured Italian marble figures of life size, representing an angel supporting a cross with one hand while the other is pointing upward, and a male and female kneeling, with upturned faces, in attitude of listening to the declaration, "Canet tuba et mortui resurgent incorrupti"—the trumpet shall sound and the dead shall be raised incorruptible.

The presence on wall, turret, and tomb, in attitude of expectancy, of that loathsome bird of evil omen—"only that and nothing more," none other being there, as in our own hallowed resting-places, to lull with melody the mourning spirit—did not enhance my estimate of a civilization and refinement which, imitating a Hindoo custom, exposed the festering remains of mortality, if not on scaffolds and roofs of houses to vultures, yet to the light of day and the air of heaven in an uncovered charnel vault, truly—

> "A thing
> O'er which the raven flaps her funeral wing."

Besides the benevolent institutions established and supported by the Beneficentia, there is another hospital, the Refugio de Incurables, containing at this time eighty-seven patients. A convent building belonging to one of the nearly extinct orders of monks, is used for the purpose, and the still lingering remnant of these religionists have charge of and support the sick, that they may thereby propitiate the Executive government to allow them to retain possession of the convent property, which a law of Peru declares forfeited to the State whenever the number of friars belonging to any one order shall be reduced below thirteen. Most of the patients in this Refuge have incurable cutaneous diseases. It is also the pest-house to which cases of small-pox are sent; and many Chinese coolies who are refused admission to other hospitals gain admission here. It is a wretched lazar-house, filthy in the extreme, without order, comforts, or any thing to gladden the fleeting moments of expiring mortality save the prospect of speedy release from suffering and neglect. The poor monks are incapable of enforcing discipline, and cannot pass from the indolence and indulgence of the past to the menial offices required for the maintenance even of necessary cleanliness.

Another hospital, that of San Bartolome, is devoted to the accommodation of sick and wounded soldiers, being supported by the national government and under its exclusive control. It is a large building somewhat on the plan of San Andres, but it is by no means as well arranged, or as orderly, cleanly, or comfortable. It has five hundred beds, and contains at present two hundred and fifty-five patients. Its generally defective and dirty condition does not indicate much regard for the cholo victims of war and exposure, however much Castilla may tickle their fancies with showy uniforms, and pet them when in health and capable of performing service in upholding and perpetuating arbitary and despotic rule.

Having spoken of the hospitals, nearly all, certainly the largest and best organized of which I have named, it may also be stated that Lima has a National School of Medicine. Although founded before, this did not go into full operation until 1855. Its officers are a dean, secretary, librarian, and curator, and a medical faculty of thirteen professors and several auxiliaries, to wit: Professors of Practice of Medicine; of Descriptive Anatomy; of General and Pathological Anatomy; of Physiology; of General Pathology; of Medical Nosology; of Surgical Nosology; of General Therapeutics and Materia Medica; of Pharmacy; of Surgical Anatomy and Operative Surgery; of Legal Medicine and Toxicology. Also a Master or Teacher of Clinical Medicine, several Auxiliary or Adjunct Professors, and an Anatomical Dissector.

The collegiate edifice is commodious and conveniently arranged, and contains an excellent museum of preparations in natural history, mineralogy, botany, physics, anatomy natural and pathological, surgery, and obstetrics. The course of instruction extends through nine months of the year, and the student is required to study five years, undergoing an examination at the end of each course of lectures, and a final examination at the end of the fifth year, which is designed to test his general attainments before he can be entitled to a diploma as doctor. A fee of four dollars is charged the student by the secretary for inscription on entering the college; the course of instruction is gratuitous, there being no charge but the inscription fee until graduation, when a fee of one hundred and twenty dollars is exacted. The college is endowed by Government with a sum of $20,000 annually, specifically derived from the import duty on ice. Independently of its precious virtue as such, the faculty are thus interested in prescribing ice as a febrifuge. The number of students in attendance on the last course of lectures was eighty-seven. The college curriculum looks well on paper; but it is due to candor to say, upon the authority of two accomplished European physicians now in practice here, that in this as in many other things, degenerate Spanish pretension exceeds largely the reality.

The *Estadistica General de Lima* for 1858, states that the Faculty of Medicine of the University of Lima is required by law to examine not only all physicians and surgeons, both national and strangers, who pay on being admitted a fee of $125, but also all pharmaceutists who pay $60, dentists $50, phlebotomists $25, and matrons $30. As many as eighteen natives and ten foreigners are said to receive medical diplomas annually. The *Estadistica* further states that there were in Lima in that year, sixty-one regular physicians, twenty-eight pharmaceutists, thirteen phlebotomists and cuppers, two male and thirteen female accoucheurs, and five dentists.

I have said that I must note things *currente calamo*, and as I happen to see them; it is therefore hoped that the narrative will be excused which puts hospitals and cemeteries before public parks and senate chambers. Whenever the chance is afforded to stroll, "I stand not upon the order of going, but go at once." But for this rule my observations would be very meagre.

Formerly the only public promenade and drive was outside of the city wall on the Callao avenue, which for about a mile had a double row of shade trees, seats, turnouts, and aqueducts, and was the great resort of citizens who sought pleasure or fashionable display. Being beyond the beat of the police, frequent robberies and assassinations caused it to be abandoned, and two other public walks, called *alamedas*, were opened within the safer limits of the city. These are both in the suburb of San Lazaro, north of the river Rimac, and access is had to them by a substantial stone bridge which spans the river. The *alameda nueva* runs three-fourths of a mile along the right bank of the Rimac, having a drive in the middle, and a double row of shade trees bounding a spacious walk on each side. Midway this alameda stands an exquisitely-chiselled marble statue of Columbus. The figure has a height of nine feet standing upon a pedestal of twenty feet. An Indian woman is represented crouching meekly at his feet, in whose hand a cross is being placed by the great discoverer, while with one of his hands raised above her head, and his eyes turned toward heaven, he seems in the act of commending her to divine mercy as he gives her the symbol of revealed truth. A granite pediment and substantial iron railing enclose the monument, which is of such rare merit as to have induced the city of Genoa, before it left Italy, to offer a large sum for it, that by its retention the memory of the great discoverer might be appropriately honored by the country that gave him birth.

A short distance from this beautiful work of art, on the north side of the *paseo*, stands an amphitheatre capable of seating more than ten thousand spectators of the barbarous bull-bait, the Spanish national holiday amusement, and the favorite Sunday entertainment of the inhabitants of the capital, especially during grand festivals; but one which, although generally attended by the higher classes, and even by the clergy until recently, is now I am assured by foreign residents resorted to by the less respectable people alone, as is also the *Coliseo de gallos*—the circus for cock-fighting—except on some extraordinary occasions. It is gratifying to find that this withdrawal of encouragement from a brutal diversion by those whose example in all communities exercises a reformatory influence over the vicious inclinations of the masses, has been inaugurated. The higher civilization which comes of the cultivation of gentle and refined sensibilities, and of intellectual pursuits and pleasures, forbids an indulgence in pastimes which blunt the kindly sympathies of human nature by familiarity with suffering and gross sensualism, and create a false standard of excellence and nobleness by elevating to the rank and honors of a hero, one who has nothing to distinguish him but the brute courage of a bull dog, or the cunning and activity of a monkey or a cat. Is the *matador* who ventures into the arena where an enraged bull is challenging him to the attack, any bolder than the dog which may have preceded him and been tossed into the air? Or is he more adroit than the monkey because he may have eluded the plunge of the infuriated animal, and driven into his victim's spinal marrow a gleaming steel which science and skill not his own furnished him? Let us hope that the partial withdrawal of Peruvians from the amphitheatre gives promise of a general emancipation of the Spanish race from indulgence in this barbarous pastime. But let not America and Great Britain denounce harshly and without compunctions of conscience the cruel diversions of other nations, complacently thanking God "that they are not like other men," when they, under pretence of encouraging the "noble art of self-defence," crowd around the prize ring, betting tens of thousands of dollars on human brutality, rejoicing in every blow that inflicts pain and disgraces their nature, and exulting at injuries that may send a fellow-man to his final account—an heir of eternity self-degraded to the level of a perishing beast seeking thus the presence of Him who made man in His own image. A Spanish bull-fight is the event of the amphitheatre in which it takes place, and is forgotten with the day of its occurrence. The "set-to of the Benicia Boy and Tom Sayers" agitated two Anglo-Saxon nations for months, took place within an hour's ride of the metropolis of boastful England, and was attended by British noblemen and members of Parliament; and its result convulsed one nation with joy, threw the other into mourning, and engendered a spirit of wide-spread bitterness and lasting animosity. Which pastime is the more inhuman—the Spanish or Anglo-Saxon? Which the more disgraceful to national character?

Another *paseo*, called the *Alameda de los Descalzos*—literally rendered the alameda of those without shoes from the convent of the "bare foot friars" situated near it—excels that already spoken of in the beauty of plan and decorations. It is at the foot of a small outshooting spur of the Andes named Cerro de San Cristobal, from the summit of which the best view is obtained of Lima at its foot, and Callao in the distance. The alameda is a long narrow enclosure with walks, flowers, shrubbery, shade trees, and seats for visitors within a handsome iron railing, and outside of it a fine carriage drive. One hundred vases on pedestals, and twelve colossal marble statues executed in Rome representing various arts, are tastefully distributed among the beauties of nature; and the arched gateway is surmounted by appropriate statuary. This park is lighted by gas at night, and it is the resort, especially about sunset, of fashionable citizens; the pedestrian promenading the interior or lounging on the marble settees, to feast his eyes on the grace and beauty flitting past him; while the handsome turnout makes the circuit of the *campo* amid dazzling glances, the envy of the ambitious, the admiration of all, achieving a triumph which its wealthy owner, inflated with Peruvian pride, vainly believes will resound through America and echo in the fashionable *salons* of Europe. At the north end of this alameda, separated from it by the width of the *campo*, stand the church of San Diego without any special attractions, and the *beaterio*—house of female seclusion—called the Patrocinio; a chapel being on one side of the latter, and the convent of the Recoleta de los Agonizantes with a small chapel, on the other side.

About three squares east of the plaza mayor is a small irregular space dignified by the name *Plaza de la Constitucion*, near the centre of which is the only ornament to distinguish it from what with us would be considered a *common* with a dirty ditch running through it. On a marble pedestal twelve feet high is a bronze equestrian statue, erected in the year 1858:

"A Simon Bolivar,
Libertador
La Nacion Peruana."

On the sides of the base are chiselled in basso-relievo, views of the battles of Ayacucho and Junin, both fought and won by Bolivar in 1824, and resulting in the establishment of South American independence. This statue was cast in Munich, and, so far as spirit and expression are concerned, great success was achieved, certainly surpassing in these merits the monument erected in memory of General Jackson at Washington; although in artistic skill, as shown by balancing the whole statue upon the hind legs of the horse in the latter monument, Mr. Mills has excelled the Munich artist, who was compelled to make the long tail an additional pillar of support in the Bolivar equestrian statue.

On the east side of the Plaza de la Constitucion is the hall of the Chamber of Deputies, corresponding to the United States House of Representatives. The exterior of the building is not imposing. The chamber in which the deputies sit is in size about ninety by fifty feet, and has a high arched ceiling and dome, giving many reflecting surfaces and consequently confusion of sound. A balustrade divides the chamber into two parts; an outer for the accommodation of spectators, who are also admitted to galleries above, and an inner and larger part of the main floor for the deputies, which is carpeted and furnished with high-backed cushioned chairs arranged in two rows on each side of the hall. The president of the Chamber and two secretaries are seated at a table at one end of the room, and a tribune resembling an antiquated church pulpit is situated on each side. The deputy addressing the Chamber occupies for the time a tribune, which elevates him above the level of his hearers.

This legislative body is now, in conjoint session with the Senate, engaged in amending the Constitution of Peru, so that an opportunity is afforded to see their proceedings; and while candor compels a condemnation of many things in this country, let even-handed justice record the fact that the deliberations of this body are characterized by an order, a decorum, and a dignity, to which the House of Representatives of the United States are too generally indifferent. The attention due to courtesy as well as to the subject under discussion, is given by all when a deputy is addressing the Chamber. There is neither reading, writing, nor talking, to tell of weariness and rudeness; no unparliamentary interruptions, nor vulgar displays of mere muscular oratory; no indecent display of legs on desks; no offensive pools of tobacco juice on the floor; and nothing to be seen of that filthy indispensable appendage of an American Congress, designated "spittoon," by an *affectation* of delicacy and refinement, which, nevertheless, tolerates the actual presence of the nuisance, and countenances its use. If it be asked what is a tobacco-chewing representative to do when in the discharge of his duties, without such a bar-room convenience?—the answer is plain. When he aspires to a seat in a deliberative assembly, which, in the experience of other countries, *does* represent the intelligence and refinement of a people, and *should* also in our own, as when he seeks an entrance into good society, a condition precedent should be the abandonment of dirty practices, as offensive to some of his associates as it is to all that better half of our race, whose comfort and pleasure a well-bred gentleman will seek to promote at whatever sacrifice of mere sensual indulgence. If a man cannot control his vulgar propensities and coarse appetites, he should remain in a suitable sphere in life, and with congenial companionship.

The Senate Chamber is situated on the south side of the same Plaza de la Constitucion, and occupies the grounds of that most diabolical of all the self-constituted tribunals which have in the history of religion claimed to have derived authority from heaven to do the work of hell. Indeed, the Senate Chamber is the identical room in which that terrible tribunal, the Spanish Inquisition, held its awful sittings, and where were pronounced its fierce decrees. The room is of moderate size, and with nothing to distinguish it as the forum of the highest legislative power of the nation, except some specimens of superior roof-panelling and carving. The Senate was not in session at the hour of my visit, and thought was left free to lift the veil of oblivion from cruelties of which this chamber was formerly the scene. Nor did it seem wonderful, that when the act of the Cortes of Spain abolishing the Inquisition was promulgated in Peru, then a Spanish colony, that the people who had long groaned under its tyranny, and trembled in perpetual fear of its secret executions, should have rushed, as if with one impulse, to revenge their wrongs by the destruction of the instruments of torture; and that they stood petrified with horror at what they beheld. And after such revulsion, on the discovery of machinery concealed amid the curtains of a canopy for moving the head of a crucified image of Christ, which was made to confront the accused, and to approve of inquisitorial judgments by solemnly bowing, it was not strange that they vented their rage by demolishing even the sacred symbol of their faith, thus sacrilegiously made the instrument of a base trick. What must have been the commingled terror, joy, and rage of those who found among the secret archives of this dreaded tribunal the recorded condemnation of friends who had long before secretly disappeared! and some of whom found, too, their own names, with the charges on which they probably would have been summoned to an awful account. When the room of torture was burst open, and there were seen a table with iron collar, and straps to secure body and limbs; with cords, axle, and wheel, to stretch, break, and dislocate the human frame; pillory, and scourges stiffened with blood; gags and nippers; netted wire with points projecting inward, of various sizes adapted to body and limbs; and finger-screws for crushing nails and bones; all, contrivances of torment, to compel agonizing nature to conform to the behests of priestly power, even to the acknowledgment of guilt although innocent; when these were revealed to them, it was to be expected that the frenzied people would break them into fragments, as they did, and cast them forth from this precinct of hell. To the disgrace of his memory, Ferdinand, in 1812, restored this institution; but it was of short duration, for the successful revolution, and independence of the South American colonies of the mother country, shortly after resulted in its permanent abolishment.

It is not surprising that the people of these countries, suffering from ecclesiastical and political despotism, those mutual supporters and beneficiaries, should at last have thrown off the yoke. But there is still more for them to do before they shall have accomplished the full redemption of human right, and vindication of human privilege. Those who will not tolerate civil and religious liberty in others, are themselves unworthy of them, and they are apt to realize the fate of those who tumble into the pit of their own digging; nor can progress be assured but by the spread of knowledge. Let Peruvians then erase from their national Constitution that article which gives an ecclesiastical precedence in a political assembly. Let them strike from it that prohibition of religious freedom which is its disgrace, and which denies to man the privilege of publicly worshipping God according to the dictates of his conscience, "none daring to make him afraid." Let them establish schools where knowledge shall be placed within reach of the humblest pupil, to the extent necessary for the just and intelligent exercise of those political privileges, which are alike his natural heritage and his duty; but without thereby inculcating a release of the citizen from the parental obligation to provide, as far as in him lies, the further means of eminent success in life; and also without devolving upon the industrious and meritorious classes burdens of taxation oppressive to them, whilst they tend to encourage irresponsibility, idleness, and worthlessness in others. And let such schools be independent of ecclesiastical institutions, and free from sectārian influences; the object and aim of which are too generally to inculcate fanatical dogmas, and partial precepts, and to poison the pure and natural fountains of liberal sentiment; thus shaping the instruments of a selfish clerical aggrandizement and power, while they unfit the pupils for enlarged and diversified intercourse. Let Peruvians watch executive power, check its efforts at consolidation of government, resist its arbitrary decrees, and teach it obedience to the popular will as deliberately determined and set forth in the organic law. Let them disband their large standing army at a time of professed peace, for it encourages aggression upon neighboring States, and thus leads to frequent foreign wars; and it is the agent of perpetually-recurring revolutions, and of Executive encroachments at home. Thus, whilst relieving themselves from excessive taxation for the support of an oppressive military establishment, increased capital would be thrown into the channels of trade, and the capacity for labor of the discharged soldier now festering in indolence, or a means of mischief, would be turned to useful account in agricultural, mining, and manufacturing enterprises. These are all languishing for assistance; in fact, many valuable products are lying useless in unopened mines, and the music of even a single factory is still unheard, because the hand of military impressment would be outstretched to seize the employés, regardless of the interests of proprietors, or the wants of impoverished families, whenever soldiers are desired for purposes of personal ambition, domestic tyranny, or trespass on neighboring nations. An American on arriving in Lima is surprised at the number of soldiers passing and repassing, and in view of home usages looks for a grand volunteer parade. But he looks in vain; these men are of the regular national army; every day their gay uniforms are seen in barracks, bar-room, and boulevard. There are six thousand of them stationed in the capital, all except the officers being cholos and negroes, ready to do their affiliated chief Castilla's bidding, whether it be to confirm him in the Presidency, contrary to the provisions of the Constitution, to punish or displace recusant deputies, or to intermeddle in the affairs of feebler republics. The Peruvian standing army is nearly twenty thousand; in time of peace greatly disproportioned to the population of the Republic.

We should not forget that the reality of war is apt to follow the creation and cherishing of its instruments, and that the price of its fierce glories is not alone the stream of human blood that deluges and desolates the land, nor the mountain of debt which for its maintenance mortgages the toil of unborn millions for generations; but religion must stop her labor of love, and science, too, stand still and cease to work for the improvement of man, and the exaltation and ennobling of human nature, that victims may be furnished to the hateful Moloch, and ignorance and passion, brutal instincts and violence, assert their savage sway, and revel in carnage and oppression. True, the reign of wickedness and wrong, the domination of selfish, inhuman, and tyrannical rulers, may not always last. The reflective historian, Alison, has said of injustice: "No special interposition of Providence is required to arrest it; no avenging angel need descend to terminate its wrathful course. It destroys itself by its own violence. The avenging angel is found in the human heart." Yet however sure the punishment of those who have wielded for evil the power entrusted to their hands, it were far better than that the innocent should suffer and the helpless perish, the multitude be borne down by misery, murder inflict its diversified decrees of death, and tyranny stalk abroad unchallenged, that the agencies of war should "sleep the sleep that knows no waking," and that the death-angel should have no access to the swift keys of that terrible organ, whose accompaniment is ever

> "A loud lament, and dismal Miserere."

The Senate Chamber is not as large as the Chamber of Deputies, and the portal looks like the gateway of an ordinary *patio* more than the entrance to the upper house of the national legislature. The room is small and unadorned, except an elaborately-carved wood ceiling. The President's table, the chairs and tribunes, conform to an extreme republican simplicity. The senators, two for each province of Peru, *are designated by lot from the Chamber of Deputies;* the latter, consisting of one hundred and six members—one for every twenty thousand inhabitants—*being appointed by an electoral college*, which *is elected by the people.* Thus a more intelligent and dispassionate creative element is interposed between the generally ignorant, unreflecting, and impulsive lower classes of citizens, and an organic part of the Government designed to exercise great influence over the welfare and destiny of the State. It is to be regretted that other and grave impediments to a successful experiment of this mode of election of the national legislature, prevent a fair comparison of it with the more direct democratic method of some other republics. Both the legislative chambers are guarded by armed soldiers, the gleaming bayonet serving to remind the members of the expediency of shaping proceedings in conformity to Executive will. Most of the public buildings in Lima are also under military guard; no stranger can fail to recognize the supremacy of the military over the civil rule.

*The administration of justice* is effected through the agency of—1. *Justices of the Peace*, elected annually by popular vote. 2. *Courts of First Instance*, in which the judge must be thirty years of age, a native of Peru, and five years a practitioner of law. The Judge of First Instance, Prosecuting Attorney, and Reporter of this court, are presented by the Superior Court in two ternary nominations to the President, who selects from these the officers of the court, whose term of service is during good conduct. Each province has one judge; some have two or more, according to population. His jurisdiction is generally both criminal and civil, except in Lima and Arequipa, where is a special judge for each class of cases, because of the greater amount of duty. 3. *Superior Court.* In this court the judge must have served as judge of an inferior court, as prosecuting attorney, or as reporter, at least for four years. There are not less than three judges in the Superior Court, with one prosecuting attorney, and one reporter; but the number may be increased according to population. In Lima there are as many as ten. In civil cases not less than three judges, and in criminal cases not less than five, must sit. There are seven Superior Courts in Peru, the judges being appointed by the President, by selection from two lists of nomination presented by the Supreme Court. The other officers of this court are also appointed during good conduct. 4. A *Supreme Court*, composed of seven judges and one attorney-general, who are nominated by the President to a joint convention of the Senate and Chamber of Deputies. To be eligible to this court the candidate must have been a member of the Superior Court eight years, or have been engaged in the practice of law during twenty years, thus securing the greatest legal experience of the country. This court in Peru, as said by Guizot, "is like the Areopagus." It is the protector of the citizen in all revolutions commonly endangering the liberty of the weaker party. The executive power may, and often does oppress, but this court never. The appointment is for life. The mode of appointing the judiciary in Peru gives greater assurance of capacity and impartiality than does the popular election of judges prevalent in many of the United States; in which partisan prostitution however debased, and conventional intrigues however unprincipled, are too commonly the passports to place and preferment, though ignorance and corruption thereby occupy stations where knowledge and virtue alone should be found, though violated law remains unvindicated, and crime stalks abroad "unwhipp'd of justice."

Besides this portion of the machinery of law, there are in Lima as many as two hundred and sixty-six counsellors, attorneys, clerks, registers, and sheriffs; certainly a large number for a population of 125,000 inhabitants.

If the character of the buildings provided for schools be considered the measure of Peruvian estimate of education, the stranger would in this respect be very unfavorably impressed; for with the exception of one academy for young ladies, conducted by several French Sisters of Charity, there are none in Lima worthy of comparison with even public primary school edifices in the United States. And yet the cost of instruction in private literary institutions is high—from five dollars per month for A B C, to thirty dollars per month for the general branches of education.

The public school system is a failure, both in regard to plan and result; and until freed from the trammels of sectarian religionism, it is not likely to accomplish the general improvement contemplated by the enlightened philanthropy in which the system originated. At the College of Nuestra Señora de Guadalupe, the children of wealthy parentage receive a better education than in the public schools; but this is by no means up to the collegiate standard in North America. The College of San Carlos, founded in 1770, and as at present organized an amalgamation of three other literary institutions, is entitled to higher commendation than any other in Peru. The building contains tolerable halls, a refectory, and a library. Law and theology, the classics, French and English languages, natural philosophy, mathematics, geography, history, and some of the fine arts, are taught. As to the University of Lima, once the chief seat of learning in South America, and in its palmy days sending forth some eminent men who were ornaments of various branches of knowledge, its buildings in the vicinity of the Chamber of Deputies, with spacious court, corridors, halls, fresco paintings allegorical of the sciences, and inscribed quotations from the classics, are the lingering monuments of what it was, but no longer is, a proud and honored seat of learning—that which best determines a nation's claim to civilization, influence, and power.

# CHAPTER VIII.

THE MARKET—SOCIAL AND RELIGIOUS DEFECTS—CLERICAL PROFLIGACY—IDOLATROUS PROCESSION—TESTIMONY OF A FRENCH TRAVELLER—PERU BEFORE AND AFTER THE SPANISH CONQUEST CONTRASTED—INFRACTIONS OF NATURAL AND MORAL LAW BRING THEIR OWN PUNISHMENT—CHRISTIANITY A FAILURE IN LIMA—NAVAL AND MILITARY INSTITUTE—MUSEUM AND LIBRARY—RELIGIOUS INTOLERANCE—PENITENTIARY—CHORILLOS—DEPARTURE FROM LIMA.

FROM law and learning let us turn to a subject of unmistakable interest to the Limeñian, and which has shared as largely of his munificence as he has of its abundance. Whatever neglect may be chargeable to those in power for failure in providing suitable food for the mind, certainly they are not to be faulted for neglecting to furnish facilities for obtaining the more substantial aliment for the stomach. Producers and forestallers are provided with a superb market-house. An entire *manzana*, a square of ground of about four hundred feet in each direction, has on its four sides a convenient, neat, and showy building, enclosing a large court, and divided into apartments opening both on the street and on the court, which are occupied by green and dry grocers, and other venders. The court faces of the quadrangular building have along their entire length handsome arcades, paved with granite slabs, and forming a covered corridor or passage way for purchasers. The court within this enclosure is paved and divided into four equal parts, over each of which is a roof supported by iron pillars, and open in the middle for ventilation. These four buildings are fitted with stalls for the use respectively of venders of meat, fish, poultry, fruit, and vegetables; all of these articles being in abundance, but at extravagant prices. For example, fresh meat not less than twenty-five cents per pound. Smoked hams, fifty to sixty cents per pound. Lard, thirty to forty cents per pound. Butter, one dollar per pound. Eggs, four to six cents each. Potatoes, superior, three for twelve cents; inferior, ten for twelve cents. Sweet potatoes, ten for twelve cents. Let it be remembered that potatoes are indigenous to Peru, and were exported thence to Europe, and the scarcity and cost of labor may be fairly estimated when such a price is demanded for a native esculent. Cabbage, per head, twelve to twenty-four cents. Cauliflower, per head, twenty-five to fifty cents. Wheat flour, for one hundred pounds, nine dollars and a half; and for a single pound, twenty-five cents. Fruit and fish in proportion. No one should migrate from North to South America for cheap living; but if prompted by other considerations thus to change residence, let him arrange to spend the Christmas holidays at the old homestead, or take it good-humoredly when he finds he must pay seven dollars for a turkey, two dollars for a chicken, and thirty-two cents per quart for milk, wherewith to compound that necessary, but most deceptive and villanous of all festive beverages, egg-nog. For coffee, thirty-seven cents per pound must be paid. Peruvian sugar costs twenty-five cents per pound. Green tea, in three-pound boxes, good quality, two dollars and a half per pound. The vegetable market is well supplied; the exposure on a stall of *black* maize—Indian corn—was a curiosity. The gifts of Flora are not equal to expectation in this tropical region, and the *pucheros de flores* of former times, tasteful comminglings of fruits and flowers, the sweet and the beautiful, were not seen. Perhaps they are not sought in republican market-places, as once in the proud days of the old monarchy in the plaza mayor, when high-born señoras graced that scene of vice-regal grandeur. Nor are the fruits equal in quality, variety, or profusion, to those found nearer the equator; although the reddish-yellow granadilla, the golden pine-apple, and gay orange, contrasted prettily with the darker fig, banana, and palta; while that queen of fruits, the chirimoya, with its slightly-indented covering looking like a reticulated green mantle, lay scattered around, to gladden the eye and give promise of customary pleasures in reserve at the American Minister's in the evening, when the unsurpassed hospitality of his mansion shall crown its rare grace and intelligence, its "feast of reason and flow of soul," with a fitting feast of this elysian fruit. It is a wonderful product of nature that suggests to the palate a combined deliciousness of strawberry, sickle-pear, and peach, with a dash of the nectarine. But why should fastidiousness forbid my naming the American Minister? True, there has been such a deterioration of qualification for diplomatic appointments in our country that it is questionable if the reputation of a man of actual worth be not damaged by the notoriety of appointment. But John Randolph Clay is not of the pot-house school of politicians, nor is he of that class of diplomatists. His public life dates back to a purer period; his character as an educated gentleman and enlightened statesman is established; and his courtesy, and high-bred social qualities, his dignity and ability, have made him popular abroad, and honored at home, by all who have sufficient patriotism to consider duty to country paramount to party fealty.

All the sellers in the Lima market are women, generally cholos. This probably results from the large number of men taken for the army, and from their fear by healthy and robust countrymen of being seized by the press-gang, if they should venture into the city with the products of their labor. The dainty stranger should not visit the market before breakfast; his appetite will not be strengthened by seeing a saleswoman flea-hunting in her dog's hairy tegument, and turning from the interesting pursuit to dip, with her hand, sausage meat for a purchaser; or by seeing another, crack between her finger nails, less agile insects taken from the head of her child who divides her attention with customers, desisting from the entertainment to assort mutton chops, possibly intended to appease his hunger, probably already sufficiently satisfied with what he has seen. The lower classes, who form the great body of the community, are regardless of cleanliness and modesty. It is not uncommon to see the carcasses of dogs lie for days in front of houses, and buzzards feasting on them, to the removal of which an entire indifference is shown by those to whom the putrefaction, it might be supposed, would be both offensive and unhealthy. Women may sometimes be seen riding astride a mule with an infant in the arms taking its primitive meal, or asleep with the pendant breast exposed to the public gaze. In fact it is rarely the case that one walks in any part of the city during the day or night, without being shocked by sights of indecency, immodesty, and immorality, too gross even to be hinted at, and disgraceful to the arrogant civilization and Christianity of the nation. If one thousand seven hundred and ninety-three priests, exercising ecclesiastical authority, and performing religious functions in this city, as published in its statistics for 1858, with the machinery therein also enumerated, of seventy churches, forty-two chapels, six hundred and twenty-eight altars, and vast power of influence and enforcement, cannot produce a better state of morals and manners, it shows either a defective system of relig ion, or incapacity and faithlessness on the part of the executors of the holy trust; and the one should be amended, the other driven forth from the sanctuary, or both be radically reformed if both be at fault. The statements of candid citizens, and of foreign residents of many years, compel the belief that the general demoralization is mainly due to a depraved clergy. The precepts of the just and conscientious few can have but slight influence in purifying the turbid channel of social life, while most of their brethren are stirring the pestilential current and wallowing in the mire themselves. If priests, taking vows of chastity and devotion alone to God, perjure themselves, obey the lusts of the flesh, and scatter their illegitimate offspring abroad, with the sole self-deluding merit of not disowning them, thus giving the brazen lie to their profession, it is to be expected that in both lying and lechery they will find imitators among those whose temporal purity they should guard, and whose eternal welfare it is their solemn duty to promote. The unblushing boldness with which clerical debauchery stalks abroad in Lima, renders it needless to put in any saving clause of declaration. The rigorous virtue and exacting morality which claim a public deference in Anglo-America, especially of the crosier and surplice, may cause a doubt of statements made in these matters; and therefore, if the obligations of truth were not imperious, I would gladly give them a coloring more in harmony with home experiences. But the representations of competent and unprejudiced persons, verified as far as practicable by my own observations, must not be misstated.

The celebration of mass at an early hour of Sunday morning, does not exempt a priest from the duty of obeying the divine command, "Remember the Sabbath day to keep it holy." And yet he may be seen on that day as on others, in bull-ring and cock-pit, restaurant and tavern, with commoner and concubine, joining in noisy revel, or looking on with complacent sanction. Nor does the going down of the sun always arrest his wayward peregrinations; for vicious inclinations being unsatiated, at that hour when the clerical robe after the holy offices of the day should be folded in the pure atmosphere of the private sanctuary, it may sometimes be seen profaned by the pursuit of street adventures, at corners with *tapadas*, its wearer in gay and lascivious conversation, or threading byways in fulfilment of a lustful assignation. We may demand in the name of Christianity, and in its own language, is he who standest in high places "instructed out of the law"—"a light of them which are in darkness"—and "teacher of others"—not to teach himself? "Thou that sayest a man shall not commit adultery, dost thou commit adultery?" "Thou that abhorrest idols, dost thou commit sacrilege?" Is it not strange that those who assert a special privilege to study and expound the Holy Scriptures, should fail to give a just interpretation, and make a righteous application of these, in their own cases? If the Bishop of Arequipa will turn to the "weak and beggarly elements of the world," if he cannot, like his great predecessor St. Paul, "contain," but must obey the carnal desires, "let him marry" as he is commanded by the Apostle, like an honorable man and consistent Christian, and not prove a stumbling-block to his more scrupulous brother. And let him not encourage the frailty of depraved disciples by a shameless example of licentiousness made public by his procurement of separate apartments in Lima for his seven concubines and his thirty-five illegitimate children, during his absence on a mission to the Roman head of the church; who, if rumor speak truth of his virtues, would spurn him from his presence if aware of such scandalous libertinism.

The streets of this capital were yesterday the scene of a procession which was a disgrace to its professed enlightenment, and an idolatrous violation of the letter and spirit of its boastful Christianity. A gorgeously-gilded throne, borne on the shoulders of negroes, partially concealed by a deep valance, supported the pontifically-attired effigy of St. Peter, its right arm moved by secret machinery being occasionally raised in attitude of blessing the throngs of deluded worshippers who bowed their heads for its benediction. And another similarly-decorated daïs, bore a life-size "graven image" of La Merced, the patron saint of the arms of Peru; elegantly arrayed in curls, coronet, richly-embroidered crinoline, and robe; pearl necklace and ear-rings, brooch and bodice, and holding in its uplifted and jewelled fingers a silver *yoke*. It was not said that the last named was displayed as a type of the enslaved condition of the people, or if it were only significant of the Church's invitation to bear its yoke "because it is easy, and its burthens light;" a fact which need not be questioned by those who would seek its indulgences, and imitate the clerical profligacy by which it is disgraced in Peru. These effigies were escorted by prelates and other ecclesiastics; and that of La Merced was preceded by six pert-looking mulatto girls—designed to represent virgins—carrying incense upon silver salvers, from which numerous censers swung by priestly hands were kept supplied, and rolled upward their perfumed clouds to tell of the adoration of her votaries. The whole procession moved to the measured chant of hundreds of the clergy, who often bowed, behind whom followed the civic dignitaries of the nation and city, bare headed and reverential; and after these came the plumed warriors, on horse and foot, with breastplate and helmet, lance, sabre, musket, and cannon, flaunting banners and martial music, guarding the saints through the city, and back to the altars of the church of La Merced, whence they came; and where they will receive, hereafter as heretofore, the petitions and vows of thousands of misguided religionists. Can popular regeneration be rationally looked for when examples of ecclesiastical profligacy are patent to the public eye, when such violations of divine precepts are practised, and such delusions devised to mislead the ignorant by those faithless ministers of Christ—

"Who grope their dull way on
By the dim twinkling gleams of ages gone,
Like superstitious thieves, who think the light
From dead men's marrow guides them best at night;
Who cheat the weak believer's blinded eyes
By nonsense heap'd on nonsense, to the skies;
And give them miracles, ay, sound ones too,
Seen, heard, attested, every thing—but true."

That it may not be supposed that I am looking at what is passing around me with prejudiced eyes, and coloring first impressions of novelties too highly, I will quote at some length from "*A Travers l'Amerique du Sud, par F. Dabadie. Paris,* 1859." This French traveller, himself a Roman Catholic, but evidently one whose sense of religious duty inculcates the sin of compromising the lofty character and capacity for good of that Church, by concealing the wickedness of unworthy disciples, says: "The religious processions of Lima are actually converted by profane women into Carnivals of Venice—ridiculous, absurd masquerades! The ceremony loses its sacred character; the tapadas absolutely making or refusing assignations with those proposing; *the assistants* absolutely compressing the waists of the tapadas more frequently than they say their prayers. . . . It is but a piece of mundane coquetry, with imposing finery and trappings. They go to the Pantheon to celebrate All Souls Day as they go to a bull-fight or opera, ogling and laughing over the very ashes of their friends, with not even a souvenir of thought or sincere prayer for the loved beings who lie in the earth. Lima is the heaven of women, purgatory of men, and hell of asses—except that one of the last mentioned cherished by the Archbishop for Palm Sunday, when he is decked out with finery and heads the procession of the day. The populace would consider their damnation certain if any one of them attempted to ride on this holiest of asses, or if they required of it any species of work, or offered it any indignity. Women consider a husband only as he may contribute to their love of dress and indulgence; interest with them is the only motive of marriage. It is a strange thing for love, that sweet passion which ennobles life, to penetrate the heart of a Limeña. Do not ask her for tears or confusion, experienced by others of the young in the presence of the objects of their devotion; neither look for that voluptuous sensation which makes a bride so beautiful and interesting at the approach of the solemn moment. She goes to the altar with indifference, and does not try to conceal it: she would underrate herself if she made her happiness or misfortune to depend on the feelings entertained toward her by her husband. What does she care about the mysterious joy between two loving beings? She has but one passion, that of display; but one imperious desire, that of living the leader of fashion. It is that, which, the day after the wedding, would take her to Chorillos; and she would even on that day annoy herself in her solitude, if required to remain at home to await her husband's return from business. This insensibility does not prevent the Limeñian from throwing herself into marriage with ardor. Although she may deceive the watchfulness of parents, yet she is anxious of complete liberty; besides, a husband represents an increase of wardrobe and jewelry-box. And so strong is this desire that many young Limeñas are humbugged by cunning grocers, who, knowing the confidence felt in the powers of St. Antonio to procure husbands, fix up an image of that saint on an altar near their shop door: on this altar the señoritas deposit their offerings of sugar, tea, candles, etc., and much to the profit of the grocer, whose stock in trade is thus disposed of, whilst it is sure to find its way back, constituting thus a matrimonial circulating medium. If the men become the slaves of the women, they must certainly be admitted to become eventually both indifferent and lazy slaves."

It may well be questioned if Mons. Dabadie is not alike ungenerous and in error, in throwing the whole burden of indifference and disregard of the joys and obligations of the matrimonial tie and domestic relation, upon the women. No one can scrutinize social habits in Lima, without becoming sensible of the fact that women are probably "more sinned against than sinning." For not only have they provocations to faithlessness, and opportunity afforded for its indulgence by sanctioned customs, but they are taught by the universally-recognized dissoluteness of men not to place confidence in them, and not to contemplate marriage as a means of happiness beyond its power to furnish an establishment, and make a woman mistress of her own actions. If notorious dissipation, debauchery, and unconquerable passion for gambling among the men of Lima, causing an abandonment of the family hearth at those hours which, after the necessary business absence of the day, should be consecrated to the duties and to the joys of home, may be regarded as some excuse for insensibility, indifference, devotion to dress, and intrigue, among the women, then do they not deserve our author's sweeping denunciation; nor should they be held up as especially criminal. And let it not be overlooked that amid the trials of solitude, and experience of the unreliability of those who should be their protectors from evil, and shield from suspicion, they are to a great extent without the religious consolations which should be brought to the sorrowing heart by righteous counsellors, to sustain them in the agonies of loneliness, suspicion, and neglect; but that in their stead, the poison of insinuation, and the pestilence of justification of guilt, are breathed upon them, even by the false prophets of their faith, who know full well

"that once plung'd in
Their woman's soul will know no pause in sin;"

and that thus they will become the dupes and victims of their own infamous designs. It would not be just to join in this unqualified condemnation of Limeñas. Women, as a sex, are purer and more virtuous than men; instinct, reason, and interest, make them so. The observing know it; the candid acknowledge it. Let us apply the general truth to the particular case we have been considering.

Mons. Dabadie continues: "In the street of San Francisco, opposite the monastery of that name, a kind of barracks is found containing quite a population apart from the rest. There, lives a class of women and children, whom one would think came in a direct line from gypsies, if their complexion did not show a variety of a thousand shades from white to black. These women are the acknowledged mistresses, and the children the progeny of the monks of the higher order, who visit them at all times, and pay them a stipend according to their means; meagrely, for the expulsion of the Spaniards from the country has impoverished the convents. 'La casa de la monjas'—the house of nuns—as the people ironically call it, is a real Gomorrah. The clerical *protectors* of the tenants who inhabit it, *willingly mistake the chambers, not having the weakness of the laity of being jealous of each other.* Do not suppose that we are amusing ourselves in speaking ill of the monks of Lima. Observe them on a festival day of great sanctity, either in the procession or in the churches, and you will have proved their barefaced licentiousness. In tedious ceremonies, brothers who have no active participation in the service, go out of the temple and smoke in the adjacent cloister, under the portico of the church, or on the sidewalk, amusing themselves with trifles. It is shocking to find them in the processions, when bearing the cross, banners, and candles, having no respect for their robes, nor for the sainted images they carry, nor for religion, nor for decencies demanded by the occasion. They shut both heart and ear to the sacred songs which ascend toward heaven. They smile at the women, who flutter about like butterflies, as the cortége is passing along; cast lascivious glances at them, and address to them words of double meaning. On returning to the church, two lines of monks are often formed at the portal, through which the crowd pass into the interior, and there too they indulge themselves without restraint in jest and sarcasm, compliment and repartee; alluring complaisant Christian señoritas, white, black, or copper-colored, and addressing to them shameless gallantries; the spectator, I will not say religious, but merely of proper delicacy, turning away in disgust from such unblushing libertinism. These abominations among themselves they are the first to expose, for in their stated elections for superiors of convents, such is the bitterness of rival aspirants and their partisans, that they publicly charge against each other infamous transactions, making known the number of their concubines and illegitimate children, and crimes which society has deemed it necessary to erect penitentiaries to punish."

Such is the testimony on Peruvian morals and religion of a French traveller, happily free from the imputation of sectarian prejudice. It is a sad truth, that many of the Catholic clergy of Lima degrade the religion they profess, pollute the altar at which they bow, and defile their sacred vestments. They debase themselves by their lewdness and general sensuality, and are exemplars of the worst of sins. Can a State be profited by maintaining such a clergy, to the exclusion of others of a common Christianity, whose presence and exercise of religious functions, if in obedience to the pure and tolerant spirit of the Gospel of Christ, might shame frailty, and purge His sanctuary of wickedness? Can the interests of religion be maintained, and its divine precepts be rightly interpreted, by violations of its sacred obligations? Can the depravity of social life be reformed by corruption? Can virtue be learned of vice? Can good come out of evil? A terrible retribution has overtaken the descendants of those who, under a professed purpose of extending the dominion of the cross, perpetrated barbarities on the unoffending aborigines of this land, at the recital of which the soul sickens. And what was achieved by this cruel crusade of a mistaken Christianity? When Peru was first trod by the Spaniard her people enjoyed a high degree of civilization, and a government and institutions securing personal safety and happiness, political tranquillity and national prosperity. Industry prevailed, agricultural wealth abounded, wonderful facilities of intercommunication were provided. Unnumbered flocks furnished fleeces for garments, and ample granaries supplied the wants of those even whom age or affliction disqualified for labor. And the nation possessed, too, a religion far loftier in its conception than a mere physical idolatry, for it contemplated in the sun the great giver of a supreme beneficence, as it is even to later finite comprehension its most glorious type. Was the Peruvian made happier or better by the change forced upon him; in that which was given him for that taken away; and especially in view of the manner in which it was effected? The truth of history, and that of the present, answer the question. Delivered over to a brutal soldiery as vassals, the shameless lust and avarice of their conquerors necessarily led to their debasement and misery; towns, villages, and private houses were pillaged, in violation of the inculcations of civilization, to say nothing of the obligations of Christianity. The rights of person and of property were so utterly disregarded as to have incurred universal condemnation since; as such barbarities in all future time, however palliated and by whomsoever perpetrated, will be reprobated by just and enlightened nations. The sacred cloisters of the virgins of the sun were polluted by grossest outrage. Temples were desecrated and plundered; granaries despoiled; flocks of the cherished llama and vicuna were wantonly destroyed; aqueducts and canals were neglected; the great national highways were suffered to fall into decay; and finally a religion of complicated mechanism, of multiplied saints apparently deified, incomprehensible ceremonies and symbols, of fierce fanaticism and intolerance, inconsistent with the teachings of Divine mercy and sacrifice for man's redemption; regarding, too, the object to be attained as justifying any means however inhuman; such a religion, *forced upon the country by a war of bloody ferocity*—not bestowed by a blessed mission of peace—to supplant one of a simple idea, emanating from a daily contemplation of the great source of light and heat, of joy, of growth, of glory, to nature; that which symbolizes beyond any other work of Creation, Supreme Power and Beneficence.

Punishment, however tardy at times, is nevertheless sure to overtake offences against humanity and right. Nor can finite man foresee the manner any more than he can the day and the hour of its coming. But it will stand confessed in its own time. And no one can now fail to recognize the deterioration that has set its seal in Peru on the Spaniard—a representative of superior man—as the penalty of violating laws which Nature has assigned for the government of her creatures. The commingling of races, while it is destroying the numerically weak, is debasing the higher standard to a level, which, under the influence also of the rivalries and jealousies of varied and conflicting mongrelism in political and social life, is rapidly sinking below that which preceded it in the progress of events. Truly a terrible retribution has overtaken the descendants of those who were guilty of gross violations of moral and natural law; not, whatever they may have professed, in the interest of *true* Christianity, which teaches obedience to both, but because their souls, guided by selfish and animal instincts, were filled with visions of gold rather than with visions of glory; least of all was celestial glory regarded, except as a means of conciliating the Church—but too ready, as it proved, to pander to their schemes of avarice, plunder, and sensual indulgence.

Christianity appears to have been a practical failure here, as in some parts of North America, where *profession* seems to have been mistaken for *fulfilment*, and where the greater the departure from its holy spirit and purpose, the greater have been the protestations of sanctity. In contemplating religionism in Lima and reflecting on that of Puritan America, one cannot fail to recognize, in the doings of the Peruvian Catholic and of the Protestant Covenanter, a like realization of ceremonialism—differing only in vain-boastful formulary—of bigotry, intolerance, selfishness, and actual ignoring of the precepts of the Prince of Peace, whose mission was one of righteousness, love, mercy, and good will to men; not, as illustrated by their history, of injustice, persecution, bloodshed, and cruelty.

Peru has its "*Institute Naval-Militar*," a conjoint military and naval academy, located in the capital on a lot of ground of very limited extent; the building, possessing neither architectural beauty, strength, nor convenient arrangement, occupying the entire space, with the exception of two small court-yards. There are forty midshipmen, and fifty-five cadets in this institution. All the branches of general education are taught except the spoken languages, instruction being given in but two of these—English to midshipmen, and French to the cadets, indicating the opinion entertained by this Government of the comparative merits of the respective nations in the naval and military science of war. Military tactics are taught from the time of entrance, twelve years of age, except artillery practice, which is reserved for the last year. The expenses of the Institute are defrayed by the Government. It was closed for several years before General Castilla's accession to power. He reopened it, and in his hands, doubtless, it proves an important piece of the machinery by which he undisguisedly enforces the edicts of his arbitrary will. When bayonets are seen to gleam at the door of legislative halls, as if to remind representatives that they have a master, and that the military is the dominant power of this pseudo-republic, and when grave senators are taken into custody until they shall record enactments in conformity to Executive dictation; when an armed soldiery pace the courts of the Presidential mansion (an anomaly in republican government, wherein the people are supposed to be the shield as well as the creator of their chief officer), and even, as I have seen, form, by lying across it, the threshold of his door, that punishment for violated law, and retribution for official cruelty, shall not reach its occupant; and when cuirassiers with flashing blade guard his steel-clad coach in its swift transit, that outraged public opinion and private wrong may not avail of an opportunity of vengeance; it will not be denied that the education and training of such instruments of usurpation, identified with his fortunes and obedient to his will, evince at least foresight, and considerate preparation to defend despotism.

Lima has also a Museum and a Library. The former, called the Museum of the College of San Pedro, is situated on the grounds in the rear of, and belonging to the church of that name. It consists of a meagre collection of specimens in natural history—principally in zoology, geology, mineralogy, and botany; some Indian mummies, implements, and trinkets; but being few in number, and badly arranged and preserved, there is no inducement for the visitor to tarry among them even if his weary limbs did not compel him to seek a seat elsewhere that cannot be found in the Museum, unless indeed he may desire to look at the historical portraits of some of the old Incas and the Viceroys, that give the walls an historical interest. There being no Government endowment of the Museum, it is not likely to have its sphere of usefulness enlarged; for the cultivation of the natural sciences in this Capital, as in many even larger cities of the United States, is not of that popular character to lead either to the search after specimens, to generous contributions, or to sufficient bequests to enlarge and enrich it.

An Academy of Design in the same building with the Museum, affords gratuitous instruction to a small number of students in this branch of the Fine Arts. The National Library, adjacent, is more worthy of attention. It was founded in 1821—the books of the University of San Marcos forming its nucleus. Subsequently the libraries of several monasteries—those great storehouses and conservatories of ancient learning, without which the "dark ages" might have embraced even the present epoch in their forbidding cycle—and some personal collections, were added. It contains now about thirty thousand volumes, in all the departments of literature and science; and possesses some very valuable old books on religious and historical subjects; those relating to the Conquest, and to Spanish Viceroyalty in South America, are great treasures. The library is public. The apartments are commodious, well ventilated, and cleanly; and are supplied with comfortable seats, tables, and writing materials for visitors. Padre Vijil is the librarian, an attentive officer and a scholar, accessible and courteous. He was formerly a popular priest of the Roman Catholic Church in Peru, but was recently excommunicated because of his support of the civil authority against encroachments of ecclesiastical power. An ecclesiastic himself, such a statement might seem incredible: but Padre Vijil is familiar with history, past and present; and possessing more than ordinary wisdom and judgment, he comprehends the true interests of religion, and the importance of keeping them free from party corruptions and intrigues, and in position to assuage the bitterness of partisan agitation, and the cruelties of civil revolution—an example worthy of imitation by many Protestant fanatics of our own country. He possesses, too, a liberality of opinion truly Christian, and a purity of life above suspicion. Such qualities of head and heart were of necessity at war with the sensualism and general sinfulness of the ministry of his Church. It is not surprising that he should have been deposed from the priesthood by his superiors, though not degraded in popular opinion. His present position is well suited to his tastes; and while he enjoys the confidence and respect of the best citizens of Peru, he is at liberty to pursue his investigations at leisure, and continue without let or hindrance his efforts in behalf of the rights of his fellow man, whether these be civil or religious.

The rapid increase of the library has made it necessary to enlarge its accommodations, and an apartment is now being fitted up which was formerly the refectory of the Jesuits, who owned this and other property in the vicinity, when, before the suppression of their order, they were in the height of power and prosperity. Judging from the magnificent proportions of this room, and the superbly-carved oak ceiling, it probably was, in the palmy days of that rich order, the scene of many a costly revel. It is strange that such a splendid banquet hall should have been recently devoted to the base uses of a wood-cellar! Yet such has been one of its mutations. And now, having been purified of sensuality by degradation and penance, it rises to the loftier office of treasuring the imperishable records of learning and science. Long may such be its noble use! And long may Padre Vijil continue its philanthropic and incorruptible presiding genius!

It may have been inferred from what has already been said, that the State religion of this miscalled Republic is Roman Catholic, and that its Constitution prohibits the exercise of any other. But it should be acknowledged that the executive authorities have lately, under the pressure of foreign diplomatic privilege, winked at the *private* worship of a few Protestant Christians. This is interpreted to mean that the Government will not prosecute them to punishment, nor hound on a fanatical populace, provided they make no open profession of their faith, no public display of their profane rites. The Protestant in Lima who seeks to worship God, obeys literally the Gospel precept—"but thou when thou prayest, enter into thy closet, and when thou has shut the door, pray to thy Father which is in secret." And can those who fulfil that injunction in sincerity and truth; who do *not* believe that righteousness is dependent on "modes of faith," but that "his can't be wrong whose life is in the right;" doubt the realization to themselves of the Divine promise, "and thy Father which seeth in secret shall reward thee openly"? It is to be regretted that the Peruvian religionist does not perceive that it is this anti-christian policy which is weakening the foundations, and shaking the pillars of his church, throughout his own and some other lands. He should know that its strength would best come of purity; of the "charity that suffereth long and is kind, envieth not, vaunteth not itself, is not puffed up;" and of the observance of the Divine commandment "thou shalt love thy neighbor as thyself"—on which, and on the love of God best shown by obedience to His will, "hang all the law and the prophets."

The Japanese worshipper of the sun, and the Turkish follower of Mahomet and the Koran, are more tolerant than the Peruvian Catholic; for the former by treaty stipulation has conceded the right of worship, according to the dictates of conscience; and the latter recently denounced the fanatical zeal of his Syrian subjects, and granted to France the vindication of the sacred observances of Christianity on Turkish soil. It would be a commendable example of consistency if Louis Napoleon would also see to it that his co-religionists of South America do not discredit their profession of faith by persecution and proscription.

Returning one Sunday morning from an ineffectual effort to find the sanctuary of Protestant Christians, I realized the truth that secrecy in their religious observances was demanded by a Roman Catholic government, in the enactment of whose laws the ecclesiastical power of the country largely participated. And when on another occasion, in company with our Minister resident, we sought by a narrow passage-way a studiously hidden room having but a simple platform for a clergyman and a few rude benches for forty persons there assembled, I should have felt humiliated but for the assurance that He also was there, who said, "Where two or three are gathered together in my name there am I in the midst of them." For what are sculptured column and groined arch, embroidered robe and jewelled altar, and all the magnificence with which wealth and power can clothe the proudest temple, compared with the glory of His Presence? What form of ostentatious ceremonial, or of merely typical presentation, can touch the heart, and reach the conscience, like the simple teaching of that "pure religion undefiled before God—the wisdom that is from above, first pure, then peaceable, gentle, and easy to be entreated, full of mercy and good fruits, without partiality, and without hypocrisy"?

Contemplating these things, the candid mind naturally inquires, with what pretence of reason can Catholics convert Ireland into a modern aceldema, in resistance to antagonist ecclesiastical prerogative; and in the United States complain of "Know Nothing" party persecutions—in both of which countries they enjoy constitutional freedom of religious opinion and worship—when, throughout nearly this entire southern continent, there is constitutionally proclaimed the "Apostolic religion;" the exercise of none other being permitted? Nor does the disgrace of this prohibition in Peru attach alone to its original legislation; for, within a few days, in this capital, the Senate and Chamber of Deputies refused, after an earnest and protracted discussion, to expunge that intolerant and anti-republican provision from the fundamental law of the state.

A building now about being completed in Lima, and intended for penal and reformatory purposes, is deserving of some notice. In the year 1853 Señor Mariano Felipe Pas Soldan visited the United States, commissioned by the Peruvian Government to examine and report upon their penitentiaries, with reference to the introduction of improvements into the prison system of Peru. It is but just to say that this investigation was set on foot and conducted by Señor Pas Soldan in a spirit of philanthropy, and with an ability honorable to his Christian character, and to the high intelligence of his pure Spanish origin. A report to his Government shows that he visited and inspected the various penal and reformatory institutions of the District of Columbia, and of the States of Maryland, Pennsylvania, New York, and Massachusetts, embracing their jails, penitentiaries, houses of correction, and houses of refuge; and that as a result of his observations, he recommended to his Government a system of imprisonment and a plan of building adapted to its fulfilment, embracing the good points and discarding the bad of the institutions he visited. In this respect his investigations resulted most happily. To the examination he brought an active, searching, and comprehensive mind; and the field before him was rich in materials, the United States having been the reformers of the old and now obsolete systems of imprisonment among civilized nations; and many of the separate State Governments having made liberal appropriations for the objects contemplated by the movement, which attracted the earnest attention and inspection of the leading Powers of Europe.

The prison edifice, planned, and now nearly finished, under the superintendence of Señor Pas Soldan, is unequalled by any penitentiary in the United States, in general design, and in special adaptation to the prison system of associated labor in silence, with personal isolation at night. The whole premises are enclosed by a stone wall thirty-five feet high, one side of which has a portal giving admission directly to that part of the building in which are situated the various offices and the warden's apartments. A main corridor leading thence, has on each side store-rooms, and from it also diverges at right angles on each side a smaller corridor, which communicates through strong iron-grated doorways with a wing, in which are contained the lodging cells, one hundred in number, for the female convicts. The main corridor then connects at its further end through two strongly-secured doorways, with a rotunda or observatory three stories in height, the upper being set apart as a chapel, whilst from the other two stories radiate five corridors, communicating with a corresponding number of wings, in which are admirably-constructed workshops, kitchen, refectory, and cells for solitary confinement of men at night. The total number of cells is one thousand. The wings are two stories high, and in their construction and entire appointments for security, comfort, and cleanliness, they surpass similar departments of all other prisons of the United States, the model penitentiaries of which I have carefully examined. It is not my purpose to dwell on details which might prove tedious and uninteresting; but it is due to candor and justice to say, that while Señor Pas Soldan gratefully acknowledges his obligations to the States visited for much and valuable information, and especially for the radiated principle, which affords the greatest facilities for the conducting of business and enforcement of discipline, yet has he, by thorough knowledge of his subject, together with architectural skill and ingenuity, planned and built a penitentiary affording perfect security, and the means of non-intercourse of convicts, and therefore likelihood of reformation. The walls are of stone and burnt brick, and are of great thickness and strength to resist the shock of earthquakes. An abundant supply of pure water from the river Rimac affords a necessary element of cleanliness and health. If the Peruvian Government, which has thus far entrusted the design and execution of this great improvement to Señor Pas Soldan, should continue to him its confidence until the consummation of his work, by the introduction of requisite discipline, it will probably prove of incalculable benefit to the State, as well as an enduring monument of his own philanthropy and patriotism.

The fashionables of Lima have a watering place, to which they resort in the bathing season, embracing the months of January, February, and March. *Chorillos* furnishes a salt sea for the Limeñas, and a "salt river" for the Limeños. Into the former señoras and señoritas plunge, and come out refreshed and beautified. *Up* the latter señoras are *rowed* by gambling pilots, who understand the shoals and quicksands of the dangerous stream, and how to give the awful *cold douche*, all but veterans in the deceptive navigation coming out wearied, wasted, and woe-begone. Germany has its Baden-Baden, America its Saratoga and Newport, and Peru its Chorillos, all useful if wisely used; all hurtful when abused. Many visit these resorts of invalids professedly for health; but mistaking the means of securing it, and worshipping at the shrine of Mammon rather than at the altar of Hygeia, they quit them, cursing the babbling waters

> "That keep the word of promise to the ear,
> And break it to the hope,"

without reflecting that theirs is the sin of omission as of commission, which has added to the afflictions of the body as well as to the burdens of the soul.

Chorillos is a town of several thousand permanent inhabitants on the sea-coast south of Callao, nine miles from Lima, and connected with it by a single track railroad. Midway between the two cities is the pretty little country village of Miraflores, in the vicinity of which the battle of La Palma was fought in January, 1855, when, by a victory of Castilla over Echenique, the former made himself nominally President, but absolutely Dictator of Peru. Castilla's triumph, it is said, was chiefly due to the bravery of an American adventurer, a Texan Ranger, who, thinking that he detected a hesitation in Echenique's advance on Castilla's retreating forces, attacked him impetuously at the head of his own company, and changed the fortune of the day. This trivial event shaped anew the destiny of the country, and established the power of a man of selfish purpose and resolute will, and as ignorant of the teachings of history and of the true principles of republican government, as he is reckless of official obligations and of constitutional restrictions on executive power.

The appearance of Chorillos is not attractive; and no hotels being provided for guests, visitors must assume the care of private residences. The town stands on a high bluff, and on the beach below bordering the sea there are many small mat-covered huts, arranged in rows and clusters, with narrow intervening alleys. These are the dressing-rooms, where bathers disrobe themselves, and don the kirtle and pant of blue flannel preparatory to taking the sea. Indian attendants accompany the bathers, who dip listlessly into very placid water without any of the slap-dash, heels-over-head accompaniments of a Cape May roller.

The art of photography has had a remarkable success in Lima. The gallery of Mr. Pease—*La Calle de Plateros de San Pedro*—contains some unsurpassed, life-like, and beautifully-finished photographs, the perfection of which has led persons to think that there is something favorable to the art in the somewhat subdued light of Lima, and in its uniform temperature, which makes it unnecessary to change the force of materials. Mr. Pease is fortunate in possessing several rare paintings purchased from old families, whose reduced fortunes from the vicissitudes of revolution compelled their sale. Among these is a Holy Family, the property of a former Viceroy, which possesses merits as a work of art so great that a French artist was sent from Paris to Lima to make a copy of it; and becoming enamored of its extraordinary beauties, he attempted stealthily to remove it, and to leave his copy in its stead. The theft was detected and nearly resulted in tragical consequences to himself. Four thousand dollars have been refused for it by the present owner. In his possession is also a magnificent and well-preserved viceregal bedstead, with the still more curious receipt for "2,000 hard dollars dated in Lima, 20 January, 1640," on the occasion of its sale by a retiring Viceroy to his successor; the vender being the *Count of Cinchon*, whose wife learned from the Indians the anti-periodic properties of the Peruvian bark, which subsequently was named *Cinchona*, in her honor. At this day it is regarded as one of the most valuable of natural productions, from which is derived the well-known quinine, in all malarious regions perhaps the greatest gift of science to man.

The statements herein made, and the reflections indulged in, are the results generally of personal observations of public things; in part derived, too, from those whose long residence in this country has made them as familiar with its condition as if they were "to the manor born." The sanctity of *private* life has not been invaded by criticism; when its hospitalities have been accepted, remarks upon its usages have been deemed a social sacrilege, and therefore avoided. But the *public* and its out-of-door life, opinions, and customs are not entitled to the immunities of the *tapada*.

In obeying the obligations that now require me to leave Lima, I feel none of the regret expressed by another traveller, who tells us that he was so fascinated by his surroundings, as scarcely to have had the power to tear himself away. To recall its past gives me no pleasure, for the history of the Spanish conquest of this country is one of blood, treachery, religious persecution, and robbery. Whether the tyranny, the butcheries, and extortions of viceroyalty, or the persecutions, cruelties, and murders of the inquisition be considered, nothing but horror and indignation attend their recollection. Nor does any pleasure come from the contemplation of more recent events, and the efforts of the country to shake off the political and religious atrocities of which it was the victim under the rule of Spain; for the daily proofs are before us that, while the professed formulary of government and its official agents were changed, the actual political spirit and results remain; that despotism and oppression are still here; and that superstition, bigotry, and intolerance, the offspring of ignorance and delusion, are now, as they were in the days of Pizarro and of his viceregal successors, the religion of the people. Of what honor to God, or benefit to man, are its proud adornment of churches, its brilliant festivals, its pageantry of processions, the startling or the dulcet tones of its hundred bells, at whose peal as in the Angelus, business, and breath almost, are suspended; what the swell of mingled choirs, with solemn pomp of ceremonial, if the charities of the Gospel are unfelt and untaught, and the spirit of divinely-inculcated love has no participation in rites which are unhappily but a vain and empty mockery of the religion of Christ? The climate of Lima may be equably mild, its airs balmy and perfumed with the fragrance of flowers—as a fanciful writer has said who was forgetful of its acequias—its fruits beautiful to the eye and luscious to the taste, but what avail these to restrain the footstep that would shun the pollution of its moral atmosphere, and escape from the vice and debauchery that boldly invade, or insinuatingly beset its path?

A last duty on shore was a sad one—to follow to the grave all that remained of Lieut. James H. Moore, of the frigate "Lancaster," who died in Lima at the residence of Mr. Naylor, an English merchant; the attentions of whose family to a stranger will be gratefully remembered by those of his countrymen who saw in them worthy disciples of Him who "went about doing good." Lieut. Moore was an officer of rare promise of distinction, faithful in duty, honorable and generous in all his relations of life. He was buried in the British Protestant cemetery at Bellavista, by the side of Captain Lambert of the British navy, who was recently murdered in the suburbs of Lima at midday, probably by robbers, who were never arrested. Lieut Moore's body, refused the use of a hearse because he was "a heretic"—although a Christian—was borne to the grave by his countrymen, attended by an English officiating clergyman, the officers and crew of the United States ship "Wyoming," then in port—the "Lancaster" having returned to Panama—the officers of her Britannic Majesty's ship "Vixen," and a number of American and English gentlemen, residents of Lima and Callao, who united, as if of one nation, in paying a last tribute of respect to the memory of a brave and accomplished officer. Sad as were the reflections incident to this loss of a fellow-countryman in the prime of life and reality of usefulness, and his burial far from the land of his love, yet did the event show those of kindred nations forgetful of past differences, and bound by a bond of sympathy, uniting in manifestations of respect for the departed; illustrating the benign influence of a common origin, language, and literature, when cherished by the relations of peace.

# CHAPTER IX.

HARBOR OF CALLAO—ISLAND OF SAN LORENZO—THE BOQUERON—EL FRONTON—VOYAGE TO VALPARAISO—SEA-COAST OF SOUTHERN PERU, OF BOLIVIA AND NORTHERN CHILE—CHINCHA ISLANDS—GUANO—RAINLESS REGION—PISCO—ISLAY—ARICA—IQUIQUI—COBIJA—CALDERA—CHAÑARCILLO—LA SERENA—COQUIMBO—ARRIVAL AT VALPARAISO.

Having bade adieu to Captain Mitchell, the gallant commander, and his accomplished officers of the United States ship "Wyoming," at anchor in the harbor of Callao, whose courtesies will be gratefully remembered, I went aboard of the British Steamship Navigation Company's steamer "Lima," bound for Valparaiso. Anchor hove and ship underway, we steered for the southern outlet of the harbor, in which, for the first time after the declaration of American Independence, the national birthday of the United States was saluted by a British man-o'-war. On Commodore Stockton sending a lieutenant to make an acknowledgment of the unusual comity, Admiral Sinclair manned his boat, and accompanied by his officers, boarded the American frigate, saying, with a sailor's characteristic frankness, "fifty years have passed since mother and child quarrelled—time enough to wipe off old scores."

An occasional phenomenon of the harbor of Callao, called "the painter," darkens all white paint about vessels in port at the time. It is thought by some persons to depend on disengaged sulphurous gas, which causes an active effervescence of the water, and results probably from interior changes taking place nearer the earth's surface here than elsewhere, and may have connection with the cause of the frequent earthquakes of this region.

The lighthouse on the north end of the island of San Lorenzo was visible in the distance, a very unusual circumstance, for as it is high enough to be in the perpetual fog that envelops the island heights at night, it is, I am assured by old traders at this port, of no use whatever. It would be well to put it lower, below the line of fog, *or put it out*, and thus relieve foreign shipping from a heavy assessment for its support.

On nearing San Lorenzo the larboard bulwarks of a Peruvian frigate were seen barely lifted above the water, showing the spot where, with all her armament and four hundred of her crew on board, she was capsized a few days since, in an attempt to put her into a floating dock for repairs when a heavy sea was on. A fine ship is probably lost to the country, which can ill afford it, and one hundred and fifty persons were killed or drowned by the accident. President Castilla was near being of the number, having gone ashore but five minutes before. Like his Scotch exemplar he seems to "bear a charmed life."

We steered across the harbor due west, and came so near to San Lorenzo before changing our course, that the steamer seemed intent on climbing its bold heights; but suddenly heading south she swept close along shore, taking as wide a berth as possible of "Callao Point Reef," and the "Whale's Back," which lifted its dark outline above the water, in bold contrast to the sea of foam that whitened its lower rocks. Emerging from this narrow channel, *the Boqueron*, the islet of El Fronton was soon passed—supposed to have been once united to San Lorenzo, but at present separated from it by a narrow and impassable strait. And now, a few detached rocks having been left to the westward, we are fairly at sea.

> "Once more upon the waters! Yet once more!
> And the waves bound beneath me as a steed
> That knows its rider. Welcome to their roar!
> Swift to their guidance, whersoe'er it lead!"

The next morning after leaving Callao we made the Chincha Islands; fourteen hours by steam from the port of departure. On these islands—three in number—are the rich *guano* deposits of Peru. The original word is *huanu*, signifying in the ancient Quichua dialect "animal dung." The word now in general use is an abbreviation of *pishu huanu*, "bird dung." The terminal syllable *nu* of the ancient dialect has been changed by the Spaniards into *no*. The European orthography *guano*, now so generally adopted as to make an effort to correct it probably useless, is erroneous, the Quichua language, which originated the name, being without the letter g.

The deposit of these islands is doubtless due to the accumulated excrement of marine animals and birds, which are seen now in great numbers. The sea-lion and the seal, both by their presence in the adjacent waters at this time, and their skeletons in the strata of guano deposited ages since, tell of their agency in its production; while myriads of birds skimming the neighboring sea in quest of its abundant fish, show that they too have been agents in the general economy of nature, by furnishing a valuable fertilizer for impoverished soil.

These islands being situated within the rainless region of this coast, furnish the richest guano known to agriculture, inasmuch as its fertilizing ingredients are not dissolved and washed away. A peculiarity of a great part of the coast of Peru, from the neighborhood of Arica to Cape Blanco, embracing about 16° of latitude, is, that rain is rarely known to fall within its limits. Stevenson, an English traveller of accurate observation, gives the following rational explanation of the anomaly: "In April or May the mists called 'Garuas' begin, and continue with little interruption till November, which period is usually termed the winter solstice. The gentle winds that blow in the morning from the westward, and in the afternoon from the southward, are those which fill the atmosphere with aqueous vapors, forming a dense cloud or mist; and owing to the obliquity of the rays of the sun during this season, the evaporation is not sufficiently rarified or attenuated to enable it to rise above the summits of the adjacent mountains, so that it is limited to the range of flat country lying between the mountains and the sea, which incline toward northwest. Thus the vapors brought by the general winds are collected over this range of coast, and from the cause above mentioned cannot pass the tops of the mountains, but remain stationary until the sun returns to the south, when they are elevated by his vertical heat, and pass over the mountains into the interior, where they become condensed and fall in copious rains. That rain is not formed on the coast is attributable, first, to a want of contrary winds to agitate and unite the particles; and secondly, to their proximity to the earth, which they reach in their descent before a sufficient number of them can coalesce and form themselves into drops."

The agricultural use of guano is by no means of recent discovery. In the time of the Incas it was employed as a manure in ancient Peru. The islands near the coast being easy of access were much resorted to by the natives, and the *guano blanco*, the fresh white deposit, was preferred, as it doubtless had the fertilizing properties in greatest strength. The mode in which the Peruvians used guano was different from that by us. A hollow or trench around the young shoots was partly filled with the manure and then covered with earth. The field was then flooded with water, which was readily done in a country freely intersected by aqueducts. But for this the radicals would have been destroyed by the potency of the guano, the saline ingredients of which were thus dissolved and diffused in the circumjacent soil, where they were subsequently sought out and appropriated by the roots without danger to their delicate organization. The field was kept submerged but a few hours.

The aggregate superficial extent of the three Chincha Islands is about seven square miles; they are designated northern, middle, and southern. The northern is the largest, and is that yielding the greatest quantity of guano, eighty feet being considered about the average depth; though a gentleman largely interested in the trade told me that he had measured it at an indicated point having a depth of one hundred and fifty feet. The original estimate of the length of time—one thousand years—that this deposit on the Chinchas will suffice for the wants of the world, is likely to prove fallacious. So great has become the demand for it, that half the deposit of the largest island has been removed already; and a considerable quantity has also been taken from the middle island. More than a hundred vessels are now lying at anchor around and between the two larger islands taking in cargo, besides many loaded and awaiting formalities of exportation in the harbor of Callao, showing the extraordinary increase in the demand for guano within a few years. Instead of fifty thousand tons being removed annually, according to the original calculation, it is now known that for three years but little less than five hundred thousand tons have been shipped per annum. And so great are the pecuniary wants of the Peruvian Government, from official improvidence and delinquency, that it is now thought that with corresponding recklessness and continued forced sale, the deposit at these islands will become exhausted in ten or twelve years. Large as will have been the aggregate revenue of Peru—probably from five hundred millions to eight hundred millions of dollars—from this source, yet there is not a country paying its quota of that immense sum for the use of guano, that will not have derived more benefit from it than this. Elsewhere agricultural skill and industry have made it tributary to a production which has resulted in blessings—developing internal improvements, affording means of education, promoting social happiness and general prosperity. To Peru it seems to have been a curse, for it pensions officials to fatten on public plunder; while it encourages perpetual revolutions, that place and peculation may reward successful treason and reckless disturbers of domestic peace. It fosters, too, a large standing army, resulting in oppression, paralyzed industry, and wars with their attendant evils. Limited to the moderate expenditure actually demanded by the administrative necessities of a small republic, how great the good that might be made to flow to the country from a judicious use of the large surplus revenue! And how brief the time would be before an intelligent and enterprising people, directed by wise and honest leaders, with such means at command, would climb or pierce the Andes; and uniting the Pacific and the Amazon with an iron band, would awake the slumbering echoes of mountain passes with the panting engine, and speak into life the dead elements of immense mineral and agricultural wealth!

That an idea may be formed of the large amount of shipping engaged in the guano trade, it may be stated that during six months of this year—1860—from April first to September thirtieth, as ascertained from the United States Consul at Callao, the tonnage of American vessels entering that port was 111,648 tons, being but 9,992 tons less than that of all the other foreign vessels together, which was 121,640 tons. The *registered* tonnage of the ships is here referred to. One-third more should be added to show their *actual* carrying capacity, which would in like proportion increase the guano thus shown to have been exported, and in like manner the value of cargoes and the amount of freight. Thus it will be seen that at thirty dollars per ton, the guano shipped in six months in American vessels from the Chinchas, and which according to Peruvian commercial regulations, must take its final departure from Callao, was worth $4,465,920, and the amount received for freight to one-half that sum. The cargo in the above estimate is considered as all guano; but it should be stated, for the sake of accuracy, that a very trifling part thus shipped was vacuna and goat skins, and Elias' sherry wine. Although the shipment of guano here referred to was in American bottoms, nearly one-third of it was on foreign account, in addition to what was exported to Europe in English, French, and German vessels. The above estimated value of guano is the price in Peru; it is twice that in the United States—sometimes even more.

It must not be inferred, however, from the above comparisons of United States and all other foreign tonnage engaged in the *export* trade of Callao, that the former enjoys any similar proportion of its *import* trade. American manufacturing and mercantile complacency may be mortified by the truth, but nevertheless the fact cannot be changed to gratify national vanity. The record shows that of the total value of imports into Callao in 1860, to wit, $8,562,957.16, the United States furnished a total of but $192,836.44; while Great Britain's proportion amounted to $2,582,109.33; that of France to $2,395,898.79; and even Germany, Chile, and Panama contributed more to the wants of Peru than the United States did.

Five miles south of the Chinchas are the two small and barren *Ballista isles;* and near them the hidden and dangerous *Salcedo rock.* Steering in shore from the Chinchas, a half hour brought us to *Pisco,* the seaport of the province and of the inland town Ica. Pisco has a population of six thousand, but there is nothing in its location or appearance deserving notice. It has the finest mole in South America, a half mile long, extending beyond the rather threatening looking breakers, and built of iron by Mr. Wheelright, a United States civil engineer, at a cost to the Peruvian Government of $450,000.

Before the abolition of negro slavery, many negroes were engaged in cotton and wine growing in this province, who still remaining here, form a worthless part of the population of Pisco, of no use to themselves and a burden to the rest of the community, most of whom are cholos. The chief merit of this act of Peru was that she was not unmindful of the equal claims of citizens to protection and justice; that she did not imitate some others of larger professions of moral and physical grandeur, and play the national philanthropist at the cost of those who aided in giving her existence and power; that she did not merge a government protector in a public robber. The debt incurred by Peru for the emancipation of the negro slaves was $3,900,000; two hundred dollars being allowed to the owners for each slave, with interest until paid. The debt is now nearly extinguished; but it will be long before the country will recover from evils that have followed the error of confounding the political slavery of the Caucasian race with personal servitude of an inferior race, between whom it is as impossible to establish a harmonious relation of equality, social and civil, as it would be for human capacity to annul the fiat of Supreme Wisdom, and recreate them with similar physical organization, moral sentiments, and intellectual endowments. Agriculture is languishing for labor; and that labor, once useful under necessary direction and control, is perishing, now that it is cast loose without the powers to sustain it in competition with a higher order of intelligence, energy, and enterprise.

The very small quantity of cotton now grown in this province of Ica, is of long staple and silky texture, and is all purchased on French account. The largest export from Pisco is the product of the vine, the *Aquardiente de Pisco*, of this district of Peru—"Pisco" as it is commonly called—the ordinary brandy of the country. A much superior quality and of more exquisite flavor, is the *Italia de Pisco*, usually known, especially abroad, by the more familiar name "Italia;" it is made from a richer grape, the Muscatel. Don Domingo Elias, a wealthy planter and once President of Peru, is also extensively engaged in manufacturing wine. It is known here as sherry wine, and after having made the voyage of the East Indies, it is considered by good judges equal to the best sherry of Spain. One hundred and twelve thousand gallons are produced annually. It readily brings three dollars per gallon. Pisco and Italia are conveyed to market on mules in large pear-shaped jars, containing from five to ten gallons each, called *botijas.*

From ten to twelve miles south of Pisco is the deep Bay of Paraca, well sheltered, and better suited for anchorage and landing than the open roadstead of Pisco, where the surf is often dangerous, and the swell so great that vessels cannot lie at the mole in safety, but lying off are loaded and unloaded by means of launches. Mariners say that the mole should have been built at Paraca instead of Pisco. The large interests and influence of Señor Elias determined its present location.

From the Bay of Paraca the coast sweeps for five or six miles to the westward, and then again to the south, forming a bold and elevated, but barren promontory—the peninsula of Paracas. On the north face of this peninsula is an image of which the following is a rude representation:

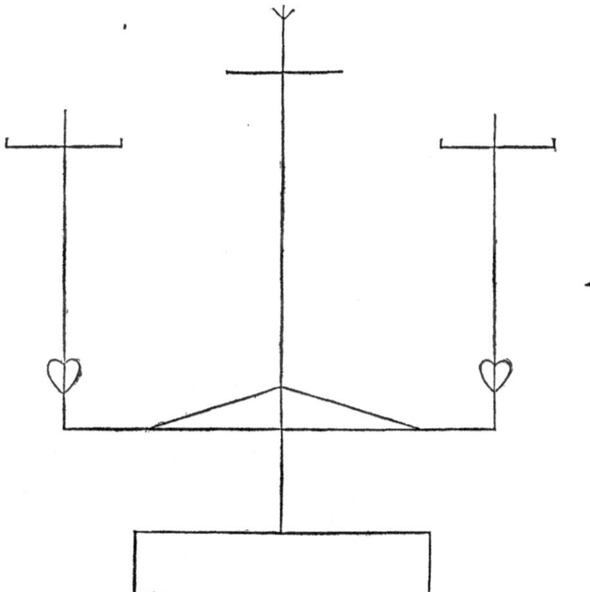

The height of the middle crucifix is not less than five hundred feet—estimated by the known height of the hill. It is plainly seen from the Chincha Islands, thirteen miles distant. It is ditched in the earth, and but for the exemption of this part of Peru from rain it would soon be obliterated. There are no records to tell at what time this symbol of Christianity was sculptured on this desolate hill-side; but tradition says that it was done in the time of Pizarro, and in a single night, by the united effort of many zealous Catholics, to impress the worshippers of the Sun with a conviction of Divine interposition, and thus by a pretended miraculous manifestation of the emblem of their faith, to win the Peruvians from idolatry. The present inhabitants of the neighborhood make annual pilgrimages to the shrine, and after deepening the impressions of the figure they drink pisco, dance the zama-cueca, and have a good time generally.

Doubling Cape Paraca we entered a channel between the promontory and San Gallan Island, two and a half miles wide, called El Boqueron de Pisco, through which the wind blew with violence, as if to dispute our passage. But a short struggle gave steam the mastery, and we soon emerged from the stormy funnel, the ocean spreading illimitably to the west, and to the east a barren hilly coast stretching southward hundreds of miles, seamed by deep ravines as we approached Islay, and streaked and patched for ten or twelve miles north and south of that town, as if with the lingering snow-marks of spring in colder regions, but here by drifts of a whitish powder blown about by the steady winds of this coast. This substance becomes fixed in some places by incrustation and admixture with other substances. After an examination of it and the phenomena attending its presence at Islay, I conclude that it is the widely distributed disintegrated lava bed, or substratum of the great desert situated between the seaport Islay and the inland city of Arequipa, thrown up and spread during ages over that extensive volcanic region. Occasionally the background of this winter-looking scene, where winter never comes, was the far-off Andes, pencilled against the eastern sky in faintest outline. From Pisco, our last point of departure, we encountered a stiff southeast trade wind, which gave us a rough sea, and delayed somewhat our arrival at Islay. Distance from Pisco three hundred and thirty miles—direction southeast.

*Islay*, in latitude 17° S., has between three hundred and three hundred and fifty houses, and a population—as stated by Mr. Gibson, resident agent of the Pacific Steam Navigation Company—of about twenty-five hundred. It is the seaport of the important inland city Arequipa, the second in size in Peru, situated from eighty to ninety miles in the interior, and having a population of forty thousand. Arequipa was the ancient city to which the Marshal Almagro returned after the first Spanish incursion into Chile, when he encountered disheartening difficulties on his mountain march south, and terrible sufferings on his retreat nearer the seacoast across the great desert of Atacama. Here, too, it was that he received information of the insurrection of the Peruvians, and the danger that threatened the city of Cuzco, from which he had departed on his southern expedition of conquest and annexation; and where he was shortly after treacherously garroted by command of his old, but perfidious associate Pizarro.

Islay is built on the brow of a rocky bluff two or three hundred feet high, of steep ascent, and overlooks a little bay or harbor, formed by the coast line on the east, a bold promontory of three-quarters of a mile on the south, and a western barrier of several rocky islets that serve as a breakwater against the ocean swell, which, however, still rolls in sufficiently strong, especially at the full and change of the moon, to render landing at the mole very difficult. Lady passengers are often put ashore from launches by means of an arm-chair or basket swung from a revolving crane rigged with suitable tackle. They are thus hoisted to upper regions like other valuable merchandise—for are they not made a marketable commodity by modern usage? Two of such, who have by graceful manners and charming esprit, won the admiration of our ship's company—an English rose-bud and a flashing jewel of the Emerald Isle—sought to startle the natives with blue eyes and the latest fashions. One of them, not calculating on an impertinent sea, all of human nature having been deferential, allowed the propitious moment for a step and a bound to pass, and in the pause was rudely assailed by a presumptuous roller that lifted her *saya despliegada* even beyond the questionable height of a Broadway parvenu. Belles, who prefer disembarking by the stairway of Islay to being triced up to the air of *yo-heave-o*, would find the *saya ajustada* a more modest though less capacious costume. The houses of Islay are built of simple materials—fewer of adobe and cane, and more of clapboard and shingle, than seen elsewhere in my Peruvian rambles. A fountain in the public square, near the custom house, receives, through pipes, a moderate supply of water from adjacent hills. Several vessels are at anchor taking in cargo—wool, rice, cinchona, and specie, in exchange for European merchandise, chiefly drygoods and iron, now lying at the landing in considerable quantities. Flour in bags of one hundred pounds—quintals—principally from Chile, is largely imported, upon which there is a duty of two dollars per quintal, not for the protection of agricultural interests, however, for wheat is not a product of Peru. Add this and four dollars per quintal for transportation on mules to Arequipa, to the first cost of the flour, and it will be seen that its citizens pay dearly for the staff of life. Music is at a high premium, too. On a pianoforte the duty is ninety dollars; and fifty more must be paid for freight to the capital of this province *between two mules.* It is not easy to decide which are the least of asses, the carriers by necessity of the physical burden, or those who submit to the civil burden of such unrighteous taxation. The pseudo-republics of this coast are strangely illustrative of oppressive government. But criticism should not be arrogant of political sanctity, for our turn may yet come to exemplify the subserviency of so-called republicans to those who have usurped and tyrannically exercised unconstitutional power. It was a novel sight to witness all merchandise, even to sacks of wheat, iron bedsteads, and bales of goods, carried on men's shoulders up a steep acclivity of two hundred and fifty feet height, from the landing to the custom house plateau, where mule caravans awaited to convey it to the interior. An Anglo-American seaport similarly situated, the entrepot for the commerce of a populous back country, would not be long without an inclined plane railroad and a stationary engine, or horse-power, for the raising of this large quantity of merchandise. The citizens of Islay talk of a railroad to the interior. They come of an ancestry remarkable for grandiloquence—none so capable of killing a question by speaking against time; this doubtless will be the fate of the proposed railroad to Arequipa. A desert to cross without water and without fuel, and having neither skill, capital, nor labor, yet Peruvians propose to build the road! Need more be said? True, the historian Prescott seems to have thought it practicable, for he says that Gonzalo Pizarro "caused galleys to be built at Arequipa, to secure the command of the seas." But if he had personally crossed, or even read authentic descriptions of the intervening desert of seventy-five miles extent, he would have known the impossibility of their being transported from that far inland city to the sea, and would have omitted a statement, in view of natural difficulties, altogether absurd.

Two remarkable excavations in the earth are found three-fourths of a mile west of Islay, near the extreme point of the promontory on which the town stands. These are enormous basins of rock, each about three hundred feet wide at the top, and two hundred and fifty feet deep, gradually narrowing to a diameter of probably one hundred feet at the bottom; circular in form, and each communicating by an aperture of fifteen or twenty feet in diameter with the sea; the water entering and escaping in unison with the ocean swells, and sending up the subdued melody of its flow from the depths below like the singing fountain of the Arabian tale of enchantment, as if to tempt the weary to cool chambers and sparkling waters, which once reached, might prove both bath and burial place. Standing above and looking at the coming and going tide through the archways of these vast wash-bowls, but little power of imagination was needed to fancy Neptune driving his variegated coursers into one of them at early dawn, calmly to make his morning ablutions away from the agitations of his wild domain. How were these excavations of rock formed? Did they result from undermining by the ocean through ages of alternate ebb and flow—assaults of tempest waves and rending earthquakes, with final fall of unsupported masses, and washing away of the crumbling debris?

All hands aboard, in obedience to the summons of the parting gun, we bade adieu to Islay, and steered from the harbor between two of the before-mentioned rocky islets, which appeared whitewashed with guano-blanco by tens of thousands of pelicans covering their castellated crags, and circling about them jealous of the intrusion near their sea-girt homes. With calmer waters than rocked us before our arrival at Islay, we again bore away southeastwardly, and next morning at six o'clock anchored in the little bay of Arica.

The town of *Arica* is in the Province of Moquegua, the most southerly of Peru—its latitude 18° 28′ S. It stands on a nearly level plain formed by the recession of the coast-range from the shore-line, and communicates with the interior by a valley which pierces the surrounding hills, affording a distant view of the Cordillera, and bringing down by its little river Azapa, when in flood in the spring, a supply of fresh water for the town and shipping. At other seasons very good water is obtained from wells. The anchorage for shipping is protected on the south by a bold rocky point six hundred feet high, from the base of which extends a reef on which the surf incessantly beats in noisy war. This extends to a low islet, from which projects another shorter reef, the whole forming an admirable breakwater in that direction. The water-front of the town is protected from the incoming rollers by a stone wall, north of which is a mole for the landing of merchandise. Still further on stands a commodious bonded warehouse and custom-house, two stories high, chastely built of stone, and faced their whole length of one hundred and twenty feet by a handsome iron colonnade. Beyond this are the capacious warehouses and offices of the Pacific Steam Navigation Company, and these are flanked at the north end by the railroad station buildings. All of these facing the harbor, present an imposing appearance. Behind them are the dwelling-houses and small stores, neat and clean, yellow or whitewashed adobe buildings; most of them one story high, fronting on streets from twenty to forty feet wide, running at right angles, and smoothly and beautifully paved with small rubble stone diversified with ornamental figures; the sidewalks being of white slabbing. A pretty market-place and three tasteful churches break pleasantly the sameness of the scene; and at the north end of the town shade trees and flower-gardens relieve the eye from the glare of reflected light. Conspicuous among the houses is the very inviting hotel of Madame Aimè—a large square two-story building, surrounded by two suites of open galleries, and a handsome garden of ornamental trees, shrubbery, and flowers. The voyager, weary of restless waters and a rolling and pitching ship, longing for the rest and sense of safety of *terra firma;* and the traveller from Bolivia, jaded, hungry, worried by mule obstinacy, and often suffering from the *seroche,* resulting from diminished atmospheric pressure in climbing even the mountain pass of Uaylillos, 14,750 feet above the sea, on brain, stomach, lungs, and eyes, may well rejoice in such a hotel as is found at Arica, and such a hostess as Madame Aimè. This town has a population of three thousand, mostly Indians and Indian half-castes. It is the seaport of this district of Peru, and also of the neighboring Republic of Bolivia, when trade is not interdicted by disagreements between the two countries. It is in communication with *Tacna,* thirty-five miles to the north-northeast by railroad, the only one of any considerable extent in Peru—the seven miles road of Callao to Lima, and the nine miles from Lima to Chorillos, really being what even a North American frontiersman would call "one-horse institutions." Tacna is the largest town and the capital of the Province of Moquegua, having a population of twelve thousand, including the residents of suburban haciendas. It is the starting point for the transmontane region of which La Pas is the capital, and the place at which preparations must be made for that tiresome muleback journey of four days. The railroad was built by an English contractor, Mr. Joseph Hagan, for a joint-stock company; but its ownership has passed exclusively into the hands of the builder and Señor Candamo, the largest capitalist of Peru. Mr. H. obtained the grant to build the road, with a Government loan of $2,000,000, and also a guarantee of six per cent. on the cost. The *vales*—bonds—of the company, held by the Government as security, were afterward sold, and they were bought by Mr. H. at forty-eight or fifty cents on the dollar.

The transaction showed two things: first, that sharp speculations are not limited to Wall Street; and secondly, that the States of South as well as of North America are doomed to be mercilessly plucked by the shrewd, selfish, and mercenary. The railroad fare to Tacna is four dollars, and half as much more is charged for baggage. The road has a gradually ascending plane; for half the distance from Arica the grade being thirty-five feet, and the remainder seventy feet to the mile.

Three ships and several smaller vessels are now at anchor in the harbor of Arica, and a large quantity of imported merchandise is lying at the mole; as also wool, copper, and tin, products of this country, awaiting exportation; and an abundance of sugar-cane, chirimoyas, oranges, and other tropical fruits and vegetables, for coastwise transportation to less favored districts further south.

On a hill, somewhat more than a mile from the town, there is an ancient burial place of the Peruvian Indians, from which many mummies have been removed by curiosity-hunters. A Government prohibition has arrested the frequent desecration of the graves; although, occasionally, a foreign resurrectionist escapes detection and bears off a snuff-colored, shrunken specimen of humanity, folded up and wrapped in coarse cotton or woollen cloth. These remains become rapidly reduced to powder when exposed to the air, and are blown abroad by the winds to fulfil other uses in the economy of nature; yet when first disintered they present an appearance of excellent preservation, which is due, perhaps in part, to nitre contained in the soil of this region. One million quintals of nitre, I was informed, are exported annually from Callao, realizing about two millions of dollars.

Taking leave of this very pretty and improving little seaport, we stood out of the Bay of Arica, doubling the surf-crested reef and steering close along a steep rock-bound coast resembling somewhat the palisades of the Hudson River. In rounding the barrier reef a glorious sight was presented, as increasing distance lifted the magnificent panorama from which we were passing; a bold spur of the Andes, bounding beyond with dark and frowning heights a nearer and brighter picture; while the beauties of town, valley, and mountain, seemed to lead the eye to the contemplation of the grandeur of the far-off summit of proud Tacora, which raised its snow-crown like frosted silver above the clouds, and bathed its icy minarets in the gleaming light of an intertropic sun. The day was clear, the air balmy, and the sea smooth and polished as a burnished mirror; all nature sought to elevate the sentiments, and rejoice the spirit; but the thought of that home, with its blissful associations, so longed for and so long lost, would wind its way among the heartstrings, and awaken sympathies responsive to its touch of tenderness.

At 11 o'clock P. M. of the day we left Arica we arrived at the next port in our route, *Iquiqui*, latitude 20° 12′ S., and laid off a short time to land passengers and freight. Of course sight-seeing was impossible, but no disappointment was felt, as Captain Bloomfield, of our steamer, familiar by long service with this entire coast, and reliable authority concerning it and its various and variegated races of humanity, informed us that "no one need desire to go ashore, for nothing but *saltpetre* would be found worth seeing." His high appreciation of this saline is accounted for by his English birth and education. Our venerable kinsman, Mr. Bull—with respect may he always be spoken of—has a wonderful *penchant* for the explosive, of which it is a chief ingredient; and no person of candor will deny that, comprehending fully its use, he has also put it to effective account. The town stands on a slight indentation of the coast, at the foot of a cliff two thousand feet high, and has huts sufficient for a population of fifteen hundred persons, who are supported by the production and sale of nitre, upward of one million of quintals, at a value of about two dollars per quintal, being shipped annually. Part of this probably finds its way to Callao before final exportation, hence a corresponding deduction must be made in the quantity already stated to be shipped from that port. The importations at Iquiqui are the necessaries of life, nothing being grown or manufactured here, or in the vicinity; even the water used is distilled from sea-water or is brought a distance of thirty miles.

It was here that the two United States vessels, "Lizzie

Thompson" and "Georgiana," delivered their cargoes of lumber and barley, and were chartered to load with guano at Pabellon de Pica and Punta de Lobos, about forty miles further south, where they were subsequently captured by the Peruvian war-steamer "Tumbez," by the special order of the central government. It was this act that led to the controversy between the United States and Peru which has resulted in an interruption of diplomatic relations, after an unanswerable exposition by the American minister, Mr. Clay, at Lima, of the facts at issue, and the principles involved in the unwarrantable seizure of these vessels. It neither comports with the dignity, rights, nor interest of neutral nations, to submit to the commercial restrictions, seizures, and losses incident to the civil strife, and revolutionary struggles for personal or partisan ascendency, perpetually agitating these Spanish-American countries; especially when belligerents, practically if not by treaty stipulations, nationalize each other by negotiations and agreements which ignore the idea of rebellion against legitimate government, and create in impartial judgment an equality of claim to national respect and recognition.

Bearing away from Iquiqui due south, we ran within three miles of that small part of the republic of *Bolivia* which borders on the Pacific, after having passed *Paquiqui*, a promontory a quarter of a mile long and thirteen hundred feet high, jutting at right angles from the bluff of four thousand feet, which for hundreds of miles rises almost perpendicular from the sea, with its dark craggy brow frowning upon the waves as if indignant at their ceaseless aggressions. Although guano may be seen in superficial patches at Point Francisco two miles north, and Point San Philippi two miles south of Paquiqui, yet the last-named place is the only important guano port of Bolivia, except Cobija, further south. Four English vessels are now loading at Paquiqui, none of the guano deposited there being shipped to the United States. It is not considered equal in quality to that of the Chinchas, in consequence of its less proportion of ammonia. The guano at Paquiqui is the deposit of birds, that at the Chinchas of the various species of seal as well as birds. Bolivia sells annually to the highest bidder the exclusive privilege of removal.

Twenty or twenty-five miles further south is *Tocopilla*, consisting of a number of small houses, and several copper smelting furnaces standing on the beach directly under a lofty metamorphic bluff, that presents at numerous points and for long distances north and south the outcropping of rich copper ore, which looks like immense metallic buttresses for the grand sea-wall of the Southern Continent. Copper is the great mineral staple of this coast for more than five hundred miles—even beyond Coquimbo. Three ships are riding at anchor close in shore; and as we pass along almost within hail of the lofty cliff, fourteen furnaces are seen in blast on this part of the Bolivian coast. We left Iquiqui at midnight, and the next day, at 5 P. M., anchored off *Cobija*, in latitude 22½° S., the only seaport for general commerce belonging to Bolivia.

This town has twenty-five hundred inhabitants, and is situated at the base of a hill from which extends westwardly for half a mile a low and rugged promontory forming the southern boundary of the harbor. The junction of the promontory with the mainland is occupied by a part of the town; a small but by no means formidable looking fortification stands on its outer point; and several furnaces in blast occupy the intermediate space, their tall chimneys giving forth the flaming token of industry and enterprise. We were landed from a launch upon a tolerably good wharf, on which stood the inevitable cholo sentinel—the unvarying sign of South American military domination—and a promiscuous crowd of all colors, a compounded multitude of races, assembled to seize upon our steamer's cargo of flesh, fish, fruit, and forage in general, which the sterile soil and almost equally unproductive waters hereabouts fail to supply; and for which these people are dependent mainly upon parts of Peru and Chile, and even to some extent on the Argentine Republic in the interior. The houses are weather-boarded, of one story, with shingle or plank roof. The streets are unpaved. Public buildings—a custom house, port-captain's office, church, and military barracks of course. In the centre of the town is a dusty plaza, on the sides of which are storehouses, and where are assembled every morning several hundred mules to be loaded with goods for the interior. The exportations of Cobija are principally copper and guano; the former amounting in value to nearly $2,000,000 annually. An idea may be formed of the cost of housekeeping here by the following prices: Fresh meat eighteen cents per pound, and if the supply be exhausted, a not uncommon occurrence, the inhabitants become vegetarians until next steamer-day; flour twelve dollars per hundred; potatoes five cents per pound; cabbage and cauliflower one dollar a head; rice and sugar twenty-five cents per pound; butter one dollar to one dollar and a half per pound; fresh water furnished by two distilleries, sixty-two cents for sixteen gallons, and if one of these sources of supply should fail from any cause the price rises to one dollar; servants wages twenty dollars per month. I shall have too much regard for any friend of mine to recommend him for the consulate at Cobija; for apart from the absence of social, scenic, and even sensual attractions, he might find it impossible to balance his debtor and credit account; unless willing to imitate a foreign functionary, who, coming off to the steamer for an expected package, and impelled by curiosity to see its contents before going ashore, unwittingly opened it and exposed to some of us a large lot of miscellaneous jewelry not intended to be seen by impertinent observers, but designed to be clandestinely introduced into Cobija *without payment of duty*. Relying on the silence of strangers who were not Government detectives, he hastily concealed the package, and was shortly afterwards observed in familiar conversation with the port-captain, who little supposed that he was interchanging official civilities with a *smuggler*. Nations owe it to justice and self-respect to see that they are represented abroad by those who will not degrade themselves, and dishonor their country, by engaging in unlawful acts against the Governments to which they are accredited.

A brief detention at Cobija sufficed for discharging freight, and we were soon again climbing the long swells of the Pacific, which lifted our steamer on their shoulders like a plaything, and let her down into their deep trough with gentleness as if they loved their favorite too fondly to deal roughly with her. The air is bracing, bringing health from the breezy south. Its coming is welcomed, and it passes on its way ladened with love for those afar off, who are ever in mind and heart. It is said that our voyage will not be varied by change of scene for a day. So let it be! There is enough in the billowy floor beneath us, and the boundless canopy above, to inspire thought and exalt the spirit. Through these we may contemplate that eternity of which they are the symbols, to which we are hastening, and the immortal interests of which it were well for us duly to weigh.

At dawn of the second day after leaving Cobija we were passing the low sandy coast of Atacama, the northern province of *Chile*—sometimes improperly written *Chili, but the former is the Chilean Government orthography*—and at 7 A. M. we entered the snug little bay of Caldera, about a mile and a half in general diameter. The town of *Caldera*, in latitude 27° S., like nearly all along this coast, is built on the southeast side of the harbor, being protected in that direction from the almost constantly prevalent southerly winds, by a promontory extending westwardly, which presents at its point a rugged breastwork of rocks than which nothing could better resist the ceaseless war of ocean swells and occasional violent storms. A substantial pile wharf prolonging a well-built stone breakwater and abutment, heavily floored, and on which is a terminus of the Copiapo railroad, forms a small inner harbor of smooth water for convenient landing of passengers at a stairway. The sandy slope on which the town stands is spotted liberally with sandstone and dark granite looking rocks. Five or six streets seem to be under municipal regulation, but these are unpaved, though the luxury of freestone sidewalks is found to prevent the pedestrian becoming stalled in sand. In my ramble over the town, eight or ten houses only were seen with *altos*, the rest having but one story, scarcely high enough for a specimen Kentuckian to stand up in. The houses are built of scantling frame, lathed with split cane, and indifferently stuccoed or roughly weather-boarded, and have slanting roofs of shingle, plank, or matted cane. A church seemed to be slowly creeping toward completion; but it is probable that by the time it is finished it will require rebuilding. If the custom of one of your bishops, as well known for political partisanship as for ecclesiastical tyranny, not to consecrate a church until the uttermost farthing is actually paid for its erection, should prevail here, it is to be feared that the people of Caldera will be regarded by some of the self-righteous as outside barbarians, inasmuch as they are not likely to have one temple *dedicated* to the service of religion. A double-towered building asserts its prerogative of architectural distinction, and imitates many a seedy aristocrat by looking scornfully through its own dilapidation at shabby neighbors, as no doubt its occupants the town officers do at the canaille over whom they rule. Strolling outside of the town, I saw but one dwarfed and sickly-looking shrub in all the surrounding waste of sand and rock. Provisions for the two thousand native tatterdemalions are brought from a distance, and fresh water is the product of distilleries. The only inducement to live here is in the opportunity for capital and enterprise to profit by working the neighboring mines of copper, and the not very distant rich silver deposits of Chañarcillo and Tres Puntas, the former of which alone has exported $80,000,000 in bar silver and crushed and crude ore, since its discovery in 1832.

An intelligent gentleman, for a time resident at these mines, who came aboard the steamer at Caldera, gave me some interesting information about them, of which the following is a summary: Chañarcillo is a village, not of houses but of caves; a hill covered with round holes, resembling a piece of wood honeycombed by worms. Twenty leagues to the south of Copiapo (which is about fifty miles east-southeast of Caldera) at the termination of a chain of mountains which extends for a long distance, varying its directions, and whose surface reflects various metallic hues, a hunter of Guanacos discovered in May, 1832, a deposit of silver of incalculable value, which in less than ten years produced more than twelve millions of dollars. There are upwards of a hundred mines now being worked, some very rich, others occasionally so, but all justifying expectation of ultimately richly rewarding the perseverance of their owners. The veins at considerable depth are richest. The works of the chief mine of Chañarcilla, called Descubredora, as much on account of first discovery as of richness, extend to a greater depth than any others; but Las Guias, La Carlota, La Santa Rosa, El Rosario de Picon, La Colorado, La Guia de Carballo, El Reventon Colorado, and several others, are also in flourishing condition. A considerable number of others, although at present not very productive, are yet valued at immense sums by their owners; and if a mine be abandoned by one party it is unhesitatingly purchased by another, who pursues the work until a fortune is made, or all that has been embarked in the enterprise is lost. Chañarcillo is one of the parts of the Republic of Chile where the greatest activity prevails, and probably for many years it will continue a principal source of its riches. In the midst of the mines is a small village named Placilla, where miners go for relaxation and frolic; and there in an hour is expended in gambling, flirtation, and drinking, the proceeds of long labor and deprivation of comfort, and the occasional nuts of metal *their consciences oblige them to purloin*, that the patron who works much less than they do *should not be unreasonably rewarded.*

It is related of these mines of Chañarcillo, that they were discovered in May, 1832, by a donkey driver, who was seeking wood, and hunting the huanaco (guanaco) at the same time for amusement. Becoming fatigued, he sat on a stone to rest, and soon perceived a projection of his seat to be formed of silver. Godoi, the poor mule driver, thus suddenly became the possessor of a secret, which, discreetly kept, or wisely imparted, would have bestowed on him unequalled wealth. He forgot the guanaco, and would have forgotten his wandering donkies had he not needed a conveyance for some of his sudden riches to Copiapo. He found himself in a difficult position; how to turn his discovery to profitable account, was the question. To obtain useful counsel, he at last confided his secret to Juan José Callejas, an old explorer and miner by profession; who, although a placer hunter of many years in the neighborhood, had not been as lucky as the poor wood-cutter. Godoi presented him one-third of the new-found riches for the benefit of his professional experience; and after having appropriated the immediately accessible cream of his discovery, Godoi sold his remaining two-thirds of title, and free from all anxieties of ownership and business, retired to taste the pleasures of riches. Although never, as a donkey driver, recognized by kindred, he soon found himself, as the affluent *Don* Godoi, sought out and courted by numerous relatives, the discovery of whom surprised him as much as the discovery of the silver mine. Intimate friends and smiling patronesses also visited and courted him, in whom he recognized those who had been before merely purchasers of his panniers of wood. Godoi, like other weak-minded persons aspiring to social position, felt obliged to return these numerous and delicate demonstrations of regard. And to show his appreciation of the efforts to please him, he threw open his house with unrestrained hospitality. Magnificent dinners were succeeded by splendid balls; these by nights of debauchery; and the always crowded breakfast board with daily gambling, followed; until ruinous expenditure resulted in impoverishment, and oil even was wanted for the lamp which lighted his footsteps to dissoluteness and disgrace. Godoi awakened to the fact that he was abandoned by pretended friends, and that the joys he had tasted as in a dream had turned to bitterness in reality. A generous friend of the explorer who had become wealthy through the discovery, on learning the misfortune and penury of Godoi, presented him a share of a single vein which yielded him fourteen thousand dollars; with which sum his benefactor induced him to purchase a farm in Coquimbo, where, profiting by the wisdom dearly purchased, and no longer trusting to the arts of the false and delusions of the wicked, he lived some years in domestic peace and happiness; and then dying, he left an example of humble but honest occupation in early life, and simple competency with industry at its close, to tell how much more real happiness they bestowed than did the great riches unregulated by moderation, useful employment, and morality, which cursed his middle age.

Eleven copper smelting furnaces are seen in blast at Caldera; and the superintendent of these informed me that several others on the opposite side of the harbor, not as strongly built, were lately shaken down by an earthquake; this, like other districts of Chile, suffering greatly from these visitations. The exportation of fine copper is eighteen hundred tons annually, worth from ninety to one hundred and ten pounds sterling per ton; but much more of regulus and crude ore are shipped. *Chanaral*, which we passed last night, fifty miles to the north of Caldera, is also an important smelting point, producing copper largely, and greatly increasing the exportation.

A railroad projected by Mr. Wheelwright, and built by Mr. Evans, both from the United States, extends fifty miles, from *Caldera* to *Copiapo*—which has a population of fifteen thousand—and then on to *Pabellon*, seventy-three miles from Caldera. This road pays a dividend of sixteen per cent. per annum. Another company has continued the road to Chañarcillo, twenty-eight miles further; but the enterprise has not proved as profitable. A fine station and car-houses, and a machine shop, are at the Caldera terminus of the road; and large quantities of ore, coal, coke, and general merchandise lying at the depot, showed an actively-operated road. Coal and coke are brought from England; the latter for locomotive fuel, the former for smelting. The southern part of Chile has large deposits of coal, but it is not so valuable for smelting purposes.

About thirty feet above the water-line of the harbor, and a hundred in shore, the low bluff near the railroad depot is excavated under projecting rocks so extensively, as to induce the belief that it was once water-washed. It sustains the opinion of ocean recession at this point.

No Chinamen were seen, as in Peru, among the tawny Chilenos, squatting on the wharf under their gaily-striped ponchos, or listlessly lounging through the streets. Slavery, little understood by the ignorant masses in its extended application to national, social, and domestic condition, and in its relations to nature's ordinances; and misrepresented by artful demagogues and fanatics, the more readily to deceive the unthinking and accomplish selfish purposes, or gratify an insane idea however hostile to the public peace, is so repugnant to these people—who do not know what freedom is except as implied by the license to stir up an occasional row, which they call revolution, and getting shot or banished for it by arbitrary and irresponsible authority—that they will not even allow the *voluntary* servitude of Coolie *apprenticeship*, temporary though it be. Is not this "straining at a gnat and swallowing a camel"?

The "Scotland," a Boston barque, has just dropped anchor alongside. She sailed from this port a few days since loaded heavily with copper, and for want of a "trunk" for its proper distribution, became strained, leaked badly, and must discharge cargo and repair. A "broken back" is sometimes the consequence of carrying copper cargo without suitable staging; and such is as fatal an accident to a ship as to a man.

Having added to our list of passengers for Valparaiso, we steamed out of harbor and headed south for Coquimbo, our next port of destination. Between seven and eight o'clock of the morning after quitting Caldera, we were off *La Serena*, a town of ten thousand inhabitants, on the coast of Chile; and at the distance of seven or eight miles looking attractively in its picturesque surroundings. It was in this vicinity that Pedro de Valdivia established his first colony, when, in 1540, with one hundred and fifty Spaniards and a few Peruvian Indians, after traversing the inhospitable desert of Atacama, he marched into the heart of Chile, to lay the foundation of the present city of Santiago. A bold enterprise, considering his small force and meagre resources, and in view of the fact that the Marshal Almagro, who had been empowered by the Emperor Charles of Spain to discover and occupy the country for the distance of two hundred leagues south of the limit of Pizarro's territory, and who had made the first attempt to penetrate Chile and bring it under Spanish dominion, had but a short time before been so discouraged in the effort as to leave the country, and return to Cuzco without prosecuting the enterprise to the extent of permanent settlement in any part of it. La Serena occupies a small plain between lofty hills, which bound the river valley, extending inland. And here for the first time for many hundreds of miles, the green garniture of earth was unfolded to our view. Church steeples were seen rising gracefully above white houses and dark trees; and although not heard in the distance, no doubt their bells pealed forth their Sabbath chimes, to call worshippers to their religious observances. The anchorage being far from shore we passed on seven or eight miles further to the recognized seaport of this district—*Coquimbo*—in latitude 30° S., which is better sheltered, with deeper water, and greater facilities for commerce.

Coquimbo has a dusty plaza, guarded from tide and roller which seek to sprinkle it, by a stone wall, beyond which projects a wharf for convenient landing of passengers and freight. On the other three sides of the plaza are frame store-houses and public offices; miserable looking shanties compose the rest of the town. These are scattered along the foot of a hill of rocks, piled in inextricable confusion, and defying intrusion from man or beast. From the deck of the steamer sixteen furnace chimneys may be counted, which, in respect to the day, are not in blast. Their foreign ownership and direction may account for this observance; for the commandment, "Remember the Sabbath day to keep it holy," is not obeyed by the coast natives.

> "The Sabbath comes, a day of blessed rest:
> What hallows it upon this Christian shore?
> It is not sacred to a solemn feast.
> Hark! hear you not the forest monarch's roar?
> Crashing the lance he snuffs the spouting gore
> Of man and steed, o'erthrown beneath his horn;
> The throng'd Arena shakes with shouts for more;
> Yells the mad crowd o'er human entrails torn,
> Nor shrinks the female eye, nor e'en affects to mourn."

Sixteen vessels are lying at anchor, loading and unloading, showing a considerable import and export trade with the interior through this place. The shipments from Coquimbo are copper—metal and ore.

A large cargo of human live stock, chiefly of the complexion of the great staple of the coast hills for five hundred miles, and uncounted baskets, bundles, and promiscuous truck, having been taken aboard, the signal sent its echoes of departure among the distant heights, and a wild rush of affrighted natives was made from the steamer for the launches clinging to her side. So great is their horror of sea-sickness, that when a voyage is inevitable, they bury themselves in berth and blanket as soon as they come aboard, and there remain, if cabin passengers, until arriving at their destination they are aroused from torpor to go ashore. A separation at Coquimbo is a scene of action and expression, of tragedy and comedy, not easily forgotten. But the wild excitement, the mingled exclamations of apprehension, terror, and warning, the boisterous joy and ridiculous gymnastics of some who gained the launches in safety, though sometimes at the cost of a wet jacket, and the wail of agonized parting of others, could not drown the hoarse word of command that rose from the ship's gallery above the din ; and the "let her go" of Commodore Bloomfield soon gave us a headway that merged the fortunes of all in the destiny of the steamer. The copper-skins of the second class speedily went to work rigging shelters on the forecastle with shawls and fancy blankets, to protect themselves from the cooler winds of the higher latitudes we are daily making ; the rocky promontory of Coquimbo, as we bore away from the harbor, looking like a huge rasp forged in Vulcan's workshop.

From thirty to forty miles south of Coquimbo a promontory of the coast is seen, sternly sterile in its aspect, and called, from its supposed resemblance to a cow's tongue, "Lingua de Vaca."

We have a beautiful day and delicious atmosphere, inspiring pleasant thoughts. I would like to put together a missive of such, but my stateroom-companion—we have filled up at the various stopping places to repletion—is so garrulously inclined and inapprehensive of my monosyllables, that an attempt to do so might disturb feelings in harmony with surrounding nature. I will go on deck and look on the great sea, ever full of sublimity and instruction.

The breeze of yesterday afternoon heightened to a gale in the evening, and through the night blew furiously from the southwest, disturbing the ocean in such a fashion as to make the horizontal the favorite position of every thing on deck and in cabin. Pedestrians are nowhere to be found, the nearest personal approach to perpetual motion—a German diplomat—having "turned in" to avoid being *turned over*. Old Boreas seems to think that nautical novices have underrated his power to toss the Pacific about. However the name may imply tranquillity, we do not now deny the Pacific's entire submissiveness to the higher power of upper air. We have been pitched, pelted, pummelled, and punished particularly and promiscuously, enough to show its ability to get up an elemental row, even in this latitude, after the manner of that "Horn" which is generally supposed to have no equal alternative dilemma. The heavy blow made it necessary last night to stand further off the coast than usual; and as the steamer's course this morning is southeast to make our destination, she is struck by cross-seas from the southwest with such force that her port state-room lights are sunk under water. All things movable are lashed, and even man descends from his high estate, or has to submit to the humiliation of being "floored." Oh! that I were a pendulum for a time, that the perpendicular, which is my anatomical right, might be maintained! Better the monotony of merely apparent oscillation, with *conscious rectitude*, than the largest latitude of motion resulting in a *sense of actual degradation.*

There is a difference of opinion about the origin of the name Valparaiso, the chief seaport of Chile, for which we are bound. While some say that the Spaniards who entered Chile from Peru, across the desert of Atacama, while seeking the sea down the valley of Quillota, first beheld here the beautiful harbor in a setting of verdure, which called forth the exclamation Val Paraiso—Vale of Paradise; others refer it to the early mariners, who, after a weary voyage were rejoiced by the surpassing scene of surrounding hills and quebradas clad in the livery of early spring, when, doubling the rocky bluff which shields the little bay on the west, they cast anchor in its welcome haven. The inspiration which so baptized the spot may be comprehended, if these bold men were as mercilessly buffeted as we were for the day before we made the port. But why this ocean should have been called *El Pacifico*, by Fernando de Magelhaens, who first entered it by the strait that bears his name, is not as easily understood, especially when it is remembered that in that famous voyage he sailed *with great storms*—"con gran tormenta"—even as far as latitude 32° 20′.

As we neared our destination, steering southerly, Concon Point was passed lying on the left, and Valparaiso Point, surmounted by its light-house, on the right; the semicircular bay stretching before us about two and a half miles long and two miles wide, with eighty merchantmen and men-o'-war riding at anchor in the port next in commercial importance to Callao on this coast. The city of Valparaiso was seen occupying a narrow crescentic beach, overlooked by numerous hills, most of which also are studded thickly with houses standing on terraces, rising above each other to the height of from two hundred to two hundred and fifty feet.

A citizen of Valparaiso relieved me from the annoyances to which strangers are usually subjected by importunate boatmen and hotel runners. Landing at a fine mole, of three excellent hotels, the Union, Aubrey, and Santiago, the first was selected for a brief residence, and fully sustained the recommendation given of it by an American resident, for comfort and attention.

VALPARAISO.

p. 193.

## CHAPTER X.

CITY OF VALPARAISO—PUBLIC MORALS—PUBLIC BUILDINGS—PANTHEON—PROTESTANT CEMETERY—FIRES AND FIRE INSURANCE—CURRENCY—POPULATION—SCHOOLS—HOSPITALS.

The plan of the city of Valparaiso was determined by necessity, not design. Embracing the semicircular harbor to which reference has been made, is a correspondingly shaped sierra, a range of hills of from twelve hundred to fourteen hundred feet high. These hills, fifteen or sixteen in number, are partially separated from each other by ravines called *quebradas*, and they are sufficiently distinct to have received special names, to wit: *Cerro Alegre*, *Cerro de la Concepcion*, *Cerro del Baron*, *Cerro de Bellavista*, *Cerro de Yungai*, *Cerro de la Cordillera*, &c.; while others, the usual resorts of sailors when ashore, have borrowed an English nautical phraseology, and are known among foreign mariners as the *foretop*, *maintop*, *mizzentop*. However experienced Jack may be in surmounting difficulties, climbing into these altitudes proves dangerous, and he often comes down with a mortifying reminder that his lonely bunk below deck is safer than a more social hammock aloft. Some of the hills are deeply seamed with gullies; others present plateaus which the hand of art has formed into terraces made accessible by steep winding paths and stairways. Long since the foot of the sierra probably dipped boldly into the waters of the bay, and was washed by ocean swells; but centuries of disintegration furnished debris of stone and earth, which has been washed from the hills by rain-torrents, and thus has been gradually formed a crescentric level belt along the water's edge, two miles in length, and of varying width, on which the business

13

part of the city has been built. So narrow is this beach between the rocky buttress of the Cerro de la Concepcion and the water line, that but a single street is found there, which, being near the centre of the elongated city, may be compared to the contracted middle of an hour-glass held horizontally; while the expanded parts of the city, extending east and west from its waist, find a similitude in the enlarged bulbs of the glass. The west end—el Puerto, the Port—is the older part of Valparaiso, where wholesale business is transacted, and where are also found the *Intendencia*, or local government house, the custom-house and public stores. The east end of this lower part of the city is the more modern, over which business improvements are extending, and is called the *Almendral*, from an almond grove that once beautified the spot. From the contracted middle, streets radiate east and west; more numerous and widely spread, however, to the east, over the Almendral, than to the west, over El Puerto, the former being larger. These streets are traversed at right angles and at unequal distances by cross streets, in most instances, indeed, mere alleys, which are little else than less precipitous continuations of the gorges of the adjacent hills. Commerce has appropriated the greater part of this level space to its own use, hence parts of the adjoining heights have been sought for as residences; and there, on ledge and hill-side, on projecting rock, and along the rims of ragged gullies, citizens have built dwellings, which, however picturesque the panorama they present from a distance, rising above each other in successive tiers like a great amphitheatre, yet are, when scrutinized closely, a confused assemblage of indifferent buildings, in dangerous and dirty localities; tottering in many instances on the brinks of precipices of a hundred feet, and in others overlooking ravines of filth which would prove sources of pestilence but for the daily hurricanes that sweep over the Sierra, and disperse the malaria at one season, and the torrents of rain which at another wash away accumulated nuisances, threatening, too, the miserable hovels that stand on their verge. An exception to this description must be made of the Cerro Alegre, improved as it is with tasteful cottages, and terraced and adorned with flower-gardens and shrubbery; where English, German, and

American residents form a distinct social community, cherishing their peculiar characteristics, promoting each other's happiness and improvement by the cultivation of literature, accomplishments, and amusements of a higher civilization; and contributing by their example of good order, industry, and peaceful pursuit of the means of happiness, to elevate the native standard of progress. This happy result of foreign and native intercourse in Valparaiso none can fail to perceive, who have mingled with Chilean families of the higher class, among whom will be found examples of rare moral excellence, intelligence, accomplishment, and refinement, however immoral, vicious, ignorant, and degraded the vulgar masses.

But the enlightened and accomplished few, and the occasional examples of domestic and social virtues, should not be regarded as furnishing the standard of *public* intelligence and morals. It would be equally just to involve partial excellences in the condemnation of the vices of the many. However painfully national sensitiveness may feel the judgment, yet truth demands the acknowledgment that *public* virtue is neither a sentiment nor an observance in Valparaiso; an opinion common among travellers, and generally entertained by foreign residents; who recognize in the frequent abandonment of the domestic circle, by old men and young, either a greater love of vicious indulgences elsewhere, or a want of attraction at home; who see in the stern discipline of the mother who marches her daughters in single file before her on the street, watchful of their every movement and look, a want of confidence in them and in others, sadly indicative of *her* unfavorable opinion of filial and of public morality; who infer from the refusal to entrust sisters to the care and protection of their own brothers, or of other near kindred, a deplorable evidence of lost faith and of profligacy in those best known to them; who perceive in the separate apartments of a large number of females without visible means of support, reasonable presumption of abandoned habits; who behold in the atrocious excesses, robberies, and murders of the soldiery, during revolutionary outbreaks, and the indulgence by them of licentious and savage passions, proofs of depravity, originating in an education of infamy, or in wicked neglect; and who recognize on the public streets, in the multiform diseases known only to a secret nomenclature, the proofs of a wide-spread depravity, associated with a recklessness of consequences or a destitution of the means of relief. The want of the latter evinces a lamentable disregard by the municipal authorities of the public health. In excuse of this neglect it may be stated that the influence of the clergy is said to have been exerted to prevent any public provision being made for the treatment of diseases incident to lewdness. A physician of eminence informed me that the medical profession ascertained an enormous percentage of such diseases; and through a commissioner appointed for that purpose, prepared and proposed to the civil authorities sanitary measures for their treatment and prevention. To their amazement they found themselves opposed by the highest functionaries of the church, the proposal being denounced as subversive of the will of God, and calculated to encourage immorality and legitimate vice. Municipal benevolence, threatened by clerical malediction, resisted kindly influences, instead of remembering that the Head of the Christian Church traced with His own hand the Divine Judgment, "He who is without sin let him cast the first stone;" and that He "went about all the cities and villages, healing *every sickness and every disease* among the people."

The hospitalities of a charming family often afforded me the opportunity of gazing from the Cerro Alegre upon the busy scene below, where ships flying the flags of all nations, and obedient to port regulations lying as if in line of battle, rode at anchor with merely sufficient length of cable to guard against accidents in a rarely tranquil harbor; while launches bore their cargoes to shore, to be carried thence through busy streets to the spacious warehouses of El Puerto. Beyond was the grander scene, where ocean spread out its heaving bosom on the one hand, and on the other the verdant *Viña del Mar* skirted with its emerald setting the snowy-crested surf that washes its foot, and the *Campaña of Quillota* in the distance, looking darkly down on humbler comrades; while a hundred miles off to the northeast *Aconcagua* lifted its proud summit more than twenty-two thousand feet toward the heavens, as if to assert its prerogative of majesty over nearly all its mighty brothers of the Andean Cordillera. It is appropriate that such a scene, showing the destiny of man fulfilled in the active enterprises of life, and the grandeur and beneficence of nature, should be outspread for the daily contemplation of those who, like the residents of Cerro Alegre, appreciate the nobleness of the former, and the lessons of humility and gratitude taught by the latter.

At the base of the mole, on which alone merchandise and passengers are permitted to be landed that smuggling may be prevented, stands the Custom-house, the upper floor of which is used as an Exchange and Commercial Reading-Room. Commodious fire-proof bonded warehouses on the beach further west, are overlooked by a not very formidable fortification on the heights above. To the south of the custom-house is the principal plaza, on which are usually seen large quantities of foreign goods undergoing inspection and delivery. Fronting on the plaza opposite to the custom-house is the Intendencia, a substantial but plain building, the official residence of the *Intendente*, or Governor of this Province, and furnishing also offices for certain subordinates. Behind the Intendencia, as also in other parts of the city, are barracks for the military, many of whom, in flaunting regimentals, are kept on hand in this so-called model republic of South America, to hold in check the turbulent spirit of this people, who are thought to be especially bold and revolutionary in their tendencies, perhaps from the influence of the free speech and insubordinate example of the large foreign element of Valparaiso. The city boasts of two other patches of ground called plazas—the Plaza de la Municipalidad and the Plaza Victoria. On the former several dirty alleys debouch; and the latter, although boasting of the contiguity of the theatre, and the mausoleum of a fountain which seems to have died of drought, shows so many traces of vandalism as to indicate a republican repugnance to the fine arts similar, with shame be it said, to our own.

Both hereditary partiality for contracted thoroughfares and a necessity to economize space, have led to the making of narrow streets, barely wide enough to allow of two vehicles to pass each other, and not then without the wheels dipping into the curb-gutters, and liberally bespattering pedestrians on the four feet wide sidewalks, from head to foot. Wretched is the fashionable señora, even in fair weather, who happens on these narrowest of promenades at the moment of passing each other of two omnibus coaches: nothing will save her from a shower of filth, but retreat through the nearest doorway at hand capable of admitting an expansion of crinoline, certainly not adapted to Spanish-American sidewalks. And in the wet season, when the streets and quebradas are filled with torrents of muddy water from the hills, an India rubber armor, or a close coach, affords the only security against a baptism ruinous alike to costume and composure. The streets are also unusually rough, from the promiscuous use of large and small stones in paving.

The business part of the town has somewhat of a European look, as well because of the height and general style and material of buildings, as from the character of goods and their display in shop-windows; and also from the great number of foreigners, their dress, language, manners, and customs, there seen. While elsewhere, the Spanish one-story or low two-story houses with projecting balconies are found, roofed with tons of red tiles sufficient to crush any ordinary framework. The humbler houses are floored with brick, and having grated unglazed windows, look cheerless, comfortless, and prison-like. Balconies are now prohibited by law, because of the combustible nature of their materials, and the narrowness of the streets, favoring the extension of fires heretofore very destructive in Valparaiso. But where these mementoes of antique architecture remain, the ostentatious closets on them—generally sought to be hidden in other countries—do not give strangers a favorable opinion of former Chilean refinement, particularly when it is considered that worshippers in these profane temples, going and returning, were the "observed of all observers."

The churches at Valparaiso are neither so numerous as at Lima, nor so violative of good taste in architectural design. In the latter city idolatry seems to be canonized even in the highways and by-ways; but in the former, religious ceremonials are seen only in the churches and at the Pantheon. Intercourse with a higher intellectual cultivation and enlightened religious sentiment, is slowly leading to the entertainment of more rational views and observances; besides which it is impossible to command deference for priestly processions in the crowded thoroughfares of business, more intent on the dominant duties of life than on the tinsel, trumpery, and pharisaical street-corner shows of priestcraft; which have no higher aim or use than imposing on the ignorant, and tickling the fancy of deluded and superstitious followers. Nine Roman Catholic sanctuaries daily assert their prerogative of constitutionally-decreed worship; while a Protestant Episcopal and a Congregational Church are graciously allowed by the Minister of the Interior to hide themselves unostentatiously within high inclosures, thus avoiding offence to national religious prejudice.

One of the many hills surrounding the harbor is devoted to burial purposes, and on it is the *Pantheon*, a cemetery of three or four acres, with adobe wall, gateway, and chapel. Here are closely-crowded vaults and graves, and many monuments of excellent design and execution, showing a higher sentiment and better taste than prevail in Peru. My visit to the Pantheon happened on All-Saints' day—called also All-Souls' day—a festival strictly observed here, business being suspended, and every Catholic considering it a religious duty to bestow votive offerings in memory of departed friends, and aid in all the ways inculcated by the Church in extricating their souls from the pains and penalties of transgression. I fell into the living current of men, women, and children, setting with a free will toward that mournful spot, to which they must soon be carried whether they will or not. They bore wreaths, bouquets, and baskets of flowers, and passed through an alley bordered by hovels, the tenants of which profited by the chance of selling *dulces*, for which señoritas have a passionate fondness; while black eyes occasionally flashed invitations from window and door to turn aside the unwary. Then winding our way up a tortuous acclivity along the edge of a ravine of pestiferous exhalations, we next ascended a steep hill-side, and finally turning abruptly to the left from the dusty ascent, we clambered along a rugged pathway which led to the cemetery gate. There stood sentinels armed and accoutred for destruction, fit representatives of the dread master they served, and whose portal they guarded—a needless service, however, for all are welcome within these domains of death, whether they come to honor or to be honored, to pray or to be prayed for, to return or to remain. It inspired sympathy and respect to see the living seeking the resting-places of their beloved and there depositing on polished marble and verdant mound the silent tokens of affection, veneration, grief, and hope. And if candor would allow, gladly would this narrative be here arrested, for there is no gratification in recording instances of pious fraud, and of superstition and delusion, although the offspring of sincere religious sentiment.

Priestcraft in all ages, and of its various modifications of faith, form, and doctrine, has well understood, that the readiest road to the purse of the believer is through his heart. The fears of the dim and uncertain future, and the lingering love and desire to secure the eternal happiness of departed spirits, respond to the talisman of an intercession, the efficacy of which has been inculcated by the artful and designing; who would not, if they could, recognize the insult to heaven in supposing that their human interposition could divert it from adherence to the righteous and eternal principles of its own moral government, and the unchanging judgments founded upon them; and which assuredly recognizes no influence to divert it from these, bought by filthy lucre. This inculcated delusion is not found here alone, but the sectarianism of other nations arrogating a higher reach of intelligence and reason, is tarnished by the same theological artifice in one or another of its various forms. It is not surprising, then, that the clergy should have availed of this sad occasion, when the sensibilities of the heart were tenderly alive to impressions, to levy contributions on superstitious credulity. In many parts of the cemetery were seen

> . . . . . "State Priests, sole venders of the lore
> That works salvation,"

with upturned eyes, or resting occasionally on the purse of the employer who stood by, mumbling prayers for the repose of the deceased, or for extrication from presumed detentions by the way, or exclusions from heaven; sometimes stopping in their orisons to ask the name of the beneficiary on whose behalf the petition was made, that by its audible announcement in the right place and at the proper time, no mistake could be made by the saint addressed as to the identical person to be benefited by the intermediation. The length of the prayer and the number of its repetitions, important conditions of successful application for celestial favor, were observed to depend on the amount of the fee; about which a little misunderstanding arose occasionally, the *Padre* generally succeeding in enforcing his own views of the contract, a very natural result as he probably reserved the right to revoke what he had done. One handsome young priest of uncommon shrewdness and business tact, and with a lurking devil in his piercing black eye, seemed to treat the occasion as affording the chance of a profitable speculation. And, as appears to be the case everywhere with the young and good-looking of the clerical profession of all forms of faith, he was an especial favorite with the ladies, who were certainly the chief victims of pious fraud here as elsewhere. The mediations of this popular Padre were always engaged several performances ahead, so great was the demand for his pleadings, the persuasive eloquence of which may have been fully known to some of his fair patrons. He was absolutely loaded down with small change, which he turned into his well-lined pockets by the handfull, like a huckster on market-day enjoying the monopoly of a much sought after commodity. In the chapel a general service was held for the repose of all the dead collectively. Occasionally there was seen near a tomb an old family servant, a wreck of better times, with rosary in hand petitioning heaven in behalf of those whose kindness in life was not forgotten in death; an unbought offering of grateful intercession more precious than the marketable appeals of the crafty and heartless.

Separated from the Pantheon by a narrow lane is a smaller burial ground for Protestant sepulture. Formerly a foreigner not of the Roman Catholic faith, had not where to lay his head when death stilled its achings. But religious intolerance has so far yielded to the benign influence of a growing commercial intercourse, that a heretic may now find interment without the friends who carry him to the grave being stoned, as in times past, by a Chilean mob; and without the probability that the body will be disinterred, and subjected as formerly to profane exposure.

Still further from the Pantheon is a Potter's-field, where the bodies of the poor and friendless are put into a pit capable of holding many hundreds. They are placed in layers with intervening strata of earth, the horrid sepulchre of decomposing mortality being left open to the day until filled, when it is covered with caustic lime and sealed with earth. Hither also a living throng of impoverished looking beings bent their steps. And here, too, was seen the false disciple of Him who went about doing good, ostentatiously displaying the crucifix, the holy symbol of self-sacrifice, but which was insulted by him who bore it stretching forth his hand to take the pittance of poverty, for naught was here but the coin of wretchedness. And what could be doled out for its piece of copper, but a modicum of even hypocritical sanctity?—the miserable victim of imposture throwing himself upon his straw that night without even so much as a penny loaf of bread to appease the pangs of hunger. Whatever the name of the festival of this day, whether "All Saints" or "All Souls," certainly they are not all saints who are the chief actors in its celebration; and as to their own souls, they will stand much in need of holier intercession to save them from the penalties of unrighteousness. Turning speedily from this last repugnant scene, I joined on the way to the city a cheerful throng who were descending the hill, apparently self-satisfied with what they doubtless deemed the good deeds of the day.

A stranger in Valparaiso will not fail to observe, immediately on landing, the heraldic looking Fire Insurance badges; sometimes three or four, representing as many different companies, being seen on a single house, showing an unusual apprehension of fire. And this is not surprising when it is considered that scarcely a day passes without an alarm; and so disastrous have been the conflagrations that property of $5,000,000 value has been destroyed in ten hours by one fire. Insurance companies are said to have preceded frequent fires here, and it is a mooted question if they are not also entitled to the priority of cause and effect. I did not see an Insurance badge or a fire-engine in Lima; and one only of the latter in Callao, and that was exhibited as a curiosity to a wondering crowd. Nor did I see a fire nor hear an alarm in either of those cities; but from North American experience it may be inferred that an opportunity will soon be afforded by the curious to test the capacities of the new apparatus in Callao. In Valparaiso, however, insurance companies, fire companies, fire bells, and fires of course, abound. Several of the first named are of foreign capital sent here for investment, and so probable is the investment to become *permanent* that the speculation may well be declined unless to gratify a disinterested desire to relieve the distresses of others. The fire companies have peculiar and independent organizations according to the nationality of their members, most of whom are foreigners. A law exempting all firemen from the performance of military duty secures the services of a sufficient number of able-bodied natives to man each apparatus. The steam fire-engine and alarm telegraph have not yet been introduced into Chile. By and by she will be taught their value. But a tug with a fire-engine attachment, and the head of water given by the elevation of the city reservoir, located two hundred and forty feet above the level of the port and Almendral, are important additions to the ordinary means for the extinguishment of fires.

Valparaiso is well lighted with gas, but it is too costly, when the large coal deposits around Arauco Bay, and the facility of water transportation thence, are considered. The street gas lamp is an improvement on that of our cities. A long-handled lighter is used for turning a cock just below the lamp, and then by pushing up with it likewise a perforated tin trap floor, hinged on one side, the flame is instantly communicated to the burner within. The lighter being withdrawn the trap falls to its place by its own weight. A moment merely is consumed, and climbing with the clumsy use of lucifer matches are avoided.

Every house has a flag-staff projecting from its front. A law of the republic requires a display of the national flag on every anniversary of the revolution of independence, an event which generally wastes a week in its celebration. Patriotism galvanized into activity by legal enactment and penalty, is not worth perpetuating.

A noteworthy and creditable social feature is that the lowest Chileans are exempt from a filthy habit of very many North Americans, embracing even some who otherwise might be considered exemplary gentlemen. No excuse of health, natural want, or refined gratification, can be made for our national vice of tobacco chewing, and spitting the offensive extraction in every place, public and private—church, counting-room, parlor, and promenade. If a visitor is seen rolling a quid about his befouled mouth, and threatening to bespatter the carpet of a high-bred Chilena, she will conclude that a mistake has been made in his introduction to her house, and withdraw under the impression that he is a "plug ugly" gone astray. Even cigar smoking is not common, the milder and less offensive cigarito alone being tolerated in good society, though never used by ladies. Vulgar women, and men generally, use tobacco in this least pernicious form.

The Valparaiso market is well supplied with fresh meats, vegetables, fruits, and groceries. A family may live here at about the cost of residence in New York.

The currency is convenient, and pretty looking, much like the United States coin. It consists of

COPPER.

| | | |
|---|---|---|
| Medio centavo, | | ½ cent. |
| Centavo, | | 1 " |

SILVER.

| | | |
|---|---|---|
| Medio decimo, | ($\frac{1}{20}$ of a Peso.) | 5 cents. |
| Decimo, | ($\frac{1}{10}$ of a Peso.) | 10 " |
| Viento centavo, | ($\frac{1}{5}$ of a Peso.) | 20 " |
| Medio Peso, | ($\frac{1}{2}$ of a Peso.) | ½ dollar. |

GOLD.

| | | |
|---|---|---|
| Peso, | | 1 dollar. |
| Dos Pesos, | (Escudo.) | 2 dollars. |
| Cinco Pesos, | (Dooblon.) | 5 " |
| Diez Pesos, | (Condor.) | 10 " |

Copper forms a considerable amount of the circulating medium of Chile. The Government has ceased to coin doubloons or their fractions since the year 1851; yet they remain in circulation and form a large part of the currency of the country. All considerable payments are made in gold, owing to the scarcity of silver, which is only used to make change; and even for that silver coin has sometimes commanded a premium of from one to seven per centum. The decimal system of currency was adopted in this country by Legislative Act in 1851, and seems to have been borrowed from France. The Peso is the unit of value, and is divided into one hundred parts denominated centavos.

In 1820 the population of Valparaiso did not exceed five thousand. Since then it has increased greatly in commercial importance, and its population is now estimated at seventy-five thousand. French, Germans, English, and Americans, contribute largely to make up this number. These are recognized as well by their business activity, energy, and enterprise, as by their fairer complexion and European costume, though in dress they are imitated by the better class of Chilenos. The natives who are direct descendants of Spaniards retain the physical characteristics of that renowned people, and the grace and dignity of deportment for which they have always been distinguished; to which is added a charming candor of address to those properly introduced to Chilean families of high social position. But the mixed race of Spaniard and Indian, who compose three-fourths of the population of Valparaiso, of all proportions of the original blood and corresponding physique, is an inferior class to the Castilian, having a less stature—although surpassing the Peruvian Cholo—a tawny skin, coarse features, straight black hair, and uncleanly and indolent habits. Most of this degenerate race are intensely sensual, and regardless alike of private virtue and public good faith. Degradation, profligacy, and poverty, are so palpable, that no candid chronicler can avoid the acknowledgment of their unusual existence. Were it not for the corporate regulation which designates one day in each week as "beggar day," and prohibits public alms-seeking on others, the principal promenade and chief business thoroughfare would be continually crowded with mendicants and afflicted outcasts.

There are a few excellent academies in Valparaiso for the education of the children of wealthy citizens, where, in addition to the usual branches of learning, the English and French languages—considered here necessary accomplishments—are well taught; but at greater cost than in the United States. The provision made for instruction of indigent children is meagre, and the public school system is a failure.

Only one charitable institution is worthy of mention—the city hospital. It has three hundred beds, and is dependent for support on individual contributions, no public provision being made for it. It is quite unequal to the demands made upon it for relief of the large number of afflicted and destitute. Separate hospitals for the care and treatment of British, French, and American seamen, are provided by their respective governments. The first named two being subject to the control of experienced and permanent officials, are well organized and conducted. But United States mariners are unfortunately subject to the evils of changes, corresponding to those of the home government, and having no reference whatever to considerations of competency or faithfulness.

Nearly all the physicians in successful practice in Valparaiso are of foreign birth and education, and most of them honor their profession by skill and conduct. Two pseudo-medical practitioners, having scarcely a pretence of patronage, resorted to the novelty of homœopathic delusion to avoid starvation—"whose tongues and souls in this are hypocrites." They now realize an infinitesimal subsistence of body, at the cost of a complete loss of conscience.

Most of the apothecaries are Germans; none of English or North American nationality. The reason assigned for this is, that the licentiating board of the University "require all candidates to produce diplomas of pharmacy; and as in those two countries none are issued, English and American apothecaries are not admitted to examination." They are in error; several colleges of pharmacy are in successful operation in the United States, affording full instruction in Materia Medica, Chemistry, and Pharmacy, and conferring a graduate diploma on every student who has attended the required course of lectures, served a full practical apprenticeship, and is found qualified on a final examination.

## CHAPTER XI.

A BIRLOCHO AND A BIRLOCHERO—HACIENDA PEÑUELAS—CHILEAN PIC-NIC—PLEASURE AND PAIN SANDWICHED.

Early on the morning of a feast day, when all business according to custom was suspended, I started in company with the United States Consul on a before-breakfast ride of twelve miles to the hacienda Peñuelas, an estate of several leagues extent. Our conveyance was a *birlocho;* before the introduction of stage-coaches the usual carriage for Santiago travel, and still often used on that and other roads. The birlocho is a heavy, lumbering chaise, consisting of a one seat body mounted on strong leather thorough braces attached behind to vertical semicircular steel springs, running on two large clumsy wheels, and having shafts for one horse. On the outside of the shafts another horse is attached by a strong rope to some part of the vehicle, a hook on the other end of the rope slipping into a ring of his saddle girth. The driver is mounted postilion fashion on the latter horse, and directs the movements of the birlocho either by pulling the bridle of the shaft horse, or by urging in the opposite direction the horse he rides against the shaft, at the same time punching the neck of the shaft horse with a formidable looking whip handle. The postilion's limbs are wrapped in leather leggings; and with bandit slouch and variegated poncho, knotted *raw-hide* whip—so called probably from habitual enactment as well as constituents—and colossal spurs savagely serrated, the birlochero, as the postilion is called, presents—doubtless to the eyes of horses—a truly terrific appearance.

Soon after starting we came to the conclusion, from our

bounds and rebounds, lateral inclinations, inflections, retroflexions, superpositions, and general churning, that if either of us should survive the morning ride, he would be likely, in fulfilment of Halstead's physiological theory, the offspring of a corduroy road slumber, to have "good digestion wait on appetite." For instead of climbing the *Cuesta* which we began to ascend just outside of the city limits, at a pace indicative of a humane regard for horse flesh, the birlochero scaled the steep ascent of one thousand four hundred and eighty feet so fast, with such recklessness of obstacles, and indifference to precipices, as showed that he had bowels of compassion for neither man nor beast. Our way was over and beyond the Sierra that overlooks the city, and like all mountain roads, this one wound with abrupt turns along the sides of acclivities, bounded on one side by overhanging cliffs, while deep ravines yawned on the other. The summit of the Sierra having been reached without death, but with the fear of it constantly before our eyes, our Jehu *peon*, apparently impelled by pride of superior daring and skill in horsemanship, redoubled his brutal onslaught on the poor beasts now dripping with sweat from their incessant effort; and plunging his rowels into the bloody flanks of the one, and plying his knotted thong on the flayed back and sides of the other, away he dashed, deaf to all appeals, allowing us no privilege of action but to hold on, shut our eyes to consequences, and pray for deliverance. Dr. Page's giant windmills crowning the heights, which once gave flour to California and a fortune to their proprietor, stood still, as if in mute amazement at the strange intrusion; while troops of dogs with loud-mouthed bay joined in the race, giving renewed impulse to the wild Chileno, who precipitated his flight down the descent. To have been at the mercy of winds and waves would have been a blessed fortune, but it was vain to pray for it; so awaiting impending fate, we

> "Became settled, and bent up
> Each corporal agent to the terrible feat."

At such a furious pace as we were going suspense was not of long duration; the plain below was soon reached, and with it came some sense of safety. But our flight was not arrested; over the level we went pell-mell, and having entered the domains of our host and bounded over three miles of his hacienda, we finally brought up at the court-yard gate. And never was a more sincere "thank God" uttered than ours at that moment.

A hearty welcome awaited us, "our stern alarums changed to merry meetings," a breakfast that honored the guests and was not less honored by them, and a laugh at the incidents of the morning, handed these over to the past and opened the way to pleasanter events that followed.

The court-yard of an acre of ground is enclosed on three sides by an adobe wall; on the fourth stands the family mansion, a quaint looking, long, one-story stucco, many roomed, tile roofed building, with an ample dining-room at right angles to the main edifice, and a balcony before and behind. Although simple and unostentatious without, the dwelling is handsomely furnished, affording both comforts and luxuries within. It was formerly the abode of religionists, as a Jesuit convent; it is now the residence of purity and sentiment, intelligence and refinement, in the accomplished family of a German and Chilena marriage. On the side of the house opposite to the court-yard is a large and handsome garden of shrubbery and flowers, of rich variety and coloring. Bounding this beyond, a crescentic border of weeping-willows and acacias is seen, mingling their dense foliage and deep shades, and passable at one point only; seeking which in my exploration, access was found to a rustic bridge spanning a crystal stream that came leaping and babbling over rocks above, as if telling a tale of pastoral life to which it had just been a delighted witness; and spreading out into a limpid lake, it dimpled and sparkled in the sunshine, seemingly laughing at its recent gambols; and then stealing away, sheltered itself under the shadowy banks, to dream of the flowers and foliage that stand there gazing into the placid depths, in rapture of their own beauties reflected from the mirrored bosom of the sleeping waters. The opposite side of the stream is set in a similar garland, passing which, and then through a queer little cane-wicker gate, of fitting lightness to swing willingly to the fairy fingers with which it is familiar, my eager foot led by the mysterious beauties of the scene, wandered on among fruit trees of rare variety, rivalling each other in profusion and richness. Culinary plants, too, were seen marshalled in rank and file on open spaces; and flowers stood by, there as everywhere—for November is the May month of this southern hemisphere—the queenly lookers on of luxuriant horticulture, lavishing their beauties on surrounding nature, and diffusing perfumed tribute on the wings of zephyrs. Along the border of a part of this abounding garden, flow the fugitive waters of the picturesque little lake of which mention was made. From this stream artificial canals escape, meandering like wayward brooklets to refresh the thirsty soil, and whisper to roses and violets, as they stoop to receive the dewy kiss, the happy dreams of recent slumbers. On another side of this Chilean Eden rise Lombardy poplars, prim and stately, but occasionally forgetful of accustomed dignity, waving their tall spires, and rollicking in the breeze in very wantonness of joy under its balmy inspiration. Beyond these was seen an outstretched prairie of several hundred acres, clad in a mantle of verdure that gracefully bent and rose again before the playful winds like ocean swells; and this changeful expanse is bounded in the distance by a rolling sierra, whose steep sides are seamed by dark quebradas. The landscape is of rare beauty, and wants nothing for its perfection but a North American forest to crown the wavy outline of the far off heights.

It was with feelings of reverence and gratitude that I turned from this outspread witness of divine power and goodness, to unite with the family and visitors of our host in their church offering of thanks and praise. There, in a tasteful little Catholic sanctuary, the two hundred *peons* of the estate joined the wealthy proprietor on bended knee at a common altar; and the heart of a Protestant, free from the trammels of intolerance, gladly availed of the occasion to offer its tribute of thankfulness to the same "Father who art in Heaven," and who, whatever sectarian intolerance and selfishness may inculcate, knows no distinction among those of His children who worship Him "in spirit and in truth." The ceremony of mass was followed by excellent admonition to an attentive audience, composed chiefly of servants to the manor born, whose general conduct, I was assured, was at all times consistent with the teaching of the Apostle, to "put away all bitterness, and wrath, and anger, and clamor, and evil speaking, with malice;" and to "be obedient to them that are (their) masters according to the flesh, with fear and trembling, in singleness of heart, as unto Christ." After the religious services of the day, it became a question how the rest of it was to be spent. This resulted in an agreement of family and friends to seek some dell among the neighboring hills, and there, with forest bower for dining-hall, and sward for festive board, to give the fleeting hour to social pleasure and enjoyment of nature.

The busy note of preparation soon resounded throughout the household, showing that all entered heartily into the spirit of the impromptu *pic-nic*, a word which has not been rendered into Spanish, but has been bodily transferred; and, unmusical as it is in our "harsh, northern, hissing, grunting guttural," it sounds melodious as uttered by the silver-tongued señoritas of this elysium. When the moment of starting came, carriages were filled with matrons and patrons, and prancing steeds mounted by the young and gay, a jovial son of merry England lifting his voice above the din of departure in the unforgotten "Over the hills and far away."

A distance of a mile and a half, in a direction opposite to that by which we had entered the hacienda, over fields, across meadows, and along a river bank, brought us to the foot of the hills, between two of which we passed; and, as our green avenue narrowed, the occupants of carriages were compelled to descend to the humility of pedestrianism, and follow a path through brake and bramble, broken for us by the equestrians who had gone before. Emerging from the chaparral, a valley was reached shut in from the surrounding world in its entire circuit, except where we entered, by hills mantled in verdure, and decked with wild flowers. An arbor of *Boldo* and *Molle*, twined with *Arrayan*, in nature's own profusion and fantastic architecture, stood on a gentle slope, sufficiently capacious to accommodate the company; and when the lingering pedestrians reached that bower of beauty, our happy predecessors were found enjoying its refreshing shade, seated on outspread shawls and ponchos; and the melody of a guitar, touched by an accomplished señorita, with the lute-like voice of her gazelle-eyed sister, were floating down the glen in harmonious unison, awaking the echoes of the sleeping quebrada.

Gazing around, and moved by the inspiration of sweet sounds, how natural for the entranced spirit to join the strain!

Here, upon Chile's land of roses,
Brightly the light of noon reposes;
And lofty Aconcagua's brow
With snowy crown is gleaming now,
Gazing upon the verdant bowers
  Reflected in his robe of sleet,
While summer in a vale of flowers
  Is sleeping beauteous at his feet;
And melody ascends to greet
  The dews his golden clouds distil;
And breathing music as they meet,
  Gives language to the sparkling rill.

Rest renewing the desire of adventure, the party turned out to *prospect* the sequestered spot for nature's spoils, and rare were the jewels that were gathered. Floral rubies, sapphires, amethysts, pearls, and the topaz, were soon woven with the emerald into wreaths, bracelets, necklaces, and bouquets; and, blooming on brows, blushing on bosoms, rioting in ringlets, decorating dresses, and flashing all over bewitching Chilenas and their embellished cavaliers, a botanist on a tour of discovery, coming suddenly into this happy valley at that moment, might have exulted at finding a *floral species of the genus homo.* And pretty were the sentiments, and oftentimes eloquent, that these mute teachers of the good and beautiful inspired. Many a thought strayed from the bright and pure scene below to the holier one of heaven; and to more than one, buds and blossoms were emblems of the translated who now bloom in the spirit-home.

"Wondrous truths, and manifold as wondrous,
  God hath written in those stars above;
But not less in the bright flowerets under us
  Stands the revelation of his love.

"Bright and glorious is that revelation,
Written all over this great world of ours;
Making evident our own creation,
In these stars of earth, these golden flowers.

"Gorgeous flowerets in the sunlight shining,
Blossoms flaunting in the eye of day,
Tremulous leaves, with soft and silver lining,
Buds that open only to decay.

"In all places then, and in all seasons,
Flowers expand their light and soul-like wings,
Teaching us by some persuasive reasons
How akin they are to human things.

"And with childlike, credulous affection,
We behold their tender buds expand;
Emblems of our own great resurrection,
Emblems of the bright and better land."

No exploring expedition ever returned home more delighted than this joyful party to the bower, from its valley and hill-side wandering; and when dinner was shortly after announced, no one was wanting in a willing and graceful acceptance of the arm offered to Doña J. and Doña T.,—Doña L. and Doña C.,—Doña N. and Doña E., &c., &c., as politeness or a more tender sentiment prompted. A peep through the leafy wall of the corridor, along which we passed, revealed the cook basting an entire *mouton* on a *cane spit* in a primitive kitchen, with servants busily arranging turkey, tongue, ham, fowl, and other accessaries of the feast. A few steps brought the guests into a natural dining saloon, its walls of dense undergrowth of *litre*, *maqui*, and *myrtle*, being columned with *boldo* and *maiten;* while a ceiling of foliage hung on spreading branches, and frescoed by intrusive sunbeams, perfected the unique architecture. It was not surprising that the urgent appeal of appetite was needed, to draw attention from the beauties of the banquet hall to the creature comforts of the banquet; and that the invitation to be seated was oft repeated, ere the snowy cloth on the sward, spread with an elegant service, and surrounded with grassy ottomans embroidered with shawls, received its share of attention.

Seats being at last occupied, the table, speedily loaded with substantials and dainties, soon attested the general joy. And it is appropriate that an American should record this, the happiest day to him since he left his northern home, in the language which furnished sentiment to the feast; for let it be added in acknowledgment of the accomplishments of the company, that with one exception, all present, from Chile and various other countries, *conversed in English*, and complimented it on this convivial occasion, by making it the vehicle of wit and repartee, of toast and response.

Dinner ended, music and the dance followed, and here the *Zama Cueca* captivated foreign guests by the spirit of its peculiar poetry; nor did we wonder, when we saw the artful feints and graceful coquetry of the dark-eyed damsel who danced it, that the cavaliers of the party were emulous of being whipped by her embroidered handkerchief.

Our estimable hostess, the venerated guide and guardian of the bright spirits, who, like unswerving satellites revolve about her domestic orbit, warned us in due time that

> "The golden bowers of Even
> In the rich west began to wither"—

and the delights of this Chilean pic-nic faded away like the declining sun robed in retiring splendor, for they seemed to gather a greater and a brighter joy as the day's bliss was coming to a close. The hacienda Peñuelas never entertained a happier party; and when the festive board of its historical old mansion echoed again, as it did, the innocent mirth and sparkling thought of its inmates, ere separating for the night they once more partook of its munificent hospitality, I thought that this reunion might justly be regarded one of the examples of diffused good resulting from that revolution, which, by releasing immense domains from entailed clerical possession, devoted them to a more general and unselfish use.

The blushing morn aroused those guests who remained all night; and while others were preparing for departure I stole away to take a last lingering look at the flowers—those "new made old acquaintances," who smile wherever met with in the wide world, and speak a welcome and familiar language to the heart. Awakened from their slumbers by the matin song of birds, and the prattling stream dimpling itself in beauty to meet the rosy day, they were taking their dewy baths.

> "To one who look'd from upper air
> O'er all the enchanted region there,
> How beauteous must have been the glow,
> The life, the sparkling from below!
> Fair gardens, shining streams, with ranks
> Of blushing flowers on their banks;"
> And golden fruits, reposing there,
> Breathing a perfume on the air.

Coffee having been served, and the good-by spoken with that feeling of sadness ever attendant on its utterance to those who illustrate, as does the family of the hacienda Peñuelas, the parental, filial, and friendly virtues, and who we never again expect to meet on earth, my companion and myself started for Valparaiso. And then it was I realized the sense of doom felt by the condemned on his way to execution; for the sight of the *birlochero* who brought us out on the wings of the wind, like Banquo's ghost, renewed the unoblivious past, and accursed the hour with dread of the future. Macbeth's fearful apostrophe

> "Avaunt and quit my sight! Let the earth hide thee!"

scarcely served to tell my horror of his presence. Gladly would I have taken the road on foot rather than have trusted again to that incarnate fiend, whose eye seemed to gleam with renewed joy of mischief. But neither appeal nor expostulation awakened in my companion kindred feelings, or disturbed his stoical equanimity: he had received a California training, and did not fear—in this case literally—"the devil on horseback." I was less fortunate; so sinking back in the birlocho, and heaving a sigh, I surrendered myself to impending fate.

The incidents that marked the conduct of the birlochero it is needless to narrate. The reënactment of the scenes of the morning before, with, if possible, a greater indifference to consequences, induced by copious imbibitions of *chicha*, was the precursor of his climax of madness, when, descending the sierra toward the city, with a rocky precipice on one side of the road, he attempted to turn a short curve at a running speed. The jerks of the birlocho's lateral slide as the curve was being turned told of imminent danger; and then the off-wheel striking an obstacle an upset began, my companion falling from the lower side of the vehicle on the verge of the precipice. It was instinctively manifest that my chance of escape lay in becoming braced between dashboard and back, and taking the chances of the birlocho, for if thrown out from the ascending side with the momentum then received, the rocky depth would have been sure to reveal a fatal sequel. Another moment sufficed to complete the disaster. Happily, a last bound of the horses drew the vehicle from the edge of the gorge, and it was capsized within a step of a nearly perpendicular descent of a hundred feet. Wedged as I was in the birlocho, I of course shared its fate, and was buried under it. My companion though much injured retained his consciousness, and dragged me in a state of insensibility from the wreck. Such restoratives as could be obtained from a kind native woman living near by, finally brought me back to sense, a most painful one of dreadful usage. It is needless to particularize injuries.

The birlochero rendered no assistance, either in disengaging me from the broken birlocho, or in restoring me from temporarily suspended vitality. Either confounded by the consequences of his folly, or disappointed in not having achieved a full success by disabling my comrade also, he is represented as having stood by unharmed—for the post-horse and rider are always safe in such accidents—and to have remained for a short time stupefied or in sullen indifference, and then to have disappeared altogether.

Fortunately, the family carriage of my excellent friend Señor Kammerer, came by from his hacienda; and two ladies, Señoritas Clara and Isabella Alvarez Condarco—may God bless them! —relinquishing their seats, insisted on our use of them; and thus I was conveyed by Dr. I. B. Gordon—United States Consul—generously forgetful of his sufferings and thoughtful only of me, to his own house; where I received kindest attentions from him, and from Dr. A. Reid, of Valparaiso, and offers of service from many American and English friends.

My injuries although painful are gradually yielding to treatment and time, and to the kind attentions of a noble-hearted American resident of Valparaiso Mr. P. A. McKellar, and his accomplished Chilean lady, to whose hospitable residence I was conveyed when sufficiently recovered for removal; and where I am now being invigorated by the pure atmosphere, and rejoiced by the beautiful prospect of a superb garden of several acres extent, often thrown open to the public. Here the lily and the rose, the cactus and the camilla, the florapondia and the siempreviva, the jasmine and the heliotrope, the honeysuckle and the hyacinth, the verbena and the violet, the malva and the mignonette, are looking up lovingly at the clustering cherries, grapes, peaches, and pears, sunning themselves above; with an occasional tall Norfolk-isle-pine, pimienta, and magnolia, standing sentry around like grenadier outposts of this Eden. On this scene, lying at the foot of a range of steep hills, and truly in my eyes a *Val Paraiso*, my chamber fronts; and from its window, while I write these lines, I regale the senses; delicious perfume coming to me on every breeze, the eye revelling on the most beautiful of nature's gifts, while birds of rich plumage and sweet song are my neighbors in an adjoining aviary; and one of them of such sad and tender note, that it seems a

> "Sweet visitant of Paradise;
> For, Heaven forgive that thought! the while
> Which makes me both to weep and smile,
> I sometimes deem that it might be
> The lost one's soul come down to me!"

And it tells me, too, of the terrestrial home, and the beloved there, and the tones of affection and sympathy which have made me forgetful of the affliction often my lot. Thus listening, and thus thinking, I fall into a sweet dream of peace, purifying to the spirit, cheering to the heart, and in every way promotive of that good result which my kind friends here spare no pains to secure. The names of these friends must be ever in my heart; and if, in the fulness of its gratitude, I have mentioned them, and spoken of things violative of that rule of publication which should hold the private relations of life sacred, and restrain me from personal allusions, may I not be pardoned? Thus ends a chapter of sunshine and shadow.

## CHAPTER XII.

JOURNEY TO SANTIAGO—CASA BLANCA—THE TWO STAGE ROUTES TO THE CAPITAL—SIERRAS AND CUESTAS—MELIPILLA—THE CORDILLERA—CHILEAN AGRICULTURE.

LEAVING Valparaiso for Santiago at four A. M., the clear stars served as lamps for the brief period before dawn. There are two modes of public conveyance between the chief seaport and the capital: one the well known American or English nine passenger, four or six in hand coach; the other a smaller four-wheel carriage for four persons, with tongue and pair of horses attached thereto, and two other horses outside of these pulling each by a single rope attached to some part of the vehicle; the horses thus travel abreast, unless there are more than four, in which case two of them may draw from the tongue as leaders, and are then managed by a postilion mounted on one of them, while a driver in the carriage holds the others in rein. Thus they act on the rule that two heads are better than one, which does not always hold good in this case as they sometimes act contrariwise, the passengers paying the penalty of disagreement. If there were no other objection to postilion driving as it prevails in Chile, it is sufficient that he does not incur the risk to which his recklessness often subjects those entrusted to his care; for he is always safe on the outside in the event of accident, and in case of the tumble of a party down a precipice he readily disengages himself and horse from the vehicle at the moment of danger, by unhooking the trace-rope from his saddle-girth. Immunity from personal danger encourages his disregard of the safety of others. I had ample experience of the recklessness of a birlochero, and therefore took the American coach, and had a sense and a realization of security. But if you should make this journey and trust yourself to the so-called French line, pay the postilion an extra fee for the privilege of tying a rope round his neck; and put a revolver in your belt. If he shows himself a dare-devil, pull the rope; and if he disregards the hint, shoot him on the spot: for if you do not kill him, the probability will be that—your doom being that of most persons—you will be more apt to see San Diablo than Santiago.

The road for a distance of thirty miles from Valparaiso is unpaved, and much obstructed by mule trains and ox-teams; the former carrying on pack-saddles wood, wheat, wool, and flour, and in panniers poultry, meat, and vegetables; the latter drawing large clumsy wagons and carts, with hugh wheels and tongue, and a body of closely-intertwined cane sides, raw-hide top stretched over bows, and floor of the same, for the transportation of merchandise in general. The usual team consists of eight oxen arranged in pairs, which pull from a yoke attached to the horns; while two extra oxen are fastened head-on behind, as well to hold back in descending the steep hills of this mountainous country as to relieve those of the team that have become weary or foot-sore. The roads are made and kept in repair by Government, and a regulation requires that the wagons shall drag behind each wheel a block, to check them when stopping on a hill-side. The drivers of these merchandise teams are like their confrères, the happily nearly obsolete professional teamsters of our own country; generally lawless in public conduct, and licentious in private morals. They display a gay poncho, and the smallest specimen of a round crown, narrow brim, straw or chip hat, tied on with a gaudy check handkerchief bonnet-fashion. Armed with a fifteen or twenty feet pole or *goad*, with iron spike point, each sceptred chief walks either before or at the side of his team, and, in imitation of more distinguished tyrants, punishes his victims according to his humor, generally contriving to get them where they ought not to be, and in the way of every traveller on the road. And unfortunate is he who meets an ascending ox-team, or a dozen of them—for they usually move in processions—when he is going down a cuesta in a birlocho at a running gait. He may take his choice between a smash up on one side, a leap down the precipice on the other, or impalement on the *intermediate horns of the dilemma*, as he pleases.

The country over which we passed looked barren, yet the soil was rich in places, as shown by heavy crops of barley, wheat, and garden vegetables, where properly cultivated. The houses seen along the road are built of light scantling or pole frames, filled in with cane or common brushwood, daubed with mud, and thatched with hay or straw. A mere shed serves for kitchen and dining-room, and half-clad families and nearly disrobed wagoners and muleteers were seen as we passed the pueblos, taking their morning meal in primitive fashion, with fingers for forks, and seated on the ground.

At seven and a half A. M. we stopped for breakfast thirty miles from Valparaiso, at the neat little village of *Casa Blanca*, containing about two thousand inhabitants; so called from a white post-house built there by Valdivia the great Spanish pioneer of Chile. At this town the road to Santiago forks, giving a choice of routes to the traveller. One branch takes a nearly due east direction, and traverses two sierras, important geographical features of this region of Chile, the *Sierra de la Costa*, which is crossed at the *Cuesta de Zapata* (*pass or depression* of Zapata), eighteen hundred and sixty feet high, and the *Sierra de Prado*, which the road passes over at the *Cuesta de Prado*, at an elevation of twenty-four hundred and twenty feet. This branch of the Santiago road is fifty miles long from Casa Blanca, giving a total distance from Valparaiso to the capital of eighty miles. The other branch of the fork runs southeast from Casa Blanca, and after passing several unimportant spurs of the Sierra de la Costa, to wit: Las Orcadas, Cuesta del Boldo, Cuesta de la Mina, and the somewhat higher Cuesta de las Hormigas, it crosses the considerable *Portezuelo de las Ibacache*, twelve hundred and fifty-eight feet high; much less, however, it will be observed, than the two lofty cuestas on the other route. This branch then seeks the valley of the *Maipú River*, still further to the southeast, and changing its course to the east at the town of *Melipilla*, runs through the gap of the Sierra de Prado which gives passage to the River Maipú, thus avoiding the tedious climbing, abrupt turns, and precipitous and dangerous descent of the Cuesta de Prado on the first-mentioned route. This second branch is known as the Melipilla road, from its passing through that town; and after turning the Sierra de Prado, it changes its course to the northeast, crosses the *Mapocho River* a short distance north of its affluence into the Maipú, and preserves the general northeastwardly direction, running frequently close along the left bank of the Mapocho until it reaches Santiago, seventy-five miles from Casa Blanca, or a total of one hundred and five miles from Valparaiso. It will thus be seen that the Melipilla road is twenty-five miles longer than the first described, or *Curicavi* road, as it is sometimes called, from its passing through a village of that name about midway between the Cuesta de Zapata and the Cuesta de Prado. But the greater safety of the Melipilla road, as well from the preferable mode of travelling it as from its avoidance of the short curves, steep descent, and fearful precipices of the other, is cheaply purchased by its increased distance, especially when it is considered that a longer time is not required to reach Santiago by this route. The French line takes the Curicavi road, while the American coaches always travel the Melipilla. After leaving Casa Blanca the latter road was found in much better condition than that nearer Valparaiso; many rich and well-cultivated quebradas were also seen as we ascended the Cuesta Ibacache; and in descending the eastern face of that pass, the mighty Andes, from fifty to sixty miles off, burst suddenly on the sight, stretching far to the north and south, marshalled like an army of giants; the imperial Tupungato towering at their head, with its snowy banners unfolded like pennons of peace from its proud domes, although the earthquake slumbered within its mysterious depths. And as we traversed the scorched and dusty plain at the foot of the Cuesta, breezes from the icy chambers of the distant Cordillera came by, to refresh us with their coolness. Pursuing our southeastwardly course between the ridge we had just crossed and the loftier one we were seeking to turn, we came to that fertile part of the valley about ten miles before reaching Melipilla, where the immense hacienda of San José is situated. This estate, of many leagues extent, belongs to Don Juan de dios Correa, the largest landed proprietor of Chile, now in involuntary *retirement* in Paris, for reasons of this *free* State. Far away were seen stretching the rich fields, teeming with luxuriant crops; while others, irrigated throughout, and enclosed by substantial and highly-ornamental adobe fences, pastured numerous herds of cattle. From this hacienda to Melipilla the country appears very productive; and this pretty little town of five thousand inhabitants having been passed at twelve and a half P. M., our route changed to the east, and continued through a highly-cultivated region, vineyards and fields of heavy-headed grain skirting the way on either hand, while leagues of graceful poplars bounded the magnificent avenue we here travelled. At the little village of San Francisco de Monte we crossed the Mapocho River, and ascended its left bank in a northeast direction through a beautiful valley, but sadly deficient in forest timber, as is all of Chile that I have seen. The Cordillera, which for some time had been hid from view, rose again before us, now that we had entered upon the great valley on which its feet had rested for uncounted ages, appearing like a castellated wall of the world, supported by mountain abutments, and crowned by a snowy parapet, gleaming in the setting sun like a silver crest, around which the wondering clouds gathered as if in adoration. How sublime the spectacle of that mighty creation on whose stupendous pillars the overarching blue of heaven seemed to rest in tranquil grandeur, dividing a continent throughout its length; reposing its head on a lap of tropical verdure, while its foot is clothed in polar sleet; separating nationalities, giving birth to vast and untold rivers, and determining their flow; yielding mineral wealth, without which labor would delve in poverty, and industry need incentive and reward, commerce languish, and the arts fail; and finally, reminding man of his feebleness and dependence, by shaking even his empires with its mighty throes!

Great quantities of shingle and boulders are found along the course of the Mapocho River; these are used in making roads and fences. Their presence shows the enormous water-power formerly in operation in the basin between the Andes and the Coast Range, to shape and distribute so extensively the rocky debris of these mountains.

The large production of cereals throughout a great part of the country over which we have passed to-day is surprising, in view of the nonusage of improved agricultural implements. The soil is upturned by a wooden plough without either share or coulter of iron, guided by a single stick handle, as in the days of the old patriot farmer Cincinnatus, for whose simple mode of tillage Chileans seem to have an abiding reverence: to the rude tongue two oxen are yoked by the horns, and the patient beasts are banged incessantly by a ponchoed peon with a long pole. Wagons of hay were seen in process of loading and unloading without a hay-fork, and by hand only; and, despite the speedy and cleanly mode of threshing by machinery, the now obsolete mode everywhere else of treading out grain by racing animals over it, is still in vogue here. The Creator has bestowed a magnificent land on these people; in view of natural gifts they have fallen short of the degree of progress they should have made; and the efforts of foreigners in their behalf seem really to fret them into jealousy; although without them Chile would scarcely be entitled to her preëminence as the most flourishing South American republic.

We reached Santiago at six P. M.—fourteen hours from Valparaiso—distance one hundred and five miles; excellent time; but we had California drivers, who knew how to handle the ribbons, and that too without hurting either passengers or teams. They were part owners of the line, and watchful over their own interests, which forbade recklessness.

## CHAPTER XIII.

CITY OF SANTIAGO—HOUSES—CAÑADA—BOTANIC GARDEN AND AGRICULTURAL SCHOOL—PLAZA DE LA INDEPENDENCIA—FALSE RECORD OF STATUARY—CHURCHES—HALLS OF CONGRESS AND JUSTICE—ECCLESIASTICAL CONTRAST—CAMPO DE MARTE—PENITENTIARY—PALACE—HOSPITALS—CHARITIES VINDICATED.

SANTIAGO, in 33° 26′ S. latitude, lies close to the western slope of the Andes, and immediately south of Cerro Blanco, Renca, and San Cristoval, foot hills of a spur of these mountains, on a plain to general observation nearly level, but having sufficient declivity to the west to allow of the free flow of water furnished by the Mapocho River to the city, and which is distributed throughout it by innumerable small aqueducts. These do not run in the middle of the streets, as do the acequias of Lima, but across the *quadras* (squares); and where they pass from one to another of these they are covered by flat stones, or iron plates. Nor are they the depositories of all the garbage, as by city regulations that is carted away at stated periods; yet enough of filth finds its way into these canals to make them in hot weather somewhat disagreeable and imperilling to health, especially when not duly covered, or when they become choked by accumulated sediment or offal.

Like Lima, the capital of Peru, so this city, the capital of Chile, has running through it from east to west, and dividing it into two unequal parts, a river, the Mapocho; which, rising in the chain of mountains to the northeast, flows first southwest toward Santiago, then westward a short distance, and then changes its course to the southwest again until it empties into the Maipú River. The portion of the city south of the river is much the larger, and embraces the public buildings, finest residences, commercial depots and offices, and places of fashionable resort generally. In the absence of any reliable recent census, owing to the evasions and denials of the poorer classes from apprehension of military impressment and taxation, the actual population of Santiago cannot be satisfactorily ascertained. It is estimated to exceed at this time one hundred thousand inhabitants, and probably may number one hundred and twenty-five thousand; to the observation of the traveller this calculation seems reasonable, as well from the crowded state of the principal streets and public places on holidays, as from the extent of the city, which covers a space of seven and a half square miles. The streets, in general of Spanish American narrowness, are not as well paved as they should be, considering the abundance of material at hand in the various conditions of rock, boulder, and cobble stone. Throughout the southern portion of Santiago they intersect each other at right angles, embracing quadras of a little over four hundred feet in each direction. These afford ample space for the expanded style of building deemed a necessary measure of safety here, as in the greater part of South America. The suburban houses are rude one-story structures, adobes, cane and mud being the materials, with thatched cane or flag roof. The residences of the better classes of citizens are substantial, commodious, and ornamental; and having strong and stout walls of well-made adobes and burnt brick, the street fronts of the finest houses in Santiago invariably have an alto. But the natives feel greater personal security in the one-story back buildings which surround the inner courts, to which access is had by a large gateway under the middle of the front edifice. It would be difficult to find anywhere more convenience, beauty, and even magnificence, than are found in a first-class residence in Santiago. This city is the capital of the wealth and fashion of Chile, as well as of its Government. Many of its citizens are the owners of landed estates and mines yielding princely annual incomes, in several instances ranging above a half million of dollars per annum; and no expense is spared by these persons either in the erection of mansions or in furnishing them. A first-class house does not consist alone of the buildings around the one *patio* (court) with which the gateway communicates; it is common to find a second patio behind the first, similarly surrounded by apartments and an open corridor, and adorned by flowers and a jet d'eau. Often a third patio and suite of apartments are found; while a fourth and even a fifth are seen in more opulent residences. The seclusion as well as safety of this arrangement, and the facility with which every branch of domestic economy may be isolated when desired, as well as the exemption from toilsome climbing of stairways, commend this style of architecture to the old, to invalids, and children, as well as to the lover of privacy and quiet. It is adapted to this mild climate where furnaces are unknown, fuel being used only by the cook, or occasionally in a brazier; and where also man is not reduced to a minimum of space by an overcrowded population.

The distinguishing improvement of Santiago, that which best serves the purpose of a landmark to strangers strolling about town, is the Cañada; so called from a species of cane or flag that grew abundantly on the banks of a rivulet which once meandered along the nearly three miles of space now occupied by this beautiful promenade and drive. The Cañada runs from east to west the length of the city, and has throughout probably two miles of its extent six parallel rows of ornamental trees. Between these are walks, fountains, and statuary; and a paved avenue on the outside affords to wealthy Santiaguinos the means of displaying on holidays, and according to fashion on Sundays and Thursdays, their fine equipages. Seats, too, are provided for those who seek refreshing breezes, sprinkled and cooled by the rapidly-flowing waters of artificial streams and jets, and where they may linger and listen to the operatic music of a full band provided at stated periods by the public authorities; while they gaze at the proud summits of the Cordillera in the east, radiant with the golden glories of a setting sun, then bathed in changeful and mellowing hues of vermilion, and violet, and purple, ere veiling themselves in darkness; and look also on the bold brow of the Sierra de Prado in the west, which seems to gather a darker frown at the transcendent majesty and beauty of its loftier brother.

Another cañada, or, as a public walk is also called, *alameda*, is situated in the northwest suburb of the city. It is two miles

CAÑADA.

p. 228.

long, and shaded throughout its entire length by rows of poplars. Not far from this suburban Cañada is a botanic garden of sixty acres, beautifully improved with drives and walks; trees, shrubbery, plants, and flowers—indigenous and exotic; rivulets and lakes; bowers, bowling greens, and hedges. A farm of larger size, for practical instruction of fifty boys in agriculture, is attached to the garden. The pupils—all of whom are *internes*—are also taught the usual branches of scholastic education, with whatever has connection with rural pursuits. Both the garden and farm are conducted at the expense and under the direction of the Government.

Among other municipal improvements for the use of citizens are seventeen fountains. These afford the only water-privilege, except by purchase of aquadores (water-carriers), who deliver it at houses, as in Lima, on donkeys. The want of enterprising capitalists or public spirit to weave the city with a network of water-pipes, leaves even palatial residences without the bountiful supply that might readily be had from the Mapocho River. Probably the speculation would prove a losing one, for the repugnance of the majority to the use of water for purposes of personal cleanliness is shockingly palpable. An endemic hydrophobia seems to prevail. Is it caused by hereditary hatred of their forefathers' Moorish oppressors, and opposition to all their usages, among which was the religious rite of ablution?

Nearly midway between the east end of the great Cañada and the Mapocho River is the *Plaza de la Independencia*, occupying the space of a quadra. A part of the plaza is enclosed by a neat iron balustrade and planted with flowers, in the middle of which, somewhat elevated, is an octagonal red porphyry basin of about thirty feet diameter, in which is a marble pedestal sculptured in basso-relievo portraying scenes and actors in the Chilean revolution of independence, supporting suitable water-spouts, and surmounted by statuary of life-size representing Liberty striking a chain from the arms of an Indian girl. This is very well as a matter of art, but not reliable as delineating truth: unhappily, productions of the chisel are as often inspirations of fancy as of fact. If ever chains were riveted upon a free-born race it was by the conquerors of the American

Indians, both north and south. Nor does the injustice and cruelty of that infliction rest with past generations alone. At this day the more exalted representatives of mankind in intellect and knowledge, and boastful, too, of a higher moral culture and religious sentiment, among whom millions of our own self-righteous countrymen stand prominent, whenever the greed of territory prompts, demand of them possessions given to their fathers long ages since by the Great Spirit. And if, unwilling to surrender their inheritance, they resist a claim repugnant to the laws of nature and God, the penalty of blood is fiercely enforced; and the remaining few, helpless and dismayed, overcome by brute force none the less disgraceful because cloaked by the purchase for a mess of pottage, are cast out to pine in grief, or to perish in want. It has been truly said by a distinguished prelate of Minnesota, that "there is not a man in America who ever gave an hour's calm reflection to this subject, who does not know that our Indian system is an organized system of robbery, and has been for years a disgrace to the nation."

Fronting on the four streets bounding this plaza, are, on the north side, several municipal buildings; on the east and south, arcades, where the chief fancy retailing is done; and on the west side the cathedral. The latter, although the metropolitan church, is still incomplete; yet there is much about it that is imposing. It is not less than three hundred and fifty by one hundred and thirty feet in size; but neither its extent nor exterior appearance indicates the effectiveness of its interior. Although there is, as in most Catholic churches I have seen in South America, a display of bad taste in the tawdry trappings and tinsel, which always detract from the grandeur of proportions, and architectural embellishments appropriate to a temple dedicated to the Most High, yet its twenty massive columns and numerous graceful arches, supporting a semi-elliptical roof, its frescoes and gildings, rich high altar, and some fine vestry paintings, do not fail to impress the spectator favorably. The walls are of dark-gray friable granite, very thick, and strengthened by massive abutments.

Behind the cathedral is the Jesuits' church—*Iglesia de la Compania.* It is large and built of dark Spanish bricks, which give it a very antiquated look outside. The interior is imposing, the high altar being of beautiful design and finish. Some of the paintings are excellent, and the admission of light from above through stained glass of the roof and an effectively-constructed dome, deepens the religious sentiment of the devotee by its unwonted and solemn influence. A great objection to this, as to nearly all Spanish-American churches, is a brick floor, on which worshippers are compelled to sit and kneel for hours, with merely a small carpet-rug (borne to and fro) to protect them from its cold and damp. When it is considered that most of the church-goers are women, that the early morning hour, and just from a warm bed, is the time usually chosen to seek preparation for the trials and temptations of the day—which, whatever may be said by captious travellers, are no greater in "good society" here than elsewhere—and that the special church-going robe, the black *manto*, is the only extra covering put on at this the coolest part of the day, it is not surprising that there should be, as I am professionally informed there is, an unusual prevalence of female constitutional weakness, and an extent of special disease among them that is considered an opprobrium of physicians. Since the above was written this Church of the Compania has been destroyed by fire during the ceremonies of the feast of the Immaculate Conception, more than two thousand persons, it is said, having perished in the flames. To any one who has seen in niches and on ledges thousands of candles, and scarcely fewer lamps, suspended carelessly from arches and ceilings of South-American churches, in illuminated celebrations, in close proximity to inflammable materials, such as artificial flowers, silk and muslin banners, curtains, and drapery, pictures, paintings, and wooden statuary, it is not surprising that this awful catastrophe should have occurred. It is hoped that the religious vanity of those of the clergy who have encouraged and participated in such displays, has been sufficiently rebuked by this terrible holocaust to prevent their repetition.

On the opposite side of the Plaza de la Compania to the Jesuits' church is the Hall of Congress; a very unpretending two-story building, not to describe which can give no offence to its members; who, doubtless, will feel very much gratified, as well for reasons of personal comfort as national pride, when the new capitol near by—which seems to have dragged its slow length along to a resting-place—shall have been completed.

On the east side of the plaza stands the Hall of Justice; a low, stuccoed, and pilastered building. The ostentation of an inexplicable wooden balustrade on the top lifts it above its legislative neighbor; though the decisions of its inner courts may not be considered as preëminent by that revolutionary and not very deferential confrére.

It is needless even to name twenty-five or thirty inferior churches, most of which are but coarse imitations of the worse features of the few more conspicuous and in better taste. A fact in reference to them of singular uniformity is their unfinished condition; and it is the more remarkable in view of the characteristic devotion of Catholics, and the liberality with which they contribute to uphold the dignity and extend the influence of their profession. The reason assigned by some for this defect, seems to a charitable interpretation of human motive incredible; but if it be true that it is, as surmised by some persons, a priestly device, the more frequently and speciously to appeal to parishioners for contributions, which are diverted from the purpose designed to the sensual and luxurious gratifications of the clergy themselves, then is their perfidy doubly wicked; for, while it shakes and endangers, by discovery and reprobation, the faith of proselytes, it would also defraud Divinity of the willing tribute of His simple-minded but sincere worshippers.

The finest of the churches of Santiago are not equal, either in architectural design and finish, or in embellishment and furniture, to the grandest in Lima. A certain sameness exists in both cities, growing out of the imperious requirements of countries subject alike to earthquakes; but beyond this, Peru exhibits more church grandeur and general opulence of decoration, especially in altar-furniture, than Chile. This may be accounted for by the accessible wealth in precious metals of Peru at the time of its conquest, and for a while after, and which was rapaciously and ruthlessly seized by the invaders, wherever found, and appropriated by both people and priests. The wild spirit of adventure kindled in Spain by the discovery of this mineral treasure, brought hosts of the needy and unscrupulous to strengthen the already powerful temporal and spiritual coalition, who did not stop at the plunder of every Peruvian shrine of its sacred jewels, and every house of its silver and gold, but tortured the victims of oppression, robbery, and lust, until they revealed their buried treasures and gave up their household gods, with their freedom and their virtue. Deducting the Crown's one-fifth of the treasure seized, which, in the early history of the conquest, was faithfully paid, whatever may have occurred when viceroyalty became firmly established and conscious of power, the Church secured directly and indirectly the larger share of the remainder; for, what it failed to obtain by self-appropriation and division of spoils, it rarely failed eventually to get the greater part of, by fees, contributions, and bequests, for its good offices in assuaging the pangs of disturbed conscience—which, in those times of violence, cruelty, rapine, and murder, were many and grievous—and otherwise comforting the distressed and the dying; while even the dead were considerately cared for at the instance of opulent friends.

It is not difficult, in view of these facts, to account for the affluence and grandeur of the churches and church establishments of Lima, which were more distinguished even before the Peruvian revolution of independence than now. But the success in the acquisition of wealth by the Church in Chile was neither so sudden nor so great. Almagro, to whom by royal warrant this part of the continent was granted for discovery and occupancy, and who was the first Spaniard to penetrate its interior, after having himself examined the country as far as the valley of Coquimbo, and despatched a part of his command further south, who explored nearly to the river Maule, abandoned Chile because it was not a country of gold, and returned to Peru, to contest with Pizarro the possession of the imperial city of the Incas; and although Valdivia some years afterward reëntered the country, establishing various permanent settlements, and passed much beyond the extreme limit of Almagro's exploration, his reward was rather the glory of daring achievement than the acquisition of mineral wealth. The metallic riches of Chile have been gradually brought to light, as its other great resources are being developed; and, accordingly, the worldly aggrandizement of its Church was for a time in abeyance to its spiritual mission. This was fortunate, for it was kept thereby freer from the corruption and vice of its more worldly neighbor, and better prepared to fulfil its great duty. The very early history of its efforts in Chile were accordingly signalized by many examples of self-sacrificing devotion to the cause of the religion of Christ. It is strange that the purification of poverty is necessary to perfect piety! With the discovery of the precious metals, came here, as elsewhere, the yearning after and acquisition of riches. The evidence of this is palpable in the structure and adornment of religious edifices; but, as before said, they are less imposing than in Lima. It is probable that greater wealth contributed also to increased ecclesiastical demoralization.

A principal public resort on occasions of national celebration by military parade and review, is the *Campo de Marte*, a level square of one hundred and fifty acres, beyond the southern limits of the city, with a wide drive and promenade, with ornamental trees on all sides, facing which, on the north, is the handsome artillery barracks; on the east and west, beautiful *cuintas* (country seats) spread over the extensive plain formerly known as the *pampa;* and on the south is the Penitentiary. A few words about the Penitentiary, in conformity with my rule of gathering by the wayside and noting as opportunity offers.

This institution is built on a principle sound in theory, and sustained by the experience of many States of North America; and yet in its discipline, and the general administration of its affairs, stopping so far short of the system professed to have been adopted, as to have utterly failed in the objects desired—which certainly should be more than the mere confinement of a human being like a wild beast. A quadrilateral brick wall of sufficient height and strength, on which thirteen guards furnished by the military authorities do duty, encloses about ten acres of ground. Immediately within this outer wall is another, enclosing an octangular-shaped space, in the centre of which is a building capable of holding only about fifty or sixty persons, which is used as a chapel. Its small size implies that religious observances are not popular with the convicts, or that Government considers the most of them too hardened to waste church accommodations on them. Surrounding this little nucleus of the prison is a many-sided paved court, from which radiate twenty-five uncovered passages, called in the prison language *streets*, the entrance to each of which is commanded by an iron gate. On opposite sides of some of these open corridors or streets, are long rows of cells extending as far as the inner octagonal wall before spoken of, against which the far end of each block of cells abuts, while the ranges of cells of adjoining streets are in contact, back to back. Each cell is seven by eight feet in size, is designed for solitary confinement at night, is strongly built of burnt brick, and has an iron-grated door opening on its corresponding street, in the centre of which is a wall sufficiently high to prevent communication between the inmates of opposite cells by conversation or signs. The whole number of cells is five hundred and twenty-five; of inmates five hundred. On other streets workshops are erected, in which the convicts are engaged in cabinet and smith work, and shoemaking during the day. This associated labor counteracts the reformatory effect of personal isolation during the night; for no provision is made, either in arrangement of the shops, or by the enforcement of a suitable discipline, to secure that moral isolation which is the chief feature of the Auburn system of imprisonment, and absolutely necessary to its success. By a singular regulation of this Penitentiary, the product of labor is passed to the credit of the convict, who receives the full proceeds of sale when he is discharged. Thus the entire expense of the prison falls on the Government, instead of the convict being required to contribute to his own support as in the United States, which is but just to the community who are presumed to have already suffered from his crimes, while it inflicts no improper hardship on the convict; but on the contrary he becomes instructed thereby in a trade that will serve him usefully when restored to society, and he also acquires habits of industry. This defective regulation, which seems to have originated in false considerations of kindness for the convict, presupposes idleness or occupation to be properly optional with him—certainly a great error in reformatory effort. For, if he be without the capacity of earning a subsistence, and have no habits of industry, what guaranty can there be that his unlawful depredations on society will not entail upon the State his continuous support? True, if he declines to work he is excluded from the shop, and confined to his cell. The enjoyments of the shop are thus considered sufficient temptation to exertion. But this implies defective discipline, affording the opportunity of companionship. And it also ignores the fact that, if the semblance of occupation is put on without actual labor, it answers the purpose to avoid confinement. The rule seemed so erroneous that doubts arose as to my proper understanding of the Superintendent's statement of the fact, but it was subsequently reaffirmed. From what was learned of the very recent neglect of all efforts to reform the barbarous system of imprisonment so long the disgrace of civilized nations, it is but just to report a commendable improvement, and it is reasonable to expect a further approach to a perfect system in Chile; particularly if the Government should place at the head of the movement such a philosophical and practical philanthropist as Señor Paz Soldan of Lima.

Although the transition from a penitentiary to a palace may not seem appropriate, as many translations from a palace to a penitentiary would be if justice were duly administered, yet my story must be told in the order of occurrences; and the opportunity being afforded to see the chief public building in Santiago, incidentally to the discharge of necessary duties, it must be noted accordingly.

The palace covers a square of four hundred feet, near the centre of the city, fronting on a plazuela by no means large enough to exhibit its architectural pretensions to advantage. Erected about sixty years since, it was intended for the residence of the Spanish Viceroy, whose court was but little less distinguished by displays of grandeur and opulence than that of his royal master. The intention being at the time to erect Viceregal palaces in both Mexico and Chile, two plans were prepared in Madrid for the buildings. But by mistake, that intended for Santiago was sent to Mexico, and that for the palace at Mexico was sent to Santiago. Before the error was detected they were commenced according to the plans received, and were so completed—the palace here at a cost of $900,000. The façade is of light granite, the order Doric, two stories in height, except at the centre, where the main entrance is, and where it rises to three stories, surmounted by a dome. Between the alto-relievo pilasters the iron-grated windows give to the edifice the appearance of a prison, which is increased by the armed sentinels at the doorway, at the corners of the street leading to it, and at the military barracks opposite. On entering the portal, a guard-room is found on the left, facing the quarters of the officer of the day on the right. Just beyond the former is a broad stone staircase, over the arched entrance of which is an inscription announcing to the visitor that it leads to the dwelling of His Excellency the President. A corresponding stairway on the right is inscribed with the notice that above will be found the department of the Minister of the Interior and of Foreign Relations. Ascending this latter stairway and passing through a vestibule, a balcony is reached surrounding a courtyard about fifty feet square, with a little murmuring fountain in the centre, emblematic perhaps of the stream of complaints flowing to the office of his excellency the Minister. From the astute mind and philosophic character of this statesman, it is probable that the latter disturbs his equanimity as little as the former. From the balcony access is also had to the offices of other members of the Executive Cabinet, to wit: to those of the Minister of Justice and Public Worship, the Minister of War and Marine, and the Minister of the Treasury, whose respective clerks are also accommodated in this building.

Occupying a considerable part of the palace will likewise be found the National Mint, the coinage of which is very creditably executed.

Of course hospitals have not been overlooked by a medical rambler. Of these, the *Hospital of San Juan de Dios*, now used exclusively for men, is the most remarkable, from its antiquity, extent, position, administration, and general usefulness. It is situated at the east end of the Cañada, on its south side, near the Church of San Augustin, and is admirably located for ventilation and view. Although the present building is comparatively of recent erection, the institution was founded in the early part of the seventeenth century, by the monks of the religious order of San Juan de Dios, who then owned the ground on which the hospital now stands, and which was formerly occupied by their convent. Some of the monks, as was the case with many of these old religionists whose monasteries in fact were the depositories of medical literature in the dark ages, possessing some knowledge of medicine, were in the habit of humanely devoting it to charitable purposes; and educated physicians being then scarcely known in Chile, they prescribed for all who applied to them for advice, and often took into their convent, and in imitation of the good Samaritan, administered personally to the afflictions of the destitute. Thus originated this great charity, honorable to its founders and honorable to those who now perpetuate its blessings to suffering humanity. As the order of monks, whose name, and the memory of whose good deeds, the hospital preserves, became extinct, the National Government took the management of its affairs; and by public appropriations and private bequests it has, from time to time, been enlarged, new buildings erected, and its general condition improved. Its glorious destiny of benevolence and usefulness, as long as mortality with its pains and penalties shall endure, will make it a monument of the philanthropy and liberality of its pious founders and of Chilean legislation, more imperishable than the bronze and marble that listlessly adorn the neighboring Cañada. All the hospital buildings are of one story, except the main front on the Cañada, two portions of which have altos. The walls are of adobes and three feet thick, securing exemption from being thrown down; roof of indestructible tile, and floors of asphaltum and burnt brick, for greater cleanliness. The buildings are arranged around quadrangular patios, there being five of these well-paved, with the exception of that attached to the front building, which is adorned with flowers and shrubbery, and a fountain with jets. Capacious galleries open on most of the courts, allowing communication between different parts of the establishment without the necessity of passing through intermediate rooms; at the same time, by the devotion of each court and its surrounding edifice to a different use, the various departments are sufficiently insulated to prevent undue interference with the peculiar duties, discipline, and management of each other. The medical and surgical wards are separate, large, well-ventilated, and clean; the bedding ample and of good quality; and the general administration under a corps of experienced, polite, and attentive Sisters of Charity, and professional attendance by educated and skilful physicians and surgeons, are such as to deserve commendation. The *botica* (pharmacy) is large, handsomely arranged, and abundantly supplied with medicines, and all needful accessories of that department, and has an accomplished pharmaceutist in constant attendance to compound prescriptions. Its arrangement of appropriately-labelled jars for keeping a supply of the various invalid beverages and most necessary decoctions, without the objectionable delay attendant on preparation when called for, is deserving of imitation in corresponding institutions in the United States. Bath rooms are numerous, and well supplied with hot and cold water; and the kitchen and laundry show a studious regard for health and comfort. The hospital has at this time more than five hundred patients; the number is sometimes as high as six hundred. This, and all other charities under the control of Government, are managed by a Board of Trustees named by the Executive authorities, composed of men of wealth and respectability, who serve without compensation. The Hospital of San Juan is the owner of certain estates, houses, and investments, the income from which, together with contributions and occasional bequests, are ordinarily sufficient for its support. If not, the public treasury is called on for assistance. The hospital statistics show the most frequent diseases to be those ordinarily classified as diseases of the chest; those of the stomach and bowels, particularly gastric fever and dysentery; and venereal affections: the latter, here as in Valparaiso, surprisingly significant by its very large proportion, of either a remarkable immorality among the lower classes of the population, or of a lamentable neglect of curative means. And as I am professionally informed, and believe also from my limited opportunities of observation, it is chiefly owing to the great prevalence of the last-mentioned class of diseases that in proportion to population an unusually large number of blind persons is met with, both in hospitals and highways. It has been eloquently said by a medical writer in the *Annales de la Universidad:* "Looking round the whole horizon, we do not find a single spot that casts the germs of epidemic miasma toward our blue sky; yet in the midst of this beautiful land we perceive death cutting down the tender plants of the generation, and striking off the young branches of the tree, leaving only the dried limbs, in whose veins flow the poisons that afflict society. The venereal disease is the prime mover of the revolution effected in the human species—the infernal contagion transmitted and transmissible. That the mortality of the country is due to it I cannot doubt, after seeing the innumerable children who have been brought to the charity hospital suffering with scrofulous syphilis." It would be happy for this country if means were adopted to interpret to the unlettered and unthinking multitude the "hand writing" perpetually obtruded before them. If this be not done, despite their fair inheritance of land and climate, the *Upas* in their midst, poisoning the fountains of public health, will bring to the nation, as to the children whose fate is touchingly proclaimed above, premature decay and death.

Another hospital is that of *San Francisco de Borja.* It is devoted exclusively to women, is eligibly situated, and consists of ten separate and distinct one-story buildings, each one hundred and thirty feet long by thirty feet wide. These are arranged in equal numbers on opposite sides of a large, open, oblong space, laid off in walks, and cultivated in flowers and shrubbery. These buildings, in which are the wards for invalids, stand in two rows endwise opposite to each other, and each building is at such a distance from those of the same side, as to allow of intermediate gardens in addition to the main central one. The whole presents a very pleasing appearance, and contributes doubtless to cheer the sadness of many a suffering inmate. It is designed to have a large and more showy edifice in front, for official as well as other occupancy; this will more perfectly shield from observation and intrusion, the present buildings and their inmates. From three hundred to four hundred patients are usually accommodated, whose diseases, with slight exceptions, correspond to the general character of those named when speaking of the Hospital of San Juan de Dios. An income of twenty-five thousand dollars per annum, from property held under charitable bequests, constitutes its chief support. Sisters of Charity are the efficient instruments in its excellent management.

The *Alms House* is another of the charitable institutions of the city, and is devoted solely to the destitute and infirm. It consists of commodious one-story adobe buildings, arranged round five patios. Sufficient ground is attached for useful and ornamental gardens, and the two hundred and sixty-five inmates of both sexes looked well-clad, clean, comfortable, and contented. The premises once belonged to the Jesuits, whose large possessions, on the extinction of that order, were wisely made in most instances tributary to the promotion of charitable objects. Sisters of Charity in this, as in the institutions already mentioned, are the administrators of the benevolent trust. To avoid tediousness I will, merely in justice to the spirit of practical charity of Santiago, enumerate briefly several other institutions having their origin in enlarged philanthropy.

Four *Dispensaries* are supported by Government, at which about fifty thousand persons are said to receive gratuitous medical assistance annually.

*An Institution of Evangelical Charity*, the expenses of which are borne by private subscription, gives medical advice and attendance at their houses to the poor, and pecuniary aid when necessary to deserving objects.

*Hospederia de San Rafael*, supported by subscription, where destitute or sick strangers are taken and provided for until they can get employment. It should be added, however, to the honor of Santiago, that foreigners are received into all the hospitals without charge; and I am assured by those who are in position to know, that if any distinction be made between them and natives, in regard to attention and treatment, it is in favor of the former.

*The Institution of the Good Shepherd*, a Magdalen Asylum

for profligate women who desire to reform. Supported by subscription.

*Casa de Maria*—for indigent girls who, from parental neglect and want, might be led from the path of virtue.

*A House of Maternity*—for charitable accouchement. Maintained at the cost of Government.

*Casa de Expositos*, a foundling hospital. And also a *Providencia*, to which the little unfortunates are removed in the event of passing through the many dangers that beset tender infancy; and where they are educated, taught some useful employment, and whence they go when a suitable home can be provided for them. The establishment of these latter charities has been regarded by some persons as a boon to licentiousness; and a voluminous writer upon Chile, who has discussed both its public institutions and social customs with much ability and freedom, if not always in the latter case with discretion, has pronounced the Casa de Expositos an "encouragement of vice." But this seems to be a reversal of the order of cause and effect; for if the vice had not been in existence and calling for the adoption of some means to mitigate its effects, such an institution would not have been thought of. It was the sequence in the order of events, a necessity growing out of antecedent depravity, with the perpetuation of which it is manifestly unjust to burden it. It would be as reasonable to condemn all the other noble charities it has afforded so much gratification to mention, which contribute to brighten a national escutcheon dimmed by undoubted defects, and such as distinguish the philanthropy of other lands, because forsooth their provision for destitution and distress may "encourage the vices" upon which these in nearly all cases depend. Profligacy, debauchery, drunkenness, bring poverty and disease. Pity beholds the sufferer, leads him to the door of Mercy, where Charity ministers to him, and says, "Go, sin no more." When the man sick of the palsy was brought to Him who went about doing good, to be healed, He first said, "Son, be of good cheer, thy sins be forgiven thee;" and then, after this Divine manifestation of beneficence, "Arise, take up thy bed and go unto thy house;" thus showing His knowledge and forgiveness of the frailty inseparable from human nature.

And it is to be forgiven not merely "seven times," according to a worldly dispensation, but "seventy times seven," in obedience to the precepts of heavenly truth, and in fulfilment of that "charity which never faileth; but suffereth long, and is kind." In human affliction, the withholding of relief would often destroy, but rarely reclaim; for the lamp of life is then too flickering to shed even a ray of hope ere it goes out in the darkness of death. The shadows of coming gloom increased by the heartlessness of man, deepen the despair that welcomes oblivion. We are commanded to imitate our Father in heaven, and to be perfect even as He is. This is undoubtedly difficult, and to some may seem impossible. Yet having been enjoined upon us by Himself, and contemplating His comprehension of our capacities, and that He is too just and merciful to require aught that we have not the ability to perform, the effort of obedience, far from being presumptuous, is but a proof of that faith which removeth mountains, and brings the blessings of goodness within reach of human attainment. And this capacity of resemblance must be conceded, in view of the illustration of Divine inculcation of love and duty: "He maketh His sun to rise on the evil and on the good, and sendeth rain on the just and on the unjust." Throned in mystery, as God may seem to a finite comprehension, His great essence is thus revealed to those who seek the light of heaven, and would become warmed with the glow in their own hearts of its immortal love. And this "*love, the fulfilment of the law*," must go forth on its benign mission with healing on its wings, lifting up the broken-hearted, and causing the wondering multitude who have lingered in error, to glorify the Omnipotent Source of such goodness, when they see "the dumb to speak, the maimed to be whole, the lame to walk, and the blind to see," whether they be "evil or good, just or unjust." This application of benevolence is especially due to this continent; for if it be true that even in older communities, where the social organization has had a longer time to adapt itself to the requirements of necessity, civilization increases human disparities, and that the more the wealth and luxury of the few, the greater the poverty and wants of the many, then are the people of this country, of deteriorated race, who compose by far the larger part of its population, entitled in a marked degree to the considerate care and assistance of those through whom such evils have come upon them. The more powerful, enterprising, energetic, and intellectually-exalted Spaniard, in the struggle for mastery, whether in dominion, government, commerce, mines, or landed estate, has achieved triumph and possession. Hence the general indigence and ignorance of the mixed race are even greater than found in homogeneous nations; and the sense of these is the more galling, from the contrast with surrounding opulence. Better for the unhappy victims of oppression and depravity had they enjoyed conscious equality and competence, even with the imputation of barbarism. The Spaniard further entailed upon the descendants of the aborigines, through force as well as example, unnatural relations, vices, and diseases, to which those primitive natives were strangers. Apart, then, from general considerations of humanity, there is justly devolved upon the affluent representatives of the Spanish race, a special trust to minister to the necessities and sufferings of those whose "vices" are the offspring of a "higher law" of civilization—accursed in this as in some other phases of human relation—rather than the product of their own simple, and, in comparison with the pioneers of Spanish dominion in America, purer natures. No additional force can be added to the obligations of humanity and religion by the consideration, but still it should not be overlooked that the day is not distant when, unless largely strengthened by immigration, the European element of Chilean population will be merged in the degenerate mixed race; or its gradually weakening power be wrenched from its grasp by rapidly-increasing social antagonism. The cherishing of kindly sympathies, and exercise of enlarged philanthropy, may serve then to perpetuate blessings to a posterity who, whatever may be the pangs of misfortune, will yet find alleviation in the memory and fruits of the good deeds of their ancestry.

## CHAPTER XIV.

DESCRIPTION OF SANTIAGO CONTINUED—LUNATIC ASYLUM—MEDICAL SCHOOL—LIBRARY—MILITARY AND MECHANIC INSTITUTES—PANTHEON—OFFICIAL AND INTERNATIONAL DISCOURTESY—SANTA LUCIA—APOQUINDO MINERAL SPRINGS—VALLEY OF SANTIAGO—RAILROADS.

THE remark was made to me in Lima by a member of the Beneficentia, that the only asylum on the west coast of South America for the rational treatment of insanity, was the one in that city. He was in error. At Santiago a Lunatic Asylum is found of large size, excellent arrangement, and admirable government. A lot of ground three hundred and sixty-five yards long by from one hundred to two hundred yards in width, is enclosed by a substantial wall fifteen feet high. A building of two hundred and fifty feet, forming the centre of the front wall, contains the administrative offices; while within, running lengthwise the enclosure, is an alley, with many long one-story buildings extending from it on both sides, arranged parallel to each other, having patios between them for exercise and garden cultivation, and from which the rooms are entered. The main walls of the building are forty inches, and the partition walls of the rooms for separate occupancy are twenty-five inches thick, both built of adobes. The strongly-framed roof, of cane and mud, as a good non-conductor of heat in summer, is further covered with tiles saturated with soap and alum, which is said to make them water-proof. Thirty-two of the cells, several of them of oval shape, are dark, and lined with quilted India rubber to prevent personal injury, for the confinement exclusively of *madmen*. And for further protection, some of these have oak bedsteads built in the wall. Warm and cold baths are liberally provided, both plunge and shower; also a swimming pond, walled and cemented, which is found an excellent hygienic means from the amusement and exercise it affords. The number of inmates at present is one hundred and seventeen. A very full proportion of cures is reported; and the advantages of the *modern system of treatment*, a gentle and tranquil deportment, and consistent firmness, with rational amusement, entertainment, exercise, occupation, and appropriate medical prescription, as contradistinguished to the *old and barbarous system of unvarying severity and seclusion*, are fully sustained by the experience of this institution. The Santiago Lunatic Asylum was built and is supported by the national government.

Chile possesses the means of educating medical attendants for these numerous hospitals. A university established in 1842, being the reorganization of one chartered more than two hundred years before, embraces the faculties of philosophy and humanities, physical and mathematical science, medicine, law, political science, and theology. The *medical school*, consisting of a full corps of professors, is in operation; the course of instruction aiming to meet as far as practicable, in the infancy of the institution, the wants of the country. To foreigners aspiring to practise medicine, surgery, or pharmacy, in Chile, the privilege is extended upon presentation of a diploma from a respectable university, and being found competent after a strict examination, both theoretical and practical, by question and answer, attack or maintenance of proposed doctrines; beside diagnosis, prognosis, and prescription; and surgical operations on the cadaver. The fees amount to $120—the travelling and incidental expenses to as much more. Owing to the delay incident to examination, the detention at Santiago grows irksome to the candidate. Usually five or six weeks are occupied in ridiculous formalities, which should not consume more than two or three days. If unsuccessful, the candidate may present himself for examination again after the lapse of six months. In pharmacy the examination is well suited to test the qualifications of candidates for license to compound and vend medicines. Ignorance and presumption, either in prescribing or administering medicine, meet with no favor in Chile. In this respect she is in advance of many of the States of North America, the *lives* of whose citizens are considered by no means as precious as *individual right to do in all things as one pleases*, for the brief time that malady or malpractice may permit him to exercise it. Besides several excellent academies, for *private instruction* of the children of wealthy parentage at high charges, Government has provided a *National Institute*, *normal school*, and many *primary institutions for public instruction*; which, although not up to the standard of merit of similar institutions in some other countries, are yet creditable to this young republic.

*A Military Institute* is also provided for the education of naval and army officers. Boys of twelve years are admitted and instructed during five years of study in the various branches of mathematics, elementary and profound, history, geography, navigation, the French and English languages, drawing field fortifications, artillery and infantry tactics, gymnastics, and sword exercises. There are sixty cadets in the Institute; but the building, which is in admirable order, and the grounds, are ample for the accommodation of many more.

Still another admirable institution supported by Government is that for instructing boys, of whom there are now five hundred in the school, in the useful *mechanic arts*. They are also taught the usual branches of scholastic education. This will prove one of the most useful institutions of Chile. It is nearly self-supportive.

Santiago has a *National Library* of 39,000 volumes, to which the public has access; a reading-room with suitable furniture being likewise provided. And in the same building is the *National Museum*, in the formation of which a French naturalist, M. Gay, had the chief agency. The ornithological and botanical departments, embracing the birds and plants of Chile, are nearly complete; as is also its zoology. Some fine specimens of Chilean minerals are in the cases; but the shells of the country are few, and present but little attraction. Altogether the collection, as representing the natural history of this country, is highly creditable. The Museum is opened to the public on one day of each week. Strangers are admitted at any time.

*The Pantheon* of Santiago, like that of Lima, is on the smallest scale, not more than about fifteen acres being walled in for the cemetery of a city whose population certainly exceeds one hundred thousand. Such scant dimensions are scarcely pardonable, as it lies at the foot of Cerro Blanco—well adapted to purposes of sepulture, but nothing else. This cemetery is a splendid speculation at the enormous charges made for *temporary* burial, the same leasehold interment prevailing here as in other Spanish-American countries, and the same horrid feature of gratuitous communism existing too. And if the immense receipts for conveyance, burial, removal, and masses, had been appropriated to the purpose, the avenues and paths of the Pantheon might have been paved with gold by this time. A little chapel within the entrance tells the visitor that its uplifted cross is "Spes unico" —the sole hope—of those who pass that portal for the last time. There is more taste displayed than in Peru, in the adornment of the resting-place of the dead; cypresses, shrubbery, and flowers abound, and there are some appropriately designed and well-executed monuments. Some curiosity was felt to see the statue of which Lieut. J. M. Gilliss (Superintendent of the United States Naval Astronomical Expedition to the Southern Hemisphere) said, one of the mausoleums "is surmounted by a nude figure of Grief executed in white marble, which, by order of the archbishop, has actually been covered with a petticoat of black cloth from the waist to the knees!" This declaration has been indignantly denied by Santiaguinos. Certainly no such attired figure is *now* seen; but a winged marble statue of Grief was observed, with inverted torch in the right hand, the left resting on an urn consecrated to the ashes of D. Juan Henrique Rosales and D. Maria del Rosario Larrain, daubed with coarse cement in a manner designed to represent a fig-leaf. Whose *vandal delicacy* is commemorated by this act I know not; but, the whole story of this offending specimen of the fine arts, and the sadness it was designed so touchingly to tell, is suggestive of the question—which is more obnoxious to criticism, the vulgar affectation of modesty that could not look upon nature with the purity that truth and virtue teach; or the misapprehension of duty which included in a formal report to the Congress of the

United States, remarks on unofficial subjects offensive to the sensitiveness of a country that had, with singular alacrity, aided in promoting the objects of that scientific expedition—of which the officer above referred to has stated that, "throughout nearly the three years of our residence at Santiago, the Government evinced the most earnest disposition to forward the objects of the Expedition, and to extend every possible consideration to its members officially and personally. Our equipments and every subsequent object for public and personal use had been admitted free of duty, a site had been prepared for our observatories, a guard had been stationed there to protect them, every necessity had been promptly supplied when sought; in short, we had been the recipients of its courtesy and coöperation from the moment of arrival at the capital." Mr. Gilliss came to Chile accredited to its Government as an officer of the United States Navy, sent on a scientific mission. As such he was received, and how treated is recorded in his own language. If the report to his Government had embraced solely observations and reflections upon the objects of the Expedition, as directed by Congress, he would have been entitled to commendation for the faithful and able manner in which he had performed his whole duty; and great benefits would have resulted, not merely to science, but to the political and commercial relations of the two countries. But to embrace in such a document descriptions of social, political, and religious customs, private as well as public; even in some instances drawn from the sanctuary of domestic life into which he had been received almost as the guest of the nation; to accompany these with criticisms often severely censorious, while jest gives additional pungency to others; and to present the whole record of science, social organization, and scandal, to the Government authorizing the Expedition, to be *by it printed and circulated as a State document*, can scarcely be regarded, when judged of either by the rules of international courtesy or personal politeness, as legitimate and civil. It is the undoubted right of every traveller to observe, record, and publish his observations and reflections; but the mode of so doing should be rightly determined, and the obligations imposed by formally accredited and officially recognized position, and private hospitality, should not be disregarded. It was with mortification that frequent remarks were heard in Valparaiso and Santiago of the discourtesy of a countryman who had been long and largely the recipient of Chilean attention and entertainment, public and private. These remarks were often characterized by great bitterness, induced perhaps by the consciousness that many of the public faults and private foibles, which had been exposed, were truthfully represented. But an equal consciousness is felt by Americans, and the remark universally made by other foreign residents here, that whatever these faults and foibles may have been, they should not have been presented to our Government as an official report, side by side with an acknowledgment of national courtesy and coöperation in the objects of the Expedition. And further, that the strange oversight, or extraordinary international incivility, should not have been perpetrated by our Government, of publishing and distributing that report as an accepted State document. "Our country right or wrong," sounds so patriotic as to have become an axiom with demagogues. But our country, justified when right—condemned when wrong, is a far more honorable aspiration of conscience, and one that candor obliges me thus to exemplify.

In this connection it may be remarked that the rocky hill of *Santa Lucia*, on which the necessary buildings of the United States Astronomical Expedition were erected, lifts its stern crest one hundred and ninety-eight feet above the city of Santiago surrounding its base, an everlasting monument, not only of the scientific enterprise which would peer into the mysteries of space, and map anew, by the trembling light of its own firmament, the southern hemisphere; but of that indomitable spirit of Spanish discovery which sought to penetrate the unknown regions of earth, and give to civilization the tribute of a vast conquest. It was on its craggy height that Pedro Valdivia, three hundred and twenty years ago, in 1541, planted the fortification, from which, as from an eagle's eyry he swooped upon the startled inhabitants of the beautiful valley at its foot; and to which he retreated when danger threatened him, to renew his energies, mature his plans, and await a more propitious moment to accomplish his bold purpose of adding a new empire to the already surpassing dominion of Spain. But for the foresight which contemplated the probable perils that would beset him, and the military sagacity that instructed him to occupy so defensible a position by his small force, the wonderful achievements of Valdivia would never have made his name famous in history; although the Spanish Monarch, it is reasonable to suppose, might have eventually subjugated that portion of Chile not ruled by the unconquerable and still unconquered Araucanian. Nor was it long before Valdivia had cause to congratulate himself on the prudence which had led him to secure a place of refuge in case of hostilities with the natives; for scarcely had he founded the town of Santiago, so named in honor of the patron saint of Spain, when the Mapochin Indians, then inhabiting that part of the valley, becoming awakened to the purposes of the invaders, attacked them, and utterly destroyed the town. But for the almost inaccessible fort on Santa Lucia, it is probable that the Spaniards would have been exterminated. As it was, they were barely able to maintain their position until reënforced from Peru.

The west side of the hill is rugged and precipitous: the summit is reached from the east by a steep, rudely-terraced path. At the outbreak of the Chilean war of Independence a battery on this hill commanded the city. It is now dismantled, to prevent revolutionists overawing the Government by seizing it. A little lower than the site of the battery is still seen the building of the former astronomical observatory, not now used as such, the instruments having been removed to the Agricultural College. A short distance from the foot of Santa Lucia, to the east, is the small, one-story, adobe, tile-covered house occupied by the conqueror of Chile more than three centuries ago. It is carefully preserved as a monument of the old Spanish pioneer. On the way from this remnant of the olden time, another relic of the past was seen—the residence of the Countess del ———, one of the few who persisted in retaining the title, with the pride and many of the customs of ancestry; among the last, that of driving four horses to her coach. Having been notified that such was the exclusive privilege of the President, she haughtily retorted, "If any more such communications are made to me I will drive *six*." This was satisfactory to supreme authority, and it was decided to "let the Castilian alone."

My remaining day in Santiago was devoted to visiting the Apoquindo Mineral Springs, about two leagues east of the city. Taking the road along the Tajamar, which follows the left bank of the Mapocho River for three miles we then passed through a richly-cultivated country, adobe walled vineyards hanging their clustering fruits around in great profusion, while olive groves and fig-tree orchards darkened the way with their deep shade. Beyond this first land belt of great fertility, the more rapid acclivity of the foot hill water-shed yielded a less bountiful supply of fruits and vegetables; and then the hacienda of the Franciscan friars, who own the Springs, was seen unfolding its vineyards from which is produced the luscious *Mosto*, a native wine resembling that of Bordeaux. *The Apoquindo Springs*, next reached, are situated twenty-five hundred and seventy-four feet above the level of the sea, and seven hundred and twenty-four feet above that of the plaza at Santiago; the latter being eighteen hundred and fifty feet above the sea level. The improvements are neither handsome, commodious, nor conveniently arranged, and consist merely of one-story adobe buildings, with projecting tile roofs, and very primitive apartments, for the accommodation of probably sixty or seventy persons. There are five springs, and seven roughly-constructed bath-rooms, within two-thirds of a circle of fifty feet diameter; the bath-pools of perhaps six or seven by three or four feet size, being sunk in the earth so as to receive a sufficient quantity of water. One of the baths is a natural basin of rock, five feet in diameter and four feet deep; the others are artificially walled. Three of the springs have water of like properties, and are used for baths alone; the other two are both emetic and purgative. But the attendants were found to be so destitute of accurate information in regard to the temperature, constituents, and medical properties of these waters, that no confidence could be placed in their statements. The following, which I transcribe bodily from an Essay on the mineral waters of Apoquindo by Professor I. Domeyko of Santiago, published in 1848, will be found more reliable:—"At the foot of the first band of porphyritic earth of the Andes, in a cheerful, pleasant, and healthy locality, some four or five streams of mineral water come from the interior of the rocks and flow down the ravine, mingling with another rivulet of pure water, without leaving in their course any deposit of salts, or saline efflorescence. The water of Apoquindo is clear, crystalline, odorless, of a very disagreeable taste, difficult to describe, and left standing in a closed vessel forms no deposit. It is neither acid nor alkaline; exerts no action upon vegetable colors; and only by boiling and concentration, presents saline substances, a part of these forming a pellicle upon the surface, while another part is precipitated. The gas evolved during the ebullition scarcely disturbs water of barytes, thus showing that these waters contain scarcely a trace of free carbonic acid.

"In three different seasons of the year I have measured the temperature of the Apoquindo waters at their flow from the crevices of the rock, principally in the two little streams whence is taken the water for drinking. The *Reaumur* thermometer marked

| | | | | |
|---|---|---|---|---|
| 30th July, 1848, | 18° 5′ R. | Temperature of air, | 17° 50′ | R. |
| 15th Ootober, 1848, | 18° 3′ R. | " | 21° | R. |
| 5th November, 1848, | 18° 2′ R. | " | 22° | R. |

[Lieut. Gilliss's *Fahrenheit* thermometer showed in the month of April in a spring on one side of the ravine 74° 5′, and in a spring on the opposite side of the ravine 74° 3′. Allowing for difference in season, closely correspondent with Professor Domeyko's report.]

"The water of the bathing well, a water for its medicinal virtues in cutaneous diseases called "itch water," has the same temperature.

"In this well there is an intermitting evolution of gas, the different sized bubbles rising from the bottom in considerable quantities; fifteen or twenty seconds rarely passing without bubbles appearing. This gas is colorless, inodorous, extinguishes combustion, is not absorbed by a solution of caustic potash, and agitated with a solution of barytes scarcely clouds it. According to these indications, this gas can be no other than nitrogen, possibly mixed with a minute portion of carbonic acid. When analyzed in the laboratory of the Institute, this gas gave but two per cent. of oxygen. This development of nitrogen gas in the midst of a fountain of mineral waters is an interesting phenomenon, and one of much importance in terrestrial physics, but is not the only one that has been observed. Berzelius found that the mineral water of Porla (in Switzerland) in a well of a yard in depth, slowly gave off bubbles of gas, composed of six parts of nitrogen and one of carbonic acid (by volume), and, according to the same chemist, it arises from the decomposition of nitrogenous organic substances. The Porla water contains neither sulphurets nor sulphuretted hydrogen, and the greater part of the substances dissolved therein consists of bicarbonates, chlorides, and organic matters.

"Longchamps, in a treatise on mineral waters published in 1834, says, that in all the mineral waters that he has analyzed, he has found nitrogen, sometimes pure, at others mixed with a little carbonic acid, rarely mixed with oxygen, and never with the latter in as great proportion as in atmospheric air. The waters of Baréges gave Longchamps four cubic centimetres of nitrogen for each litre of water, but these waters differing from those of Porla are sulphurous; they contain sulphur and sulphate of soda with considerable silica, which has led Longchamps to think, first, that the bases were found in a metallic state in the interior of the globe (Davy's hypothesis) combined with sulphur or chlorine; and secondly, that the sulphate of soda came from the conversion of sulphuret of soda into sulphate, by the action of the oxygen of the air introduced by rains into the crevices of the rocks, filtering through the pores and cracks.

"Anglada also, in a memoir upon sulphurous and warm mineral waters (1831), says, likewise, that all waters containing or giving out sulphuretted hydrogen contain nitrogen, which gas, according to Anglada, owes its origin to the air carried along by the waters in their course, and the oxygen of which is absorbed by the sulphur of the sulphurets in solution.

"The Apoquindo waters do not belong to the class of which Longchamps and Anglada treat. In them there is no trace of sulphur in the state of sulphuret or hydrosulphuret, and even the amount of sulphate of lime is very small. This water by its composition resembles that of Porla; but that which is most notable in the water of Apoquindo is, first, the great quantity of salts contained in it, amounting nearly to the *maximum* contained in the most saline and active waters. Secondly, the great proportion of chloride of calcium contained in this water, greater even than that of Cauquenes. And, third, the almost complete absence of free carbonic acid, and of carbonates.

"Herewith is the composition of the Apoquindo water taken from its source, compared with the analysis of the Cauquenes water, showing both great analogy and concentration:

COMPOSITION OF EACH 1,000 PARTS BY WEIGHT.

| | Drinking Water of Apoquindo. | Cauquenas Water. |
|---|---|---|
| Chloride of Calcium, | 2.165 | 1.929 |
| " Sodium, | 1.177 | 0.821 |
| " Magnesium, | 0.034 | trace |
| Sulphate of lime, | 0.052 | 0.041 |
| Iron and alumina, | 0.020 | 0.009 |
| Silex, | 0.035 | 0.020 |
| Organic matter, | trace | trace |
| Total of saline contents, | 3.483 | 2.820 |

"The same water, brought to the laboratory well corked and sealed, gave by ebullition, in an experiment conducted with great care, seventeen to eighteen cubic centimetres of gas in each litre or cubic decimetre of water. But this gas analyzed, gave a more considerable proportion of oxygen than that contained in the free gas of the basin of "itch water," although the said proportion was not more than one-fifth or one-sixth part of the volume of gas evolved in the ebullition of these waters.

"I have also sought in the Apoquindo waters for the presence of iodine or bromine, using for the former chloride of palladium, and for the latter the ordinary method, but have been unable to discover the slightest trace of either substance.

"The water of the basin in which baths are taken, contains also the same salts as the drinking water, with the difference that the said salts are found in less considerable proportion than in the latter, perhaps in consequence of some pure spring water running near the basin mixing with the mineral water. The mineral water of the basin contains but 2.037 of the salts in a thousand parts; much less it will be seen than the water taken where it escapes from the rocks. Reflecting on the results of this analysis, it is seen:

"1. That if the energy and medicinal virtue of waters depend upon the quantity of salts contained in them, the water of Apoquindo must produce effects at least as prompt and manifest as that of Cauquenes. There would remain only the determination of the possible influence of local circumstances, of air, temperature, and hygrometric state of the atmosphere of the two places, upon invalids.

"As far as the height above the sea-level is concerned, it is nearly the same in both localities; that of the Cauquenes baths being, according to my barometric observations, eight hundred varas (the vara is about thirty-three inches, English measurement), and Apoquindo nine hundred and thirty-six varas above the level of the sea.

"2. Nearly the whole of the dissolved salt consisting of common salt and chloride of calcium, the latter forming about two-thirds of the entire matters in solution; this chloride ought to be that which produces the principal effect upon invalids using the water.

"3. It is seen that the Apoquindo waters and that of Cauquenes are analogous to each other in nature, and form perhaps a class of mineral waters distinct from all those known on the old continent. This class of waters, whose peculiar character consists in the great quantity of chloride of calcium contained in them, arises in the midst of formations precisely identical in a geological point of view; and it is not less interesting to observe that the electro-positive elements which most abound in the said waters, are those which also abound in the variegated porphyries and zoolitic rocks predominating in such localities.

"It is desirable, in consequence of the now ascertained character of the Apoquindo water, and of the important facts collected by certain physicians of the capital from their use of it, that the Government, or the municipality of Santiago, should erect bathing establishments and other suitable accommodations for invalids at these springs; and also a hospital for the poor, whose frightful mortality should stimulate the zeal of patriots, and the humane."

It is hoped that the extract above quoted has not proved too long and scientifically minute to command perusal. Apart from the useful information it imparts, it shows that Chile is not without residents of scientific attainments who are active in making known its resources.

Since the publication of Professor Domeyko's essay, some improvements have been made; but still these are not either as extensive or convenient as are demanded by the wants of the large population within a distance of seven miles, to thousands of whose afflicted, it is believed by the best informed physicians of Santiago, these mineral waters might prove of great advantage. The present buildings are located on the gradually-sloping foot of the mountain, the valley of Santiago lying unfolded below, spread with grass and grain broken into dimples by sportive zephyrs, while sunshine and shadow chase each other over its fair bosom. Long avenues of Lombardy poplars like military hosts stand marshalled in columns, and olive groves reveal their deeper verdure to give variety to the picture. Across the carpet of green and gold the Mapocho River takes its winding way, as if a subtle serpent seeking elysian bowers. And far away in the distance the Sierra de Prado lifts its dark form and sharp crest against the western sky like an impassable wall; whilst behind, the towering Cordillera raises its head in grandeur, and in pride of the surpassing scene unrolled at its foot. It is not without cause that the Santiaguinos dispute the origin of the name Valparaiso with their commercial neighbor, and refer its etymology to Valdivia's soldiers, who, on going to the coast from this beautiful creation, exclaimed to the founders of the seaport who were boasting of *its* beauties, "Va al Paraiso"—go to paradise—meaning their enchanting valley.

On our way back to the city the opportunity was availed of to look at the *Tajamar* (breakwater), a wall of nearly three miles length on the south bank of the Mapocho River, built at the instance of the great benefactor Portales, to protect the city against inundation when the river is in flood. The wall is twenty feet high and from five to six feet thick. The river is spanned by two bridges; one of them of substantial masonry, six hundred and fifty feet long, supported thirty feet above low water on eleven strong arches. This space is demanded to give passage to this wild mountain stream when swollen.

No more proof is needed to show that Chile is in advance of its neighbor Peru, in the enterprise necessary to develop natural resources, than is found in its railroads and telegraph lines, now in operation or in process of construction. The latter country has but the Lima and Callao, and Lima and Chorillos Railroads, seven and nine miles long respectively; and the Arica and Tacna road of thirty-five miles length. Chile can boast of, *First*, the *Caldera and Copiapo* Railroad, seventy-four miles in length; originally built to Copiapo, fifty miles, and subsequently extended to Pabellon, twenty-four miles further; the whole having been finished in 1856 by an English and Chilean company at a cost of $2,500,000, under American construction. Its transportation of copper ores is heavy. *Second*, the *Pabellon and Chañarcillo* Railroad, which, although in fact an extension of the first mentioned, was built and is owned by a different company. Its length is twenty-four miles; it was finished in 1859 at a cost of $800,000. The main business of the road is the transportation of copper and silver ores. *Third*, the *Valparaiso and Santiago* Railroad, length one hundred and ten miles; finished to Quillota, thirty miles, at a cost of $7,000,000; thence to the capital under contract, and now being pushed forward after considerable delay resulting from political revolutions of the country, and conflicting personal interests striving to divert the road from the route originally decided on by the able American engineer, Mr. Campbell, whose high sense of duty and undeviating integrity and self-respect, led him to resign his position in the employment of the Chilean Government, rather than swerve from his convictions of right, or submit to the intermeddling of the ignorant and selfish. His successor may be more politic and accommodating in unimportant matters, but will be compelled to endorse the surveys and recommendations of Mr. Campbell by their adoption. For, unless the valley of the Quillota River (more appropriately called *Aconcagua*) is pursued to the point at which that stream is joined by the *Tabon* River, and thence southeastwardly along that river to the *offshoot of the Andes*, forming by its westward stretch across the great interior valley of Chile an intermontane link with the Coast Range; and unless that *spur* of the Andean Cordillera is crossed at the *Cuesta of the Tabon*, of only twenty-six hundred and fifty feet height, with the Tabon River rising on one side flowing northwardly, and the *Zampa River* rising on the other side flowing southwardly, to *conduct the road to the Mapocho River, and by a slightly deviating line and unsurpassed grade* to its eastern terminus, Santiago is likely to be visited from the seaport yet several generations, by ox-teams, French diligences, and American stage-coaches. Mr. Campbell may await the approving verdict of the nation. The pedestal of his monument is erected—the column will soon be placed upon it.* *Fourth*, the *Southern* Railroad, from Santiago to Talca, one hundred and forty miles; finished to Rancagua, fifty miles from the capital, at a cost of $3,900,000; and now under contract and progressing to San Fernando, thirty-one miles further. *Fifth*, the *Cañada* Railroad, which is merely a city passenger branch of the last-named road. Its double track was laid two miles along the outside of the fashionable Santiago promenade, at a cost of $74,000. It is a profitable investment for the owners, the fare being a decimo, and no official perquisites—in railroad parlance "stealings"—by the conductors. This self-paying operation, to which the attention of railroad stockholders in North America has been directed of late as the great cause of small dividends, or no dividends at all, is prevented in the Cañada city railroad by the passenger being furnished with a metallic check in return for his fare, and on leaving the car he deposits the check in a locked box at the door. The number of checks informs the agent at the end of line, who alone holds the

* Since the above was written the Santiago and Valparaiso Railroad has been completed on the line of survey indicated. Its length is one hundred and fourteen and one-quarter miles; and the running time between the termini is eight hours.

key of the tell-tale, how many fares the conductor has received. Besides the above roads, there are projected one of nine miles from *Coquimbo to La Serena*, and another of forty-five miles from *Tongoy to Ovalle*, the latter certainly to be pushed forward with energy, and speedily completed under the superintendence of Mr. J. A. Barnard, civil engineer; a fellow-citizen who honors his own country by serving Chile with rare fidelity and professional skill. *Telegraph lines* are in operation between Santiago and Valparaiso, Santiago and San Felipe, Santiago and Talca, Caldera and Pabellon, Talcahuano and Concepcion.

I start to-morrow for Talcahuano by the land route to avoid awaiting the steamer at Valparaiso. The journey will be long and wearisome, but the attractions of the great valley will probably repay one for any endurance of fatigue, exposure, and deprivation. As to *danger*, it might be as well, were it not too late to effect it, to consider the expediency of obtaining a life insurance in accordance with the Chilean custom, to wit: for a specified time, the insured person *living* for the period named to *receive* the amount of the policy; if he should die all is *lost*, but as life is already gone the money can be of no moment to the one *most interested*. The Santiaguinos consider it an excellent method of providing a marriage settlement for a daughter, who being insured in childhood, on surviving, does not become a bridal beggar; and whose chances of matrimonial bliss are proportionably increased. If she should die, the relief of the husband from the burden of support cancels the loss of insurance.

As the hotel *watch*man is invariably on the corridor at my hour for rising, enjoying his early morning *nap*, he cannot be relied on for an early morning *rap*, and I shall have to "*call*" *myself*, to be in time for the southern train. Hence as it is now midnight, this last Santiago *despatch* must be abruptly closed. And in bidding you good-night, I will also say good-bye to the *Hotel Ingles*, that one of the three inns of the capital at which tolerable accommodation has been found, although water and towels are sadly needed, and bells also, or an indicator, to prevent the unceasing calls from the galleries, which make of the patio a bedlam from morning to night.

# CHAPTER XV.

SOUTHERN RAILROAD DEPOT—GREAT INTERIOR VALLEY OF CHILE BETWEEN THE ANDES AND COAST RANGE MOUNTAINS—MAIPU RIVER—ANGOSTURA DE PAYNE—LANDED ESTATE, SUFFRAGE, TREASON, INTOLERANCE—RANCAQUA—CACHAPOAL RIVER—BATHS OF CAUQUENES—REQUINOA—RIO CLARILLO—RENGO—ANGOSTURA REGULEMU—SAN FERNANDO—RIO TINGUIRIRICA—COUNTRY CONVEYANCE—EL DESCABEZADO—RIO TENO.

On a bright December morning, at a cost of a *decimo* (ten cents), the usual Santiago hack-hire, and the cheapest probably in the world, I reached the southern railroad station directly south of the west end of the Cañada, with time to spare to take a look at its buildings; and where I was shortly after joined by the United States Minister to Chile, who was to be my *compagnon du voyage.*

A substantially-enclosed space of sixty acres contained the following buildings, erected with reference to capacity, convenience, and durability, unsurpassed in the northern States: Besides a commodious edifice in which are the various offices of the company, there are a first-class railroad station proper, three hundred by ninety feet in extent, with iron columns, rafters, braces, and corrugated iron roof, all of best finish, made in England for erection in Santiago. A circular engine-house, constructed entirely of iron, one hundred and sixty-eight feet in diameter; also made in England at a cost of $60,000. It is capable of accommodating sixteen engines, nine of which are now built and in use, nearly all American, manufactured by Rogers & Co., of Paterson, New Jersey; and found on full and fair trial to be superior in power and speed to the English imported locomotives, which they have superseded. A machine shop one hundred and twenty by fifty-five feet, of brick and adobe, with projecting corrugated iron roof; the machinery all

American; the workmen Americans, English, and natives. A car shed three hundred and fifty by forty-five feet; a double, open colonnade supporting an iron roof. A freight house two hundred and eighty by thirty-eight feet, thick adobe walls, with close fire-proof shutters and corrugated iron roof.

The water for the use of this station is brought three miles, from the Mapocho River, in iron pipes laid for this special use. There are few railroad stations more complete or better arranged, or as cleanly and orderly, as this of the Southern Chile Railroad Company; and its appearance gave promise of good management in the working of the road on which we were about to trust ourselves to the care of American engineers, certainly with more confidence than can be felt in the wild Chilenos, who dash down the neighboring cuesta as if the question of human endurance were the problem of their lives, which they were daily engaged in solving.

The cars being well filled with first, second, and third-class passengers, at a cost respectively of one dollar and a half, one dollar, and half a dollar, for Rancagua, a distance of fifty-four Spanish (fifty English) miles—the third-class passengers outnumbering both the others—we started in a southerly direction up the valley, because with the ascending scale of latitude; the Andes on our left to the east, and the Coast Range on our right to the west, about twenty-five miles asunder at Santiago, but approaching nearer at some points while they recede at others, an average width of the valley being probably about eighteen miles.

In thus designating the boundaries of the great valley which stretches to the south from three hundred and fifty to four hundred miles, it may be stated that from twelve to fifteen miles north of *Tupungato*, the imperial peak of this region, which is but little north of east of Santiago, the Andes throw off a mountainous chain westwardly called *Sierra de la Dehesa*, which pursues its somewhat flexuous course under the local names of *Sierra de la Gualtatas*, and *Sierra de la Meza alta;* on the last is the *Cumbre de Tabon*. It is near this important cumbre—over which, by the surveys of our countryman Mr. Campbell, the Valparaiso and Santiago Railroad will have to cross with a two feet higher grade than that with which the Baltimore and Ohio Railroad crosses the Alleghanies—that this offshoot of the Andes changes its course to the southwest, and reaching a point twenty-five or thirty miles southeast of Quillota, divides into two chains, one of which, the less of the two, continues on in a southwest course under the names *Sierra de la Viscacha* and *Sierra de Zepata*, and then westwardly running out to the seacoast just north of the Maipú River, after having given numerous spurs which traverse the Province of Valparaiso. The other, and more elevated chain, passes almost due south, under the name of *Sierra de Prado*, several times spoken of before, and forms the western boundary of the great basin in which Santiago is situated, while the great Andean Range itself forms the eastern boundary. It is at a somewhat depressed part of this Sierra de Prado, and yet at a height of twenty-four hundred and twenty feet above the sea, that the well-known Cuesta or Pass is found through which the traveller by one of the routes finds his way to the capital, and the descent of the steep zigzag declivity of which causes him so much terror. It is this last chain, the Sierra de Prado, which pursues its way as the *true coast range* south of the Maipú River, and far on even to the Province of Valdivia; and by this name I shall call it, avoiding that of *Cordillera*, as applied to it by a few writers, and restricting that term solely to the backbone of the Andes, according to the invariable usage of the natives. Certainly the word *cordillera*, which signifies *a chain*, is specially applicable to the *greatest mountain chain of the world.* Thus, too, will be avoided the confusion resulting from its application to the comparatively limited chain of the coast, unless a suffix is always added, as the Cordillera de la Costa.

The plain over which the railroad passes south of Santiago presents occasional isolated hills, otherwise the surface seems nearly level, a slight declivity to the west being manifest by the flow of water in the innumerable small canals by which the whole region is irrigated—these being supplied by the great Canal de Maipú in its passage from the river of that name to the Mapocho; and further on by the Maipú River itself, and then by the many streams in their passage from the great mountain chain toward the sea. The railroad excavations invariably exhibit a substratum of boulders, cobble, and smaller rounded stones, and these are seen in cuttings of thirty-two feet depth, showing the long-continued, extensive, and powerful action of water in breaking up the mountain debris thrown off by earthquakes, frost, and avalanche, and rounding and spreading it over immense surface and to great depth. They are interesting questions to consider, if this be the result of mountain streams swollen into torrents by heavy rains and thaws, spreading widely and shifting their channels from time to time from this cause, and from terrestrial convulsions which often induce surface changes? Or if consequent on agencies at work ages since, when the ocean itself may have stretched forth a giant arm into the interior of the continent, washing the base of the Cordillera on the east, and of the Coast Range on the west? Or if incident to these combined causes?

However unfitted for agricultural uses this stony valley undoubtedly once was, it is now very productive, and is constantly being made more so by the deposits of soil and fertilizing elements brought down from the mountains, by numerous rivers, and distributed by small aqueducts over every square mile of this section of Chile. The recovery of this shingly neighborhood from sterility, is the result of recent enterprise.

The road to San Bernardo, nine and a half miles, is bordered by beautiful quintas, and rich pastures where immense herds of cattle driven down the valley are fattened for the Santiago and Valparaiso markets. Beyond San Bernardo vineyards cover thousands of acres, and olive and fig orchards now beautify lands which a few years since were nearly valueless, but through irrigation and culture have become exceedingly fertile. Leagues of graceful *alamos* (poplars) lift their tall spires on every hand, serving the varied purposes of shading avenues, bounding estates, fencing, fuel, and building. The certain and rapid growth of this tree from the planting of a mere twig, fits it especially to the wants of the country, which through this region is almost destitute of natural timber. Many of the large estates are enclosed by high and thick adobe walls, perforated thickly with air-draught openings, which might serve admirably for musketry loop-holes in the revolutionary encounters of the Republic. The walls are tile-capped, to prevent rain washing and climbing. The adobes are made by ploughing the soil, and flooding it with water from a canal; the water then being drawn off, cattle are turned on to tramp the ploughed soil into mud, which is then mixed with straw and tramped again, then moulded in troughs of a suitable size, and exposed to the sun to bake. Such is the most convenient and the usual material for mansion and fence on the best haciendas.

The announcement of our approach to the Maipú River attracted the attention of passengers to the outer world, the Chilenos from their cigaritos, with which they beguiled the tedious hours and poisoned the inner atmosphere, and the five Americans aboard from their books and papers—none others were reading or noting. A traveller along the west coast of this great continent cannot fail to notice the absence of one *special American "institution;"* the *token* of enterprise, activity, intent, inquiry, power, knowledge—the *proof* of *progress*—the *newsboy!* On the landing, at the station, on car and steamer, in hotel or street, the same Dead Sea of mind is found, with no daily literature, no magazine, no quarterly, no guide-book even, absolutely nothing to stir up the passive elements of moral being. If the shrill voice of that young merchant of civilization —for that is the commodity in which he deals—could be once heard awaking the echoes of this fair garden of the world, the hopes of nations would be cheered by the promise of its actual freedom and development; for it would be the proof that the now fettered press had burst its chains, and stood forth in the majesty of its might, guaranteeing to man the realization of his lofty destiny.

The bridge over the Maipú, one of the finest rivers of Chile, has eleven spans and a total length of eleven hundred feet; it is built exclusively of stone and iron, timber not being used for railroad bridge purposes, in consequence of warping and cracking from the long-continued dry weather of summer. The heavy rains of winter finding it thus twisted and cracked, swells it again by unequal absorption into shapes at variance with railroad necessities. An American traveller cannot look at such splendid monuments of science and skill as this bridge, and corresponding works on this road, without feeling proud of his countryman, Mr. Evans, their constructor; who, while contributing to the prosperity of Chile and to the development of its natural resources, nobly illustrates the enterprise and capacity which have placed his country among the most progressive of nationalities.

The floods of the Maipú wash down from the mountains great quantities of limestone, which is gathered by the peons when the swollen river subsides, and burnt in limekilns along the banks, furnishing an excellent building and agricultural material, as likewise that required for the *compulsory whitewashing of houses on the occasion of the annual national celebration.* This stream also deposits a sediment which grouts the shingle along its course with a natural cement, making the banks in many places impervious to water for a thickness of ten feet.

Up the valley to the left of the road, along which the Colorado, the northeast branch of the Maipú, descends, the summit of Tupungato may be seen lifting its snowy crown in imperial grandeur twenty-two thousand four hundred and fifty feet above the sea, wresting from Chimborazo its ancient celebrity, and disputing with Aconcagua, Llimani, and Sorato, the preëminence of altitude on the western hemisphere.

It was on the plains of the Maipú, but a few miles east of the point of passage of the river by the railroad, that the decisive battle was fought which secured Chilean independence; the Spanish army six thousand strong, in perfect discipline, and flushed with a recent victory on the banks of the Maulé, having been here, within a few days' march of the capital, encountered by six thousand five hundred Chilenos in April, 1818, and defeated with great slaughter; two thousand of the royalists having been killed and wounded, and three thousand five hundred made prisoners—nearly the entire force.

The Maipú River pursues its way to the Pacific through the great portal of the Coast Range, of which mention was made in describing the Melipilla road to the capital. The plain over which the road passes to the south of the river Maipú, is much encroached on by mountain spurs; and, after passing the Angostura River eighteen miles south of the Maipú by a fine tower-bridge of three hundred and sixty feet, it becomes reduced to a mere gorge, where the Andes come down in the bold hill of Chiyi, twenty-five hundred feet high, to within ninety or a hundred feet of a lowlier spur of the Coast Range. The river flows northwardly between the two, and the railroad cuts the toe of the Coast Range spur—the whole gorge being swept by the river when swollen. This is the celebrated *Angostura* of the Southern Railroad—the word signifying *narrow pass*—and is sometimes called Angostura de Payne to distinguish it from another Angostura further to the south.

A few miles beyond is the Convent of Mostazal, erected by Don Pedro José Luco who married his own niece by permission of His Holiness the Pope, on condition that he would build and support this convent on his hacienda in mitigation of the sin. Near the convent is the *haunted bridge*, on the character of which for the supernatural, an adjacent hydraulic ram, erected for the supply of a railroad tank with water, exercised a controlling influence; for when it was put in operation, the simple and superstitious natives, ignorant of its presence and action, thought its continued pumpings the moanings of an evil spirit in the bridge, and sought the mediatorial offices of the Padre of the convent, who came with paraphernalia, retinue, and expurgatorial prayers, to exorcise it. But the ram being incorrigible, and continuing to pump, the spirit was supposed to be too much for the good father; who, in consequence, was about to lose his hold on the faith of his flock, when one of the railroad engineers, dreading the loss of the padre's benign influence, explained to him the mystery of the spiritual phenomenon, much to his edification and unconcealed merriment, and thus he was speedily restored to the confidence of his rebellious parishioners.

The great valley soon resumes something of its former width, and at the distance of nine miles from the Angostura, the northern boundary is reached of the magnificent hacienda de la Compania of Don Juan de dios Correa, containing ninety thousand acres of land. This gentleman's estate of San José, on the Melipilla road, of one hundred and twenty thousand acres, has already been spoken of. With such an example of landed proprietorship, the remark of an intelligent foreign resident is not surprising, that, excepting the cities, and quintas owned by wealthy citizens, and the mines, the whole landed estate of Chile belongs to about three hundred persons. The effect of this, hitherto, has been to make this Government an actual oligarchy. For as the right of suffrage, by law, is in those citizens only who have attained the age of twenty-five years who can read and write, those who possess real estate of a certain value, and those who have an employment the income of which must be equal to the annual rent of such estate, estimated at not less than one dollar and a half per day, it must be evident that, as not one-fifth of the inquilinos or peons, who compose the great body of the rural population, can read and write, and as their daily wages rarely amount to a medio peso (a half dollar), they have but one chance of voting, and that is by a *fictitious* property qualification conferred on them by the proprietor of the estate on which they live, and for which act of grace they, of course, deposit the ticket furnished to them by him. The extent of this power is exemplified by the fact, that Señor Correa is said to have mustered into service, in a fortnight, two thousand of his retainers for revolutionary purposes. It is not wonderful that the Government should have found Paris a safer residence for Señor Correa than San José, and that he should have been recommended to that school of *stern republicanism* to learn obedience to its behests. Nor is it surprising that such a feudal system, and the perpetual jealousies of rival aspirants incident thereto, should lead to intrigues, combinations, and revolutions, for personal and partisan aggrandizement; that treason to the State, not obedience to the Law, should be the rule. In the political convulsions of the Spanish American Republics, this treason to the State is as frequently the act of those holding the reins of government, as those striving to wrest them from their hands; for the usurpation of powers not granted by the written Constitution, is as much treason to the State as the violation of special enactments for its safety under that fundamental law. And the apology for arbitrary acts by an existing organization of government, that they would also become the rule of action of successful revolutionists, is a plain avowal of a purpose of despotism under the hypocritical pretension of free institutions. As to the motto on the gold coin of Chile, "equality before the law," it is a national falsehood. Such a condition of citizenship is impossible, with the two hundred and forty-nine thousand nine hundred and fifty-two square miles of territory, parcelled out among only three hundred of its one million and a half of inhabitants. And if any thing more were wanted to prove the declaration a coined lie, it is found in that Article of the Constitution proclaimed in these words: "*Article* 5.—La religion de la Republica de Chile es la Catolica Apostolica Romana con esclusion del ejercicio publico de qualquiera otra." "The religion of the Republic of Chile is the Apostolic Roman Catholic to the exclusion of the public exercise of every other." Was there ever a more barefaced profanation of political principle? A *Republic* declaring its own *intolerance!* A prohibition of religious liberty, the dearest right of mankind, by *the fundamental law* of a country just released from a foreign yoke, and professing to have established free institutions!

But it is not without hope that the friend of Chile looks forward to the day when, "by reason or by force," as is proclaimed by another of its representatives of value, these antagonists to progress will disappear before a more liberal spirit. Recent legislation contemplates the final abolishment of the law of entail, and the liberation of the landed estate of the country from its present limited control, that it may become tributary to the happiness and welfare of the many, instead of to the princely wealth and power of the few. Already an enlightened statesman and patriot, whose administration of the interior and foreign relations of the country is distinguishing this epoch as the proudest and most prosperous of Chilean history, has decreed that the words of the Constitution, "exclusion of the *public* exercise of religion," do not prohibit the *private* exercise of religious rites according to the dictates of conscience; and, accordingly, two *enclosed* Protestant churches have been recently dedicated to religious worship in Valparaiso. That city and Talcahuano have also burial-places for Protestant dead, where friends may consign them to earth without danger of personal violence. And already the young men of Spanish descent are returning home from foreign colleges and travel, bringing the knowledge, and imbued with the liberal sentiments of other lands, to give a nobler impulse to the destinies of their own. And the young women of Chile also are discovering that Protestant foreigners are worthy of their confidence and affection; and the sooner prohibitions to such marriages by a narrow-minded clergy are removed, the sooner will the country realize the advantages of an infusion of moral and social elements surpassing in purity and power those of the degenerate Hispano-Indian race composing four-fifths of its population.

A law lately passed by Congress confiscates the property of all persons instigating or participating in revolutions, to defray the damages incident thereto. This, it is professed by its advocates, will exercise a salutary influence in restraining causeless disturbances of the public peace; while it cannot prevent a general uprising of the people, demanded by the public good, when arbitrary and unconstitutional powers are exercised by faithless agents. But it cannot be denied that such obstructions placed in the way of so-called factional disturbers of the public peace may also prove impediments to popular movements for necessary reforms. The objects of ambition are generally veiled by plausible pretexts; and the path of progress has been constantly barricaded by despotic power with similar obstacles. The friends of free institutions should be too jealous of their privileges voluntarily to surrender them in cases of doubtful expediency, at the instance of crafty aspirants, or from impulses growing out of apparent emergencies. It should be candidly admitted, however, that personal ambition and antipathies, and ecclesiastical love of power, more frequently produce the factional struggles in Chile miscalled Revolutions, than do considerations of political principle or national policy; and hence the readiness with which combinations are formed between rival leaders and parties of opposite professions, for the purpose of achieving the displacement of those in power by revolutionary movements; which, if successful, result in renewed struggles among themselves, and new alliances of antagonistic elements to strengthen the chances of triumph. The maintenance of principles regards with suspicion a compromise dangerous to their purity, and to a triumph which can only be permanent, if it repose on untrammelled virtue and right. And the opinion of intelligent foreign observers is, that it is very rare to see a really disinterested and pure patriot, engaged even remotely in the political disturbances of the country. Such are well aware that it is not by duplicity, dishonesty, affiliation with ecclesiastical selfishness and intolerance, and factional intrigues, that they can hope to establish the success of sound political principles and constitutional liberty. A victory gained by such means, is like a nectared draught that turns to poison on the lip, and results in an immediate and perpetuated struggle with former coöperationists whose only hope is in distraction, and who will labor as untiringly for the overthrow of one party as of another who will not relinquish to them the rewards of success. It may be for these reasons in part, that the distinguished gentleman now at the head of the Department of the Interior, Señor Antonio Varas, has positively refused to allow his name to be presented to the nation as a candidate for the office of President of the Republic—a refusal deeply regretted by enlightened and patriotic Chilenos, and universally by foreign residents, who have seen in Señor Varas' able, consistent, just, and firm administration of the affairs of his office, proofs of great sagacity, and a rational ground for belief that under his Chief Executive guidance, as a statesman and patriot, Chile would continue to prosper, as she has for several years, in an unprecedented manner. Office can have no allurements for such a man, whose high intellectual resources can always confer on him eminence and happiness; who may not choose to be suspected by any of having exercised his official functions for ulterior purposes of political advancement; and who may be unwilling to sacrifice a jot of principle to policy and expediency. But when such considerations result in such conclusions, it is a misfortune for the people whose condition imposes them.

The defile of Angostura de Payne having been passed, the valley is seen to widen again to the east and west until the hacienda de la compania of Señor Correa is reached. On this estate is an isolated and remarkably steep hill of three hundred and fifty or four hundred feet height, accurately described by

Lieutenant Gilliss as presenting a "surface covered at intervals of a few feet with a network of lines intersecting each other diagonally, not unlike paths made by goats." He adds: "The regularity of their intersection, however, would forbid such a supposition," leaving the appearance an unexplained phenomenon. But the mystery of Lieut. Gilliss ceased to be such to us when another side of the *Pan de Azucar* (sugar-loaf) was brought into view; a large number of sheep being actually seen browsing, as they climbed and descended the hill obliquely, the numerous paths decussating each other, and intercepting quadrilateral spaces, producing the network appearance spoken of, from the base to the summit. The mysterious lines are sheep-paths—nothing more—although in a land of many wonders. Despite the mathematical postulate, that a straight line is the shortest distance between two points, a sheep has an instinctive notion that the old saw "the longest way round is the shortest way through" has some truth in it—and that the shortest way to reach the top of a hill is spirally; and a continuous corkscrew thence to the base again, unless the sheep be a very clumsy worker, must give "regularity of the intersections," however incredulous the philosophical inquirer.

Having crossed this immense estate with its rich pastures, and its fields of heavy-headed grain, spreading out their tens of thousands of acres of agricultural wealth, traversed near the line of the railroad by a macadamized avenue bordered by poplars for half a league, presenting an unsurpassed perspective to the mansion of the wealthy haciendado embowered in shade-trees at its further end, we soon arrived at the station of *Rancagua*, the present terminus of the Southern Railroad, fifty-four miles from Santiago—time three hours and a half. Taking one of the several vehicles jockeying for passengers on the plain of shingle, on which we slipped and slid in ridicule of equipoise, we rode to the town, a mile off.

The literal "*carry-all*" in which we were literally *all carried*, was unmistakably antiquated, and looked as if it were the time-honored remains of a Spanish gift to some Purumancian Indian chief, whom the invaders endeavored to inveigle into submission before resorting to force, and to have drifted down to later days with the ebb and flow of aboriginal fortune, to have floated on the tide of revolution, weathering military outbreak and civil commotion, and to have descended from its exalted function of conveying royalty through all mutations of time, to the final humble office of transporting railroad passengers to and from the ancient town of Rancagua. Our "coach" had wheels, body, and tongue, but they were not such as usually distinguish that honorable vehicle; for the wheels, besides exercising the independent revolutionary proclivities of the people, from their unequal size, bore but little resemblance to such, except in the presumption that they *had once* been round. The body had neither doors nor curtains; and from its loss of substance and general dilapidation, it was shrewdly suspected that the reverence in which it had been held as a remnant of royalty by those who mourned over the monuments of departed greatness, had led to its gradual passing away from the prevalence of an endemic passion for relics. And the tongue was as much like a cow's as a coach's; broad, and pliant enough to penetrate the anterior air-holes of the vehicle by retroversion, if the mulish beasts attached to it had not, with characteristic stubbornness, refused to accommodate themselves to its abortive efforts. Three asinine rozinantes *roped* abreast, and driven by a *Roto* attired in a somewhat more affluent than Georgia costume, for *he had* a chip hat, something more of a shirt than a collar, and the dependencies of breeches, conveyed us after varied pummellings and prodigious efforts, through a mile of dust and loose cobble stone to the *Hotel de l'Union*, a one-story adobe building planted in the midst of muddy-looking huts, that seemed as if they were being borne down by the trouble of a superincumbent load of tiles. The estimated population of Rancagua is from four to five thousand, mostly of varying copper shades.

The objects attracting attention on entering the capital of the Department of Rancagua, to which the advent of a railroad should have brought something of improvement in social condition by this time, were, besides shirtless urchins, and in emulation of Constantinople, countless dogs—the undoubted equals of that class of people everywhere whose incapacity for refined and intellectual pleasure gives congeniality to the companionship of brutes: first, the interesting ceremony of kissing a little wooden saint, for which blessed privilege the holy father who was its custodian and carried it through the street, levied upon each person a tithe—the equivalent of an American missionary "tis-but;" second, the registering of voters and issuing the certificate of qualification; third, the church, riddled by bullet-holes patriotically preserved, to show where General O'Higgins with a few Chilenos made a stout defence against a superior force of Spanish royalists, through whom he afterwards cut his way.

Our stay in this town was too short to allow of wanderings, which would have paid poorly for the loss of necessary refreshment, and imperious appetite decided in favor of casuela, fish, eggs, beefsteak, mosto—all good, as were also the bread, butter, and coffee; hence Rancagua must be reported more favorably of than appearances indicated. Twelve dollars purchased a seat in the French Company's coach, driven six in hand by a Californian, and at meridian the route was resumed toward Talca.

It was a pretty picture that greeted the eye, as passing from the town, luxuriant gardens and fields were seen decked in the choicest livery of summer; while the Cordillera, clad in its snowy mantle, overlooking the genial valley, told that winter still reigned in those upper regions. A ride of a mile and a half brought us to the *Cachapoal River*, which, from its origin within the Andean Chain on the slope of the *Cruz de Piedra* cluster of mountains rising to the height of seventeen thousand feet, is fed even in the dry season of summer by melting snows, and hence is even then abundantly supplied with water; while at times, either from heavy rains in the region in which it has its numerous sources, or from unusual thaws, it becomes greatly swollen, its torrent spreading over a vast extent of surface, and devastating the whole country along its banks. The expanse of boulders and gravel visible on every side, shows its capacity of wide-spread mischief, and the power it must possess thus to break up, round, and sweep away millions of tons of rock from mountain quarries. The waters of this river reach the Pacific by the Rapel River, into which it empties. The Cachapoal was crossed by a fine bridge erected for the passage of the Southern Railroad, which is finished to this point although not yet run beyond Rancagua.

It is up the valley of this river, about thirty miles east of Rancagua, nearly three thousand feet above the sea, and within the Andean foot, that the *Baths of Cauguenes* are situated. They are celebrated in Chile for the possession of medicinal properties, and especially for the cure of rheumatism, secondary syphilis, and chronic cutaneous eruptions. The baths are not easy of access, the road being rough, acclivitous, and in many places narrow and dangerous, making the sure-footed mule necessary; and the too sick for such a means of conveyance, and the timid, are carried on an extemporaneous ambulance or hand-barrow, called *langarillo*, formed of four poles lashed together with thongs near their ends, over which a rawhide sacking is stretched. A visitor who returned from these baths during my sojourn in Santiago, and who had great faith in their virtues, from his having been cured in ten days of an inveterate syphilitic rheumatism, informed me that the springs are three in number, from which eight or ten baths, sunk in earth terraces below each other, are filled; each bath being separately sheltered by a thatch cabin for privacy. The temperature of the water varies from 100° to 120°, according to the time required to fill the bath. The composites of lime are the chief elements of the water. The accommodations, formerly consisting of a few rude cabins, are now being increased by the erection of a commodious hotel; and the proprietor is also having the most difficult and dangerous part of the road to the springs improved. To obtain the full benefit of the water it is necessary, besides applying it externally, to drink of this *rather warm* beverage, considering it is distilled in a snow-covered retort of the Andes.

About two miles south of the Cachapoal is the *Rio Seco*, formerly the principal bed, but now only a branch of the first-named river—the old channel having become greatly obstructed by rocks and trees swept from the mountain by floods. Although named *dry*, the *Seco* presents quite a full and turbulent appearance from the unusual thaw of this hot day. The road south of the Rio Seco is as level as a floor, and naturally paved with shingle, which from long use has been broken and consolidated like a macadamized turnpike. Well-cultivated fields, rich alfalfa pastures, with an occasional vineyard, and what closely resembled apple orchards, but proved to be methodically-planted Espinos, enclosed by substantial adobe or boulder fencing with parapet of dry mud or tiles, bounded our wide avenue; which was enlivened by mule trains, country carts, and herds of fat cattle on their way to market. These evidences of thrift and industry, with the newly-constructed bed of the Southern Road, now ready for the rails, winding its way within sight through adjacent fields, made our ride of nine miles to the village of *Requinoa*, interesting and cheering. An equal distance further on brought us across two little *esteros* of limpid water, *Tipaum* and *Mendoza*, to the beautiful *Rio Clarillo*, which, having received the two before-named crystal streams, seeks the Cachapoal, with which it unites before that river pierces the Coast Range of mountains. The distinction made by the natives between the Estero and Rio is, that the former rises from springs near the foot of mountains, and except in the rainy season, is always placid and clear; while the latter rises within the mountains, and even in the dry season, from the melting snow, is usually swollen with a turbid and often impetuous torrent.

Near the Rio Clarillo is the town of *Rengo*, containing about two thousand inhabitants, and consisting of straggling houses bordering the roadside for more than two miles, thus enabling the traveller in transit to see to best advantage whatever of external attraction Rengo may possess. We certainly entered this town with pleasing anticipations; for, we plead guilty to a pardonable weakness of our sex, and were eager to catch the first glance at the pretty señoritas who live in travellers' tales, and of whom an American astronomer has recorded that, "what most elicits the attention of the passer is the handsome features of the women." But either our smitten countryman's retina retained the lingering impressions of those celestial orbs which had been nightly winking at and coquetting with him as he lovingly gazed at them from the summit of Santa Lucia, and he mistook them for the terrestrial satellites man loves to have revolve about his path, "on whom" the poet tells us "than on the lights above there hang more destinies;" or we were most unfortunate in making our observations during an occultation, for we strained our vision in vain for a realization of blissful anticipations. It was finally voted that *this part of the Report of the United States Naval Astronomical Expedition* was an error of observation, resulting from an ocular illusion, and that we should be guilty of a libel upon some other parts of Chile if we imputed to their social heavens the possession of less brilliant constellations.

Beyond Rengo the road becomes somewhat more undulating, and about six miles from the town passes over the slightly-elevated termination of a spur of the Andes, which for some time had been noticed gradually encroaching upon our route. Crossing this, we entered the *Angostura Regulému*, a second narrow pass formed by the Andes and Coast Range, throwing off lateral spurs which approach within a hundred yards of each other. A creek, the Estero de Regulému, winds along the southeast foot of the Andean spur, and passes through the gorge in a northerly direction, and preparations are in progress to throw over it a railroad bridge of three hundred and fifty feet length. This is the last point at which we saw the advancing work of the great Southern Road, for the completion of which Chile should put forth all her energies, as upon it will depend the development of the resources of her truly magnificent interior valley. A narrow part of the valley was now traversed for a distance of about two and a half leagues, when we crossed the *Rio San Fernando*, an arm of the *Rio Tinguiririca*, embracing an insular tract of land on which stands the town of *San Fernando* (a contraction of St. Ferdinando), in latitude 34° 35′ S., where we arrived at 4 o'clock P. M., glad to find that it was not inundated by this wild mountain stream, which in heavy rains and thaws holds the inhabitants in constant apprehension.

The population of San Fernando is variously estimated. If the Department of Colchagua, extending from the River Cachapoal to the Teno, and from the Andes to the sea, of which it is the capital, is correctly reported as having from ten to twelve thousand inhabitants, San Fernando probably contains half the number. The plaza is a mere common; the streets, with few exceptions, are unpaved; and the houses, low, untidy, and unsightly, might, with few exceptions, be called wretched mud huts. "Carpentier's Hotel," of which the owner of the stage-line is proprietor, and to which we were of course carried to get the *grub*—nothing more—singularly *included in the stage-fare*, we found to be a mean and miserable hovel, without even pretence of decent accommodation about it. Dinner without dishes, and a chamber without comfort or cleanliness, were the realities of "entertainment." A tin pan of *casuela*, *fiery with aji*, for the inner-man; and a flag-mat bed without sheets, and a patched coverlid like Joseph's coat of many colors, for the outer-man, were the sum and substance of our "fare included;" that horrible *gratuity*, which precluded even the poor privilege of grumbling. An infinitesimal portion of the fiery broth served to allay any desire for its further acquaintance; and even had our couch invited it, slumber would have been a stranger to our eyelids, from fear of the tons of tiles visibly threatening us from above with entombment on the spot. Long before the peep of day we were in motion, and at 4 o'clock A. M. we bade adieu to San Fernando, rejoicing in the belief that we should never again become the victims of its contract of hospitality.

It was a balmy morning on which we rode over the wide level bed of shingle spread to the south between the town and the Rio Tinguiririca, which has its source in the snows of the extinct volcano of San Fernando; and there, amid a vast waste of stone traversed in places by brooklet arms of the river, which waywardly left it to return again after strolling awhile in coquettish adventure, birds of gay plumage were welcoming with matin songs the rosy dawn that leaned upon the snowy crest of the Cordillera, looking into the twilight valley like a blushing bride over her nuptial couch. It was a picture of rare beauty; and well might that silvery orb, in all ages the recognized queen of planetary brilliancy and grace, linger as she did in the azure canopy above, when all her sister stars had passed away, as if unwilling to withdraw her gaze from so fair a scene. A drive of about three miles brought us to the principal channel of the river; and it was well we attempted its passage in the early morning, for even then it was running riot from its swollen flood of melted snow from the previous day's heat, and which had not subsided entirely during the night. On the afternoon of the day we should probably have found it impassable, its course being short, and quickly affected by thaws. The baggage was removed to the top of the coach to be above the reach of water, and our team of six horses being increased by the addition of two more, under the guidance of a postilion, they dashed forward, and by dint of persevering effort under whip and spur, and wild hurrahs, sometimes plunging and floundering, at others swimming, and occasionally thrown down by the huge boulders swept along by the fierce current—the rumbling noise of which could be heard as they rolled along the rocky floor of the river—they finally succeeded in landing us safely on the opposite side of the ford. Rough as was the road over which we passed for half a league beyond, and until we got fairly off of the plain over which doubtless this river had from time to time shifted its course, yet was it welcomed after escaping from the furious Tinguiririca.

The country soon again presented a higher degree of cultivation, fields of wheat, barley, and alfalfa, covering the valley, which, along this part of our route, has a width of from twelve to fifteen miles. And here, too, as further north, the fruits brought by the early emigrants from Europe thrive luxuriantly, the mild and uniform climate producing almonds, olives, grapes, pomegranates, and figs, as also quinces, apples, pears, plums, cherries, and peaches. The dried peaches of Chile exceed in deliciousness any found in North America; and it may probably be said with truth, that the *Huasco* raisins surpass any produced in the Mediterranean for delicacy and lusciousness; as much so, perhaps, as the *Yungai* coffee of Bolivia excels in richness of aroma and flavor any of the world, not excepting the famed berry of Mocha. The Yungai coffee crop is small, and very costly. In the Valparaiso market it readily commands from three-quarters to one dollar per pound.

Such was the genial temperature and general beauty of sursoundings of our morning drive, that we had no difficulty in appreciating the appropriateness of the name of the aborigines, who at the time of the Spanish invasion occupied this district of Chile: *Promancians*—more lately corrupted into Purumancians—signifying "people of delight," as we are informed by the supplementary notes to the Abbé Don J. Ignatius Molina's

History of Chile, "being derived from the beauty of the country which they inhabit." Substantial walls of boulders enclosed the haciendas and quintas bounding the road; having a thickness of four feet at the base, gradually diminishing to the height of five, sometimes being cemented, and with a corresponding parapet. The farmers of this region profit by the geological changes consequent on earthquakes, which often shift the course of rivers; the extensive deposit of stone thus brought from mountain sources, furnishing them secure and enduring fencing. Over this whole region a network of canals for irrigation was seen; hence a dry season gives the haciendado no uneasiness, for the adjacent Andes have always a supply of snow for summer consumption; and these also furnish enriching mineral deposits, to renew exhausted fertility from careless cultivation and unalternated crops.

Leaving the unimportant village of Chimbarongo on the right, we passed on to the crossing of the creek of the same name, the fertilizing waters of which traverse numerous aqueducts. Weary with looking on feudal dependents of the varied degrees of guaso, inquilino, and peon gañan, who, with their female companions of Indian tints and corresponding social position, had since we left San Fernando monopolized the highway with their mules and ox-carts, it was to us as cheering as it was charming, to behold the representatives of higher rank, in three fair young señoritas with pretty blonde faces, rows of ivory in ruby settings, and eyes like brilliants beneath arching brows of ebony, who looked from their *carreta* as it moved solemnly along to morning mass, at the village church near by. May the orisons they offered to heaven procure for them pardon for the heartache they gave some of our companions, although it cannot be said artlessly, for their furtive glances and winsome smiles revealed the intent of mischief. The *carreta* honored by these houris, is the *country* coach of Chile for parties of pleasure, social visiting, and going to church. It consists of a cart, or in deference to its high office we will say carriage body, ten or twelve feet long and five feet wide, the sides of which are sometimes boarded and painted pale blue or yellow, but nearly always interwoven cane or flag is the material; and the top, arched high enough to allow a moderate sized lady to stand up, is similarly made, the cane or flag-leaves being interlaced tightly and thickly, to make it water-tight and a good non-conductor of heat. The floor is plank or ox-hide, and the seats are arranged along the sides, cab-fashion, that the occupants may face each other. Little *barred* windows intimate the necessity of guarding the precious freight from being stolen by waylaying lovers, If you happen to be looking toward one of these at a time that a señorita is peering through it, so luminous will it appear, that you might readily suppose it the focus of a calcium light. Curtains before and behind secure seclusion or otherwise, according to the humor of the inmates. The body is mounted on two large, clumsy wheels, running on a wooden axle, and, being unfamiliar with lubricating substance, they indulge a propensity for hideous creaking to "fright the souls of fearful adversaries" contemplating a foray. A tongue, sometimes looking like a young sapling transferred in its native state from the forest, has a cross-piece at the unattached end having on its under surface two slight concavities, which, being placed on the heads of two oxen, is lashed to their horns by rawhide thongs. When there are many passengers, or the company is ambitious of extra style, two additional oxen are placed in front, pulling by a rope attached to the tongue. The *carratero* (carter or coachman), attired in a variegated blanket hung on his shoulders, his head protruding through a slit in its middle, called a *poncho*, and short-legged white trowsers of an amplitude sufficient to induce the belief that they might have descended from Moorish ancestors on one side, with a little sugar-loaf chip or straw hat, without brim or band, and armed with a fifteen feet lance-headed pole, walks in advance of his reflective steeds, significantly displaying for their due regard the emblem of authority, and instrument of punishment for waywardness and transgression. "The ox knoweth his owner" we are told by the prophet Isaiah; but it is manifest that the declaration was intended to apply to the ancient representative of that observing beast only, and by no means was designed to impeach his capacity of improvement under modern instruction; for it is placed beyond question that the Chilean ox knoweth likewise, and full well, his owner's *peon*, to whose unswerving requirements he is meekly submissive, measuring his movements in strict conformity with the carratero's appreciation of his own comfort, convenience, and dignity; which, it cannot be disputed, is unalterably conservative, and opposed to the shifting and troublesome tendencies of a discontented, and in his judgment *rather fast age.* Such is the fashionable equipage of the interior of Chile, an attempt to supersede which by more convenient and rapid means of conveyance, except in, and immediately in the neighborhood of large cities, is considered an unworthy encouragement of foreign innovations, derogatory to social interests, and dishonoring to Chilean nationality. But I have wandered from the most agreeable part of the theme, from the lovely freight to the lumbering conveyance. How it was that the fair spirits within this *prison-van* did not take "the wings of the morning," and fly over the glad earth clad in green and garnitured with flowers of bright and beauteous hues, was a mystery. Perhaps an antiquated duenna was ensconced in a corner of the vehicle, who held them in unwilling bondage. If so, they had only to have intimated their grievance and they should have been set free, and the ancient representative of domestic tyranny who guarded them have been ducked in the canal running through the adjoining meadow, as a punishment for doing what no governess in this country is expected to do—*watch her young mistress too closely.*

A short distance beyond, the road turning to the east became a wide avenue, passing through a hacienda of great extent and fertility, and bordered by Lombardy poplars thickly planted and of luxuriant foliage, causing a twilight within its walls of verdure. Again pursuing our southerly course, several miles further on we reached a less attractive region of *a higher level* than that part of the valley over which we had been travelling, and hence not intersected by canals as are the lower surfaces. This elevated tract stretches from the Andes to the Coast Range, a distance of sixteen or eighteen miles, and ten or twelve miles across in the direction of the road, and is more uneven, and studded with numerous small isolated hills varying in height from twenty to fifty feet, looking like volcanic blisters on an uplifted surface, as if an internal effort had been made to connect the two mountain chains by a great cross-link, which had failed for want of sufficient upheaval force. This tract, known as *Los Cerillos de Teno*, was in time past infested by highwaymen, the hills serving as watch-towers whence the approach of travellers could be seen for several miles, and behind which the robbers concealed themselves until proximity made escape hopeless. A more thickly-populated adjacent country, and the efforts of Government to arrest and punish offenders, have given to this section of the Province of Colchagua a better reputation than it formerly had; although a sole remnant of the bandit tribe may possibly have existed in a wayside *Roto*, who had evidently been imbibing liberally of *Chica*, and seemed ambitious of a general breach of the peace and a passage of arms with our postilion in particular.

Away to the southeast forty or fifty miles, an extinct volcano —*El Descabezado*—was seen lifting its decapitated trunk more than thirteen thousand feet, and standing forth in grandeur of massive proportions from the clustering peaks that stretch away to the north and south, as if he scorned support even in his headless condition. Over his bold shoulders the snow mantle fell in graceful folds, here and there being thrown aside by the blast to reveal some noble outline of figure; but dropping lower, as if in boastfulness of hardihood he thus proclaimed to his loftier brothers of Aconcagua and Tupungato, that eternal snow with him measures from three thousand to four thousand feet more of depth than with them. A gap in the lower Andean ranges showed the point at which the river *Teno* was pouring forth its flood; and we were soon destined to renew our morning experience of the effect of a summer-day's sun upon a snow mountain stream; for shortly after, when we reached that river, we found a French travelling coach that had passed us some miles back, and several ox-teams, standing on the bank contemplating in dismay the furious torrent, which seemed to indicate an impossible passage. What was to be done? The Frenchmen did not show any signs of advance. The great Emperor's "allons" did very well for national glory, but "allez" in their estimation suited better their personal safety. They evidently had made up their minds that some others might *be*, although they should not *talk*, braver than themselves. As to the Chilenos, they appeared to be striving by sundry solicitous coaxings to institute an initiative consultation with the oxen; but from their inflexible silence and immobility, they evidently designed to throw the *onus* of this *water* question on the carreteros, avoiding all responsibility and danger too if possible, and wisely concluding, no doubt, that it was sufficient for them to *bear the burden on land.*

Our gradually reduced stage-load consisted now of an Englishman, who was a member of the Valparaiso bar, intelligent, courteous, and fearless; a Californian who had crossed the plains, hunted grizzly bears, and encountered the greater danger of canvassing the State for the gubernatorial office—need more be said? and a third inside passenger, whose Anglo-Saxon ancestors entered land in the colonial province of Maryland under the patent of Lord Baltimore two hundred years ago, and who could not repudiate the moral force of the race from which he sprang, if he tried. Our driver, of California mettle and nerve, called out as soon as he had taken his survey of the scene, "What say you, gentlemen, shall we try it?" It would have been hopeless to wait for the melting of the Andean snow, the supply was rather large, and centuries of summers had vainly expended their hottest efforts to reduce it; retreat is becoming an obsolete English word, and Americans refuse to revive it; so the answer was a unanimous "aye." The baggage being again transferred to the top of the coach, and preparations made for an escape from it and a buffet with the torrent if necessary, two powerful oxen trained to the service were put in the lead of the six horses; as well for the advantage of their steady draught, an indispensable quality when unseen boulders are to be encountered, as for their unswerving obedience to direction, thus serving to keep the horses from becoming unmanageable from fright of the tumultuous waters. While the driver skilfully guided his team, the postilion, an experienced *carretero*, stripped to the buff, mounted his spirited charger, and with goad in hand took his station beside the pair of oxen in the lead. Several smaller branches of the stream were thus crossed, all serving to reduce the main river from which they escaped, and a rough bed of shingle being also passed, we then plunged into the turbid flood which rushed by in volume and speed, as if a mountain lake had burst its barriers. For a time it seemed as if we were likely, instead of pursuing a circuitous land route to the Pacific, to seek it by the shorter and less tedious channels of the Rio Teno, and the Rio Mataquito into which the first-named empties; and we soon found it necessary to mount to the higher altitudes of the coach, which sprung a leak and threatened to bilge, sometimes floating and at others attempting lateral somersets, Noticing this latter gymnastic proclivity, our pilot steered an oblique course across the stream so nearly in the direction of the current as to present the back of our extemporaneous pontoon boat instead of the side to its force. By this manœuvre it received a momentum that assisted the crossing, and in from ten to fifteen minutes we, more frightened than hurt, landed on the opposite side of an unquestionably dangerous looking river of two hundred and fifty yards width, in its swollen condition. Our own joy on reaching shore in safety was scarcely greater than that of the French travellers left behind, interested spectators of the experiment; for they saw in the favorable result a promise that they might risk its repetition with impunity, and "allons" now became doubtless the animated word of command to their postilion, although we did not wait to see whether or not they received a cold bath in the icy waters of the Rio Teno.

## CHAPTER XVI.

ROAD COSTUME—CURICO—RIO LONTUE—PRIMITIVE HABITATIONS—SOCIAL CONDITION—POLITICAL UTOPIANISM—INCONSISTENCY AND CRUELTY OF FANATICISM—MOLINO—RIO CLARO—TALCA—RIVER MAULE—LONCOMILLA AND ITS FRATRICIDAL BATTLE—RIVER PUTAGAN—LONGAVI AND CERRO FLORIDA PEAKS—MIRAGE—RIO ACHIHUENO—PARRAL—ARRIVAL AT SAN CARLOS.

RESUMING our journey, the road led for a mile or two over a rough and barren tract, and then the country presented an appearance of agricultural wealth; a rich soil and teeming crops bounteously irrigated, and long lines of the alamo bordering the road, which itself was thronged with happy people, pedestrians, equestrians, arrieros, and carrateros. The road costume is peculiar, and may be reduced to four essentials for each sex, that is of the nine-tenths of the population seen in travelling, who have the ring of the Indian *copper;* the one-tenth of Caucasian *silver* is not in common circulation. The dress of the men consists of a little conical straw hat, *minus* the apex; a *poncho*, resembling a gaudy venetian carpet with a longitudinal slit in the middle to pass the head through, bound with bright ribbon, and hanging from the shoulders around the body down to the hips; a graceless garment befitting its sluggish Indian inventors, but an incumbrance to one who values the privilege of manhood to use his arms. To the Chileno, from the inquilino to the roto, the poncho is bed, board, and broidery; for he sleeps on it, eats from it, and often spends the wages of a year to procure one of bright colors with which to decorate his person. A pair of trousers, which would be both more symmetrical and useful, if some of the material were taken from the width and added to the length; and finally, spurs of terrific proportions secured to the heels, sometimes through the intermedium, at others independently of, the less necessary appendage a pair of shoes. The women have invariably two long black hair plaits hanging down the back; a gay shawl worn à l'Espagnole, one end thrown gracefully over the shoulder, or à la tapada to conceal the greater part of the face when concealment is a merit or coquetry dictates the cunning device; a skirt à l'antique—innocent of inflation; and the gaudiest-colored shoes obtainable. From this it will be perceived that parts of our road were not without a considerable display of human butterflies, although the variety of species was not great, the *yellow* and *red* evidently predominating.

By the sight of a large cross on a hill we became aware of our approaching a town; and in a few minutes more, doubling the hill, we passed along a prettily-shaded alameda, and landed at the principal hotel of *Curico.* While breakfast was being prepared we strolled about the town, containing about five thousand inhabitants; a public promenade of nearly a mile, planted with poplars, and aqueducts of limpid water running down their long avenues; houses without taste or variety, except that some were built of adobes and others of mud-daubed reeds, occasionally whitewashed, and squatty enough to warrant the belief that their enormous tile roofs were slowly crushing them to the earth; unfinished churches without external architecture, whatever may be said of internal sanctity; adults burdened with ennui, and children not burdened with books, or any sense of obligation to use them, made up the sum of observations, from which we cheerfully returned to something more agreeable to hungry travellers—an excellent breakfast—except the butter, which from the abounding alfalfa pastures of the neighborhood ought to have been golden, fresh, and of rich flavor, but was pale, and old enough to vote at the coming election for President of the Republic, were it not for the constitutional disqualification of *poverty.*

A hearty meal despatched, seats were resumed in the coach, and a productive country of four or five miles having been passed over we reached at meridian the *Rio Lontue,* heading in the snow mountains of Las Llamas, in the vicinity of the Planchon Pass; from the mountain of which name, as also from those forming the group of the extinct Peteroa Volcano, it receives a part of its tributary waters. Although this river at the crossing is divided into several arms, which flow separately over a shingly valley two miles wide, yet its principal stream was so swollen, deep, and rapid, from recent thaws, that no attempt to ford it had been hazarded for several days. The continuous route was therefore interrupted by stopping the coaches on the opposite banks of the river, and transferring passengers and baggage over an Indian hanging bridge, for an exchange of conveyances. This bridge, although of much more rude materials, is nevertheless constructed on similar principles with the suspension bridge of other countries. Two strong timbers, forked at the upper ends, are planted five or six feet asunder, perpendicularly and deeply, on each bank of the river, and connected by a cross-piece lashed to each. Timbers of equal strength, but less height, planted somewhat further from the stream, give secure attachment to two cables made of raw-hide, which supported in the forks of the main timbers are thrown across the river. From these strong horizontal cables, are suspended vertically numerous raw-hide ropes or thongs, which are attached to and support long poles that thus traverse the direction of the stream; upon these last rests a flooring composed of lighter cross-pieces, filled in and closed up with cane, branches, and reeds, of sufficient quantity and strength to bear the weight of a man, and even a mule or horse. Not having lateral braces, and being very elastic, our hanging bridge required care in crossing, to avoid a bath in the Lontue, of nearly freezing temperature, from the icy fountains of the Cordillera.

Shortly after resuming our route on the south side of the river, we crossed a considerable and the last arm of the Lontue, the Rio Seco; and although a few well-cultivated haciendas were seen, the general aspect was that of unthrifty husbandry, and a greater disregard than further north, of the means of irrigation at the disposal of the inhabitants. The fencing, sometimes made of trees or posts, sparsely filled in with dead acacia branches, at others consisted merely of dry brush. Many of the habitations along the roadside are in the fashion of Indian lodges, with but a single opening answering the threefold purpose of door, window, and chimney. These huts are made of brush, cane, or flags, lashed or rudely twined into a coarse matting; and having but one apartment, with earthen floor, for the whole family, and visitors too, if any should tarry at night. Even the hovels, one remove from savage design, possess no higher claim to be considered the dwellings of a civilized race; for apart from the wattled walls of reed and brush, sometimes daubed with mud, to be washed off by the first heavy rain, with thatched roof of flags or straw, the occupancy of but one apartment in sickness and health, by day and by night, and by all ages, sexes, and conditions, huddled promiscuously together, showed a shameless disregard of the decent observances of life. It is to the interior of Chile that the traveller must come, to see the actual national condition—social, moral, and political. It is not as represented by the limited better race and class of the few of its cities, where accumulated wealth, means of education, and intercourse with foreigners, have chastened and refined those within whose reach these gifts have been placed, that we are able to comprehend the status of the people at large; but by looking upon the populace as it is mainly constituted, of jornaleros, guasos, peons, and rotos, its dependent and laboring classes, by whatever name these are known, who possess but in a few instances even a mite of fee simple property, no coequal political rights, no education, no justly remunerative pursuit, no chance of preferment here, and no hope of a hereafter, as they are taught to believe, but that which a privileged priesthood may choose to give in return for the fee wrung even from the hand of toil and want, that has just grasped the poor reward of daily labor, or grubbed a pittance from some corner of its master's estate. Aye, *master!* For if not so technically and in the phraseology of statute law, he is so by the stronger law of fact, resulting from the tenure of estate; and the *peon* and such like, the serfs of the country, can no more shake off their servitude—their *slavery*—than they can dispense with the morsel of food that sustains life, and for which they are dependent on the employment, or the bounty, of the great landholder or the miner.

In Chile, as elsewhere, capital will rule; and he who wields it *is master*, however politic it may be to suppress the term, for fear of giving offence and producing troublesome antagonisms. To say nothing of the dominant power of English wealth in influencing the destinies of other nations, it is sufficient, in illustration of the truth, to refer to the undeniable influence of capital in controlling the elections in our country, and even *mastering* the honest public will by giving to it a Presidential *master*. When fully examined and understood, the problem of free government, as presented in most modern republics, exhibits some strange features; and the self-delusion of the multitude who are its boastful supporters, and its victims too, becomes manifest.

The traveller who has sense enough to consider the political question of human rights, in its application to beings of a like race and natural endowments, without being carried by transcendental philanthropy to the absurd length of insisting that a goose having wings can soar as high as the eagle, and is entitled to wheel in loftier space with that imperial bird; or to the equally foolish extreme of affirming that an ass (not a human ass) is as swift as a horse because he has the same number of legs, and movable ears; such a traveller, unprejudiced by the errors of education, seeking truth, and open to rational convictions on a practical question; who sees the negro, in his appropriate relation of servitude and dependence to the Caucasian, submissive as a child, affectionate in his instincts, imitative of others, looking for guidance, and obedient although inclined to indolence; will not find the term *master* of such horrible import, when applied to one who, being of the master race as ordained of God, can direct him in the path of usefulness to himself and others. From an imperial master of the same race of mankind to a schoolmaster, so many gradations of station are perpetually obtruded on us to which that word of relative supremacy is applied, that the sensitiveness must be strangely abnormal that will take offence at its application to one of superiority in the scale of natural being, whether he be the Caucasian master of a Negro, or the Caucasian master of a Peon. It was not, then, with censorious purpose that the remark was made when I drifted away from my narrative, that the Peon has his master in Chile. Nor can he shake off his *absolute*, although not nominal *slavery*, so long as the Spaniard approaches to numerical equality, preserves himself from deterioration of blood, and remains true to the nobler spirit and instincts of his race. But the boastful pretence of free institutions, and the hypocritical show of hatred of the condition of slavery, which will not allow even the semblance of it presented by a temporary coolie apprenticeship, is, under the circumstances of actual social and political condition, deserving of a share of the reprehension due to the high priests of anti-slavery elsewhere; who, for the liberation of the negro from a condition of servitude, sanctioned by the Law and the Prophets, by Christ and the Apostles, by the example of all nations, and the constitutional compacts of their own land, would glory in a carnival of the flaming torch and bloody hand; in the midnight murder of men and women of their own race, and the worse than murder of virgin purity; in the assassination of the feeble and unresisting, decrepitude already tottering on the verge of the grave, and helpless infancy just come to breathe new love into human hearts. And yet with complacent inconsistency and cruelty, these deluded propagandists of freedom crush under the wheels of the same political juggernaut the lingering representatives of aboriginal liberty in America; thirst for the blood of those who refuse to be their "hewers of wood and drawers of water," and insist on living in the land their fathers gave them; and from the Rock of Plymouth to the Father of Waters, applaud an Executive decree of death against hundreds of unresisting children of the forest, who, whatever the offences against civilization of their untaught nature writhing under a sense of gross wrongs, still surrender to those who claim to be the special representatives of civilization and Christianity, and hence are bound to "deal justly and love mercy."

Chilenos should not allow national sensibility to become unduly wounded at an exposure of social and political condition, by those who certainly manifest no uncandid disposition to conceal their own defects, or to complain that others have been quick to detect, and ready to criticize them. However errors may be presented, either to private or public cognizance of those interested, it is the part of wisdom to mark and mend them. The most influential inhabitants, those favored by fortune and rank, have probably not chosen to forego ease and comfort, and examine where alone they may be seen, in filthy suburban hovels, and in the miserable lodges and huts of remote provinces, the social destitution, moral debasement, and political corruption or utter abnegation of the lower classes. They should not be offended at the wayside observation which perceives, and the spirit of frankness that reveals these; the one not being impertinently curious, nor the other unfriendly. Had my visit to Chile been restricted to its seaports, I might have doubted the correctness of a description representing accurately its physical grandeur, fertility, and general resources, as seen since leaving Valparaiso. And yet with such gifts of a beneficent Creator, a moral degradation has been found of wide prevalence. It must be understood that these remarks apply to the unfortunate many, in birth and poverty; not to the favored few, of blood and wealth. The absence of home comforts, the disregard of domestic relations, the renunciation of matrimonial, parental, and filial ties, the ignorance or indifference to moral restraints, and the disregard of Christian precept by a general profanation of the Sabbath; the day specially selected for military drill, drunken debauch, gambling, cock-fighting, and horse-racing, heretofore seen, were again observed during this Sunday drive to Talca; the road being enlivened by a Government registry of voters *under military supervision*, horse-races, general licentiousness, cock-fights, dog-fights, and low gaming, from pitching coppers, through various grades of hazard, up to monté. Such are the blots upon the body politic, patent to all who choose to read the record unfolded before them; and for the existence of which, in a country professedly Christian, there must be some censurable cause operating upon the social organization. Whether this results from the deterioration incident to amalgamation with an inferior race, whose baser characteristics maintain the ascendency, or be consequent on some radical defect in the political framework fastening upon society the evils of ignorance, civil disqualification, and an exclusive or defectively administered church, are questions not to be discussed *currente calamo.* But they deserve the unprejudiced investigation and profound reflection of the leading minds of Chile, upon the determination of which the destinies of a magnificent country greatly depend.

Passing through *Molino* with a large plaza and a little street, where voters were again seen being registered under *military surveillance,* the first town through which our road ran in the *Province of Talca,* beginning at the Rio Lontue and extending south to the Maulé River, we came, four or five miles beyond, to the *Rio Claro.* Crossing this, we soon entered upon a rough and sterile tract, with but few mere patches of cultivation; and such continued to be the characteristics of the country nearly to the city of Talca. Many of the hills were very steep and it often became necessary to assist our team of six by the attachment of an extra horse; a service rendered by an outriding Chileno always in attendance. The Chilenos are fearless and skilful horsemen, and would make a formidable cavalry if mounted on horses of sufficient weight. Those of Chile are too light, although they are well trained to the charge by a custom of riding them under the spur against strongly-supported transverse poles, and against each other breast to breast; and so vicious does a horse become at times by this training, that he will spring suddenly against an approaching horse and dismount the rider before he can guard against the shock.

About fourteen miles south of Molino is the *Quebrada de la Marca,* noted for the excellent *chicha* furnished at its famous *posada,* a *horn* of which, for the want of a goblet, proved refreshing to us on a hot day.

At *Chagre,* where we changed horses, apparently about thirty or thirty-five miles due west of El Descabezado, the stones of which the fences are made present nothing of the characteristics of the scoria found about Los Cerillos, but are lighter even than indurated clay or sand; its exceeding lightness and great friability, as well as its grayish-white color, warranting the belief that it was formed of the ashes of a volcano—perhaps Descabezado, when active—agglutinated by rains falling on successive lamina, and sun-dried, producing a stone as light as pumice. This whole region abounds in it, not a boulder being visible. A great part of the land along our route of to-day being incapable of irrigation, is barren, desolation reigns around, and there is nothing of immediate wayside scenery to give interest to the ride. Travellers were few, a pack-train and herd of cattle with an occasional horseman scarcely serving to relieve the oppression of loneliness; and but for the Cordillera, with its unrolled panorama of grandeur and magnificence, bounding the vision to the east, and Peteroa, Descabezado, Nevada de Chillan, and Piedra Azul, extending over eighty or ninety miles of space, standing in bold relief beside their less imposing compeers, piercing the skies with icy pinnacles, and lifting on high their domes of everlasting snow, pencilled with silvery light, or mellowing in softer radiance or darker shadow, as jealous clouds concealed their beauties from the sun; but for these eternal oracles of God, that speak conviction to the human mind, calming its doubts and confirming its faith, and that awaken the sleeping emotions of the heart to strange delights, there would be no temptation to repeat the ride from the Rio Claro to Talca. Having crossed the unimportant streams of Chagra and Panque, and passed for a short distance somewhat better cultivated fields near the city, we found ourselves, at six P. M., dashing over paved streets and skirting the Plaza de Armas, to the fashionable but rather humble-looking hotel which faced one of its sides.

*Talca* is about one hundred miles by the road southwest by south from San Fernando, in latitude 35° 14′ S. It was founded in 1742, and is much nearer to the Coast Range of mountains than to the Andes, being but a few miles from the foot of the former, from which it is separated by the Rio Claro in its southerly stretch, to empty into the River Maulé. Being the capital of the province of the same name, it has a considerable population, estimated at fifteen thousand; and it is the point to which the Southern Railroad is tending, and, it is supposed, will be made its southern terminus. The policy would be short-sighted that would arrest that improvement short of the Bay of Concepcion or the Biobio River.

A minute description of Talca would not repay one for the perusal. It may be imagined from what has already been said of other second-class Spanish-American towns. Rectangular streets badly paved, or not paved at all; a plaza, with or without a fountain, according to the facility of getting water, and sometimes a fountain to commemorate the want of it; the plaza being usually surrounded by the public buildings and municipal offices, and the grand theatre of religious and military displays, revolutionary and other riotous movements; an alameda shaded by Lombardy poplars; squatty houses of indifferent materials, rude construction, and without architectural design; and unfinished churches. The *personnel* are equally characteristic, and consist in the main—exceptions being undeniable, and the nobler because of surrounding degeneracy—of a lazy, bigoted, crafty, and selfish priesthood; and an ignorant, indolent, superstitious, and impoverished population. In the winter a more refined and intelligent class of inhabitants is found in Talca than at other seasons, the haciendados of the province with their families resorting thither for amusement and the facility of social intercourse, which cannot be enjoyed in the country in bad weather and at the distances they reside from each other. Still, the influence of this temporary accession of a higher education and morality is but partial in its effects upon the mass of society, and exercises no control whatever over the more powerful agents who so signally fail in their great office. The "bell of agony" (thus religiously known) was heard to echo for hours from the church-tower the expiring groans of one who for long years had been *par excellence* the recognized reprobate of the community, venerable in vice and weary of wickedness only because he was going where profligacy and lust could no longer give joy to sensual appetite, and who now, at the final moment, was shrived and purified of sin by virtue of liberal bequests and the saving grace of a wafer, conveyed to him in a clerical *coach of state* through the streets, at the approach of which every head bowed and every knee bent; while the military, as if in burlesque of the benevolent mission, saluted this transubstantiated "Prince of *Peace*" by *presenting arms* as it passed along. Such scenes were not calculated to establish confidence in the reformatory influence among the clergy of a partial secular enlightenment, nor to give a traveller a high opinion of Talca religionism.

The Hotel l'Europe, at which we stopped, was built in conformity to the Continental rule—a one-story, quadrangular edifice, on the sides of a patio, to which access was had by a gateway. On the sides of the court were the dining-room, chambers, and billiard-rooms—the last an indispensable in the humblest inn—while a parlor is rarely seen, and a reading-room never. Brick floors, commonly met with in the chambers of interior Chile, are neither agreeable nor healthful; their board ceilings are safer than the heavy stucco with which ours are loaded, and the falling of which sometimes proves dangerous to life. But the partitions of our middle-class houses are preferable to those of corresponding houses in Chile, both for security and privacy; for muslin, however prettily covered with paper, will neither shut out a thief nor the snoring serenade of a neighbor, whose inheritance of evil

> Burthens e'en the tranquil night with discord
> And murder of sweet sleep.

The regular nine o'clock P. M. dinner was excellent, as also the 10 A. M. breakfast, both sustaining the reputation of this town for abundant and cheap food; which, it is said, has heretofore induced many families of diminished incomes to resort thither, causing Talca to be called at one time, in derision, "the bankrupt colony."

Although at the season for visiting the Baths of Chillan a public stage-line is run two or three times each week south of Talca, yet, during eight or nine months of the year, persons travelling south of this city are compelled to take a private conveyance. This was our necessity, and with the aid of some fellow-countrymen found permanently residing here, we succeeded in hiring a *carretela*, two postilions, and ten horses, to carry two of us to Tomé, nearly two hundred miles, for four ounces—about fifty-seven dollars of our coin. Full time being taken to visit the chief points of interest, we bade adieu to a city which in the civil war of 1859 was for a time the headquarters of the Revolutionists, had been strongly fortified, barricaded, armed, and provisioned, and, to the surprise of most of those who had become involved in the movement, was surrendered with scarcely a show of resistance. Bribery sometimes becomes a great military strategist, and is supposed to have achieved triumphs in Chile as elsewhere.

Our carretela was simply an old-fashioned *cab*, with square body, standing top, seat on each side, and door behind, mounted on two wheels, with shafts for one horse; in the case of the carretela another horse being attached on the outside of the shafts *birlocho fashion*, for the use of the postilion, who guides both horses. Eight loose horses were driven along by another postilion, and these furnished relays. It was an odd way of procuring *fresh* horses, but the only one of getting any at all, as none could be obtained on the route. The poor beasts had a hard time, for being left free, and availing themselves of their supposed privilege to range, they strayed from the road to pick the wayside grass, and were driven from side to side, and sometimes over extensive plains by their roto persecutor, thus passing over double the distance they would have done by confinement to the direct route; and when their turn came to go into harness, they were no more fit for duty than when taken out. Such is one of the inveterate customs of Chile, which we took the liberty of commenting on in English—a condemnation intelligible to our Chileno drivers might have resulted in our abandonment on the road.

After having lost the grateful shade of the Alameda, and a wide poplar bordered avenue by which we left Talca, we crossed an inhospitable plain presenting nothing of verdure but that of scrubby espinos to relieve the barren scene; although the valley far off to the east, near the converging head-waters of the Maulé River, is rich and well irrigated artificially. Even the grand outline of the Cordillera, so long the object of admiration and wonder, seemed fading away to the southeast as we sought the Coast Range, along the eastern foot of a spur of which—the Cerro Chivato—we passed many huge granite boulders bounding the road; and finally crossing a hilly offshoot of the Range, we entered the rocky valley of the *Maulé River*. As we descended the hill, the river was seen with its deep and impetuous torrent nearly a mile wide, a short distance above Los Perales, the usual head of navigation; with large numbers of pack-mules and cattle standing on its banks, awaiting their turn to be ferried across. We were now thirteen miles from Talca, without an inn or decent habitation of any kind in which to seek shelter; and it was by no means agreeable to learn that we might be detained many hours on the hot shingley river bank, or in the dried brush rancho near by, a very pest-hovel of abominations, ere we could get to the opposite side. But we determined to shorten our detention if possible.

A traveller in Chile soon learns the meaning of *yapa*, and its wonderful efficacy in accomplishing results. It is uncertain if the above is the correct spelling of the word, or if it may not rather be *llapa*, from "Llapar—to add an additional portion of quicksilver in extracting metals." But whatever the orthography, the well-understood signification is, something given for which a return of favor is expected—in our vernacular, *a bribe*. Foreign residents here, very arrogant of their own incorruptibility, impute to Chile the special indulgence in the practice the word implies. But if they had a little more candor, they would admit that it is rather an epidemic than an endemic vice; that like cholera, no communities escape it, and that it often prevails most extensively and fatally where the science of government, commerce, and manufactures, claim to have elevated the human race to the highest rank of virtue and refinement. Be this as it may, we can testify that Chilenos are in the path of progress and civilization as determined by the above test—the yapa worked as a charm on the Maulé. We were put aboard of the next launch with deferential consideration; our extra horses having been previously driven into the stream to "paddle their own canoe," a wild Chileno on a trained swimmer whooping them before him with frightful yells. And when they were seen struggling with the furious current, sometimes disappearing beneath it, at others rolled over like huge boulders, and finally swept a mile down stream before landing, it was suggested that "the other side of Jordan" was probably not more difficult to reach than the south bank of the Maulé. However, the excitement of novelty often blunts the sense of danger, and we "shoved off," under the auspices of ten breech-clothed, but otherwise nude boatmen, with integument of the color of well-tanned sole leather, stretched over splendidly-developed muscles; ready for pushing, poling, rowing, steering, swimming, or any other kind of river service that might become necessary. And a hard time they had, for once in the channel, and fairly within the power of the impetuous torrent, away we went down stream with a speed of twenty knots, despite the vigorous efforts of our watermen, who could do no more for the time than to keep the bow of our trembling craft head-on toward an eddy below, formed by a sand-bar from the opposite bank, into which happily our pilot succeeded in shooting her; and by rowing and dragging along shore, we were finally landed in safety, well pleased at the opportunity thus offered, to transfer from our pockets to the palms of the Chilenos, the yapa now due—for unlike a process of gold mining, in this of *undermining*, the product is obtained *before* the *quick*-silver is applied.

Most of the inhabitants of the Provinces of Talca and Maulé are half-breeds and other mongrel descendants of the ancient Promancians, the courageous, robust, and warlike tribe of Indians who occupied this part of Chile before the conquest; and who defied and successfully resisted the efforts of the Peruvian Incas to subdue them, as they did likewise the subsequent invasion of the Spaniards under Almagro; and who failed to preserve their liberties, from a too generous confidence in the seductive promises of Valdivia, at a still later period. This conqueror having artfully stimulated jealousies and resentments against their neighbors, and using one to aid in the conquest of another tribe, thus succeeded in subjugating all except the wiser and invincible Araucanians. The fine physical development, boldness, and activity of our boatmen well illustrated the superiority of their aboriginal ancestry.

Having now entered the Province of Maulé, of which the river we had just crossed forms the northern boundary, we pursued our route over a level and sandy country for a short distance. The soil, although still thin, appeared more productive, but without the irrigation commonly found further north. Passing a posada, and some prettily embowered rustic cabins, where were seen soldiers in gaudy uniforms reclining in the shade of large willows trimmed so as to look like immense umbrellas, we soon after came to the mill, the crystal stream of which was crimsoned with blood by the fratricidal battle of Loncomilla, in 1851, which will ever remain painfully memorable in the annals of Chilean revolutions. It was a consequence of the discontent incident to a Presidential election, considered by many illegal in the means, and false in the declared result. After various military movements on the part of the opposing forces this battle ensued, for the number engaged in it one of the bloodiest of modern times; in which citizens of the same country, and the same religion, were arrayed against each other; father against son, brother against brother, relatives of all degrees engaged in deadly strife, the manœuver of combat being disregarded and military discipline forgotten in a ferocious hand to hand fight, in which the glittering steel gave no quarter, and night only stilled the panting efforts of human rage. Of eight thousand men engaged in the battle of Loncomilla, it is stated that less than three thousand were capable of bearing arms on the morning after darkness arrested the carnage, a result attesting the peculiar bitterness of civil strife. General Bulnes, in command of the Government forces, would gladly have escaped the next day with his shattered remnant of one thousand, if he had possessed the means of crossing the Maulé River. Summoned to surrender by the victorious General Cruz, commander of the revolutionary army, Bulnes contrived, by prolonged discussion of terms, to gain time for the secret action of emissaries, who, it was then supposed, and is now generally believed, succeeded in bribing some of the leading revolutionists, whose treachery and desertion compelled General Cruz to retire from a field actually won, and of which he remained master on the night before, and eventually to enter into a treaty terminating the war, in which his party obtained no greater rights or privileges than they had previously possessed. That General Cruz was duly aware of the cause of his misfortune, is shown by one of his despatches, in which, although he declined to "criminate any individual," he proclaims his "disappointment as dependent upon causes within his own camp;" and adds, that he had "counted on the co-operation of others, who failed him in the hour of need—his successes being inexplicably reversed."

It was an instance of perfidy not surpassed by those with which every chapter of the history of Spanish conquests in America teems; and supports the opinion of some, who believe that the ancestral disregard of good faith is imitated by their posterity.

Five or six miles south of the battle-field we crossed the *Putagan River* at high-water mark, a branch of the *Loncomilla*, which empties into the Maulé a short distance west of the ferry. Having mounted the steep southern bank of the Putagan, we bore south-southeast across a treeless plain, fourteen or fifteen miles in extent. This was uncultivated, level, and allowed an uninterrupted view of the nearer Coast Range, and more distant mountain scenery nearly due east from this point, with the Longavi and Cerro Florida, wrapped in their white mantles, standing like giant spectres among the lowlier peaks of the Cordillera. Although our road lay over an unwatered and barren plain, the foot of the Andes could be seen skirted with a broad belt of verdure, indicating mountain streams and their enriching tribute. Far in the distance ahead, a mirror-like expanse of water appeared across our route, and trees suspended above it as if in mid-air. It was a *mirage*, for as we approached it disappeared, and having, after two hours of weary travel, descended forty or fifty feet from the higher level we had traversed, and come to the clear and tranquil *Rio Achihueno*, we had no difficulty in accounting for the illusive picture of a lake and trees which the pencil of refraction had sketched in the air above to charm us with its beauty. Although wide, and in some places deep, the Achihueno was forded in safety, our postilion appearing to be familiar with the signs of depths and shallows.

Ascending to the table land on the opposite side, and changing horses, we struck across another sterile plain of equal extent with that left behind. With the exception of one small vineyard, the vines of which clustered about a little brook that strangely distilled its limpid waters midway this desert, a boon to the thirsty traveller, there was not a spot of verdure to relieve the expanse of barrenness.

The setting sun took leave of us as we pursued our way across this desolate plain, but still gilded the mountain tops after having left the lower world in shadow, and as a last sign of departing glory touched with a roseate ray the lofty brow of the Cerro Florida. It was a scene of transcendent beauty "that seen became a part of sight," for the rare privilege of beholding which we bore unmurmuringly the discomfort and danger of being benighted on this waste. Our destination, *Parral*, fifty-five miles from Talca, in latitude 35° 42′ S., was not reached until after 10 P. M. The latter part of the route was unseen, and of course nothing can be said about it, except that sundry severe joltings and sudden "backing and filling" indicated that a more rugged country was passed at the conclusion than at the commencement of our day's travel.

On entering Parral, old-fashioned lanterns, dimly lighted by tallow candles, were seen hanging from the fronts of all the houses, in obedience to municipal regulation, serving to light us to the posada selected by our postilion, where we obtained a miserable meal and as mean a bed in an out-house; but even these were welcome to hungry and wearied travellers.

Although up with the dawn and ready for the road, one of our postilions, who was a "Jack of all trades," found it necessary to turn blacksmith and shoe some of his horses, having provided himself for emergencies before leaving Talca. The detention enabled us to look at Parral, stare at the natives, and be stared at. As many as two thousand persons of all shades of humanity, down to the sable servant, the politically presumed equal and undoubted familiar of our landlady, are accustomed to stow themselves in the not numerous, nor commodious, nor ambitious tenements of this town; the amphitheatrical cock-pit having better design and finish than most of the houses, no doubt in consideration of the brave bird's courage and endurance entitling it to higher distinction. The unpaved streets looked like a continuous kitchen from primitive wayside fires; while olive-hued damsels, innocent of toilet, stepped softly about in unsandalled feet, clothed simply in the mystic garb which asks no aid of art, because most artful in that it half conceals, yet half reveals fair maiden charms. Had they tendered us a cup of the savory coffee they were preparing for the morning beverage, to detain us strangers for inquisitive regards, the acceptance would not have been waived for want of corresponding curiosity. *Carretas*—ox carts—too, were creeping along,

AN OX-CART.

ladened with small round stones, probably for paving the court-entrance of some village grandee. Carts, did I say? But not such as are thus designated in the north. Nor drays, as seen there. Nor chariot either. Yet more like the last as pictured by the pencil of art than any vehicle of modern civilization. The Chilenos manifest a decided preference for the classical in some things—or is it merely an insuperable prejudice against foreign innovation? Their adherence to the old Roman plough has been spoken of—a knee of hard wood with two oxen attached to it through the medium of pole and horns, by which the ground is scratched two or three inches deep; a most effectual cultivation to prevent the market being overstocked with cereals. Perhaps this will account for the regulation of the price of wheat by the few proprietors of landed estate, to suit their own views of value. The ox-cart consists of a square or oblong frame with a dried ox-hide bottom, resting on a wooden axle running on two low solid wood wheels, from two to two-

and-a-half feet diameter: from the want of iron tires these wheels are worn irregularly, and are rarely a perfect circle. A rude tongue, or its substitute two poles attached near the ends of the axle and uniting before so as to intercept an isoscelës triangle, being secured to the horns of the oxen, elevate the cart somewhat in front, dropping it behind like the old Grecian chariot; the resemblance being increased sometimes by the addition to the cart of an oval or square wicker body, like a china-ware crate open behind. In this the freight is stowed, and when unloaded the driver there indulges in drowsy meditation. In regard to the team the classical resemblance fails; it certainly would not have been crowned for speed at the Olympic games. The carretero's head-gear is changed from the fashions of northern Chile. From Talca to this place, and so on toward the Biobio, it is a coarse felt, color blue or black, of conical shape, but with the apex slightly flattened in. It is called a *maulé*, from the province where it originated and is still used. One might suppose from its shape that it is worn in honor of El Descabezado, which rises and sets in the minds of the people of this province as the wonder of creation. They are excusable; Englishmen would think so too if it looked down on Windsor palace.

Beyond Parral the soil looks dark and rich, but the want of water must be sensibly felt in a country where there is no rain for seven or eight months of the year—embracing the spring and summer, when most needed for agricultural purposes. In the southern hemisphere, it must be remembered, the spring commences the twenty-second of September, summer in December, autumn in March, and winter in June. Good crops of wheat and barley were seen during our morning ride; and had they been sown sufficiently early to obtain the occasional showers of early spring, they would have been heavy. From twelve to fifteen miles south of Parral we came to the clear and placid *Perquilaoquen* River, which was forded without difficulty. We were now in the *province of Nuble*, the ninth in the series passing southwardly from the extreme northern province of Atacama; and changing our direction to the south by west, we saw, after going a few miles, the first post and rail fence we had yet met with, indicating our proximity to timber; the great want of which is a sad deprivation to Chile. This sign of thrifty husbandry was a pleasant sight, after the wearisome leagues of trenches and wretched brush hedges by which we had been passing. Then we came, a little further on, to luxuriant fields of the cereals; maize sown broadcast, beans and other garden vegetables, and vineyards, which continued to border the road until after a ride of thirty miles from Parral we came in sight of the bright red tile roofs of *San Carlos,* looking gaily out from among the deep green foliage of ornamental trees which embowered that neat little town, giving it an air of cheerfulness and comfort we chose to take as tokens of assured welcome and hospitality to travellers, who had keen appetites for an eleven o'clock breakfast.

## CHAPTER XVII.

PROHIBITION OF THE CULTIVATION OF TOBACCO—SAN CARLOS—THE VINE—WHEAT—RIVER NUBLE—CHILLAN—BATHS OF THE CORDILLERA—NEVADA OF CHILLAN—RIO ITATA—CUESTA PARALES—RAFAEL—ARRIVAL AT TOME.

THERE is one vegetable to the growth of which the climate and soil of Chile are well adapted, and will produce of fine quality, the production of which is prohibited under heavy penalty, even to the small extent of supplying the personal wants of the planter. Government has monopolized the trade in *tobacco*, and appoints agents to regulate the importation and sale of it. Of course the revenue from it is large in a country where the cigarito is used freely by the men, and women too of low degree; the human breath and clothing, the breakfast and dinner table, the hotel, coach, car, street, all places being polluted by its offensive exhalations. It would be difficult to determine which is the more valuable source of revenue to the State, the above, or a like monopoly of the sale of playing-cards. It is a severe criticism on the condition of Chile by its own Government which practically avows that more revenue can be raised from its vices than in any other manner. As little sympathy as those are entitled to who are taxed on a vile weed that natural taste abhors, and a stringent education of which is required to constrain it to tolerate the poisonous product, yet it must be acknowledged that it is an anomaly of republicanism which punishes a citizen for cultivating on his own land an article, the use of which by its own reservation of sale, the Government appears to consider commendable and proper.

The town of San Carlos is in the Province of Nuble, nearly on the intersection of latitude 36° S. with longitude 72° E. It contains about four thousand inhabitants, and is surrounded by one of the best vine-growing districts of Chile, the wine made in this vicinity being perhaps equal to the celebrated *Mosto of Cauguenes*, produced about twenty miles to the northwest in a somewhat more hilly region.

The growth of the vineyard throughout Chile, and especially in the Provinces of Maulé, Nuble, and Concepcion, the climate and soil of which are remarkably adapted to the purpose, is only second in value to that of the cereals. *Chacoli*, *chicha*, and *aguardiente*, products of the grape, are the favorite drinks of the common people; and *mosto*, a wine, when properly made, of rich flavor and excellent body, is not only extensively used by the wealthier classes in Chile, but is often in demand for exportation. The above-named drinks may be thus described: Chacoli is much like cider, and is the unfermented juice of the grape; chicha is made by boiling chacoli, which hastens fermentation, each kettlefull remaining over the fire until scum ceases to come to the surface; aguardiente is distilled from the pulp, skin, and seed, left from the manufacture of chicha, with a portion of freshly-expressed grape-juice. Mosto, the choicest drink, is made according to the received methods of the best wine producers of France and Germany. None of these are brandied except when exported in fresh casks. Our breakfast at San Carlos was graced by Mosto, equal to choice Burgundy, at twenty-five cents per bottle! It would be well for North Americans if they could substitute this delicious beverage of the South for the fire-water which consumes them while it is consumed. We testified by deeds to our host—more significant than words—our appreciation of his excellent beef, mutton, coffee, and bread of surpassing quality, for which Chile is famous. I have not seen an indifferent loaf since my arrival at Valparaiso.

Our carretela being in readiness, we left San Carlos with a grateful appreciation of its excellent fare, and better men physically for the enjoyment of it. As we crossed the plaza the judges were seen sitting there in state registering voters, in the broad glare of day, as if boastful of the openness and fairness of proceedings. There was no challenging, no intimidation, no bullying, no fighting over the inviolable privilege. It was in this instance certainly a tranquil and dignified procedure, becoming the preliminary arrangements for the exercise of an inherent and sovereign right—none daring to make its possessor afraid; and one worthy of imitation by many of our own countrymen. Our road continued south by west across a district where extensive, well-enclosed fields of heavy-headed wheat were sporting their golden waves. It was a scene of agricultural wealth, reminding us of the magnificent prairies of Illinois, when, near harvest, they seem to heave and swell with luxuriant crops. This may justly be considered a teeming granary of the republic, where wonderful fertility and cultivation are exhibited through leagues of our progress. The policy of those public agents would indeed be short-sighted, which, with a knowledge of the resources of this great interior, would fail to penetrate it with the Southern Railroad, now winding its sluggish way through its first and second chief divisions, soon to rest, if rumor speak true, in the Province of Talca. With immense reaches of bowling-green, scarcely a swell of earth requiring the hand of the leveller, and water convenient of access, this magnificent valley seems specially adapted for a railroad from the capital to the Bay of Concepcion; and even beyond, if the heroic Araucanian should ever be cheated or bullied out of his possessions. And while it would reanimate present industry and startle new enterprise into life, none can doubt its own rich reward of employment. With vast regions yet awaiting judicious agriculture, irrigation, and improved implements, to repay to an inconceivable extent the hand of labor, no portion of the earth producing finer or more abundantly of cereals; bounded by hills adapted to the vine, of suitable climate, and affording unsurpassed pasturage for sheep; with water-courses wasting a power equal to the wants of all the factories of England, and mountain timber, and immense deposits of coal to the south; what should prevent the great valley from distributing throughout its own limits, and beyond them, its flour, wine, woollens, building-materials, and fuel?

A ride of fifteen miles brought us to the *River Nuble*, a wide, clear, and strong stream; and at the point of our crossing, with depth sufficient to allow of light-draught steamboat navigation. The Nuble heads in the Andes near the celebrated hot baths of Chillan, the waters of which it receives. A ferry-boat put us on the opposite side, and having ascended the steep bank, we passed over a country not as remarkable for fertility and cultivation as that on the north side of the Nuble; which, having a lower level, had doubtless, from changes of channel and overflow, derived its great fertility from the enriching deposits of that river. But still the growing crops looked promising, and our day's journey had lost none of its interest, when, seven miles from the ferry, the steeples of Chillan were seen lifted above surrounding trees, to tell us we were near our resting-place for the night.

*Chillan*, in latitude 36° 12′ S. and longitude 72° W., is the largest town in the Province of Nuble; and having a population of twelve thousand, is perhaps the fifth in size in Chile—Santiago, Valparaiso, Talca, and Concepcion, being larger. It is regularly laid out, and, except its suburbs, is well improved, the streets being wider, the alameda prettier, and the houses better built and neater, than are found in any of the towns south of Santiago. The two large churches we visited are more chaste, and more nearly finished than those seen elsewhere; showing appropriate regard for the external of piety, while internal ceremonies were impressive and sincere. The inhabitants are considered more agreeable and intelligent than those of most parts of the republic, except in regard to the few highly educated; by intelligence is meant sprightliness and vivacity, for the public schools, it is stated, are not well patronized. There is a marked improvement in the appearance of the people, the complexion showing a larger infusion of the white element than is observed in other parts of the interior. During an afternoon and evening stroll about town, more of the Caucasian characteristics of fairness and feature, more of chasteness in dress, and elegance of deportment were seen, than in any city of Chile in proportion to the population.

An excellent hotel dinner, with superb mosto at *twenty cents per bottle*, was furnished us. And to give you a proof that the interior Chilenos are yet a very primitively honest people, it may be said that in no instance during our valley journey were we charged more than two dollars each person for dinner, lodging, and morning coffee. Our Roto postilions took care of themselves, according to contract—one charge covering all expenses; the safest and most satisfactory arrangement to be made by a stranger. Of their board I can say nothing. As to their lodging, they invariably threw themselves on their ponchos on the gallery outside of our door, to guard us, or—it might have been—to keep us from running away, and to seek the rest usual among peon servants, who snatch it as they best can, in stable or corridor, on hay or poncho, and blanket if obtainable, without giving their employers any of the solicitude felt for negro slaves in North America.

From sixty-five to seventy-five miles from this town, nearly due east, are situated what in other parts of South America are known as the *Baths of Chillan*, but here are called the *Baths of the Cordillera*, from their being within the great mountain range of the Andes. The baths have such celebrity that it may be interesting to hear something about them; but as my engagements did not allow of my visiting them, I shall be compelled to give a translation of some of the most important facts relating to their location and virtues, taken from a Spanish medical monograph obtained here:

"It is said that in the beginning of the last century, a friar of the religious community of San Juan de Dios, having heard from some of the inhabitants of that part, that hot water flowed from amidst the snow, at the proper season of the year visited the springs, and judging that they might be of service, went there every summer with persons afflicted with diseases deemed incurable, who were said to have obtained great relief, until at last in one of his excursions he was assassinated. The spot in which nature has placed the springs, is overtopped and sheltered by that grand mass whose summit lords it over even conspicuous parts of the Cordillera. This Colossus, judging from the geological nature of the ground, from the numerous places whence smoke escapes, and especially from the many mineral springs of hot and cold water, charged highly with principles the result of volcanic action, appears to be a volcano; extinct for the time, in consequence of some fearful terrestrial convulsion and change, which closed its crater; the products of the volcanic action still going on, being conveyed to other active volcanoes in the neighborhood by subterranean passages, when a sufficiency of the compounds elaborated within is not discharged by the numerous breathing holes which surround this gigantic closed crucible. However this may be, from twenty to twenty-five leagues from Chillan, surrounded by nearly inaccessible hills, at the point where all vegetation ceases and the region of perpetual snow begins, a small spur exists of an irregular elongated shape, composed of broken stones upon a sort of unctuous clay, and which separates two torrents; on this the most central point of the Grand Quebrada, the bathing establishment is located. Of the geological nature of the soil little is known; on examining a vertical section of the hill to the north of the baths, it appears to consist of a thick layer of porphyritic aluminous non-volcanic semistratified rocks, from which some impure ferruginous waters flow, settling in immense masses of granite, some of colossal dimensions, some entire, others decomposed, united by a hard volcanic clay, shaded at intervals with different colors, and which appear to form the foundation. To these follow a thick layer of conglomerate rocks of an ashy gray color, feldspar, burnt clay, native sulphur mixed with earthy substances, different kinds of scoria, heaps of small pumice stones, and even true black and porous lava, all sufficient indications of the volcanic origin of the soil due to convulsion, which had taken place in long passed epochs. The surface of the soil presents peculiarities. The borders of the pools which surround the bathing establishment are composed entirely of round stones; the mineral springs of both water and vapor arise in certain hollows, the circumference of which (seen to be sprinkled with powder, if not with crystals or needle-like pieces of sulphur separated during the ebullition) of an obscure gray clay, in some places yellow, which results from the disintegration of the feldspar, which latter by itself forms the entire surface of these cavities exposed to the constant action of fire; from whence it results that the ground in the immediate neighborhood of the springs is exceedingly hot. In its general nature the soil appears to be an amalgam of vegetable earth, very porous and much burnt, mixed with small friable angular stones, white mud mixed with different shades of a yellowish red color, with sulphate of lime, and an unctuous marl arising from the decomposition of different minerals. It may well be said that the sulphurous acid, the uninterrupted evaporation of water, the sulphur, and above all the direct action of an internal heat communicate to the soil, soft in some places, hard in others, a very uncommon character worthy of the observation of the curious, as well as of the savant. The zoology and botany of a spot, habitable only for four months in the year, affords little of interest. They are limited to a few lichens and mosses, and animals of an inferior class which may be attracted there only for that brief period. The waters in most common use for general purposes come from various parts. They are cold, clear, without smell, slightly styptic, kept a day they become turbid and insipid from the deposit of oxide of iron and escape of carbonic acid. They are easily recognized from the red deposit of iron on the surface over which they flow, and contain a small quantity of chloride of sodium, a base of carbonate of iron, and a little carbonic acid. They increase the appetite, improve the digestion, and although somewhat constipating they animate the frame, give color to the cheeks, and occasion sensations of perfect health. The mineral springs are numerous. They are sulphurous waters. Near them are several which give out steam saturated with sulphurous acid, sulphur and sulphuretted hydrogen, and are useful as vapor baths; and not distant from these are five or six springs, one of them of a sulphuro-ferruginous nature; the rest sulphurous but cold, some containing more alkaline sulphuret, more or less iron, carbonate of lime, or soda, &c. The temperature of the springs differs greatly, some nearly reach the boiling point, others are cold. Those most used range from 40° to 50° Reaumur (equal to 122 to 154½° of Fahrenheit). The sulphuro-ferruginous 30° Reaumur (99½° Fahrenheit). The cold sulphurous 8° Reaumur (49½° Fahrenheit). The mountain torrent 0° Reaumur (freezing point Fahrenheit). The water of the spring known as the cauldron is 80° Reaumur (boiling point of Fahrenheit).

"The chemical analysis of Professor Domeyke gives the following constituents, viz.:

| | |
|---|---|
| Sulphuret of Sodium, | 18.00 |
| Sulphate of Soda, | 10.00 |
| Chloride of Sodium, | 2.00 |
| Carbonate of Lime, | 50.00 |
| Carbonate of Soda, | 8.00 |
| Sulphate of Magnesia, | 1.01 |
| Iron and alum, | 4.04 |
| Silex, | 5.00 |
| Organic matters, | 0.09 |
| Azote, Carbonic Acid, | Inappreciable." |

It would appear from the temperature of these waters that a patient may be frozen or boiled at his option; and by intermediate temperatures a certain cure is promised of the following diseases: "*Rheumatism*, muscular and articular; white-swelling, gout, lumbago, pleurodynia, abdominal muscular rheumatism, uterine, and diaphragmatic. For treatment of *diseases of the skin* these waters are remarkably applicable and satisfactory; in eczema, acute and chronic herpes, scabies, impetigo, tinea, acne, crusta lactea, porrigo, ringworm, prurigo, lepra, lupus. In *syphilis* they have been found powerfully curative, although some physicians consider that sulphur and its preparations are indicated only in those cutaneous affections which do not depend on syphilitic taint; but experience shows that they do not only cure the symptoms of constitutional infection, but also contribute to make them appear when suspected, simplifying them in severe cases, assist the good effect of mercurial treatment, and generally repair the bad effects produced by the improper administration of mercury in cases in which it might under judicious medical advice be considered contra-indicated. *Blenorrhagias* of long duration have yielded to the baths in from fifteen to twenty days. Venereal ulcers, primitive and consecutive, have yielded to the bath in less than twenty days; whilst it cannot be denied that it is inapplicable to some extensive syphilitic ulcerations, although pain in the bones often yield to it when nothing else has been found efficacious. These baths have been found serviceable also in some forms of paralysis not dependent on lesion of the brain or spinal cord. The separation of osseous sequestra is facilitated by them, and old wounds often heal with wonderful rapidity in the Cordillera. They are unsuited to consumption in its advanced stages, and to acute affections generally; but pulmonary catarrh, and often asthma, are greatly benefited. They are also serviceable in affections of the gastro-intestinal mucous membrane; functional disorders of the stomach, chronic gastritis. Chronic diarrhœa and dysentery generally yield to hip baths and enemas. The scrofulous, rachitic, and scorbutic diatheses are greatly improved by the waters of the Cordillera. Gonorrhœa, non-saccharine diabetes, spermatorrhœa, leucorrhœa, uterine catarrh, hæmorrhoids, diarrhœa dependent on hepatic derangement, and severe discharges of various forms, have been greatly relieved or cured by these baths. Many other affections are curable by the use of the mineral sulphurous waters, but which we classify as of probable cure only, since the observations which we possess are but few in number, or carelessly noted. Nineteen cases of very persisting neuralgias of various kinds have been carefully recorded as permanently cured; and spasmodic affections, headache, epilepsy, hysteria, uterine spasm, and convulsive movements of the limbs. *Chronic* inflammations are very amenable to treatment in the Cordillera. Of hepatitis, metritis, cystitis, gastro-enteritis, laryngitis, we have forty cases noted. In menstrual derangements the baths have acquired great reputation, also in sterility and impotence. In old ulcers, caries, necrosis, and in affections of the bladder, in glandular affections and local œdemas, they are equally efficacious. These mineral waters are contra-indicated in all classes of fevers, in acute inflammations generally; they are inapplicable to hæmorrhages, congestion of the brain, as well as all *organic* affections of the heart and of other viscera. The waters are administered as drinks, and externally as baths, general or partial; as lotions, fomentations, douches, enemas. The vapor baths are used externally and by inhalation. The alkaline sulphuretted mud is used externally by friction, anointing, and poulticing. It must be allowed, however, that the pleasing impressions of travel, separation from business, from long-continued effort, and from habitual cares; the pure bracing air of the Cordillera, the influence of hope and expectation of cure, separation from the depressing influences incident to remaining where disease originated and has long continued, regular exercise, methodic regimen, and rest, coöperate greatly in producing a successful result of the treatment by the internal and external use of these extraordinary mineral waters."

I have no comments to make on the long extract, the perusal of which may have been repaid for the time given to it, for it will have been perceived that professional men of the country are not insensible of the duty devolved on them of thoroughly investigating the qualities and effects of the valuable agent nature has placed in their midst doubtless for wise purposes. Corroborative testimony has reached me casually from several sources, of the wonderful efficacy of the Chillan Baths of the Cordillera.

After a night of as grateful repose as that of the peon at my chamber door, it was a pleasant sight at dawn next morning to see the boiling kettle offering up its vapory incense from a little adobe hearth ostentatiously built in the patio; a few fragments of charcoal, economically used in a country of not redundant fuel, sufficing to furnish coffee before commencing our last and most fatiguing day's journey to Tomé.

At 6 A. M. we left, with feelings akin to regret, this pretty town with pretty women, and a beautiful country bordered by magnificent mountains, like a bright jewel in a setting of gold, for the Nevada of Chillan, the pride of the Nublean Cordillera, gilded by the rising sun, was seen in the east rolling off the massive covering of morning clouds from its hoary brow, like a giant awaking from his slumbers; while the Coast Range in the west lifted its burnished crest proudly above its mountain foot, that rested on a carpet of verdure outspread beneath. Our direction was southwest over an avenue leading from the town, which was wide, level as a floor, and straight as an arrow for probably five miles. It was trenched on each side and embanked, serving the double purpose of draining the road in the rainy season, and protecting from intrusion at all times the fields of luxuriant vegetation that bordered the way. Every day's observation adds to the conviction that this great interior valley of Chile might be made the granary and the vineyard of South America, by the construction of improved modes of inter-communication, readier access to the soil by labor, and a superseding of the present rude modes of agriculture, the primitive plough, the reaping hook, the *trilla* (tread-mill), the winnowing by hand, and such antiquated procedures, by the subsoil plough, horse reaper, thresher, and fan, alternation of crops, and the many improved methods accessible to every people ambitious of agricultural excellence.

A rolling prairie followed the level avenue, and then the Chillan river, twelve miles from the city. Crossing this clear but moderate-sized stream, the road became rougher, and we soon began to ascend hills of sufficient height to indicate our near approach to the Coast Range, over which our route lay. Along this part of the road many ox-carts were overtaken, heavily laden with wool on the way to Tomé for exportation; and the poor oxen becoming stalled in the deep sand troughs of the outcropping hills, endured terrible inflictions of the goad from brutal carreteros.

At twenty miles from Chillan the postilion counselled us to take advantage of the last opportunity that would be presented for breakfast; so stopping at a roadside casa-posada, of by no means tempting exterior, our repast was ordered—"whatever they could give us." One dish was certain to be placed before us, according to the custom of the country; and that conviction was strengthened by the outspread red peppers sunning themselves in the yard, as if they were not sufficiently hot without the addition of solar caloric—a sight to make one wish himself near an ice-house. Very soon after, the chickens were heard screaming for help, but in vain, for the bowels of compassion were all on our side—they were speedily guillotined, and on the way to *casuela*, the favor being granted them of sitting in the pot on some of their own eggs, mixed with varied vegetables, of divers properties and abundant quantities. As if several hours' boiling did not suffice to make the compound sufficiently heating, an incendiary portion of the red-hot pepper known as *aji*, was added—the element and essence, sum and substance, of vegetable phlogiston; and well might the weird sister who superintended this decoction of caloric, as she threw in the last fiery ingredient, have exclaimed:

> "For a charm of powerful trouble,
> Like a hell-broth boil and bubble!

The casuela was at last *tabled*—not after the form of an obnoxious proposition in a deliberative assembly, but in all the "pomp and circumstance of glorious war" . . . upon human endurançe. What was to be done? Strive or starve? Fast or feast? Be consumed by hunger or by fire? The horns of the dilemma were before me, and suicide by either not being a venial crime, or an agreeable contemplation apart from moral considerations, I seized the alternative of the red-hot compound in one hand and cold water in the other, and proceeded in the experiment by the rapid application of water to fire in process of deglutition, to supply a natural want, and yet prevent an otherwise probable combustion. Though rashly undertaken it proved successful; and the inner man being thus fortified at least against freezing, we again took the road, and at twenty-seven miles from Chillan reached the Rio Itata, a clear, placid, and beautiful stream between two and three hundred yards wide, in places appearing to have considerable depth, which we crossed on a rudely-constructed raft of logs. This river rises in the Andes near the thirty-seventh parallel of latitude, and flowing in a northwest direction separates the provinces of Nuble and Conception, until it receives its principal affluent, the Rio Nuble; it then changes its course to the west by north, which it holds to the Pacific Ocean.

The Itata is the eleventh river we have crossed since leaving Santiago—to which the largest river in Chile, the Biobio, subsequently seen, may be added—the majority of them of large size and rapid current; and all of them *having their sources in the Andes, running westwardly through the Coast Range*, and emptying directly, or in some instances by a union of two, *into the Pacific Ocean.* To these might be added smaller streams, tributaries of the above, flowing in the same manner from the Andes westwardly toward the Pacific. It may well create surprise then to learn that Dr. J. J. Von Tschudi has stated—"Travels in Peru translated from the German by Thomasina Ross, London, 1847"—after remarking (page 292) that he will "call the *western chain the Cordillera,* or the coast mountains; and the *eastern chain the Andes,*" that (page 295) "I have in my last chapter observed that *the Cordillera* is the point of partition between the waters of the *Pacific and the Atlantic Oceans.* All the waters of the *eastern* declivity of the *Cordillera,* all those which have their source on the level heights, and on the *western* declivity *of the Andes,* flow from thence *in the direction of the east,* and work their way *through the eastern mountain chain.* Throughout the whole extent of South America there is *not a single instance of the Cordillera being intersected by a river.*"

Now, bearing in mind that Dr. Von Tschudi has premised that he denominates the *Coast Range* the Cordillera—(in which he differs from the natives)—and the emphatic manner in which he declares that it is *the partition between the waters of the Pacific and Atlantic,* and that there is "*not a single instance of its being intersected by a river,*" it may be supposed that my astonishment was great at finding *exactly the reverse the fact,* so far as relates to that large portion of interior Chile and its numerous rivers seen by me.

But for the prefatory sarcasm upon other authors by the translator of Dr. Von Tschudi's book, that he, "disclaiming any intention of making one of those travelling romances with which the tourist literature of the day is overstocked, has confined himself to a plain description of facts and things as they came within the sphere of his own knowledge," it would have been inferred from his general narrative, that he had *not been in Chile beyond Valparaiso,* and as very justly remarked by Lieut. Gilliss of the United States Navy, "had been prevented from seeing much beyond the range of hills surrounding its bay"—the *part,* sometimes described for the *whole,* by voyagers along the west coast. And so far from supposing that Dr. Von Tschudi designed to indulge in the *fiction or extravagant invention of statements,* in which "*romances*" consist rather than in the pleasing, fervid, and embellished style in which actual observations, and their incident trains of thought, are presented, it may be inferred from the general accuracy of his Peruvian descriptions, so far as I may judge, that his error in regard to the rivers of Chile resulted rather from some *inexplicable, though honest misapprehension of facts.*

Leaving the Itata River, we crossed a succession of outlying Coast Range hills, some of them rugged and steep, with intervening valleys partially cultivated, with but few houses deserving the name of human habitations—brush-built huts being the shelter in which the people burrowed; and when they were seen in clusters, reminding us of the "bush-meetings" often seen in our Southern States, when, after harvest, planters indulge the negroes in their preferred and favorite hard-working religious revivals, and fanciful mode of "getting good." These well ventilated dwellings may do for temporary occupancy in hot weather; but if the slaves of the States were compelled to live in them in winter as are these freemen of Chile, they would soon sigh for the cozy quarters and cotton comforts of the old plantation, and the quebradas would echo with their touching melody—

> "Oh! carry me back to old Virginia,
> To old Virginia's shore."

A small stream crossing our route showed the loose, glistening sand-shoals, indicative of gold diggings among adjacent hills, which subsequent information confirmed the existence of, but not of California richness. Eight or nine miles of very broken and but partially cultivated land, brought us to the foot of the *Cuesta Parales*, the chief *pass* by which the Pacific is reached at this part of the Coast Range. The elevation, although less than that of the Cuesta Prado west of Santiago, is yet so great as to make the ascent steep, tedious, and dangerous, the abrupt serpentine windings being overhung by threatening cliffs, and overlooking precipices frightful to the timid, and even startling to the bold. But the view from the summit repaid us for the toil and apprehension of the ascent. At our feet was spread out the vast expanse of hills and valleys, over which we had passed after leaving the Rio Itata, deeply scarred with ravines from mountain torrents, ribbed with bald ridges that had stood unchanged the tempests of unnumbered ages, and embellished in sheltered nooks by patches of verdure that lent their emerald charm even to the awful majesty of desolation. Beyond was the bright, the beautiful, the bountiful Eden of Chile. And in the far east, the waving outline of that transcendent Cordillera, which had been our "cloud by day and pillar of fire by night," whose mysterious power had swayed the heart and filled it with strange joy, wonder, awe, and an unchanging worship, in that it is the everlasting symbol of the incomprehensible sublimity of its Creator.

Changing horses, and also the snail's pace at which we had climbed to the top of the Cuesta, to a gait more suitable to the necessities of our long journey, we hurried along the summit road of about eighteen miles, smooth, nearly level, and much like the old national road over our Alleghany glade region. On each side of the way were many well-timbered and cultivated glens, and even the vine was seen in some places in luxuriant growth. On this upper summit road we saw several trains of pack mules, and counted two hundred and thirty-three ox-carts carrying produce and merchandise to and from Tomé, the sea, port of this region of the republic; wool in large quantities, wheat, and mosto, from the interior, and return loads of hard ware, groceries, and drygoods. How much better than this creeping carreta would be the more commodious wagon and powerful team, so long the mountain ship of the Alleghanies, and now of the far west sierras of North America? Sluggish oxen, pulling by the horns a miserable apology for a dray, mounted on a pair of wooden wheels that might be mistaken for the heads of flour barrels but for their thickness, flapping about like the wings of a surfeited condor, striving to fly without the power to lift its overloaded carcass, must give way to some more expeditious means of interior exchange of commodities, if Chile expects to profit by her extraordinary natural advantages.

Before coming to the western slope of the Coast Range we passed *Rafael*, a village of seventy or eighty houses, located in a picturesque little glen, looking like Oakland of the Maryland

Alleghany glades region, now being sought in summer by the residents of Southern States for its sequestered beauty and coolness. I remember well the clear atmosphere, invigorating air, and delicious sense of enjoyment of that retired mountain village of the once proud colony of Lord Baltimore, for they are linked with the enduring recollection of a man met there, shattered in health from the cares of State, and apprehensions of the departing glory of our country, and prepared to lay down his life for the perpetuity of its nationality, if the gathering storm which seemed to be threatening could thereby be allayed. His large perceptions, comprehensive knowledge, calm and analytic reason, clear judgment, moral courage, inflexible purpose, and resolute will, united with a winning earnestness and sincerity of manner, led to a belief that if events which seemed to be shaping a crisis in our history should bring about that calamity, and find him on the theatre of action, his great mind, pure heart, and just sense of right, would place him in the front of those who will do battle for the constitutional liberties of his race.

We now changed our course to the southwest, and a short distance beyond Rafael were compelled to leave at a wayside posada two of our horses, broken down by continuous travel. As the long shadows told of coming evening, we began the precipitous and dangerous descent of the mountain, which was done with such fearful speed that in an hour we reached Tomé at its foot, standing on the Bay of Concepcion, the largest and most secure harbor of Chile. Long before we reached the western declivity of the Coast Range, one of our drivers becoming uncontrollably exhilarated by aguardiente or chicha, which despite our necessary precautions he contrived to imbibe on the way, we considered that personal safety required that he should be degraded from his alternate post of postilion to that of exclusive horse-drover. His potations fitted him well for the vociferous occupation, and his yells and whoops caused the mountains to echo as if they were engaged in a drunken carnival. Thanks to the care and expertness of the other, our journey, ordinarily estimated to be four hundred miles, was accomplished without an accident; and, while we did not forget the golden gratuity received by him with a grateful surprise, showing that with such the peon's palm is not familiar, we gave him a written acknowledgment of his faithfulness and dexterity, that other travellers might avail of his good qualities, and he also be rewarded for his worth.

In, it might almost be said, our flight—so rapid was the descent of the Cuesta—occasional glimpses were caught of the ocean spread illimitably to the west; its rejoicing waves seeming to clap their hands, and greet with welcome the messengers who brought with them tidings of their great brothers of the Cordillera, awhile before seen by us lifting their proud heads for the wreaths of clouds woven in the busy loom of the Pacific, and borne to them on "the wings of the wind."

## CHAPTER XVIII.

TOMÉ—TALCAHUANO—BAY OF CONCEPCION—BAY OF VINCENTE—PAPS OF BIOBIO—RIVER BIOBIO—SIERRA VELLUDA—VOLCANO OF ANTUCO—CITY OF CONCEPCION—COAL MINES OF CHAMBIQUE, LOTILLA, AND LOTA—PENCO.

Tomé, in latitude 36° 40′ S., is situated at the foot of the Coast Range of mountains, on the northeast shore of the Bay of Concepcion, which shall be described hereafter, and four miles to the east of its main entrance. This flourishing little seaport contains four thousand inhabitants, a few neat among many indifferently built houses, and several *bodegas*—large warehouses—for the storage of wheat, wool, and wine, the principal products of the neighboring rich provinces of Concepcion and Nublé, brought here for exportation. Flour, manufactured in the vicinity, also enters largely into the exportation of Tomé. Here, too, are received large importations of foreign merchandise for the interior, particularly for the provinces above named, and for the southern departments of the province of Maulé. For purposes of general commerce Tomé is the chief seaport of this part of Chile, both from the ready access to it from the ocean, and from its intimate interior relations, while *Talcahuano* at the southwest part of the same bay is a greater resort for whaling vessels, in consequence of the greater facility afforded by its tranquil waters for the transshipment of oil, and for refitting. The former of these towns is increasing in size and importance; while the latter, long the favorite resort of mariners, seems to be on the decline; its streets, when we crossed the bay ten miles to it the day after our arrival at Tomé, presenting a deserted appearance, and none of the commercial activity that characterized its bustling little neighbor.

A small plaza, a fountain, and alameda, and a pantheon which has a semblance of Christian charity, in that it tolerates a Protestant cemetery in its neighborhood, with a ceaseless clatter of cracked church bells faithfully pummelled with stones by noisy religionists; these seem to put forth a quasi pretension to superiority for Talcahuano over its ambitious and enterprising little neighbor Tomé.

But to observing foreigners it is apparent that unless a greater degree of stability is secured in the administration of the Government of Chile; unless the perpetually recurring outbreaks of revolution can be prevented, and greater attention be given by public functionaries to the cultivation of the arts of peace, and to the development of natural resources; and further, unless there shall be effected a permanent good understanding with the neighboring warlike Indians, who have defied the power of the republic as they did that of Spain, and who effectually paralyze the hand of agricultural industry and mining enterprise to the south of the Biobio River, closing, too, avenues whereby Talcahuano and Concepcion, of which the former is the natural seaport, are cut off from interior trade; unless these desirable results can be secured no prospect of commercial resuscitation can dawn upon this declining city; no chance be afforded of its profiting by the advantage it possesses in its safe and capacious harbor, over every other seaport of the republic except Tomé, on the same magnificent bay.

With some friends in Talcahuano a visit was made to adjacent heights, to obtain a view of surrounding points of interest. The range of hills to the west of the town stretch northward, forming the peninsula bounding the Bay of Concepcion on the west, and terminate at the distance of seven miles, in *Tumbes Point.* The most elevated of the hills is called *Sentinela*, from three hundred to four hundred feet high, situated at the base of the peninsula, and was formerly occupied by the old Spanish fortification, "Castilla"—which commanded the harbor and city of Talcahuano; and with the circumvallation bristling with cannon stretching across the foot of the hill behind the city, from the *moro* on Concepcion Bay across to the Bay of San Vincente to the south, commanded also the entire land approach to the city, as well as the Bay of San Vincente itself. This was the fortification to which the Spanish General Osorio made his escape with only one hundred of his followers, after his disastrous defeat at the battle of Maipú, before spoken of; and where he remained until the following September, 1818, when he destroyed the fortifications and sailed for Callao with the men-o'-war and merchantmen in port, and all the royalist families of this province who could raise money to accompany him, the prospect of maintaining the Spanish power in this part of Chile being considered hopeless. But two places were thus left unsurrendered to the Republicans; these were Valdivia and Chiloe in the extreme south, which were captured in 1820, freeing the country entirely from Spanish possession, with no probability that its reconquest would ever again be attempted.

From the Sentinela may be seen to the east and below, the irregularly oval Bay of Concepcion, ten miles long and seven wide, and a depth of water and capacity sufficient to accommodate the entire naval and commercial marine of the republic, where, and where alone in Chile, if the entrances were properly fortified, they would be safe from capture by a stronger maritime power. The town of Talcahuano is on the southwest shore of the bay; Tomé on its northeast; Penco and Lirquen on its southeast; and the island of Quiriquina, three miles long and one wide, like a natural breakwater, protects it on the northwest toward the ocean, leaving two entrances, one between the north end of the island and the main land, the chief passage about three miles wide, and a smaller one a mile wide, between the south end of the island and Tumbes Point, the extremity of the peninsula bounding the bay to the west. To the south of Sentinela, beyond the little Bay of San Vincente at its foot, may be seen from that height those two mamillary eminences called the Paps of Biobio, nearly one thousand feet high, which form the remarkable and well known landmarks to mariners on this coast; and south of these the mouth of the Biobio, the largest river of Chile, navigable for steamers of fourteen inches draught a distance of one hundred and twenty miles. From thirty to thirty-five miles further off in the same direction, the island of Santa Maria is visible protecting the Bay of Arauco, on the shores of which are the towns of Coronel, Playa Negra, Playa Blanco, Lotilla, and Lota, all famous for the inexhaustible supplies of bituminous coal in their immediate vicinities, and from which large quantities are shipped; an article of vast value to Chile, for without it the steam marine of this coast would become oppressively costly, the copper interest languish, and furnaces cease to realize to their proprietors the immense wealth contributing largely to the general welfare. Still further off stands Arauco, one of the earliest colonial settlements, now, as then, contributing to hold in check the aggressive and revengeful spirit of the unconquered aborigines. Following the windings of the Biobio River to the eastward, as seen from the Sentinela, the eye rests on the white walls and waving alamos of *Concepcion*, deemed immaculate by its boastful citizens, with the village of San Pedro on the opposite bank. And away in the dim distance in the same direction the Sierra Velluda was observed lifting its snow-clad summit above the horizon, with its less lofty but fiery consort of Antuco at its side. Active as the latter is known to be, the sentinel from this natural watch-tower might be pardoned for attributing possible ocular illusions at so great a distance to volcanic phenomena; and unwonted refractions of light to reflections from the mirrored surface of the picturesque lake, which, in its fearful sport, that volcano has formed to cool its burning sides. It is known that the volcano of Antuco within a recent period poured out a flood of fire which crossed the bed of the River Laja; and by congelation this lava walled in the river, forming thus by the accumulated waters a lake, which, I am informed by Col. Blakey, the intelligent United States Consul at Talcahuano, who visited it in December, 1859, now covers an extent of surface twenty-one miles long by from two to six miles wide, forming in adjacent valleys miniature bays, and insulating smaller detached summits, making of them islets covered with verdure, the resorts of innumerable water-fowl. It is not without reason that the inhabitants of the province through which the river runs into which this stream formerly flowed, are apprehensive that the dam of lava, deep and wide as it is described to be, may give way from enormous pressure, or from slower but not less certain causes, and overflow the country in its course, producing great destruction of life and property. For scarcely a quarter of a century has passed since a flood of the Cachapoal River, separating the provinces of Santiago and Colchagua, was attended with such results in the month of December—the summer of this region—when there had been no rain to account for it. And the Government of Chile sent an able engineer, Señor Condarco, to investigate the cause of so extraordinary an occurrence; who, after a diligent prosecution of his labors in the Andes, finally discovered that the natural embankments of a mountain lake had given way, from the great accumulation of water incident to an unusual thaw, and sent down the torrent that laid waste the country below.

Our enjoyment of the outspread magnificence of sea and land was interrupted by the notice that friends, who had preceded us to the *hacienda de Tumbes* at the northern point of the peninsula, were delaying breakfast for us. A bracing ride along the undulating ridge in the early morning air, with the sunny bay gleaming in silvery ripples that danced in very joy of the balmy breeze that kissed their dimples, on our right; and the broad ocean, breaking its blue swells to bathe the rocky shore in showers of foam, on our left, soon brought us to our destination. Although the mansion of the hacienda had not been occupied for some time by its owners, we were not long in perceiving that where the will exists Chilenas have a ready, pleasant, and effective way of extending hospitalities. From this new standpoint we soon discovered that, although some objects of interest that had contributed to recent gratification were unseen, yet we were repaid for their loss by the sight of others; and among these we recognized one of the majestic mountains of the Cordillera, for days an object of admiration and wonder while descending the great valley, inspiring a feeling akin to reverence in the memories of the past; and now again seen, looming above and beyond the Coast Range to the east-northeast, with his snowy cowl drawn over his head, as he lifted it proudly and peerless above other gigantic monuments of surrounding nature. I had almost touched the hem of the glittering garment of the Nevada de Chillan; and now that his bold lineaments were again beheld even at the distance of one hundred and forty miles, I longed to lay the tribute of adoration on the shrine of such unchanging grandeur.

A summons to the morning meal dispelled the pleasant retrospection, and approaching the antique, tile-roofed, Spanish mansion, looking down on the thatched reed outhouses, as superciliously as a proud old Castilian or a modern upstart pretender, we found the repast tastefully spread—as only these *Caucasian* señoritas understand the art of—under a *ramada* or temporary portico, erected for the occasion, to give us the interest and comfort of out-of-door scene and air. It was built of *olivilla* and *mardoña* rustic posts, supporting similar rafters; and roofed, and walled on the exposed side, to shelter us from the sun, with twined and thatched *Chiquen* and *Avillana* branches and leaves. *Casuela*, the first dish of a Chilean breakfast, soon tempted with its savory and provoking aroma a saucy appetite; but I had over-estimated my ability of endurance when I hastily sought to appease it; for the first appropriation of the liquid flame to the wants of the inner man, while it brought a practical illustration of the "fire that is not quenched," brought also tears to my eyes. And when a mischievous señorita on the opposite side of the table, observing my internal combustion, wickedly tendered me an additional portion of the accursed *aji* to season the broth "*more to my taste*," I thought of the streams of lava consuming Antuco, and the lake of icy waters he had gathered for their extinguishment, and felt a sympathy coming of realization of fiery affliction. A repetition of the indiscretion was not indulged in, and it was a source of joy when the cause of torture was removed, and a dish of *mote con leche*—husked wheat boiled in milk—came to soothe with its demulcent properties my blistered throat. This reinstated confidence, and with becoming gusto a bumper of Champagne prepared the way for an unequalled *mouton*, served by the peon cook upon a natural spit of *maqui*. And that we might not slight any appendage of this extraordinary quadruped, his feet fried in butter with flour and eggs, were next grandiloquently trotted on the table as *Patitas de Cordero*. Duly disposed of, with suitable contributions of vegetables, unequalled bread, and alfalfa butter fresh from the churn, strawberries next appeared, nearly white, being but slightly blushed on the sunny side, with minute purplish seed sprinkled like beauty spots over the surface, and weighing *eight to the pound!* That number quartered filled the largest-sized dessert plate, and, smothered in cream, was a repast of itself befitting surrounding scenery. The flavor of the Chile strawberry is perhaps a shade less rich than the best of our garden cultivation. But while you may talk of biting a cherry to express infinitesimal division if you choose, do not borrow the hacienda dė Tumbes strawberry the size of a hen's egg, for your figure of speech to a Chileno; unless you design to have your knowledge of natural products impeached, and your metaphors ridiculed for their absurdity. Coffee followed, of Bolivian growth and flavor —the best in the world—and then the curling smoke of the cigarito threw its oblivious influence around to mar or make a further joy, as might be determined by natural or perverted taste. Fearing, shortly afterwards, from certain significant signs, a purpose to "kill us with kindness," the stranger guests took leave of new made Talcahuano friends, and we literally "vamos'd the ranche."

The city of *Concepcion*, the capital of the Province of the same name, is but nine miles southeast by east from Talcahuano, the road between them lying over a nearly level sandy plain, with the Bay of Concepcion on its north side, and the river Biobio on the south, the distance between these latter being about five miles; the road crossing this isthmus in a diagonal direction, to reach the city of Concepcion, which does not lie on the bay as might be supposed by its name, but upon the north bank of the Biobio from six to seven miles from its mouth. The location of Concepcion on the largest river of Chile, and so near to the ocean, might lead you to the belief that it is an important seaport; but that river, although navigable for light-draught boats to a greater distance, is obstructed by sand-bars at and within its mouth, rendering it impracticable for navigation of large vessels; and hence Concepcion is without foreign commerce, and dependent on Talcahuano as a port of entry. Its imports and exports are carried, by the slow conveyances of the country already described, across a nearly level plain admirably adapted for a railroad; and on which one would be built in six weeks in North America under the pressure of a like necessity.

The population of Concepcion is estimated at from twelve to fifteen thousand. It is difficult to obtain satisfactory information on this point anywhere in South America; as well from the unreliable basis of the census, as is the case in these countries where ignorance conceals the truth from fear of some ulterior design by government officials, as from the fact that whatever statements are published often embrace the population of the department with that of its chief town. The streets are regular, wider than in any other city of Chile, most of them well paved, raised in the middle, with side gutters, and with good sidewalks of brick or board. A handsome plaza adorns the city, on which is erected a splendid mausoleum to a lost fountain, or perhaps to commemorate one that was *never found.* It consists of a bronze fluted Corinthian column with classic capital, upon a pedestal supported by four colossal mermaids, trying certainly very ineffectually to blow limpid streams from sea-shells held to the mouth; the whole being surmounted by a statue of Ceres, with sheaf and sickle, emblematic of the agricultural character of the province. Its height is nearly fifty feet; it was cast at Munich, and is a creditable monument of the taste and liberality of the municipality; although it cannot be denied that its cost appropriated to the introduction of pure water, would contribute more to the health and comfort of the inhabitants. On one side of the plaza stands a large cathedral, unfinished of course, and has been for one fourth of a century. Jolly priests, with "fat capon lined," might become less demonstrative of good living, if churches had expended upon them the liberal bequests designed for their completion. Doubtless the unction is laid to the clerical soul that omniscience knows and approves the pious offerings, but is indifferent to the application, needing neither decorated arch nor columned portico to perfect His glory; and hence his servants, the administrators of the trust, are excusable for diverting them to their own creature comforts. The traveller through South America is often guilty of the sin of believing that if there were not so many priests, there would be more and better religionists; fewer saints, fewer sinners; not so much selfishness and sensuality behind the altar, more charity and spirituality before it. On the opposite side of the plaza to the cathedral stands the Intendencia, a capacious and handsome government house in process of completion. On a third side the extensive *portales*—arcades—of General Cruz, the favorite citizen of Southern Chile, and nine years since the nearly successful leader of the revolutionary party in overthrowing the Government. The fourth side is occupied by shops, plain, but neat and cleanly, as are most of the houses in the centre of the city; while the precincts, like those of all Spanish American towns, present with their reed, brush, and mud hovels, and tattered and half-naked populace, a repugnant spectacle of squalid poverty and filth.

In passing the *Casas de Ejercicios* to-day, I remembered that I had not noted these *houses of spiritual penance*, to be found in all considerable communities in this country. The clergy, who no doubt are in position to know full well the extent of prevalent wickedness, not only think it necessary that such establishments should exist, where sinful flesh shall self-inflict punishment by stripes, pinchings, hair jackets, hard beds, hard fare, and no fare at all, for moral delinquencies; but also, that it shall be made to *pay stated fees* according to possession of worldly wealth, for the privilege of this exorcism of evil, under proper physical instruction, in authorized institutions. Strange as it may appear to rational minds, these *religious penitentiaries* are sought by crowds of pious sinners, during the season of Lent especially; who abandon for nine days their homes, and all the obligations of domestic duty, to engage in a system of self-castigation, laceration, and deprivation, which accomplishes nothing more than the lifting of one load of conscious wickedness from their souls, that they may the better bear that which is in contemplation for the future.

Besides a beautiful drive, promenade, private gardens, and shade trees, Concepcion has in its flourishing college and excellent academies, ornaments of still higher merit. In no part of Chile does the literary education of young ladies receive more attention.

This city is built in the valley of Mocha under a spur of the Coast Range of mountains; but, for the sake of more desirable elevation, as well as for the convenience of deeper water on the Biobio, it would have been better placed on a higher plateau a little west of its present site; where it would also have been nearer to the Bay of Conception, and to that of San Vincente. With extensive and fertile provinces surrounding it, abounding in mineral and agricultural wealth beyond the pretensions of any other part of Chile—for immense coal-fields are located but a few miles south, and millions of acres of virgin soil in its vicinity await but their redemption from Araucanian control and the stretching forth the hand of industry to yield rich productions of labor—with mountains of metallic treasure still acknowledging savage sway, and an unused water power ample for large manufacturing enterprise; what but the fostering and protecting care of Government, the energy and industry of its own citizens, and capital, and foreign skill, are wanted, to make Concepcion what it is designed by nature to be, the great city of the Republic, and its commercial, if not its political emporium? And especially would this destiny become realized, if, as sound national policy dictates, the Southern Railroad now in progress down the great valley should be continued to this point, affording an outlet for its great productions, and means of obtaining with facility for the undeveloped interior the improved implements, machinery, labor, instruction, and example of emigrants from countries that have the lead of Chile in the arts of civilized life.

The following facts relating to the coal mines in this vicinity, will give some idea of the importance of Concepcion as a commercial and manufacturing point. Lota is situated on the northeast side of Arauco Bay, which is about twenty miles wide, an inlet of the Pacific Ocean but little south of the mouth of the Biobio River. On this bay are situated also Lotilla, Chambique, Colcura, and some other towns.

The principal coal mines now (1861) being worked are Chambique and Lotilla, the yearly products from which are about 72,000 tons, and increasing; and it is thought by many that the quality is fully equal to the English coal, as it burns with great freedom, and generates steam rapidly. The coals from these mines supply the English and other steamers on this coast, and are also shipped to the ports of Coquimbo, Huasco, Caldera, Chaneral, &c., for the smelting of copper ores. They are also exported to Peru and California. The price at the mines is $5.50 to $6 per ton delivered on board vessels. The company has built an iron mole three hundred feet in length, at the end of which is a drop from which car-loads of two and a half tons each can be lowered into vessels moored there. Vessels of twelve hundred tons have been thus loaded in two days. In addition to this improvement, a steam crane is used for discharging copper ore, and for the shipment of fire-bricks.

There is also an establishment for the manufacture of fire-brick, the clay being obtained in the mines, from which 30,000 are said to be turned out per week, at $30 per thousand delivered on shipboard. They are considered superior to the English fire-brick, and supply the northern parts of Chile, and also Peru. A smelting establishment with five furnaces is also in operation here, and it is the intention of the company to erect others. The copper ore is brought from the northern ports in return for shipments of coal.

Carboncillo (small coal) is used in the smelting, refining, &c., of ores, and for the manufacture of brick. Coal is found at these mines from one hundred and five to one hundred and twenty yards below the surface. At the Lota mine the tunnel is two hundred and seventy yards long. The Chambique coal is raised from below by a steam engine, and being deposited in cars they are drawn by horse power to the seashore.

The mining company has also an extensive machine foundry, blacksmith and other shops, where all necessary castings are made. There are six hundred employés in the various departments.

Although the Lota coal makes more smoke, it will raise steam in shorter time than English coal.

There is a vein of superior fire-brick clay about four feet in thickness under the vein of coal. The principal mine is that of Lotilla; in it there are three seams of coal now being worked: the first is fifty yards beneath the surface, with a thickness of four feet; the second, forty yards lower, averaging two feet ten inches; the third, nine yards deeper, is four feet ten inches thick, under which is found the fire-clay. The dip of the vein is westerly seven inches to the yard. About thirty inches above the third vein is found a bed of fossils, as regular as the vein of coal itself. These coal fields are very extensive, and it is estimated that at the present rate of working, seventy years will be required to exhaust them. There are several other mines of less extent and value. Colcura is about one league west from Lota; formerly flour was manufactured and shipped from this place. Timber is abundant in its vicinity. It is situated at the foot of the Cerro Villa Gran, well known as the scene of a fierce battle between the Spanish invaders under General Villa Gran, and the unconquered Araucanian Indians, who still maintain their freedom in this vicinity, despite the arts of diplomacy and the power of their enemies.

The location of Concepcion it is reasonable to presume will eventually invite trade; its climate is very salubrious, but like many other cities of Chile it has suffered greatly from earthquakes. That of 1835, which shook Talcahuano nearly to pieces, three immense sea-waves washing away what the trembling earth had spared, also laid Concepcion in ruins. And Penco, seven miles off on the southeast shore of the bay, over whose unhappy people the arm of the destroying angel seems ever to have been outstretched, was at the same time crumbled into dust. We rode over to see the remains of this town, once the pride of the Spaniards, from the fine harbor on which it stood, and its neighboring gold washings. It was founded by Pedro Valdivia in 1550, and at *that time called Concepcion*, which name it retained through all its vicissitudes of fortune *until* 1764, when it was *transferred* to the present city of Concepcion on the Biobio, already described, which *was then founded. Penco*, as I shall, to avoid confusion of terms, call the town first founded by Valdivia under a different name, is as before stated on the southeast shore of the Bay of Concepcion, near the mouth of the little river Andalien, on the southeast shore of the Bay of Concepcion, and consists at present of about one hundred and fifty adobe houses and reed huts, with several bodegas for storage of wool and wheat brought from the adjacent country for exportation. With the exception of the old fortress, which has chiselled upon two of its faces, with the arms of Castile, the numbers 1686 and 1687, indicative it is presumed of the periods of its commencement and completion, and the stone walls of which—from five to ten feet thick—are gradually disappearing to be used in other structures, rather than from natural causes or terrestrial phenomena; we looked in vain for the "ruins" and the "fallen walls of temples and fortifications," so graphically described by a distinguished fellow-countryman in 1854. *What he saw* has been correctly and instructively presented, to the extent reasonably to be expected of a stranger whose opportunities are usually somewhat restricted. But in reference to these "ruins," as in some other matters about which from failure to examine for himself he has relied upon the statements of others, he was greatly misled. The only "ruins" we could find were those of brush huts, undeniably passing away with tolerable speed; and the probability is that by next month the place that knows them now "will know them no more forever." And as to the "temples," "fallen" or standing, they certainly escaped the scrutinizing search of four Americans, two of them Californians, who "prospected" Penco through and around for relics of the past. I remember to have read this poetic description of the ruins of old Concepcion to which I refer, with profound interest at the time of its publication, and felt badly treated when the illusion was dispelled, and the fact was realized that Penco would not disinter some mournful mementos with which to repay the long pent-up sympathy in her behalf.

But although the proofs are not seen, having been crumbled into dust, washed away by the inundating wave, or appropriated to recent building purposes, Penco has been peculiarly a victim of desolation. Having been abandoned by Villa Gran in 1554, after his terrible defeat at Marigueno, it was burnt by the victorious Araucanians. Rebuilt by the Spaniards in 1555, it was shortly after captured by the young but formidable Indian chief Lautero, then only nineteen years old, who put to death the inhabitants and again destroyed the town. Lautero was the young

Araucanian, who, we are told, when but sixteen years of age, rallied his flying countrymen at the battle of Tucapel, changed a defeat into a victory, and made a prisoner of Valdivia, who commanded the Spaniards. An Indian Ulmen, high in authority, having no confidence in the peaceful protestations of Valdivia for the future, despatched him with his war-club, and thus terminated the life of this extraordinary man, who had with a mere handful of soldiers penetrated the heart of Chile for more than one thousand miles, overcoming the resistance of the natives and natural obstacles at every step of his progress; and having added a vast empire to Spain, had at last his triumphant career suddenly brought to a close through the agency of an Indian boy taught to believe that life was valueless without liberty, and who set an example of heroism to his faltering countrymen that made them invincible even by the before unconquered Spaniard. The deeds of the young chieftain Lautero were shortly afterwards visited with terrible retribution. While encamped on the banks of the Rio Claro on his way to assault Santiago, he was attacked by Francisco de Villa Gran, whom he had previously defeated at Marigueno, and slain, with every man of the six hundred Araucanians composing his army.

Penco was in 1557 rebuilt by Garcia de Mendoza, and fortified so strongly as to resist an Indian siege of fifty days. But after the defeat of Loyola its governor (nephew of the founder of the order of Jesuits) when on his return from a visit to the interior in 1598, the Araucanians again succeeded in capturing and destroying it. Again rebuilt, it was in 1730 swept away by earthquake and inundation. And once more restored by the Spaniards, it was doomed to another destruction by earthquake in 1751; the inhabitants flying for safety to the neighboring hills in time to avoid death from the inrolling sea, which washed off with its retiring wave every vestige of habitation. For thirteen years the inhabitants remained undecided in purpose, and finally the majority of them resolved upon building the present city of Concepcion seven miles off, on the Biobio River, in what they considered a more secure place at least from the ocean wave. A few of the people, with affections still clinging to the scene of former varied fortunes, ventured to construct temporary habitations, thus perpetuating the geographical identity of a spot distinguished by extraordinary vicissitudes of fortune.

About three miles to the north of Penco is the fisherman's village of Lirquen, occupying a wide-mouthed quebrada. A flour mill near by gives employment to a busily-disposed little stream, that comes tumbling headlong down the valley as if eagar for occupation.

The number of vessels arriving at the ports on the Bay of Concepcion, viz., Tomé, Talcahuano, Penco, and Lirquen, for one year, ending 1st April, 1860, was four hundred and forty-two; of which two hundred and twenty-eight were foreign ships. Having described the surroundings of this fine bay, I now glide over its placid bosom, with my face turned toward my native land: which, however rich the resources of this lovely Chile; however blest in its physical advantages by the Hand of a Beneficent Creator; however beautiful its valleys, sublime its mountains, fertile its plains, numerous and enriching its rivers, bounteous its minerals, salubrious its climate, diversified its scenery; however calculated to charm, still cannot draw affections from that northern home! For is it not a land of civil liberty, political equality, and religious toleration? Without the blessings of which what are soil and scenery? What were hills even of silver, or mountains of gold?

## CHAPTER XIX.

VOYAGE COASTWISE NORTHWARD—CONSTITUCION—COPPER PRODUCT OF CHILE—SAILING VESSEL TO CALLAO NOT AS RELIABLE AS STEAMER TO PAITA—GULF OF GUAYAQUIL TO TUMBES.

Aboard of the staunch American steamer "*Biobio*"—Commander George N. Rogers—we stood through the principal entrance of the bay to the north-northwest, between Quiriquina Island and Loberia Head, and shortly after changed our course due north, and passed Cullin Point and Coliumo Head, the coast trending first a short distance east, then south, and then returning on itself to form the small Bay of Coliumo, which affords secure shelter for coasters in heavy southwesters. It is back of this bay that the coal strata of Chile are first seen, which stretch to the south as far as the Island of Chiloe, upwards of three hundred miles.

From Coliumo Bay, for fifty-six miles north to Cape Carranza, and even to the mouth of the Itata River, the shore line is high and partially wooded. Off Cape Carranza the rock is found, about three-fourths of a mile from shore, on which the Chilean war-steamer was wrecked in 1856 with a loss of four hundred lives. Seventeen miles further north, in latitude 35° 20′, close in shore is a rock of imposing size, from its Gothic appearance known as La Iglesia—the church—an opening like a doorway of corresponding architecture, contributing to the resemblance. And from half to one mile beyond are two pyramidal rocky masses, the one named Las Ventanas, from its window-like openings, the other Piedra Lobos—being the resort of seals; they mark the mouth of the River Maulé. The Cerro Mutün on the south bank of the river recedes in such a manner near its mouth, as to enclose a semicircular plain on which stands the town of *Constitucion*, often provincially called Maulé, from the river. Constitucion has three thousand inhabitants, a dirty plaza, unfinished cathedral, indifferent one-story houses, bodegas, and ordinary corporate buildings. It enjoys the trade of the largest portion of the Provinces of Talca and Maulé; but until greater enterprise, industry, skill, and capital are brought to the development of these fine portions of the republic; until the natives seek to put to better account the long neglected gifts of nature, and Government renders more accessible and safe this harbor, Constitucion cannot reap the great advantages its relative position as a natural entrepot would give it. From Constitucion north the boldness of the coast diminishes until near Algaroba Point, when it becomes cliffy with high land in the neighborhood. About Curauma Head are high cliffs also, and beyond it the land rises steeply to the ranges of that name; in the distance, if the weather be clear, the Campana (bell) de Quillota, six thousand two hundred feet, being seen; and even the far-off Andes may sometimes be discerned, with the majestic Aconcagua in surpassing altitude. A few miles past the heights of Curauma is Curaumilla Point, and seven miles further Valparaiso Point bounds the bay of that name, two hundred and fifty miles from Talcahuano, making an aggregate of three thousand miles of the Pacific shore of South America from Panama to the Bay of Arauco; all of which, and even further south, is traversed by a continuous line of British steamers. The only opposition is on the short route from Valparaiso to Arauco Bay, by the North American steamer Biobio, Capt. Rogers, a thorough seaman and familiar with the navigation and interests of this coast. What will be the result of individual competition on a partial route with a wealthy corporation that aims at monopoly, and a connected line to support it, must depend on the disposition of those interested in trade to maintain it at remunerative rates of passage and freight, rather than patronize one which, whatever liberality it may show when constrained by opposition, is sure to recognize in them only contributors to its oppressive exactions whenever it shall be in position to exercise exclusive control.

One of the most valuable products of Chile is copper. It may be useful to give the substance of information derived from one thoroughly conversant with the subject, in reference to the extraordinary richness of Chile in this metal. The following table will show the exports in a given period of the various forms of bars, regulus, and ore:

STATEMENT (*in copper and contents*) *of the Exports of Copper Bars, Regulus, and Ores, from Chile, from* 1848 *to* 1857, *inclusive.*

**Tons of 22 quintals.**

| | 1848. | | | | 1849. | | | |
|---|---|---|---|---|---|---|---|---|
| | Bars. | Regulus. | Ores. | Total. | Bars. | Regulus. | Ores. | Total. |
| England,......... | 1590 | 1193 | 654 | 3437 | 3087 | 1406 | 314 | 4812 |
| United States,..... | 2780 | 887 | 75 | 3742 | 3938 | 185 | 225 | 4348 |
| France,........... | 1532 | 3 | .. | 1535 | 741 | .. | .. | 741 |
| Germany,......... | 27 | 234 | 172 | 433 | 112 | 27 | 154 | 293 |
| | 5929 | 2317 | 901 | 9147 | 7878 | 1618 | 698 | 10194 |

| | 1850. | | | | 1851. | | | |
|---|---|---|---|---|---|---|---|---|
| | Bars. | Regulus. | Ores. | Total. | Bars. | Regulus. | Ores. | Total |
| England,......... | 3247 | 2570 | 389 | 6206 | 2865 | 1219 | 374 | 3758 |
| United States,..... | 4256 | 263 | 100 | 4619 | 3552 | 355 | 143 | 4050 |
| France, .......... | 833 | .. | .. | 833 | 59 | .. | .. | 59 |
| Germany,......... | 300 | 119 | 1 | 420 | 99 | 202 | 33 | 334 |
| | 8636 | 2952 | 490 | 12078 | 5775 | 1776 | 550 | 8101 |

| | 1852. | | | | 1853. | | | |
|---|---|---|---|---|---|---|---|---|
| | Bars. | Regulus. | Ores. | Total. | Bars. | Regulus. | Ores. | Total. |
| England,......... | 3215 | 3112 | 1468 | 7795 | 714 | 2080 | 2158 | 4952 |
| United States,..... | 5753 | 435 | 531 | 6719 | 4184 | 531 | 1213 | 5928 |
| France, .......... | 103 | .. | .. | 103 | 98 | .. | .. | 98 |
| Germany,......... | 459 | 409 | 159 | 1027 | 754 | 302 | 178 | 1234 |
| | 9530 | 3956 | 2158 | 15644 | 5750 | 2913 | 3549 | 12212 |

| | 1854. | | | | 1855. | | | |
|---|---|---|---|---|---|---|---|---|
| | Bars. | Regulus. | Ores. | Total. | Bars. | Regulus. | Ores. | Total. |
| England,......... | 1987 | 2819 | 3269 | 8075 | 4419 | 6255 | 3439 | 14113 |
| United States,..... | 4589 | 426 | 670 | 5683 | 2207 | 127 | 1045 | 3379 |
| France, .......... | 962 | .. | .. | 962 | 972 | 27 | .. | 999 |
| Germany,......... | 282 | 688 | 107 | 1077 | 611 | 545 | 633 | 1759 |
| | 7818 | 3933 | 4046 | 15797 | 8209 | 6954 | 5087 | 20250 |

| | 1856. | | | | 1857. | | | |
|---|---|---|---|---|---|---|---|---|
| | Bars. | Regulus. | Ores. | Total. | Bars. | Regulus. | Ores. | Total. |
| England,......... | 986 | 7964 | 3864 | 12814 | 2133 | 10976 | 4138 | 17247 |
| United States,..... | 3684 | 1775 | 1151 | 6610 | 1995 | 1517 | 1286 | 4798 |
| France, .......... | 1431 | 112 | 131 | 1874 | 1566 | 62 | 28 | 1656 |
| Germany, ........ | 124 | 133 | 583 | 840 | 322 | 943 | 540 | 1805 |
| | 6225 | 9984 | 5729 | 2938 | 6016 | 13498 | 5984 | 25498 |

N. B.—In the above statement *bars* are considered as *fine copper*, *regulus* as *half copper*, and *ores* as such, of unspecified richness.

The *exports* from Chile for 1858, and the first nine months of 1859, collected from authentic sources, were, to wit:

| | Quintals. | | Quintals. |
|---|---|---|---|
| Regulus, 1858,........... | 427,662 | Giving fine copper, | 215,757 |
| " To Sept., 1859,.. | 279,842 | " " | 136,217 |
| Total,.............. | 707,504 | Total copper contents, | 351,974 |

Or about 50 per cent. for the average ley.

| | Quintals. | | Quintals. |
|---|---|---|---|
| Ores, 1858,............. | 1,013,216 | Giving fine copper, | 220,443 |
| " To Sept., 1859,.... | 515,122 | " " | 136,605 |

Or about 22 per cent. for the average ley.

Of the whole imports of copper into England in 1858, it is satisfactorily ascertained from Parliamentary returns of that year, that Chile supplied 56 per cent.

In estimating the effect of the copper production of this part of the world upon the copper interests of commerce at large, it must be stated that Bolivia, adjoining Chile, exports copper largely, which for all business purposes is the same as if it was sent from Chile, for it is chiefly produced by Chile enterprise; that is, by labor and capital of people living in Chile, either natives or foreigners. Hence the importance of considering Chile as a copper producing country, in all interested calculations relative to this article. If all the exports of Bolivia and Chile were sent to England, which is admittedly the great copper market of the world, they would compose 70 per cent. of her entire imports; and including her own production and that of Ireland, with that of the rest of the world, the importation from Chile and Bolivia would amount *to one-half of all, both imported and produced.* The truth is that, with copper riches perfectly fabulous, Chile has been too much overlooked by commercial statisticians. There is *one mine alone* in the Province of Coquimbo (Tamayo), belonging to a private individual, which produces annually more than six times the entire imports of copper into England from Spain; and nearly as much as the imports into England from Australia and Cuba put together. Yet this mine has not been publicly noticed; nor has that either in the north of Atacama recently discovered, and belonging to another private individual, which yields as much copper annually (7,000 tons) as is imported into England from Spain and *all other countries*, except Australia and Cuba. *These two Chile mines together produce as much copper as is imported into England from every other country in the world, except Chile herself!*

But in estimating the importance of the Chile supply, it must be remembered that she exports largely to other countries as well as England, which influences the English market in two ways: first, by finding its way into England *indirectly*, but being credited to the country whence it last came; and secondly, England, being the great copper market, whatever supplies Chile sends direct to other countries diminishes by so much the demand of those countries in England.

The exact exports of copper produced by Chile and Bolivia in 1858, were:

| | Quintals. | | Quintals. | | Tons. | |
|---|---|---|---|---|---|---|
| Bar Copper,............ | 189,181 | containing | 183,610 | or | 8,346 | Pure Copper. |
| Regulus,............... | 431,181 | " | 217,340 | " | 9,879 | " |
| Ores,.................. | 1,219,616 | " | 263,183 | " | 11,963 | " |

Of these there were sent to England—

| | Quintals. | | Quintals. | | Tons. | |
|---|---|---|---|---|---|---|
| Bar Copper,............ | 93,867 | containing | 91,051 | or | 4,139 | Pure Copper. |
| Regulus,............... | 333,642 | " | 170,245 | " | 7,738 | " |
| Ores,.................. | 807,132 | " | 163,185 | " | 7,417 | " |
| Pure Copper,...................... | | | 424,381 | | 19,294 | |

In other words, of all the copper product exported by Chile and Bolivia to all parts of the world in 1858, there was sent to England, in the shape of—

| | |
|---|---|
| Bar Copper, about.............................. | 50 per cent. |
| Regulus, " .............................. | 77 " |
| Ores, " .............................. | 62 " |
| Altogether in Pure Copper,.................. | 64 per cent. |

Leaving 36 per cent., or 10,894 tons of pure copper for other countries. These statements would seem to indicate that the production of Chile must rule the copper market, and point out the importance of its consideration by all engaged in the trade.

A practical miner and smelter, who recently made a careful reconnoissance of the new copper region in the north of Atacama, says that "the copper in this district may be measured by leagues," and the mines being near the coast are not so subject to the controlling influences upon mule transportation, of an arid country and an absence of culture—want of water and grass. And but a few days since, a gentleman who had been in that vicinity informed me that the copper ore did not lay in veins but was piled up in inexhaustible hills, from which it was literally dug down.

Number of furnaces in the Province of Capiapo 59—of which 26 are working, and 33 suspended for repair and otherwise.

Number of furnaces in the Province of Huasco 30—of which 18 are working, and 12 suspended.

Number of furnaces in the Province of Coquimbo 63—of which 11 are working, and 52 suspended.

The loss of copper from furnaces not in operation is 16,160 quintals per day.

To avoid detention at Valparaiso by awaiting for the next steamer, I took passage on the ship "Caroline Reed," Douglas, master, bound for Callao, and getting out of harbor to be becalmed within sight of the city for twelve hours, it was not until next day that a south-southwester came along which carried us before it cheerily for a couple of days. Baffling winds then followed, and finally almost a dead calm, and we were doomed from the 27° to the 24° of south latitude to encounter almost literally the condition described by Captains Parker and Fitz Roy, when, after saying that the winds from September to March generally blow from the south-southeast to southwest, yet add that, "sometimes during the summer, for three or four successive days, there is not a breath of wind, the sky being beautifully clear, with a nearly vertical sun." Indeed during six days there was at times not sufficient motion of the air to give the ship steerage way, and she wallowed in a glassy sea at the mercy of the lazy swells; while occasionally, she crept along as if afraid of disturbing the slumbers of the marine insects which had extinguished their phosphorescent lamps, usually illumining this part of the Pacific coast. The only noise that disturbed a quiet like that of Nature's death was the clatter and swash of the ship's pump, at frequent intervals, giving notice that she was not seaworthy. Before the end of this voyage the passengers had reason to regret the confidence they had reposed in the declarations of the captain, who was also part owner, and who, by a large show of outward sanctity, managed for a time to conceal what afterwards proved to be absolute rascality. By the testimony of two intelligent French passengers, this vessel was ascertained to be leaking badly immediately on getting to sea from New York. Having received a coat of paint and tar after doubling the Horn, she was to be sold on speculation in the Pacific, to the bottom of which she will probably make her next voyage. It is not my purpose to write a tale of grievances, however annoying to others less favored than myself. But having some experience, I may advise others preparing for a voyage, to assure themselves beforehand of the condition of the ship and her supplies, and also the character of the master—his nautical knowledge, honesty, and regard for the decent observances of life. The usual winds at this season finally befriended us, and in fifteen days from Valparaiso we anchored in Callao harbor—distance fourteen hundred miles. The voyage in this direction is often made in much less time.

The British steamer Lima was taken a few days after for Paita. We passed the unimportant little seaports on the Peruvian coast, of Huacho, Sape, Casma, Samanco, Santa, Huanchaco, Malabrigo, Pacasmayo, Lambayeque, no one of them worthy of special description, and reached Paita in two and a half days. At several of the towns above named, and at some other parts of the Peruvian coast, landing is effected with difficulty, and only to be accomplished both by passengers and for merchandise, by *Cabillitos;* which are bundles of reeds, lashed together and turned up at the bow, and being very light are thrown from the top of the surf to the beach, when the boatmen jump off and carry it beyond the next breaker; or a stronger and larger raft called *Balsa* is often used, made by lashing together logs of the cabbage-palm, with a platform of thick boards or logs raised about two feet, on which merchandise is placed. These often are provided with a large lug-sail, and they may frequently be seen going up and down the beach, and through the surf, with impunity.

Of Paita I have nothing to add to a previous description. It is a wretched compound of clerical licentiousness and popular indolence and corruption, seasoned with a spice of foreign mercantile craft. I saw the robed priest tie his game-cock at the church door, where he crowed a chorus to a solemn mass celebrated at a cost of four hundred dollars, for the repose of the soul of a deceased citizen, who it was understood was to be absolved from all his sins, including that of cheating his doctor —as the unfortunate medico himself said; while the passers-by, indifferent to what was going on within, saluted the edifice by taking off their hats and making a profound salaam, as they hurried on, some of them to the neighbouring cock-pit, others to the mole to gape at the shrewd stranger embark and disembark the commodities of Paita trade, and the Yankee whaler transship his oil that he might bear away for another "catch."

The bark "Dominga" being up for Tumbes, whither I was bound, I despatched business at Paita and sailed thence with her master Thomas Lee, who, after recent experience, I was rejoiced to find united the deportment of a gentleman to the qualifications of a seaman. Doubling Point Parina and Cape Blanco, we steered north-northeast up the Gulf of Guayaquil; and two days after, the wind having died away, we came to anchor six or seven miles west of Malpelo Point, in latitude 3° 29′ south and longitude 80° 30′ west, a sailing distance of one hundred and thirty miles from our port of departure. The following day bringing no signs of a breeze, Captain Lee and myself took the ship's boat, and coasted within a mile or two of a low shore covered with scrubby trees, and rimmed by a continuous line of breakers; which, stretching further out at the Point broke high and wildly over the reef, growling a fierce warning not to venture too near. Six miles northeast of Malpelo Point brought us to the *present* mouth of the Tumbes River, in latitude 3° 21′ south, and longitude 80° 17′ west, off which, vessels touching here for supplies of wood, water, and fresh vegetables, usually anchor. Formerly the river emptied into the so-called Bay of Tumbes, nearer to Malpelo Point; but heavy freshets in the rainy season occasionally change the channel, and at present its principal mouth is found, as before stated, six miles from the Point. An American ship and a bark were seen lying at anchor in the open roadstead off the mouth of the river, which is about three hundred yards wide; and across it is a sand-bar, on which in stormy weather there is a furious surf, making the entrance dangerous even to well-manned and managed boats. We were fortunate in our passage over the bar without getting swamped; an event for mutual congratulation, when, just within the surf, we saw several sharks, and many alligators, for which this river is noted—apparently awaiting with impatience the breakfast of which doubtless they would have been gratified to have had us to form the foreign dish. Half a mile within the river is striving to make for itself a new channel across the low sandy peninsula which separates it from the gulf on the west side: the next freshet may accomplish this cut off. At high tide the breakers are even now seen to roll across the intermediate tongue of land, and mingle their foam at this part of the stream with the turbid current of the Tumbes. One mile above, the river becomes narrowed to fifty or sixty yards, the dark rich alluvial banks being covered in places by a heavy growth of *Mangrove*, while in others they are entirely concealed by dense thickets of intermingling verdure. The tortuous stream, doubling upon itself at every few hundred yards, precluded the view beyond; so that our progress was constantly revealing new scenes and objects of interest and beauty. Birds of gay plumage, rivalling the tropical verdure and flowers in richness and brightness of coloring, welcomed us with strange song; and the flag-roof bamboo huts, but little larger than dove-cots, raised on posts five or six feet from the ground for protection against venomous reptiles and inundation, stood in small clearings to show that the humble occupants of these ranches enjoy the beauties and the rich productions of this tropical garden as well as their lordlier neighbors Don Mariano and Don Somontes; whose magnificient *chacras*, adorned with the cocoa, lime, orange, plantain, and banana, and shaded by groves of the algaroba, guachapeli, amariyo, secca, cedro, and charan, bordered the river, in whose mirrored bosom they gazed on their own reflected charms. These country-seats showed affluence and taste.

It was at the plantation of the latter gentleman, Don José Somontes, about three miles up stream, that we stopped to procure horses to go by land two miles to the town of Tumbes, thus avoiding the more tedious river route against the current —by which the town is seven miles from the gulf. Horses were furnished, but not until a promise was exacted to return and partake of the hospitality of his house. Having been ferried over the river we struck across a level, and at a short distance from the river-bank an indifferently cultivated plain, for one and a half or two miles, which brought us to the modern town of *Tumbes.*

## CHAPTER XX.

MODERN TUMBES—RUINS OF ANCIENT TUMBES—GULF OF GUAYAQUIL—ISLAND OF EL MUERTO—ISLAND OF PUNA—GUAYAQUIL RIVER—CITY OF GUAYAQUIL.

TUMBES has a population of about three thousand, there being but few of the pure European blood, more of unmixed Indian descent, and still a larger portion of mongrels. The houses differ from those heretofore described in that a greater number of them are two-story buildings; not because earthquakes are not both frequent and severe on this part of the continent, but from the facility of procuring cane and bamboo as building materials, which readily yield to such terrestrial motions and shocks without falling. Posts of *algaroba*—commonly known as iron-wood—crotched at the upper end, are planted deeply in the ground. These, simply divested of bark, are used of their natural shape, as from the metallic hardness of the wood no plane will make an impression on it. And for the same reason, no nail being capable of penetrating it, the cross timbers are lashed to the uprights by *withs of passaya bark*, and twigs of the *bejuco;* both of them being strong, pliant, and more durable than hempen rope. The walls are made of interlaced bamboo sticks, plastered with mud, and sometimes whitewashed. The ceiling is of board, or muslin; the roof, framed of large guayaquil cane, hollow and light, is crossed thickly with bamboo for the support of a thick flag thatch; and the floor is made of large guayaquil cane, partially split into small ribs in such manner as to allow its being spread out like a board with a bamboo substratum, on cane rafters, forming a compact, cool, and elastic, though rather noisy material to walk on. The light fantastic toe may not trip on it—

"Nor stealthy pace
Toward his design move like a ghost"—

whatever its purpose, without detection. The rude algaroba pillars within the best-built houses, are sometimes covered with marbled paper, as are also the walls, and put on quite a show of style. The form and adornments may be peculiar, but certainly neither iron nor marble can be stronger than the algaroba column. The projecting roofs are supported by posts in front of the houses; and when many of these adjoin, a continuous arcade is thus formed which protects pedestrians from sun and rain. Sidewalks and streets are unpaved. May other travellers visiting this town meet with as kind friends as I did to extend to them private hospitalities! The *Posada* of Tumbes is a wretched counterfeit of an inn. If your dinner were cooked under your own eye, superintended by a greasy mulatto wench whose fat hung about her in folds, and who with the same wooden spoon stirred, tasted, and stirred, *ad infinitum*, during the interesting process, the various dishes designed for your use, with a view doubtless of seasoning them *to your liking*, do you think you would *like* them at all? Of course you would pay for the culinary exhibition, and the natives would be amazed that you had left the meal untouched; and perhaps you would be somewhat surprised yourself, after having felt an hour before as if no number of dishes of fish, flesh, and fowl could stagger your appetite. It was necessary to work day and night, in order to finish business in time to reach Guayaquil for the next steamer thence to Panama. But how to get to Guayaquil, was a question not easy of solution. Two means were possibly attainable—to hire a small one-masted river "bunque," or "chata," with one large square sail, and no shelter but that of a thatched arch open before and behind; or procure a row-boat capable of carrying sail if the wind should favor. The latter alone could be relied on; for if becalmed, the bunque would fail to arrive in time for the steamer, and two or three weeks would elapse before another opportunity would be afforded of sailing for Panama. After some trouble, a boat and four rowers were hired to carry me to Guayaquil, for fifty-six dollars; but no temptation would induce the crew to start short of a day's preparation; and it was determined to occupy that interval in visiting the ruins of the ancient Peruvian Temple of the Sun, on the site of the old city of Tumbes, now called *Corales*, where Pizarro first landed in Peru in 1527. Our projected adventure made it necessary to cross the river Tumbes, which we had ascended a few miles by boating the day before, and which may be navigated by canoes eighteen or twenty miles beyond the town, where its falls interrupt further progress, although, heading in the Andes it has a length of seventy-five or eighty miles. This river was the former Spanish line of separation between the Viceroyalties of Lima and Quito; and hence between the States of Peru and Ecuador, although the former has for some time claimed to the Macara, about twenty miles further north. Since the accession of Castilla to power, he is ever ready to make this an excuse for intermeddling in the domestic affairs of Ecuador. This disposition on the part of Peru has led to a proposition of General Flores for a union of the States of Ecuador, New Granada, and Venezuela, for common defence against the aggression of more powerful neighbors, which would effectually arrest the encroachments of Castilla.

Having crossed by the ferry-boat, we found on the opposite side of the river horses in waiting, which had been provided by L. G. Sanford, Esq., United States Consul, and Dr. R. M. Columbus, a graduate in medicine of a North American University; with whom, and several other friends, I started for the ruins of the temple, after having refreshed ourselves at the chacra of the hospitable Don Manuel Rodriguez, with a luscious draught of cocoanut water, fresh from trees growing in profusion on the river bank. To see a native almost walk up the perpendicular trunk of a tree without any thing adventitious to assist him, and pluck the pulpy and juicy fruit from the tufted top seventy or eighty feet high, would lead you to think that he had been taking lessons of his fellow-countrymen of the monkey tribe.

Our road was westwardly, and deep with dust, for it was the dry season, and no rain had fallen for several months. Several well-cultivated chacras skirted the way, until we came to a very heavily-timbered Algaroba forest; the trees looking as if they were the memorials of ages that had gone before us, and had been moulded of iron, or been hewn from dark imperishable rock. Tropical vines were seen clambering up their knarled and stalwart trunks, clothing them in verdure, and clinging with feeble tendrils to brawny limbs; while iris-hued flowers bloomed along the wayside, fit companions of the birds that flashed their rich plumage from bough to bough.

About five miles brought us to the old bed of the river Tumbes, now dry, and since the change of its channel only occasionally containing water when the river is greatly swollen by heavy rains. Crossing this, dry-shod, we mounted the opposite bank of thirty or forty feet, and passing some bamboo houses sparsely scattered over a level of a half mile, came to hills, skirted by the remains of an aqueduct eighteen or twenty feet wide, and seven or eight feet deep. Along this we rode, circling the hills, the sides of which, in many places, appeared supported by dilapidated walls, built of large boulders in some places, in others presenting the distinct rectangular outlines of large adobes, seamed with shingle or cobble stones. Some of these may have upheld superincumbent structures now no more. On crossing over some of the least elevated of the hills, small quadrangular stone foundations were observed, as of houses; while the larger size, and perfectly regular and level surface of other places, indicated the probable existence there of streets and public squares. A mile and a half from where we crossed the old bed of the river, we came to the foot of a hill from one hundred to one hundred and fifty feet in height, commanding a fine view of the surroundings. Off to the west, five miles distant, *El Punta Garrita* formed the northern termination of a range of hills, the *Padarones*, which, stretching away to the southward, throws off a smaller spur to the eastward, upon the several eminences of which the ancient city of Tumbes was built, supposed to have had one hundred thousand inhabitants. The hill on which we stood is the northernmost of the spur, and is isolated from the rest by a narrow space bounding its southern foot. To the north of this isolated hill, four miles distant, is plainly seen the Bay of Tumbes, in which Francisco Pizarro cast anchor when he first feasted his eyes on this land of promise. And spreading out from the Padarones Range on the west, to the river Tumbes on the east, a distance of ten miles, is a level plain, which, in the days of the Incas, was watered by innumerable small canals, fed by the large aqueduct circling the hill-sides before described, that tapped the Tumbes River at a height sufficient to distribute water to the town, and the outspread plain before it. Nor is it surprising that the beauty, fertility, and wealth of bountiful nature and human industry unrolled before him, should have filled the Spanish intruder with amazement; and that he should have become inspired with visions of the magnificent conquest that this transcendently beautiful portal of Peru opened to his imagination.

On the level summit of the hill which we had ascended and carefully explored, were seen parts of a symmetrical quadrangular wall of great thickness, seven hundred and fifty feet long and four hundred and twenty feet wide, enclosing the remains of massive walls, abutments, and arches, nearly all prostrated, rent, and crumbling, under the combined influence of human and natural causes; earthquake, fire, and storm aiding the hand of man in the work of destruction. There still are visible, however, some large adobe blocks, with intermediate water-washed stones, doubtless from the gulf shore; the size of these blocks justifying the presumption that they were parts of massive walls. Portions of walls, too, of the thickness of from five to six feet, are standing supported by huge abutments; and a descent of fifteen feet below the present general surface level, at one spot exposed a perfectly symmetrical arch of four feet radius, with a part of the wall supporting it on each side, in an excellent state of preservation. Near to this arch a tottering wall, resting against neighboring fallen masses, exhibits on its exposed side two well-proportioned and unbroken niches; once, possibly, adorned with images of gold or silver.

Mr. Prescott says, in his "History of the Conquest of Peru," in describing ancient Peruvian architecture, in it "there is no appearance of columns or of arches, though there is some contradiction as to the latter point. But it is not to be doubted that, although they may have made some approach to this mode of construction by the greater or less inclination of the walls, the Peruvian architects were wholly unacquainted with the true principle of the circular arch reposing on its key-stone."

This is an error, for the arch seen by myself and friends amid the ruins of the Temple of the Sun, at the site of old Tumbes, so far from being a mere "approach to this mode of construction by the greater or less inclination of the walls," and showing that the "Peruvian architects were wholly unacquainted with the true principle of the circular arch reposing on its key-stone," *demonstrates their perfect comprehension of its principles* at the time of the building of that Temple, its circular sweep and key-stone; and shows its entire independence of "greater or less inclination of the walls," and that it rests upon those of accurate perpendicularity as columns of support, as in the architecture of our day.

And this observation sustains the statement found in the translation by Francis L. Hawks, D.D., LL.D., of the work on "Peruvian Antiquities, by Mariano Edwardo Rivero and James Von Tschudi," viz.: "A general error among most historians, as well the ancient as the modern, is the opinion that the Peruvian architects had not attained to the construction of arches and vaults; for in many *Huacas* of stone we observe vaults very superiorly constructed." And further: "In some of the larger edifices you meet also with vestiges of arches, but it is certain that their application was quite limited." It may be added, that the publication of Rivero and Von Tschudi is the ablest authority extant on Peruvian architecture, and embraces the results of the most extensive researches that have been made in modern times, by personal examination and study of Peruvian antiquities.

The great extent of the building which occupied this eminence, as indicated by the ruins, would justify the supposition that, as stated by Rivero, the Temple of Tumbes was among the most sumptuous of the nation; that at Cuzco, perhaps, alone surpassing it in size and richness. It embraced, probably, besides the chief section dedicated to the supreme *Numen*, the sun, chapels for the worship of the moon, the stars, the thunderbolt, the rainbow; another section for priestly deliberations, and finally one for those entrusted with the alternate weekly religious services. And in the same enclosure there was, no doubt, one of the "more than two hundred" royal palaces erected for the use of the Inca, in his journeyings between Cuzco and Quito; and also one of the monasteries of the Virgins of the Sun.

And well might the religious devotion of the Peruvians consecrate to the uses of the sanctuary and its servants, an eminence of peculiar adaptation for beholding and worshipping the first glorious emanations of their rising god; and for witnessing the proofs of his beneficence, in the rich productions of the magnificent garden spread far and wide, at the foot of the holy habitation of his golden and jewelled image.*

Our ride was continued over other parts of the spur of hills before referred to; and showed, in the artificially levelled surfaces, prostrate and broken walls, vestiges of the foundations of houses and drainage-trenches, the still lingering proofs of a large city having once occupied these heights. Some distance further south, one hill appears to have been set apart for burial purposes; large urns of classic form, with large mouths, being found there, some of them containing human remains in a sitting posture with the chin resting on the knees. In one instance we traced the root of a giant cactus penetrating an urn, where it had revelled on the dust of mortality, and flaunted above the desecrated tomb its crimson-flowered banner in token of triumph.

The traveller cannot look upon the still lingering proofs of the greatness and prosperity of the ancient Peruvians, about the site of Tumbes of old, without deploring the sordid passions, the love of gold, the fanaticism, which under pretence of extending civilization sent forth as missionaries those who were ignorant of its benign influences; to inculcate a Christianity, too, sadly

* The author has recently been informed by Dr. Columbus, that in 1862 himself and other citizens of Tumbes and vicinity formed a company for the exploration of the ruins of this temple. From thirty to forty laborers were occupied in the work of excavation for more than two months. It resulted in the discovery of one large central apartment, surrounded by many smaller rooms communicating by corridors, and having a large portal on the east, toward the rising sun, near which were several arches well preserved. The walls were painted in red, representing Indians and animals. The rooms had evidently been filled by gravel, conveyed from the seashore for the purpose of concealing the sacred treasures, &c., from the Spaniards. Many gold and silver images of animals and plants were also found, of great value; and also earthen vases of bright colors and beautiful design.

affiliated to the superstition it denounced, and more intolerant and vindictive than the idolatry it despised. Missionaries who carried misery into this once peaceful and prosperous land, caused its rivers to run with blood, its fruitful fields to become desolate, its public policy, wisely adapted to the necessities of the people, to perish, its domestic joys to wither, and a general ruin to its vast empire of ten or eleven millions of people, and eight hundred leagues extent from Quito to the river Maulé, to follow in the track of the invader, whose sole rule of action appears to have been the enforcement by bloody inculcation of his arbitrary will, and the appropriation of the property and the liberty of these people to the gratification of his mercenary longings and his unrestrained lusts. The page of history presents no such deed of perfidy as the capture of the Inca Atahuallpa, and the slaughter of thousands of his unarmed retinue, when that monarch, unsuspectingly confiding in the good faith and hospitality of Pizarro, visited him at his quarters, to honor and welcome him as the ambassador of a foreign prince. And the climax of unequalled treachery was completed, when, after engaging to free the monarch on the payment of one room full of gold and two of silver, he received and retained the ransom, worth more than sixteen millions of dollars, and then strangled him by the garrote—thus repaying friendship and hospitality by seizure, imprisonment, robbery, and death. When the apologists of Pizarro attempt to shield his crimes, and excuse his acts of cruelty by his religious zeal and holy purpose of extending the dominion of the cross, they may well be answered, that the religion was unworthy of adoption that required for its extension that the wife of the Inca Manco, then a prisoner in Pizarro's power, should be "stripped naked, bound to a tree, and in presence of the camp be scourged with rods, and then be shot to death with arrows!" This cold-blooded brutality—*and to a woman*—should brand his name with eternal infamy. And it was such deeds of inhumanity that finally deprived him of all sympathy, when retributive justice meted out to him a violent death, at the hands of his own cheated and incensed contemporaries.

No one, when recalling the past, and reflecting on the present condition of this country, can fail to see in the degenerate posterity of its conquerors, the indisputable deterioration of race, by admixture of blood with an inferior and more numerous Indian population, destined probably, at no distant day, to absorb it altogether; the impairment of the higher intellectual and physical attributes; the substitution of indolence for activity; of cunning and intrigue for ability and boldness; of perpetual revolutions, war, and bloodshed, for stability, peace, and safety; proofs of the "just recompense of reward" which has overtaken both national and individual wickedness.

On our return from the ruins of the Temple and other sacred edifices, whose gigantic remains are still telling the history of the past—although Mr. Findlay, in his "Directory of the Pacific Ocean," says these "are now nowhere to be seen"—an opportunity was afforded to look at the few cane huts scattered about and occupied by listless inhabitants, the impoverished successors of those who dwelt in the once proud city of Tumbes, whose very name has been taken from it, with its riches. And yet even amid their present poverty, there are proofs among the natives of a pride cherished by the traditions of ancient affluence. This is shown in the persistent refusal, even by the humblest of the Indian descendants of this district, to use any but the precious metals for many of their domestic purposes, whatever other deprivations they may have to endure. My companions on this excursion, to prove the correctness of the statement, stopped at the wretched looking cane ranche of Julian Rosillo, having one earthen floor room for the joint occupancy of himself, wife, three nearly naked *chiquitos*, and such visitors as might choose to partake of his hospitality. Some *maize chicha* was asked for, which required a spoon for stirring. It was brought in a silver vessel, and with a silver spoon of purer metal than that used in more refined society. A *yapa*, and the promise of another when he should visit town, enabled Dr. Columbus to purchase the spoon, who presented it to me as a proof of the consistent adherence of poverty to some of the usages of ancestors; among whom gems and gold were the common ornaments, and silver the familiar metal in domestic use.

The shades of evening fell over it as we returned through

the Algaroba forest, and I did not remain long in modern Tumbes when we crossed the ferry, but proceeded on to Santa Rosa, the beautiful chacra of Don José Somontes, where my boat was to overtake me with Mr. Sanford, who had kindly offered to be my fellow-voyager to Guayaquil. A cordial welcome was extended to us by Don José and his charming family, who offered every temptation of hospitality to prolong our visit. And certainly if the refinements and elegancies of life, and the graceful entertainment of an accomplished family, could have prevailed over a sense of public duty, many days would have been given to the delights of Santa Rosa. It is strange upon what rare spots of intellectual and moral excellence the traveller occasionally comes, in his passage over the great social waste of South America. In other instances where superiority was observed, foreign contact was recognized, and its influence was evident. And here also the sensitive and sympathizing nature of Caucasian descent, was magnetized by the spiritual power of that exalted agency which the mere accident of occasional commerce brought into operation.

Our boatmen's song as they descended the river, came floating, first faintly to us on the still night air, and then more distinctly as they approached Santa Rosa, warning us that the hour of our departure had arrived; and near midnight, taking leave of a family and friends whose kindness enshrined them in grateful memory, we went aboard our boat and pulled down the tranquil river, reposing in the clear moonlight, with nothing to disturb its peaceful bosom but the measured motion of the oars, as dipping in the silvery water they rose again, letting fall the crystal drops that sparkled like diamonds as they returned again to their quiet slumbers. An hour sufficed to put us alongside of the Bark Dominga, in the offing, on board which we found a welcome berth until daylight. At six A. M. we cast loose our little craft—a frail one for a voyage of nearly a hundred miles—and turned her head toward Guayaquil.

That large ocean expanse known as the Gulf of Guayaquil, is geographically considered as extending from the sea to a supposed line drawn from Malpelo Point in Peru, to Punta Salinas, the southwest end of the Island of Puna. Between these two points, the southern or main branch of the river Guayaquil is described as emptying into the gulf. But any one contemplating the characteristics of the estuary presented here, might be forgiven if, in his ignorance of geographical distinction, he mistook the river for a part of the gulf itself; for the Island of Santa Clara (Amortajada or El Muerto), which, like a shrouded corpse, lies a dead sentinel taking his eternal sleep at the post of duty the mouth of the river, is nineteen miles from Malpelo Point on the one hand, and seventeen miles from Punta Salinas on the other, making a width of thirty-six miles; while the wave, the swell, the general ocean turbulence, and sea monsters, are ever present to add to the deception of the voyager.

Pulling northeast by north, in eight hours we came off the Punta Arenas of Puna Island, and a southwest breeze striking us here, we took in oars and set a mainsail, going before the wind at the rate of eight knots, coasting the south side of the island its entire length of twenty-eight miles without seeing a house or the sign of cultivation, until doubling Punta Española near its northeast end a neat cottage peeped out from its island wilderness.

It was upon this Island of Puna that Pizarro landed on his second voyage to Peru, to await the passage of the rainy season and the arrival of reënforcements, before penetrating into the interior of the country of the Inca for the purposes of plunder and subjugation. He found the island well cultivated, and blooming with cacao plantations and various tropical products, and inhabited by a warlike race of Indians who received the strangers in a hospitable manner. But a suspicion of Pizarro that the natives designed resistance to his arrogant assumptions of control over their dominions, led him, with characteristic treachery and cruelty, to seize and slay a number of their chiefs, which brought on immediate hostilities; and the watchfulness and implacable spirit of revenge on the part of the islanders keeping the Spaniards in a perpetual state of alarm, they hurried their departure and crossed over to the main land, but not to find the same manifestations of friendship as at their first visit. Distrust had evidently taken possession of the minds of the Peruvians in the mean time; a scene of desolation was presented for the contemplation of Pizarro, the city of Tumbes was nearly deserted, dwellings were destroyed, and the great Temple de spoiled of its golden ornaments and jewelled images, which Spanish avarice had only left untouched on their first discovery, that they might be made an easier and more certain prey when the necessary force was obtained.

It is surprising how completely this fine island of Puna, once inhabited by a numerous tribe of Indians, and the seat of an abounding agriculture, has become deserted, and reverted to a condition of original nature—the domain almost solely of the deer and the wild hog, as we were assured by our cholo boatmen.

Extensive sand-bars were passed close in shore, on which myriads of water-fowl were collected; and whole armies of pelicans stood there, in lengthened line, erect, mute, meditative, and disciplined, like soldiers on parade; unintimidated by our approach, and as if prepared to resist any act of aggression. Their martial appearance entitles these birds to the name of Tumbes soldiers, which American whalers have applied to those that bivouack and drill on the flats of that river.

Doubling Point Mandinga, the northeast end of the island, and the few huts called the town of *Puna*, on our left, we steered northwardly for the channel of the river on the west side of Great Mondragon Island, and, night having overtaken us, we found the contents of our provision basket refreshing, and then wrapped in blanket-shawls we laid down in the stern of the boat. With the young moon peeping coquettishly from behind silken clouds to watch over us, and light the shadowy river, we soon fell asleep—for myself—to dream of alligators and river-robbers, of whose ferocity and desperate deeds in these unsettled revolutionary periods our timid boatmen had not failed to narrate for our entertainment many frightful tales. At midnight, favoring gales died away, and our sail being furled and mast unshipped, the measured stroke of the oars as they struggled against an ebb tide and a strong current, was the serenade of a weary night. Propitious dawn came at last, to disclose the features of the river bank, the dim outline of which alone could be seen during the night. This was low, and supported an impenetrable wall of rank verdure—trees, shrubbery, vines, and flags, being closely twined and matted, and studded with wild-flowers of great variety and brilliancy of coloring, giving shelter to birds of rich plumage offering their matin service of sweet song to the coming day. The interest incident to constantly varying scene, yet always of rare beauty, marred only by the occasional sting of the *sancudo* or *jegen*, a diminutive knat, which, unlike the mosquito, gives no musical warning of its attack, was brought to a sudden and nearly tragical conclusion. An alligator, unseen by us before in the turbid stream, seized an oar and nearly pulled one of our rowers overboard; by the assistance of others the man was saved, but the blade of the oar was crushed to fragments. The fright of the boatmen gave wings to our little craft for a few minutes, and although the voracious monster could not overtake us, he pursued us with sufficient perseverance to make us sensible that if overtaken our fate might be that of others who have been upset and destroyed in the river Tumbes by these formidable reptiles.

A gradual bend in the river as we ascended from the north by east to north-northwest brought into view in the distance the *Cerro de Santa Ana* and the *Cerro del Carmen*, at the foot of which stands the city of Guayaquil. We approached it by the main channel between the western bank and the Island of Santai, opposite the city. Near the city the river banks are low, muddy, slimy-looking, spotted with an uninviting crop of alligators awaiting anxiously the chances of a breakfast to be furnished by some morning bather, and rapidly narrowing until at the city the stream is scarcely a mile wide. Several square-rigged vessels and steamers, with many bunques, chatas, and river rafts, were lying at anchor and along shore. Seeing the British flag flying from the stern of one of the steamers, we made fast to her, and going aboard found she was the British Steam Navigation Company's boat "Anne," to sail for Panama the next day. I bore letters to her commander, Captain King, who gave me a hearty English welcome, and at once made me feel at home on board.

We were twenty-nine hours making the run of ninety-seven miles, from the roadstead of Tumbes to Guayaquil; subject, it is true, to some risks and discomforts, for neither the foggy miasmata of night, nor the heat of a tropical sun by day, were pleasant realities; nor did river pirates, either of the human or reptile class, afford agreeable subjects for contemplation.

The *City of Guayaquil*, so called from its original cacique *Guayas*, in latitude 2° 12′ S., and longitude 79° 52′ W., is the principal seaport of the Republic of Ecuador, contains twenty thousand inhabitants, and is situated on the west bank of the river of the same name, at the foot of a hill from two to three miles long, four hundred feet high, and having four distinct and characteristic elevations above the general height of its elongated crest. At a greater distance off from the city, to the west, is another higher range of hills, the Cerro de Chongon, which is separated from the before-mentioned height by a narrow level tongue of land that connects two extensive savannas—one situated northwest of the hills, the other stretching several miles southwest and south of the city. The last of these savannas has become memorable in the revolutionary annals of Ecuador, as the plain across which General Flores recently turned the position and defences of General Franco, and achieved an easy victory, after having been foiled for several months in numerous attempts to capture Guayaquil.

This city extends north and south about a mile; its main street, about sixty feet wide, fronting the river and protected by a strong stone wall, forms the chief business mart and promenade, under the name of the *Malecon*, or Alameda. It is poorly lighted at night by numerous oil lamps, which, if they are of no public use, are at least a public expense, and serve to convince the people what they need, by contrast with the brilliant gas-lighted stores that border one side of the great thoroughfare, and lend to the corporation their excess of splendor until ten o'clock, when night spreads her sable wing unhindered over the Malecon. Several streets running parallel to the river are intersected by many others at right angles, most of them being unpaved; and such as have a rough apology for a pavement would have been "more honored in the breach." Numerous ravines descending from the hill pass through the city to the river; and being the receptacles of filth and offal, must, except when washed out by heavy rains, become very offensive.

The houses are very different from those seen elsewhere. Most of them are higher, many having three stories, and framed of the heaviest and strongest timber—in which Ecuador abounds. But it is manifest that, if instead of restricting themselves to perpendicular and horizontal framing exclusively, their builders were to use ties and braces also in the construction of houses, an equal if not greater strength would be secured with much less consumption of material. A balcony to the second-story of each house, projecting over the sidewalk, supported by a rude colonnade, with a plain arch thrown from one column to another, gives the appearance of a continuous arcade in all the streets, and shelters pedestrians both from sun and storm. When a third-story is built it projects beyond the second, and forms either a room or open or curtained balcony, as desired. And as an immensely heavy tile roof, of six pounds to every eight square inches, in all cases projects even beyond this, it follows that a considerable portion of the street is shaded by the overhanging building. Another feature of these more commodious houses, described by an old resident, is, that in their joint-occupancy the lower story is always used for store-rooms and shops; the second floor is as invariably occupied by tenants of recognized frailty; while those of reputable character and unimpeached virtue pass the doors of the sinners to the higher apartments, conventional usage conceding to them the merit and the post of honor nearest heaven. There are no gardens, or even yards, and closets or corresponding conveniences for health and decency, are novelties; the consequent debasement of domestic habits, the disregard of delicacy and cleanliness, may be inferred.

The population of Guayaquil is essentially Indian; that is demonstrated wherever you wander, through and around the city, by the copper color, straight black hair, small dark twinkling eyes, high cheek bones, flat occiput, and sinciput bevelled to the low forehead, small stature, and graceless gait; with indolence, indifference to instruction, and superstition. And if, in some instances, admixture of Caucasian blood has brought with it a measure of intellectual and moral improvement, in others amalgamation with the negro has degraded the Indian below even the standard of his original nature. Most of the soldiers seen in passing the barracks, on duty at the prison and at the guard-house, were negroes. An idle military life, and inflated sense of self-importance, are congenial to their lazy inclinations and love of show; their ignorance and incapability of appreciating the principles and blessings of constitutional government, make them ready and fit instruments of usurpation and arbitrary power; and their brutal nature adapts them to deeds of cruelty, and to the hireling task of disturbing the public peace, and murdering those especially whose attributes of superior race they cannot hope to rival, and whom therefore they would destroy. But for the prompt movement of my cicerone in turning aside the bayonet, I should have been pinned to the wall of the guardhouse by one of these black ruffians, for simply looking in the gateway as we passed by. My guide told me that personal safety was more secure with a darker complexion, a white skin being cause of mortal offence to them.

There is one college in little more than nominal existence; and *one public school, with forty pupils*, who receive instruction from a foreign teacher; while *one hundred priests in seven churches* solemnize daily masses, without, as is said, an inculcation of good will and charity toward Protestant Christians, beyond the concession of burial when dead; but without the privilege of the humblest building where two or three might gather together in His name who is the God and Father of us all.

I learned from an intelligent source that in this, as in all the other South American countries, nearly all those young men who are ambitious of education seek it abroad, most of them spending several years in France for that purpose; and it was further stated that they generally return home regarding Voltaire rather than the clergy as authority for religious subjects. Indeed, educated men, and those of the highest respectability and influence, have no respect for the church, nor do they attend its ceremonies, except from policy on rare public occasions. They plainly perceive the fact that the priest, ignoring the Deity in practice, puts himself in His stead in regard to actual prerogatives and authority, and the deference and obedience due to Him. And although in early life they are taught to regard His teachings with reverence, yet the experience of more mature years exposes the worthlessness of the whole scheme as devised and maintained for the benefit of a selfish and too commonly licentious clergy. Women cling to the formulary, some from love of the virtue which if preached from the pulpit is sadly violated in practice; others from idle ceremony, a solemn mockery of both mind and heart; others again from ignorance and superstition; although the great mass, the lower classes of these, are unrestrained in their depravity, and as acknowledged by the candid of the clergy, do not hesitate to rob and cheat the curate himself—who, it is no libel to say, they have learned is not immaculate.

A newspaper publication has been projected at Guayaquil, and the benighted people were a few days since startled by the full blaze of a weekly a foot square. I saw a copy. It has a portentous look of an early doom, for it contains a criticism of a recent executive proceeding!

From the top of the Cerro de Santana, at the foot of which lies the northern or old Spanish part of the town, the two large affluents, the *Bodegas* and the *Daule*, may be seen rolling down their muddy torrents from the north to unite at the base of the Cerro to form the river *Guayaquil*. Both these branches are navigable for light draught steamboats a considerable distance into the interior; the larger stream, the Bodegas, to the distance of eighty-five miles. Rafts were seen descending both streams, on which were built family huts, and storehouses containing *cacao*, the great product of the country, on its way to market. This height having several pieces of artillery upon it was recently stormed by General Flores, after he had penetrated the city from the opposite side by a strategical movement. From the steep and otherwise difficult ascent an American would have considered such a feat impracticable, if Franco's men had stood to their guns. But the redoubtable darkies did not stop running until they had pitched down the precipitous descent on the opposite side from their enemy, and plunged up to their necks in the river, where, revolutionary ardor becoming cooled, they cheerfully capitulated.

At the eastern foot of the Cerro del Carmen is situated the ostentatious Pantheon, to which I last night saw a señora, *but four hours dead*, borne to a hurried interment, on a bedizened hearse, driven by a liveried postilion in gold lace and cocked hat, and lighted by many lanterns carried by a procession of chattering boys of all sizes, colors, and costumes, who seemed to consider the ceremonial of sepulture a clever amusement. And not far off is the little spot where Protestants are now allowed burial, *but without the performance of religious rites.*

To the northeast, from eighty to ninety miles off, may be seen on a clear day the snow-clad summit of Chimborazo, twenty-one thousand two hundred and forty-two feet high; consecrated by the genius of Humboldt, and long venerated by tyros as the greatest of mountains; but sadly fallen from its high estate, since science has announced the greater altitudes of the lofty peaks of the Himalayas in Asia, Sahama and Perinacota in Peru, Llimani and Sorata in Bolivia, and Tupungato and Aconcagua in Chile.

The industry of this town is confined almost entirely to the extensive manufacture of cigars from native tobacco, showing a large growth and consumption of that weed; and the cleaning, by means of large perforated ox-hide sieves, of the cacao, another and valuable product of Ecuador. The latter is extensively exported, as are also Panama hats, baled in hide *zurones* of fifty dozen each; sarsaparilla, cinchona (Peruvian bark), called by the natives cascarilla, and orchilla weed, now used in Europe as a valuable dye. Ecuador abounds in fine timber, several species of which are largely exported. A merchant in the lumber trade kindly exhibited to me specimens of many of these. Besides the light and dark canes extensively used for building purposes, there are the *Madera Negra* (black wood), not excelled in durability even when exposed to weather. After having been planted in the earth as posts for houses for one hundred years, my informant told me that he had found this wood perfectly sound. *Guayacan* of like qualities with the last mentioned, but of lighter color. *Algaroba*, a dark and very heavy wood, commonly called from its weight and impenetrability, iron wood. *Amaria*, the most beautiful veined wood of this country, used principally for ornamental furniture. *Figuiroa*, of a dark brown color, close fibre, receives a fine polish, and is used for the interior of buildings. *Roble*, Guayaquil oak, of a white color, and used also for building purposes. *Suche*, of a beautiful yellow, close fibre, and susceptible of polish, used in building. I saw columns for the interior of the cathedral being made of this wood to replace others, which, I was assured, had been destroyed in a few years by the ravages of very destructive large white ants. *Guachapeli*, something like North American white oak, used principally in ship building. Knees of any curve or angle can be had of this timber. *Maria*, used principally for masts and spars; these can be obtained of any desirable size, but the tree grows in mountainous districts, and the transportation to market is very costly. *Manglé* grows near salt water, is tall and straight, but is too heavy for ordinary uses; the larger trees are frequently seen three feet in diameter and one hundred and fifty feet long, and are used for keels of vessels; the smaller are used for house rafters. *Palo de Vaca*, a very hard, close-grained wood, used chiefly for furniture, being susceptible of a high polish. *Moral*, of a light yellow color, grows to a great length, and is very durable. *Guasango* grows on the seacoast, is very hard, and much used when great exposure to weather is to be encountered. *Pachiche*, very durable, and used chiefly in the construction of water-tanks and wells. *Ebony* is scarce and highly prized. There are also other woods, the names and uses of which I had not the opportunity of learning. But these are sufficient to show the importance of Guayaquil as a timber mart. The market for the sale of meats, fish, vegetables, and fruits, is well attended by sellers and buyers. The vegetable kingdom is especially well represented on the stalls. But the hour of departure having come notings were abruptly brought to an end. Going aboard the steamer she slipped her moorings, and in a short time Guayaquil faded in the distance, and was soon garnered in memory with other parts of this southern hemisphere.

## CHAPTER XXI.

CAPE ST. HELENA—CAPE SAN LORENZO—MANTA—MONTE CHRISTI—ESMERALDAS—ISLAND OF MORRO GRANDE—TUMACO—TRUE BOUNDARY BETWEEN THE PACIFIC PROVINCES OF ECUADOR AND NEW GRANADA—ISLAND OF GORGONA—BUENAVENTURA—BRITISH PACIFIC STEAM NAVIGATION COMPANY—DEFECTIVE CHARTS OF THIS PART OF THE COAST—NEW SURVEYS NEEDED.

At dawn next morning we were steering between the islands of Puna and El Muerto; and when, pursuing a north-west course, we stretched further out into the Gulf of Guayaquil, the close resemblance of the latter island to a shrouded corpse became very apparent. At six P. M. we doubled St. Helena, one hundred and sixty-six miles from Guayaquil, the northern limit of the Gulf, a bold, barren, and distinctive head-land extending far out into the ocean; and connected to the coast line by a long, narrow, low, sandy tongue of land. Bearing away to the north by west, we kept on that course during the night, leaving the Isle de la Plata on the west, and passing Cape San Lorenzo. Then changing our course to the eastward we anchored next morning in the open roadstead of the little town of *Manta* nearly two hundred miles from Cape St. Helena, having one large store-house and about forty huts for a population of one hundred and fifty or two hundred people. This is the sea-port of two interior towns; one, also called *Manta*, being an Indian settlement four or five miles to the southeast; and the other, and larger town, *Monte Christi*, containing a population of fifteen hundred, situated nine miles to the eastward, at the foot of a hill of the same name, fourteen hundred and twenty-nine feet high. The exports of the port of Manta are hats, orchilla weed, starch made from the *yuca*, which is of two species, viz., the iatropha manihoc, and the iatropha curcas—the former produces the starch, the latter is a valuable esculent; caoutchouc, and cacao, products of the adjacent country. The hats generally known in commerce as *Panama* hats, are not made in that place, which is merely an entrepot for their collection and exportation. Nor is the name *Guayaquil*, sometimes applied to these hats, more correct as relates to their manufacture—their being sent from that place to Panama is a mere incident of trade. They are all made in this province, from the *leaf of a palm* known here by the name of *Rampira.* The leaf is about a yard long, and one-third of an inch wide, and is torn into shreds of straw for use; and according to the quality and fineness of this straw, and the skill in plaiting, is the price set upon the hat. The finest hat occupies many months in the manufacture. The value ranges from two dollars to one hundred dollars each, according to quality. Dr. Rubio, an intelligent physician of Monte Christi, informed me that many lives are annually sacrificed by the manufacture of the finest hats, owing to the long-continued bent position of the workman producing pulmonary disease. Good palm straw is grown in the districts of Monte Christi and Santa Elena, but the best in that of *Jipijapa* (pronounced *Hippihappa*); and the so-called Panama hats of all the various qualities, are manufactured in Jipijapa, Monte Christi, Manta, and Santa Elena, all in the Province of Manabi, in the Republic of Ecuador. Hats of this material cannot be made elsewhere, for a prohibitory penalty attaches to the exportation of the unmanufactured straw. So much for commercial accuracy. A country of no large pretension to manufacturing skill and production might be conceded the small credit it is justly entitled to.

The hat market is held in the places named, at night. The purchaser, who is generally a merchant buying on speculation, goes to the market-place, usually the plaza, and taking his seat with a lantern in one hand, as well to attract attention as to examine the quality of the hats, he jingles a bag of specie, which alone is current among these primitive people; who, as some of us think very sensibly, disbelieve that the prolific and perishable production of a paper mill can be as valuable as the more limited and unchanging issue of nature's golden depositories.

The Indian vender, attracted by the light, and the popular music of all countries, comes to sell, and asks four times as much for his goods as he intends to take. The purchaser offers less than the actual value, which, being refused, he increases by decimals until it gradually reaches one-fourth of the price demanded, when the bargain is closed. An Indian considers himself a good salesman to have obtained a greater price than the purchaser first offered; and the buyer would undoubtedly be entitled to a *fool's cap* instead of a Jipijapa hat, who would give the price originally asked.

A sufficient time is usually afforded by the detention of the steamer at the port of Manta to allow passengers an opportunity to ride over to Monte Christi. Several Guayaquil hat merchants landed at Manta, and having taken in freight and gone aboard, we hove anchor, and again bore away northerly one hundred and fifty-eight miles, which brought us, the succeeding day at two P. M., to the mouth of the river Esmeraldas; just within which, on the south bank (latitude 1° 4′ north), is the small town of the same name, with a population of about three hundred, Indians and mixed breeds.

When not turbid from heavy rains the water of this river is of a deep green, hence its name, as explained by some persons; while others refer it to a mine of emeralds on the south side and not remote from the river, which once yielded a large number of these gems—the pure waters,

> "As on they flow,
> Catching the gem's bright color, as they go."

But the superstition of the natives, who believe that it is guarded by a dragon dealing in thunder and lightning, has for a long time deterred them from working it, and even from guiding the more courageous into its neighborhood. Las Esmeraldas might derive its name also from the rich green of its picturesque hills, which lift above and around their terraces clad in unchanging verdure, from the perpetually alternating sunshine and shower of an endless summer. The contrast between the seacoast of Ecuador north of Manta and of New Granada, and that of Peru, Bolivia, and Chile, is very marked.

The former presents a continuous wall of trees and shrubbery, covered with luxuriant foliage, courting the sweet sea-breeze and shading the billow that sports at its foot; while the latter stretches away in sterile slopes, or raises its rocky and metallic buttresses to hold the ocean at stern defiance.

After a brief detention, we steamed out of the harbor of irregular and doubtful depth, with the same care that was required on entering, to avoid the dangerous bar at its mouth; and standing away to the northeast, found ourselves early next morning passing to the west of a group of islands in latitude 1° 51′ N., and longitude 78° 46′ W., the northernmost of which —Morro Grande—we doubled by steering east and then south, passing close along its eastern shore for about five miles, through a narrow channel between the island and the mainland. Having reached its southern end—Morro Chiquito—a fourth of a mile to the south of which, on the island of *Tumaco*, stands the town of that name, we dropped anchor in the almost completely land-locked harbor.

Less than a hundred yards from shore, off the northwest end of Morro Grande, stands a tall and graceful rock sculptured by nature's hand, lashed by envious billows that break abashed at its base. It is *El Virgencita*—the little virgin—like the being whose name it bears, a type of loneliness, subject to the buffetings of rude surroundings; and a strange beauty it has in its desertion, for a chaplet of verdure rests on its summit, and festoons drop gracefully around, like ringlets from a maiden's brow.

The whole Island of Morro Grande is an emerald thicket—trees and shrubbery completely mask it—leaving a mere rim of clearing near the shore for the bamboo huts of the indolent, half-clad mulattoes and zambos, who have but to stretch forth their hands, and take from the cocoanut-palm, the banana, plantain, mango, orange, and other fruit trees, the food and beverage that bounteous nature brings to their very doors.

The town of *Tumaco*, off which the steamer is now riding at anchor, is said to have a population of one thousand. From its small number of cane and bamboo houses, one would not suppose that it contained half that number; but these natives have a great facility of packing in a small space; the artificialities of civilization have not made much progress in Tumaco, although by a government decree in 1844, it was declared a free port until 1861.

It is its past history, however, and not its present condition, which gives to this Island of Tumaco its interest for the traveller. When Pizarro, during his second voyage of discovery, determined to explore the interior of the continent in the vicinity of the Rio de San Juan, while Almagro returned to Panama for further assistance, he sent his sagacious and resolute pilot Bartholomew Ruiz (who did not receive his full share of the honor of these bold adventures) to prosecute discoveries along the coast to the south. It was then that Ruiz discovered the Island of *Gallo* now called *Tumaco;* and it was but shortly after that he fell in with the strange craft, known ever since as the *balsa* of these countries, on which he found a number of natives; and among them those two from the Peruvian port of Tumbes whom he took aboard of his vessel and detained, and from whom the information was obtained which led to the subsequent discovery of Peru. When Pizarro, rejoined by both Almagro and Ruiz, prosecuted his further voyage along the coast, and reaching the thickly-populated neighborhood of Tacamez, in the Bay of St. Matthew, found that he must have reënforcements, and again sent for these to Panama, he determined to avail of the insular, and therefore more defensible position of the Island of Gallo, on which to remain until the arrival of assistance. And here it was that the remarkable deed occurred which stamped Pizarro, even in that age of hardy and brave adventure, as a man of extraordinary courage, indomitable energy, and unswerving perseverance. For when the Governor of Panama, discouraged by the failure thus far to discover the land of Peru—the famed, but by him and most of his contemporaries, then considered fabulous region of gold—and deploring the loss of many Spanish cavaliers who had embarked in the enterprise, sent orders for the return of the expedition; Pizarro, still borne above misfortune by confidence in its original purpose, determined to prosecute it to the end, to suffer every exposure, deprivation, and hardship necessary for its accomplishment, and to dare official displeasure rather than abandon the enterprise. With his sword, tracing a line from east to west on the sand of *this island*, otherwise obscure, but thus made historic by a deed which ennobles human nature, and has done more than any other act of his life to dignify his character, he called to his comrades, and said: "On that side are toil, hunger, nakedness, storm, desertion, and death; on this side, ease and pleasure. There lies Peru with its riches; here Panama with its poverty. Choose each man what best becomes a brave Castilian. For my part I go to the south." Stepping across the line he was followed by thirteen only of his companions, including his heroic pilot. The remainder returned with the governor's messenger to Panama.

Such is Prescott's record of the act of Pizarro. But Mr. Arthur Helps, in his history of the "Spanish Conquest in America," published since Mr. Prescott's "History of the Conquest of Peru," says that the foregoing statement is "according to the invincible passion for melo-dramatic representation which people of second-rate imagination delight in, those especially who have not seen much of human affairs, and who do not know in how plain and unpretending a manner the greatest things are, for the most part, transacted." As Mr. Helps tells the story, it was the commander of the vessel sent to convey the Spaniards back to Panama, who, "pitying the straits to which Pizarro was reduced," drew a line on his vessel, allowing that terrible conqueror and those who chose to follow his desperate fortunes to withdraw beyond it. Mr. Helps' book proves him to have delved deeply into old records. He certainly has a curt way of disposing of distinguished authority; and one feels disposed to regret that a doubt has been thrown over Mr. Prescott's effective representation, and that the beautiful coloring of moral grandeur he has given to it should have been thus dimmed.

Be this as it may, certain it is that, deserted but not dismayed, delayed but not doubting; abandoned by the timid and the heartless, for it was with difficulty that they begged even a small portion of ship-stores to support life; and without the means of prosecuting their voyage, but sustained by brave hearts, and undiminished confidence in long-cherished hopes, and with faith in their compatriots Luque and Almagro, the little band of undaunted spirits awaited for seven months the coming of private succor from Panama. Twenty-five leagues north of *Gallo*, and five leagues from the continent, was the island of *Gorgona*, also discovered by Ruiz, which, being better supplied with water and fruit, they determined to reach if possible. And having accomplished this on a raft constructed for the purpose, they there remained until a small vessel was despatched to them, with which these fearless and unsubdued spirits once more pursued their trackless way over an unexplored ocean, in search of El Dorado, to which, slowly but surely, accumulated presumption as undoubtedly pointed in their opinions, as inductive philosophy resting on assured facts to certain conclusions.

Except by that of the discovery of the western world, the record of this constancy, devotion, courage, and final success, is not surpassed by any which adorns the proudest page of Spanish history. And if its object had been solely the glory of discovery, the opening of mutually advantageous commercial avenues, the extension of the blessings of a higher civilization, or of "peace and good-will to man," Pizarro, as the moving spirit of the great achievement, would have placed his name among the most renowned of earthly benefactors. But, animated by avarice; impelled by a cupidity whetted to the keenest relish, and craving for possession; dreaming dreams and seeing visions of gems and gold in his excited imagination, until their fancied existence was regarded as a demonstrated fact, the discovery of which was to entitle him, in his opinion, to the right of estate, without reference to other human ownership; he failed to recognize after wards, in his relations with the unhappy victims of his invasion, the righteous principles of justice and mercy, and thus branded his own name with the infamy of most shameless perfidy, robbery, and murder. The events of the conquest, recorded by the unprejudiced pens of Spanish historians of that period, point to the general fact that the condition of the Peruvians at the time of the discovery showed a singular freedom from vice; they were mild, docile, industrious, and placed by the policy of government beyond the possibility of destitution or of want; public prosperity and personal happiness prevailed throughout their empire, until the lust of conquest, stimulated by the love of gold, and encouraged by a bigoted fanaticism, rather than restrained and guided by the benign influences of a pure and exalted religion, broke the spell of enchantment which had long rested on the country beneficently—however despotic the sway—and swept over it as with a tempest, carrying dismay, desolation, and death to every habitation.

The river *Rosario*, coming from Ecuador, and receiving the Caunapi branch which flows from New Granada, empties into the sea opposite the Island of Usmal, a few miles northeast of Tumaco. The Rosario is represented on some maps as the division line between the above-named Republics. But such an assumption, of necessity throws Tumaco under the Government of Ecuador, off the coast of which it would in that case lie; while in fact it has always been recognized and governed as a part of New Granada. And I have the assurance of a very intelligent Spanish citizen of New Granada, who lived for some time in Tumaco, that the true division line between the Pacific Provinces of these two countries is the river *Carchi*, which empties into the ocean a few miles southwest of Tumaco.

Our detention here was short, and putting to sea again we headed for Buenaventura, passing at midnight the *Island of Gorgona*, in latitude 2° 58′ N., five or six miles long and half that width, said to be a paradise of tropical verdure. As already stated, it was to this island that Pizarro and his brave comrades came from Tumaco to await the expected assistance from Panama, before he could prosecute his discoveries. Here now live a German and his Granadian Eve, literally insulated from the world, the New Granadian Government having bestowed the island upon him for services during its war of independence. We ran close to this Eden, the blue wave dancing joyfully around it, its dark undulating outline distinctly defined in the clear moonlight showing the depth of shadow of its perennial luxuriance, and the air breathing balmy summer "wafted from that happy isle."

Very different have been the experiences of weather in my southern and northern voyage. That to the south besides being attended with constantly diminishing temperature, was at times very boisterous and rough; while pleasant breezes, with the exception of a few days of calm off the coast of Chile, have served on the return to temper agreeably the increasing heat. Somewhat more than a day's steaming brought us to the Bay of Buenaventura, in latitude 3° 50′ N., and running eight miles up the Buenaventura River, with a varying width of from one to two miles, but a very narrow channel for navigation, we anchored, at 2 P. M., in the pretty harbor of the town of Buenaventura: distance from Tumaco one hundred and sixty-eight miles. Here clouds and water-spouts gather, to make it at all times the place *par excellence* of modern deluges. We thought, on entering the harbor, from the unclouded sky and clear atmosphere, that there would be an exception in our favor, and that one day of the three hundred and sixty-five of the year would pass without rain. But as we were leaving our anchorage in the evening, the storm rolled up its dark masses, and the lightning flashed its signals to tell that Buenaventura was to sleep that night as usual under a wet blanket.

One-half of the New Granadian navy was lying at anchor in this port: to wit, a schooner mounting six guns. It was said that she was guarded every night by fifty *soldiers*, from an apprehension that the revolutionists intended to *swim* off and take her by surprise! The other half of the navy—another schooner—had sailed, probably to some place of greater security!

The town is at the northeast part of the harbor, and has an insular position between the Rio Buenaventura and one of its affluents, the Rio Daguire. The Rio San Antonio and Rio Cayman also empty near by, aiding in the formation of that water expanse called the Port, which extending to the southwest under the continued name of Rio Buenaventura, finally empties into the bay eight miles further. The town formerly contained five hundred people, but the commander of the schooner stated that the requirements of military service in these troublous times, together with revolutionary desertions, had reduced the number one-half. No addition to our freight or passenger list was made here; and it may be remarked that there has not been thus far any great manifestation of commercial activity, or of pleasure travel on the route of this boat. If any North Americans are looking to this coast with reference to the establishment of steamer lines, let them carefully examine the various routes before embarking in the enterprise. At present the British "Pacific Steam Navigation Company" have the nearly exclusive steam navigation of the west coast of South America. From Panama to Valparaiso they have a continuous line of splendid boats; the fare from Panama to Callao being one hundred and sixty dollars, and from the latter port to Valparaiso one hundred and thirty dollars: returning, the fare is twenty dollars less in each case in consequence of the usually favorable winds shortening the time of voyage in this direction. This line stops at but few ports on the route. But intermediate lines of smaller steamers run respectively from Panama to Guayaquil; from Guayaquil to Callao; from Callao to Valparaiso; from Valparaiso to Puerto Monte in the far south of Chile; and these call at all the smaller ports on the coast where there is any trade, or any prospect of developing it. Some of the intermediate routes are unprofitable, and such necessarily are a burden upon the continuous and more profitable line, which carries the greatest number of passengers and the largest and most valuable cargoes at the highest rates. On two of the shorter intermediate routes opposition boats from the United States are now running; and it may be that these experimental lines, if entirely successful, will form the nuclei of a continuous opposition steamer line along the whole coast. But a careful examination of the proposal, and good judgment in the decision of the question, will be required, as well as staunch and fast boats, and skill, punctuality, and an accommodating spirit in their management, to justify the undertaking. The "Pacific Steam Navigation Company" have at this time a fleet of twelve steamers; the length of their line of travel is nearly four thousand miles, and the ports at which they stop on that long route upwards of fifty; and it should be stated, to the credit of the chief manager, Mr. Petrie, of Callao, and of the commanders of the steamers, that on no corresponding steamer route in the world, especially in view of the want of light-houses, and the prevalence of fogs on this coast, have so few disasters occurred. The steamers are of the first class, strong, well-appointed, commodious, and comfortable; the commanders skilful, attentive, and polite; the officers generally, faithful and orderly, and the lines are run with singular punctuality.

Many nearly naked products of practical amalgamation, of hues well suited to the occupation, having coaled the steamer, we hove anchor at six P. M., and stood westwardly until fairly clear of the entire coast; and then we bore away west-northwest, and finally north-northwest for Panama, three hundred and forty-five miles distant.

The observations of the first and second days out showed the warping influence of unlooked-for currents upon our direct course, and illustrated the necessity of multiplied examinations, and further study of the ocean drifts of this part of the Pacific—in the opinion of navigators much needed. But few parts of the coast of the western hemisphere are as unimportant commercially, at present, as that embraced within the termini of this steamer route—Guayaquil and Panama. The ports are but little resorted to, and its exclusion from the familiarities of trade renders the ignorance of its harbors, shoals, rocks, winds, and currents of less practical importance now, although it may be regretted in the future.

The English Admiralty surveys of Kellett and Wood have not been repeated nor verified by others; and though more correct in many particulars than the old Spanish charts, yet they are regarded by some experienced seamen as imperfect. It might prove a useful question both for the North American and British Governments, to determine if some of their naval vessels had not better be employed in verifying or correcting the above surveys, and adding further observations for publication, than in yachting about classical seas familiar to every schoolboy, or lingering in inglorious ease about harbors where manly service degenerates into capering "nimbly in a lady's chamber to the lascivious pleasing of a lute"?

The acknowledgment should be made, however, that in the matter of surveying foreign coasts and harbors, the British Admiralty are governed by a wiser policy, and exact more active service at the hands of their naval officers than the United States Navy Department. This may depend upon longer official service of executive authority, and therefore larger experience and more comprehensive knowledge and appreciation of marine necessities and duties. Certain it is that in unsurveyed harbors, or where the surveys are of doubtful accuracy, and sometimes for the improvement of young officers in this branch of service even when further information is not actually needed, British commanders detained long in port are expected to form surveying parties for actual duty. And I am assured by those conversant with such matters, that many an officer is able to trace his promotion, and the subsequent special favor and confidence of his Government, to official records of his competency, activity, industry, perseverance, and accuracy, when engaged on such duty in the early years of his professional life.

It is an unfortunate fact that some of our finest specimens of naval architecture, the appearance of which in numerous foreign ports would give to the unreading and ignorant a proper appreciation of our national power, are required to linger ingloriously in harbors that might be named, until the original anchorage, it has been ironically suggested, has undergone a geological change; and a heaving of the anchor embedded in a glassy stratum would have warranted the supposition of a vitrification of the sand bottom by volcanic heat, but for the not irrational intimation that long accumulating ale and champagne bottles had something to do with it. And this naval inactivity has not even the apology of a useful incidental employment to palliate it; which, while it would promote personal health, official efficiency, and professional improvement, would advance also the interests of general commerce, contemplating the development of the natural resources of the Pacific Provinces of Ecuador and New Granada.

Our progress was retarded by head-winds and cross currents. The latter, in particular along the coast of New Granada, our commander thinks are but imperfectly understood. In this field of inquiry there is need of the inspiring influence and suggestions of our own Maury to give impulse to investigation, his assiduity in collecting and collating its results, his analytic mind to unfold the secrets of nature, and his comprehensive intelligence to simplify to others her phenomena, and frame rational theories and sound rules of practice.

## CHAPTER XXII.

NEGRO SLAVERY—ITS ANTECEDENTS AND CAUSE IN SPANISH AMERICA—CONSEQUENCES OF EMANCIPATION.

In returning to the starting point of my southern tour, mind busies itself with a retrospection of the incidents and observations of the interval. Among other things, the condition of the negro, and the influence he is exercising on the social and political state of the countries visited, having been inquired into, have led to reflections reasonable in one whose own people are interested in that subject.

In New Granada, Ecuador, Peru, and Chile, as well as in the other *Spanish-American colonies*, negro slavery existed and became an *inheritance of the ensuing Republics.* Indian slavery likewise existed under the Empire, although in a letter of Cortez to the Emperor Charles the Fifth he says: "*Considering the capacity of the Mexican Indians* it appears a grave thing to compel them to serve the Spaniards." Nevertheless, the pressure of necessities of revenue and importunities of followers, compelled him, as he further says, "to place on deposit to the Spaniards the lords and natives of these provinces." This was the commencement of that system of servitude in Mexico known as the "encomienda," and which was subsequently extended to the other countries discovered and colonized by the Spaniards. True, the Emperor issued an order that no Indian captive was to be held as a slave "throughout his dominions;" and an historian of that period regards this "a considerable step in the up-hill work of humane legislation," although he withholds all comments on the numberless cruelties, oppressions, and exactions, which placed the Indians in a far *less humane relation* than would have been a wisely and benevolently ordered system of servitude. Subsequently Ponce de Leon was sent to Mexico as *residencia*, and he was instructed to inquire into the subject of encomiendas, and "in case he should determine that the Indians were to be given in-encomienda, he should then consider whether they should remain as they were, or be given as vassals or by way of fief."

In 1533 Charles "authorized the granting of encomiendas *in Peru;*" and on the appointment of Antonio de Mendoza as Viceroy of Mexico, we are told that the Emperor secretly gave him the power of dealing with the subject, which shows that the question was still open as regarded the inhabitants of New Spain. In 1535 Charles the Fifth undertook an expedition against Tunis. It cannot be proved that that expedition had any influence on the fate of the Indies; but in the next year a law was passed which may have been due to the want of money at home, or to the want of attention to colonial affairs. This was the *law of succession* proclaimed at Madrid in 1536, which gave encomiendas for a second life, and was applicable to all the Indies. Thus, an actual personal, as well as political enslavement of the millions of natives of these newly-discovered countries was established, subject only to the laws of *repartimiento*, which assigned the specific service and its duration.

The countries thus enslaved embraced among them the two great centres of Indian civilization, Mexico and Peru; not the Peru of our day, but that of the Incas, extending from Quito to the Maulé, nearly two thousand five hundred miles. Both inhabited by races whose intelligence, customs, social and political institutions, by their general advancement and adaptation to the wants of the people, surprised their discoverers. It was a usurpation of dominion in the West, and a subordination to its own selfish purposes by Spain of teeming millions of people, having no parallel except in the aggressive and appropriating policy of Great Britain in the East. Although conquered and controlled by Spanish hardihood, prowess, and superior agencies of war, yet from approximative physical and moral equality of the Indians to their conquerors, intercourse by marriage and otherwise was not insuperably repugnant to the instincts of the higher race, and thus resulted in great part that extensive mongrelism which is the most striking characteristic of the present population, and which, from the interest of neutralization and accumulation of power and influence, has overthrown the system of servitude founded in the first instance upon the greater diversity of race.

Owing to the rapid disappearance of the Indians in some of the Spanish colonies, particularly in the West India Islands, from depressing influences and harsh treatment, a royal grant allowed the importation of negro slaves to supply necessary labor. Many of these in time found their way to the continent, and thus another element of mongrelism was introduced on the great theatre of Spanish-American practical amalgamation. For although the gap between the extremes of the human races—the Caucasian and the Negro—could not readily be filled; not merely because of instinctive repugnance, but because of the operations of natural law, which counteract the violations of the ordinances of God, who determined the distinctions, relations, and purposes of His beings, in the development of plan has created "every thing after his kind," and has also provided to preserve them thus; yet the existence of the intermediate Indian facilitated the temporary closure of it. The Indian's approximation to the White on the one hand, gave to their hybrid offspring a higher vitality than could be possessed by the mulatto; and his corresponding approximation to the Negro on the other hand, gave to that hybrid offspring also a higher vitality than that possessed by the mulatto. And taken in connection with the greatly preponderating aboriginal element in the populations of the Spanish-American countries, the *imperious self-preservative law of nature*, if European and African immigration should be arrested or greatly restricted, will surely assert its power and restore the native blood to its original state, and surrender again to its representative man the control of his own destiny.

This event appears likely to be hastened by the abolition of negro slavery since the achievement of the independence of the Spanish-American colonies. For his emancipation, by freeing him from the control of a master capable of regulating his actions for their mutual good, handed him over to the debasing mastery of his own passions, which, by the universal testimony of the intelligent and candid citizens of these countries, are precipitating his extinction.

Successful in its effort to shake off the political oppression of the mother-country, the Caucasian race, which originated and was the chief agent in executing the scheme of colonial independence, has in its organization of government and modification of law, merged the question of domestic bondage, as applied to an inferior race, in the general proposition of political slavery considered in its relation to equals in creation. In the Spanish-American republics some apology may be found for this in the wide-spread mongrelism already referred to, which shaded away the marked differences of original race, temporarily elevating the lower at the cost of the higher organization; and where but few were left untainted by deterioration, scrutiny was deprived of a motive for activity. And if, by some, distinctions were readily observed, the policy of interest, or aspirations for place and power, taught them silence and submission to the many; who, however degenerate, had become through numbers the controlling element of the State in its new form. It is not surprising that mongrels should overlook the inferiority of one of the elements of their own ancestry. Their ignorance of natural laws governing the physiological relations of races blinded them to evils which could not fail to become aggravated by the social equality necessarily resulting from the exercise of equal political rights by the Negro. The intensity of their new-born zeal for freedom made them reckless of acts destined to deprive invested capital and useful enterprise of necessary labor, and in its stead to increase the burdens of society by idleness, poverty, debasement, and consequent disease. They failed to foresee the additional corruptions, social convulsions, and perpetually recurring political disturbances, certain to follow an equal grant of civil rights to those who, from inherent defects, know not how to use them for the general good, and hence become ready instruments of evil, of usurpation, oppression, persecution, and revenge, in the hands of the designing and wicked. Deterioration and its inherent prejudice, and the want of means of knowledge, made them ignorant of the causes of the human degradation in their midst, and the increased debasement to which the abolition of negro slavery and the elevation of that lowest type of man to equal political and social privilege with the highest, must necessarily lead. From emancipation and legal equality, the tendency is unavoidably to social level, mingling of blood, hybridism in the direction of the preponderating element; and after a long endurance of punishment consequent on the perpetration of crimes against the laws of organization as decreed by the Creator, an ultimate extinction of the feebler race, a reparation of the outrage inflicted on nature, and a return to the original type.

Certain physical differences of color, hair, form, feature, are manifest to all. But of the brain, the seat of mind, and of its associate nervous apparatus, and their physiological laws and manifestations of nobler being, the lower races know nothing; and the uneducated even of a higher are too often ignorant from neglect of investigation or the force of unreasoning prejudice. And yet these are distinctive and peculiar in the races, and as undoubted to those who seek for truth and knowledge, and are not the victims of a conspiracy against exalted nature, rational freedom, and progress, as are the physical differences above named to the thoughtless looker-on.

But it is strange that so many to whom information is accessible, and who have the capacity, have failed to apply inductively certain well known facts. Let them compare peoples of Caucasian origin, of any period known to history, with what we know of the Negro. Can any such examples be pointed to among the former of such degradation and debasement as are presented by the latter? Does the history of man, since the flood, furnish the record of a White community without some recognition of a Supreme Being; without law, order, or government, as the explorations of travellers have shown to be the fact in many instances among Negroes? Has any such Caucasian monster been known as the Negro king of Dahomey, shown by a late discussion in the British Parliament to celebrate his "grand *customs*" by sacrificing two thousand persons, and collecting in a pit their human blood sufficient to float a canoe? and who, by the testimony of Lord Palmerston, was accustomed to "ornament his palace with the skulls of his victims sacrificed on these occasions." When Adahanzen died, two hundred and eighty of his wives were butchered before the arrival of his successor, and the remaining wives were buried alive. At the "Yam customs" every noble sacrifices a slave; and scarcely has one barbarous and bloody custom been abandoned from the earliest period of which any thing is known of them. Is there any historical or traditional account of any family of the White race being found, as in the case of some Negro tribes, habitually naked, and without shelter for women and children other than a hollow tree, or a covering of bushes, as provided even by the Nshiego Mbouve ape; without some manifestation of religious sentiment, or form of worship; without some social organization; without some knowledge of agriculture, and mechanical skill beyond the making of a wooden spear or bow and arrows? Yet in such a condition millions of negroes have been found during past ages, and are still being brought to the knowledge of civilization by European travellers in Africa. Surely it will not be pretended, for it cannot be maintained, that this near relationship to brutal nature is dependent on the influence of slavery, when these negroes have shaped their own destiny, and most of them roam as free as the ourang outang that disputes with them the dominion of their wild empire. Happily for the advocates of diversity of race, and the equal diversity of mental and moral power, the white man has been a stranger, and his influence unfelt in interior Africa. The negro has been left to determine without control the problem of human disparity. In no instance has he made any near approach to the arts, sciences, literature, religion, or any of the manifestations of a higher civilization of the white race. On the contrary he has grovelled in ignorance, sensuality, and savagery, in their most revolting forms. From the period of the destruction of the plain of Sodom, when its cities and inhabitants, as "an example, suffered the vengeance of eternal fire," because of their "giving themselves over to fornication and going after strange flesh," the race of Ham has illustrated the low instincts of brute nature. And writers, both sacred and profane, Moses, the prophet Ezekiel, Herodotus, Sonnini (authenticated by the great biblical critic

Adam Clarke), Gale, Bochart, and Herne's recent Researches, bear testimony to the bestiality of the negro: the làst-named author adding that there are districts of country in Africa in which apes and baboons live in the mud-huts of the negro natives, as if members of the same community.

It would be difficult to conceive a finer climate than that found in the republics of New Granada, Ecuador, Peru, and Chile; in many parts of these countries it is actually delicious. Throughout the most of this great extent of continent the soil is surpassingly fertile, the products necessary to man's comfort and luxury, flourishing, with even imperfect culture—such as sugar, cacao, coffee, the cereals of all kinds, rice, maize, cotton; and fruits of every description, luscious and nutritious, growing spontaneously and bountifully, making of the country a vast Eden, were it not for the indolence and debasement of the people. Man alone is not as decreed by his Creator. Overstepping the limits of His assignment—an offence pardonable in an ignorant and degraded being, who has no knowledge of the laws of reproduction, and no prompting but animal instinct coupled with a vague sense of improvement—the Spanish conquerors of America committed treason against their race; for, it involved the destruction of its supremacy, its absolute debasement; and is compromising now the peace and prosperity of these countries, and the permanency and extension of Republican government. Unfortunately, the first settlers of the colonies were mere adventurers—usually the outcasts and moral lepers of society—and those of Spanish America never exhibited the restraints of self-respect, and preservative instinct of race, through which the Anglo-American has more perfectly guarded his integrity. The former, therefore, amalgamated with the Indian in all the colonies; and repugnant as the Negro may have been to him, from low sensualism and generally vicious habits, the Spaniard intermixed with him too, to the still greater degradation alike of his own moral and physical nature. It should be said of Chile, that the last deterioration exists there, notably to a much less extent than in the countries north of it. The climate of that country is colder, and less adapted both to the negro and to slave-labor; hence fewer negroes, fortunately for that State, were carried to it; and a happy consequence of that exemption from his presence is perceptible in its superior population to that of any other South American Republic I visited. But wherever the negro, and the negro compound are found, freed, as they now are by acts of emancipation, from the control of superior beings, there have they become the victims of their own crimes, indolence, and sensual appetites; which, although in the West India islands where they are the dominant race, are returning them to a state of barbarism, as has been fully shown by abundant published testimony, yet in the continental countries above named are bringing about their extinction. In the mean time, until that is accomplished, they are destined to be disturbers of the public peace, tools of military tyranny, thieves, murderers, vagabonds, blots on the body politic. But still, so long as they remain on the stage of action, as heirs of "impartial freedom," to *such* is confided in part the experiment of self-government, on the result of which the hopes of loftier man depend.

From the existing stand-point the eye of earnest desire cannot look beyond and behold a cheering promise of the future, so far as the questions of self-government and of constitutional liberty rest for their solution, with the Pacific Republics of South America. And this results chiefly from the deterioration of nobler faculties, and the impairment of the capacity of higher race for the fulfilment of the trust created and confided to it by nature. Regardless of the imperious mandates of destiny, whose violations never fail to decree their own punishment, and faithless to the duty of preserving in its purity, elevating, and ennobling that exalted humanity from whom they sprang, they have betrayed their high calling, become common levellers, seek to degrade that glorious emanation of Supreme Wisdom they should guard, and impiously defame the temple at whose altars they were appointed to minister.

Humanity, fashioned by the Creator, cannot be improved by the devices of man; and political government, reposing upon the ordinances of that creation, and upon the precepts of Divine Revelation, as did that which was framed by a strange wisdom and bequeathed to us by Washington and his compeers of immortality, and which served for a time as the model of later republics, could not be violated without danger to the whole fabric once securely resting upon it. Thus it is that a consequence of disregarding nature's laws, and wise political arrangements in conformity thereto, is seen in the deplorable condition of the countries of which we have been speaking, and of others of Spanish settlement.

While the Southern States, Cuba, Porto Rico, and Brazil, with slavery entailed on them by the acts of others, have enjoyed, through an intelligent and benevolent direction of it, an extraordinary degree of prosperity, and mutual happiness and reciprocal benefits have prevailed, what is the condition of other countries in which it has been attempted to abrogate the distinctions of natural and civil law? It would be true to say that while in all deterioration and evil have resulted, in most of them the freed negro is sunk in moral corruption, and is absolutely rioting in his own ruin. Even if it were appropriate in this connection to dwell on what has not passed under my special observation, the well-known facts would render it unnecessary to refer to distracted, desolated, impoverished, and perishing Mexico; to torn, wretched, and insignificant Central America; to savage Hayti reverting to heathenism, and becoming a waste, where the sugar-cane and coffee-tree once flourished in unequalled luxuriance; to Jamaica and other English islands, blasted in agriculture, ruined in trade, and only kept from sinking into the same pollution and barbarism with Hayti, by the pride and power of the misguided Government which impoverished thousands of its prosperous, educated, refined, and loyal white citizens, and blighted fair gardens of tropical agriculture, that it might gratify the vain-glory of a mock philanthropy by restoring to the negro his native right of indolence and licentiousness, and tickle the fancy of "groundlings" with a *show* of love of liberty and equality, while it takes special care to concede even to these white dupes but a *meagre* privilege of *political right* and a *stern realization of social degradation.* But the obligations of personal narrative and observation demand that I should point to New Granada, ever harassed by revolution, and trembling on the verge of dissolution; one part of it the victim of one military dictator, while another part groans under the oppression of a rival chieftain—both lawless, both cruel; and such is the universal national impoverishment, that, but for the annuity of an American railroad across the Isthmus of Panama, the Presidential usurper who may happen to hold the capital for the time, would not have the means of paying the expenses of his official state. Why speak of Ecuador, known rather as the territory on which Chimborazo frowns, and where Cotopaxi pours forth its volumed flame and ashy cloud, and heaves and rends the earth, as if in punishment of man's neglect of this glorious and perennial garden of earth; where truly he has paid no tax of human effort to improvement—no tribute commensurate with Supreme Beneficence? And Peru! Has even its ancient grandeur survived modern humanitarianism? Where are its unequalled roads and magnificent canals? the happiness and prosperity of its contented millions? Will the evidence of a Spaniard be taken against the policy of his own countrymen, whose precepts taught and example illustrated the wickedness of disregarding the distinctions of the Almighty? He had no grievances to redress—no sense of injustice to dictate false representations. He had received his portion of plunder, for he originated the saying, "he plays away the sun before rising," by losing at Cuzco the golden image of the sun of the great temple, in one night's gambling. What says this witness, Capitan Mancio Sierra de Leguizamo, in his last will and testament? "We found these kingdoms governed in such a manner that throughout them there was not a thief, nor idler, nor a vicious man; neither was there any adulterous or bad woman. The lands, the mountains, the mines, the pastures, the houses, the woods, were governed and divided in such a manner that each man knew and kept to his own estate. There were no lawsuits about property. The affairs of war did not hinder those of commerce, nor those of commerce those of agriculture. In every thing, from the smallest to the greatest matter, there was concert and arrangement." He then adds, "the Spaniards have destroyed people of such good government as were these natives of Peru." And what have flowed from amalgamation and its consequential political and social equality of antagonist races? Is it necessary to answer the question after what has been already said of this republic? Scarcely has it taken a position among the family of nations, when it is found to be hastening to premature decay. Religion is a thing of form. Morality has no national existence. Virtue, like the diamond, is buried, and unrecognized in overshadowing darkness. Personal safety and justice have no guarantees. Agriculture, in a comprehensive sense, has ceased. Commerce languishes. The political rights of the citizen are not respected by public authorities. Literature and science are not of personal knowledge or of practical utility, and in the library of Lima "sleep the sleep that will know no waking" in the near future of Peru. Government is the football of military usurpers. Free government and self-government are popular illusions, while despotism stalks abroad guarded by mail-clad cuirasseurs, as brutal as they are black, whose sabres carry on their points the answer to all remonstrances and appeals for redress against arbitrary power.

And the State, despite extortionate exactions, would become bankrupt but for the deposit of guano which ancient Peruvians bequeathed as an everlasting legacy of fertility; but which the present Government is thrusting upon the market of the world with the improvidence of a spendthrift, who has mortgaged his estate for the means of indulging the profligacy of to-day, though beggary may be the doom of to-morrow.

It would be wise for all who are interested in the question of the correlation of the races, to examine with a view to the ascertainment of truth, and to consider dispassionately the experiment by others of political and social equality, and thus supplant closet speculations by a practical knowledge, which alone should be relied on to determine how far it is meet that a Caucasian freeman should become not merely debased in blood, but also a bondman of labor to the negro. Thus far reliable testimony sustains the conclusion that when this inferior element of society is liberated from disciplinary and intelligent control, his native tendency to still greater degradation drags him, and others whose destiny may be inseparable from his, down to ruin. Occasional instances of *mongrels* educated by extraordinary effort, are not to be regarded even as exceptions to the rule of *negro* inferiority, certainly they do not disprove *free* negro depravity. Vice, crime, and pauperism devolve upon white laboring classes evils incident to the development of these in their midst, from whatever cause; and while the burden of their own support becomes increased by the withdrawal under a system of free negroism of productive laborers from pursuits to which they are, and whites are not adapted, their burden of taxation likewise becomes increased by additional expenses of prisons, alms-houses, and other penal and charitable institutions, demanded by the social condition referred to.

Better, far better than these, or than the war of races coming of them—whether waged by nature or by the vindictive passions of man—that the counsel of Paul the Apostle of Christ should be taken, and that slaves should be taught to "be obedient to them that are (their) masters according to the flesh, with fear and trembling, in singleness of heart, as unto Christ. Knowing that whatsoever good thing any man doeth, the same shall he receive of the Lord, whether he be *bond* or free."

We are in the Bay of Panama, a hundred miles wide at its mouth, from Cape Garrachina on the east, to Cape Mala on the west; and nearly seventy miles in length, from these wide-spread arms to the city of Panama, which stands at its head. Steering up the bay, the archipelago of the Pearl Islands is seen to the eastward, about fifty miles from Panama. This archipelago, including rocky islets, is numerous. The Isla del Rey, the principal of the group, is seventeen miles long and ten wide. This is one of the most valuable pearl fisheries of the world, the product being $150,000 annually to the divers. The profit of the pearl merchant is still greater.

These Pearl Islands stand off the mouth of the Gulf of San Miguel, an arm of the Bay of Panama, and remarkable in the history of America as being the watery expanse to which Vasco Nuñez de Bilboa was conducted from Darien, when, acting on information derived from the Indians, he undertook the journey which resulted in the Spanish discovery of the Pacific Ocean on the 25th September, 1513. Travellers, in making the journey from Aspinwall to Panama, will sometimes have pointed out to them, near Panama, the height from which Vasco Nuñez first saw the great ocean spread illimitably at his feet. But it is not to be seen on that line of transit. The isthmus was first crossed by the Spaniards at least a hundred miles to the south-east of the line of the railroad; and among the rich presents at that time made to them by the Indian Caciques living on the shores of the Gulf of San Miguel, were two hundred and forty large pearls, derived doubtless from the neighboring pearl fisheries.

Francisco Pizarro accompanied Vasco Nuñez on this first expedition to the Pacific; and it is stated also that he was present at an earlier period when Nuñez was informed by the son of the Cacique Comogre, that by traversing the great sea, of which the Spaniards were then for the first time informed, to the southward, they "would find a land of great richness where the people had large vessels of gold, out of which they ate and drank; where, indeed, there was more gold than there was iron in Biscay." And doubtless it was the information thus received that led to the subsequent arrangement at Panama between Pizarro, Almagro, and Luque, which resulted in the discovery and conquest of Peru.

There are the white caps tossing their silvery spray over the dark sea-wall of the depot of Pacific treasure, now, as of old. And there are the towers of its crumbling churches. And there dips the cross of St. George on the "Anne" in salutation; and now the stars and stripes of the "Lancaster" in response.

We have been nearly nine days in making the voyage from Guayaquil. Rather a tedious voyage it would have been, but for its novelty, off of the usual route of travel, and the fine social qualities of our commander, Captain King, than whom a more skilful seaman and agreeable companion has never been baptized by the "white sea-foam."

## CHAPTER XXIII.

VOYAGE FROM PANAMA TO SAN FRANCISCO—PACIFIC COAST OF CENTRAL AMERICA—GULF OF TEHUANTEPEC—MEXICAN COAST—ACAPULCO—ATMOSPHERIC CHANGE OFF THE GULF OF CALIFORNIA—COAST OF LOWER CALIFORNIA—SANTA BARBARA ISLANDS OFF THE COAST OF THE STATE OF CALIFORNIA—GOLDEN GATE—ARRIVAL AT SAN FRANCISCO.

"The morn is up again, the dewy morn,
With breath all incense, and with cheek all bloom,
Laughing the clouds away with playful scorn,
And living as if earth contain'd no tomb—
And glowing into day; we may resume
The march of our existence; and thus I,
Still on thy shores, fair Isthmus! could find room
And food for meditation, nor pass by
Much that might give us pause, if ponder'd fittingly."

But this may not be. However beautiful the attractions of this sunny clime; though the fascinations of the verdure-adorned ruins of Panama, and of the remembrances of its past history are difficult to overcome, and the hospitalities of friends hard to escape from, yet the obligations of duty are imperious, and I return from the South of the Spaniard's descendant to seek without delay the North of the descendant of the Saxon. A golden key in both cases opened the portal of a new region to the tide of emigration, which flowed in the one through a channel of rapine, lust, and cruelty, to present degeneracy, and civil and religious oppression; what is to come of the other and later, setting steadily and sternly to meet the coming current of the Mongolian and Malay, on the glittering strand of California, is yet to be revealed.

Without waiting for the steam-tug which conveys the railroad passengers from the depot wharf to the San Francisco steamer in the offing, I put myself as ofttimes before, under the care of my good friend Flag-Officer Montgomery, and crossing at high tide the reef which surrounds the peninsula on which the town is built, and which at low water is bare for half a mile, went aboard the "Lancaster," bearing that veteran officer's blue pennant, to take leave of friends who were the first to greet me with a cordial welcome when coming from the far-off South, and now gave me the *adios* of countrymen when about to seek the distant North.

Domiciled aboard the steamship "Golden Age," I found her to be one of the largest and fastest on the Pacific, and much superior in all her appointments to those on the Atlantic end of the line, with accommodations for from one thousand to twelve hundred passengers. A large family to be cared for during a long voyage; and yet all seem contented and happy—good order, discipline, and regard for the comfort of passengers characterizing the government of our new sea-home. The commander, Captain Watkins, being asked the secret of his success, replied—"If such I have, it is due to a constant effort to command myself—the first duty of those in authority." Every day this model officer inspects his ship, with the same scrutiny observed on board a man-o'-war by its executive officer.

Late in the evening we stood out of the Bay of Panama under an easy head of steam, the rollers lifting their golden crests as they encountered the onward movement of the ship, whose dark way was thus brilliantly illuminated by the gleaming phosphorescence for which this harbor is noted when agitated.

Early next morning found us doubling *Cape Mala*, the southwestern point of land bounding the Bay of Panama, and we pursued a varying westerly course along the coast of *Azuezo*—a province of the State of Panama—during the day; lofty hills in the background advancing their gradually diminishing swells clad in tropical verdure, to bathe in the blue waves that broke in foam at their feet. Evening brought us off the *Island of Coiba.*

Beyond this, although our course bore west-northwest and northwest by west, corresponding to the trend of the coast, and not a great distance from it, we only occasionally saw the dim and apparently barren outline of the remainder of Central America. The skies were clear, and the breezes as if wafted by a lady's fan, until on a line with Lake Nicaragua, over whose bosom the northers from the Gulf of Mexico reach the Pacific, less shorn of their strength than where mountain barriers are interposed. Here a stiff gale disturbed the sea somewhat, but by this time the voyagers had learned to bear a little rough and tumble, and there were no candidates for sea-sickness and sympathy.

On the fifth day out from Panama we rounded Guacalate Bar, and entered the Gulf of Tehuantepec; and on the sixth coasted within ten or twelve miles of its mountain shore, ready to take advantage of friendly shelter under the lee of the Coast Range, if the winds, which in winter particularly often come fiercely through *La Chivala Pass*, should disturb uncomfortably this notoriously riotous gulf. During the more tranquil summer the course of the California steamers is in a direct line across the mouth of the gulf, from Guacalate Bar to Port Angeles, the headlands which mark east and west the geographical mouth of this wide indentation of the coast; a route by no means safe when a violent winter norther, blowing through the mountain gap, sends a rough sea against the incoming ocean swells. The strife of waters at such a time is described as being terrific.

Port Angeles having been passed at nine P. M., we steamed within three or four miles of the dark mountainous shore of Mexico during the night, sensibly feeling the deprivation of the refreshing breeze which came to us during the previous day through the gorge of Chivala, invigorating intertropical travellers, and causing the very billows to dance in joy of the delicious dalliance. During the entire seventh day we skirted a low sea-shore, resting against an undulating mountainous background, sometimes raising on high lofty and distinctive peaks; and at six P. M. made Point Diamant, a bold rocky cape, which marks the entrance to the Port of Acapulco, although the immediate pillars of the narrow inlet to that fine harbor are Bruja Point on the east, and Griffin Point on the west—Griffin Island lying a little further seaward, and dividing the entrance into two channels, the "great" and the "little," both of which having sufficient depth of water for vessels of the largest draught.

The harbor is as nearly land-locked as possible to admit of ingress and egress, and is about three miles long and one wide; but only the smaller west end, called the Bay of St. Lucie, is ordinarily used for anchorage, on the north shore of which stands the *City of Acapulco.* The anchorage is commanded by a fort built on a small tongue of land at the entrance of the inner harbor, and looks as if it might once have been a fortification of considerable strength, though now greatly dilapidated, after the fashion of every other great work, whether road, bridge, church, or fortress, since Spanish America threw off the government of the mother country.

Although nearly encircled by land, and ordinarily regarded as affording perfect shelter for shipping, yet hurricanes of fearful force sometimes sweep over the surrounding mountains, causing vessels to drag their anchors. Nevertheless, from the facility of access, great depth of water even within a ship's length of shore, freedom from bars, rocks, currents, and heavy swells, this harbor must be regarded as one of the finest on the Pacific coast; and from its nearly equidistance between the Pacific termini of the California route, it will probably continue to be, as it is now, the chief intermediate coal and provision depot of this steamship line.

The city of Acapulco is in latitude 16° 55′ N., and longitude 99° 48′ W., fourteen hundred and forty miles from Panama, has an estimated population of perhaps twenty-five hundred; lies at the foot of steep hills ribbed with rock, partially mantled with shrubbery, belted below with the broad-leaved banana and the plumed cocoa-palm, presenting a picturesque tropical scene, doubtless especially pleasing to those returning from the northern regions of quartz rock and pine. The streets are narrow, irregular, and bordered by mean-looking, low, one-story, mud-bedaubed, whitewashed houses, with roofs of red tile or thatch projecting over uneven sidewalks of a height above the level of the street, that in the event of a trip and tumble would lead an unlucky night-walker to think that he had gone on a voyage of discovery into a cellar. But the stranger may be comforted by the assurance that whatever other pitfalls may lie in wait for him—with which all seaports abound—cellars are not of the number, for earthquakes forbid these ready-made graves in volcanic countries; so that Pat and his shovel have no chance of employment hereabouts—there being besides neither railroads nor canals—unless with characteristic pluck he attacks the bowels of Popocatapetl and Orizaba, in search of the phenomena of terrestrial convulsions.

The scene presented at night on landing from the steamer, was novel and exciting. Lifted high and dry on the sandy beach by a gentle roller, the moment of its retirement was seized to leap from the launch and escape, ere another should catch the loiterer, and inflict the penalty of a foot-bath for trespass on ocean's skirt. Opposite the landing stands a large shed, with latticed and palisaded sides, dignified by the name of custom-house. It is the depository of the few goods destined for the interior, whither they are conveyed on mules. This rude public store bounds the sandy plaza on one side, two other sides of which are occupied by petty variety stores, dirty-looking eating houses and dramshops, while the fourth is dignified by the cathedral, a one-story adobe building, with a squatty tower from which came the ceaseless clatter of an afflicted bell, which—like some "Scribes and Pharisees" at home, who make a virtue of *dis*obeying the Divine injunction to "go into their *closet* and pray to their Father who is *in secret*," and who for "a pretence" make long prayers every day in the week in public places, and according to a published programme—stood at the street corner, and in the absence of any devotee within the sanctuary, continued noisily responsive to a murky saint, who pummelled as much piety out of its cracked sides as burthens the souls of some sanctimonious sinners who thank God that they "are not as other men." Senseless as seems this perpetual din of bell-metal in Spanish America, it may yet be, in the absence of positive harm, a more acceptable service in the eye of heaven, than the frequent teachings in our own land of a desecrated pulpit, which awaken in the human heart the wildest passions of fanaticism and intolerance.

The plaza is the market-place, where were seen flowers, fruits, and shells, on mats spread on the ground, with the venders squatting or standing about, seeking purchasers. The whole was fantastically arranged; and the gay and varied intertropical coloring illuminated by many candles made quite a pretty scene, the novelty of which was heightened by the dark-complexioned flower-girls, who familiarly button-holed a readily detected stranger, and dropping a bouquet in his bosom, hinted payment in his country's coin, "un *dime*." The intimation was irresistible, coming from descendants of the Aztecs, the ancestry of many of whom could be recognized in their diminutive size, delicate conformation, approximative Indian features and complexion.

Most of these people live upon the products of sale of such trifles to the Americans *in transitu*, who land at Acapulco for a few hours, during the coaling, watering, and provisioning of the steamer. Their general appearance and their houses indicate poverty. But their wants are few, and readily supplied in a warm climate by skirt, shirt, pants, sombrero, thatched shelter, spontaneous fruits and nutritious roots. They take no heed for the morrow, what they shall eat, nor wherewithal they shall be clothed—and the only instance I heard of in which this scriptural precept was departed from was that of a French-Yankee—a lusus naturæ—who, following in the wake of the American army from Matamoras to Mexico, remained in the latter city for a while after the treaty of Guadalupe Hidalgo, and finally drifted to Acapulco. Here, with the combined smartness, shrewdness, and skill of both his inherited and adopted nationalities, he is successfully conducting the only restaurant where unsurpassed chocolate, and good squabs, eggs, and sherry-cobblers, can be had; and here, with the assistance of an active little helpmate of a wife, who shows her partiality for shirt and trousers by wearing them, he is rapidly laying up treasures on earth.

Many half-naked, dirty-looking, idle negroes were seen sauntering about, indifferent to the chance of employment afforded by the entrance into port of the "Golden Age," and that of the downward bound steamer which came in a few minutes after. They are the worthless survivors of an industry that existed before the abolition of negro slavery in Mexico, when, under the direction of the superior intelligence and energy of Spanish masters, the fertile valleys beyond the coast range of mountains gave to commerce their rich productions.

As our launch skimmed over the placid bay on our return to the steamer, with the bright torches of rapidly plying boats flashing their long lines of light across the glassy surface, the dip of the oars letting fall as they rose again phosphorescent drops as if of molten gold, and moving in measured harmony to the prolonged cadence of a colonial Castilian tongue, the memory of that historic period was awakened, when, floating on these still waters, guarded by yon fortress, and embosomed within these lofty surroundings which hid them from the eyes of the bold buccaneers Drake and Anson, lay those treasure galleons lading with the immense riches of this, one of the two most magnificent dependencies ever owned by an earthly power—dependencies, strong in their affections for the mother country, and which now might have been the brightest jewels of her crown, had wisdom directed the administration of her high trust of sovereignty, and the just rights coming of equal race been conceded. But recognizing no law but the dictate of selfishness, no restraint within the limit of despotic will, no justice but that of tyrannical prerogative, royalty finally broke the bond of love which had held these colonies to Spain; and every effort to restore the political union by the sword, served but to alienate more entirely their affections, to provoke a fiercer resistance, and to arouse an intense and enduring hatred. It is a fact significant of evil, when nations become forgetful or regardless of the lessons of history. Government, however constituted, is too apt in the exercise of power to overlook the rights of the governed, and thus arousing in the aggrieved a determination of self-protection and resistance, it often aggravates the evil by the application of coercive measures, alike unjust and unwise—at variance with the inculcations of a benign religion, stimulating to human passions, destructive of social peace and prosperity, and even of the foundations of the political fabric. A union of government and people essential to national welfare, or of the different parts of a great empire, whether of original association or colonial, can only be secured by mutual confidence, equity and affection. A political union of States, to be permanent, must result from attraction, not from compulsion. True, the latter may enforce it for a time, if of sufficient power; but it is the welding of an iron despotism, and although it may not be sundered on the instant, the slower assaults of time and the corroding influences of discontent and aversion, will eventually and surely destroy it.

On reëmbarking we found several of the Mexican church party on board, who were escaping from the reëstablished liberal Government. It is remarkable how imitative the officials of so-called free Governments are becoming of arbitrary rulers. Illegal arrests, decrees of banishment, military executions, and practical repeal of all constitutional rights, are as common in this distracted country as under any known absolutism.

During the eighth and ninth days out from Panama, the bold shore of the Mexican States of Guerrero, Michoacan, and Colima, along which we passed, appeared but a few hundred yards off, giving a feeling of safety to timid travellers. Great depth of water is always found on the Pacific coast, where mountain ranges approach close to the ocean; shallows invariably skirt the low lands. Noon found us opposite the extinct volcano *Colima*, twelve thousand feet high, and thirty leagues distant, but distinctly seen towering loftily above the peaks of nearer spurs. At evening we were abreast of *Manzanilla*, a small seaport from which the specie of the adjoining country, and particularly of the large interior *city of Colima*, is shipped in the California steamers once a month, in return for merchandise, from San Francisco and Europe. During the night we were approaching Cape Corrientes, the eastern point of the Gulf of California, from which at eight A. M., on the tenth day, we took our departure across the mouth of the Gulf. At night it became much cooler, and on the evening of the eleventh day of our voyage, as we neared Cape St. Lucas, in latitude 22° 52′ N., the low temperature made a change from linen to woollen clothing necessary to comfort. It is on this part of the California route that many passengers suffer impairment of health from neglect of necessary precautions. From the relaxing effects of heat on the physical frame, and predisposition to disease incident to malarious exposure during an intertropical transit, detriment to health may reasonably be looked for when the atmospheric temperature falls suddenly from 90° to 60°, unless warm clothing be put on, habits of temperance observed, and night air on deck be avoided.

The large *Island of Margarita*, nearly closing the mouth of *Magdalena Bay*, showed its bold outline off our starboard side on the afternoon of the twelfth day. Shortly after a dense fog prevented a sight of *San Lorenzo Point* in latitude 24° 50′, and enveloped us in a veil of such thickness that a ship under full sail was unseen until she swept under our bow like the flying Dutchman—" a moment seen, then gone forever." An instant later and she would have gone down, and not known what sent her there.

A deep bight indents the coast of Lower California north of Point San Lorenzo. Having stood across this northwest half west on the thirteenth day out, we steered along the west side of the large *Cedros Island*, in latitude 28° 21′ N., the two small *Islands of Benito* lying off our port side, lifting into the air their little pinnacles and domes in miniature imitation of mountain scenery.

Our route lay now north-westwardly across another deep indentation of the shore line, always a pleasant departure from the low shore to those who know that the charts of the coast from Panama beyond this point, although of London publication, are made up from old Spanish surveys, and equally unreliable individual sources, and are not issued on government or admiralty authority. It is discreditable to the United States, that in the navigation of a coast in which they have the largest interest, in life and treasure, both its naval and commercial marine are dependent on such imperfect foreign guides; and that they are constantly liable to shipwreck from unknown sunken rocks and shoals; and to impediments of navigation from imperfectly understood currents. It is mortifying to reflect that there have been officers of their navy who might have conferred benefits on their country and the world, and acquired professional reputation, if actively engaged in coast-survey duty; who, under existing regulations and usages, have been victimized by ennui, disabled by diseases of indolence, or prematurely incapacitated by intemperate habits and artificial excitements, and have been finally "retired" from service discredited, if not disgraced.

At nine A. M. of the fifteenth day from Panama, we made the well-known group of *Santa Barbara Islands* off the coast of the State of California; the dark outline of *San Clemente* showing its seventeen miles of peak, undulation, and elevated level at the distance of thirty miles on our starboard bow; while the dangerous *Cortez shoal*, whose breakers were concealed by a dense *fog bank* that lifted its black wall above the sea in a manner to cheat a landsman with the belief that he was under the lee of a bold bluff, lay some fifteen miles away on the port side. The archipelago of Santa Barbara lies off that part of the coast where are situated the towns of San Diego, Los Angeles, and Santa Barbara, and consists of eight islands, destined to play a conspicuous part in the future activities of this coast.

In fair weather the northwardly route of the California steamers is usually inside of this group, not merely to avoid the current setting southwardly to the outside of the islands, but to take advantage of its supposed sweep around their south, and upward set along their east sides. In the thick fogs, however, which are frequent, the danger of running ashore is great; and consequently the outward route is usually selected by careful commanders, at the cost of a somewhat longer passage. The through steamers do not now, as they did formerly, stop at the ports above named; of course we did not see *Dead-man's Island* at the mouth of San Pedro Bay, the port of Los Angeles—so called, not because of its resemblance to a shrouded corpse, as in the case of El Muerto in the Gulf of Guayaquil, but because there lie buried many Americans whose lives were lost in the service of their country in the war with Mexico, and who found a resting-place on this sea-girt spot, for protection against the ravages of the coyote, a species of wolf that infests the mainland, and, like the hyena, revels on human remains.

In the afternoon we ran along the seaward side of San Nicholas, a sterile-looking island. The Island of Santa Rosa loomed up dimly in the distance towards evening; and after dark we passed on the west side of San Miguel, the outermost of the Santa Barbara archipelago. The lighthouse on *Point Conception* of the mainland was seen in the small hours of the morning of the sixteenth day, beaming forth an ever-cheering welcome to the mariner; and *Point Arguilla* was passed about five P. M., after which a low, sandy, and barren-looking shore at a few miles distance was coasted for thirty-five miles to *Point San Luis Obispo*, from which to *Point Sur*, in latitude 36° 20′ N., eighty-five miles further north, the shore a mile and a half off, looked bold, rugged, seamed with deep ravines, occasionally disclosing a green valley from the early sprouting wild oats, and of a height varying from a thousand to fifteen hundred feet; ex-

FORT POINT AND THE GOLDEN GATE.

cept where the two small bays of *Esteros* and *San Simeon* indent the coast, where it is lower and edged with verdant ranches. Point Sur being passed at ten P. M., the wide mouth of the *Bay of Monterey* was crossed during the night, and at daylight next morning—the seventeenth day—an unusually long voyage because of our having in tow from Acapulco a disabled steamer, we were off *Point Anno Nueva*, thirty-eight miles beyond which brought us to the rocky *Point San Pedro;* thence the coast line dips slightly to the eastward, and ten miles further we entered that celebrated inlet to mineral and commercial wealth, the *Golden Gate*, which, in eleven years, has excited a greater interest, and become better known to nations, than any other geographical point on the map of the world in a like period. Two miles and a quarter wide at its entrance, between Point Bonita on the north and Point Lobos on the south, and extending eastward a distance of two miles and a half, with a bold, abrupt, rocky shore on the left as you enter, and a somewhat lower and undulating shore line on the right, there is a gradual diminution of the width of the passage, until one mile only separates Fort Point on the south, on which stands a formidable fortification, and Lime Point opposite, the northern pillar of the narrow inlet, a spot somewhat renowned in the annals of senatorial speculation. These two and a half miles of funnel-shaped entrance form the magnificent portal appropriately called Golden, for through it the white-winged messengers of the sea are perpetually passing, bringing the riches of commerce, and bearing away the wealth of exhaustless mines. Four miles within the gate, guarded midway the channel of the bay by another fortress of great strength, which crowns the *Island of Alcatraz*, there is brought into view, on doubling *North Point* to the right, the young Queen City of the Pacific, occupying a level space reclaimed from the bay at the foot of steep hills, whose crescentic sweep belts a dense mass of substantial buildings; while scattering houses climb the surrounding heights, showing the resolution and perseverance with which the citizens of San Francisco are surmounting the natural difficulties of placing here the emporium of western commerce. Such she is, as attested by the forest of masts swaying to and fro, responsive to the swell of the proud waters whose chief adornment they are, and giving to the winds the banners of a varied commerce, destined ere long to swell to an unsurpassed trade with five hundred millions of people of Eastern Asia and its adjacent islands, long a sealed volume in the history of national intercourse and progress.

For a distance of several miles before entering "The Heads," as the outer limits of the funnel-shaped mouth of the Golden Gate are called, the crowning hills of the otherwise black and bleak-looking seashore lifted up their cultivated fields, to look out upon the expanse of ocean as if to challenge a comparison of its azure beauty with their own rich emerald. And telegraph poles, too, standing at intervals upon the wavy summits of distant heights, outlined against the sky like mile-stones on the highway of advancing civilization, with stations and lighthouses; and all around below, swift pilot-boats, hovering about a fleet of inward and outward-bound vessels, pursuing their silent and trackless way; these served to tell us that we had passed from the dominion of the Spanish-American to that of the Anglo-American; from the proofs of degeneracy coming of mixed breeds, to those of the exalting influence of preserved purity of superior race; from the region of indolence and sensuality to that of industry and intelligence; from countries of oppression and intolerance to one, let us hope, of unchanging liberty, liberality, and law.

## CHAPTER XXIV.

CITY OF SAN FRANCISCO—BAY OF SAN FRANCISCO—BAY OF SAN PABLO—MARE ISLAND—STRAIT OF CARQUENEZ—BENICIA—SUISUN BAY—SACRAMENTO RIVER—CITY OF SACRAMENTO—COAST RANGE MOUNTAINS—FEATHER RIVER—MARYSVILLE.

It has required but a brief survey of surroundings to bring me to the conclusion that my mode of journalizing must be changed. An old America has been seen "of gray and leafy walls, where Ruin greenly dwells," and where moral sense seems irresponsive to the inspiration of a lofty civilization. In examining what "Young America" is doing with that part of the hemisphere into which he is infusing a new life, and the resources of which he is developing in a manner to astonish the world; where change and progress are written upon every thing, and the realities of to-morrow may contradict the descriptions of to-day, we must deal more in generalities than specialities. In this manner alone will my California narrative of what I saw, avoid the ridicule to which it might otherwise be subjected by the presentation of "dissolving views," whose realities, apart from nature, are merged in other scenes as the eye rests upon the picture. But a few years have passed since this State was peopled by a few wild Mexican half-breed herdsmen, who roved over ranches bounded only by mountain ranges, or the streams which broke from their untrodden solitudes, to wander through immense plains, and who slaughtered tens of thousands of cattle for hides and tallow alone. Now four hundred thousand inhabitants, nearly all of Caucasian nationalities, led and stimulated by American example and success, are disembowelling the earth of its mineral treasures; developing unsurpassed agricultural wealth, and establishing the means of free intercommunication between all parts of the State, and with neighboring territories. Looking at San Francisco, the traveller beholds apparently insuperable barriers to improvement disappearing as if by the touch of an enchanter's wand—lofty hills vanishing before the steam-paddy, which sends its trains of railroad cars to fill up marsh and shallow; wooden buildings of earlier date seeking suburban retirement with wheel and lever, to give place to storehouses of iron and granite; palatial residences springing up as if by magic, embowered in shrubbery and flowers; hotels of metropolitan dimensions, succeeding each other with a rapidity of construction showing an extraordinary flood of travel and pressure of demand; eighty-three thousand people, a dense mass of busy artisans, enterprising merchants, and men of varied professions, cultivating the arts of peace, promoting the interests of trade and of social happiness, and establishing the empire of knowledge and civilization, where, but twelve years ago, the eddying sand, sporting in the gale that rushed through the wind-gap of the coast range, built its mimicry of nature's grander scenery undisturbed by man's intrusion; and where the wavelet, unbroken by the rollicking oar, kissed the silent shore with silver ripple.

Standing upon Telegraph Hill, or upon Rincon Hill, the north and south horns of a deep crescent of hills, the concavity of which was formerly a harbor where vessels rode at anchor and discharged their cargoes, and looking down upon the warehouses, foundries, and machine shops, now occupying the entire space, pushing the water front to a straight line from one extreme point to the other, the observer is amazed at the immense results of labor and perseverance in a brief time. Yet San Francisco must be regarded as in a transition state, for here linger still many mean-looking houses, the mementoes of its days of hurry and hardship; ungraded, unpaved, or defectively planked and dangerous streets; badly built and unfinished wharves intercepting filthy pools, the receptacles of garbage and offal, and sources of evil to a magnificent water front, which should be carefully guarded for the uses of the vast shipping destined to adorn it if it be not destroyed by neglect or unwise legislation. Sand hills and drifts also remain in populous thoroughfares, recalling experiences of desert travel; and pioneer customs of all sorts, illustrative of enterprise and adventure, intentness, selfishness, rudeness, recklessness, jostlings, and general *abandon* of go-ahead-a-tiveness, ignoring collaterals and consequences. But while we trace in these San Francisco *as she was*, yet can we not fail to contemplate her *as she is to be*, in the wide and well-paved avenues seen in the rapidly improving parts of the city, bordered by substantial edifices and fancy stores filled with the products of Asia and its isles, competing with the manufactures of Europe and America for the golden prize that California holds forth to the trade of the world. As seen, too, in the scattered clusters of architectural residences which would grace the "west end" of Atlantic cities, adorned with gardens of perennial foliage, and flowers that never cease to bloom; in the improving material, style, and arrangement of public structures; in beautiful churches looking from surrounding heights upon the outspread proof of man's progress, and the improvement of his moral nature which they have had their share in elevating; in the uninterrupted, abundant, and cheap supply of pure water, flowing from distant sources to every door, a spring-tide of health and enjoyment, when but a few years since a draught was a costly boon; in well-lighted streets; in an efficient police to control the disturbing elements of society, without, as formerly, *inconsistently trampling law under foot to punish lawlessness*, thus justifying in practice what it professes to denounce, and violating the sanctity of a principle which is the only sovereign of a freeman, and, professing to obey which, he cannot disregard in practice without the establishment of a precedent, eventually detrimental to the cause of constitutional liberty. We see the foreshadowing of her future in city passenger railroads, places of rational amusement, and public gardens of unusual attractiveness; in markets of great variety, abundance, rarely equalled quality, and moderate prices—the fruits and vegetables generally of California attaining a wonderful growth, and the salmon of its waters being unequalled; in numerous, excellent, and cheap restaurants; in public schools, libraries, asylums, hospitals, and an active fire department. In all these the growth of twelve years—no, not more than nine years, for this city has been three times nearly, and twice entirely destroyed by fire—we have proofs of a creative and reproductive power, which entitles San Francisco to the post of honor for unequalled activity, enterprise, and success. And in them we read also the signs of her magnificent destiny. Diligent inquiry and observation have led me to the conclusion, that the *luxury* of living may be had here for a family at about a third above New York prices. Those who are content with the *necessaries* of life, and of industrious and provident habits, cannot fail of acquiring competence and comfort, with the probability of their experience transcending any moderate expectation. As to men unembarrassed by families, it may be confidently asserted that, nowhere in the United States can such live at as small expense as in San Francisco, provided they are willing to occupy furnished rooms, and take their meals at restaurants unsurpassed for excellence and unequalled for cheapness.

For the purpose of visiting some part of the mining and agricultural regions, a fare of one dollar was paid for a passage which formerly cost thirty, to Sacramento, on board a steamer of speed and accommodation equal to a North River boat. Casting loose at four P. M., our route lay northward up the Bay of San Francisco, the uninhabited island of *Yerba Buena*, destined to play a conspicuous part in the future annals of the city, lying to the right, and serving as a partial wind-screen for the town of *Oakland* on the east side of the bay, against the blasts, which, during the summer months, come fiercely through the narrow entrance of the harbor. To this island, called Yerba Buena by the Spaniards from its production of a peculiar plant, the later Saxon settlers gave the less euphonious name Goat Island. But this and like efforts to despoil the Spaniards of an incidental honor of discovery and occupancy is not likely to prove successful, for their footprints are too deep to be effaced from the new world; and their renown will continue to be proclaimed through all time, by the sublime language that speaks from its mountains, valleys, and rivers—from every sea, island, and headland.

Further on than Yerba Buena, and to the left of the steamer route, is *Angeles Island*, of several hundred acres extent, separated from the western shore of the bay by the narrow, but deep *Racoon Strait*, through which flows a strong tidal and river current, to be duly considered by vessels entering the harbor on an ebb tide, to avoid being driven on the south shore of the inlet. The island shuts from the view of the ascending navigator of the bay the little harbor of *Saucelito*, off its west side, where formerly whalers of the North Pacific, and subsequently the founders of San Francisco, obtained supplies of fresh water. Thirteen miles from the city, on the west side of the bay, just after passing an insular "Red Rock," stands *Point St. Quentin*, on which is built the State Penitentiary; and about three miles to the northwest of this, at the head of a snug little harbor, the village of San Rafael is seen nestling in a pretty setting of verdure-clad hills. A short distance north of Point St. Quentin is the narrow entrance to the *Bay of San Pablo*, a differently denominated part of that beautiful expanse of water usually known as the Bay of San Francisco. The passage is bounded on the east by *Point San Pablo*, and on the west by *Point San Pedro;* two rocks near the former and two near the latter called *The Brothers* and *The Sisters*, by a little stretch of fancy, may be regarded as being occupied in the pious duty of washing the feet of the apostolic fathers. Many rocky islets scattered over the face of the bay add to its picturesque scenery; and the back ground of the shores being offshooting spurs of the Coast Range of mountains on both sides, adds to the beauties of the scene by their graceful undulations, and especially when their foothills are clad in the livery of early spring. The Bay of San Pablo looks like a rapid and muddy embouchure of the great Sacramento River, bearing the floods of its turbid tributaries to the ocean through a vast valley of the Coast Mountains. Steering northeast, *Mare Island* was soon reached, on which is located a United States navy yard, embracing extensive shops, storehouses, and a sectional dry dock. A strait separates the island from the main land, on which, opposite to the public buildings, is the old town of *Vallejo*, now inhabited by most of the workmen of the navy yard, and a remnant of the former Mexican population. *Napa* Creek, which drains a part of the fertile valley of the same name, and affords water communication by steamboat between that rich country and San Francisco, empties into Mare Island Strait a short distance above the town of Vallejo. Leaving all these to the left of our route, we passed eastward through the *Strait of Carquenez*, six miles long, and varying from three-quarters to two miles wide, communicating with *Suisun Bay*. On the north shore of the strait stands the town of *Benicia*, so called in honor of the wife of the brave old Mexican frontiersman, General Vallejo. Benicia is fifty-eight miles from San Francisco. It was here that it was for a time intended by interested parties to establish the commercial emporium of the Pacific, and also the capital of the State of California. But the laws of trade, too imperious to be over-ruled, elected San Francisco for the former; while the machinery of party, moved by a controlling personal interest, decreed that it was advisable to expend the State appropriations in the erection of legislative and executive buildings where there was a probability they would be washed out occasionally by an over-flow of the Sacramento River—a process of purification known to be needed by the experienced in partisan legislation and political corruption. Benicia has several fine academies; there are also in its immediate vicinity the extensive machine shops and foundries of the Pacific Mail Steamship Company. A fleet of their steamers was seen moored along shore. The United States Pacific Military Headquarters, consisting of barracks, arsenal, magazine, and storehouses, are located near the Steamship Company's works. Opposite to these, on the south side of the strait, is the neat little town of *Martinez*, the county-seat of Contra Costa.

It was night when we passed from the Strait of Carquenez into Suisun Bay and the Sacramento River, which, having been ascended during the dark hours, remained a sealed book until a subsequent opportunity was afforded to see its generally low and level banks of rich soil, but liable to overflow in high water. We reached the city of Sacramento at 2 A. M., a ten hours' run of one hundred and twenty miles from San Francisco.

The city of Sacramento is situated immediately below the junction of the American River coming from the east, and the Sacramento River flowing from the north; and is built principally on the east bank of the latter, south of the former river.

These rivers are greatly swollen at this time, from heavy rains and the spring thaw of the Sierra Nevada snow. The highest water hitherto known here was in 1854, when it rose to twenty feet above low water. It is now equally high, and threatens to submerge the plain on which the town is built. In December, 1861, a flood of these rivers did overflow the levee and inundate the city; and in the following month, January, 1862, an unprecedented rise to twenty-four feet above low-water mark, converted the city and adjacent country into a vast lake, flooding every dwelling and store, destroying probably millions of property, and rendering communication impossible except by boats. The Sacramentinos must be made of pretty resolute stuff, if their purpose to make this city the capital of the State can survive such a drowning out.

The streets of Sacramento are laid off at right angles, designated by letters and numerals: they are wide, mostly unpaved, with plank sidewalks, covered with shed awnings in the business part of the town; and a plaza of abundant mud and dirt, reveals a lingering attachment to Spanish American fashions. Most of the houses are weather-boarded frame, and the suburbs are far from prepossessing; but there are substantial stores in the heart of the city, and some fine brick dwellings with pretty flower-gardens, for which the Sacramentinos seem to have a passion.

The present capitol building furnished by this county for the use of the Legislature, is unworthy of the character and resources of the State; but a new one is in process of erection at a probable cost of half a million of dollars, the foundation walls of which are already up, and which it is expected will be finished in about three years, unless the Sacramento and American Rivers—not originally consulted in the premises—should decree otherwise. Whether the omission to take into consideration the influence which these important agents might exercise on the question, was dependent upon the want of wisdom and experience in the Legislature, usually the attendant on mature age, I know not; but certainly if there was an old man in that honorable body, he could not be distinguished among the stalwart-framed, ruddy-complexioned, and dark-haired members.

Indeed, it is rare to meet with a wrinkled brow and venerable locks anywhere. The young, the vigorous, and the resolute appear to have taken possession of this new land, which is rapidly becoming the active theatre of that civilization destined to confront and conquer the errors and prejudices of Asia.

Taking the seven A. M. boat for Marysville, we found on board that human speciality *the newsboy*—long lost sight of. He has scaled the Rocky Mountains, and awakened the echoes of the Sierra Nevada with his startling summons. His next leap will be to the Hawaiian Islands; and then may Buddha and Joss shake on their shrines, for it will not be long before Japan and China will respond to an influence more powerful than that of the missionary.

Having ascended the Sacramento River fifteen or twenty miles, the Coast Range Mountains could be seen in the far west, a portion of the chain breaking into spurs as it approaches San Pablo Bay, some of them passing along the west side of the bay, while others descending obliquely along its head seek the Strait of Carquenez, and leaping it form the great Mount Diablo Range, which runs along the east side of the Bays of San Pablo and San Francisco, through the counties of Contra Costa and Alameda, to unite again in the far south with that chain which, in consequence of its bordering more closely the seacoast on the west side of the bay, properly retains the name Coast Range. It is thus by the connecting Gabelan spur, that the subdivisions of the great northern Coast Range, which separate to embrace the Bays of San Pablo and San Francisco, again coalesce; and after having by their reunion formed the southern boundary of the magnificent valley of Santa Clara, pass on to receive still further south the gradually approaching Sierra Nevada. It is in the Coast Range that those breaks are found, at Bodega, the Golden Gate, Monterey, and San Pedro, well named *wind-gaps*, through which the sea-breezes seek the great interior basin, thus mitigating the extreme summer heats which would otherwise be insupportable.

On each side of the Sacramento River the overflowing water was seen, as we ascended it, covering the adjacent country in many places from ten to fifteen miles, giving the appearance of a succession of lakes. The tributaries of this great river are all similarly swollen, and the destruction of property on their banks must be immense. Fleets of bridges, fences, flumes, and crops passed us, and even an occasional house was seen launched on the swift current, "bound to San Francisco and a market." Orchards, vineyards, gardens, and thousands of acres of rich bottom lands are under water, and probably ruined by the deposits of sand and clay brought down from the mining districts and spread abroad by the flood.

About twenty-five or thirty miles above the capital the Sacramento River receives one of its largest affluents, Feather River, which we ascended, and found also to be rolling down a swift tide of turbid water, thick with sediment from the gold-belt of the mountain region, the great source of sand-bars and general lifting of the river bed and obstruction of the channel, thus impeding steamboat navigation, as well as injuring seriously the agricultural interests of the State by increasing the liability to overflow.

The discovery of the precious metals has done much for California by attracting immigration, and leading to an examination of her other resources. But it is feared by some of excellent judgment, that the permanent interests of the State are sustaining great detriment by the injury to navigable water-courses incident to mining and consequent flooding of valuable lands, by the diversion of labor from agriculture, by the cherished spirit of speculation and improvidence, and their common attendant demoralization, and by the abnormal attraction of professional men, including professional gamblers and professional idlers, resulting from a continuance of the golden enthralment and the supremacy of the mining interests. California is capable of producing cereals far beyond the demand for home consumption. From July, 1860, to March, 1861, she exported two million six hundred thousand bushels of wheat, and of barley a very large quantity. As to potatoes, the whole Pacific coast of America could rely on her without apprehension of disappointment. Why should she send millions of dollars abroad for cured meats, butter, cheese, wines, dried fruits, tobacco, rice, when her river bottoms can produce abundantly of corn, and oak forests furnish thousands of tons of mast for fattening hogs; when her luxuriant valleys can pasture innumerable herds; when her hill-sides, basking for months in a warm and rainless sky, would rejoice in the vine and grow jocund with the grape; and when a virgin soil and propitious climate await but the hand of the husbandman to fill it with the richest rewards of industry, however applied? It is manifest that the greatest want of California is labor.

Large timber is only occasionally seen along the river banks, and this differs from that of the Atlantic States, in the gnarled and scraggy appearance of the trees. The usual inhabitants of these forests are the *Digger Indians*, whose lodges—if such they can be called, which are merely hollow mounds of earth into which they burrow through a hole—stand in clusters of five or six, giving shelter to the most wretched-looking of the native race, whose food is the acorn and such esculent roots as they can dig from the earth, seasoned occasionally with a worm or grass-hopper; and whose clothing, if clad at all, the tattered cast-off garments of the miner, picked up on the wayside.

*Marysville*, at the junction of Feather and Yuba Rivers, was reached in eight hours and a half from Sacramento—distance about seventy miles. Rapidly accumulating deposits in the rivers may soon make it necessary for this town to rely upon railroad communications for its prosperity, which it has hitherto had as much from the facility of receiving its supplies of merchandise by the Sacramento and Feather Rivers as from its proximity to many of the richest gold mines of the State. Marysville is the chief town of Yuba County, the most important in the northern part of the State, and possesses an extensive area of the finest mineral and agricultural lands. The town is situated on a nearly level plain, sufficiently above high water to protect it from river freshet, except those few parts in the vicinity of sloughs. Its present population is six thousand. The streets are wide, intersect each other at right angles, are unpaved, and designated alphabetically in one direction and numerically in the other, which facilitates the finding and recollection of places. The sidewalks are paved, and substantial brick buildings occupy the business part of the town, while the dwell ings in other parts are of brick or frame in cottage style, and have fine gardens. Several churches are well designed and substantial, as is also the court-house; and well-conducted hotels are found, in number and accommodation equal to those of some Atlantic cities with twenty times the population. Marysville is lighted by gas, and is entitled to be considered a neat, well-ordered, and prosperous town, creditable to its inhabitants, and giving promise of a growth and influence correspondent with the destiny of the State. Already two railroads are being built; one to connect it with Folsom and thence with Sacramento, and whatever improvement may penetrate the great valley of San Joaquin to the south, or climb the Sierra Nevada to the east; and the other to run to Benicia or to Vallejo, as may be determined; in either case giving a more certain, frequent, and a shorter communication with San Francisco—the steamboat connection between those places and the commercial metropolis being always uninterrupted. A third road is being projected to Oroville in the interior. It would have been pleasant to have lingered longer in this fresh and vigorous little town, where, in my "prospecting" California, I found "a nugget of pure gold" in one of the truest of friends and best physicians who ever emigrated from his native State of Maryland. But duty would not wait on pleasure, and the "word which must be and hath been," had to be spoken.

# CHAPTER XXV.

BIG BUTTE—MOUNT SHASTA—YUBA RIVER—TIMBUCTOO—HYDRAULIC GOLD MINING—ROUGH AND READY—GRASS VALLEY—QUARTZ GOLD MINING—AUBURN—AMERICAN RIVER—ALABASTER CAVE—FOLSOM—CHINESE.

As we left Marysville the *Big Butte* was seen thirteen miles to the northwest, lifting its dark brow nineteen hundred feet above the surrounding plain, on which it stands a majestic and lonely monarch, as if proclaiming to its giant brother of *Shasta*, visible one hundred and fifty miles off in the far north, and fourteen thousand three hundred and ninety feet high, that they alone reign within the great interior valley of four hundred

DISTANT VIEW OF MOUNT SHASTA.

miles extent, which lays its tribute at their feet. The following is from the pen of a gentleman of Marysville, an hour spent with whom, where all surroundings were bright and joyous, was, in his own language, like

> "sunlight on
> The golden streams that through the valleys glide."

Genius can weave no more fitting wreath for Shasta's imperial brow:

> "Behold the dread Mount Shasta, where it stands
> Imperial midst the lesser heights, and, like
> Some mighty, unimpassioned mind, companionless
> And cold. The storms of Heaven may beat in wrath
> Against it, but it stands in unpolluted
> Grandeur still; and from the rolling mists up-heaves
> Its tower of pride e'en purer than before.
> The wintry showers and white-winged tempests leave
> Their frozen tributes on its brow, and it
> Doth make of them an everlasting crown.
> Thus doth it day by day, and age by age,
> Defy each stroke of time—still rising higher
> Into Heaven!
>
> "Aspiring to the eagle's cloudless height,
> No human foot hath stained its snowy side,
> Nor human breath has dimmed the icy mirror
> Which it holds unto the moon, and stars, and sovereign
> Sun. We may not grow familiar with the secrets
> Of its hoary top, whereon the Genius
> Of that mountain builds his glorious throne!
> Far-lifted in the boundless blue, he doth
> Encircle, with his gaze supreme, the broad
> Dominions of the West, that lie beneath
> His feet, in pictures of sublime repose
> No artist ever drew. He sees the tall,
> Gigantic hills arise in silentness
> And peace, and in the long review of distance
> Range themselves in order grand. He sees the sun-light
> Play upon the golden streams that through the valleys
> Glide. He hears the music of the great and solemn
> Sea, and over-looks the huge old western wall,
> To view the birth-place of undying Melody!

"Itself all light, save when some loftiest cloud
Doth for a while embrace its cold forbidding
Form—that monarch-mountain casts its mighty
Shadow down upon the crownless peaks below
That, like inferior minds to some great
Spirit, stand in strong contrasted littleness!
All through the long and summery months of our
Most tranquil year, it points its icy shaft
On high, to catch the dazzling beams that fall
In showers of splendor round that crystal cone,
And roll, in floods of far magnificence,
Away from that lone vast Reflector in
The dome of Heaven.

"Still watchful of the fertile
Vale, and undulating plains below, the grass
Grows greener in its shade, and sweeter bloom
The flowers. Strong Purifier! From its snowy
Side the breezes cool are wafted to 'the peaceful
Homes of men,' who shelter at its feet, and love
To gaze upon its honored form, aye standing
There, the guarantee of health and happiness!
Well might it win communities so blest
To loftier feelings, and to nobler thoughts—
The great material symbol of eternal
Things! And well I ween, in after years, how,
In the middle of his track, the ploughman,
In some sultry hour, will pause, and, wiping
From his brow the dusty sweat, with reverence
Gaze upon that hoary peak. The herdsman
Oft will rein his charger in the plain, and drink
Into his inmost soul the calm sublimity;
And little children, playing on the green, shall
Cease their sport, and, turning to that mountain
Old, shall of their mother ask, 'Who made it?'
And she shall answer, 'God!'

"And well this Golden State shall thrive, if, like
Its own Mount Shasta, sovereign law shall lift
Itself in purer atmosphere—so high
That human feeling, human passion at its base
Shall lie subdued; e'en pity's tears shall on
Its summit freeze; to warm it e'en the sunlight
Of deep sympathy shall fail;
Its pure administration shall be like
The snow immaculate upon that mountain's brow!"

Crossing to the south bank of Yuba River, we pursued an easterly route, with that river frequently in view; first over a level tract of country not remarkable for cultivation, and then over low foot-hills, some of which were very rugged, and most of them bearing marks of mining claims, ditches, diggings, and flumes, with endless heaps of washed boulders, cobble, and gravel, showing the enormous labor and wealth that have been expended in prospecting and placer mining in this county. If there has been a correspondent expenditure in the other auriferous regions of the State, the aggregate, if so appropriated, would have been sufficient to have placed California in railroad communication with the valley of the Mississippi long ere this. A drive of eighteen miles brought us to *Timbuctoo*, a town in the eastern part of Yuba County, of from four thousand to five thousand inhabitants, in and around it, engaged in mining and kindred pursuits.

The mode of mining chiefly pursued here is that called *hydraulic*, which consists in washing down the gold deposits by projecting against them streams of water, and then directing the sediment by water currents through wooden troughs, called *flumes*, where the particles of gold become disengaged and detained by riffles of quicksilver. This mode of mining was first used at Nevada in 1852, but the primitive arrangement of rawhide hose and wooden pipe has been since much improved on; and wherever it is applicable the results, as compared with the early processes of *pan, rocker, and long-tom*, are remarkable for increased production. We were conducted over the extensive and rich Antoine claim by a resident of Timbuctoo, largely engaged in mining. The claim is located, with twenty-four others, on Timbuctoo Hill, having a height of five or six hundred feet, and a diameter of about one mile at the base. This small mountain, which by its large yield of gold has proved one of the richest deposits in California, was once *placer*-mined over its entire surface; and now, for that which is imbedded deeply within, is being so rapidly disembowelled by tunnelling, and undermined and washed away by streams that have been turned from their channels for this purpose, that it is computed that in from two to three years the whole will be levelled to the bed of the adjacent river, and where the mountain now stands will be found naught but a plain of boulders. Indeed there are geologists who believe that this will be but a return to its original condition, and that it is in fact an upheaval of a water bed, as it is formed of corresponding rock of various inclinations, washed into holes similar to those of the present bed of the Yuba River, mingled with rounded stones of all sizes, and with gravel and sand.

After clambering over enormous quantities of boulders, the refuse of flumes scattered broadcast at the foot of the hill, we penetrated an artificial cleft in the rock and hard cement, of great length and depth, through which water and rolling stones were rushing with the noise of a mountain torrent. Having ascended this gorge in constant danger of falling fragments from the ragged walls above, and slipping and sliding over an unctuous pathway, we emerged upon a plateau fronting which was a perpendicular bluff of gravel and boulders, sand and clay, resting on a substratum of hard white cement. This bluff was one hundred and thirty-five feet high, from three to four hundred feet wide, and against its base, men clad in india-rubber cloth, standing sixty or seventy feet off, were directing four streams of water from pipes of three-and-a-fourth inch nozzles. The water thus used is furnished to miners by a canal company, and is conveyed in canals and flumes a distance of thirty miles. The cost of water for the Antoine mine is eighty dollars per day, and, including other necessary charges in the working, it foots up an aggregate expense to the proprietors of eleven hundred dollars every ten days. The product amounts to three thousand dollars for the same period—the "run," as it is called, at the end of which a cleaning up takes place—that is the boulders which have become jammed in the flume are removed, the amalgam is taken out, retorted, and quicksilver replaced in the flume preparatory to another run.

The head of water gives a pressure of from seventy to one hundred and forty feet, and it is conveyed from the reservoir through a thirty-two inch diameter riveted boiler iron pipe, thirteen hundred feet long, to a rubber hose of seven inches diameter, from which it is thrown, as before stated, with such force that four streams produce a rushing and crashing of boulders like the roar of a cataract. The spectator realizes the might of these streams when, after a process of undermining for a few minutes, he sees thousands of tons forming a terrific land-slide of rock and earth, fall with deafening crash. The disintegrated mass subject to the continued play of the pipemen, is gradually washed at the Antoine mine into a deep cut which traverses the plateau, and thence through a cleft of an adjacent part of the hill to a strongly-braced wooden trough having a rapid fall. This is the *flume;* it is about five feet wide and three deep, and five or six hundred yards long. Across the bottom are placed blocks of hard nut pine, four or five inches thick, intercepting small spaces well packed to prevent leakage, into which quicksilver is put, which attracts the particles of gold rushing along the flume with the mass of debris, forming an *amalgam,* which, from its metallic weight, rests securely in the little spaces between the blocks until the expiration of the run, when it is carefully collected, and the gold and quicksilver separated by heat. Eight hundred pounds of quicksilver are used at the Antoine mine during every run of ten days, from which some idea may be formed of the immense quantity consumed in the State, and the importance of the almost simultaneous discovery of that metal with gold in California.

The cost of opening the Antoine claim was seventy-five thousand dollars before operations could be commenced. The day for picking up gold on the surface of the earth has gone by, and the investment of large capital is now required to bring about the remunerative results rarely to be secured without the adoption of improved methods.

Hydraulic and quartz mining—the latter yet to be seen—I am informed are attended with many accidents from falls, land slides, and rock blasting ; perhaps in no equal number of operatives as among miners, are the services of the surgeon so frequently required.

Next morning we started for Grass Valley, a quartz rock gold region, eighteen miles distant in Nevada County. The usual passenger conveyance of this country of rough and deeply-rutted roads in the wet season, is what is here called a mud wagon, a wider and more capacious vehicle than the stage-coach, with a body resting on stiffer springs, and not so high, hence less liable to capsize. Passing *Sucker Flat* and *Empire Ranche*, three miles brought us to *Morney's Flat*, where are found numerous still productive claims. The road is precipitous and rocky, and the hill-sides are seamed with ditches and tail-washings, the great canal of the Excelsior Company before referred to being sometimes seen in its earthen channel, at others leaping by aqueducts, supported on trestles fifty feet high, over wide valleys. Ruinous as these arteries of impoverishing sediment now prove to agriculture, the time will probably come when the glittering attraction shall have ceased to exist, that they may become converted into means of irrigating vineyards and other fruiteries, destined to flourish throughout this foothill region, the soil and climate of which, in the judgment of residents, are well adapted to their cultivation. And who can doubt the more extended and enduring benefits that will come of this nobler industry? Immense rocks were occasionally seen bounding the wayside, their sides and feet washed by mountain torrents for centuries, standing like buttresses of iron supporting massive walls and defying the vain assaults of storm and flood, while above the accumulating moss of long years gave a look of venerable grandeur to their stern brows. Sometimes a pretty opening revealed itself, verdant in grass and foliage, like a picture of youth in an antique frame; and the neat cottage, flower garden, and cultivated field near by, told that gold had not engrossed all thought and labor. A toll-gate was not wanting to exemplify man's adherence to usage, rather than to demonstrate improved highways in these outcroppings of the Sierra Nevada. But a truer sign of progress was the tiny thread of the telegraph stretched through the wilderness, and beyond the mountain limit that nature for ages had assigned to man's empire, to unite the extremes of a continent in instant intelligence, sympathy, and interest. Stately pines waved their graceful heads, and lordly oaks—live, white, red, and black—stretched abroad their brawny arms, while extensive undergrowths of manzanita, buckeye, and chaparral served to shelter the wild tenants of the forest, occasionally startled by our intrusion. Nor were spring's wild flowers wanting to heighten the beauty of the scene. Nature's gorgeous embroidery of crimson, and yellow, and purple, was spread on the sunny hill-side; while pink, and blue, and white nestled in shady nooks, to tell that no part of earth is left by the Bountiful Giver of Good without these beautiful emblems to remind us of the lovely and pure departed.

> Thanks for the gift of flowers—
> For the bright, loving, holy thoughts, that breathe
> From out their perfumed beauty, like a wreath
> Of sunshine on life's hours!

Thanks for the wayside handwriting of goodness along the garden path, to teach childhood its earliest lesson of Supreme Beneficence, and inspire its heart with the love of beauty and sweetness, brightness, joy, and gentleness; and that puts its record for man on rock and hill, forest and field, mountain and valley, that he may be taught "whatsoever things are pure and lovely—to think on these things"! And that seeing all perish too, and fall before the wintry blast, he may also be reminded of his own passing away!

Twelve miles east of Timbuctoo we came to *Rough and Ready*, a small mining village of little else than shanties—from its rocky surroundings certainly deserving of the first half of its name, and not less entitled to the last from the ready manner its inhabitants are said to have of deluding the unwary with the idea of profitable investment in gold claims, more remarkable as stone quarries. Hundreds of acres of boulder and gravel, and leagues of useless ditches and diggings, showed the vast expenditure of time and labor in prospecting, and on abandoned claims—the victims of disappointment doubtless being often the children of luxury and refinement, whose dreams of affluence having faded into realities of penury and destitution, becoming the hirelings of more fortunate speculators, to avoid starvation. California has been the theatre of diversified experience, and no part of it has seen more suffering and disappointment than this. Rugged and Rascally would have alliterated as well, and been equally euphonious and as truthful a name as Rough and Ready —appropriate as that is. The road beyond, though not as rocky, continued miry from heavy rains, and Grass Valley was not reached until 4 P. M.

The town of *Grass Valley* is the second in importance in Nevada County, and has a population of five thousand. The stores are substantially built, and contain an abundant supply of goods; and the dwellings, many of them pleasantly located on the gently-swelling hills bordering the valley, are tasteful and surrounded with fine gardens. Among the latter may be seen the cottage built and occupied for a short time by Lola Montes, the erratic, cast-off mistress of Bavarian majesty, who appears to have girdled the earth almost with coquetries and liaisons, and at her final hour to have been canonized as a saint by New York piety. Placer gold mining was for a time successfully conducted in this vicinity, but the accidental discovery of gold-bearing quartz in 1850, soon led to the erection of mills, first driven by water power, and subsequently, as the extensive gold quartz deposits were developed, steam power was found necessary to meet the great demand for those agents in the separation of the precious metal. Within the space of five miles square as many as sixteen quartz-crushing mills have already been erected, doing custom as well as private work, and thirty-five steam pumps are also engaged in freeing the mines from water, and in raising rock. As quartz mining is one of the two improved methods in use for the procurement of gold in California—the hydraulic having already been spoken of—a brief description of this may be given.

At certain distances beneath the surface of the earth in the gold region, a layer of rock is found. After the first hap-hazard period of surface scramblings, scratchings, and scrapings, the fact was stumbled on by the early adventurers, that the gold, from its superior specific gravity, gradually precipitated itself down to the rock, and was often found occupying its crevices and depressions in such great quantities as to lead to a system of "coyoting"—in California miner's phrase—or subterranean burrowing after the rich deposits; and when the bed-rock was at a great depth a more extensive and scientific system of tunnelling and barrowing, and sometimes even railroad horse-car conveyance, was introduced for the purpose of securing the treasure earth, for sluicing or such other means of separation as were most accessible. The next step in discovery was that of the rock wealth itself, occasionally outcropping, but generally at a considerable depth, and was followed by the sinking of shafts to hundreds of feet in some instances, and blasting. The quartz rock thus separated was first raised by hand and horse power, and now in many cases by steam. When brought to the surface and carried to mill, it is there broken into smaller fragments by hand labor with hammers. Many persons now regard this quartz rock as the "mother of gold," and that the precious metal was first formed in or with quartz; and by the exposure of the latter to water, terrestrial chemical agencies, and atmospheric influences, disintegration has ensued, and the gold thus liberated has been distributed abroad by physical agencies. The rock differs greatly in the quantity of metal it contains in different localities—in some mines paying but a small profit over the expenses of working them, while in others the proprietors are speedily enriched. After quarrying the auriferous quartz and breaking it into fragments two or three inches in diameter, the remaining process for obtaining the gold consists in pulverizing the rock, and separating the metal from it. This is accomplished by shovelling the broken rock into a sloping box that serves as a *feeder*, down which it slides into a *battery* of iron, in which are arranged numerous heavy upright iron *stampers*. These stampers are lifted by "cams" or arms, attached to a revolving iron shaft turned by water or steam power. As each stamper reaches a certain height it is released by the continued revolution of the shaft, and falls with its weight of several hundred pounds upon the quartz resting on the iron bed-plate of the battery, which thus becomes speedily reduced to powder. If the dry process be adopted, an arrangement of machinery for subjecting the powder to the operation of amalgamation with mercury is used, and reduction of the metal by retorting then follows. But if the more common mode of wet crushing be adopted, a continuous supply of water is furnished to the battery, by which the finely-crushed powder is washed through a part of the battery along which a vertical wire sieve is arranged to prevent the coarser particles from passing until sufficiently pulverized. Other smaller streams of water outside of the battery bear the semi-fluid mass which has escaped from the battery down an inclined board plane, on which are spread woollen blankets. These entangle that portion of the tailings that is richest in gold, and at stated periods they are removed and washed in vats or tanks containing water. The sediment is scooped from these tanks into another receiver called an amalgamator, where, by a revolving cylinder armed with spirally-arranged blades, it is freely mixed with quicksilver, and the amalgam thus formed is duly retorted, the pure gold obtained, and the mercury reclaimed by vaporization and condensation. The refuse of amalgamation, and that portion of the semi-fluid powdered gold rock which has escaped from the blanket trays, are conveyed to a large iron basin called a *Chile mill*, in which are two heavy iron wheels or rollers, connected to and kept in circular motion by a revolving pivot shaft. In this the quartz sand is again subjected to further pulverization and amalgamation with mercury.

Such are the chief features in the method of obtaining gold in Grass Valley and its vicinity, the prosperity of which is mainly dependent on quartz mining. The munificent results of enterprise and investment of capital, in the extraction of gold even from the foundation rock of this region, have been so wonderful in some instances that a statement of them would seem like romancing. It were better that we should leave Grass Valley than take the hazard of this imputation; merely adding that although the search after the precious metal has hitherto engaged the attention of the inhabitants hereabouts almost exclusively, yet are they now becoming sensible of the agricultural resources of this part of the State, and manifesting a disposition to promote the comforts and secure the luxuries of life, by a cultivation of all the fruits of a temperate climate, which are said to thrive here in a remarkable manner, by raising heavy crops of the cereals, and by promoting the growth of the vine, which it is thought will soon yield one of the richest products of California in remunerative quantity and quality.

Instead of taking the public stage for Folsom we hired a private conveyance, that we might deviate from the direct road for the purpose of seeing a somewhat remarkable cave recently discovered in El Dorado County. Our route was due south from Grass Valley, first twenty-four miles to Auburn, the county town of Placer County, with about fifteen hundred inhabitants. The road was deeply cut by numerous heavily-loaded six and eight horse wagons, and was bordered in many places by fine timber, various kinds of oak, manzanita, and magnificent pines a hundred and fifty to two hundred feet high, and from three to four feet through at the butt. Bear River, a considerable affluent of Feather River, was crossed sixteen miles from Grass Valley, and teamsters in arrears of toll for crossing the fine bridge that spans it, were reminded by the publication of their names on a placard at one end of the bridge, to "pay up like men, and have their names blotted from the book of remembrance."

Two miles from Auburn we left the main road to Folsom, and passing two and a half miles to the east, and scarcely as far to the south, crossed the north fork of the American River, after its confluence with the middle fork, by a fine suspension bridge, at the formerly somewhat famous mining locality, more significantly than classically named *Whiskey Bar*. Striking there the Georgetown road, a further distance of two miles, brought us to the cave. The entrance to the "Alabaster" or "Coral" cave is near to the roadside. A guide accompanies visitors with necessary lights. A reception room is first entered, of thirty or forty feet length, sixteen or eighteen feet width, and ten or twelve feet height, having walls of dark slate stone and an unsymmetrical arched roof of veined limestone with petrified water streaks. From this antechamber the explorer passes into a larger room, probably a hundred and fifty feet long, with an average width of seventy-five, and a height varying from ten to twenty feet. The floor of uneven slate rock, interspersed with irregular masses of crystal limestone, supports several short columns of similar marble. The ceiling is of white limestone, permanently streaked with gray and yellow clay penetrating water frescoes, while stalactite crystal pendants hang from its arches in great variety of size, shape, and color. Over the entrance to this grand cathedral is a projecting platform of rock fifteen or twenty feet wide, and extending nearly across the room, which is the orchestral gallery. Through a passage thirty or forty feet long by eight wide, near which Nature has placed a chaste marble baptismal font, we entered a crystal chapel of exquisite beauty. It is oval shaped, about a hundred feet long, thirty wide, and twenty-five feet high. Its walls and ceiling are frescoed with permeating water stains; the former being also richly decorated, pilastered, and pannelled with crystal limestone frostwork, resembling varied forms of coral, floss, scalloped and spiculated shells, moss, leaflets, and multiform frosty vegetation; while the marble ceiling, repeating this beautiful sculpture, is hung likewise with crystalline stalactite pendants, giving it the appearance of a magnificent vaulted chandelier studded with myriads of diamonds. Toward the lower end of the chapel the arched roof opens into an irregular oval dome, the deep shadow of whose interior contrasts strangely with surrounding splendor. Near the entrance to this apartment is a rude stone stairway, by which the visitor may ascend to what is called the pulpit of the chapel. This stands on a pedestal of limestone, and looks like an oval-shaped mass of alabaster, seven or eight feet high and three or four in diameter, of rare chiselling and graceful proportions, from the lower part of which falls an inimitable semi-transparent drapery of like material. The appearance of this chamber when illuminated by torches is gorgeous, and reminds one of the gem-lit idealities of romance. It was natural to feel the inspiration of such a sublime revelation of Supreme Power, and excusable to strike a chord where for thousands of years silence has reigned, none having awakened the sleeping echoes of this sealed solitude.

Cavern of the crystal hall,
Gleaming with a mirror'd wall,
Say, who hung thy sparkling roof,
Weaving in its frosted woof
Nameless gems of radiant hue?
Strangely carved and frescoed too!
Who, thy coral cornice made?
Who, thy marble fount arrayed?
Whose the sculptor hand did trace
  Types of forest and of sea,
Leaf and shell of wavy grace
  In thy ceiling's imagery?

Who upheaved yon shadowy dome—
Older than imperial Rome—
O'er thy alabaster throne,
  Wrapped in marble drapery?
Silence muses! He alone
  Robed in light man may not see,
Who the vault of Heaven hung
  With a diadem of gold,
And around its glories flung
  Ere His night its stars unroll'd!
Lo! the mystery of God,
On the rock thy foot hath trod,
Traces there the Truth Divine;—
Mortal read! Before His shrine
Bow thy knee! "*The work is Mine!*"

There being no hotel immediately at hand we proceeded on our way without further delay, one mile bringing us to the El Dorado valley turnpike, and then ten miles to Folsom, crossing *Bald* Mountain Ridge, so called from its entire destitution of trees, composed of rolling hills with an extensive substratum of limestone. From this elevated ridge a fine view of distant scenery is had, especially of the great Sacramento valley, unfolding in the spring its mantle of verdure at the foot of the mountain, with Sutter's Buttes in the distant northwest, and Mount Diablo in the southwest looking proudly down on the scene of beauty. Having descended the ridge, the mining district of Nigger Hill was passed, a half mile beyond which, by a wire suspension bridge two hundred feet in length, we crossed the south fork of the American River—at a point twenty-eight miles west of where gold was first discovered in California on that stream—and entered the town of *Folsom*, on its left bank, in Sacramento County.

Folsom has a population of twenty-five hundred persons, many of whom are Chinese, a people thus far seen in considerable numbers wherever we have been in this State. They are diligent seekers after the precious metal which has attracted them from their far-off home, and are usually found working the abandoned claims of others in the primitive methods of pan and cradle; preserving their national habits of dress in loose coarse cottons, long queues, skull-caps, or little peaked felt hats, and slip-shod shoes; they eat rice, drink tea, and the people hereabouts say steal pigs and poultry. Most of them are hired in China by capitalists for a term of years. The capitalists pay all their expenses, farm out their labor for their own benefit, and according to contract send them back to China at the end of the specified term, *dead or alive*. They seem to be conceded hewers of wood and drawers of water, the slaves in fact of California.

Although there are gold diggings about Folsom, they are not as rich as those found elsewhere. Valuable granite quarries in the immediate vicinity are worked to great advantage. And it is the great central point from which the lines of travel diverge to all parts of the State, north, east, and south—a place of hurry, bustle, and excitement—without temptation to tarry; and hence after a night's rest we took the 7 A. M. railroad train for Sacramento, and passing over a thickly-settled and well-cultivated level country, a distance of twenty-two miles, reached the capital in time for breakfast and the noon steamboat to San Francisco, where we arrived at 10 P. M.

# CHAPTER XXVI.

TRIP TO THE SOUTHWARD—WEST SIDE OF THE BAY OF SAN FRANCISCO—SAN BRUNO—SAN MATEO—REDWOOD—VALLEY OF SANTA CLARA—TOWN OF SANTA CLARA—SAN JOSÉ—EAST SIDE OF THE BAY—WARM SPRINGS—OLD MISSION OF SAN JOSÉ—CENTREVILLE—ALVARADO—ALAMEDA COUNTY—SAN LEANDRO—OAKLAND—CONTRA COSTA COUNTY—ITS COAL BEDS—MARTINEZ—PACHECO—MONTE DIABLO—CARBONDALE AND ADJACENT COAL MINES.

NEXT morning another exploration was proposed, this time in a southerly direction on the west side of the Bay of San Francisco, through the counties of San Francisco and San Mateo, to the Valley of San José—also called Santa Clara, from its being in the county of that name. Starting from the city of San Francisco in the 12 M. stage-coach, we skirted for eight miles the bay shore, the road winding also along foot-hills of the Coast Range, sometimes over their slight acclivities, at others along the level margin of little water-inlets, and in places stealing from green slopes barely sufficient space along which to wind with cautious step above the tide that washed their rocky base. Luxuriant quebradas bordered the road-side, and wild flowers were scattered broadcast over the miniature prairies we sometimes crossed. Many well-enclosed ranches were seen, and herds of fat cattle revelled on the vernal grass. Fifteen miles from San Francisco the coast-station of *San Bruno* unrolls its cultivated fields for the traveller's admiration. And the village of *San Mateo* at twenty miles' distance from the city, in natural scenery, vale and lawn, grove and streamlet, and in the decoration of art, in cottage, garden, path, enclosure, flowers, shrubbery, and general culture, presents a picture of beauty rarely equalled.

The "dirt-road" over which we travelled, must become very

heavy and slow of passage in the wet season; but a railroad, for the building of which the requisite sum has already been subscribed, will soon place San Francisco and San José in uninterrupted and rapid communication.

Considerable live-oak and post-oak timber was seen on this part of the route; and immense droves of cattle were passed on their way to the market of the metropolis, where, I was informed, the price ranges from one to five cents per pound on the hoof, during the entire year. As we approached the village of Redwood, so called from the valuable timber of that name in the neighboring Coast Range Mountain, myriads of ground squirrels were seen—said to infest many regions of California, and to be very destructive to crops. Redwood is thirty miles from San Francisco, and lies in a fine agricultural district.

As the village of Mayfield, at the distance of thirty-five miles, was approached, the bay, which had been for some time lost sight of, was again seen a few miles to the east, with both ranges of the Coast Mountain, one on its east, and the other on its west side, plainly in view, embracing a valley which, as the bay becomes rapidly narrower toward its lower end, appeared on the west side to grow wider as we progressed toward the south, and to become continuous with that of Santa Clara; which soon after unfolded its surpassing beauty and agricultural wealth for our admiration until evening closed in just before reaching the town of Santa Clara, distant from San Francisco fifty miles.

The present neat and flourishing little town of Santa Clara, of 1,500 inhabitants, is the seat of the old Catholic mission of the same name; the first established in the interior, after and beyond that of Monterey, and which afterwards fell under the ecclesiastical jurisdiction of San Francisco. The establishment of the mission was due to the Jesuits; but on the suppression of that order by the Spanish Government, it fell into the hands of the Franciscans, nearly all of whom connected with it having died, the archbishop transferred it again to the Jesuits, who by the events of political revolution were permitted to hold it, and, under a constitution guaranteeing religious liberty, still have it in possession. But these transfers of jurisdiction by no means imply a corresponding conveyance of domain; for, throughout the varied contests and alternate successes of rival factions, following the attempt of Santa Anna, in 1835, to centralize the Government of Mexico, down to the final success of the federal party, one purpose animated all administrators of the government in reference to the missions; and that was to secularize their extensive property, and abrogate all but strictly spiritual privileges. Even before they were stripped of their possessions and influence, the Fathers, rightly interpreting the signs of the times and foreseeing the catastrophe, became indifferent to the care of their immense estates, neglecting their cultivation, recklessly slaughtering their cattle for hides and tallow, and carelessly granting away their property, or selling it for trifling sums of money. In the final proceedings of 1845, which effectually destroyed the original organization of the missions, the government distribution of the proceeds of sale or rent, assigned a specified amount to educational and charitable uses. The good which has come of this proceeding is strikingly illustrated by the successful establishment of the Santa Clara College—a literary and scientific institution, ably and successfully conducted by the Jesuit order of the Catholic clergy; in which the youth of California may acquire a thorough classical, mathematical, philosophical, and generally accomplished literary education, without the risk and cost of travel to the Atlantic States. A visit to the college and an examination of all its departments, showed an excellence of arrangement, order, neatness, and cleanliness of buildings and grounds. Reception, study, recitation, reading, music, and drawing-rooms; dormitories, baths, and refectories; kitchen, bakery, infirmary, and pharmacy; mechanical shops, armory, and gymnasium; library, laboratory, and philosophical apparatus; vineyard, garden, and playground; all are as perfect as neatness, liberality, good taste and good judgment can make them. If this college is to be taken as a sample of the means of education California is furnishing her children, her citizens must become as distinguished for intelligence as they now are for hardihood and enterprise. It was gratifying to recognize the evidence of public appreciation of this institution in the large classes in attendance. The healthy and delicious climate of this beautiful region of the

State, seem to fit it peculiarly for the residence and physical and mental development of youth. Hence other educational institutions have been founded in this and the neighboring town of San José. Among the most flourishing of these is the University of the Pacific, with a college of arts and sciences in operation at Santa Clara, and—it may be noted here—a medical department successfully conducted in San Francisco by physicians of distinguished reputation.

Three miles from Santa Clara, on the site of the old *pueblo* of San José—a settlement of retired soldiers of the *presidio*, with other white settlers, on a land grant of the fathers of the mission—stands at present the beautiful *town of San José*, one of the most flourishing in the State, and in the centre of an agricultural district unsurpassed in the world for productiveness. An avenue connects the two towns—wide, perfectly graded, shaded by two rows of willow and cotton-wood trees, closely resembling a South American alameda. In the days of the old friars, who paced its paths in meditative and prayerful mood, four rows of ornamental trees mellowed the bright sunlight with their deep umbrage; but the flood of Anglo-Saxonism, as it rolled onward to the region of gold, uprooted many of these long-cherished objects of affection and pride, and the vandal axe laid others low to feed the camp-fires of reckless pioneers. It is gratifying to observe that the better taste and more considerate care of the present inhabitants are striving to preserve the remnant of the chief ornaments of this handsome avenue. Within a mile of San José, on the south side of the avenue, the Agricultural Society's grounds, covering a hundred and sixty acres, are situated. Every necessary building is connected therewith for the purposes of its establishment, and in the completeness of their arrangement they would not suffer in comparison with those of the Atlantic States. San José has five thousand inhabitants; the streets intersect each other at right angles; they are wide, well graded, and gravelled. The stores are substantially built of brick, and well filled with merchandise; the dwellings of weather-boarded frame, are tastefully designed, and nearly all have flower and fruit gardens; the churches are many, and as in Protestant countries generally, of as great diversity of style as of forms of faith, each striving to outdo the other in external show, as it is hoped their living sectaries do in internal righteousness. Education is at a premium, and the Catholic young ladies' "Colegio de Niñas" is a model of management.

The celebrated Almaden quicksilver mine has its two remarkable veins of Enrequita and Guadalupe about twelve miles from San José, in the west range of the Coast Mountain, which forms the western boundary of the valley of Santa Clara; while the Mount Diablo range of that mountain, descending on the east side of the Bay of San Francisco, forms the eastern boundary of that valley, its northern limit being the bay, and its southern limit the Gabilan spur, a connecting link near San Juan, about forty-five miles south of San José. The valley of Santa Clara, though not on so grand a scale as the great interior valley of Chile, yet reminds the traveller of parts of that great basin in its mountain walls, its picturesque scenery, its wonderful fertility, and delicious climate free from extremes of temperature. Although there is a steamboat plying between Alviso landing, eight miles from San José, at the head of a slough branching from the foot of the bay, and San Francisco, we preferred returning thither by the land route, that we might see the country on the east side of the bay. Our route crossed Cayote Creek a short distance northeast of the town. Passing over a level part of the county of Alameda at eleven miles from San José, we ascended a moderate foot-hill of the eastern Range to the first station—the Warm Springs—a watering place of considerable resort for San Franciscans. Continuing on nearer to the mountain than to the bay shore, at fifteen miles we entered the seat of the old Catholic *mission* of San José, a spiritual establishment and jurisdiction entirely distinct from the *pueblo* of the same name already described, which was a village of the populace, as contradistinguished from a settlement of priests. A few crumbling adobe buildings, a dilapidated tile-covered church and convent, are the only mementoes of this once rich and flourishing ecclesiastical establishment whose formulary of external observance was the religion of the simple natives, whose unnumbered cattle covered the rich savannas extending for leagues along the bay shore, whose flocks whitened the adjacent hills, and whose will was the sovereign law of the land during the dominion of Spain in America. It is in this vicinity that *Mission Gap* is found, the mountain pass through the Range by which communication is had between this district and the great interior basin.

The extent of level land between the Mount Diablo Range and the Bay of San Francisco, is far greater than that between the Coast Range proper and the west shore of the bay. The soil, however, on both sides is of equal and great depth and fertility, and the probability is that the waters of the bay formerly covered the whole surface of the valley from Range to Range, and that their retirement within the present limits left the rich alluvial deposits, the agricultural wealth of which Spain showed that she was duly sensible when her Government sought to encourage their cultivation for the supply of her Pacific marine, by a liberal bestowment of land grants to emigrants. Five miles beyond the old mission we passed through the pretty little village of Centreville; and still further five miles we saw in the distance, off to the left of the road, and near the bay shore, the small town of Alvarado, in water communication with San Francisco. The agricultural capacities of this part of Alameda County, and of the still wider part of the valley further north, are represented to be unsurpassed, and this we found confirmed by the continuous unfolding of affluent fields and meadows, abounding gardens, and luscious vineyards.

At the distance of thirty-five miles from the town of San José the village of San Leandro, the county seat of Alameda, was reached, sitting prettily on the bank of San Lorenzo Creek, at the foot of the Mountain Range. Seven miles more of flat country, requiring much drainage, brought us to *Oakland* in Contra Costa County, the Brooklyn of San Francisco, situated immediately opposite to that city, on the eastern shore of the bay, ten miles distant, and in free communication with the city by a steam ferry established and still conducted by Mr. Charles Minturn, one of the most enterprising citizens of the State, to whom California is chiefly indebted for the introduction of many facilities of travel. The name of this appendage to the commercial metropolis is derived from its magnificent groves of live oaks, which are not merely ornamental, but really subserve a useful purpose for parts of the town, in screening them from the fierce winds that in the summer come through the gap of the Golden Gate, and to the force of which Oakland is especially exposed. There can be no doubt that this town is destined to play a conspicuous part in the future of Pacific commerce, in which San Francisco will be the chief actor.

A necessary product of every commercial and manufacturing country is coal, for the generation of steam. The enterprise of California has been held in serious check for some time by the high cost of this element of prosperity, most of it hitherto used having been shipped from great distances, chiefly from Bellingham Bay in the north, and Chile in the far south. Recent geological explorations, however, have resulted in the discovery of valuable coal beds in Contra Costa County, and I was led, by the general interest felt in the announcement, to examine how far they were likely to realize the promise of important results made for them.

The afternoon boat for Sacramento landed a San Francisco friend and myself at the little town of *Martinez*, opposite to Benicia on the Strait of Carquenez—heretofore spoken of—where we spent the night at an excellent hotel. Next morning we took the road toward Mount Diablo, a drive of five miles bringing us to the hastily put together town of *Pacheco*, containing four or five hundred people, in a valley of twelve by seven miles, much of the land being still in a state of nature; some of it being a portion of an old Spanish grant of nine leagues to Señor Pacheco, who, desirous of keeping intermeddlers at a distance, refuses to sell any part of his vast estate. He occupies an unpretending rough-cast adobe mansion, with many natural, but no artificial surroundings of beauty, unless a bee-hive bake-oven can be so considered, which occupies a conspicuous position before the front door. The old Mexican is said to have been, from some unexplained cause, singularly exempt from the nuisance of *squatters*, a free and easy class of humanity, indigenous to the United States. But the remark does not apply to the quadrupeds of that denomination, for millions of squirrels were seen as we crossed the estate, sitting in squads on their haunches, and chattering as if in consultation about our intrusion, and then, on nearer approach, darting into their burrows with as self-satisfied a discretion, and quite as much intelligence as a Digger Indian dodges into the hole of his earthen habitation. On climbing the Big Sulphur-Spring Hill, beyond the Pacheco grant, we saw traces of coal; and soon came upon the *Peacock Claim*, where we found a tunnel two hundred and thirty-five feet long through slate and rock, with a declivity of thirty-six degrees, into a five feet and a half vein of excellent bituminous coal. The nearest point of shipment for this coal is the *Embarcadero* of Pacheco; the difficulty of conveyance to which, together with the labor and cost of mining and raising the coal, will make the speculation of working this claim unprofitable. Crossing the ridge of fifteen hundred feet height just beyond the Peacock Claim, a fine view was afforded of far-off objects, and especially of the Sacramento and San Joaquin valleys, the Strait of Carquenez connecting the extreme arteries of inland navigation with their great heart, and the long mountain ranges mellowed by distance; itself being overlooked by the near *Monte Diablo*—

Stern in loneliness—
Standing apart from smiling slopes and glades,
Which, clothed in verdure, seek t' embrace the foot
That rudely spurns the beautiful caress:
Lifting its darkened brow with scornful mien,
And lofty pride, o'er nature's timid gaze,
That upward looks as if in fearfulness.
Ages have scarred its bare and blackened sides,
And set their seal e'en on its haughty head;
And yet it stands in conscious grandeur still—
Defiant symbol of lone majesty—
As when Creation, with mysterious wand,
Touched the foundations of the circling earth,
And lifted them above surrounding things.

On descending the eastern face of the ridge, and at a height of twelve hundred and fifty feet above the level of the sea, we came to the "Cumberland" coal mine with a vein of four and a half feet thick, where we found a tunnel four hundred feet long, six feet high and five wide, strongly timbered—for protection against crumbling slate—with eighteen shoots at right angles connected by cross tunnels, and communicating with air-shafts for ventilation. The perfect grade of the mine allows of an easy removal of the coal by rail; more than a thousand tons have already been sent to the San Francisco market, where it brings twelve dollars per ton; and the farther the miners proceed, the harder and richer is the coal. About three-quarters of a mile beyond, the same vein has been opened at "Black Diamond" mine, being four feet thick and somewhat harder than the Cumberland. No timbering is required at this mine, in consequence of the sandstone rock formation which makes the tunnel self-supportive. About a mile off, the "Adams," "Clark," and "Cruikshank" mines are also furnishing coal of excellent quality; and it is expected that when a projected railroad is completed to the shipping point, aspiring to the metropolitan name New York, five and a half miles distant, near the confluence of the San Joaquin and Sacramento Rivers, coal will be delivered in San Francisco at a greatly reduced price, in large quantity, and of a quality equal to any imported into that market. A thriving little village—*Carbondale*—is being built near the mines, which promises to rival in business activity, black dust, black hands, black faces, black deeds, and black guards, its Atlantic namesake. It is situated one mile and a half northeast of Monte Diablo—the sight of which alone repaid us for our day's ride of thirty-two miles to the coal region and back to Martinez, where we arrived in ample time for the call of the evening Sacramento boat to San Francisco.

## CHAPTER XXVII.

EN ROUTE TO THE GEYSERS—VISIT THE STATE PRISON AT POINT ST. QUENTIN—PETALUMA CREEK AND TOWN—SONOMA—VINEYARDS—CHINESE LABOR—VALLEY OF LOS GUILICOS—VALLEY OF PETALUMA—SANTA ROSA VALLEY AND TOWN—RUSSIAN RIVER AND VALLEY—HEALDSBURG—THE GEYSERS—QUICKSILVER MINES—GEYSER MOUNTAIN.

A TRAVELLER who has but little time afforded to him for sight-seeing must not tarry long in one spot, but keep on the move. Happily the points of interest are so numerous in California that one cannot go in any direction without being repaid for adventure. Among the many curiosities of this State are the Geysers—spouting springs of boiling water in Sonoma County. Those of Iceland near Mount Hecla have been regarded as among the most remarkable of phenomena. I availed of the few remaining days before sailing for the Hawaiian Islands to visit the not less wonderful Geysers recently discovered here.

Taking a fine steamer of Mr. Minturn's line to Petaluma, we proceeded up the bay, passing among other places heretofore mentioned the State Prison at Point St. Quentin; which, unless greatly improved in buildings and discipline, will scarcely repay one for the delay of a visit. In the erection of buildings, no special design appears to have been adopted with reference to the introduction of either the improved Auburn or the Pennsylvania system of prison discipline. The prisoners mingle freely in shops, dormitories, and cells; uninterrupted intercourse seemed to be the rule, and criminal education, disorder, and danger of outbreak, are necessary results. This disregard of moral isolation and reformatory effort is the more to be regretted because of the bold, daring, debased, and dangerous social elements, to a large extent the refuse of other countries, introduced into this State by its unusual attractions; and for the control of which a more than ordinary judicial strictness and penal infliction are demanded. The practice of leasing the labor of the convicts to the highest bidder, or to some favored partisan, has also hitherto been at variance with reformatory result; for discipline is not likely to be enforced by a lessee intent alone on profit. The realization of this fact by the present able Executive of the State has led Governor Downey to cancel existing contracts, and to take the management of the prison, both disciplinary and industrial, into the hands of the legitimate authorities. It is reasonable now to anticipate better results, morally and financially, to the State. The presence of a strong guard of musketeers, and artillerymen with several twelve-pounders loaded with canister, on the outside of a prison-wall twenty feet high, to intimidate the convicts who might scale it, is certainly a sad commentary on the efficiency of the prison discipline. With such models of penitentiaries for study as can be found in some of the Atlantic States, there should be no ignorance here on the subject of their construction and management.

Passing from the Bay of San Francisco into that of San Pablo, we crossed the latter bay in a N. N. W. direction and entered Petaluma Creek, one of its affluents. Eight miles from its mouth and thirty-one from San Francisco brought us to Lakeville, a passenger and merchandise depot of a country rich in grass and grain, and with "cattle on a thousand hills." The creek, which at its mouth is about half a mile wide, rapidly contracts above Lakeville to a hundred and fifty, and in many places to fifty yards. It is very serpentine and has numerous miniature bayous which are favorite haunts of water-fowl. The banks of the stream are low, of dark rich loam and clay, often caving in when not matted by *tule* roots, from the swash of steamboats that frequently almost touched them, so narrow in places is the channel. Here, as elsewhere in California, the absence of barns denotes an invariably dry autumn, during which the harvested grain is stacked and thrashed in the open air. Five miles above Lakeville the navigation of the creek is interrupted; and here passengers for the town of Petaluma, in Sonoma County, land and are conveyed to their destination, two miles further, in stages.

*Petaluma* is a flourishing and fresh-looking town of twenty-five hundred people, and the point of divergence of numerous routes of travel to the surrounding interior country. As a fair specimen of this, the Sonoma Valley was selected to look at. A Kentuckian, a rare sample of nature's noblemen, was my cicerone. Two or three miles in an easterly direction brought us to the foot of a not very elevated ridge dignified by the name of Sonoma Mountain, ascending which by a good road, in dry weather, the magnificent Sonoma Valley was seen from its summit stretching to the eastward as far as the Napa spur of the Coast Range Mountain, which separates it from the like beautiful and fertile valley of Napa, in which are some of the finest farms of the State, and also the medicinal springs that have made Napa the fashionable watering-place of California. While descending the eastern slope of Sonoma Ridge, an opportunity was afforded to see a *rodero*, a Mexican custom of driving up herds of wandering cattle, lassoing, marking, and branding them. On such occasions notice is given to neighbors, that they may attend for the identification and protection of their like property that may have strayed from their ranches; and, if they choose, to partake of the dainty of cruelly caught and primitively cooked "mountain oysters"—always found in great abundance where many calves are herded. It is a scene of intense excitement. Thousands of almost wild animals are crowded into one corral; and being run down by fleet horsemen—especially dexterous when they happen to be remnants of the old Mexican tribe—are twined by the unerring lasso, flung, hacked by the rudest rhinoplastic surgery, forming superfluous noses, abbreviated ears, and cervical pendents of strange shape, and otherwise degraded, cauterized, and branded by the red-hot iron, sinking deep into the quivering flesh and hissing an accompaniment to the cries of the suffering victims; while the frantic bellowing of the surging herd around startles the very air with fear, and fills the inexperienced spectator with commingled terror and pity. Mr. S——, on whose ranche this barbarous enforcement of property identification was practised, was one of the twelve Americans who, on the anticipated outbreak of the Mexican war, undertook, and, as it resulted, successfully achieved, the hazardo[illegible] adventure of seizing General Vallejo in his bed at Sonoma, and making prisoners of his guard of thirty soldiers. The stars and stripes were relieved from the responsibility and odium of the fillibustering procedure by hoisting the pioneer flag of a grizzly bear, *progressive*—more significant than if *couchant*. The property that came of this daring deed to Mr. S—— has an extent of twelve thousand acres of virgin land, on which there now range fifteen thousand sheep, five thousand cattle, and six hundred horses.

Sonoma Valley is seen to great advantage in descending Sonoma Mountain, shut in by that spur on the west, and that of Napa on its east side, the valley extending north and south twenty miles, and having an average width of about six. The central part, with a declivity to the south barely sufficient to give necessary flow to the water of Sonoma Creek which meanders through it, is an agricultural garden of wonderful luxuriance; while the bordering slopes lift up their vineyards, as if to dispute with Los Angeles their boasted preëminence of producing the nectared grape of California. In the middle of the valley stands the little village of Sonoma, which is slowly changing its Spanish American habits and habitations for Anglo-American customs and cottages. The opportunity was availed of to visit, near to the village, the extensive vineyard of an enterprising Hungarian who is doing much to promote the cultivation of the grape in California, and whose manufacture of wine amounts to two hundred and fifty thousand gallons annually. He has four hundred and fifty acres of his estate of five thousand planted with the vine, one hundred and sixty being in full bearing at this time. A superb cellar of low temperature is made in the side of the mountain, in which are stored large quantities of excellent still white wine, champagne, port, sherry, and also brandy of native production.

Chinese labor is employed on this vineyard. These people are more docile and manageable than the whites, and they can be had at lower wages—the usual wages being twenty dollars per month and find themselves, while the white laborer demands thirty dollars and his board also. A Chinese agent makes the contract for his countrymen, and receives the pay on their behalf, a single failure in the punctual stated settlement of which renders them totally worthless; otherwise great confidence may be felt in their industry and fidelity until they have accumulated what they have learned to call their "pile"—which is three hundred dollars for each person—when, considering themselves rich, most of them become indifferent to this land of promise and long to return to the flowery kingdom. It is not the least interesting of the novelties of this country of strange sights, to see sixty Chinese laborers—the number employed in Col. Harasthy's vineyard—engaged in their well-disciplined work, dressed in wide blue cotton pants of abbreviated pattern, corresponding jacket, and high peaked cane or leaf hats with brim of transcendent width, peering out of their little almond-shaped eyes at the passer-by, and chattering an unintelligible lingo with inveterate volubility, as if vocal utterance were an essential accompaniment to physical labor. Their sleeping apartments and furniture, and kitchen arrangements, are neat and orderly; and they are represented to be remarkable for personal cleanliness, two baths daily, before and after the day's work, being commonly used.

Sonoma Valley contracts at its north end to a narrow pass, by which it communicates with the valley of Los Guillicos, three miles long, and one and a half wide, which in turn is continuous with that of Santa Rosa. The valley of Los Guillicos, set in a circlet of hills, is a little elysium of seclusion, covered with verdure and orange-colored wild flowers, forming a rich carpet of green and gold. The sole proprietor of this magnificent estate is well fitted by courtesy and liberality to dispense its munificent hospitality. If one were disposed to repine that another, rather than he, is the owner of this bright spot, the remembrance of Tennyson's "Two Voices," while looking forth on its beautiful nature might make him a happier man:

A still small voice spake unto me
"Thou art so full of misery
Were it not better not to be?

"Thine anguish will not let thee sleep,
Nor any train of reason keep;
Thou canst not think, but thou wilt weep."

A second voice was at mine ear,
A little whisper silver—clear,
A murmur, "Be of better cheer."

Like an Æolian harp that wakes
No certain air, but overtakes
Far thought with music that it makes,

Such seemed the whisper at my side:
"What is it thou knowest, sweet voice?" I cried.
"A hidden hope," the voice replied:

So heaven-toned, that in that hour
From out my sullen heart a power
Broke, like the rainbow from the shower,

To find—although no tongue can prove-
That every cloud that spreads above,
And veileth love, itself is love.

And forth into the fields I went,
And Nature's living motion lent
The pulse of hope to discontent.

I wondered at the bounteous hours,
The slow result of winter showers:
You scarce could see the grass for flowers.

I wondered, while I paced along:
The woods were filled so full with song,
There seemed no room for sense of wrong.

So variously seemed all things wrought,
I marvelled how the mind was brought
To anchor by one gloomy thought;

And wherefore rather I made choice
To commune with that barren voice,
Than him that said, "Rejoice! Rejoice!"

Returning to Petaluma, the next morning we started for the Geysers, near the division line between Sonoma and Mendocino counties, passing in a northwest direction up the valley of Petaluma, its well-fenced fields, covered with luxuriant crops of wheat, barley, and oats, and its numerous vineyards indicating great fertility. Occasional groves of live and scrub oak were seen, but timber is not abundant. This valley, lying between the Petaluma and Sonoma ridges—spurs of the Coast Range, running in a southeastwardly direction—has a length of about twenty-five miles, and an average width of between four and five. West of the former ridge lies the Bodega country, celebrated for its production of potatoes, unsurpassed in quality and quantity, the coast fogs favoring their growth throughout the dry season of the interior.

A drive of sixteen miles brought us to the flourishing little town of Santa Rosa, the county-seat of Sonoma—certainly now undeserving Bayard Taylor's designation of a shabby place—embosomed in a superb valley of the same name, well cultivated, through which we passed in a still northward direction. This valley of Santa Rosa is wider than that of Petaluma; its timber also is more abundant, and of larger growth; the patriarchal oaks of the forest shaking in the wind their venerable locks of long gray moss, to tell of their heritage of centuries. Crossing the Russian River, a clear, wide, and strong stream, fordable only in the dry season, we entered the Russian River Valley, and swept along its magnificent bowling green, until, at the distance of fifteen miles from Santa Rosa, we passed through the town of Healdsburg, of four or five hundred people, built in the shade of a large grove of madrones and oaks. The Russian River Valley is the third in the ascending series from the bay shore, which in fact form but one continuous whole—with occasional narrowings from encroaching spurs of the opposite ridges—of like physical characteristics and fertility, and should be called by but one name. Although thus far the proofs of agricultural industry have been seen scattered on either hand, still the great expanse of uncultivated land along our road shows the pressing want of labor to develop the latent resources of this as of other parts of the State. And labor will be had by the governing class who have wrested this wonderful country from the Mexican. Of what race, hue, and relation it will come—whether it will be furnished by peon, serf, coolie, Hindoo, or Moor, as controlled by Spanish-American, Russian, Englishman, or Frenchman, or will be had of the negro, must remain a question for time to settle. But labor will be sought of some complexion and form, either ebony, copper colored, or questionable tint, and of personal or *equally objectionable political bondage*, to bring about the grand results awaiting its application in this magnificent field, on which the light of human progress is now dawning.

Less than a mile beyond Healdsburg the plain is studded with many volcanic blisters, isolated and grass-covered, except at the summits, several of which are crowned with rock laminated vertically, as if burst through by upheaval force. Winding along a somewhat rougher road in a still northerly direction, four miles further brought us again to the Russian River, which for a while had been lost sight of, and which we recrossed to the east side. A gradual climb of two miles up a winding acclivity brought us—seven miles from Healdsburg—to the roadside house of John Ray, who gave us a hospitable but very homely backwoods reception. Travellers in the Geyser Mountains who do not tarry at Healdsburg, to which point a public conveyance may be had, usually stop at Ray's for the night. But finding a pack-mule driver on our arrival about to start thence for the Geysers, we determined to avail of his guidance over the uncertain mountain path. Hiring fresh horses and leaving our buggy we took the saddle at 6½ P. M., and started with the loaded pack-mule in the lead, followed by his mounted driver, my companion next, while I brought up the rear of the single file in which our narrow way compelled us to travel. This mountain journey at night was a bold undertaking for the uninitiated; but he, who with brief time at his disposal would see the wonders of a new country, must not count the cost in comfort and the risk of danger.

In a quarter of an hour after starting a thick coast fog came sweeping along, rendering the gathering gloom of evening an almost impenetrable darkness. And when, shortly after, it condensed into heavy rain as we ascended the steep and dangerous Geyser Ridge, our guide expressed his fear that, as inexperienced mountaineers, we had probably undertaken an adventure we should regret, and advised our return. But we knew "no such word as fail," and, already wet to the buff, declined to discuss the proposal to turn back. Onward we went, over rock and ravine, moor and morass, amid trees and through chaparral, as it seemed to me from sounds and scrapings; for night had gathered her black folds around, veiling all things, while the rain pelted us with momentarily increasing fall, as if in punishment for obstinacy. Of surroundings nothing could be seen by man, whatever the instincts of our beasts may have taught them. I was sensible only of darkness and drenching, water-spouts and weariness, plunges, stumbles, and multiplied inflictions of twig and thorn on face and limb, and of the necessity of keeping a tight rein to prevent my horse from falling, holding on, ignoring consequences the consideration of which would have encouraged timidity, and plying my spurs diligently to avoid falling too far behind those in advance, and thus being left to spend the entire night in the mountains with the uncertainty of being able to extricate myself even by daylight.

Four hours and a half of time and twelve miles of such a ride brought us to the Geyser Hotel; and it cannot be denied that, when we dismounted, wet and weary, we were of opinion that nothing to be here seen could repay us for the discomforts and risks of a storm-night in the Geyser Mountain.

"Tired nature's sweet restorer" and a good breakfast contributed much to renew hopeful anticipations, and we started on our tour of observation next morning with buoyant spirits.

From the plateau on which the hotel stands, facing north, and looking down a rugged bank of ninety-seven feet, a bold, rapid, and clear stream—Big Sulphur Creek—is seen below dashing over a bed of rocks with noisy revelry, whose note is the ceaseless serenade of the sleepers of the mountain house near by. The opposite bank of the creek is formed by the foot of Geyser Ridge, on which lie the objects of interest that are the attractions of this remarkable region. Descending from the plateau, the stream was crossed by a foot-bridge resting on natural abutments and piers of massive rocks. Having attained the north side of the stream opposite to the hotel, we entered the mouth of a cañon debouching at that point, in which are situated several bath-houses. Leaving these to the left, the bank of the cañon was ascended to the right, and, following a path running northeastwardly about twenty paces, a bold spring of strongly impregnated sulphur water of a temperature of 110° Fahrenheit was found, which through suitable pipes flowed to the bath-houses below. Ascending still in the same direction, the large ravine or gulch called *Devil's Cañon* was seen off to the left, formed of two branches which circumscribe a large, irregular, and entirely insulated mound of commingled red and white sterility, which, in the vocabulary of the place, is set down as the *Mountain of Fire.* Leaving this also on the left, and proceeding toward the east about eighty paces, we came to a depression of uneven surface, rocky, and bounded on one side by a reddish colored earth embankment. Numerous basins at the foot of this contain water of various inky shades, and in every degree of ebullition, accompanied by hissings and puffings of escaping vapor which rises to the height of a hundred feet. These are the *Devil's Wash-tubs*, and, in a space of about eighty or ninety feet circuit, there are ten of them of different sizes, from a few inches to several feet diameter, surrounded by ledges of friable reddish clay blackened on the surface. Large quantities of sulphur, alum, magnesia, ammonia, and oxides of iron are found in this vicinity, some of them of beautifully crystalline form. We did not linger long at his infernal majesty's laundry, for the tremblings of the crust on which we stood—certainly not in the mind of Macbeth when he apostrophized the "sure and firm-set earth"—and its insupportable heat to the thinly shod, together with the subterranean rumblings and grumblings as of discontent at intrusion into this out-house of Pandemonium, made it uninviting, and we moved on thoughtless of the adage that one may "jump out of the frying-pan into the fire."

Retracing our steps a few paces toward the north of the Mountain of Fire, in a shallow ravine were seen two clefts of nine or ten inches, and two feet asunder, in the side of a stiff clay and unctuous rocky bank, giving vent to volumes of steam with roaring noise mingled with that of deep subterranean boiling. These are known as the *Devil's Tea-kettles;* and tradition has it that, so strongly were the Indians of this region imbued with the superstition of the Evil Spirit's abode here, that death was deemed the certain penalty of trespass—a belief and apprehension in *no sense* partaken of by their white brethren, whose latter-day progressive temerity seems rather to court the privilege of exploration of Satan's undoubted dominions. About seventy feet southwest of the Tea-kettles is a depression of the surface twenty or twenty-five feet deep, and nearly forty in diameter, rimmed by a considerable quantity of iron slag and scoriæ of all kinds, and thickly traced with brimstone, alum, potash, and magnesia—having also about it several minute steam vents. This spot is called the *Crater;* it is on the summit of the Mountain of Fire, and probably was once the seat of remarkable terrestrial phenomena. Even now a stamp of the foot gives resounding proof of dangerous hollowness; and holes made by forcing a walking-cane a few inches through the unresisting earth gave vents for escaping vapor indicating close proximity to a steam-boiler, that might at any moment give the curious investigator an undesirable elevation.

Passing from the Crater in a west by north, and then in a northwest direction, and descending from the Mountain of Fire, we wound around the head of the Devil's Cañon, passing on the way a little spring rivulet of pure and cool crystal water, looking strangely out of place in this region of boiling inky pools. A short distance further brought us to a pretty grove of *Shittim trees*, where the heated and wearied wanderer may tarry and rest, and determine, if it please him, if these furnished the timber of which "Bezaleel made the ark of shittim-wood" as commanded. A colossal boulder—fit mile-stone for the surrounding scenery—will direct the explorer a few paces further to a babbling mountain brooklet, which at the crossing mingles its pure stream with the offensive waters of a sulphur spring at that spot. Forty paces of rugged pathway brought us to *Avalanche Arbor;* an enormous land-slide having occurred here recently, precipitating thousands of tons of rock from the mountain summit above, and thus relieved the lover of the picturesque from future danger in his wanderings about this secluded spot. The arbor has several massive rocks on one side and a magnificent bay-tree on the other, with its low-hung thick-spreading branches and dense foliage, forming a bower for those who would meditate in solitude and shade on the mysterious powers at work beneath them. Hastening on, a few steps brought us to another little brooklet dashing on from the mountain above—like thoughtless youth in a reckless career—unaware of the polluted fate awaiting it in the Devil's Cañon below. And here is found the place of *temporary memories*, where a magnificent colonnade of trees is marred by the carvings of the vulgar, capable of no other power of making their perishing names known than by burdening a beautiful nature with the disgraceful catalogue.

The explorer a short distance beyond comes suddenly on a projecting rock in a rapid state of disintegration, standing about two hundred feet above the bed of Devil's Cañon; from which, facing the south, he looks into the depths below with emotions of awe and terror, mingled with wonder and delight. At his feet he beholds a scene of decomposing forces—of death and desolation—the proofs of a power transcending previous conceptions; while in the distance, beyond Big Sulphur Creek, that winds along the foot of the ridge, he sees a fresh creation; rolling hills, clad in richest livery, fanned by waving groves, and at their base man's beautiful handiwork—his temporary abode—embowered in live oaks, firs, pines, madrones, and alders, and garnished with the adornments of the garden, presenting a contrasted picture of production and life. Grass, foliage, and flowers beyond, breathing the vapors and gases of decomposing nature at his feet, the creative elements of growth, of verdure and bloom. Here may science study lessons on a scale of vast grandeur, while in the scene an immovable stumbling-block in the path of scepticism is also recognized.

Descending into the cañon by a steep and narrow-ledged track, safe, however, for the courageous and sure-footed, we passed on the way that fearful exhaust-pipe of subterranean steam called the *Steamboat Geyser*. Here the escaping vapor issues from a hole about two feet in diameter, nearly midway the height of the right wall of the cañon, and in the midst of a large quantity of clinker and slag. The noise of this emission is terrific—a continuous, tremulous thunder, of commingled shrill hoarseness, running through the gamut of a thousand Mississippi high-pressure steamers in rivalry of explosive discord. The column of steam shoots with resistless force to a height of more than one hundred feet, visible in the face of the noonday sun; and, in the cool air of early morning, it lifts its white cloud even five hundred feet above the cañon, to meet the first beams that glance over the adjacent mountain-spur, and form of its baptismal mist a rainbow—a harbinger of promise even in this scene of desolation.

This is undoubtedly the greatest steam-vent of the wonderful terrestrial boiler within; although, in truth, the walls of the Devil's Cañon present several hundred small blow-holes of steam, as if the vast generator were riddled with perforations, making of the whole cañon a huge vapor-bath.

A short distance below the great steam-pipe, and directly beneath the *Devil's Peak*, from which the view before spoken of is had of the entire cañon, an *alum spring* is found—a rock pot one foot and a half in diameter, of black, powerfully astringent boiling water, from which arise the most offensive of gases, sulphuretted hydrogen, and steam, as from other springs, of different properties, in this vicinity. Huge masses of amorphous rock, of all colors and shades, slimy and slippery, track the way of the explorer; but he who would see the Geysers must surmount these obstacles, or he will have accomplished but a part of the object of his visit, and have realized imperfectly the sublimity and terrors of the place. If he pause here to debate the chances of peril or escape, increasing timidity may determine him to turn back; but he should bear in mind that the descent of this valley of the shadow of death is easier than a returning ascent; and he had better imitate Bunyan's "Mr. Greatheart" and push ahead than get involved in the difficulties of "Mr. Timorous," trusting to the helping hand of some good friend "Faithful" if he should "slip by the way." Many demons will seem to menace him with hissing, wheezing, whistling, roaring, rasping, rumbling, puffing, and moaning; but he must stop his ears to sounds, and trust to quick sight and steady nerve to put him through in safety. From a little below the Alum Spring the rocky obstacles increase in number, size, and confusion; and the panting, heaving, and throbbing of the earth appear to threaten a breaking up of its solid structure. If, baffled in surmounting the impediments in your path—the heterogeneous components of which have been melted, mingled, and baked in the eternal fires beneath—and, faltering, you stand with suspended breath on the groaning and trembling crust; or you hurry on over yielding substance, softened by the boiling water bursting forth all around, threatening a solution or sinking of the surface on which you plant your heated foot; or, displacing a stone, you open a new vent and suffer the painful contact of scalding steam and gas, giving warning of dangerous proximity to fearful agencies of mischief; if, with such experience, one fails to recognize the neighborhood of Tartarus, he is not likely to become a believer in ancient mythology.

If the attention of the adventurous explorer can be withdrawn for awhile from the bolder features of the surroundings, from the steep sloping cañon walls at the narrow bottom threaded by the little mountain stream from above, now the *Pluton Creek* of smoking waters, to their height of from two to three hundred feet, stained with red, rust, slate, green, ash, and the many colored marbling of nature's wonderful art; from rock, and stream, and bubbling pool; it may be directed for awhile with well-repaid interest to the less striking, but equally instructive specimens of strange chemistry sent forth from the vast laboratory beneath, and lying along the rugged pathway. Sulphur of all qualities and forms, from the delicate feathery crystal to the crude mass, is found on every hand, and alum, magnesia, lime, iron, ammonia, and varied salts, with acidulates of vitriolic strength, as the indiscreet at times determine by cauterized tongues and burnt garments.

Proceeding on, the puffing and panting of the *Locomotive Engine* is heard on the left of the descent, as if impatiently testing its capacities ere starting on the race before it; the earth around it shaking in sympathy as with the tread of a giant. And lower still, on the opposite side of the ravine, with a smoke-stack open in the front, is the *Witches' Cauldron*, a rock-pot seventeen or eighteen feet in circumference and of unknown depth, filled nearly to the brim with a fetid, Stygian, semi-fluid, sooty substance, boiling, bubbling, and swashing in terrific commotion. Opposite to the cauldron is *Pluto's Pulse Glass*, a stone cylinder of six or eight inches diameter, communicating with interior steam passages, and throwing up its intermittent jets of scalding fluid occasionally to the height of several feet, its greater or less activity being doubtless dependent on the accumulation and condition of tension of steam in the subterranean reservoirs and their channels of communication. But for the great vent of the Steamboat Exhaust-pipe already described, the safety-valve of which is always open, it is probable that the Pulse Glass, Witches' Cauldron, and all other pools in which rising vapors are condensed, and which are merely kept in a state of ebullition or jet by the *vis a tergo*, would themselves become steam-vents of more or less power. The *Devil's Bake Oven*, a short distance farther down the cañon, consists of an excavated vertical rock with an overhanging ledge, within which invalids have sometimes taken sulphur vapor-baths formed of escaping steam from the foot of the rock. The bath is had without cost, except that of a partial parboiling; and a gratuity is also afforded to the lover of physic at a spring near by, of a dose of Epsom salts dissolved in chalybeate water. After passing the region of hot-baths and steam-baths, a narrower part of the cañon is reached where the commingled waters, duly tempered by admixture of hot and cold currents, and medicated by various elements, acid, alkaline, sulphurous, and ferruginous, precipitate themselves over a rock five feet high into a pebbly basin, a superb tepid douche-bath, such as the invalid can nowhere obtain from the hand of art. A few steps farther down the pathway by which the stream is dashing, the cañon is roofed by two large bay trees that have fallen across it, resting their limbs on the opposite sides, while their roots still cling to their mother earth and to vitality. The close and high walls and thick leafy ceiling, give to the cañon a twilight shade even in brightest day; and this spot might have been considered, in the early classical age, the favorite resort of the bride of the presiding genius of the place—the ruler of Avernus. Having rested in *Proserpine's Grotto*, the explorer then proceeds a few paces to the *Elysian Bath*, a rock-girt pool twenty feet long by five wide, in which the temperate water of the smaller ravine which bounds the east side of the Mountain of Fire—and in which is a chalybeate alum spring, said to be a specific in chronic ophthalmia—mingles with the warmer water of the great cañon; and he who has not, when exhausted by intense excitement, and wearied by long clambering, plunged into such a blissful and renovating stream, knows not the greatest luxury of life. The water of this pool is conducted to the bath-houses already spoken of, for the use of those who forego the delights of the elysian bath rather than encounter the terrors of night in the Devil's Cañon.

Having thus made the circuit of the chief points of interest, and partaken of an excellent dinner, we started again with our guide a hundred yards up that bank of the Big Sulphur Creek on which stands the hotel. Opposite to us numerous steam vents were seen on the mountain side, and dark sulphurous streams tracked it, the foul overflowings, probably, of the Devil's Wash-Tubs situated above. These streams it is proposed to unite and convey across the creek in an aqueduct, for the supply of bath-houses on this side of the creek, more accessible to invalids, who thus—and by the use of a pure white sulphur water of agreeable coolness for drinking, found near the hotel, at the foot of the plateau on which it stands—will be relieved from the discomfort and effort of seeking the waters at an inconvenient distance. It may be stated in this connection that about three-quarters of a mile, on the opposite side of the creek above the hotel, there is another very large white sulphur spring, very closely resembling the famous Greenbrier White Sulphur Spring in Virginia. Turning in the opposite direction, we now proceeded down the creek on its left bank, and nearly half a mile below crossed to the opposite side by wading, for the want of a bridge or boat. A quarter of a mile below the crossing we climbed a hill covered with heavy-headed wild oats of rank luxuriance, and then descended its opposite declivity into a glen shaded by a thick grove, a mile and a quarter from the hotel. Here is a large spring of black sulphur water, the escape of which from the earth is unattended with noise, and which, when it mixes in an adjacent pool with a pure cool stream coming down the little valley, yields a white sulphur precipitate which gives the water a milky appearance. This is the *Indian Spring*, famous as a place of resort for the sick of former neighboring tribes, who feared to approach the more tumultuous and threatening Geysers, believing as they did that intruders there became the victims of the Evil Spirit who controlled the inextinguishable fires within. The afflicted Indians, generally suffering from rheumatism, were wrapped in blankets, steamed over the hot spring, and then, divested of the blankets, were plunged in the tepid pool, from which they were conveyed in dry blankets to their temporary lodges on the high ground in the vicinity.

The value of the waters of the California Geysers in the medical treatment of chronic rheumatism, chronic liver affections, and some eruptive diseases, cannot well be overestimated, and doubtless time, with intelligent observation and research, will determine their adaptation to a wide range of human afflictions. Many of the most celebrated medicinal springs of the world find here, within the space of a few hundred acres, their counterparts, both in properties and temperature, medical and thermal characteristics. But there are required capital, enterprise, good judgment, professional investigation and skill, to apply properly this vast laboratory of nature—to adapt it to public wants and to give profit to its proprietors. Unless the Geysers shall be made more accessible by an improved road for vehicles, the sick, those who most need the restorative virtues of their waters, will be unable to reach them; and unless proper facilities are provided when there, for their convenient, safe, and skilful application, benefit cannot come to the patient seeking relief, nor pecuniary gain to the owners, whose patronage must come of such success.

Willing to leave the examination and decision of the question, whether the varied phenomena of caloric witnessed here are the results of volcanic or of chemical action, to the scientific gentlemen whose official duty it is to solve the problem, and whose capacity and opportunity fit them for the task, and having had sufficient exercise to forego the temptation of trout-fishing and a bear hunt, thrown out by our obliging landlord to detain us among these highlands of the Coast Range, we bade adieu to the Geysers, duly sensible of the indisputable claims California is rapidly putting forth for recognition as a land of wonderful natural curiosities, as well as of vast natural resources.

After having ascended the steep hill that bathes its foot in

Big Sulphur Creek, and bounds in part the deep gorge through which that stream rushes wildly in places, in others meanders as gently as if courting repose after a tiresome race, we came, at the distance of more than a mile, upon that narrow ridge of nearly two miles' length, called the Hog's Back, presenting in some parts a mere spine for our bridle path, bounded on each side by precipices, the knowledge of which would not have contributed to diminish the apprehensions of our fearful adventure over the same road two nights before. A short distance to the right of our way, among other objects of interest, were seen abrupt red-colored bluffs, abutting in ravines of the mountain spur, and which mark the locality of the *Geyser quicksilver* mines, represented to produce an exceedingly rich cinnabar. On this same route, three or four miles northeast of Ray's Station, are the *Pine Flat* mines, where extensive deposits of pure quicksilver are found in the rock. It is thus seen, that California is not dependent on the Almaden mines for the necessary supply of this metal in her gold-mining operations.

Somewhat less than a mile from the Hog's Back, on our return, brought us to the foot of Godwin's Peak, one of the loftiest of the Miakmus or Geyser Range, which walls in the Russian River Valley on the east. The peak is three thousand four hundred and ninety feet high, and from its summit, which may be reached by a rugged side-path, through dense chaparral, an extended view is had of numerous mountain spurs and glens at its foot; of the Coast Range in the distant west, with its foot dipping in the blue ocean, while its long line is lost to the sight in the far-off north and south; of Mount St. Helen's to the southeast, with its transcendent form of symmetry and grace; and of the valleys of Napa, Sonoma, Los Guillicos, Petaluma, Santa Rosa, and that of Russian River, threaded by its silver stream, all unrolled below and presenting a continuous picture of bright verdure, broken only by occasional deep shades of relieving forests.

From Godwin's Peak to Little Sulphur Creek—a mountain trout stream of considerable size, two miles from the Peak and six from the Geysers—the road has a rapid descent. And thence to Ray's, six miles farther, after a slight acclivity, it becomes declivitous again, but with a general improvement of condition most acceptable to returning excursionists. We were glad to exchange wearied nags for our buggy and fresh horses, and with but little delay were soon making good speed along the bowling greens seen from the top of the mountain; and over which, ere long, a railroad will probably convey the passenger still more fleetly from the Russian River region to Petaluma. The distance from Petaluma to the Geysers is fifty miles. Returning to San Francisco by the next day's steamer, our passenger ship for Honolulu was found ready to sail, and I forthwith went aboard. But as, on my return to San Francisco from the Hawaiian Islands, an opportunity was afforded to visit the Valley and Falls of Yo-Semite, it is deemed best, for the sake of connection, to vut here upon the record what I saw of them.

## CHAPTER XXVIII.

ROUTE TO THE YO-SEMITE VALLEY—STOCKTON—KNIGHT'S FERRY—STANISLAUS RIVER—TUOLUMNE RIVER—DON PEDRO'S BAR—COULTERVILLE—CHINESE IMMIGRATION.

Nearly every country can boast of some great attraction in nature or art inviting the investigations of the learned, or the transient observations of the passing tourist. The disinterred remains of the buried past, the crumbling monuments of antiquity, and the imperishable proofs of its genius and power, have caused Egypt and Europe to be tracked for centuries by the footsteps of the curious. While the highlands of Scotia; the vales of fair Italia, looking on which, "full flashes on the soul the light of ages;" and the grand old mountains of Switzerland, the unscaled fortresses of freedom wrapped in everlasting snows, and shaking from brow and shoulder the avalanche and the *mer de glace*, the coronet and robe of grandeur and might, with tranquil valleys sleeping at their feet lulled by the music of countless waterfalls—the commingled mysteries of the sublime and beautiful—have awakened the enthusiasm of travellers, and inspired the pen of genius to record the strange companionship and the sovereignty of nature.

Europe may well rejoice in its scenery, as well as in its civilization. But the Creator has placed elsewhere also, in this great world of ours, the proofs of His Power, and annual discoveries in this latest of territorial acquisitions show that California is not left without these voiceless teachers of truth. Among these is the Yo-Sem-i-te Valley in Mariposa County, among the foot-hills of the western slope of the Sierra Nevada, two hundred and fifty-two miles from San Francisco. The route to it from that city is by steamer one hundred and twenty-five miles to *Stockton*, a flourishing town of four thousand inhabitants in the interior on a slough of the eastern arm of San Joaquin, the second river in size and importance of the State;

SAN JOAQUIN RIVER—MONTE DIABLO IN THE DISTANCE.

thence by stage-coach to Coulterville, or to Mariposa, or to Big Oak Flat, at which places the public conveyance stops, and another must be sought. The Coulterville route is preferable for economy of time, cost, distance, and for greater comfort.

Starting from Stockton at 6 A. M., an hour after our arrival by the boat, with a fine team of horses, fair samples of California size, speed, and bottom, we travelled first east by south, and then east-southeast, over an extensive tract of bottom lands of alluvial deposit, bearing abundant testimony of rich growth. Seventeen miles of unpaved road, parched, cracked, and dusty, in the long summer drought, brought us to a rolling and less fertile district, with fewer evidences of thrifty husbandry; and at thirty-six miles from Stockton we came to *Knight's Ferry*, a town of about a thousand inhabitants, at which a fine bridge is thrown over the Stanislaus River, the clear waters of which from the Sierra, flow over a rocky bed onward to the San Joaquin to be lost in its ever turbid current.

Abandoned diggings, sluices, flumes, gravel banks, and heaps of boulders, showed how diligent had been the search for gold in this vicinity. Beyond the river the country is still more rugged, the road to the Crimea House on Kentucky Ranche fourteen miles from the ferry, being skirted for a long distance by upheaved laminated rocks of various sizes, looking like tombstones of a vast cemetery, some as if designating the graves of giants, while others modestly marked the resting places of infancy. From the Crimea House the coach continued on the main stage-route in a northeast direction to *Sonora*, while we in a small mud-wagon took a southeast course, passing over a much more hilly country, and crossing the beds of many small streams which have existence only in the rainy seasons. At ten miles from the Crimea House we reached the Tuolumne River, heading in the Sierra and flowing west to the San Joaquin of which it is one of the large branches. The little town of *Don Pedro's Bar* has grown up at this crossing from placer and river mining, which, not being among the most profitable of such operations, is chiefly in the hands of Chinamen; and as they were seen shovelling, and rocking their cradles on the river banks and shoals, for the discarded remnants of wealth borne away by more fortunate enterprise, a curious fellow-traveller inquired whether the river had given their integument, or it had given the river, a dingy hue? From the Tuolumne River the road is more mountainous, frequent foot-hill spurs being encountered stretching westwardly from the Nevada and giving steep ascents to climb, and gorges and ravines to be threaded by narrow defiles, or turned by tedious windings, for fourteen miles to *Coulterville*, where we arrived at 9 P. M.—in fifteen hours from Stockton—distance seventy-four miles.

At Coulter's Hotel we were received, in the absence of the host, by a fine specimen of young America but thirteen years old, who registered our names, ordered supper, and showed us to our chambers, with remarkable intelligence, and much more politeness than is usually observed by older employés of these frontier caravansaries; in which mankind are regarded as a live lumber, without feeling or claim to comfort, and under an obligation to submit to rudeness, neglect, and extortion. The town, situated in a wild mountain gorge, where gold was found as early as 1849, has three or four hundred inhabitants, exclusive of Chinese, of whom there are about as many more, in and around it, engaged in sand washing with cradle and sluice, along the little creek that flows through the gulch.

Public opinion here, as in other parts of the State, is divided in regard to the character of Chinamen, and the desirableness of their immigration. While some Americans denounce them as petty thieves, and otherwise troublesome interlopers whose notions and habits are at variance with those of the whites, and whose inferiority of race unfits them for social and political equality, others contend that among them are to be found numerous and remarkable examples of probity and intelligence, and that in the general their morals are not of a lower grade than those of other immigrants, while the vices in which they indulge are not more degrading, and the crimes of which they are guilty are neither as atrocious nor brutal as those perpetrated by Europeans and Americans. Perhaps, from natural organization, the Chinaman is neither as capable of touching as low a degree of debasement as the Caucasian, nor, on the other hand, of mounting to the same height of moral and intellectual excellence. There are between forty and fifty thousand Chinese in California, and their proportion of criminals in the Penitentiary is less than that of the white population. But this fact is merely sufficient to warrant a conclusion of comparative convictions, not of actual criminality.

Chinese labor certainly constitutes a prominent element in the development and promotion of the material interests of this State. Unlike the Caucasian, the Chinaman must work or starve. No provisions of corporate charity, sectarian benevolence, or more enlarged associate philanthropy, are made for him, and "root pig or die" becomes the law of his denizenship. The avenues of most profitable and honorable employment and enterprise are, except to a limited extent in the field of commerce in San Francisco, closed to him by the jealousies of the dominant race, so that he falls of necessity into the hiatus of hardship, where other productive industry will not come, and which, but for him, would be left unfilled. Thus he becomes the house servant, the field and vineyard hand, the general laborer or Asiatic Irishman, the follower in the wake of the white miner who has appropriated the golden nuggets, and discarded impoverished sands; and he re-digs abandoned placers, and drains and washes neglected river-beds, seeking industriously their scattered and less valuable deposits, which, in the aggregate, however, contribute largely to the moneyed wealth of the State. For, by the payment of passenger fare to and from California, of freight of Chinese supplies through American shippers, and of their import duty, of steamboat and coach fare to the interior, along many of the routes of which they are the greater number of stage travellers; their outlays for transportation of goods by wagons, for State license of four dollars per month each for the privilege of mining, for house and land rent to American owners, and for provisions to farmers—for these purposes currency is given to a large amount of gold, which, but for Chinamen, would lie useless in gorge and stream. But although these facts would seem to indicate the impolicy of overlooking the general results of labor, however applied, in the narrow contemplation of temporary selfish interests, there is another view of this question of Chinese immigration of far higher importance to the race into whose hands this fair land has fallen, which should not be disregarded, and that is, how far it will comport with the preservation of that highest type of mankind, with the protection of its exalted physical and mental attributes, to concede equal political privileges to the eastern Asiatics with whom the American has now been brought face to face, who could spare to California more millions of people than the population of the United States, and not be sensible of the loss; and who, thus becoming the governing class, and through a consequent social equality the producers for a time of a hybrid race, would finally, by an inevitable law coming of numerical strength, extinguish every trace of the nobler type of man. With this nobler type now rests the determination of his own future destiny, and the preservation of his purity and exaltation, by disregarding a false humanitarianism and a fanaticism which impugn the distinctions of the Creator, and by the adoption and enforcement of laws for their protection. A commercial intercourse mutually advantageous to China and California, and to some extent industrial interchanges, may take place compatibly with a justly administered natural law of self-preservation. But if, as appears to be the fact now, differences of opinion are to exist among Californians in regard to the status of the Chinaman, a question might be put here of equivalent import with that especially interesting to another part of America, *i. e.* if the white race cannot agree *about* the negro, will it ever be able to agree *with* him?

Coulterville is the terminus of the public stage line, and the tourist must here seek other means of getting on to the Yo-Sem-i-te. Fortunately he will find here excellent horses at the livery-stable of Messrs. Smith & Scott—just and reliable persons—who furnished me a suitable outfit, and all the information necessary to make a safe and satisfactory trip. True, it was discouraging to learn from a returned excursionist, that the homicide of an Indian by a white settler in the neighborhood of the valley, and a manifestation of hostile intentions on the part of the tribe, had induced the whites to leave the two houses kept there for the accommodation of visitors. But Mr. Thomas W. Long, a resident of Coulterville, and a fearless son of the "old Kentucky State," experienced in frontier life, kindly offering to accompany me, it was determined to go forward and feel the way, and next morning we started to make an easy day's ride to the stopping place for the first night—"Black's."

Our east by north road was ascending from Coulterville, eighteen hundred feet above the sea-level, to the Yo-Semite, which is said to be twenty-three hundred feet above the sea. Five saw-mills within seven miles of Coulterville, furnish four millions of feet of lumber annually for the supply of the Tuolumne and Merced Valleys. At ten miles a trail alone marked our route, and that in places was quite indistinct. At twelve miles from Coulterville there is a "cave" about a hundred yards to the left of the path, which would scarcely be considered such but for the close board fence that shuts in its front, and gives to its interior the necessary "dim religious light," on which some sensational guide-book yet to be printed will go into raptures, to lighten the purses of California tourists. A short distance beyond the trail enters a dense forest of fine timber, seen also skirting the road in places before reaching this point; and winding over steep rocky hills for more than a mile, a slightly rolling surface was reached, covered with trees twined with vines, and sheltering a thick undergrowth. Pines, stately and straight, still clinging to their favorite green, stood round, mingling with lordly oaks clad in the yellow and nut-brown foliage of autumn; with dogwood and wild honeysuckle dressed in gayer hues of scarlet and crimson; while crystal rivulets leaped across, or ran murmuringly by our pathway, courting a willing admiration of their wild music, and tempting, too, the thirsty palate.

At seventeen miles from Coulterville a pretty glen, surrounded by pine-covered hills, was reached, two narrow defiles opening into it from opposite directions. And near the border of a streamlet that seemed fondly to linger in the sequestered spot, so placid was its flow, we found the unpretending but hospitable house of Mr. Black, at which we put up for the night.

Here it was ascertained that the Yo-Semite Valley was deserted by white visitors, and that no persons were there but some straggling Indians of a Digger tribe, engaged in gathering their winter subsistence of wild roots and acorns. The information previously received of the killing of an Indian, and the meditated revenge of his friends upon the whites, was also confirmed; but it was accompanied by the gratifying intelligence, that at the instance of an influential frontiersman they had been induced to await a promised trial and punishment of the offender by due process of law. Mr. Black having been assured, by a friendly Indian, that under these circumstances no retaliation on the neighboring whites need be feared for some time, we determined to continue our journey; and the proprietor of the first cabin built in the valley for the accommodation of visitors having placed it at our disposal, we hired a pack mule, and having procured of Mr. Black the necessary creature comforts of food and blankets for the trip, were en route again early next morning for the great valley, with the addition to our company of another Kentucky volunteer, Mr. James Lamb, whose knowledge of this region and its native tribes was a guarantee of safety, and who proved an adept in managing the domestic economy of our future cabin household.

It cannot be denied that the charge of unjust and cruel treatment of the Indian race by our countrymen is truthfully made. Inferior to us in blood, in culture, and in power, the original possessors of the land, and ever ready to extend the hand of hospitality and friendship to the stranger who came to them in the spirit of peace seeking benefits; sufferers, too, from the vices of civilization, more studiously taught to them than its virtues, they deserve at our hands as a people, an extension of the most benign policy, and individually protection, charity, and mercy; instead of which they are the victims of systematic fraud, persecution, and frequent atrocity, rapidly leading to their extermination. The murder of an Indian at the hands of a white man, if not magnified into a merit, receives no punishment; but the killing of a white man by an Indian, whatever the mitigating circumstances, calls for the blood of the offender, and brings a new curse upon his tribe; while the kidnapping of Indian children and selling them to service in California, has been made the subject of newspaper comment in San Francisco, and they are sometimes seen *unaccountably* in domestic employment, the stealing and carrying off of a white child by the Sioux or Chippewas, fills the whole land with lamentation, and calls for a Presidential decree, sacrificing a hecatomb of human victims. Shall we continue thus indifferent to the inculcations of justice and mercy, and wilfully incur the retribution which in some form or other will surely follow?

Our route from Black's was up Bull Run, well known as the old Indian trail to the Mono Lake region, on an important "divide," more easily travelled in winter and earlier in spring than others on which the snow is heavier and lies longer. A short distance brought us to a deep gorge between ridges, covered with pitch and sugar pine, the latter so called from its yielding a sugar of turpentine, which is both purgative and diuretic, cedar and black oak timber, charred bark of standing trees, many black and fallen trunks, and the ashy earth swept of undergrowth and grass, showing the wide desolation resulting from careless camp-fires. The feet of the ridges were washed by a clear, cold stream, that ran flashing over a smooth and continuous rock channel, along which we passed between four and five miles, whence a less precipitous and wider avenue led to *Deer Flat*, six miles from Black's, a prairie level of about two hundred acres, with a log cabin, shovel, pick and pan, indicating a miner's residence. Half obliterated *blazes* marked the trail beyond, which passed, six miles further, over a shaded hazel-green, and which soon became rugged, and wound tortuously among ridges, heading ravines, and passing over low hills, but with a gradual ascent, until, seventeen miles from Black's, we reached the highest altitude between Coulterville and the Yo-Semite, whence can be seen the white cliffs fifty miles distant, marking the head of the Stanislaus River in the Sierra Nevada, and, where the timber allows, the course of that river, and the dividing ridge between it and the Tuolumne River. A mile further brought us by a slight descent to a level of three or four hundred acres, called Crane Flat, where we procured grass and water for our horses, and where a little untenanted clapboard house, "pro bono publico," and a grove of pines and cottonwoods, offered to us the temptation to rest and lunch.

A splendid forest of pines, both pitch and sugar, firs, cedars, and black oaks, overshadowed the trail beyond, many of the former lifting their heads two hundred and fifty feet above us, their massive trunks of seven and eight feet diameter, standing as straight as monumental shafts. The beauty and grandeur of these trees are marvellous, and yet I am told by my companions, that thus far we have but entered the vestibule of the great forest temple, which California for ages has been building for the worshippers of these giant monarchs of vegetable nature. It is painful to witness the ravages of fire, commonly the consequence of neglect to extinguish that which cheered a night's bivouac, and sometimes of purpose to uncover hidden game, on this magnificent timber. Often a blackened and limbless trunk was seen standing like an iron column of incomparable proportions. And then again a shaft prouder than Pompey's pillar, whose root alone the same destroyer had touched with withering blight, dropping its bark and branches, and bleached by the sun, from which no friendly foliage now screens it, lifting on high its seeming marble to perpetuate its own great memory. While occasionally the scene was made instructive by one of these voiceless types of majesty, sapped by natural decay, folding around itself an evergreen winding-sheet of moss, to tell that though material forms may change, elementary life does not perish, and thus reminding the passer-by of the "mortal that must put on immortality."

The trail from Crane Flat continued very tortuous, and the trees along it were frequently seen to bear the nearly obliterated crucial blaze of the old Mexican pioneers. The undergrowth, too, in many places was observed to be flattened and matted together so closely by the weight of winter snows, as to form perfect shelters for wild animals, and such dangerous coverts for the dreaded grizzly, that they are often designedly burnt along the line of the trail, to get rid of their fierce denizens.

About eight miles from Crane Flat, and three from the highest point of the trail, and fifty or sixty yards to the right of it, the first glimpse is caught, through an opening in the trees, of the Yo-Semite Valley in the distance. A sensational writer, after the fashion of eastern guide-book authors, calls this the "Stand-Point of Silence;" but, as if to contradict his own designation of the spot, he seems to have fallen into quite a *loquacious* fit of rapture over it. The truth is, that at the distance, none of the grand features of the scene are visible—the valley appears to be nothing but a vast misshapen cleft in the earth's surface, and rather calculated to disappoint expectation. It is a mistake to strive to manufacture a preliminary enthusiasm and sentiment over it. The Yo-Semite should be left to create its own impressions on the mind and soul when they come, as they will in due time, within its mysterious influence. "Good wine needs no bush." We were aware of the importance of reaching our destination before nightfall, and the knowledge of the many miles yet to be travelled warned us not to linger on the wayside. Two miles further brought us to a headlong and sparkling little mountain-stream called Cascade Number One, and another mile to Cascade Number Two, which raced over its rocky bed as if eager to reach first the Merced River, for which we were all bound, though not exactly by the same route. Beyond a rugged little elevation, we came again on a level trail which soon forked, a finger-board telling us that the left led to the Mono Lake gold district, fifty or sixty miles to the north-east, while the other, a half mile further, brought us to the

DESCENT INTO THE VALLEY.

commencement of the steep descent into the chasm we had been long and weariedly seeking. And here we realized the fact that the Yo-Semite was not a valley of gracefully curving and sloping boundaries, a waving tracery of verdure, but an awful cleft of the earth, ten miles long, of varying depth from three thousand to five thousand feet, whose perpendicular granite walls, so near were they, looked as if about to reunite and close the vast terrestrial crevice, into whose dark depths we peered in vain for the revelation of its wonderful creation. This colossal cañon can be entered readily only at one point at its east end, and from either side of its western outlet. As we came to it upon the Coulterville trail, we made the descent from the north side. The path is winding and precipitous, the angle of inclination being not less than thirty degrees, and in many places as great as forty-five. Nearly all explorers dismount and walk, as well for personal safety as to relieve their horses from the distressing shoulder-weight of their burdens. Half way down, a main fork of the Merced River, which for ages has flowed through the valley, is heard lifting its wild music from its bed of giant boulders, as if rejoicing at its prospect of escape from prolonged imprisonment, to run through natural meadows a few miles to the west, whose wild luxuriance is their smile of welcome to its coming. Two miles of descent brought us to the bottom of the abyss, which shall be described as it unfolded itself in our further progress; its physical features as these may be presented by language, not the impressions of its inconceivable sublimity, which can be written upon the soul only by the wondrous manifestations here displayed of Almighty Power.

## CHAPTER XXIX.

### YO-SEMITE VALLEY.

Arrived at the foot of the trail, down which so rapid is the declivity that it is difficult to avoid running—a pace that would be indulged in with the certainty of a flying leap over the cliff that borders one side of the serpentine path—a river is seen making its escape through a narrow gorge to the right, while to the left, so little north of east that it may with sufficient precision be said *eastward*, the valley of Yo-Semite stretches in dim distance and perspective for ten miles, with a varying width of from three-quarters of a mile to one and a half. But in consequence of the mountain height of its perpendicular granite walls, the valley really appears to be but a few hundred yards wide. Its level floor spread with a carpet of wild grass, and adorned with groves of pine, fir, alder, oak, cedar, cotton-wood, willow, and ash, is threaded throughout its entire length by a stream, clear and cool, from the snow fountains of the Sierra Nevada—a mirror in whose crystal depths the bold features of surrounding grandeur are reflected with wondrous distinctness; while every blade of grass that borders its banks, and the overhanging boughs, seem pencilled on its transparent bosom.

One of the first objects arresting the attention on reaching the foot of the valley by the north trail, is the waterfall nearly opposite on the south side, called, not inappropriately, "Bridal Veil." It is also known, by those who prefer the Indian nomenclature for the chief objects of interest here, as the "Pohono Fall," from an evil spirit supposed to exercise a malign power over a little stream of the same name that rises ten or twelve miles to the southward, and, crossing the Mariposa trail, hurries on to form this waterfall, by leaping over the edge of the cliff, pitching its continuous jets downward nine hundred and fifty feet, that break into mist and float like waves of gauze to the rocks beneath, which have for ages been gradually lifting higher their colossal abutment to meet the falling spray. The avalanche of foam at first plunges with arrowy speed, then seems to rest an instant, then starts again on its flight; clothed, too, in varying tints, as sunshine paints the rainbow on the fleecy drapery, or shade reveals its snowy purity. Wondrous as is this magic veil, yet is there a fascination in the majestic rocks which look down from their gray heights upon this scene

RIVER SCENE.

YO-SEMITE VALLEY.

of beauty, that draws the gaze upward to their stern and unmoved features.

POHONO—OR BRIDAL-VEIL FALL.

A short distance west of the waterfall stands a bold cone of granite nearly three thousand feet high, like a watch-tower at the entrance of the valley. And near it to the east is a perpendicular bluff two thousand nine hundred feet high, crowned with spires and minarets several hundred feet higher, giving a tapering grace and architectural finish to the grand substructure. The special names applied to these by some tourists are in bad taste. To call the whole group "The Cathedral Rocks" is sufficient to distinguish them from others of like interest.

On the north side of the valley, opposite to the Bridal Veil, is a truncated mountain of granite three thousand six hundred feet high, projecting boldly beyond the general line of the valley wall. It is massively buttressed, and standing at its foot and looking up at its stern brow, it seems as if about to plunge forward and fill up the vast chasm at its foot. The size of "Tu-toch-ah-nu-lah," or "El Capitan," as it is also called—the captain of the grand array of columns that uphold the northern wall of the valley—may be judged of by the fact that it occupied a quarter of an hour to ride at a brisk trot round its base. The mercantile marine of America, England, and France could be loaded with its debris, and the tonnage of the world could not carry El Capitan itself.

TU-TOCH-AH-NU-LAH—OR EL CAPITAN.

The trail above this point leads to the river, which is crossed by ford or ferry according to the stage of water. "The shades of night were falling fast" when we reached it, and we notified our wearied nags by a reminder of the spur that further particular observations would be deferred until another day. As darkness gathered its deeper folds within the depth profound along which we sought our way in some perplexity, the kindly stars shone forth with unwonted brilliancy, and the brow of the valley, darkly outlined against the azure sky, became radiant with a jewelled coronet. A fire-glow in the distance, and then the wavy line of burning grass, gave notice that Indians were in the valley clearing the ground, the more readily to obtain their winter supply of acorns and wild sweet potatoe root—"huckhau." This unwelcome discovery was soon after confirmed by the barking of dogs, that came echoing from the walls of this grand corridor in startling reverberations. Then we came to camp-fires, and blanketed warriors, squaws, and pappooses, standing and squatting around them; their swarthy features discolored with ashes, in token of mourning for the murdered member of their tribe. Silent and unmoved, they scarcely gave sign of noticing our intrusion. A hundred yards from their bark and brush lodges, stood the cabin of which we were to be the occupants during our stay in the valley—a rude clapboard frame of two rooms, liberally ventilated by defective carpentry—the hastily-abandoned cooking utensils, table, benches, and unbedded bedstead, of which, with a few other traps, we found to have been undisturbed by the untutored savages without; an immunity that perhaps would not have been conceded to them by *civilized* barbarians, under like circumstances of destitution and provocation. It was an omen of good neighborhood, which we sought to strengthen by smoking the calumet of peace, and bestowing a few favors in return for information of a suitable meadow in which to picket our horses, and for wood, and a fagot from their camp-fire wherewith to make our own. Coffee, slapjacks, and broiled ham passed rapidly through the process of cooking to that of digestion, which did not wait long on the mountain appetite, coming of our rough ride of thirty miles from Black's—our stopping-place the night before—to the foot of the valley, and six miles beyond to the cabin. And then, wrapped in our blankets, we laid down to sleep;

and then, to dream; and such dreams! Of cañons, and cataracts, and copper-skins! But this is to be a narrative of *what I saw*, not what I fancied.

We rose with the dawn; that is, with the dawn that came down into the deep valley, while the first rays of the rising sun were tipping with radiance the spires and pinnacles around, which seemed to be lifted into mid-heaven to catch the first coming of the glorious emanation. A little to the west of north "Eleacha" raised its three cones, called "The Three Brothers," three thousand four hundred and thirty-seven feet, to receive their golden crowns. While to the south, immediately behind our cabin,

ELEACHA—OR THE THREE BROTHERS.

"El Sentinel," a symmetrical needle of granite standing like a lone sentry on a battlement three thousand two hundred and seventy feet high, keeping his watch and ward of unknown ages, welcomed the warm glow of morning that chased the clouds of mist, which rolled upward to his brow from the matchless waterfall of the "Yo-Semite," on the opposite side of the val-

EL SENTINEL.

ley. Just east of that waterfall another spire, three thousand two hundred feet high, was also burnished by the first rays of the still unseen sun.

Despatching our morning meal, cooked by a camp-fire of grateful warmth to us in the cool atmosphere of this mountain region, and saddling up for our day's work, we started for the waterfall in view, the point of interest next in the order of the ascending series. The valley was crossed from the south to the north side by fording the stream meandering through it. In autumn this may be done in several places, but not when it is swollen by winter rains or the spring thaw. To approach near enough to realize the great height from which the water leaps, we were compelled to dismount and clamber for some distance over huge rocks that had from time to time fallen from the cliffs above.

The Yo-Semite waterfall and the valley are so called from the tribe of Indians formerly occupying this district of country. The name is said by some to mean *Great Water*. It has been attempted recently by fastidious etymologists to show that *Yo-Hamite* was the name of the tribe, who alone for a time are supposed to have known, and to have held the key of entrance to the valley. But the designation Yo-Semite given by the first white explorers who visited it, appears to be too firmly fixed on the public mind to be unsettled. Nor, so far as I can ascertain, are there any sufficient reasons why it should be changed, while consequent confusion and uncertainty should forbid the attempt. On the score of euphony nothing would be gained by the change.

The stream which forms this waterfall heads in the Sierra Nevada, nearly twenty-five miles off; and although in the dry season it dwindles to a brooklet, forming in truth but an insignificant cascade in volume, yet when in full flow in winter and spring, and even in June, as I am assured by one of my companions who has several times crossed it, it is fordable with difficulty, and pitches a torrent over the precipice, forming an unrivalled cataract. It is not by a single bound that the flashing sheet of foam reaches the valley that clothed in beauty welcomes the sparkling tribute. First plunging perpendicularly fourteen hundred and ninety-seven feet, it then rushes madly through a cañon having an angle of fifty degrees, and a total perpendicular of four hundred and sixty-two feet more; and as if impatient of partial restraint, it leaps again at another bound of five hundred and eighteen feet into a rock-walled basin, whence floats on the undulating air the wild music of its rejoicing to a whispering gallery in the vaulted cliff, which echoes it with startling distinctness.

There is some diversity of statement about the height of this

YO-SEMITE FALL.

and other objects of interest in this valley. The measurements here given are taken from the record kept at the valley. Mr. Long, one of my companions on this excursion, who was formerly engaged in surveying this and neighboring counties, considers them correct. The whole height of the Yo-Semite waterfall thus given, is two thousand four hundred and seventy-seven feet. But it should be said that Mr. Hutchings, in his published "Scenes in California," states the height to be two thousand five hundred and forty-eight feet. Either measurement makes it the highest waterfall known. The cascade of *Orco*, in the Alps, having the greatest fall of which we have any record, has a less height by seventy-seven feet than the least measurement given of the Yo-Semite, while that of *Evanson*, also in the Alps, is only twelve hundred feet high; the *Falls of Tequendama*, on the River Funza, near the plain of Santa Fe de Bogota, but five hundred and seventy-four; and that first discovered by Gonzalo Pizarro in his famous expedition to Quito, on the *River Napo*, a tributary of the Amazon, rising near the volcano Cotopaxi, in Ecuador, and heretofore considered the highest in the western hemisphere, but twelve hundred feet high. In regard to the last-mentioned estimated height of the *Falls of Napo*, it may be added that Mr. Prescott, in a note to his "History of the Conquest of Peru," says in reference to it, that he "finds nothing to confirm or to confute the account of this stupendous cataract in later travellers, not very numerous in these wild regions. The alleged height of the falls, twice that of the great cataract of the Tequendama in the Bogota, as measured by Humboldt, usually esteemed the highest in America, is not so great as that of some of the cascades thrown over the precipices in Switzerland. Yet the estimates of the Spaniards, who, in the gloomy state of their feelings, were doubtless keenly alive to impressions of the sublime and the terrible, cannot safely be relied on."

Until the yet untrodden solitudes of the Himalayas shall reveal a loftier claim to distinction, the Yo-Semite waterfall may at least be recognized as entitled to the palm of altitude, however inferior to Niagara in might and majesty. And yet there is a sense of the vast and infinite, as well as of the transcendently beautiful, realized by the mind when gazing on the long line of flashing foam that seems to shoot from the vaulted firmament, and sparkles with countless gems; and which touches the valley's skirt only to mount in clouds of silvery spray, that falls again in misty baptism upon the emerald scene below.

Passing up the valley, its granite wall, having a gray color in some places, especially on the south side, is nearly white in others. This is more marked on the north side, which is exposed to the direct rays of the sun. Everywhere it is veined with water-marks by melting snow rills holding discoloring substances in solution, so that, in places, it may be compared to the marbled facing of a vast uncovered corridor. Three miles east of our cabin, and nine miles from where we entered the valley, or great cañon, as it deserves to be considered, it forks; or perhaps it would be more correct to say, that at this point it appears to be formed of two cañons of less size, which, running in different directions, converge here. One of these comes from the northeast, the other from the southeast by east; but the latter, after having a short distance up received another cañon coming from the south, which is thus designated, changes its own direction and assumes that of the main cañon or valley, running from the east by north, being in general grandeur of features, extent, and interest, as well as in direction, the representative and continuation of the main cañon.

Just before reaching the entrance of the northeast cañon, in passing up the valley, the north wall is seen spanned by a majestic arch, of perhaps fifteen hundred feet radius; and beyond, at the exact point of divergence of the gorge, an immense semicircular pilaster of granite nearly three thousand feet high, stands like a mighty pillar to support, with the arch near by, the peerless North Dome, towering above in symmetrical grace and grandeur to the height of three thousand seven hundred and twenty-nine feet. The proudest dome of religious power, that of St. Peter's, would fail to touch with its topmost cross lifted to four hundred and thirty feet, even the vaulted pediment on which that of the Yo-Semite stands in everlasting majesty:

"Simple, erect, severe, unchanged, sublime—
Shrine of the Indian—temple of the gods
To whom he bowed—spared and blest by time;

> Looking tranquillity, while falls or nods
> Arch, empire, each thing round thee, and man plods
> His way through thorns to ashes—glorious dome!
> Shalt thou not last? Time's scythes and tyrant's rods
> Shall shiver on thee—sanctuary and home
> Of nature's sanctity—purer than that of Rome!"

The northeast cañon is five or six miles long, and has an average width of about half a mile; it is through this cañon that the shortest and best trail from Mariposa to the Mono Lake region lies. A small stream, rising twelve or fifteen miles toward

NORTH DOME AND SEMI-DOME OF TISSAACK.

the Sierra, comes down the gorge, and is the north branch of the middle fork of the Merced River, which flows through the main valley. This north branch forms a picturesque little "Mirror Lake," a short distance before reaching the mouth of the northeast cañon. It is near this miniature lake that the best view can be had of the "Semi-Dome of Tissaack," which faces on the southeast the entrance of this cañon, and looks as if a mountain of granite, higher than Monte Diablo the lone monarch of Contra Costa, lifting its head of imperishable rock four thousand nine hundred and sixty-seven feet, even into the clouds, had been riven from summit to base, and one-half removed, leaving the other standing, clear, cold, stately, stupen-

MIRROR LAKE.

dous; the most wonderful of all monuments of the massive masonry of creation. When you behold the clouds flitting across its changeless face, far below its bold and barren brow, you realize its loftiness; but its own voice of power, that calls back in tones of thunder the peals of the tempest, and repeats the prolonged reverberations of answering peaks, alone can tell the vastness of its strange sublimity. There shall it stand and gaze while time may last, into

The Mirror Lake, where stars and mountains view
The stillness of their grandeur, and the hue
Imperishably pure beyond all things below,
Traced in the crystal wave of cold Nevada's snow.

When about to pass from the head of the great valley or cañon into its other branch, the southeast cañon, one cannot fail to have his attention arrested by the immense bluff forming the south wall; rising to the great altitude of four thousand four hundred and eighty-four feet, supported by an unbroken, smooth, and in many places polished abutment, itself having a height of two thousand five hundred feet, an angle of elevation of at least seventy degrees, and an extent in the direction of the valley of a mile. Taken in connection with the North Dome and the Semi-Dome of Tissaack, these three objects, arranged round the head of the great valley, form perhaps, as a distinct class, the most striking features of this wonderful panorama of nature.

On entering the southeast cañon, a continuation is found of the level meadow spread across the main valley, presenting almost a park-like appearance in places, from the clusters of trees, especially along the banks of the middle fork of the Merced River which flows down this cañon. Horses must here be tethered; and fortunate will he find himself who has been well-trained to the rough pedestrianism of further exploration. The Merced, which we have already seen receives a little tributary from the northeast cañon called the North Branch, is joined also in the southeast cañon, a mile from its entrance, by a South Branch, which comes to it from that direction down a narrow, rocky, and almost impassable gorge, along which it rushes in wild tumult, after having plunged by an unbroken fall, according to the valley record, of eleven hundred feet from the vertical cliff of the unscaled terminus of the chasm. This third waterfall of the series, enumerated from the foot of the valley, is called the "South Fall"—by some the Indian name "*Tooluluwack*" is retained.

Near to the confluence of the South Branch with the Merced River, the southeast cañon changes its course and runs east by north, the direction of the main valley, of which it is regarded as the continuation. It is but little over a half-mile wide at this point, walled in by mountain cliffs as elsewhere, and it diminishes rapidly in width to the Vernal waterfall a mile further. The trail is steep, one thousand feet of elevation to the mile of distance, paved with boulders and fenced with fallen rocks, many

TOOLULUWACH, OR SOUTH FORK FALL.

of them exceeding in weight the twenty-five thousand tonnage of the Great Eastern; some too, burdened with the names of would-be immortals—dolts still more leaden.

Forest shaded, wild and varied,
  The beauties are of this defile;
And flowers there perfume the air
  That never felt the sun's warm smile:

while the swift river speeds onward, flashing and foaming over its granite bed, a continuous rapid, seeking with eager haste to join the sparkling streams that fling their crystal tribute into the vale below. The trail finally terminates at a narrow ledge running for a short distance along the face of the south wall of the cañon, and at a considerable height above the channel of the river; this leads to the foot of a perpendicular precipice over which the "Vernal Fall" pitches its fleecy jets six hundred feet into a pellucid basin, clothed in befitting rainbows. The showers of spray, falling perpetually upon the scanty soil around, nurtures an endless verdure that has given the name to this beautiful waterfall—

"That mounts in spray the skies, and thence again
Returns in an unceasing shower, which round,
With its unemptied cloud of gentle rain,
Is an eternal April to the ground,
Making it all one emerald—how profound
The gulf! and how the giant element
From rock to rock leaps with delirious bound,
Crushing the cliffs, which, downward worn and rent
With his fierce footsteps, yield in chasms a fearful vent!"

VERNAL FALL.

Here would the footsteps of the explorer be arrested, but that ladders have been erected which, with an intermediate platform of the cliff, afford the means of scaling it, and looking in safety from behind a granite parapet down on the shadowy scene of the frightful abyss stretching in dim perspective beyond.

NEVADA FALL.

It must not be supposed that in surmounting this precipice the upper level has been attained. On the contrary a new scene is unfolded to the view, a secret chamber where worshippers at the inner shrine alone intrude; whose everlasting walls, crowned with beetling battlements, for unknown ages were unscaled save by the wild symphony of the crashing cataract and tumultuous rapids, which roll their notes of revelry over peak and pinnacle to cheer the coming of Nevada's flood.

This upper gallery of the cañon is wider than that part through which it must be reached. At its east end, less than a mile from the Vernal Fall, is situated the "Nevada Fall," formed by the middle fork of the Merced River, rising in Lake Tchnayia in the Snowy Sierra, and casting its first tribute into the Valley of Yo-Semite at this portal, over which it shoots, rapid as the light, a sheet of foam, beating the air with dewy wing ere falling on its granite bed. As if to commemorate the grandeur of surrounding nature, a pyramid of two thousand feet stands near the waterfall, by the side of which the largest of Egypt would sink into insignificance. The laughing stream, broken into dimples by the sportive breath of its own zephyrs, hastens from its rocky basin, dashing over the massive fragments of mountain debris, and then darts through an exquisitely formed natural granite aqueduct, to spread itself like a floating apron of silver tissue over an inclined plane as if of polished marble, down which it glides into the placid bosom of a miniature lake; where, so tranquil is its face, it seems to sleep ere taking its "Vernal" leap and resuming its race in the cañon below.

Oh! thou Nevada! in thy coolest wave,
Of the most limpid crystal that was e'er
The haunt of Indian nymph, to gaze and lave
With loved and loving Nature—thou dost rear
Thy grassy banks, whereon the ancient seer
Sought the Great Spirit in the peaceful water—
Gentle, serene of aspect, and most clear.
May e'er thy river, unprofaned by slaughter,
Be mirrored bath for Freedom's favored daughter!

The mysterious influence of this spot held us with charmed spell, until the slanting beams of the setting sun touched but the summit of the great Pyramid with a departing glory, and warned us to descend to the lower cañon before its fast coming twilight should deepen into night.

As we sought our cabin in the bosom of the valley, the young moon arose to add her testimony to the unrivalled grandeur of Yo-Semite; crowning its domes with subdued radiance, tracing a silver cornice on its brow, and pouring a liquid light into its depths to woo the spirit to a fitting worship.

# CHAPTER XXX.

MARIPOSA MAMMOTH TREES—TOWN OF MARIPOSA—BEAR VALLEY—ADJACENT QUARTZ GOLD MINING—MERCED RIVER, ITS GOLD DEPOSITS—SAN JOAQUIN AND SACRAMENTO RIVERS AND THEIR TRIBUTARIES DRAIN THE AURIFEROUS REGION—GREAT INTERIOR BASIN OF CALIFORNIA.

TAKING leave of our dusky neighbors, who did not seek, yet accepted with becoming spirit our surplus provisions, slowly and sadly we passed down the valley—for here are the oracles of a higher wisdom than man's—and at early dawn sought the Mariposa trail, by which we proposed to return circuitously to Coulterville, visiting the most remarkable of the groves of California Big Trees on the route. At the perpendicular height of fifteen hundred feet in ascending the steep acclivity, a fine view was afforded of the tout ensemble of Yo-Semite, and among these the *South Dome*, some distance behind El Sentinel, appropriately so called because of its relative position to the others, and not visible at all from within the main valley. About four miles up the trail, which skirts for a short distance the vast cañon, the last and perhaps the most comprehensive view was obtained of this "temple not made with hands"—whose transcendent architecture of everlasting walls and columns, spires and minarets, towers and domes,

> "Came of the fiat that gave instant birth
> To the fair sun and his attendant earth"—

and among whose imperishable arches swell the mingling symphonies of joyous floods, a ceaseless anthem at the shrine of Him who "hath made His wonderful works to be remembered."

About a mile beyond the point at which was taken the last, long, lingering look of this most marvellous scene, the trail crosses the Pohono Creek, rushing fleetly on to weave with mysterious art, in airy loom, the gauzy fabric of the "Bridal Veil." The well-beaten trail was across the ridge dividing the South from the Middle Fork of the Merced River, and proceeded in a southwestwardly direction up, down, and around secondary hills, covered with forests of magnificent timber that would, if within water conveyance of the sea, become a source of wealth to this State but little less valuable than its mines of gold. At the commencement of the route the Sierra Nevada was often seen lifting its bleak and barren peak on high, patched even through summer heats with sheltered snow drifts. Many grassy openings, too, were seen in the wood-land; one of these known as the *Big Meadow*, five miles from Pohono Creek, resembling a glade of the great Alleghany Mountain—where man and horse may well refresh themselves for their further journey; that is, if the former has been as provident for himself as nature has been for the latter. At ten miles from the Big Meadow the descent from the general upper level of the "divide" commences, and two miles more must be passed of steep declivity before the South Fork of the Merced, a bold, clear mountain river, is reached, which is crossed by a strong corduroy bridge. The left hand trail, within a quarter of a mile, leads to "Clark's Camp;" this was the first habitation seen by us since starting from the Yo-Semite—distance, including five miles within the valley, twenty-seven miles. The "Camp" consisted of one log cabin of primitive size, structure, and uses; one apartment being alike kitchen, bed-room, and parlor, for the hermit occupant—a man wedded to sincerity and solitude; of that commingled sense and sensibility which spurn the social unrighteousness they will not imitate, and often shun, by seeking the companionship of pure and undissembling nature. The frequent intrusions of wayworn travellers of the Mariposa trail on Mr. Clark, induced him to put up a tent for their use as a refectory, and another for a dormitory in common for sleepers who may not prefer to sit on a big log before the camp-fire all night, and perform the pantomime of "nid, nid, noddin." He received us with the easy politeness and unaffected welcome characteristic of nature's noblemen; and doing the duties as well as the honors of the hermitage, we were soon enabled to appreciate the facility with which an earnest purpose can accommodate itself to the prompting of hospitality, and the obligations it imposes. Weariness and watching, with which our journey to and fro and our three days of valley wandering had made us familiar, were both appetizer and anodyne, and made the homely fare sweet, and a rude cot refreshing. The cock's clarion summons, of unwonted shrillness in this clear and tranquil air, called us forth to break the ice for our morning wash; and then to luxuriate in the glow of a camp-fire that knew no restriction of fuel where fallen forest trees were cumberers of the ground.

Breakfast finished, we saddled up for the "Mariposa Mammoth Trees," our guide in the lead disdaining dependence on a horse, and with his unerring rifle in hand to replenish his larder with a bear, should one cross his path; his head uncovered by hat, though well lined with knowledge; and his heart responsive to generous emotions, and humane impulses, though beating under a check shirt solely. First, over a wild meadow, and then in a southeastwardly direction up a gradual ascent of probably twenty-five hundred feet above the bed of the South Fork of the Merced, we rode five miles, when a slight descent brought us suddenly upon the remains of a mastodon of the vegetable kingdom. It lay, as if to challenge amazement, at the threshold of the forest whose wonderful precincts we were about to enter—measuring seventy-five feet in circumference at its butt, and two hundred and fifty-nine feet in length to an end of its trunk, marked by the ravages of fire. There have been three groves of these Mammoth Trees discovered and explored in California. One, of a hundred and three trees, within an area of fifty acres in Calaveras County, discovered in 1852: a second, that I am now describing, discovered by Mr. Galen Clark our host and an exploring companion, and then situated in Mariposa County—hence its name—but now embraced within the limits of the new County of Frezno, and containing six hundred and thirty trees in its two subdivisions, covering a section of land of six hundred and forty acres: and a third grove, also in Frezno County, about eight miles south of the last named, discovered also by Mr. Clark, called the Frezno Grove, and numbering about five hundred trees. Another considerable grove is said to have been found about twelve miles east of the Frezno Grove, on the head waters of the San Joaquin River.

While some botanists consider the Mammoth Tree as forming a new genus, others regard it as belonging to the family of Taxodiums, and have designated it "Washingtonia gigantea." The wood of the Big Trees is of a light reddish color, not dense, and so devoid of sap moisture as to appear seasoned as they stand. The bark is from a foot to a foot and a half in thickness, and nearly as light and dry as cork. The nearest approach to them in general appearance, but not in size, is presented by the Arbor Vitæ cedar, of which numerous fine specimens are found in the vicinity; yet the bark of the cedar although of the same cinnamon color, is more deeply furrowed longitudinally, while its limbs are more numerous and branch from the trunk lower down, and the Big Tree foliage resembles more closely that of the pine. The author of an "Overland Journey to California," says he "believes these trees now bear no seed-cone, or nut, whatever they may have done in Scipio's or Alexander's time, and there is no known means of propagating their kind." And in an explanatory note, adds: "I saw no cones on any of the giants, though they were season." Mr. Clark, one of the discoverers, and the guide and guardian of the Mariposa Grove, expressed his surprise at this statement, pointed out to us numerous seed-cones on several of its patriarchs; and in further correction, while it showed his accuracy of aim, raised his rifle and brought one of them to the ground from the brow of the "Grizzled Giant." Mr. Clark has a standing order from the dealers in seed in San Francisco for all the cones he can furnish, to supply the great demand on foreign account for public and private parks. While America is negligent of all means to preserve from destruction by fire this great connecting link of the ancient world with the present, Europe is studious of efforts to perpetuate the grandeur of its creation, in her own soil. The author above referred to says also that he "did not perceive a single young tree coming forward to take the place of the decaying patriarchs." This was not surprising, if his examination of the grove was as hurried and imperfect as that of the Yo-Semite. There are all growths, from the *birchen rod* in

SEED-CONE AND FOLIAGE OF THE MAMMOTH TREE.

size to the stalwart tree; and the former might be appropriately applied to the shoulders of one, who, by his own acknowledgment, arrived at the Yo-Semite at one o'clock A. M. and left it at two P. M. of the same day, thirteen hours only being devoted to sleeping, breakfasting, dining, and—Oh! marvellous man!—to exploring the Yo-Semite! Mr. Clark expressed the opinion that these trees once had extensive existence in the Nevada Range of Mountains, and that they had been nearly all destroyed by earthquakes and by the fires of olden tribes of Indians. Will not California devise some means of preserving the remaining bequest, of which she has become the residuary legatee?

There are other kinds of trees scattered about—firs, pines, and cedars, beautiful specimens of their species, but pigmies by the side of the giants of which we have been speaking; the undergrowth in fact of these forest mammoths. The size of the remains of the "Prostrate Monarch" at the entrance of the grove has been referred to. The following are my own measurements of a few others, among the most conspicuous met with in our ramble. That known as the "Grizzled Giant" measured, at three feet above the ground, ninety feet in circumference. The "Faithful Couple," united below and separated above, have a circumference near the earth of ninety-eight feet. Another tree near by, a short distance above the ground gave a circumference of ninety-one feet. The "Riding School," still standing, although much burnt inside as well as outside, has a *diameter* within, of thirty-three feet in one direction, and thirty-four feet in the opposite. Our three horsemen rode through its charred doorway and trotted around its interior. The "Great Western Smoke Stack," burnt down to a height of fifty feet, and charred within and without, measured eighty-four feet in circumference. The "Grizzly's Den"—known as the former haunt of a bear—a partially burnt trunk broken into two pieces by falling, formed the section of a tunnel of twenty-five feet length, at eighty feet from the stump, through which we rode with head-room to spare. Another fallen trunk, partially burnt at one hundred feet from the roots, leaving an arch above like the span of a bridge, afforded sufficient height for a horseman to ride under without being able to touch it with the tip of his finger, though standing in his stirrups. A tree of beautiful proportions which had escaped the scathing flames, measured, a yard from the ground, ninety-seven feet in circumference. The prostrate remains of the "Forest Mastodon," nearly destroyed by fire, were examined with great care and interest. Its diameter at the butt by accurate measurement is thirty-three feet, divested of sap-wood and bark. Add two feet on each side for these—a minimum allowance for a tree of this size—gives a diameter of thirty-seven feet; which multiplied by three and its proper decimal, shows the circumference of this monster tree, fairly above the swell of its roots at the surface of the earth, to have been *one hundred and sixteen feet and ninety-seven one hundreths*. Nearly a hundred feet of the trunk still remains; which, with the trench supposed to have been formerly occupied by that part which has been destroyed, and a presumptive estimate of its branching portion, justify the conclusion that, when it stood the monarch of this forest, its height probably exceeded four hundred feet. It was observed that these lingering monuments of past ages occupy a basin of the ridge we ascended to reach them, where they have been sheltered from fierce winds; which, in consequence of their great height and weight they could not have so long withstood, on hill-side and summit. Numerous family groups of two and three trees, doubtless having sprung from the same seed-cone, are found, which contribute to diversify this forest scenery.

We returned to the camp shortly after nightfall; and the next morning parting from our host with a respect which strengthened with our stay, we struck a nearly due west course for the town of Mariposa, twenty-five miles distant, crossing first the South Fork Ridge, in descending which glimpses were caught of the undulating outline of the Coast Mountains from sixty to seventy miles distant; while the magnificent growth of pines, cedars, and balsam firs, long our finger-posts of altitude, gradually disappeared, and were followed nearly altogether by oaks in the Chowchilla Valley. The author of an "Overland Journey" was astray of geographical accuracy when he stated that from this point his "range of vision extended *south* to the Tulé lake, or immense morass *in which the San Joaquin has its source*." Whatever former guess-work may have represented, it was established at the time of his writing, by United States "Explorations and Surveys for a railroad route from the Mississippi River to the Pacific Ocean," published by Congress, that the San Joaquin River rises *in the Sierra Nevada*, *east* of the point indicated, *not south in the Lake Tulare;* nor does it at any part of its course approach nearer than probably fifty miles of the lake. My engineer fellow traveller informed me that a late State survey, made to ascertain if the lake and its morass could be drained by a canal into the San Joaquin, resulted in the discovery that the reverse would occur if the canal were dug, the lake occupying a lower level than the river, as far as the confluence of the Merced River with the latter. King's River, which rises but a few miles from the source of the San Joaquin in the Sierra Nevada, actually flows southwestwardly into the lake.

In crossing the dividing ridge west of Chowchilla Creek, we observed, as in some other parts of California where oaks and pines are found in the same localities, the singular results of the industry and providence of *El Carpintero*—so called by the Spanish settlers—the carpenter of the feathered family: the trunks of pine trees having their soft bark bored over the whole surface except near the ground, as if with brace and bit, by this California wood-pecker, which is seen in autumn with its red, white, and black plumage, gleaming in the sunshine, the busiest of the busy, foraging about and depositing in every hole an acorn. It has been denied by some that this *cache-ing* is to be regarded as an instinctive storage of food for future use. But such objectors attempt no explanation of this invariable habit of that bird; while the argument that the acorns often remain unconsumed is without force, for if the crop has been very abundant, and the ground uncovered by snow, there is no need of the provision stored away. But even in that case, the worms formed in the acorns in the spring, are used as food especially for the young bird. The Mariposa hermit, a close observer of nature, is my authority for this statement.

Mariposa Creek succeeded the "divide" on the line of our route, along which were seen unsightly heaps of boulders and gravel, scarred hill-sides, and trenches, destructive of the beautiful face of nature, while they mark the untiring search for gold wherever water could be made tributary to its disengagement from earth and stone. How widespread the surface from which the soil is being removed, and where quartz is being pulverized in countless tons, to pollute the crystal streams, fill up the channels of rivers, and form flats and bars in the straits and bays of this State! A mile and a half further brought us to the town of Mariposa—distance from Clark's Camp twenty-five miles—with a population of four hundred persons, chiefly engaged in mining and furnishing supplies to miners.

We found a good hotel at Mariposa, at which we rested for the night. Next morning we started for Coulterville, twelve miles and a half westwardly to Bear Valley, and thence the same distance in a generally northwest direction to our destination. Nothing worthy of mention was seen on the now well-travelled road to the village of Bear Valley. A short distance beyond it we began the long and steep descent to the Merced River, passing through the Mariposa gold quartz mining property, the title to which, bought of a Mexican by Gen. Fremont, *as a cattle ranche on the fine bottom lands*, the latter, prompted by "prudential considerations," is said to have "engineered" so as to embrace a gold quartz vein, *subsequently discovered in the adjacent hills.* A very precipitous and dangerous looking railroad track of several miles, conveys the rock from its quarries to mills for crushing and the other necessary processes of separation of the metal. There are seven mills on the estate, two run by water and five by steam-power, making a total of one hundred and sixty-eight stampers. The gold product of this estate has been represented to be large, though there are many persons in California who believe that to promote political aspirations it has been greatly overstated, while the almost universal opinion is, that whatever may be the product, it all passes into the hands of mortgagees, the property being so heavily encumbered by debt as to be profitless to the nominal proprietor, who thus is seen in more ways than one to have "held a barren sceptre in his gripe." The estate was designated by the old Spanish settlers, and is still known as *Las Mariposas*—the Butterflies. It has certainly proved a butterfly to Gen. Fremont, with gilded wings, too, which bear it off to beautify the gardens of other persons.

An occasional opportunity has been afforded on this road to see the primitive Spanish-American method of quartz crushing by the *rastra*, which consists of a circular trough paved with flat stones, in the centre of which is an upright revolving shaft, through which a horizontal pole passes, a short end being chained to a heavy granite block within the trough, while the longer end serves as a lever by which a mule on the outside drags the heavy stone around the circular trough, and reduces to powder the gold-bearing quartz, broken as for the stamping mill and thrown within. Quicksilver thrown in amalgamates the gold particles, while the pasty pulverized quartz flows off with the water turned in for the purpose. The more expeditious iron stamping-mill has nearly entirely superseded *el rastra.*

Descending the south bank of Merced River from the Mariposa mills, the method of turning the course of large rivers to explore the bottom for gold was seen. Dams are built, the river of course not being in freshet, and the entire stream is thus diverted into canals along the river bank, or into strong flumes built above the middle of the bed of the stream. Undershot waterwheels, placed over these, are turned by the flow of the artificial currents, and by means of horizontal shafts work pumps to keep the river-bed free of water. Thus every pocket and crevice may be searched for the golden deposits washed down from the hills, or worn from their bases, and from the outcropping quartz rock which sometimes traverses the river-bed. Sluices and amalgamation, as already described, finish the work.

Four miles down the Merced was crossed by a ferry-boat. Thence by the north bank of the river a great part of the way, the road with slight improvement might be travelled in a buggy to Coulterville, where we arrived at 5 P. M., and left at one next morning by stage for Stockton, which we reached at 3 P. M., with an hour to spare before the starting of the steamboat for San Francisco. We descended the San Joaquin, which, with the other principal river of California, the Sacramento, and their numerous eastern tributaries, drain the auriferous region, and run through the great interior basin of the State, which has a length of three hundred and fifty miles, and a breadth varying from fifty to seventy; and finally after flowing, the San Joaquin north, the Sacramento south, they meet midway, to mingle their ever muddy streams, and make their way westward through a gap of the Contra Costa and Mount Diablo Coast Mountains, and then between them and the San Francisco or Coast Range proper by the Bays of San Pablo and San Francisco, and finally by the Golden Gate to the Ocean.

San Francisco was reached early next morning, the trip to the Yo-Semite and the Mariposa Big Trees being not hurriedly made in thirteen days.

# CHAPTER XXXI.

## VOYAGE TO THE HAWAIIAN ISLANDS

REGULAR Liners profess to run between San Francisco and Honolulu; but the fulfilment does not always correspond with the profession, hence passengers often avail of chance traders for that voyage to avoid detention, and the extortion of monopolists. The clipper ship "Rapid" sailing under the Danish flag, was up for Hong Kong, via the *Hawaiian Islands;* and being bound myself

> "From the orient to the drooping west
> Making the wind my post horse, to unfold
> The acts commenced,"

I took passage on board of her for Honolulu, the capital of the islands. The Hawaiian Kingdom, a constitutional monarchy, and acknowledged independent government, conducts its functions and maintains its international relations, under that name, derived from its great island of Hawaii, which forms two-thirds of its territory; and thus designating the group—Hawaiian Islands—it is, to say the least of it, an impertinence in foreigners to insist on calling them Sandwich Islands, a name having no fitness beyond that too common among Anglo-Saxons, coming of self conceit, national vanity, or the motive of personal interest prompting a servile flattery. Because Captain Cook, the discoverer, desired to manifest his gratitude to his patron, the Earl of Sandwich, is no sufficient reason to the rest of mankind for the unwarrantable presumption. And as to the incorrect orthography *Owhyhee* for Hawaii, if pardoned in view of misapprehension at the time of the discovery, it certainly should not be perpetuated in any of the geographical publications of the present day.

A steam-tug would have carried our ship to sea in less than an hour, but between baffling winds and flood tides she did not get outside of the "heads" without such assistance for more than a day after we went aboard. Parsimony in this matter is sometimes bad policy, especially when the chances are considered of being beached in beating through "The Gate" under a compulsory pilot law, whose often incompetent agents are the offspring of party machinery, and who a week ago succeeded in *piloting three vessels ashore.*

Our good ship once fairly out, bore away southwest by south, and sprung upon her long course of from two thousand, to two thousand two hundred miles to Honolulu, according to her steerage, under a stiff west by north breeze at a speed of nine knots, which was increased next day to ten knots. Most of the passengers paid the usual tribute to Neptune, and manifested their sympathy with his reckless and upheaving ocean by correspondent deeds. Even the Chinamen, of whom there were many on board, who had before crossed the Pacific in quest of golden favors, were, after being duly purified of sins against their national dietetic usages, compelled to seek in the ship's hold the forlorn hope of relief afforded by darkness and a bunk. A few days of favoring wind wafted us to the "horse latitudes" of seamen, about 30° north, more appropriately called by Maury, the "Belt of Calms of Cancer." And here we were destined to realize the truth of that distinguished savant's theory of atmospheric circulation as applied to this tropical region; and it was gratifying while reflecting on the illustration before us, to read in the last number of Blackwood's Magazine, which formed a part of our mental sea-stores, the following well-deserved compliment. Contrasting Captain Maury's *Sailing Directions* with the British *Manual for Naval Officers*, the reviewer says: "How different it is in the American work before us! Here is a subject, in the abstract hopelessly dry, treated in a manner that, from the opening of the book to its close, never tires; and we shut it with a determination to know more of the many interesting features of the ocean. The American hydrographer, in nervously eloquent language, has summed up the evidence of man upon the laws governing the great watery element called ocean, and of the atmosphere which envelopes it, and well describes the close affinity between the two. He dwells upon the temperature of each, and its life and death creating consequences—of the winds which blow over the surface of the waters, and of the climates through which they together roll. Not only does he treat of the animate and inanimate products of the sea, and of the currents which circulate through its waters, and impart life and action to its uttermost depths; but to Captain Maury we are indebted for much information—indeed for all that mankind possesses—of the crust of the earth beneath the blue waters of the Atlantic and Pacific Oceans. Hopelessly scientific would all these subjects be in the hands of most men; yet upon each and all of them Captain Maury enlists our attention, or charms us with explanations and theories replete with originality and genius. His is, indeed, a nautical manual, a handbook of the sea, investing with fresh interest every wave that beats upon our shores; and it cannot fail to awaken in both sailors and landsmen a craving to know more intimately the secrets of that wonderful element. The good that Maury has done, in awakening the powers of observation of the officers of the royal and mercantile navies of England and America, is incalculable."

Such candid compliment is as honorable to the reviewer as to the reviewed. How superior to the jealousies and detractions of a narrow-minded national antagonism!

Truly did we, at this part of the voyage, verify the declaration of *the* preacher—"The wind goeth toward the south, and turneth about unto the North; it whirleth about continually, and the wind returneth again according to its circuits." For on entering this *mar tranquilla*, we found that the passage winds which had thus far swollen our welcoming sails, had either folded their wings in sleep, or like their feathered comrades, weary of following the patient vessel on her changeless course, or obedient to natural laws, had started on their upward and homeward stretch to cool themselves again in polar regions; leaving us to the careless sport of the ocean swell, whose "rise and fall" like that of railroad stocks, gave little promise of realization of hope to those most interested—the representatives of *bona fide* investment. We spent four days, including a Sunday, in a patient waiting for the desired activities of the morrow; faithfully observing that Sabbath according to the approved formulary of some self-complacent sanctimonious communities, whose sleep on that day, at home and in church, is the rule of practice, as well as the *least* committed offence against God; interrupted it may be by occasional reflections on a meditated speculation, or on a less venial scheme of mercantile fraud, or of political fraud or partisan atrocity, devised in moments of professed sanctity, to be matured and executed regardless of divine inculcations.

A breath of air scarcely recognized by the *dog-vane*, a barely discernible surface current, and passive swells moving in gentle undulations in the same direction, finally *hove* us over the southern edge of the *calm belt* in latitude 26° north, and the gleesome *trade wind* from the northeast came whistling through the rigging to cheer with its merry strain, and remind us that nature has her unvarying compensations. The flapping sails of the "Rapid," answering to the summons, swelled in graceful curve; while spars bending, and cordage tightening under the inspiring impulse, away she darted again; and many a thought was given as we were wafted by the steady trade wind—the mariner's constant and unfailing friend—over the blue bosom of this majestic ocean, to the incidents of discovery which have invested it with a strange interest, and even romance. And from thought of the adventures of Cook, La Perouse, Adams, and Vancouver, it was natural in a specially utilitarian age, and under the influence of contact with Californian energy and progress, to reflect on the rapidly-developing wants of this vast theatre of commerce, and on the results to flow to the nationalities on its borders, when they shall be brought by projected enterprises into free intercourse with each other. England and France bursting the chain which fetters Asiatic trade, while also engaged in opening another and shorter avenue of intercourse with the hundreds of millions peopling that great continent and its neighboring islands; while Russia and America, with the same object in view, seek to remove oriental prejudice and suspicion by a more persuasive appeal and policy; California too bringing to her shores the misguided victims of restriction, to realize the advantages of commercial interchange, and a new and extended field of industry.

How exalted must be the spiritual enjoyments of the early navigators who discovered the Pacific islands, if permitted to behold the part they are fast taking in the development of human intercourse! Depots of supply, dock-yards of repair, life-buoys of the shipwrecked, resting-places of the weary, finger-posts for the doubtful, and truly emerald spots of hope and promise to the mariner, causing his eye to beam with joy as they rise upon his sight, and moisten with sadness as they fade again from view. And none of them are more important in this pledge and reality of usefulness, than those of the Hawaiian group; standing as they do midway between Panama and China, and on the route, and one-third of the distance between the most enterprising and the richest portion—whether in regard to mineral or agricultural resources—of the Pacific front of America, and that opposite coast of Asia, the productions and treasures of which, fabulous as they are represented in oriental tales, may be surpassed by the results of an impulse imparted to industry by contact with European and American civilization and improvement, science, skill, and enterprise.

Our voyage is not wanting in variety. We are happy in having a polite and intelligent commander, Captain Möller, a Dane, and a Danish crew, quiet, sober, orderly, obedient, and active seamen. Besides the cabin passengers, there are more than a hundred Chinese on board; yet such is the attention to cleanliness, ventilation, and general good management, that we would be insensible of their being fellow-voyagers, but for their occasional presence on the forecastle, in quaint blue nankeen jacket and wide trowsers, queue long enough to tickle their heels, religiously preserved through all vicissitudes of fortune, and without which disgrace would attend their return to their native land; with conical hat, or skull-cap, and a demure demeanor, quite puritanical in its type. The study of their habits from the use of chopsticks in eating to the oblivious enjoyment of opium smoking, for which many of them, like our whiskey drinkers, will mortgage body and soul, served to vary the monotony of the voyage, which was also spiced by the varieties of a sea not always pacifically inclined, whatever its name may imply; for old Ocean, disposed to assert for a time its prerogative of capriciously administering penal inflictions, reminded me of the rough discipline of a pedagogue—may his committed cruelties, as well as his omitted duties, no longer rise in judgment against him!—who once *reined* and *ruled* in my native town. The words are to be taken literally, for he achieved a perfect success in *restraining* the young idea, by beating the pupil with a *ruler* he was thus familiar with the use of, in a manner that dwarfed any germ of knowledge that may have taken root in his aching brain. Our experience in latitude 23° N. was like a practical boxing between seas coming from two opposite points of the compass, alternately trying which could hit the "Rapid" the hardest blow, and produce the greatest consternation in state-room and cabin. Going directly before the wind, with no opposing force to steady the ship thus receiving lateral shocks, the largest latitude of rolling ensued, with a consequent vacation of berths, in disregard of the proprieties of toilet. As to the performances of the dinner-table, when the curtain rose on that "comedy of errors," the manner in which dishes danced, castors capered, plates polka'd, claret chassé'd, decanters dos-a-dos'd, and all, including the passengers, finally participated in a promiscuous ho-down, those only can judge of who have been actors in such a scene. Fortunately a day of such infliction was all we were at this time called on to endure, or despite the steward's precautions of table-racks and sand-bags, the "Rapid's" entire pantry would probably have served to exemplify the poet's "wreck of matter."

The propitious trade-wind bore us to the north of the island of Hawaii, not seen in the distance, against the highlands of which it "caromed," rebounding with diminished force on our port side. With less of headway we then skirted the islands of Maui and Molokai, and passing through the channel between the latter and Oahu, were caught up again by a spanking breeze and wafted along the breaker-bordered shore of that island, lofty hills rising in the background to bathe their brows in the vapors of the northeast trades. But a brief space elapsed ere passing Coco Point, when a pilot coming aboard off the little crescentic Bay of Waialae, he took the helm and doubled the bold headland of Diamond Point, an extinct volcanic crater abruptly terminating a range of hills running from the interior toward the sea. From this point, five or six miles from Honolulu, the shore line for nearly that distance was seen prettily bordered by the tropical cocoa and tutui trees; the ocean swells breaking over the coral reef, and rolling their white fringe up the yellow sands to kiss the feet of those waving banners of peace that cease not to welcome the weary mariners of all countries. A remarkable entrance through the reef to the harbor of the capital has been left by nature, a tortuous channel a mile long, from one hundred and twenty to two hundred and twenty yards wide, the least depth of water being twenty-two feet, opening into a port of perfect security, with room for two hundred vessels. The fact that an entering vessel would have to sail in the "wind's eye" coming down the Nuuanu Valley, and incur the risk of going on the reef, has made a steam-tug a necessity of navigation for safety. We threw it a hawser when it puffed its high-pressure salutation across the bow of the "Rapid," which, furling sails, surrendered herself to the blustering little craft, and passing from the deep blue of ocean to the green of soundings, and then through the milky-tinted waters of the submerged reef, bounded on each side by a more superficial coral bank, we anchored in the inner harbor on the thirteenth day of the voyage from San Francisco.

# CHAPTER XXXII.

HAWAIIAN ISLANDS—HONOLULU AND ITS ENVIRONS—HAWAIIAN CUSTOMS—THE KING—A VULGAR DIPLOMAT—HONOLULU SOCIETY—PUBLIC BUILDINGS—NUUANU VALLEY—THE PALI—WAIKIKI—LEAHI—WAIALAE—WAIALUPE—MANOA VALLEY—OAHU COLLEGE—MISTAKEN SYSTEM OF EDUCATION—PUAHI.

THE Hawaiian Islands are grouped in a somewhat crescentic form, with a convexity presenting to the northeast, and lie between the parallels of 18° 50′ and 22° 20′ north latitude, and west longitude 154° 53′ and 160° 15′. There are eleven of them, of which three are but barren rocks and uninhabited. The other eight, named from northwest to southeast, are Niihau, Kauai, Oahu, Molokai, Lanai, Maui, Kahoolawe, and Hawaii. The whole embrace an area of nearly sixty-one hundred square miles, of which Hawaii contains two-thirds, its superficial extent being four thousand square miles.

Although Hawaii is most distinguished for size, agricultural capacity, and physical grandeur, Oahu, from its more central position, and from the influence of general maritime interests and trade, has asserted political supremacy, and on it is the capital of the kingdom, *Honolulu*, a name implying, it is said, "on the back of, to leeward," because it is beyond the mountains, and protected by them from the northeast trade-winds.

No equally small part of the New World has been so minutely described as the Hawaiian Islands. The Pacific commerce has sought their welcoming harbors wherein to fold its weary wings, while whalers, worn with toil, have gladly escaped from polar storms, to rest and refit in their genial atmosphere. The mariner has ofttimes told his tale of wonder, and awakened in the homes of civilization a peculiar interest in the beings who people these fairy isles. The American missionary, too, has penetrated their every nook, and unwilling to hide his light under a bushel, has multiplied and magnified descriptions to superfluity. If to these sources of information the labor of the historian be added, for Hawaii has now a *recorded* past, and the official reports of scientific explorers, it may well be supposed that the proposal to write any thing new on this subject would be hopeless, especially if undertaken by one who but skims the surface before him, with an eye rarely withdrawn from an object of special duty. But the figures of the kaleidoscope please, although each turn of the toy, while it destroys one illusion, gives no trace of connection with another. Each presents its distinctive attraction, and comes of a separate creation. Thus it is with what is presented in the rapidly-changing scenes before me, novel, perhaps, and exciting, though disconnected and valueless; sketched, too, by a rude artist. Yet in some respects it may be the turning of the kaleidoscope at least for *my amusement*.

The Hawaiian Islands are indisputably of volcanic origin, and present accordingly the bold and diversified features of that character of creation. They seem to have been uplifted from the ocean successively from northwest to southeast, Kauai having been the first in the order of appearance. And this opinion is supported by the fact that that island, while it has but two visible craters at its southeastern part only, all the others, which doubtless formerly existed, being obliterated by age or concealed by forests, possesses also in proportion to its size a greater proportion of arable land, deeper soil, and more vegetation. Oahu, the next island to the east, presents more numerous and palpable proofs of volcanic action. Maui lifts its magnificent crater of Haleakala, worthy of being called by the natives "the house of the sun," more than ten thousand feet above the sea to attest its origin; and Hawaii, the last and greatest of the insular series, still exhibits in fearful activity the sublime agency to which its creation is due. It is probable that these islands are in truth the loftiest volcanic peaks of a sub-oceanic mountain range, stretching from Niihau and Kauai, in the extreme west, to Hawaii, in the southeast. Oahu, on which we first landed, is dignified by the residence of Hawaiian majesty; it is forty-six miles long and twenty-five miles broad. Here is the capital and chief commercial town, Honolulu, standing on the southern shore of a plain stretching nine or ten miles east and west, and varying from one to two miles wide, at the foot of a corresponding mountain range, which latter is cleft in twain by a deep gorge, continuous with the beautiful Nuuanu valley that debouches at the back of the town. The plain is overlooked to the east by Diamond Head, and to the north by Punch-bowl Hill, two now extinct craters, the eruptions of which doubtless in past ages formed them, as shown by the substrata of lava, ashes, and cinders, overspreading the deeper coral formations, mingled with sea sediment, bones of fishes, and marine shells. The accumulated mineral and vegetable decay of centuries has covered the plain and the valley, which opens upon it, with a rich soil, the cultivation of which forms a setting of flowers and verdure to the capital.

Honolulu presents features in strange contrast, while some are such mere shadings of diversity as to make it difficult to determine in what the difference consists. On landing, the traveller is surprised at the many signs of European civilization in men, manners, and pursuits, for the Caucasian is seen to have transplanted himself here with his social habits, and his mechanical, manufacturing, and mercantile enterprise. While gazing at the busy scene, in disdain of servile labor, stand the sorrowing descendants of the once haughty and happy islanders, listless spectators of doings in which they can only participate as slaves, subject to the will of those who with specious promises have lured them to corruption and decay, and whom they have learned to regard as the destroyers of their race. True, mongrelism is filling up the gap; and while it is approximating the extremes of physical characteristics, is also moulding the weaker nature into conformity with the customs of the stronger, or is crushing it out by that process of extinction which comes of vices inculcated in greater proportion than virtues. Many houses of modern style, commodious and convenient, are seen, built of dressed lumber, or of coral rock quarried from the ocean-bed around the island, where those busy little

HONOLULU.

architects, the reef-building polyps, have been through long centuries rearing those wonderful sea-walls. But the native hut, with its thick wall and roof of thatched grass, admirably adapted to exclude the tropical heat of day, and the cool air of night, is still seen to assert its claim of priority, while the rival tastes of Old and of New England are struggling for predominance, both, however, engrafting on their styles the essential verandah of the tropics. A regard for the beautiful of nature is observed, too, many of the residences being embowered in shrubbery and flowers, and some of the gardens are enriched by exotics of wonderful beauty and great variety, preëminent among which for variety and beauty are the extensive parterres of an Irish lawyer and a German physician,

> "Whose sandal groves and bowers of spice
> Might be a Peri's Paradise."

The population of Honolulu and its suburbs, as shown by a late census, is fourteen thousand, including two thousand seven hundred foreigners. As the latter are shaping the political destiny of the natives, so likewise are they striving to direct their religious sentiments and social customs.

The Government of the Hawaiian kingdom is a constitutional monarchy, formed upon the model of that of Great Britain, being vested in a king, house of nobles, and house of representatives, while many of the features of its judicial system, as well as its customs and municipal organizations, are borrowed from those of the United States. The first constitution adopted in 1840, guarantees liberty of conscience in religious opinion, and the new laws of King Kamehameha III. provides that "all men residing in this kingdom shall be allowed freely to worship the God of the Christian Bible according to the dictates of their own consciences." These are in conformity to the spirit inculcated by the faith of that religion; and it would have been well for its interests, and for the welfare of the people it was intended to redeem from error, if Protestant missionaries had in all things been as consistent in practice as they professed to be in doctrine, and thus exemplified the graces of charity. As to social customs, these in part still illustrate the past. With many of the natives there is a transition affectation of habits and manners, grotesque in the extreme, while some have overcome entirely their repugnance to foreign arrogance of superiority, and strive to excel their exemplars in the absurdities of modern fashion. Europeans and Americans, at first shocked at the sight of nude specimens of mankind, soon became reconciled to the study of physical development; and the illusion of a fig leaf, in the "mamucki"—breech-cloth—of women, and "maro" of men, with the native brown complexion, aids in the conciliation of delicacy by heightening the fiction of bronze statuary. With some an interest is felt in even a closer investigation, for the Hawaiian figure, particularly in the young, in consequence of freedom from the restraints of dress, and from free indulgence in the aquatic sports of the surf, is generally faultless. The inhabitants of the towns being in closer contact with foreigners, are more subject to their example and influence; hence in these, even among the poorest of the populace, some kind of garment is worn in most instances; by the men, "kanakas," a coarse cotton shirt and trowsers; the women, "wahines," wearing a calico slip, the gaudier the color the more prized, falling loosely from a yoke at the shoulders, and without girdle or gathering. Thus simply and singly attired, the wahines might by the stranger be thought unattractive, but their profuse raven hair, usually bound by a gay bandelet of feathers or *ohia* blossoms, softly expressive dark eyes, pleasant countenance, erect figure, graceful and steady carriage, coming of unsandal'd feet, soon command for them that admiration of the gazer, more commonly given than sought. It is on the occasion of an equestrian gala-day that a Hawaiian belle shows to the greatest advantage. Saturday afternoon is the time usually devoted to feats of horsemanship and general racing. Honolulu is in the saddle on that day—that is if saddles can be had; if not, the barebacks of all horses, mules, and donkeys are sure to be in demand, without reference to caparisons; the steed, however, may not complain of this *naked* exposure, for his rider is often in the same dilemma. Urchin and adult seem emulous literally of "kicking up the greatest dust," and the principal avenues of the town, and the plain east of it, become as invisible in the distance as if twilight had fallen upon them. The mariner nearing the southern coast of Oahu during such a revel, might well suppose that the crater of Punch-bowl Hill had awakened from its long sleep, and was again belching forth its clouds of ashes over the devoted city. Nor is the kanaka and his youthful rival of the same sex, those alone who at such times display feats of skill, daring, and fleetness. The wahine disputes with them the palm of superiority, and as, *astride* of her flying steed, she startles the timid stranger with her boldness and address, her voluptuous bust bending forward in graceful curve, supporting an undaunted head bound with a brilliant bandeau, and her "tie," a riding-robe of orange or crimson calico encircling the waist, hips, and legs, and thence suspended, waving on each side like triumphal banners in token of confident victory, a new-comer, unused to such scenes of excitement, may justly concede to her surpassing horsemanship, and its attendant intensity of animation, an admiration they never fail to challenge. The innovation of side-saddle, with its awkward pommel, embarrassing riding-habit, stiffened corsage, cravat, and jockey cap, may seem very civilized, but unlucky will she prove who thus caparisoned undertakes a tilt of equestrianism with a wild wahine, as free and as fleet as the trade-wind that fans her open brow.

The domestic economy of the Hawaiian who contemns foreign fashions is very simple. A grass hut of one or two apartments serves for shelter; a split lauhalla leaf mat for bed and ottoman, calabashes for cupboards and bowls, and *poi* as the standard national food, compose the chief, and in most instances the only requisites. Poi is a dish prepared from the root of the *taro* (arum esculentum) somewhat resembling the potato in consistence and nutritive properties. These roots are beet-shaped, from six to ten inches long, and three or four thick. They have an acrid and pungent taste when uncooked. This is removed by baking or boiling. It is when subjected to the former process in a shallow excavation of the earth lined with heated stones, and covered by the same, and subsequently reduced by a stone pestle to a pulpy mass, which is allowed to become sour by fermentation, that it forms the staff of life of these islanders; who, however they may relish roast dog, pig, and dried fish, on the occasion of a "luau," or feast, when intensest sensualities rule throughout the night, yet return again to the pleasures of poi with renewed zest; and as they stir their fingers in the calabash to secure its portion of the precious paste, ere poising it with wondrous dexterity above the uplifted mouth awaiting to receive it, seem radiant with joy that they are not as that unnatural part of mankind, who prefer forks to fingers, and pudding to poi.

But it must not be supposed that the cultivation and refinement of modern civilization has no observers among these swarthy islanders and their lighter-hued descendants. The king and queen are well educated, intelligent, and courteous ; of dignified manners, becoming their position ; and possessing a proper appreciation of the influence of their example over their people. The king has excellent judgment, good taste, kindness of manner, and affability in social life ; and on occasions of state, a calm, thoughtful, self-possessed, gentlemanly, and impressive deportment, commanding respect and admiration, and which far surpasses in appropriateness the ostentatious awkwardness and rude arrogance of some who are, unfortunately for their more pretentious nationalities, appointed to represent these at his court. On the occasion of an official presentation, it was with mortification that several Americans witnessed the reception of a Commissioner, newly accredited by their Government, whose vulgarity was signalized by a Bowery costume of the rowdiest style, by repeated expectorations of tobacco juice at the foot of his majesty, to whom he was addressing a speech in the name of the President, and by his emphatic announcement of gratification that "during the short time that had elapsed since his arrival in the kingdom he had been surprised at much that he had seen, and especially by the fact that he had found the people of these islands not to be half as savage and heathenish as, from what he had heard and read, he expected to find them." Kamehameha IV. doubtless considered himself sufficiently revenged for this insult, by the self-disparagement of the American Government in the appointment of such a representative ; and appreciating his own self-respect and dignity too justly to notice the impertinence, could not have failed to observe also in the palpable mortification of the late Commissioner, of the Flag Officer of the Pacific Squadron and suite, and of others present, a sufficient commentary on such official blackguardism. To account for this diplomatic *faux pas*, it may be mentioned that the incumbent, in his emigration from the northwest to Oregon, had always *kept ahead of civilization*, and that his occupancy of the chair of a frontier partisan newspaper, could scarcely be expected to fit him for ministerial duties. If, however, such are to be regarded by the appointing power as proofs of fitness for positions of delicate and responsible trust, the United States must expect an estimate to be put upon them by foreigners, corresponding to the characters of those they accredit abroad.

The better educated few of the Hawaiians, especially the women, mingle on terms of equality with foreigners in their social circle at Honolulu; nor is that circle disparaged by the association, for in the lighter graces of fashionable life, music, the dance, sprightly conversation, and pleasing deportment, it would have been difficult at the private entertainments and public assemblies I attended, to have selected among their Caucasian sisters more attractive examples of these than were presented by some of the *fairer* specimens of Hawaiian belles.

Churches are sufficiently numerous, and worshippers profess as diversified belief, and maintain their opinions with an intensity of bigotry and bad logic, conformable with the example of the teachers who train them. But of religion in these islands something may be said when other opportunities shall have been afforded to obtain full and satisfactory information. The royal family have a preference for the profession of faith and the ritualism of the Church of England; and at their instance a Bishop of that Church, under the auspices of Queen Victoria, was sent to the Hawaiian Islands in 1862 formally to establish and "further the good work of the English mission." This has been the cause of a most extraordinary manifestation of jealousy and ill temper on the part of the Rev. Secretary of the American Board of Commissioners for Foreign Missions, who in a recent book (1864) on the Hawaiian Islands, designates it "a breach of that courtesy which is due from one Christian body to another," and charges further that "in the hour of their victory a body of professed allies comes to us from the land of our fathers, with the evident intent, if it be possible, of taking possession of the field." Really such contracted feelings are unworthy of the professed objects of the enterprise in which the Rev. Secretary boasts of having been long engaged.

The royal palace scarcely deserves the name. It is a plain but commodious building, the chief material being the coral rock which borders the seashore. The grounds are ample, adorned with trees, shrubbery, and flowers, substantially enclosed, and guarded by sentinels in showy uniforms.

A monument of the king's good taste and liberality, as well as of his humane regard for the welfare of his subjects, is a large, admirably planned, and well-conducted hospital, in which gratuitous accommodation and medical attendance are furnished to those whom poverty and disease have made fit objects of sympathy and care. The Government buildings, whether national or municipal, deserve no special notice.

A principal object of natural curiosity on this island, is the *Pali*—a precipice from six to seven miles from Honolulu, at the north end of a vast gorge of the central mountain chain which traverses the island from east to west throughout nearly its whole extent. The traveller may make the trip on foot or horseback—the latter being preferable unless he is a good pedestrian. Leaving the city in a northerly direction the Nuuanu valley is soon entered, the ascent of which from its southern expanded embouchure, at first gradual, soon becomes steep; while the sloping foot-hills nearer the plain on which Honolulu stands, become lost in the nearly perpendicular mountain heights, which, as the Pali is approached, encroach upon the rapidly-narrowing pass like giant walls, covered with all shades of shrubbery and wild grass, that preserve a perpetual verdure from the ceaseless distillation of the clouds always hovering about the lofty summits overhanging the valley.

The pretty villas of foreign residents that stud the wider part of Nuuanu valley nearer the city, give place beyond to the grass huts of natives, past whose doors mountain rivulets hasten with merry note, giving welcome tribute to groves of Koa, Tutui, Hibiscus, and Lauhala, sparsely scattered along the way; and to the simple and patient people, who desire no sweeter beverage, and who by little artificial canals divert them from their course to water their sunken beds of *taro*, returning them again to their natural channels to be similarly used by each successive cultivator of that indigenous plant, which is both bread and meat to the Hawaiian. Small cascades occasionally seek the admiration of the passer-by; while one waterfall, that of *Keahuamoo*, of more pretension than the rest, challenges the excursionist some fifty or sixty yards off to come and look at it tumble from a perpendicular rock of fifty feet height, into a pebbly basin beneath. The road becoming narrower and rougher, finally leads to a rocky ledge, turning round which to the right, a scene alike beautiful and grand is so suddenly brought into view as to excite mingled awe and admiration. Standing upon a small volcanic rock plateau, the trade-wind rushing through the narrow gorge through which it is approached, with a fierceness that endangers his foothold, the spectator sees so near that his brain grows dizzy at the sight, a fearful precipice—known on this island as the *Pali*—of six hundred feet nearly perpendicular height from the plain at its foot; the latter falling gradually as it stretches away to the north many miles even to the ocean, so as to give the Pali an elevation above the sea-level of eleven hundred feet.

The picture beyond is placidly beautiful. Sward and hillock, grove and streamlet, hamlet and pathway, nature's wildness and man's culture, blend in tranquil harmony, and present a landscape of rare attractions; enclosed to the south by a crescentic sweep of the mountain chain; and far seaward as it softens in the distance, limited by a changeful edging of snowy foam, that touches the dim outline with a new and fadeless charm. And then, as if nature designed to startle man by her contrasted creations, gazing upward he beholds overlooking even his own elevated standpoint the frowning peak of *Konahuanui*, proud and unbending, as when first the central fires lifted it four thousand feet above the sea, to bathe its brow eternally in the trade-wind's misty breath. And on the opposite side of the narrow gorge, the pointed basaltic rock shaft, *Nuuanu* nearly rivalling Konahuanui in magnitude, and surpassing it in stern and stately grandeur, looks scornfully too on the tranquil valley of Kolau, and as the blast howls through the wild defile at their feet they seem thus to give utterance to their contempt of its humility.

A rough, circuitous, and steep path, along the face of the

cliff on the east side of the Pali, is the avenue of communication with the district beyond the precipice. Over this the natives pass to market with the products of Kolau, principally carried in huge calabashes swung in netting from the ends of a shoulder pole. The existence of this pathway, in the opinion of some persons, refutes the tradition, commonly believed, that it was over the precipice of the Pali that many warriors of this island were driven, and thus perished, after their defeat in a battle which was fought near the cascade of Keahuamoo for independence, against their invader Kamehameha the Great. But it is altogether reasonable to suppose that many might thus have perished in the confusion and panic of a general rout, from the crowding of persons in the narrow pass and on the small plateau of the Pali, all of whom could not escape by one steep and contracted pathway.

The unvarying Borean blast that bursts through the narrow gorge formed by the riven mountain for more than two-thirds of its height, and sweeps down the Nuuanu valley to temper the tropical heats of the capital, together with the daily recurring showers which cover with perennial verdure that valley and the mountain heights, are phenomena suggestive of inquiry, and may be accounted for by the northeast trade-wind finding itself hemmed within the vast crescent formed by the northern face of the mountain chain, which thus becomes an expanded funnel to gather and direct the steady gale with the force of a hurricane through the contracted neck of the Pali pass; the condensation of moisture drank by the trade-winds in their long ocean passage, being due in part as well to partial compression within the northern arc of the mountain, incident to impeded escape, as to contact with the colder objects of an elevated region.

The Hand of the Creator, among these everlasting records of His power, paints day by day with the sunbeam on the shower, the arc of His Covenant of Mercy. How happy the native race, fast passing away before the malign agencies directed by their more powerful fellow-man, if they can see in this symbol the promise of a more blissful destiny hereafter! Then will they, as they gaze in wonder and devotion at its imperishable radiance, seek to preserve in the retirement of nature, away from the haunts of civilized vice, their simple and unvitiated habits. And as they cultivate the verdant plain below they will recognize in its productiveness the goodness of Him who planted their land with abundance; and behold there also the proofs of His power and design in the miniature mountains scattered broadcast, evidently the remains of those cones of eruption often seen in the craters of active volcanoes, sometimes disappearing, but finally becoming monuments of previous phenomena, when other outlets occur and the elements of destruction cease to overthrow them. It is probable that the whole plain between the Pali and the ocean was once an immense crater, of thirty or forty miles circumference, the southern semicircular rim of which only is now visible, the northern having been destroyed by unrecognized agencies, and buried in the depths of the sea that now rolls its surf above the sunken ruins.

In years gone by the whole seashore of Oahu was an unrestricted bathing-place, where the guileless islanders sported in the surf, seeking health and vigor from the alluring waves. Modern ministers of religion, assuming, often as unfortunately as gratuitously, to interpret and enforce modern civilization, now wielding a power wrested from the ancient Hawaiian priesthood, have *taboo'd* the universal custom, and proclaim the sin of ablution—except according to the gregarious usages of a fashionable watering-place, consequently the *tropical* island of Oahu has now its duly appointed bathing *season*, and its duly assigned bathing-place. *Waikiki*—interpreted *spouting water*, from the rollicking breakers' feathery foam—about three miles eastward of Honolulu, is the renowned spot at which its dusky denizens "do congregate," when dust and dirt have sufficiently accumulated, according to the established code, to make a general washing appropriate. A drive over a good road through surburbs of grass huts, among taro patches, and across salt marshes that might by moderate enterprise and industry be converted into productive rice fields, soon brings the visitor to a cocoa-nut grove, within and beyond which, on the seashore, are the cottages for the accommodation of the bathers, who provide themselves with bed and board in the absence of hotels—a lucky necessity for those who need dietetic restrictions and renovation, rather than the poisonous pandering to the palate of these modern caravansaries. Nearly three miles east of Waikiki and beyond the old native village of the same name, projects the bold promontory of Diamond Head—the Hawaiian Leahi—among the most conspicuous and distinctive objects of this island, and once seen by the mariner remaining an unforgotten landmark. Diamond Head is an extinct crater, about a thousand feet above the sea at its highest point, and may be ascended by any one of moderate strength and perseverance. A volcanic pit, two hundred feet deep and probably three-fourths of a mile in diameter, is found at its top, lined with vegetation, except at the middle, where a small freshwater lake is formed.

A ride round the Head enables the excursionist to see its massive buttresses, and the deep channels of its ancient lava streams; and scattered about its foot beds of volcanic rock mingled confusedly with coral, forming a barrier to the encroaching sea, the tides of which, however, flow among the gigantic fragments, uttering their hoarse song of triumph over its long since extinguished fires.

Off the eastern face of the headland, in the sands of the seashore, beyond the reach of ordinary high water, an immense trench is found, in which lie innumerable human bones piled in indiscriminate confusion, and in every degree of disorganization; some few of them being perfect in structure, and bleached by the sun, where disinterred by the northeast wind, forming interesting ethnological specimens. Are these the remains of the victims of war in the earlier battles of Kamehameha, who landed at Wiakiki, and Kalanikupule, the king of Oahu, for the possession of this island? Or do they mark the resting-place away from the homes of the panic-stricken people, of thousands who were suddenly swept away by some epidemic pestilence?

Further along the shore, the few hamlets of *Waialae* are seen nestled in a pretty grove. And a short distance beyond, the grass huts of *Waialupe* cluster near the high hill of Mauna Loa, from the southern foot of which a ridge extends still farther southwardly to the bold and lofty cape named *Coco Head*, the eastern boundary of the beautiful bay of Waialae, of which Diamond Head, already described, forms the western.

Returning to Honolulu across the ridge which unites Diamond Head with the highlands of the interior, an opportunity was afforded of seeing nature in her rugged garb of crumbling scoria, shapeless porphyry, and basaltic boulder, in strange and perplexing contiguity. It is a mantle of mysterious texture, covering the probably yet unstable crust beneath, and may well deserve the investigations of those who seek in such testimonials the revelations of Nature. The lover of panoramic display may also from this elevation behold unfolded around him a scene of rare variety, and of wondrous beauty and sublimity. To the east, the dimpled waters of Waialae Bay seem joyful in the protection of the embracing shore which throws its verdant arms around, that tempests may "not visit them too roughly." To the north the verdure-clothed mountains look out from the misty cowls that wrap their lofty heads, gazing as if in pride upon the bold Leahi in the south, planting his fearless foot against the sea, defiant of its power, while far away the waves roll on their countless battalions, tossing their "spouting water" over coral barricades, and retiring to renew again the ceaseless assault; and to the west, beyond an outspread plain of man's adornment, Honolulu, mellowed into queenly beauty in the distance, is seen to rest against the shadowy mountains of Waianae, behind which, as I beheld the enchanting scene, the sun was sinking to its rest, clad in a gorgeous livery of clouds.

Having crossed Telegraph Ridge, so called because it is the signal station of vessels approaching Honolulu from the east, the valley of Manoa was seen to the right, slumbering in the deep shade of forest green, emulous of the rich emerald of the mantled earth, over which the crystal water was weaving a web of streamlets, whose limpid tribute gave to the spot a fresh and lasting charm. A footspur of Tantalus Hill seeks ineffectually to bar the entrance to Manoa's grateful shades and inviting solitudes. Happily these are open to the wearied pupils of Oahu College at Punahou, established in 1842 as a school for the children of missionaries only, but subsequently, in 1848, enlarged for the accommodation of others, both foreigners and natives, and finally in 1856 chartered by the Hawaiian Government as a college. The buildings, plain but comfortable, and grounds neatly kept and cultivated in shrubbery and flowers, lie near *Tantalus* Hill, a spot no doubt deemed well chosen by some who tread the academic groves at its foot, and who, despite their efforts to drink of the waters of knowledge, find, like that mythical personage, the refreshing draught ever to retire from reach.

The course of instruction takes a wide range for a school so recently organized, and the pupils exhibited excellent attainments at a public examination held during my visit. Both boys and girls are educated at this college, separate buildings being provided for their accommodation. But a striking difference is observable between the white and Hawaiian children, the former in general having the wasted physique and thoughtful countenance of close study, mind cultivated at the expense of body; while the latter looked cheerful, healthy, and fully developed. By and bye, as the pressure of discipline is brought to bear on them more forcibly, the artificialities and restrictions of a false system of training will hurry them, too, along the path of destruction crowded by their unhappy race, since puritanism first undertook to enforce its harsh and uncompromising decrees. Once during the torture of the public exhibition, when the mental cords seemed to quiver and crack with tension, a calisthenic interlude relieved the strain, and showed that the graceful girls, who went through their changeful drill and manœuvre, with Zouave-like precision, to the varying music of their own voices, both grave and gay, had in their hearts a fountain of happiness and joy, whose sparkling flow it were wickedness to restrain. And long will "a sigh in the heart," of which little Nell's enchanting melody told the plaintive tale, linger with the stranger who on that day had awakened within him slumbering and sacred memories. It comes alike of an ignorance of the laws of health, of mistaken morals, and of an austere and absurd religionism, to bind the young by a rigid formulary of thought and manners, that fetters or destroys every impulse implanted by beneficent nature for its own wise purposes. Neither measured movement nor sauntering is exercise, any more than loafing is work, or fancy dreaming is thought. Yet exercise is essential to well-developed forms, bright eyes, clear complexions, active limbs, sound lungs, and a healthy and vigorous brain, as well as to cheerful spirits. It is exercise the young need and must have, if they are to fulfil the nobler destiny awaiting them; the exercise of all youthful creatures of whatever kind, free, unrestrained, gleesome, and intense. And he whose great privilege it is to shape for manhood and womanhood the beings who are to redeem the obligations of their creation—he who burdens a sensitive, aspiring, and intelligent mind, with the cares of an afflicted and feeble frame, through narrow and erroneous views of religious duty, commits a fraud upon his fellow-creature, and violates a natural right.

The last object of interest on the route of my return, as it was also the first on my leaving Honolulu in the morning, is Punch-Bowl Hill, a more expressive than elegant name for the Hawaiian *Puahi.* It is an extinct crater, somewhat east by north of the town, and in its suburbs. It is not more than five hundred feet high, and is easily ascended at its less precipitous side. A concavity occupies the top, having a diameter of nearly a half mile, the decomposing lava and earlier vegetable formations affording sufficient soil for pasturage, on which goats and cattle were seen browsing, happily insensible that Punch-Bowl might, like some other well-known craters, suddenly become the recipient of ingredients too hot for a refreshing beverage. This hill was once the site of a fortification intended for the defence of the capital; the position is a commanding one, and by modern military engineering and a large expenditure of treasure, could be made impregnable from the sea. A few old and indifferently mounted cannon are all that remain of its equipment, and these seem to be preserved for the sole purpose of saluting foreign men-o'-war coming into the harbor, and for occasional salvos in honor of Hawaiian royalty.

# CHAPTER XXXIII.

DEPARTURE FROM HONOLULU—ISLANDS OF MOLOKAI AND LANAI—LAHAINA—SEAPORT OF THE ISLAND OF MAUI—TEMPTATIONS OF RESIDENCE—TEMPERATURE—SIMPLICITY OF NATIVE HABITS—ADVENT OF THE WHITE MAN A CURSE TO THE NATIVES—UNITED STATES CONSULS AND HOSPITALS IN FOREIGN COUNTRIES—OFFICIAL MALFEASANCE.

The object of my visit to Honolulu being accomplished, duty forbade the gratification of a wish to linger longer among the attractions of this politically chief island of the group, and in a commercial sense, as before stated, its most important, for it is the principal resort of the great whaling fleet of the Pacific, which in the palmy days of whaling was sometimes represented in the harbor of Honolulu by more than one hundred vessels, valued, with their cargoes, at ten millions of dollars, riding at anchor within its protecting reef. Such prosperity, however, is not likely to be realized in the future, although Oahu may retain its relative commercial importance, for the rapidly-diminishing "catch" of whales, owing to their disappearance from the seaman's favorite fishing grounds, together with the growth of San Francisco, and the opening of other Pacific ports, are working revolutions in trade, and affording depots of supply and transshipment that cannot fail to operate disadvantageously upon the shipping interests of the Hawaiian Islands, so far at least as relates to this particular source of their prosperity.

Leaving Kauai to the northwest, an island of great salubrity and agricultural capacity, the first in the order of creation of this group, as it was also the first in that of modern discovery, we steered in the little Hawaiian steamer "Kilauea" out of the harbor of Honolulu, bound for Lahaina, another port at which the United States have a resident consul. The king was aboard with some of his courtiers, on their way to another part of his dominions, where, in accordance with usage, he proposed to spend a part of the summer. Puahi thundered its farewell, repeated long and loud in the echoing caverns of Konahuanui, while the crowd of natives on the pier sent after their beloved monarch the boisterous tokens of their devotion. The king himself seemed touched by their attachment, and as he waved his hand in adieu, ennobled his sovereignty by the undisguised tenderness of human nature. Both in his official and personal relations, Kamehameha IV. shows much intelligence on general subjects; and while preserving at all times a becoming dignity, his manners in social life are characterized by a winning yet always courteous affability.

Fading in the distance as we bore away to the eastward, Oahu looked like an emerald set upon the heaving bosom of the ocean; and as the sad strain of a fellow-passenger floated on the breeze to mingle with the plaintive melody of the sea, it gave a sense of mournful reality to the poet's inspiration—

"Still the blue wave danced around me
'Mid the sunbeam's jocund smile,
Still the air breathed balmy summer
Wafted from that happy isle;
When some hand the strain awaken'd
Of my own, my native shore,
Then 'twas first I wept Oh! Naxos,
That I ne'er should see thee more."

Night closed in upon us before entering the channel between the islands of Molokai and Lanai, so that nothing of them was seen but their dim outlines, as the Kilauea rolled and pitched through a sea, roughened by a northeaster coming fiercely through the Molokai-Maui passage. But no disappointment was felt at the deprivation when, after the lapse of twelve hours, we anchored in the roadstead of Lahaina at daybreak, and looked back at the former, still in view, presenting no special features of interest; and the latter, whose look of tame sterility might well account for its almost total depopulation. It is the presence of these islands in the vicinity, and that of Kahoolawe still further off, to the southeast, that makes the roadstead outside of the reef a safe anchorage; except when winds and seas come unusually strong from the undefended south, when vessels have some difficulty in holding on.

Lahaina is celebrated for her fearless and skilful watermen, who besiege every newly-arrived craft with offers of service, and put passengers ashore either in a canoe or a whale-boat, and over the crested breakers or through a narrow channel of the reef, according to the spot at which a landing is desired. While riding in conscious security upon the curving swells, and listening to the melody of the natives' vowelled language, which

> "Sounds as if it had been writ on satin
> With syllables that breathe of the sweet south,
> And gentle liquids flowing all so pat in
> That not a single accent seems uncouth,"

the stranger cannot fail to have the charm of his immediate surroundings heightened by the scene he is approaching. Nearer to him stretches the bright seashore edged with rippling foam; the quaint hamlets of the islanders with interspersed buildings of more modern style, dotting a higher level, seeking the south wind's daily tribute that cools the tropic sultriness. Cocoanut, plantain, banana, breadfruit, tutui, koa, and lauhala trees, are scattered through the town, and cluster in groves beyond, tempering with grateful shade the unclouded sunlight of a level plain extending to the green foot-hills of the interior highlands of the island; while the last lift their steep and scraggy brows to catch the welcome vapors of the "trades," and quench the thirst of the green valleys that deck their rugged sides. Many and magnificent are the revelations of natural scenery, in which the stupendous and the lowly commingle in harmony, presented by these insular sportings of volcanic power.

Lahaina and its adjoining district have a population of about three thousand five hundred, the proportion of foreigners being less than at Honolulu. The island of Maui, of which it is the chief town, is forty-eight miles long and thirty miles broad, and is estimated to have a population of eighteen thousand. The town consists principally of one long street running parallel with the shore—a few cross streets, being avenues of communi-

LAHAINA.

cation with the country, having but few houses upon them, and soon degenerating into rugged lanes, strewn thickly, as well as fenced, by lava rocks of all sizes and shapes; while the streets themselves, marvellously paved with an unknown depth of reddish dust, would constrain the utterance of Hamlet by the white resident, when regarding his Hawaiian neighbor—"to this complexion we must come at last"—were it not for the luxury of a breaker-bath gratuitously brought to his threshold by beneficent nature.

To the stranger strolling through the environs of Lahaina the acknowledged fact becomes confirmed, that this formerly prosperous seaport is on the decline. Dilapidated houses and fences, neglected taro patches, abandoned premises and banana orchards, neglected sugar-cane fields, and a general return to the wildness and waste of tropical vegetation, meet him in whatsoever direction he may go; to show that demand has ceased, and that labor, no longer rewarded for its toil by the whalers who formerly sought supplies and the facilities of transshipment at this port, has lapsed into a neglect and indifference coming of the consciousness that a half acre taro patch, well lined with beaten clay to make it water tight, will furnish food enough for a family of five or six persons with an expenditure *of but two hours effort per week*, including the time consumed in preparing the poi. When commerce has failed to stimulate production, excite and direct industry, and develop the usual beneficial results—accompanied unhappily with their evils too—of contact with civilization, mere religious missionary enterprise addressing itself to the idealities of human nature, has done little else than substitute one form of bigotry and intolerance for another, although it loudly proclaims the praises of its beneficent achievements, which the disinterested, close, and candid observer here, fails to realize. Practical virtue rather than theoretical, and a religionism adapted to the improvement of man's condition here and thus affording the sole promise of happiness hereafter, and that, illustrated by example as well as taught by precept, must form the foundation of any rational hope of beneficial proselytism.

The soil and climate are well adapted to the cultivation of sugar cane, cotton, and the vine; and the natural growth of the banana and bread-fruit, with the cheapness of labor when not oppressive—one dollar per week for a man, and half that sum for a boy, who furnish their own food consisting of poi—offer strong temptations of residence to the possessor of a small income. And to the valetudinarian, especially if afflicted with pulmonary disease, these are increased by the trivial deviations of temperature; the *highest mean temperature of an entire year*, as shown by a carefully kept meteorological table, having been 83½° Fahrenheit, while the *lowest* was 66°—the mean variation being thus seen to have been *but* 17½° *through all seasons*—a deviation from absolute uniformity *far less for the whole year*, than frequently occurs in most parts of the United States on *a single day*. Perhaps, however, the contrast of climate between the two countries will appear more striking, by presenting the annual variation 17½° of this island, in opposition to that *common* in the States—from *zero to blood-heat*.

It may be stated that the extremes of temperature at Honolulu are certainly not greater than they are at Lahaina; while during one year, a meteorological table published by R. C. Wyllie, Minister of Foreign Relations, shows that the variation at the former place was less than the above mentioned. It must be added, however, that the changes of temperature are more sudden at Honolulu than at Lahaina, induced by the gusts of wind which frequently reach the city by the Nuuanu Valley from the gap of the Pali, charged tóo as they often are with mist or rain. This fact should not be overlooked in making a choice of residence for health by those of extreme sensibility to even slight vicissitudes.

It is probable that ere long these islands will become places of resort for invalids from the rigors and vicissitudes of an American climate. Indeed the lives of many have already been preserved by a residence in their genial atmosphere; and some were met with whom no temptations of social rank, political position, and accumulated wealth at home; no seductions of continental pleasure, fashion, and refinement, could allure from the balmy airs and the delicious physical existence of these elysian islands.

The appearance, habits, and dress of the native inhabitants of Lahaina resemble those of the Honolulans. Those most frequently in contact with foreigners imitate partially their usages; most of them, however, cling to the customs of their fathers. Happily these are inexpensive; an almost gratuitous repast is spread for them by creative bounty, and the simplicities of costume, or none at all, suffice for the exigencies of weather; a cotton slip is a woman's abundant wardrobe, and breeches are a superfluity when the absence of imperious foreigners leaves the wearing of a tapa (bark cloth) maro, a sufficient observance of the modesty of nature.

It is well that the Christian duty divinely inculcated "I was a stranger and ye took me in," is practically observed here, otherwise, in the absence of publicans, the visitor would fare badly. The citizens generally, both foreigners and natives, are found willing and anxious to contribute to the comfort and pleasure of all respectably accredited travellers. An Englishman, now a Hawaiian citizen and judge of this district, politely tendered to me the hospitalities of his house, and I am indebted to him for many attentions and much information. But the claims of nationality made me the guest of a fellow-countryman, and here, as at Honolulu, with a noble-minded Virginian, I am made to realize the fact that in distant lands the ties of a common country are synonymous with a bond of brotherhood. My apartments are in the palace of the former Queen Keopuolani, standing on the seashore in a grove of shade trees, and looking out upon the breakers as they lift their white crests above the coral reef, and roll their flowing tide within, to form a fitting bath, formerly for the queen and her maidens, and now for one who, however much they and their people may have been traduced by the designing, uncharitable, and vainglorious, believes that they have been "more sinned against than sinning."

The palace may be described as a specimen of the better class of native houses. It is from forty to fifty feet square, and built of strong round posts several inches in diameter, and eight or ten feet high, planted in the ground three feet apart, and inclining very slightly inward. The upper concave ends of these receive horizontally-placed timbers, and on these rest rafters, forming the frame of a high-pitched roof, the posts, beams, and rafters being lashed together, and the latter to the ridgepole of the roof, which rests on two or three stronger and taller posts, in the middle of the building, by ropes and twine of twisted cocoanut fibre, vines, and tough grasses. Small poles representing lathing, are similarly tied crosswise the posts and rafters, to the outside of which are secured large banana leaves, that serve as a rude wall-paper, and then eight or ten inches thickness of thatching, formed of pandanus or sugar cane leaves, or bundled or plaited grass, for walls and roofing. In front, the thatched roof is made to project over the doorway, and being supported by columns of small undressed tree trunks, presents the appearance of a rustic portico. Stripped of its thatching, my residence would look from the interior like a huge bird-cage; in its completeness it resembles on the outside an architectural hay-rick. Since the palace passed into the possession of foreign plebeians it has been modernized, three apartments being partitioned off, having as many windows, and it can likewise boast the luxuries of floor, tables, chairs, and bedsteads. When sheltering sovereignty the necessary domestic economy demanded but one large room, and the mat-covered earth sufficed for sitting, eating, and sleeping. To Hawaiian royalty of the past, lulled by the song of the melodious sea, there were needed "no perfumed chambers nor canopies of costly state," and its lowly couch gave a blissful rest unknown to him of England, who sighing said,

"Uneasy lies the head that wears a crown."

But the same even tenor of content and obliviousness of ill are not the realities of the present day. The ceaseless moan of the surf as it rolls its fitful tide over coral beds, and whispers sighs upon the golden strand, seems in the silence of the midnight hour, when sleepless memory calls up the traditions of the Hawaiian, and justice weighs the deeds of his fellow-man, like a plaintive wail of the gentle and confiding natives, because of conscious degradation, and for the independence and happiness fast passing away before foreign aggressions, innovations, and constrained customs not adapted to their wants, nor promotive of their enjoyments. Impartial observers are saddened by the reflection that the missionary has given them no equivalent for their deprivations, and for the promiscuous evils of which they have been made the victims by the *vanguard* of civilization, too commonly the *worst of barbarisms*, because of its commingled power and wicked disregard of all law, human and divine. The test of excellence is in the result of effort. Are the natives purer and happier, more truthful, industrious, honest, hospitable, prosperous; have they increased in number and in good works since the advent of the white man? Or are they not simply more subservient to the selfish purposes of the crafty and avaricious foreigner; more deceitful, mere formalists in religion to deceive the preacher and acquire influence through his favor, perseverance, and adroitness? Are they not disappearing before a moral pestilence as destructive as the plague, and which has brought in its train as grievous physical evils? The affirmative of these questions is painfully true. If the depopulation of these islands to the *extent of four-fifths since their discovery*, and, under the operation of like causes, the probable *extermination of the remainder* in the next twenty or thirty years, and *a consequent* abolition of paganism, are to be regarded as proofs of proselytism and redemption from habits and customs fearfully and extravagantly pictured to horrify Christendom, certainly the efforts of the missionaries and their profane confrères must be regarded as having proved eminently successful.

Although an abundance of sawed lumber is now brought to these islands from Oregon, and used by foreigners for building purposes, yet the natives prefer grass huts, commonly, however, of less size and more simple structure than the queen's house above described, the kitchen consisting of the capacious outside and a cook-stove of heated stones.

Foreigners, both at Honolulu and Lahaina, are abundantly supplied at small cost with vegetables by natives, who daily bring to the houses in large calabashes, bananas, melons, plantains, potatoes, figs, grapes, taro, and even pŏi for those who fancy finger-dipping according to the fashion of the country.

A school at Lahainaluna, two miles from Lahaina, for the education of native boys, is said to be in successful operation. It is conducted on the manual labor plan, as well to assist in the support of the institution, as to give the pupils a knowledge and habits of industrial employments.

There is at this port, and also at the capital, a hospital for distressed and destitute American seamen. Into the condition and management of these, and of those on the west coast of

South America, my commission required me to examine. There is one other yet to be visited, which is an acknowledged exception to the practice of frauds and abuses prevalent elsewhere, and the investigation and correction of which have long engaged the attention of Government. Probably the history of no commercial nation furnishes such gross examples of violated duty as is presented by the United States consular administration of the *relief trust* at the above places; a fact the more disgraceful because the humane intentions of Congress are endangered thereby. It has been my duty to consider the remote, as well as the proximate causes of this official malfeasance; and the acknowledgment is demanded by candor, that the prevalent practice of appointing incompetent persons to consulates, and the system of indiscriminate rotation in office, which seems to have become incorporated with the administration of public affairs, are the probable and chief causes of the evil.

The British and French Governments, and I am informed the Sardinian also, exact especial requirements for the consular office. Knowledge of general commerce and commercial law, clerical qualifications, and acquaintance with the language of the nation to whom he is accredited, as well as grammatical accuracy in his own, are, together with assured good character, necessary pre-requisites for the consular office, after having served a prescribed term as consul's clerk. And when once appointed to consulates of inferior rank and importance, the certainty of retention and promotion in office are held out as incentives to official improvement, industry, and integrity. Thus these countries, in justly rewarding merit, secure to themselves competent and faithful service.

It is the opposite of this usage, the appointment of United States consuls without reference to special qualifications, and too often despite recognized incapacity, questionable character, and immoral habits, that leads to the defective and discreditable performance of duty. Further, the periodical removal of these officers merely to reward clamorous partisans, invites to all possible appropriations of forbidden pay and perquisites of office, and leads to a system of bribery on the part of subordinate employés, who can well afford to pay the wages of dishonesty from exorbitant receipts.

And in proportion to the brevity of the official term, and the distance from supervision, has been the recklessness of official delinquency. The door once opened by a predecessor to successful peculation without detection and punishment, his successor having no hope of reward for fidelity in expected retention beyond his four years of appointment, imitates the example that has been set him, and seeks to realize as speedily as possible a sum sufficient to meet the contingencies of the future. A result correspondent to that commonly witnessed in South American republics, consequent on frequently recurring revolutions and official changes incident thereto; each successive band of rulers, harpies of the State and creatures of a day, indulging in the grossest abuses, frauds, and peculations.

The passage of a law by Congress years since, authorizing the appointment of consular pupils, indicates the opinion then entertained by the members of that branch of the Government, that a suitable education was a necessary pre-requisite for the office of consul. And the excellent regulations relating to consular pupils contained in the "Manual for Consuls," is significant of the importance attached by the framers of that code to a proper education of candidates for that office.

Unfortunately no appropriation has at any time been made by Congress for fulfilling the law so wisely enacted, and hence the benefits to the country, of which it gave promise, have not been realized. It is not the promulgation of an opinion through legislative enactment alone, however indisputably sound, that will secure practical benefits. And a sense of duty will compel me to say in a final report, that unless legislative and executive action go hand in hand, to the end that the country may secure the services of honest, capable, and faithful agents, any abstract plan of service which may be proposed, of efficient and economical relief of distressed and destitute American seamen, will fall short of the objects designed by the Department of State in instituting the investigation with which I have been charged.

The question to some may seem absurd—Is political liberty compatible with good government? Yet foreign experiences, as well as some at home, the recollections of which are by no means calculated to strengthen democratic faith, frequently obtrude the inquiry. The sister republics of the South, who have with us entered on the work of asserting and maintaining popular rights, are perpetually distracted with revolutions, entailing upon them evils, than which no monarchical despotism could inflict greater. The specialty of service of our own Government abroad, coming under my examination, has, in the opinion of all who have knowledge of what is passing, become synonymous with a system of licensed plundering and stupid blundering; while the tendency at home, in the general and local administration of public affairs, is to deterioration, ignorance, and corruption. This avowal will be thought by the time-serving, impolitic, and may be denounced by demagogues as unpatriotic. It is at least consistent with *upright principle*, at all times a nobler motive of action *than policy*, and as to *patriotism*, the fearless expression of *truth* in regard to national evils is among the best proofs of *it*.

It is certainly a mortifying consciousness that our countrymen have so far degenerated since the days of their fathers, who gave them both liberty and law, as well as example how to perpetuate them. And it is perhaps because of departure from professed principles of political faith and virtue, and a resort to despicable and degrading expedients, that the ignorant masses might be used for the attainment of party triumphs, that this lamentable state of things has been brought about. For when the unenlightened multitude are taught, as they have been, by their superiors in knowledge, that trick is a warrantable, and often a surer means of success than truth, cunning better than consistency, policy than principle, and even violence than virtue, and that these concessions are made to them as possessors of numerical power, they do not fail to profit by the lesson, and thus become, through demagogues catering to their low instincts, dictators of the future destiny of the country. Leaders of parties who can find a merit in a coffin hand-bill, hickory tree, sledge-hammer, hard-cider barrel, log cabin, or Uncle Tom's cabin, must expect eventually to realize their level with the agrarian mob to whom such arguments are addressed; and, in the general scramble for place, and its honors and profits, they should not be surprised if muscle triumphed over mind.

And this result has been hastened in the United States by the culpable indifference to passing events which are shaping the future life of the nation, of the misnamed conservative classes of the people, whose devotion to the accumulation of money—truly when government springs from the people, the "mammon of unrighteousness"—and the inglorious ease and selfish indulgences which come of it, has been so deadening that it seems as if they would not awaken to the fact that they have an interest in the political condition of the country, and should participate in a jealous supervision and control of its government, until it may be too late to avoid their virtual if not absolute disfranchisement.

Not only do the festering elements of political and social disorganization, at work among the uninformed native population, and even better educated fanatics, yet slaves of passion, prejudice, and impulse, require it, but the onward flood of rabid republicanism from abroad, the foreign refuse radicalism, long pent up and once set free, submissive to no restraints of reason, acknowledging no deference for constitutional obligations, imperiously demands of the more enlightened, reflective, and discreet citizens, the exercise of those conservative duties necessary to hold in check the spirit of destructivism seeking to set aside the precepts of the wise and the inculcations of history. And if the duty shall not be fulfilled, the United States will probably soon learn, that by urging too far the doctrine of popular sovereignty, by pushing to excess a single principle irrespective of correlative duties, however true in itself, and however valuable its wise application, conclusions may follow which will amount to the overthrow of the principle itself, and thus tyranny be made to trample on popular rights.

Once more in the periods of time the experiment of democratic government is being tried. We of America must bear our individual share of responsibility connected with it, and withhold neither action nor testimony bearing on the question. However mortifying then the confession, it must under the obligations of truth and candor be made, that it has been my misfortune to have presented constantly recurring proofs of national degeneracy, in the low state of morals, manners, and capacity of American officials abroad; and unless the causes leading to this and other like evils, coming of a flagrant system of political levelling, and disregard of undeniable distinctions and the inculcations of duty and wisdom, shall be reformed, the page of history will probably soon record another decline and fall of a a great nation.

## CHAPTER XXXIV.

VOYAGE TO HILO, ULUPALAKUA, HALEAKALA, MOLOKINI, AND KAHOOLAWE—INTERINSULAR CHANNEL—ISLAND OF HAWAII—KAWAIHAI—HAWAIIANS ORIGINATED THEIR OWN RELIGIOUS REFORMATION—FAILURE OF FOREIGN MISSIONARIES IN DIRECTING IT—BOLD SEASHORE OF HAMAKUA—WAIAKEA BAY—HARBOR AND TOWN OF HILO—MAUNA KEA—MAUNA LOA.

THE rosy dawn of an unclouded summer morning revealed the steamer Kilauea at anchor in the roadstead of Lahaina, awaiting passengers for Hilo and intermediate ports. Going aboard at 8 A. M., but few cabin passengers were found, all foreigners, except two, who were Hawaiians of noble rank. The *deck-load* of natives was numerous, perhaps two hundred, from infancy to premature decrepitude; the former not in the usual proportion to adult age, as observed on other occasions, for the connubial relation is less fruitful than before the advent of civilization, and the latter has not given the natives the knowledge and the means of care of offspring.

Partial observers say that the fewness of children is owing to the use of abortives, and to improper violence in aid of accouchement. If these practices were of native origin, like effects should have sprung from like causes, and these islands would have been depopulated long since; and if of modern introduction, it becomes a rational and just inquiry before indulging in harsh censure, how far may the teachings of strong-minded women of our day, and of itinerant lecturers to ladies exclusively, on the laws of life and reproduction, and their regulation, have been deemed worthy of propagation among the heathen, with the other articles of faith and practice taught by zealous disciples of the school of progress? It will scarcely be admitted by any one who has witnessed the rapid revolutions of the "hub of the universe" and its radiating spokes, that Hawaii has travelled faster than New England. The schoolmaster is proclaimed to be abroad, and the schoolmistress, too, and it is boastfully asked who furnishes them? None will deny "By their works ye shall know them." Anatomy is no longer a mystery; the hand of maiden modesty, forgetful of the primal law, lifts the veil of its nakedness, that by the familiar use of virtue it may become fashioned into nature itself. Alas! for the purity of virtue taught in the school of a model artist. Physiological law, too, has become common law, so that physicians, still clinging to the ancient ethics of their profession, are often made to blush from indignant shame, at questions repugnant alike to delicacy and morals; and yet, with the possession of forbidden knowledge, America shows no sign of becoming childless.

The above charges against the Hawaiians, as a nation, I have the authority of many fair-minded foreign residents for saying are slanders, whatever individual exceptions, as in the case of others, may have occurred to give color to them. There are other causes in operation to produce barrenness, diminish births, and hurry prematurely to the grave those who are born, about which intelligent resident physicians agree. The most common among these is that scourge of lust, to which the islanders were strangers until introduced among them by the pioneers of civilization, as if to clear a path for the readier ingress of another race; and which, in their ignorance of remedies, cursed them, and has continued to curse their children's children to the present generation, sapping the foundations of health, poisoning the fountains of procreation, and interrupting its processes if begun. Along with this may be mentioned, as destructive of infantile life, the prevalence of epidemics formerly unknown in the islands, or of which there are no traditions; a growing disregard of the preservative instincts of race, under a conviction of increasing national degradation and subjection to foreign impositions; and a want of suitable hygienic and strictly medical provision, against the ravages of diseases brought to their shores by others, and of which they have no knowledge. Hence it is unjust to cast upon these hapless people reproaches, due rather to the self-righteous intruders among them, always prone to "behold the mote in their brother's eye, but consider not the beam in their own."

Our deck-passenger companions of voyage are natives, and the majority of these are loafers, who having realized a dollar—the unvarying fare, for such freight—by the sale of pig or poultry which has grown to their hand without the labor of production, spend it in the habitual luxury of idleness, or of passive motion, calculating upon unbought fish and poi enough to preserve animal existence, when landed at the end of their money's worth of travel. These are literally *deck*-passengers, and have none of the comforts or conveniences furnished for such on the California steamers. The deck is their bench, board, and bed; on it they sit, eat, and sleep. Small is the spot allotted to those who pay the cabin fare of eight dollars from Lahaina to Hilo, certainly not large enough to "turn your partner." Calabashes of food and water, with a miscellaneous mixture of humanity, a few flashily bedizzened with ribbons and bugles, others prouder of natural charms, monopolized the remainder of the deck so entirely that the hand-rail was the bridge of transit fore and aft.

Coasting along the southern shore of the island of Maui we soon passed from under the lee of the western highlands, and across the mouth of the watery inlet that nearly divides the low hour-glass contraction of the middle of the island, which unites the smaller west district to the larger, known as East Maui. As the mariner hugs the southern shore of East Maui, he again finds the mountains shutting off the northeast trade-wind, and placing him, when without the aid of steam, at the mercy of calms, currents, and swells. And here, if weather-bound, the impoverished looking little village of *Ulupalakua* will receive him, off which the steamer stops to land passengers destined for that neighborhood and for the remarkable volcanic mountain *Haleakala*—house of the sun—seen rising behind and above the village to the height of ten thousand two hundred feet; its extinct crater having a circumference of nearly thirty-five miles, holding within its concavity of two thousand seven hundred feet depth, cones of scoriæ from five hundred to six hundred feet high, and in it London might be buried entire, while St. Paul's steeple would dwindle into insignificance.

Passing Ulupalakua and leaving the rocky islet of Molokini to the southwest, and farther off in the same direction the island of Kahoolawe, used as a sheep and goat range by the present worthy chancellor of the kingdom, we bore away southeasterly across the channel between the islands of Maui and Hawaii. This may be considered the Pacific counterpart of the English channel. The northeast trades blowing between these islands as through a funnel, and glancing from their respective highlands, becoming fitful and baffling, aided by changeful currents and a swaggering swell for which these passages are noted, cause short chop seas, rough and boxing, well calculated to test the powers of endurance of even veteran seamen. The right kind of a sea and the right kind of a craft, are the necessary provocatives of sea-sickness, and one is apt to find them after long seeking. Our captain said that many an "old salt" who had belted the globe, finally paid tribute to Neptune in passing this part of his dominion in our jumping Jenny of a steamer, which is always out of time to the ocean polka, and keeps bobbing up and down like a fishing-cork in a wind ripple; and twisting, wriggling, and rolling, in incalculable variations. But for the mildness of the climate this interinsular navigation would be attended with great hardships to seamen compelled to keep the deck on sailing vessels. Storm, sleet, and snow, would be cheerless accompaniments to the roughness and delay in beating about these channels.

Closing in under the lee of Hawaii we coasted its west shore southerly twenty miles more pleasantly, and by moonlight entered the little bay of *Kawaihae*, to land freight and passengers at a town of the same name. It was a rare picture presented by the nearly full moon peering from behind a fleecy cloud, like beauty from its silvery veil tossed aside by the capricious breeze, and crowning with softened effulgence the summit of *Mauna Hualalai* in the background, lifted ten thousand feet to meet the radiant gift. While scattered lights of the villagers, who were startled by the shrill signal of the steamer, threw their long rays upon the shaded shore-bound waters, as if in rivalry of the moonlit billows in the clear offing, that danced in pride and joy of the sublimity that looked down upon them.

Returning on our track during the night, we found ourselves at sunrise next moring doubling Kohala Point—the north cape of Hawaii—and having landed some of the live cargo at the town of Honoipu, the steamer bore away east by south with the island full in view, grass huts, and stone-enclosed patches of land rarely under cultivation, being seen bordering the rocky beach; but beyond, the country is without houses, and shows none of the usual signs of agriculture. Stone landmarks and walls, and dilapidated foundations of houses, were seen with a good glass, far inland; but the once numerous inhabitants have disappeared before, what, paradoxical as it may seem to us now, truth requires should be acknowledged as the *desolation of civilization;* but which a more enlightened, pure, and merciful, a less selfish and pharisaical future, will probably regard as proof of a *barbarism*, more fruitful of evil to its unhappy victims than that under which they increased and multiplied. The population of these islands, estimated by Captain Cook in 1779 at four hundred thousand, and corroborated by other voyagers, the accounts of old natives and the indications of the country, was found, by the census of 1860, to have been reduced to sixty-nine thousand eight hundred. And even if the opinion of the American historian of the Hawaiian Islands be correct, that the estimate of their discoverer was "vague," and that one of "three hundred thousand would have been nearer to the truth," still the ravages of contact with so-called civilization, have been well calculated to check further self-glorification, and teach a lesson of humility; especially in view of the fact, that extraordinary missionary efforts from the year 1820, when the population was computed to be at least two hundred thousand, have not contributed to arrest the withering blight of an arrogant, but pernicious and false philanthropy, stimulated rather by lust of conquest, power, and profit, than by a disinterested love of fellow-men, and fast hurrying the Hawaiians to destruction.

It seems to be overlooked that the duty of uprooting heathenism does not require an extermination of the heathen. Neither is it imperative, nor the most successful means of inculcating religious truth, intolerantly to denounce and tyrannically prohibit usages not incompatible with it, indeed harmless in themselves, interwoven with national existence, adapted to the simple nature of the people, and contributing to their happiness and perpetuity. The severity of discipline of the Puritan, in domestic and social life, and his rigid exactions of conformity to a harsh and repugnant religionism, made up of a formulary of long prayers and long faces, and an austere inculcation of unending penalties, have not assured the holiness of those who have drunk deepest of their bitter waters. How then can the stranger, even of a false faith, be expected to draw from such a Dead Sea creed and practice the precious draught of eternal life? Better, far better for him, had the professed disciples of a new dispensation borne in mind the divine precept—"neither circumcision availeth any thing, nor uncircumcision, but faith *which worketh by love.*"

It is by no means a pleasant duty to condemn the acts of American missionaries, especially in view of the favorable opinion generally entertained at home of their labors, founded of course mainly upon their own representations, promulged in every form of speech and publications, by their sectarian partisans; accompanied, too, at times by a fulsome adulation as violative of good taste, as it is detrimental to their cause in the estimation of people of good sense.

The gentleness, kindness, charity, and excellent judgment, as well as purity of life, of some of these laborers, and the unquestionably upright motives of action of others of less moderation and prudence, should not preclude the expression of a candid opinion as to the general means and agents of regeneration, formed from visible results, and from views entertained by many impartial observers long resident in the islands. The interest felt by all philanthropists in the spread of truth and knowledge, as means of promoting the welfare of mankind, demands that nothing should be withheld calculated to enlighten the public mind as to the enterprises undertaken for these objects. It is impossible to witness without condemnation the ecclesiastical domination extensively exercised over the natives; the virtual bondage in which these are held by those whose professed object it is to confer benefits. To *confer* benefits! Aye—but *not* "without money and without price." For which "tithes of mint, anise, and cummin" are *exacted*, while "the weightier matters of law, judgment, *mercy, and faith*"—the faith of the Apostle "shown by works"—are omitted. It is a violation of the plainest dictates of humanity, and assuredly of the precepts of Christianity, to levy and importunately collect, a tax on the paltry production, or pittance, of the poor native, for purposes of selfish display or accumulation. Yet such is the usage of some missionaries, though under cover of a motive designed to sanctify the deed. The natives often express disbelief in the sincerity and benefit of any scheme for their improvement, associated with such acts. And they sometimes shrewdly suggest, that the contributions professedly exacted of them "for the spread of the gospel and the love of God," much more frequently spread the missionary's table with luxuries, and gratify his love of a fine house and showy furniture; while the poor natives *are taught* to partake of their primitive poi, and repose on the ground floor of their grass hut, and to offer thanks morning and evening in "long prayers," and "vain repetitions as the heathens do," *for these merciful dispensations.* Verily might they be pardoned if, from sad experience, the victims of such hypocrisy, feeling the necessity of divine interposition, also prayed that they might "Beware of false prophets, which come in sheep's clothing, but inwardly are ravening wolves."

A perversion of truth is unhappily not an unusual resort of those who seek to magnify their works, and obtain an influence and reward transcending desert. The Hawaiian islands, from their remoteness from the great centres of observation and knowledge, have afforded a ready theatre for mystery and misrepresentation in religious matters. A common error pervades the public mind of America—how propagated it might seem invidious to suggest—that the suppression of human sacrifices, the taboo (a priestly interdict), and idolatry, among the Hawaiians, is due to the labors of missionaries. While it would be unjust to detract from any deserved praise of others, it would be equally wrong to strengthen a delusion having its origin in a selfishness unbecoming the professed objects of the missionary enterprise, and calculated to mislead the humane in future undertakings, at the same time that it would contribute to the withholding from an unfortunate people the credit to which they are entitled, for a bold and spontaneous movement to arrest the cruelties and superstitions of barbarism, and lift themselves from degradations in which a priestly government, cunningly devised and despotically enforced, had sunk them.

It is a fact of historical record, universally accepted, that the missionaries did not arrive in Hawaii until March, 1820. The great King Kamehameha died nearly a year before that time. It is also matter of history that although he continued through his reign his devotions to idols, yet he "acknowledged their worthlessness, and doubtless viewed the system as a powerful engine of government, *more of politics than piety mingling in his later views*." It is further stated that "toward the latter period of his reign, a general laxness in regard to the taboos began to prevail," and that "in lieu of human victims, a sacrifice of three hundred dogs attended his obsequies." What shook his faith in the religion of his ancestors is unknown. Whether some faint tradition of centuries, telling of shipwrecked strangers who worshipped an unseen God, and of which present historians profess to have traced some probabilities; or some word dropped, or look or sign carelessly made by still later transient but profane visitors of the coast was told to him, and thus put in motion the secret springs of a mind of great activity and power, as shown by the achievements of his reign; or some inherent and mysterious agency of thought or spirit startled conviction, and shook the foundations of the false faith in which he had been educated, it cannot be doubted, in view of well-established facts, that the light of truth had dawned upon him, although the required policy of government, as illustrated by the history of more enlightened nations, veiled it from general recognition.

And these views are supported by subsequent events, for we find that those who it is reasonable to suppose received their first impressions, if not their matured opinions from him, his queens and his son Liholiho, who succeeded to the throne after the death of Kamehameha, acted more defiantly of priestcraft, and after a temporary hesitation on the part of the son, boldly renounced pagan ceremonies. Kaahumanu, the favorite queen of the deceased sovereign, in November, 1819, cast aside the idol of the new king, Liholiho making no objection; and subsequently the latter deliberately violated the sacred interdict which forbade the sexes feasting together, by seating himself at the table of the female chiefs, partaking of their food, and directing them to do likewise. Mr. Jarves, in his History of the Hawaiian Islands, gives the following description of what ensued: "The highest had set an example which all rejoiced to follow. The joyful shout arose, 'the taboo is broken! the taboo is broken!' Feasts were provided for all, at which both sexes indiscriminately indulged. Orders were issued to demolish the heiaus, and destroy the idols; temples, images, sacred property, and the relics of ages were consumed in the flames. The high priest, Hewahewa, having resigned his office, was the first to apply the torch. Without his coöperation the attempt to destroy the old system would have been ineffectual. Numbers of his profession, joining in the enthusiasm, followed his example. Kaumualii having given his sanction, idolatry was forever abolished by law, and the smoke of heathen sanctuaries arose from Hawaii to Kauai. All the islands uniting in a jubilee at their deliverance, presented the singular spectacle of a nation without a religion."

Such was the reformation begun and in progress in Hawaii, when on the 20th of the following March, 1820, the first missionaries arrived; and the historian proceeds to say further that "the cheering intelligence of the abolition of idolatry, and the favorable condition of the native for the reception of a new religion, reached them that evening. Hewahewa (the chief priest) was cordial in his welcome to his '*brother priests*,' as he called them. He possessed an uncommon liberality of mind; *five months before* he had counselled the king to destroy the idols, publicly renounced heathenism himself, and acknowledged his belief in one Supreme Being, and said that he knew 'that the wooden images of our deities, carved by our own hands, were incapable of supplying our wants, but I worshipped them because it was the custom of our fathers; they made not the *kalo* to grow, nor sent us rain; neither did they bestow life or health. My thought has always been—Akahi waleno Akua—nui iloka o kalani—*there is one only Great God dwelling in the heavens.*'" In the far-off islands of the sea this Hawaiian priest believed with the prophet Jeremiah, "that the Lord is the true God, he is the living God, and an everlasting King." And that "the gods that have not made the heavens and the earth, even they shall perish from the earth and from under these heavens." Thus, through Christian testimony, is traced the downfall of heathenism in Hawaii, by an *inherent* power of reformation. What the great chieftain failed fully to accomplish himself, the surviving inspirations of his spirit did, through the will of his son, sustained by the faith and devotion of woman, to whom the world has often been indebted for the success of reformations, and aided by the prophetic counsel and countenance of one of the purest representatives of priesthood, from whose life many of our day might take lessons of disinterested goodness; one who, surrendering an almost unlimited power with the paganism thus prostrated, and without the aid of that preaching which was "to the Greeks foolishness," laid hold of the great truth that confounded their wisdom, and set at naught their vaunted philosophy.

In the face of such facts, now becoming more extensively made known through the candid criticism of fair minded and disinterested persons, it may well excite surprise, and even bring reproach on a cause worthy of approval in itself, that the supporters and partisans of these missions should have spread abroad the error that through them Hawaiian paganism perished; and that the special agents of the trust should have disingenuously countenanced, by a failure to correct, the perversion of truth.

Giving to the noble Hawaiians already mentioned, and to those official natives who coöperated with them, the exalted praise which is their due, for having stricken down the heathen rites of idolatry, human sacrifice, and the taboo, and which, by the Government machinery of centralized power, they could effectually and speedily do, the most that can be claimed for the missionaries, is their subsequent aid in trampling the ruins in the dust, and giving direction to the future religious belief of the people. And surely this might have been deemed sufficient honor, if the latter duty had been wisely and faithfully performed, in strict fulfilment of the Divine commands they professed to obey, and the righteous precepts it was their duty to teach. How far their practice conformed to the obligations of their religious profession, may, in some other particulars than those already adverted to, be remarked upon hereafter. In the mean time the opinion may be expressed, that if, apart from the cardinal truths of religion, which cannot be moulded to suit the diversities of man, the missionaries had adapted their system of moral training, duty, relations, and pursuits, more in consonance with the simple minds, amiable disposition, passive nature, and innocent pastimes of the natives; and if they had labored more assiduously and successfully to control their own countrymen who visited the islands for commercial and maritime purposes, and used the arts, the power, and the resources of a superior race to gratify an infamous licentiousness; and who sought by every mode of craft and corruption to cherish and strengthen their own idolatry of the almighty dollar, as repugnant in its practices and damning in its effects as that abolished idolatry of heathenism, the fall of which was hailed by the shouts of applauding millions: if such had been the aims of missionary effort, happier results, it is believed by many foreigners resident in the islands, would have been secured than can now be rightfully claimed.

It might be well to consider if Christianity and civilization ought not to be regarded as convertible terms—expressive of personal purity and a righteous performance of duty here, contemplating a hereafter of endless joy and exalted being. If this be conceded, and the deeds of the latter conform to the known precepts of the former, we cannot fail to recognize the "law of love which worketh no ill to his neighbor," and the observance of which the Divine Author of the Christian religion proclaimed to be an essential of goodness and celestial approval, as the sole and imperative rule of action, in shaping the destiny of those over whom the modern spirit of progress has usurped control.

Having passed the district of Kohala, that of Hamakua, to

the southeast, presented a seashore bluff of black, brown, and gray laminated lava rock, appearing porous, and washed into caverns by the incessant beating of the waves. And still further in the last-named district the coast is faced by a rock of more uniform dark color, cf from one thousand to two thousand feet perpendicular height, looking like an iron barrier against which the huge swells rolled and broke, flinging their spray high into the air to meet tiny waterfalls leaping from their dizzy heights, and seeming like silver threads pencilled on the rocky wall. At Waipio one of these picturesque cascades springs from a height of fifteen hundred feet, back to the maternal bosom of the sea, from which in mantling clouds it had been borne on the wings of the wind, to bathe with genial showers the hoary brow of Mauna Kea, and break the silence of shadowy solitudes that clothe his rugged sides, with murmuring melody or shouts of joy, as on it hurries to join again the revelry of winds and waves.

At the foot of a steep bluff which divides the outlet of Waipio valley into two parts, a *large, towered* missionary church has been erected for the accommodation, I am told, of twenty to twenty-five families living in the valley ; and on the upper level about three miles further to the southeast, is seen another towered church, with but three houses between the two, and none beyond the last church that a good telescope revealed. What these two churches have been built there for is beyond rational conjecture, unless, indeed, as telegraphs, to notify the passing voyager that the missionary is abroad; certainly a sufficiently well-attested fact at home, both by pulpit and press, as also by the ceaseless calls for contributions in aid of missions in foreign parts, which many now think would be better appropriated in converting the citizen heathens of our own country. When it is considered that this sparsely-populated district of Hamakua—one of the six into which the island of Hawaii is divided—has thirteen churches, it will probably be thought by many a poor widow and shoeless child, who gave their hard-earned pittance for "the spread of the Gospel among the heathens of the Sandwich Islands," that these islanders have been superabundantly supplied with the means of grace, and that it will in future be wiser to be more gracious to themselves, and not allow either a one-idea fanaticism, or the specious appeals of self-interest, to make them miserable about the "lost souls" of those who, there are reasons for believing, were happier, and better too, before than since intruders came among them, to introduce diseases from which they had never suffered, vices of which they were ignorant, and discontent with a form of governmental landed proprietorship, adapted to their wants and parental in its character, and which taught them by precept and example a provident industry, and not to fail to prepare for the wants of to-morrow by planting to-day. The indifference to cultivating the soil, the innumerable neglected taro patches, and abandonment of cocoanut-tree planting, prove how unwise was the policy hastily introduced and pressed to adoption by foreigners, of releasing an unprepared people from the influence and control of their higher chiefs, and handing them over to listlessness and indolence; or to a dependence on the chances of subsistence resulting from traffic with or employment by whalers, who have for some years found it to their interest to resort to these islands, but who may at any time for a like reason forsake them, convenience or gain attracting them elsewhere. Indeed, the strange disappearance of whales from former fishing regions, and the great facilities offered to shippers to seek the great Pacific port of San Francisco, are already operating unfavorably on the whaling interests of the Hawaiian Islands. It is not every change that brings improvement; nor are the usages, the modes of control, and reforms of one race of mankind always adapted to another of different nature and capacities. It would have been wiser, then, if the few foreigners had duly weighed these truths, and also that it was the good of the many, the natives, which deserved the first consideration, and was to be most materially affected by proposed changes. Experiments involving a total revolution of government and morals, and the relations of mankind subject to these, having no support of experience, are of doubtful propriety. But when these come of speculations at variance with the distinctions of nature, and violative of laws enacted by her, they prove not merely hazardous, but sooner or later disastrous in their results. The fate of the Hawaiians will probably exemplify the correctness of this position.

Steering more southerly along the coast of the district of Hilo during the evening, at midnight we doubled Makakanaloa Point, and again changed our course to the south-southwest, passing up *Waiakea Bay*, in extent from the point above named on the north, to Leleiwi Point on the south, twelve miles, and from the line of these points on the east to the head of the bay westwardly, eight miles. It was to this bay, known and called by the celebrated Vancouver, as by the natives before him, *Waiakea—broad water*—that the less appropriate personal name of the English navigator Capt. *Byron* was given, on the occasion of his subsequent visit to it in the British frigate "Blonde." This is a cheap custom of transmitting one's name, in the absence of any deed deserving remembrance; and many a humble headland, hill, and rivulet would be "more honored in the breach than in the observance" of it, especially by English and American explorers, who have a ridiculous fancy thus to apply their unmeaning "harsh, hissing, grunting, guttural" cognomens, even to the suppression often of native appellations, both expressive and euphonious.

A submerged coral reef extends from Cocoanut Island on the south, to within half a mile of the north side of the bay, leaving a passage of that width for vessels of the greatest draught; and there is within the reef a harbor of one and a quarter by two miles in extent, in which ships of any size may ride at anchor in perfect security. On the west side of this harbor stands the town of *Hilo*, and on the south the little village of Waiakea, a crescentic beach bordering and lying between them, on which the breaking surf looks in the distance like a fringe of frosted silver.

The quaint-looking thatched houses, with others more modern and of tasteful design, having ample grounds and gardens, rise above each other on an inclined plane on which Hilo stands, embowered in tropical shrubbery and trees. Among the latter are the broad-leaved banana and the deep-shaded bread-fruit, above which the tall cocoanut waves its graceful branches, welcoming, as I looked on the beautiful picture, the first coming of the sweet sea-breeze of the morning, whose genial breath cheered the chilled bud, and gave brighter bloom to the blossom, rudely shaken by the cool night wind from the mountains. Hilo is the gem of Hawaii, and sublime is the surrounding in which it is set, when at early dawn the coming voyager looks above and beyond it, his eye resting on the majestic *Mauna Kea*, thirty-five miles to the north of west, raising upward, 13,953 feet, its bold turrets defiant of storm, and its proud pinnacles seeming to pierce the lightning's dwelling-place. And when, turning to the south of west, he beholds the surpassing dome of *Mauna Loa*, sixty miles distant, and having a base diameter of like extent, rising in grandeur to a height of 13,760 feet, illumined by the coming sun yet below the horizon; while hills and valleys are unrolled beneath, clad in verdure of darker and richer hue, from the shadow in which they still repose.

It stands,
A mighty mount—transcendently sublime.
The very sun, as though he worshipp'd there,
In homage lingers on its dome of snow,
Gilding the radiant roof as if with gold;
And through its strangely column'd corridors,
And o'er its vast volcanic capitals,
Shedding the glory of his tropic beams.
An everlasting temple, thus it seems,
Lifted above the shadowy earth, that spreads
Before its still unfinished porticoes
An emerald carpet for its worshippers.

And long and clear will also remain the remembrance of Mauna Kea's surpassing majesty, when, shortly after the sun had risen above the sea, gathering clouds from the northeast came rolling by, and the grand old mountain in stately sovereignty folded them as a mantle about his brawny shoulders, and lifted his cold brow above, bound with snow and ice, that gleamed in the golden sunlight like a burnished coronet.

From witnessing the grandeur of creation, to thoughts of the Power of the Creator, is a natural transition; and from emotions incident to a human appreciation of these, I was startled by the summons to go ashore. Passing from the anchorage to

HILO.—MAUNA KEA.—MAUNA LOA.

p. 554.

the beach in a shore-boat, I was borne through the surf on a native's shoulders, the Hawaiian Government having left Hilo without wharf or mole; and the town not yet tolerating a hotel as a practical reflection on its hospitality, I was taken in charge by Captain T. Spencer, an American resident, on whose generosity I can safely trust for pardon for this mention of him; and who is the impersonation of outspoken opinion, commercial enterprise, and belief in the "manifest destiny" of a country he will not forswear for local advantages of Hawaiian allegiance, as some Americans have done of more noisy and intolerant patriotism.

## CHAPTER XXXV.

TEMPERATURE—AGRICULTURAL PRODUCTIONS OF HAWAII—MISSIONARY INTERMEDDLING IN POLITICAL AFFAIRS—RECORD OF PURITANISM—MISSIONARY INTOLERANCE AND PERSECUTION.

OCCUPYING a commanding site with extensive grounds on the principal avenue of the town, the hospitable residence of which I became unexpectedly a guest, was found replete with comforts and luxuries. A bath of extent and depth for swimming, to which a mountain stream brings its crystal tribute, and verandahs, on which the refreshing sea-breeze never cease to blow, except to rest when cooler airs from the snowy heights of Mauna Kea come down at night to brace the nerve of sleep, make weariness a name, and cause forgetfulness of being in a tropical climate. My examination of a carefully kept thermometrical record showed 81° Fahrenheit to have been the highest temperature of the year in this latitude of 19° 42′, while 55° marked the lowest temperature of several years, that of a well-remembered and exceptional cold day; thus, embracing this altogether unusual low temperature, the thermometrical range has been but 26°. In speaking of the climates of Honolulu and Lahaina, statements were given of the diversities of *mean* temperature at those places respectively. That a comparison of temperature may be fairly made, it is necessary to add that the observations of Dr. Rooke showed the *maximum* temperature of one year at Honolulu to have been 86° and the *minimum* 62°, the variation being 24°; and at Lahaina a meteorological journal of the Rev. Mr. Baldwin gave for a like period 87° as the *maximum* and 61° as the *minimum* temperature—variation 26°. Thus it is seen that while the absolute *extreme variation* of temperature is precisely alike at Hilo and Lahaina, that at Honolulu is set down at 2° less—a difference undeserving of consideration as affecting the question of comparative advantage for invalids. The Pali hurricanes which sometimes reach the last-named city, causing more sudden vicissitudes, are certainly to be regarded as of greater importance; and the quantity and frequency of rain throughout the year at Hilo may make a residence at Honolulu and Lahaina more desirable, at least to the extent that this fact may bear upon the particular case. But in some other respects, and especially for surpassing loveliness of nature, Hilo and its vicinity are without a rival in these islands. Verdure is the unchanging mantle of earth—green of endless shades, in grass, shrub, vine, and tree, the chief adornment, gemmed with flowers of richest hues.

A ride through the adjacent country reveals the bread fruit, bananas of the Hawaiian, Tahitian, and choice Chinese species; the orange, lime, pineapple, cocoanut, and guava, taro and arrowroot, and also the coffee-tree and sugar-cane.

The coffee-tree, apparently hopelessly destroyed in these islands by a blight which first appeared in 1857, and which the Hon. R. C. Wyllie, Minister of Foreign Affairs, expressed to me an apprehension would not recover, it was gratifying to find on my arrival at the island of Hawaii, was presenting in many instances a vigorous growth and an abundant crop of berries, with no sign of the insect producing it, which had suddenly made its appearance. A very intelligent physician and naturalist, Dr. Hillebrand, of Oahu, remarked to me that it was probable an antagonist and more powerful insect would appear and prey upon and destroy the present insect causing the blight. This is not an uncommon experience of botanists, and there are indications that it may be realized on this island. The Hawaiian coffee has a fine flavor, by some thought to rival that of Mocha, and to be inferior only to the Yungai coffee of Bolivia. Its successful cultivation would add greatly to the wealth of this kingdom.

The sugar-cane is of sure, rapid, and rich growth, eight and nine years being here the limit of its productiveness; a longer time, however, it is said, than on the other islands of the group.

There are four sugar estates on Hawaii, seven on Maui, and three on Kauai, producing nearly five thousand tons of sugar annually, of the finest quality, for home consumption and the California market. Large tracts of land suitable for sugar-cane planting are to be had on this island at from two to five dollars per acre. Some of these are convenient of access to the port of Hilo, a consideration of much importance in a country where good roads, it might almost be said with truth roads of any kind, are a great desideratum. Some of the most fortunate adventurers in this branch of industry are Chinese. It may be that their success is due to the greater facility with which they can obtain laborers from among their own countrymen. The difficulty of securing certain and reliable labor has no doubt deterred others from engaging in the business.

The district of Hilo is the most fertile of this island, and best adapted to the growth of sugar-cane, and the northern part of the district, that above the Wailuku River, surpasses the southern in both depth and richness of soil. This river appears to have been the limit of the later volcanic eruptions from Mauna Loa, which on the eastern side of the island appear not to have passed north of its bed. While the slumbering, or perhaps extinct volcanic action of Mauna Kea, has left that region of country, north of the river, long undisturbed; subject only to the changes of surface incident to decomposition and vegetable growth and decay, creating and ripening a virgin soil, which may be irrigated to any desirable extent by descending mountain streams, and which requires but the application of skill and industry to produce remarkable results in any branch of agriculture. If the primitive habits of the natives must be abolished, and their inclinations constrained, it is experienced and scientific representatives of labor that are most needed. This kingdom is dotted all over with *officials of foreign birth*—legislative, ministerial, judicial, magisterial—indeed generally administrative. But, for the good of the country, *for every one such* in the service of the Government, there should be *one hundred* well informed and faithful *laborers*, engaged in developing the agricultural resources, not in consuming its vitality, its capital and its credit, and endangering its hypothecation to the world's banker, to whom a Pacific may be as desirable as an Atlantic Bermuda, for money to defray the expenses of a government transcending its receipts: laborers to set the poor natives, now subjected to an irresistible revolution, an example of industry and practical morality, and to teach them how to avert threatened ruin.

Besides the production of sugar and coffee, of large crops of potatoes, both sweet and Irish, and of nearly all the garden vegetables grown in the United States, I have seen cotton of excellent staple growing wild and neglected; and responding to indifferent cultivation, choice wheat, tobacco of approved quality, and an experimental crop of rice that would have been considered satisfactory in Carolina or China.

As to the grasses, their luxuriant and perennial growth on this island, and also a genial climate, are shown by the fact that cattle and sheep brought here by Vancouver and other navigators in the latter part of the last century, multiplied so greatly as to have become valueless except for hides and tallow, and running wild and without ownership, were lassoed and slaughtered by thousands to supply the California demand incident to its recent great immigration.

The town of Hilo has a population of about one thousand. It has two churches, occupying commanding positions, and rivalling each other in size and display of towers; these form the showy architectural features of the town when approaching it from the sea. They both sprang from missionary enterprises, the one being Catholic, the other Protestant; but from the manifestations of sectarian animosities, it would seem as if the Christian duty of charity and brotherly love had not been duly inculcated therein. I have heard a theological controversy between two excited parties of natives on the street, in which warlike, if not convincing words, were freely bandied; and fearing that something harder and more effective in ending the dispute might follow, I speedily placed myself beyond the reach of knock-down arguments. Such disgraceful scenes result from the too common intolerance and denunciation of the pulpit, shamefully perverted from its sacred trust to the engendering and stimulating of prejudices and passions in the ignorant and deluded people, who come to "gather grapes" but are given "thorns;" to pluck "figs," but find "thistles."

How far antichristian lessons were taught, and to what extent missionary intermeddling with the affairs of political government in these islands once existed, are questions so intimately connected with the propagation of the Gospel, and with a just exercise of human rights and the prevalence of free principles, as to deserve some notice from one not interested in propagating erroneous statements. Next to the grain of mustard seed of civilization, presumed rather than proved to have been planted in Hawaii through a Spanish shipwreck, the germ of which is supposed to have been strengthened by the subsequent discovery of Cook, and occasional visits of commerce and curiosity, came the first systematic attempt of the American missionaries to Christianize the islanders. Their movement was regarded with great interest, general civilization and commerce anticipating good results from it, and America especially contemplating a further extension of liberal and elevating principles of self-government, as a natural consequence to follow the benign influence of a true Christianity. The Foreign Secretary of the American Board of Commissioners for Foreign Missions favors this view by saying that "the Protestant community on these islands is responsible for *self-government* in all matters of the church, as well as in all matters of the State. It should be held to this." * The establishment of enlightened views of government, conformable to those of the political constitution of their own country, depended in part upon the faithful administration by the missionaries of their special trust, as assuredly did the bestowal of religious truth, for which the natives were awaiting, having, as already shown, on their own motion deposed the idolatry of their fathers.

True, it was not appropriate for the missionaries to interfere in political government, and they were expressly instructed by their superiors in authority to "withhold themselves entirely from all interference and intermeddling with the political affairs

* The Hawaiian Islands, under missionary labors, by Rufus Anderson, D. D. Boston, 1864.

and party concerns of the nation," and from following, as the historian of the Hawaiian Islands has pointedly expressed it, "the example of the Jesuits, and creating at once a church and state." Adopting an opinion of Mr. Jarves, who, however, it is to be regretted for the sake of his own reputation, too often sinks the historian in the partisan advocate of the missionaries, but from whose pages, nevertheless, I shall draw material facts, although our conclusions will sometimes differ widely, it must be admitted that the prohibition of the missionaries from intermeddling in political affairs "was a good rule." Yet if we were disposed to grant their obedience to this instruction, they must still be held accountable for any injury sustained by sound political principles and practice, resulting from a *failure to inculcate*, both by precept and example, *the Divine lessons of the Founder of the Christian religion*, the observance of the rules of *justice* and *love*, instead of that *hatred and all uncharitableness* which are as fruitful sources of *political* as of *social evil.*

But did not the missionaries commit political sins as well as omit religious duties? Authentic records declare that the principal rulers of the islanders "were favorers of the mission and converts to Christianity." That the Queen Regent Kaahumanu, "in the days of her heathenism, a cruel, haughty, and imperious woman—the glance of whose angry eye carried terror to all her obsequious and crouching vassals, not a subject, however high his station, daring to face her frown," became a convert to the new faith, and "warmly attached to the missionaries, the same activity and firmness which were infused into all her former acts being manifested in her subsequent government. That the machinery of the old system, which centred all power in the hands of the chiefs, in whom it may with propriety be said the nation was individualized, was brought to aid in the moral reform. The will of the rulers being the will of the populace, the revolution that followed was not surprising." To this startling account of despotic machinery the historian adds, "The rulers had providentially become Christian," a sufficient consideration it would appear in his judgment to justify the extreme exercise of tyrannical power; and he then further states, what must certainly be regarded as an unfortunate commentary on his text, though announcing a very natural result of such an antecedent, "its pure (Christian) doctrines were manifested in the lives of *a few* of all degrees, but with *the mass it was an external habit, like the clothes borrowed from civilization.*" Nor is it wonderful that the missionaries were led from such data to exaggerate the moral revolution they presumed they had inaugurated; and that they misunderstood what they supposed was the "perceptible influence of Christianity upon the acts of the Government, and *the character of the nation.*"

About four years after the arrival of the missionaries a charge was made against them of meddling in governmental matters—a charge sustained by the general opinion of foreign residents expressed in my hearing, and of which the historian of the Hawaiian Islands says, "so far as their influence affected the chiefs *this was true.* That they gave advice in emergencies when asked, is evident from the humane influence they exerted, and the encouragement they afforded the loyal chiefs in the late rebellion at Kauai." Although even this unsophisticated apologist of most of their acts, condemning them for calculating timidity and two-faced-ness, states that "*they were not always sufficiently frank and open in it,* and shrunk unnecessarily from encountering boldly the opposition when their assistance would have been serviceable to the chiefs, or they rendered it in too cautious and *noncommittal a manner* for it to avail much at a crisis, though *it effected much in the general issue.*"

The historian proceeds further in proof of the political association of priests and people, although he strangely, and, as we think, ungenerously charges the illiterate and simple-minded authorities with the errors of execution—"in the early stage of their career the strong attachment of the rulers for their teachers, *and the inseparable policy of the Government with the religion it fostered,* caused its precepts to be felt in *every political movement; the missionaries were truly and rightfully the active causes.* No more positive proof exists of the hold which the mission was acquiring in the affections of the Government, than the aid furnished in furtherance of their views. So far as the missionaries were faithful to their cause they *became identified with Government;* for it was only to them, and the transient visitors of intelligence at the islands, that the chiefs could safely apply for disinterested advice." And again, in detailing the proceedings of a general council at which it was proposed to reduce certain gubernatorial edicts into a national code, it is stated that "two years before, an attempt had been made to introduce a municipal code of a similar character. The regents had invited some of the *missionaries to be present at the council at which the several clauses* were to be discussed."

With such evidences of intermeddling in the affairs of Government by the American missionaries, furnished by a historian prone to strain criticism, if not historical accuracy, to a partial judgment of their acts, it is not surprising that a general discontent should have arisen among foreign residents who thought their proceedings at variance with the professed objects of a religious enterprise, calculated to mar the benevolent designs of its originators and patrons, and to convert it into a machine for the accomplishment of selfish, fanatical, and unhallowed purposes. And it was reasonable to expect that English, French, and American resident officials, with such facts patent to them, would unite with others in an expression of disapprobation; and as was the case, even to manifest a spirit of antagonism to a cause, the professed agents of which were engaged in procedures determining a governmental policy and purposes greatly to be deprecated.

Nor should such opposition have been regarded by the advocates of a two-fold missionary scheme—political and religious—as a "wholesale condemnation of creed or sect," as has been said. Differences of opinion as to the expediency of measures may be honestly entertained; and a belief in personal incompetency, in errors of judgment and practice, does not justify a charge of infidelity, or denominational hostility.

But how stands the question with reference to the other side? Are the missionaries free from the attaint of intolerance and persecution? Has their conduct presented an example of consistent profession and practice? Have their lives illustrated a benign Christianity? That they were sent to establish; and to do which the secretary for Foreign Missions says, more than one million of dollars have been expended, while, by the testimony of one of their most eloquent friends, "in the course of six years preaching he had admitted but a single individual into the church"—so few were the *really converted and deserving.* Let us seek an answer to the questions; and in so doing we may ascertain some additional reasons for the signal failure of the scheme—as one of *absolute good*—exemplified by the above fact, and others heretofore mentioned.

The attention of the Roman Catholic Church in France was drawn to the Hawaiian Islands as a desirable field for the propagation of their faith, and in 1827 several missionary priests were despatched thither, two of whom arrived at Honolulu; and, as stated by the *historian*, in language for such an authority remarkably indicative of partisan feelings and ungoverned prejudices, "with an effrontery that showed a sad want of moral principle," insisted on remaining; although by command of the haughty and imperious Queen Regent, the favorite convert of the American missionaries, the proverbially "new and *good* Kaahumanu," an order had been given "*for their expulsion.*"

Although these missionary priests are thus charged with a "sad want of moral principle," yet the same author, and upon the same page of his book, strangely declares, that "they appear to have been men of *simple and pious habits*, desirous of effecting good in accordance with the mandates of their Church. Had they been dropped among an entirely heathen tribe, *their zeal, instructions, and purity of lives, would have won respect, and success crowned their labors.*"

And a kindly appreciation of these "simple and pious priests" appears to have been entertained at first by the American missionaries also, for it is said of them that they furnished the former "with copies of their works in the Hawaiian tongue to enable them to prosecute their studies."

But when it was found that a small congregation was gathered by the priests, who conformed to their communion, and that occasional converts were made among the natives who attended their instruction, then, as we are told, was "*strongly urged upon the Government* the impolicy of allowing the introduction of this new religion, about worshipping images, and dead men's bones, and taboo on meat." And then also, as is further and rather censoriously recorded by the historian, "some *with more zeal than propriety taught the Government* of the long and bloody persecutions of Europe, the inquisition, crusades, papal supremacy, and all the iniquities of its most corrupt age. These sunk deep into their minds, and their fears, magnified by ignorance of history, conjectured like evils for their dominions. As the proselytism of natives slowly progressed, and the Romish mission gave indications of permanency, the Protestant missionaries by force of argument, teaching, and all the influence they could lawfully employ, endeavored to arrest its progress. Sermons defending the theology of Protestants, and *attacking the dogmas of the hostile Church, were uttered from every pulpit; tracts* gave further circulation to their opinions, and *a war of discussion was commenced and actively pursued. Government lent its aid*, and *unfortunately for the principle, though necessarily for its support, Church and State were more closely united than ever*"—a sentence expressing in brief apposition as candid an admission of what all liberal minds deplore, as solemn a truth, gross a falsehood, and lamentable a consequence, as ever fell from the pen of an author. The Reverend Secretary for Foreign Missions in his book already referred to, in the face of such facts unblushingly declares that the missionaries have abstained from "interference with the political affairs of the nation." And in comparing the operations of missions he says that, certain writers have "overestimated the successes of Romish missions and their comparative power, in the same field with missions," by him designated as "of the evangelical or *Puritan stamp.*"

It would have been a praiseworthy example of Christian candor, calculated to direct more justly the action of Hawaiian rulers, if the American missionaries of that time, while telling them the faults of others, and with extravagant harangues exciting them to acts of persecution, had revealed also the frauds and violence, the bigotry, intolerance, duplicity, and shocking barbarities, practised by the *Pilgrim Puritans* from whom they sprang; whose chartered privileges—merely those of a mercantile company—were granted in the royal hope, unhappily disappointed, that their example would *win* the aborigines of New

England to the knowledge and obedience of the only true God. Such was the "royal intention and the adventurers free profession."

But it seems not to have suited their selfish purposes to make known that the worst of Romanist offences against the spirit of Christianity have been sternly imitated by Protestant fanaticism. It was not told to the islander, whose ignorance it was the profession of the missionaries to enlighten, that the Puritans clandestinely and illegally transferred a charter, to be subsequently perverted to purposes of heinous oppression and crime, in a far-off country where observation and authority could not readily reach them.*

Nothing was said of the disfranchisement of all who refused to burden their consciences with that covenant, the fell spirit of which instigated the enactment that "none should be admitted to the liberties of the commonwealth (of Massachusetts) but such as shall be members of some of the (Puritan) churches within its jurisdiction." And no matter what their material interests at stake in the community, they had no security of property or person, but became, from want of "covenant grace," a degraded caste.

The Hawaiians were not told that the criminal law of Puritanism, when popery had not yet intruded on its sanctified domain, was steeped in blood; that witchcraft, blasphemy, adultery, perjury, conspiracy, cursing or smiting, rebellion of children against parents, and such like offences—*strangely found in its holy precincts*—were deemed deserving of the same penalty affixed to the crime of murder. Even the islanders, whom it was sought to purge of heathenism, would have stood aghast at the relation of such a code, and trembled with forebodings of the sanguinary carnival which would have been inaugurated by its adoption among them. Nor did the American missionaries, in denouncing the other iniquities of popery, think the wicked insinuation worthy of notice, that a Puritan censorship of the press had been deemed necessary to the purification of "the cradle of liberty."

Neither was it told, with suitable commentaries, that whipping

* See Historical Review of the Puritan Government in Massachusetts, by Peter Oliver, Boston edition, 1856.

*even naked through the streets*—banishment, fines, imprisonment, branding, bodily mutilation by cutting off the ears and boring the tongue with a red-hot iron, the pillory, selling into slavery, and even the gallows—punishments coming of bigotry and intolerance, disgraceful to the model mission of "a Puritan stamp" were inflicted upon men *and women*, for *religious opinions*, for which they were accountable to God alone; and imposed by those, too, who claimed to have freighted the ships in which they fled from their own country to raise altars in a wilderness, with that most precious of human rights, *liberty of conscience*. The cruelties of Puritan "persecutions, inquisitions, crusades, and supremacy," would have been but a fair offset to those of European Catholicism proclaimed to the Hawaiians by the American missionaries; and certainly as appropriate a theme for pulpit denunciation. They did not sketch, even in outline, the horrors of the exterminating wars prosecuted against the rightful possessors of the soil, by those who had it ever on their lips, that theirs was the mission to "Go into all the world and *preach the gospel* to every creature." Nothing was said of the Puritan plea of Christian right "by the grand charter of God," to despoil the Indian of his forests, fields, and waters. Nothing of the sad fate of the Pequod tribe, who, as the Pilgrim Winthrop afterwards said, "had done Massachusetts no injury," and yet every warrior and old man of whom was slain, the women being distributed *as slaves*, and the male children *sold* to the Bermudas. Nothing of the cold-blooded murder of the two great Narragansett chiefs; the perfidious resolution "to blot out that tribe from existence, although the ink with which a treaty of peace had been ratified was scarcely dry," the merciless slaughter of nine hundred warriors even when defence of their homes and their lives ceased to be maintained, and the horrid burning of the captives, old men, women, and children. Nothing of the deliberately predetermined extermination of the Wampanoags, hunted like wild beasts by the dropping shots of the chase; nor of the fate of their King Philip's son, "the last of the race of Massasoit—that kindly and kingly entertainer of the Pilgrim Fathers—who was sent like a brute without a soul, to toil *in slavery* under the burning sun of the Bermudas."

Fortunate indeed, would it have been for these simple, trusting, and faithful children of nature, if, like King James of England, they had known those with whom they were dealing. "My son," said that monarch addressing Prince Henry, "take heed of the Puritans, very pests in the Church and Commonwealth, whom neither oaths nor promises bind, making their own imaginations the square of their conscience"—then would not one hundred thousand human beings have been sacrificed in fifty years, to gratify a ferocious fanaticism; nor would their land have become crimson with innocent blood nor reeking with the fraud of false-hearted intruders.

And fortunate would it have been for the Hawaiians if American missionaries had presented the two pictures in candid comparison; *that* they did *not* draw of *Puritan* intolerance, fanaticism, and cruelty, with that by them so vividly portrayed of Catholic bigotry, folly, and persecution; then might the rulers of these misguided people have avoided the perpetration of persecutions, for which their only excuse is to be found in the disingenuousness of those whom they trusted.

It is not surprising that the unfair and persistent efforts of an established mission to control a centralized power for selfish purposes should have inaugurated what was subsequently called "the persecution;" nor that, as a consequence, the party in the state hostile to the Government, should have been increased by the accession of many previously indifferent observers of the controversy, who were prompted by liberal and generous sentiments to side with the oppressed. But this manifestation of sympathy strengthened the resolutions of intolerance, and inflamed the imperious Kaahumanu; by whose command the "natives were forbidden to attend the religious services of the Papists." The arbitrary will of Kaahumanu, directed by the missionaries, who availed in all things relating to their interests, of the Kamehamehian policy of supreme control and unquestioned domination, was not to be resisted; and accordingly, Government *imposed fines and imprisonment* upon converts to Catholicism. The history of that period shows that such converts "were confined and set to work making stone walls, repairing roads, and fabricating mats, aggravated by filthy lodgings, bad food, and the contempt and rudeness common to the lowest orders particularly of natives, with whom malevolence to the unfortunate had always been an active principle. They were punished for their idolatry, and they who repeated the offence five times, either by worshipping at the chapel or indulging in their old rites, *were obliged to remove the filth of the fort with their hands.* Romanists to the number of thirty men and women were incorporated in the ranks of *common malefactors*, and from time to time *for several years made liable to similar punishments.*"

The partial historian of this persecution for conscience' sake, unblushingly attributes the "*mildness*" of this inhumanity, in comparison with the harsher punishment which would have attended such offences a few years before, to the "*humanizing spirit of the Christianity*" *introduced by the missionaries.* The saving clause of the sentence, is in the *kind* of Christianity *thus introduced.* But at the inauguration of the new faith, it would have been more appropriate that some other name had been taken, and that the religion of the meek and lowly one of Bethlehem had sprung and flourished of its own benignant spirit, and not from the rankness of evil passions; had come at its own time and in its own way, with healing on its wings, not to be smitten by the rude blasts of persecution; had made known its own messages of peace and good will to all men, and not have been shamed by curses and cruelties meted out to the oppressed. If Christianity had come thus, not only the intolerance of Romanism, which American missionaries had enriched the Hawaiian tongue with new epithets to denounce, but intolerance in all matters of religious faith, would never have raised its head. And if a purified and enlightened public sentiment and not the inhumanities either of legal enactment or of arbitrary will, had been the means of reformation, the historian would not have been required by truth reluctantly to acknowledge in reference to the above-recited punishments, that "there were individual instances of missionaries whose minds, illiberalized by sectarianism, looked on with reprehensible apathy."

Meanwhile, the pair of patient priests, protected as they believed by the panoply of truth, and sustained by an inward consciousness of duty, pursued their path of piety so meekly and uncomplainingly, so entirely in harmony with the merciful and loving spirit of the Gospel they professed, that a conviction of their goodness coming of a true religion, seized upon many, and they still gained converts, despite the inflictions of the civil authorities, controlled by fanaticism. Embittered by their continued success, a misguided Government next determined to send them out of the country; and as they declared themselves without the means of going, they were by direction of the rulers in 1832, forcibly put on board of a vessel and banished. An act which the historian—Mr. Jarves—pronounces "*for barbarians*, a humane consideration;" strangely overlooking his previous record of the priests' "simple and pious habits, their zeal and purity of lives;" and also that he had called the rulers, *Christians*, and pronounced the Queen Regent's "character so entirely altered, and her deportment so consistent with the principles of her faith, that none could doubt its sincerity." Who were the "barbarians"? The priests, or the princes? And will Mr. J. inform us further, in what consists the "humane consideration" of *banishment for religious opinion?*

# CHAPTER XXXVI.

CONSEQUENCES OF MISSIONARY ERRORS AND PERSECUTIONS—MISSIONARY DUTY—MISSIONARY CONTRAST.

THE Kamehamehian rule of government—arbitrary decrees and punishments—the handmaid of the American missionaries in these islands, was not restricted to the catholic clergy alone. We are told by Mr. Jarves that Kuakini, the brother of the self-willed Kaahumanu, and her governor of Oahu, being "fully equal to the task of subduing the impertinence of lawless whites, his rigorous enforcement of the letter of the law gave cause of offence to many foreigners." Briefly told, his agents rudely entered private houses, seizing and carrying off forbidden beverages. Horses were forcibly taken from owners who rode on Sunday. Armed bands paraded the streets and violently suppressed houses obnoxious to puritanical ordinances. It is not surprising that under such an enforcement of fanatical despotism, the annals of that period should present the acknowledgment "that the strong arm of Government was not capable of infusing order and sobriety into a dissolute population; that secret means of indulgence were sought out; that the governor's measures met a strong opposition, and many continued to be evaded." That it should have been declared that the apparent moral condition was entirely owing to the absolutism of the chiefs; and that the historian of the time was compelled to say, "that this was partly true, *no missionary could deny.* They numbered but few *real* converts, though they justly claimed the amelioration of manners, the desire of instruction, and much of the gradual change for the better, to be the result of their labors. Still following the example of the rulers, it had become *fashionable to be of their belief; all important offices were in their hands, and interest* more than intelligence conspired to produce an *outward* conformity to morality. While numbers, *to the best of their abilities*, were Christians, *thousands joined their ranks from unworthy motives;* perhaps in no instances have the united cunning and mendacity of the Hawaiian character been more strikingly displayed than in *their stratagems to deceive their religious teachers.* By fraud, by even giving up much-loved sins, and by ready knowledge of the Scriptures, many managed to become church members, because by it their importance was increased, and their chances of political preferment bettered. This is too Christian a practice for civilized men to wonder at. *Deceived by appearances the friends of the mission exaggerated their success.*" With the obligation of presenting such a record upon him, it is remarkable that the historian should at any time have attempted to gloss his subject. It was at this time that a condition of civil and moral anarchy is stated to have prevailed throughout the islands; schools were deserted, teachers relapsed, congregations were thinned, excesses abounded, several churches were burned, and in some places idolatry was reinstated. And this result has been referred by the apologists of missionary errors to the sweeping away by others of moral restraints and municipal regulations in a well-ordered community; and that in the face of the above-cited acknowledgments of fraud, falsehood, and hypocrisy, assuming the mantle of morality and piety for despicable and mercenary purposes; of admitted inhumanity and tyranny that could not fail to kindle a spirit of resistance; and of conceded religious persecution, the offspring of fanaticism and the parent of evil. Could it have been rationally expected that people would fall in love with the demon of all-uncharitableness, equally repugnant with the idolatry they had repudiated? Rather might we suppose that they thought—*If these white priests who claim to have been taught of God, can teach us no better precepts than these, no purer and nobler principles of action, nothing more deserving of reverence than that religion which we have voluntarily discarded as worthless and wicked, they cannot be reliable interpreters of what the "One Great God dwelling in the Heavens" considers pure and good.*

*He cannot have revealed Himself unto them, as they profess; they are but "blind leaders of the blind."* And truly was it said, that in 1836 the missionaries had carried the nation to a point when it became necessary for new influences to operate, for the accomplishment of desirable results which they had been unable to reach. And why? Because "the strenuous opposition to the progress of the Gospel was gradually changing its character, and settling into a political animosity to the chiefs; who had unfortunately and unwisely submitted to ecclesiastical control, and shaped their governmental policy according to ecclesiastical dictation." Because, as candidly confessed by the historian of Hawaii, "laws, people, and government, partook of the puritanical caste of their religious teachers."

Such was the lesson taught by the missionary experiment up to this period that a change of programme was demanded; and such, comprehensively expressed—the puritanical character of the movement—was the cause of the failure of the work of religious civilization. It became necessary to regenerate individuals through personal conviction and purification, rather than to move the unwieldy and passive multitude through arbitrary authority; to obey the Founder of Christianity, and "seek the lost sheep of the house of Israel—to heal the sick, cleanse the lepers, raise the dead, cast out devils," instead of courting "Principalities and Powers," and devising political engines full of human conceits to move the unthinking and indifferent masses in conformity to despotic will, that the missionaries might make "Christendom resound with their triumph," and magnify their achievements.

Subsequently to these events, information having been conveyed to the banished priests that in consequence of an understanding between the king and the commanders of a French sloop-of-war and a British frigate, they could return to the islands, these clergymen in 1837 again visited Honolulu, in a vessel under English colors; but much excitement having thereupon ensued, their reëmbarkation was ordered by the governor, and a proclamation of perpetual banishment was issued. To this the priests entered formal protests before the English consul, who counselled a disregard of the edicts of Government. Forcible expulsion followed, and also a severe ordinance effectually to prevent the introduction of the Catholic faith. The historical record of those events shows that "a number of the natives were arrested and confined for their adhesion to the doctrines of the priests. They manifested a dogged obstinacy to the authorities, and a contumely which brought upon them unnecessary severities. They were few, ignorant, and powerless; the menials of the governor frequently apprehended them when they were detected in the exercise of their (religious) rites, and carried them before him."

Soon after these occurrences, the Hawaiian rulers, now entirely under the influence of the missionaries, who unhappily considered their interests at variance with all others, and secular views and policy as necessarily of Satan, determined upon the appointment of the Rev. William Richards, one of the American missionaries, as "chaplain, teacher, and translator of the Government;" and the year 1838 marked the epoch when the missionaries emboldened by previous successes, and the rulers pleased with the executive bauble gilded with novel usages, determined to throw off the cloak which had but illy concealed previous relations of cause and effect, lay aside further disguise, and establishing an official connection, thus fearlessly proclaim the union of Church and State. Mr. Richards' act, ostentatiously proclaimed, of "dissevering himself from the mission by the advice and consent" of his missionary brethren, was a device too thinly veiled to prevent detection, if a cover were designed. It was plain to all disapproving of the step, that the relations of sectarian interest, sympathy, motive, purpose, and plan, remained the same as before; and that the ostensible disassociation but strengthened their bond, by enlarging their power, and confirming their obligation to each other. Profession is not always to be regarded as the test of sincerity. We have already seen that the missionaries were instructed by their patrons in the United States "to withhold themselves entirely from all interference and intermeddling with the political affairs and party concerns of the nation." The taking of office under Government by one of the mission, was therefore a violation of his sacred trust. Mr. Richards intended to occupy office, either *true* to the cause of the mission, or *false* to it. If the former, then he forfeited the confidence reposed in him by the lords of the vineyard, who had commanded him not to sow thistles among grapes—not to bring upon their cause the odium of moving in political matters; and that his connection with the Government was considered as bearing that complexion, is shown by the act of disseverance deemed necessary by the missionaries. And if, on the other hand, he designed to abandon the spiritual objects of the enterprise for selfish and temporal purposes, then unhappily he must be numbered among those of whom Christ said, "He that entereth not by the door into the sheepfold, but climbeth up some other way, the same is a thief and a robber."

We leave to others the determining of Mr. Richards' true position, after reading that page of Hawaiian history on which it is recorded that, after the missionary power became paramount, and the Rev. Mr. Richards had taken office under its modest title, "*his influence on the foreign policy of the chiefs became considerable, and in it he was sustained by his brethren.* Each missionary was generally the friend of some chief living in his neighborhood, and over whom he imperceptibly acquired that influence which moral confidence is sure to engender, so that without knowing exactly how it was, he felt himself powerful in his little field. *The missionaries being united in policy, were thus enabled to affect the tone of the public councils, through the voices of their individual friends.*"

As shown by the records of the time, other members of the mission are designated as wielding great influence; but it is not necessary, beyond the general testimony already presented, to show the responsibility of the American missionaries for many errors of the Government, to do more than to name one more personal example, that of the Rev. Mr. Bingham, referred to by Mr. Jarves, as "long known by the soubriquet of King Hiram, who had acquired great prominence in the affairs of the mission, enjoyed the confidence of the chiefs, and was devoted to the cause in which he had embarked. But it must be acknowledged he possessed *a tenacity of opinion and a sectarian zeal,* which at times separated him in some degree from his friends, and marred his usefulness."

With this foreign sectarian influence and intemperate zeal at work, stirring up the bitter waters of strife, engendering prejudices, and exciting evil passions and religious intolerance, it was but reasonable to look for international difficulties. It was not to be expected that repeated persecutions of her subjects, under whatever pretexts, would be submitted to by France without interposition; and hence those proceedings which subsequently modified the policy of the Hawaiian Government, released it from the shackles of bigotry, and shaped it in accordance with the liberal spirit of the age, developing in truth the new era, the dawn of which was contemplated by a sensible intimation that the missionaries were unable to carry the nation beyond a certain point—one that every enlightened mind will admit, having been once reached, wiser counsels were demanded to shape its future.

In 1839 the French frigate "Artemise" arrived at Honolulu, her commander, Laplace, having been instructed by his Government to put an end to the ill treatment to which its citizens had been subjected in the Hawaiian islands. His complaint stated that the rulers of the islands had been misled by perfidious counsellors, that French subjects had been made victims of unwarrantable persecution, and in violation of the usages of civilized nations had been forbidden the exercise of their religion, while Protestants enjoyed every privilege; "for these, all favors —for those, the most cruel persecutions."

Captain Laplace was certainly wrong in saying, as he did in his manifesto, that "among civilized nations there is not even one which does not permit in its territory the free toleration of all religions," unless indeed he designed to exclude from the pale of civilization certain nationalities, especially of South America, in which he should have known religious freedom is not allowed. But Catholic intolerance in those countries should not be imitated by others who condemn it; and as he was not himself the representative of a national religious exclusiveness, we should not quarrel with his efforts in behalf of religious freedom, however we may differ with him on a point of fact.

The commander of the "Artemise" demanded that French citizens should be permitted to enjoy the privileges granted to others; and that a guarantee for the faithful performance of the engagement entered into should be given. As the consequence of a refusal on the part of the Hawaiian Government was to be an immediate declaration of war, asylum and protection was offered on board the French frigate to friendly foreigners. But in the tender of such to the American consul at Honolulu for his countrymen, the French commander expressly stipulated, and I refer to it in proof of the *political* character of missionary proceedings, that he "did not include in this class the individuals who, although born in the United States, make a part of the Protestant clergy of the *Chief* of the Archipelago, *direct his counsels, influence his conduct, and are the true authors of the insult given by him to France.*" "For me," he further said, "they compose a part of the native population, and must undergo the unhappy consequences of *a war which they shall have brought on this country.*"

"Deplorable" as this demand has been pronounced by the Rev. Secretary for Foreign Missions, and ungenerous as considered by others, in view of the feebleness and incapability of resistance of the Hawaiians, yet it surely does not become Americans, the special advocates of civil and religious liberty, to deny the justice of the French claim to be placed on a footing with others. And as to immunity to perpetrate a wrong, the weak have no more right to it than the strong. They are equally at fault for acts of injustice, and should be subject to a like penalty. It is a sickly statesmanship that concedes the claim of the feeble to violate with impunity the unchanging principles of international right.

The Hawaiian rulers had set a bad example in granting no privilege of conscience to their helpless people; and having adopted the rule that *might* made *right*, in their own Government, they were not entitled to complain that a machinery corresponding to that of their old system, which centred all power in the hands of the chiefs, and which was approvingly claimed to have been "brought to aid the moral reform," the machinery of arbitrary will and power, should also have been brought to bear upon them to enforce equity.

The display of naval power, with the purpose to use it if necessary, led to the wise decision to secure peace on the terms demanded. A treaty was entered into between his Hawaiian Majesty, who had passed from his wardship to the throne as Kamehameha III., and the commander of the frigate on behalf of France, when the latter sailed from Honolulu, after having received from the foreign residents opposed to the missionary policy of the Government a letter of thanks, containing the following significant passage: "We are willing to hope that the horrifying realities of persecution and torture for conscience' sake, will, by your firmness and justice, have been forever crushed, never again to show its hydra-head; and that the simple and confiding children of nature in these islands, so long deluded by designing and interested counsellors, will see the necessity of immediately retracing their steps, and taking a manly and nobly disinterested example you have set them for their guide, that the blessings of freedom, of peace, and prosperity may be henceforward the interesting portion of these hitherto deluded people."

Thus we see that it was left for the representative of a professedly Roman Catholic country to plant and maintain religious freedom in a field first occupied by American Protestant laborers, and where they had sown the seed of a spurious Christianity, to take root in the evil passions of human nature, and produce the bitter fruits of malevolence, discord, and persecution. Under the blighting shadow of such a tree the hopes of a people seeking regeneration must have perished. And it is a mortifying reflection for Protestant Americans that their missionaries, born and bred under a political constitution *forbidding the passage of any law* "respecting an establishment of religion or prohibiting the free exercise thereof," should have failed to bear to others that glorious decree of human wisdom and of human privilege, with the blessed inculcations of peace and good will toward all men.

The remarks upon Protestant missionary intolerance in these islands are consistent with the condemnation of like illiberality in the Catholic clergy of some other countries herein spoken of. Sectarianism, creeds, and confessions of faith—"winds of doctrine"—may both pleasantly and profitably be passed unheeded. It is only violations of the common rights of humanity, and of the Christian principles upon which they profess to build their respective churches, that it is deemed a duty to expose. If Protestants condemn "the example of the Jesuits in creating at once a Church and State," they must not expect their imitation of it to be approved by the impartial and just. Let them not be "forgetful hearers of the word," but treasure *for practical uses*, rather than for the vanity of pulpit oratory and sensational declamation, the sublime instruction, "For with what judgment ye judge ye shall be judged; and with what measure ye mete it shall be measured to you again." "First cast out the beam out of thine own eye, and then shalt thou see clearly to cast out the mote out of thy brother's eye."

If the "poor heathen" is to be benefited by religious projects of civilization, the executors should remember that though they "have the gift of prophecy and understand all mysteries, and all knowledge, and have all faith, *and have not charity*, they are as nothing." *Not the cheap charity to bloated wealth of alms-giving*, unattainable by *righteous poverty*, but that to which all may aspire, both rich and poor, which the apostle tells us "suffereth long and is kind, envieth not, vaunteth not itself, doth not behave itself unseemly, thinketh no evil, endureth all things," and *exceeds* in righteousness even *faith*, the cherished foundation of the Christian's reward, and *hope*, without whose blessed promises his earthly probation would be drear and desolate. The "Poet's Creed," read in the "Polynesian," is true, every word of it:

"I hold that Christian grace abounds
Where charity is seen; that when
We climb to heaven 'tis on the rounds
Of love to men.

"I hold all else named piety
A selfish scheme—a vain pretence:
Where centre is not, can there be
Circumference?

"This I moreover hold, and dare
Affirm where'er my rhyme may go—
Whatever things be sweet or fair,
Love makes them so.

"Whether it is the sickle's rush
Through wheat-fields, or the fall of showers,
Or by some cabin-door a bush
Of ragged flowers.

"'Tis not the wide phylactery,
Nor stubborn fast, nor stated prayers,
That make us saints; we judge the tree
By what it bears.

"And when a man can live apart
From works, on theologic trust,
I know the blood about his heart
Is dry as dust."

If higher and nobler motives of action cannot be presented to mankind than those which spring from selfishness, malevolence, and vengeful passions, to induce them to change their religion, truth might well stand by heedless of the result of the effort. Happy in the possession of a delicious climate, and a bountiful nature bestowing a rich return to moderate industry; easy, healthful, hospitable, with unrestricted means of gratifying his sensuous inclinations; and an absolution from pains and penalties for nonconformity to the selfish decrees of a priesthood, whose taboos were abolished and absurd theology exploded by the highest in authority, it may well be doubted by the philanthropist if the Hawaiian derived any actual advantage in the substitution for these of polemical subtleties he could not comprehend; petrified creeds impenetrable to his perceptions; conflicting interpretations by professed disciples of a common Christianity, and therefore stumbling-blocks in his way; mutual denunciations, persecutions for conscience' sake, and punishment of himself for his inability to determine who of his white brothers was right and who wrong, while each professed to be the only true interpreter of the new faith. In view of existing facts the Rev. Secretary for Foreign Missions may well say that "the shadows were perhaps never darker than they are now, even while we are raising the cry of victory." Nor is it surprising that with such antagonisms in operation, Christianity became polluted by an almost universal hypocrisy; and that to this day, as recognized by every intelligent observer, and acknowledged by the disinterested and candid, a conformity to a Christian church requirement and ceremonies is to be regarded rather as the cloak of pride, interest, stratagem, and deceit, than as the garment of sincerity and true piety. Witnessing this shameful corruption of morals, and contemplating its causes in the gross perversion of the real objects of the missionary enterprise, one is reminded of the warning of Jesus to the multitude, "Wo unto you, Scribes and Pharisees, hypocrites! For ye compass sea and land to make one proselyte; and when he is made ye make him twofold more the child of hell than yourselves."

The sincere friends of this much-abused people hoped for them a better return for the kindness and hospitality extended to the discoverers and other early voyagers to these islands; and especially was it due to them, in view of the many and irreparable evils brought to their homes by vicious and heartless guests. There are many foreign residents who frankly acknowledge the force of the obligation, and who think that if missionary efforts are to be continued the Divine injunction should be remembered, that "Not every one that saith Lord, Lord, shall enter into the kingdom of heaven, but he that doeth the will of my Father which is in heaven." And what is that will? "Thou shalt love the Lord thy God with all thy heart, and all thy soul, and all thy mind. This is the first commandment, and the second is like unto it—*thou shalt love thy neighbor as thyself.*"

Love is the golden thread interwoven with the whole woof of Christianity, as it came from the Hand of its Divine Author; and man is not in his proper relation to his Creator, nor to his fellow-man, until, discarding the stony theology of sectarian dogmas and creeds, he goes fearlessly forth to fulfil, in its simplicity and truth, the *Law of Love.*

My information, derived from several Protestant sources, was that the Catholics are more successful in making proselytes than Protestants; and this was accounted for in part by the facts that in their domestic habits the priests have adopted the simple and inexpensive customs of the country, their genial demeanor and benevolent offices are better adapted to the native notions of goodness, and they do not levy on their church members assessments; this conduct establishes confidence in the disinterested character of their purposes, and in the sincerity of their professions; while, on the other hand, the large families of most of the Protestant clergy requiring for their support, and the gratification of the vanities of personal and household display, a much larger expenditure, has led in some cases to a system of church taxation and levy on labor considered by many natives oppressive, and indicative of an unchristian seeking after treasures on earth rather than a patient waiting for those more precious in the world to come.

This great success of the Catholics in these islands, reminds us of the more glorious results attendant on the mission of priests than on that of the Puritans in North America. While the former, through the benign influence of genuine religion, and a reasonable conformance to the outward life, simple habits, and natural instincts of the Indian, possessed themselves of the door of human nature, *the heart*, and by kindness, sympathy, persuasion, and rational appeal, passed through it to the inner seat of his convictions; the cold, unbending, unpitying, and uncompromising disciple of puritanism, sought to attain the same end by dictatorial harangues on *election, justification, and sanctification*, unintelligible to themselves and incomprehensible to their hearers; and by harsh decrees, fierce denunciations, and finally by the practical enforcement of death and damnation. The results of these two systems of proselytism are matters of record. The former, introduced by the French Franciscans, on the rocky shores of Maine, was subsequently borne thence along the great valley of the St. Lawrence and the lakes, even to that of the Father of Waters, by the Jesuits; winning the confidence and love of the untamed savage, guiding him to the peaceful contemplation of truth, and along the path that leads to eternal life. While the latter wrote in blood the record of aboriginal repugnance, and of their own persecutions, oppression, and final extermination of a race whom they professed to seek with the

Gospel of Peace, but in fact destroyed with the weapons of war; and when at a later day they seized the happier fields of Catholic missions along the St. Lawrence and the lakes, there too they blasted the fair face of a benignant Christianity, by the terrors of uncompromising heartlessness, intolerance, cruelty, and selfishness. As a New England historian * has asked in regard to the contrasted spirit of the missions of that day, equally applicable to the missions of which we have been speaking in the Hawaiian Islands—"Can we wonder that Rome succeeded and that Geneva failed? Is it strange that the tawny pagan fled from the icy embrace of Puritanism, and took refuge in the arms of the priest and Jesuit?"

* "The Puritan Commonwealth, by Peter Oliver." Boston, 1856.

# CHAPTER XXXVII.

WAIAKEA—WAILUKU RIVER—SACRED GROVE AND RUINS OF A HEIAU—WATERFALL OF WAIANUENUE.

AMONG the most useful and best conducted of the benevolent institutions of these islands, is the Manual Labor School at Hilo, under the superintendence of Mr. and Mrs. D. B. Lyman, to whom great credit is due for its judicious organization and excellent arrangements. It was conducted for a time under great disadvantages, but was incorporated in 1848, and obtained from the Government a grant of forty acres of land, on which the present buildings are erected. The main building was afterwards destroyed by fire, and in 1856 was rebuilt at the expense of Government, aided by contributions from resident foreigners and natives, and from the American Board of Foreign Missions, who also pay the salaries of the principals. The edifice is plain but commodious and neat, occupying a healthy and commanding position. Well cultivated lands, tasteful houses, and gardens surround it, with the bay stretching away before it to wed the ocean that forms the distant horizon; and three lofty extinct craters rise in the rear, now clad in verdure, yet serving to remind the young Hawaiians, who dwell in their shadow, that their fatherland was upheaved from beneath the deep sea that now surges against its rocky shores, in vain efforts to recover its lost dominion. The average number of pupils is about sixty, who are selected from the common schools of this island, and who labor from three and a half to four hours per day. They cultivate and cook their own vegetable food, furnish their own bedding, make, mend, and wash their own clothes, and perform some minor mechanical labor, the proceeds of which pay for the animal food they consume. Their academical instruction is in the Hawaiian tongue, but they are taught also the English language on payment of a small fee, which is said to be charged for the purpose of prompting to productive industry. This is one of the foreign enterprises for the benefit of the natives, which must be pronounced popular and successful.

Rather more than a mile from Hilo, on the south shore of the harbor, stands the ancient village of *Waiakea* consisting of eighteen or twenty thatched houses, commanding a fine view of natural scenery, and so well protected by the natural breakwaters of reef and rock as to show that the old Hawaiians had a prudent consideration of safety, as well as a nice appreciation of the picturesque and grand. The soil of its vicinity is very rich; and with Mauna Kea crowned with eternal snow towering in majesty before it, while Mauna Loa, to the left, lifts its everlasting dome to the heavens in surpassing grandeur; with old Ocean rolling his restless breakers against the opposite and distant shore, bordering a verdant landscape, the tide moving with gentler swell to kiss its own sheltered beach, and a climate distilling an atmosphere of balm, no spot perhaps on these islands offers greater natural inducements for residence, to taste and affluence.

Foreign residents are not insensible of the value of this harbor to commerce. And if a proper consideration were given to this fact by the public authorities, Hilo would probably become the emporium of the Hawaiian islands: for not only is its harbor the largest, deepest, and easiest of access, but its pilot and port dues are less, with no expense to be incurred for a steam-tug, as in the case of entering the port of Honolulu against an invariable head wind, and through a narrow, sinuous, and dangerous channel of the surrounding reef. This island too, from its greater size than all the other islands of the Hawaiian archipelago together, and from its fertility, and frequent showers over a great part of its surface, furnishes the largest quantity of supplies for shipping, always cheapest where grown. And its relative position making it more accessible to vessels from the east, coming down with the northeast trade wind, and not liable to become becalmed as on the lee side of other islands, or baffled by inter-insular winds and currents, would seem to point out Hilo as the port most likely eventually to become the intra-oceanic stopping-place of the California and East India trade on its outward passage. But a brief time was required to finish official business here, and while awaiting a return passage an opportunity was afforded to visit several objects of interest in the vicinity. Among these is the river scenery of the *Wailuku—water of destruction*—so called from frequent suction and drowning of bathers in a whirlpool, although perhaps no people in as high a degree as the Hawaiians, possess the natural gifts of fishes. This river is twenty-five or thirty miles in length, and of considerable size, formed mainly of the melting snows and rains of Mauna Kea, and flows eastward to the ocean, into which it empties about a mile and a half from the town. A bridge spans it near its mouth, a half mile beyond which, and close to the seashore as it stretches northward from the mouth of the river, is seen what is traditionally considered a sacred grove of trees; and near by, a large quantity of stones, which, on like authority, are regarded as the ruins of a former *heiau.* These temples were usually built near the sea, or on elevated sites forming conspicuous objects, and the absence of similar stones in this vicinity, which on the contrary presents an unbroken surface of soil on one side, and ocean expanse on the other, indicates that these must have been brought from a considerable distance and by great labor; such as was not likely to have been given to any other than a religious object, in a country where large or substantial edifices of any other description are not known to have been erected in the olden time, and where grass houses, it is believed, were alone used for dwellings. Many of the stones now seen here are large, and each one must have required the united effort of many persons for its movement; but they were in their natural state and without any marks indicating the uses to which they had been put. They were lying in confused piles, as if massive walls had fallen in detached parts at different times, and they occupied a high hill, affording an extensive view of land and sea. This opinion of these ruins is sustained by the better preserved remains of such structures found in other parts of the island, of which we have authentic accounts, in which the thick and high stone walls are seen to have outlived the perishable buildings within, used merely as priestly or idol residences, and which were constructed of materials not more durable than those ordinarily used by the people at large.

The grove, not more than fifty paces from the stony ruins, occupies an oval space of about two hundred by one hundred and fifty feet. A majestic *ohia* stands in the middle, lifting its stalwart trunk aloft and stretching its giant arms abroad, as if to protect trees of smaller growth, the more yielding bodies and pliant limbs of which had been bent and intertwined, while yet young, so thickly and inextricably as to form an overhanging roof of foliage, and a dense surrounding wall of trunks, branches, twigs, and leaves, impenetrable to intrusion except where a rude portal is found on the side next to the ruins of the temple, by means of which access is had to the interior of the grove.

Whether this was a place of retirement in moments of priestly relaxation, or for meditation on subjects connected with their holy functions, or in some manner associated with the sacrifice of human victims of frequent occurrence before the reign of Kamehameha the Conqueror, but discontinued by him, as were other usages of idolatrous worship, there are now no means of determining. But the grove is rapidly passing into neglect and decay, with a discontinuance of the uses, whatever they were, to which it was devoted; as are all others of the ancient sacred places rapidly crumbling into ruins, under the decisive measures adopted for the abolition of idolatry by Liholiho at the instigation of the high-priest Hewahewa.

Having returned to the south bank of the Wailuku, and ascended it a mile and a half, the river was seen from the cliff that walled it in, coming from the west through a narrow cañon and forming a rapid of between one and two hundred yards; it then pitched over a precipice to the depth of a hundred and four feet. The basin below and its surroundings presented a scene of marvellous beauty, and we sought it by descending a lateral ravine, observed to open below a short distance down stream. An obscure trail was found leading between high and nearly perpendicular walls of rock, trellised and festooned by the climbing *hehoi*, the thick foliage and pendant nuts of which frescoed and nearly concealed them. Through a network of promiscuous undergrowth, the meshes of which were closely interwoven by an unending season of vegetation, a way was forced, up and down and around rocky fragments, the more startling and perplexing because nearly concealed by the dense jungle through which we broke and crashed until suddenly brought to a stand-still, or a tumble over a fallen fern-trunk, forests of which were scattered around to challenge the over-confident footstep. Through this labyrinth of obstructions, veiled in twilight—for even the mid-day sun could not penetrate the closely-walled and covered aisles through which we sought a winding way that reminded us of childhood's solutions of the

WATERFALL—WAIANUENUE.

Trojan problem—we groped along, finally reaching the mouth of the ravine which opened below on a bed of volcanic rocks, where we gladly seated ourselves to look on a scene of rare beauty and sublimity, that fully repaid us for the vexation and fatigue endured in reaching it.

Facing the waterfall—appropriately called *Waianuenue*, signifying rainbow water, from the iris that spans its mist when the sun sends its long risen beams into the deep recess, to cool themselves in this rarest of nature's rock-encompassed baths—the sparkling flood is seen to take its fearless leap of more than a hundred feet over a broad ledge of rock, vertically cut and faced as if chiselled by the hand of art. Split in twain by a projection resembling the architectural dental of a marble entablature, the descending water breaks into foam, which, reuniting, forms a wavy column as of snow, whose myriads of minute flakes fall and vanish in the deep and dark waters below—looking deeper and darker from the shadowy surroundings of rock and verdure of this wild gorge. This waterfall has about the volume of that at Niagara known as the "Centre Fall," and like the precipice, too, over which it shoots, this is excavated behind the falling sheet into a deep cavern; which, however, surpasses the "Cave of the Winds" of the Centre Fall in beauty, from its vaulted wall and roof being lined with moss, the rich green of which, contrasted with the snowy foam, gives another charm to this bathing place of zephyrs.

The basin is oval, with diameters of about two hundred and one hundred and fifty feet; enclosed, except at the outlet, by a perpendicular wall of rock a hundred and fifty feet high, hung with a tapestry of vegetation, and corniced with flowers, over which a tropic foliage sports in the breeze.

From this rare chamber, in which the wearied waters seem to sleep, they finally flow placidly through a narrow portal, after having glided around the base of a basaltic column. This colossal shaft is formed of immense superposed hexagonal and pentagonal blocks, rising to a height of a hundred feet above a graduated peristyle of compactly-adjusted pillars of like formation, similar to those of the famous Giants' Causeway in Ireland, and forming a fit pediment for a monument that suitably commemorates the grandeur of creation which it proudly overlooks.

We turned from this enchanting abode of solitude with the feeling, that the spell put on our hearts by the religion of nature there taught, would long remain.

## CHAPTER XXXVIII.

VOLCANO KILAUEA—JOURNEY TO IT—LUXURIANT VEGETATION—HAWAIIAN HIGHWAY—FATE OF THE HAWAIIAN—PULU—DOME OF MAUNA LOA—KILAUEA.

THE object of surpassing interest in Hawaii, indeed one of the wonders of earth, is the *Volcano Kilauea.* To visit it, some preparation is necessary; for neither on the way to it, nor when there, are bed and board to be had; hence a blanket, food, et cetera, must be provided at Hilo, where precise information can be had of your purveyor as to the essentials of comfort. A sure-footed and hard-hoofed horse must be provided, otherwise he should be carefully shod for a road that looks as if it had been paved with iron for half the distance. And the excursionist should be particular in the selection of a competent and faithful guide, who will also carry baggage and provision in two large calabashes hung by netting from the ends of a shoulder-pole. My experience justifies my speaking favorably of *Kaihikaoli*, a native Hawaiian living in the suburbs of Hilo. Since my trip to Kilauea I have heard that Mr. Hitchcock, an enterprising citizen, intends to provide relays of horses, and better accommodations on the road for visitors.

Suitably equipped and provisioned, and with Mr. Lyman, principal of the native manual labor school, as my intelligent companion, I started for the volcano on a delicious summer morning; pursuing a southerly course over a rugged trail, through tangled shrubbery of *oi*, *amau-mau-fern*, *ti*, and *guava*, with the silvery-leaved *tutui* trembling like the aspen in the background. At the distance of rather more than four miles we entered a forest, through which a wide avenue three miles long has been cut, along the greater part of which is a causeway nine feet wide, built of volcanic stones, with gigantic fern logs thrown across corduroy-road fashion. This causeway facilitates travel over an uneven, and in places, marshy surface, but it is overgrown by rank grass and weeds.

The principal timber of this forest is the indigenous *ohia* from fifty to seventy feet high, looking much like the oak, but without its distinctive brawniness and strength. The *tutui*, dressed in bright green foliage, seeming brighter by contrast with surrounding dark verdure, and with the deep shade of the spreading *lauhalla* upheld by its numerous props, and having long lancinated leaves resembling those of the pine-apple radiating thickly from the ends of branches, and forming a canopy of umbrellas, giving shelter to the traveller against rain and sun. The long leaves of the lauhalla tree—the Hawaiian pandanus—smoke dried, trimmed, and split, are used for making the coarser mats of the country, in common use. *Ferns* abound in great variety; the *amau mau*, distinguished by the beautiful architectural scrolls into which its tender branches and young leaves are coiled for protection, and the *pulu fern* with its scrolls cased in silken armor to guard them even from winds that might visit them too roughly, being most remarkable for luxuriance. But in all this dense growth of vegetation nothing surpasses in grace and beauty, and in instructive lesson too, the depending *ie*, which twines its golden vine around the stalwart trunk, and clasps with tiny tendrils the rough bark of the *ohia;* while its long and delicate leaves, springing spirally like those of the lauhalla from twigs, expand into sun-shades to shield while they adorn the stern form to which the creeper clings. An emblem of the feeble, lovely, and tender, who, while they seek support of ruder man, yet throw around him their own graces, and strive to shield him from unkindly influences. At seven and a half miles from Hilo—three hours in time—we emerged from the forest, and dismounted in the shade of a cocoanut grove for refreshment.

Again in the saddle our course lay next west of south over a path choked with wild grass, and across a plain on which the amau fern and the ti struggled for dominion; the latter mingling with the former for miles, looking like a wilderness of

Indian corn as it swayed its sapling stalks to and fro in swaggering merriment, and gave the slender leaves of its tufted tops like banners to the breeze as if in boastful triumph over its rival. But as the road showed diminishing soil and signs of impoverishment four or five miles further, the fern shook its nodding plumes as master of the field, a few scrubby ohias, like sentries, standing guard in the distance. A tuft of the ti leaves was the flag of truce in the former wars of the islanders; and from its root an ardent spirit called *oholehau* is distilled, resembling whiskey in color, strength, and flavor, and once much used by the natives for its intoxicating effects. The root possessing considerable saccharine juices, has also been used for food in times of scarcity; and the leaves make wrappers in cooking according to the native mode of baking, and for taro and stiff poi in travelling.

From the tenth to the twelfth mile our road was like the proverbial one to Jordan—hard to travel. The almost daily rains, and animals following each other in the same tracks, make deep holes with intervening ridges, perplexing to the poor beasts and dangerous to riders. The former sometimes stick fast on this part of the route, and the latter occasionally plunge headlong into a mudhole, and to extricate themselves are compelled to "follow in the footsteps of their illustrious predecessors." Where the fern is the sole vegetation a waste of lava is seen, with no soil but that which exists in the clefts and crevices of the metallic-looking crust. Beyond this as far as fifteen miles and a half from Hilo the surface is a slightly-inclined plane, apparently of iron, modified by small elevations and depressions, ridges and chasms, metallic-looking plates broken and bent, and of various shapes; swells, wavelets, and ripples, some circular, others serpentine; as if a black tenacious fluid, in every condition of obstructed flow, had become suddenly solidified. Compared with the reality on a previous part of the road it was a transition from soft to hard, and after debating the question we were left in doubt of the relative advantages of mud and metal as materials for road-building. At the end of this stage of our journey—fifteen and a half miles from Hilo—we came to the stopping-place for the night; time, seven hours and three-quarters; gait, a walk nearly all the way, and a slow one too, the guides on foot carrying from forty to fifty pounds each of baggage and provision, in calabashes two feet in diameter, absolutely distancing our horses.

Of half a dozen thatched huts we selected the largest, and dismounting and giving our horses to the guides to be tethered and grassed, we entered, without any notice being taken of our intrusion by the native occupants; one of whom, engaged in pounding and kneading taro, had his nakedness very partially hidden by a much abridged garment—the shortest specimen of that mystery which has neither definite form, fit, fashion, nor right to be recognized, and even to name which is forbidden by the fastidiousness of an affected refinement, except when the plaintive "song of the shirt" sometimes touches our heart-strings. Another native similarly attired, with the vague addition of a "maro"—a Hawaiian device which has superseded the primitive *fig-leaf*—was transferring poi from one calabash to another, making a dipper of his hand. And a third, a gray-haired old woman in long loose slip, was occupied in assorting the vegetable ingredients of a decoction, slowly and thoughtfully, as if preparing "a charm of powerful trouble" for some miserable martyr. Perhaps she belonged to the sisterhood of modern medicine. Like the "strong-minded" new-lights nearer home, she

"Looked gravely dull, insipidly serene,
And carried all her wisdom in her mien."

It was an agreeable reflection that we were not dependent for the creature comforts of food on the manipulated poi before us. But the contemplation was not pleasant of a platform of logs—a "hikiee"—occupying nearly one-fourth of the room, on which was spread dried fern leaves and a mat for our bed; the common bed of the country, as it was to be our bed in common. Nor were our anticipations of "balmy sleep" enhanced by the knowledge that seven kanakas, including our guides, and three wahines, were to be joint occupants of the one apartment of the hut for the night. Necessity is a great leveller, however, and teaches the wisdom of adopting a practical philosophy and conforming cheerfully to imperious circumstances. So, after discussing the merits of a rough road as a surpassing appetizer, over a cold chicken and a cup of tea—for the making of which we found a kettle at hand, the only cooking utensil on the premises—we wrapped ourselves in our blankets and courted the slumber tendered by a corduroy bedstead; after having concluded that the lady who undertook a journey to the volcano showed neither wisdom, love of adventure, nor amiable adaptability to unavoidable requirements, who, on reaching this halfway house, and seeing no American hotel elegances, would not enter, but burst into tears, and, like Rachel, "refused to be comforted." Ladies must forego a sight of the world's greatest wonder, or forego crinoline, and turn bloomer in dress, daring, and disregard of the customs and conveniences of fashionable life.

The lurid light of the Lake of Fire, when at night we looked abroad, was seen reflected by the overhanging clouds in the distance; and a throe of that vast mystery which sensibly lifted our platform of logs, made us think that our Hawaiian hotel, although in truth "built on a rock" of lava, might nevertheless be readily toppled over. The novelties of our situation, with the anticipations of the coming day, made sleep a stranger to my eyelids that night; and seeing the swarthy figure of a native crouching by the fire that glimmered from a shallow pit in the middle of the earthen floor, rolling its smoke upward to escape through the thatched roof, and observing his painfully thoughtful countenance, which seemed to tell of memories of the past of his race, and meditations on the fate that awaits it, as the tide of Caucasian civilization rolls on to bury it beneath its resistless surges, my mind, following a similar train of thought, recalled the strange vicissitudes of nations who had risen, flourished, and fallen; and a profound sympathy for the doomed Hawaiian before me came of the reflection, that then my own country, surpassing in its progress to prosperity and power all that had preceded it, was endangered by a convulsion which would shake it to its centre, and might shatter it into fragments.

Never was the day more cordially welcomed than when, looking forth, the morning was seen successively to put on its garments of gray, and roseate, and gold; and coffee, our own, of course, and cold viands having been taken, and four reals each paid for the novelty, if not the luxury of a hikiee, we mounted at six A. M., and rode over a rough causeway of volcanic clinker and coke, with fern trunks laid crosswise, for somewhat more than a mile; then followed a rocky pathway, paved as if with the broken castings of numberless iron foundries.

At twenty-two miles from Hilo we entered a dense *ohia* forest of large growth, with the *pulu fern* also in great number and size, some of them twenty feet high, and from one and a half to two feet in diameter. The *pulu* of commerce is obtained from this fern, and is extensively used as a substitute for feathers and hair, in the making of beds and mattresses, and stuffing of sofas and chairs. In the natural state the pulu forms a snuff-colored silken envelope for the young and tender branches of the fern, which grow from the top of the stalk or trunk, forming beautiful scrolls until of sufficient strength to supersede the older branches and leaves that droop on all sides like graceful plumes. In gathering pulu the natives cut from the top of the fern trunk the tender scrolls in mass, then strip off the soft fibrous wrapper that protects them, which they loosen by picking, and expose for several weeks on platforms to the rain and sun. From two to four pounds are gathered from a full-sized tree. When perfectly cleansed and dry, it is bagged and sometimes baled for shipping, and is much sought after for the California market.

A mile or so of woodland shade was a pleasant relief from a warm sun, and then a better road, over which we travelled at a faster gait than our previous snail's pace, soon brought us, at twenty-five miles from Hilo, in full view of Mauna Loa in the distance before us, with snow-banks scattered over its magnificent dome like an emblazonry of pearls. So vast are the proportions, and so grand the outline of this wonderful structure of creation, that by scientific explorers who have ascended to its summit it was found to possess a horizon of its own.

Cheered by the prospect of a speedy end to a wearisome trip, we cantered along an excellent bridle-path, the first we had met with, and at ten A. M., four hours in time from our stopping-place of the night before, and twenty-eight and a half miles in distance from Hilo, we came suddenly and while riding over an apparent level surface to an immense pit of about nine miles circuit, sunk nearly seven hundred feet in the earth, walled throughout almost its whole extent by perpendicular rocks, floored as if with black marble, and rolling up from more than a hundred vents of cone and chasm dense clouds of smoke and steam, to tell of the terrific fusion below. It was *Kilauea!* and well may the visitor hesitate to dismount in such fearful proximity to the most wonderful active volcanic crater of which we have authentic history.

A few yards from the rim of the abyss stands on a slightly-elevated plateau an unoccupied hut, built for the accommodation of visitors, who are charged two dollars each per day for the use of it, by a native who accompanies them from the stopping-place of the night before for that purpose, and who furnishes a mat to lie on. This may be called extortion, but foreigners have earned this penalty of imposition. In the olden time hospitality was religiously practised by Hawaiians. With them "the string of the latch was never pulled in;" every house was a shelter, every mat a resting-place for the weary, and every calabash of poi was open to the traveller, without recompense of reward; and those informed of these matters assure me that such is still the usage of the remote interior; but wherever the influence of foreign example has frequently reached, there a correspondent greed of gain has been engendered; and, as in the case of foreigners, extortion is the more gross and glaring from their irresponsibility to any restraining public opinion, and from eagerness to accumulate and depart, so with the native, understanding the foreigner's practice and motives, he plucks freely to-day the bird that will not roost under his roof to-morrow. The vicious examples of our countrymen have been much more influential for evil among these people, than their precepts have been for good.

Like the usual habitations of the country, this volcano hut is built of the lightest materials, and in a manner to adapt itself to, rather than resist the terrestrial tremblings and shocks to which from its situation it is constantly liable. Rustic posts and light cross-timbers, with walls of thatched *fern*, lined with long flag-looking leaves of the indigenous *uki*, and roofed with *pili* grass; the materials of wall and roof being bound to *aho* lathing, which is also similarly fastened to the posts by *ie* and *huihui* vines, that make excellent cordage; thus constructed, lightness and elasticity are secured. Even if thrown down, the weight could not injure the occupants.

While our attendants were finding grass for the horses, and preparing lunch, a stroll to the rear of the hut showed us several vents under a low bank, from which volumes of steam were issuing and condensing on overhanging and adjacent rocks, forming little crystal pools, from which water for culinary purposes was obtained, and where chickens wrapped in leaves may be readily cooked by steaming.

Several hundred yards further west, under a continuation of the same bank, but at this point presenting a steep bluff, that by some visitors has been described as an outer rim of the crater, but which cannot be traced in continuity around it, there is an immense sulphur mound, with offshoots and facings of the bluff of the same substance. The whole surface in this vicinity seems studded with apertures and crevices, from which sulphurous gases and vapors escape, and where may be collected rich specimens of feathery and acicular prismatic crystallizations, of a light yellow color. Some of the finest and largest tetrahedral pyramids are found under the superficial crust, but in consequence of the suffocating atmosphere and great heat, especially near the apertures, the pursuit of these is not often persisted in.

Further to the west on the same level, large cracks and even chasms are seen, traversing a considerable extent of surface, from which columns of steam ascend, which, condensing as it rises, falls in showers to nourish the grass and flags in the vicinity, and form little pools of water for the thirsty traveller. At times, indeed, so great is the quantity of vapor that it forms a dense cloud, concealing completely the neighboring bank of the crater. The surface openings of this neighborhood, often hidden by vegetation, and sometimes covered by a thin and friable crust of lava that gives way under slight pressure, demand of the excursionist great caution in his rambles even during daylight, and at night enforce a confinement to the small space of this upper level immediately about the hut in which he lodges.

In the same direction and at the distance of about a mile and a half from the house, the highest point of the rim of the crater is reached, from which the best view of the *tout ensemble* is obtained. If it be not designed to make the entire circuit, and unless more than four days are given to the excursion, points of greater interest should not be neglected for this by the general and unscientific explorer; it is better to return to the starting point for refreshment, and to be ready as we were at meridian for descending into the great abyss, whose revelations, however appalling and terrific they may be, serve but to strengthen the desire to penetrate more deeply into nature's mysteries. It is a remarkable fact that the most timid and apprehensive at the commencement of the exploration of Kilauea, become insensible of danger during its prosecution, such is the strange fascination of even its frightful features.

I was informed by my companion, Mr. Lyman, and also by Mr. Coan, another intelligent observer of the phenomena of this crater, that so sudden, frequent, and great are the changes occurring in it, that a visitor is apt to become distrustful of the statements of his predecessors. Hence it was determined to disregard the descriptions of others, and examine the features of the changeful scene presented at the time of our exploration.

Standing on the northeast rim of the crater and looking into and around it, a first thought was its unlikeness to the general notion of a volcano derived from those with which travellers and readers are more familiar. No lofty elevation was seen, with steep conical acclivity and narrow truncated top, from the open mouth of which ashes and stones were being thrown. But a vast cleft or pit—*Lua Pélé*, Pélé's pit—four thousand feet above the sea, on the nearly level flank of Mauna Loa, which soars ten thousand feet above it, was before us, seven hundred feet deep, egg-shaped, somewhat more than three miles long, and two and a half wide at its larger end. Blackness seemed to reign within, and stupendous ruins to floor it, as if some great city within its bosom had been consumed by fire, leaving a charred and smoking wreck and fitful flames to tell of the mighty conflagration.

A feeling of disappointment is said to be experienced by many on first beholding this crater. The same remark applies to visitors to Niagara. Nature fails sometimes to produce impressions on the instant, correspondent to her wonderful creations. But a final acknowledgment of the surpassingly marvellous and fearful cannot be withheld by those who come to look on this work of her hands.

At the northeast rim of the crater, the point usually selected for the descent into the abyss, the visitor, imagining himself standing on the front cornice of a vast cathedral, like a Grecian temple, without dome, tower, or roof, and looking directly down three hundred and fifty feet, sees below a plateau extending from side to side, and half a mile in width, covered with vegetation as with a carpet. This may be regarded as the orchestral gallery, beyond which and about three hundred and fifty feet lower still, is seen the dark marble floor of the great temple stretching away two and a half miles further, and pierced near its extreme end by a lake of fire, whose illumined smoke rises as if from an eternal censer to Him who was alike the Divine Architect and Builder.

Descending to the plateau by a rough and steep declivity, in doing which the free use of hands was necessary to prevent too rapid locomotion, and shrubbery, roots, and rocks proved excellent substitutes for a handrail, we crossed over it by a tortuous path, carefully avoiding holes and chasms that beset the way. On this plateau are found scrubby ohia and sandalwood trees, dwarf ferns, and a creeper of the same family, called by our guides kukaeuwau, together with ohelo bushes bearing berries of a blended red and yellow color, and of size and taste somewhat like the cranberry, but sweeter. They are very grateful to the palate of a wearied and thirsty explorer. These berries were formerly held by the natives sacred to the uses of Pélé, the then worshipped goddess of this volcano, who was supposed to wield its terrible agencies of fire, and thunder, and lightning, at will; and into whose fearful abode every native in passing threw some of the berries gathered above, as a propitiatory offering. Until this was done the tasting of the fruit by a native was deemed sacrilege. At the commencement of the religious reform of these islands, the daughter of the King of Kauai, a chieftess of highest rank and excellence of character, is said to have been the first native, not only to descend into the crater, but to eat of the ohelo berries freely, and without offering any to Pélé, in condemnation and contempt of the idolatry then doomed to extermination.

From the plateau above spoken of, explorers usually descend to the lava floor of the crater, and proceed directly to its greatest attraction, the lake of fire. But to save time and toil, and yet not fail to look at every thing deserving of attention, our guides left the beaten track and led us close to the east wall of the crater, towering several hundred feet above us. Warned not to linger for fear of falling crags, we soon reached a path up a steep cliff of probably two hundred or two hundred and fifty feet height, along which we hastened, and then proceeded a quarter of a mile further on a level bed of clinker and cinders, to an old crater known as *Kilauea Iki*—small Kilauea—in contradistinction to *Kilauea Nui*, which is the great crater.

The Kilauea Iki, which is a short distance removed from and to the east of the true volcano Kilauea, is not now active; and it is the last of a series of extinct craters stretching from the seacoast in the district of Puna, up to this point. It is a deep pit, like that of which we have been speaking, with walls but little less elevated, though more sloping, and now covered with vegetation. In shape, as viewed from above, it is elongated, and contracted in the middle like an hour-glass. Its lava floor is of a black color, and of comparatively recent formation, an eruption having occurred in 1832, at the level of our standpoint near the western end of its southern rim, which divided into two streams, one of which flowed into and floored anew this crater, while the other ran westward to the great Kilauea, and plunging over its lofty wall formed a cataract of fire, one of the most awful of nature's displays of might and grandeur, which faced the cliff of several hundred feet height, as if with iron, leaving above and below its ineffaceable footprints in the everlasting billows of its majestic torrent.

Crossing this bed of lava in a southerly direction, we ascended about fifty or sixty feet from Byron's ledge—the gigantic partition wall between the two craters—to the upper level on its southern side, and skirted the eastern rim of the large crater for nearly a mile, over volcanic stones, clinker, coke, and cinders, and descending gradually a sloping surface; and finally we slipped and slid down a steep bank to the depth of two hundred feet, over beds of clinker and cinders, sometimes leaping from rock to rock, or coasting over an ashy or pasty soil in a more humiliating posture. The bottom of the crater was thus reached at the only place of descent except that by which persons usually go down from the plateau or gallery already referred to; and it landed us near an enormous sulphur bank on the southeast side of the crater, that looked like an abundant magazine for all earthly purposes of war and pharmacy. Various earths and salts —such as gypsum, aluminous, magnesian, and ammoniacal sulphates, are also found mingled with this chief element and product of fusion, or incrusting neighboring crags. The heated surface on which we stood, and surroundings of steam and deleterious gases escaping from vents, and permeating the sulphur bank itself, which looked like an enormous tumulus of variegated lime in process of slacking, soon reminded us that curiosity might not be gratified, certainly without great discomfort, and possibly danger.

From this deposit of sulphur we struck across the solid lava in a southwestward direction. And as I stood for the first time on the dark floor which, recently in a state of fusion, was then cast into its present form by the hand of Omnipotence, I felt an awe even at the threshold, befitting a human intrusion into such presence. My description may fall short of the reality of the scene, yet it must be attempted to preserve the thread of the narrative. However even the surface over which we toiled, clambered, and leaped, appeared, when first seen from the upper rim of the crater, yet viewed from below it looked like a tempest-tossed ocean that had become frozen, blackened, and burnished; in wavy outline in some places, in others lifted and broken by resistless forces into fragments which became fixed again in grandeur of chaos. The river of Niagara in winter faintly images the wild disorder, its icy crust crashing and crumbling before the mighty torrent, which piles the whirling masses on high, or bears them in strange confusion welded again with seams of frost. Wherever we turned our steps, cracks, fissures, and chasms, traversed the floor of consolidated lava, from many of them sulphurous vapors, gases, and smoke issuing; while some of the larger vents revealed, far below, a sea of molten lava in the terrific throes of its red agony, and breathed forth vast volumes of steam to tell what would be the convulsions of earth but for these safety valves. The access of water to immeasurable alkaline and earthy bases in a state of igneous fusion, generating a resistless pressure of steam, together with liberated sulphurous gases, would probably blow Hawaii to atoms, but for the millions of openings that allow of their harmless escape. In many places immense cakes and blocks of lava, thrown on end and partly embedded in substrata, formed impassable barriers; in others they were submerged, making deep trenches and pits, which compelled a deviation from direct progress. Sometimes we encountered cones and domes from twenty to forty feet in height, upheaved by subsurface agencies, and increased from time to time by fresh projections of liquid lava, cooling and forming successive laminæ, which were pierced by apertures making of them huge chimneys for the escape of hot and stifling gases from the vast laboratory beneath. And occasionally these structures were seen to have fallen in by their own weight, or to have been undermined by flows of the fiery torrent, leaving their jagged and craggy foundations of more solid lava rock surrounding the ruin, to warn the explorer of the awful abyss below. Many fissures and chasms were recognized by the fresher and more cellular lava, to have been perfectly closed by a welling up and partial flow of the consolidating fluid. And wide spread over the surface in several places, was observed the spongy and bronzed layer of an eruption that occurred but a few months since, showing the extent to which the boiling flood had flowed from these lava ducts, and diffused itself in wavelets and ripples, and in coiled, or in smooth and even currents of more porous and lighter lava known as the *Pahoehoe*, or satin stream.

The laminæ thus formed have become so numerously and thickly superposed of late years, and the great floor of the crater has been so much upraised by the lava tide beneath, that the wide ledge, which it has been stated once projected like a black marble mantle from the wall of the crater throughout its entire circuit, at a height of three hundred and forty-two feet above the bottom, and which was particularly described in 1840 in the Report of the United States Exploring Expedition to the Pacific, if it has not fallen and thus disappeared, is now either buried beneath the present floor, or by submersion has been melted down, except at the western wall for a small extent; where a shallow black line is seen, like the wash-board of a room, showing itself slightly above the floor as it is now found.

Still pursuing the same general direction over the more recently solidified lava, that crackled under the feet like light snow in frosty weather, we came, within about half a mile of the narrowest southwest end of the crater, to massive piles of gray, slate, and black colored rocks, solid and compact, having evidently been subjected to great pressure, and overhanging an oval chasm of about one thousand by seven hundred and fifty feet diameter, bordered by a narrow black rim which looked like a shelf projecting inwards from the bottom of the surrounding rocks. Many of the latter of great size and weight, craggy and toppling, threatened to fall and crush the black ledge at the foot of the cliff; the whole ruin indeed as well as ledge seemed of uncertain stability, in the presence of the resistless forces palpably at work in its vicinity.

These rocks in 1851 formed the colossal foundations, walls, and abutments of a dome, built by volcanic power, which at that time spanned the chasm now seen. The wonderful structure was described to me, by one who then saw it, to have been on a scale of transcendent grandeur, and to have been surmounted by several conical chimneys for the escape of smoke, gases, and sometimes flame. But falling from its own ponderous weight, or having been shaken into pieces by that dread power which raised it as if in sport, there is now revealed again, what for a brief time was hidden, a lurid lava flood, which, as we gazed upon it, boiled and bubbled with fearful activity, spouting its crimson streams and heaving its fiery crests high into the air, rivalling the sun with brilliant coruscations. And responding to the deep pulsations of earth's mighty heart it surged to and fro, swallowing up and melting, as if they were flakes of snow, the adamantine rocks of the adjacent cliff, that fell upon its bosom, and dashed its gleaming spray against the surrounding walls to run down in streams of startling contrast with their blackness, as if it sought to burst or burn the barrier that confined it; under which, indeed, on the side opposite to that were we stood, could be seen consuming fires illumining deep caverns, and enlarging the domains of the terrific element.

It was the "Lake of Fire" on the brink of which we stood; and contemplating its red glare, and terrific commotion, the excited fancy might well compare it to that of Revelation, into which, "whosoever was not found written in the Book of Life, was cast." I was told that sometimes the Lake of Fire rests for awhile, motionless and noiseless, apparently sleeping, with a leaden looking scum like a silken coverlet, upon it, and causing disappointment to the expectant explorer. But as beheld by us, it was fearfully aroused, tossing its huge bulk from side to side, and lashing its fiery flood into heaving billows, that wrapped around and under them, to disappear in an instant, the thin film that feebly strove to hide its terrific features from view; vindicating its claim to be considered the wonder of both the learned and unlearned, the cause alike of awe in the civilized religionist, and terror to the superstitious heathen.

And its contemplation inspired profound reflection, as well as intense emotion; for it is the palpable manifestation of that element, which, flung into space in the morning of time, when this planet was "without form and void," had whirled around its axis, and circled in its orbit for untold ages; moulding into shape, crystallizing, and consolidating its original materials, with which, too, the destiny of man is linked, on which the temporal objects of his creation are enacted, and whence, a nobler longing and conviction tell him, he may rise to a more exalted and immortal being.

It demonstrates, also, the geological truth of internal fusion, for it is the welling up of that ocean of fire on which the crust of earth is floating; and within this crater the lava flood and its transformations illustrate also, from time to time, the wondrous phenomena of terrestrial development. Here may be seen in miniature the gradually-encrusting surface, and the consolidating rock; the upheaved mountains, and intervening valleys; rolling prairies, and outspread plains; ravines, and river-beds. And although in this grand dissolving view of nature —representing the imperceptible transition from chaos to order— the reality of barrenness still predominates, and rocky cliff, cone, chasm, cavern, pinnacle, parapet, tower and turret, bare and black, present the striking features of the slowly-unfolding panorama; yet, when disturbing agencies allow, the type is also seen of that advent of morning and evening, when, in the long generations that have gone before us, God said, "Let the earth bring forth grass, the herb yielding seed, and the fruit tree yielding fruit after its kind;" for, in sheltering crevices, the pioneer fern is seen timidly to lift its scarcely-recognized form, and tremblingly look abroad over the dark dominion on which it has been the first to plant the banner of vegetable life.

Dense volumes of smoke and steam rise from the lake of fire, and from neighboring cones and vents, and are wafted from the explorer's usual standpoint by the prevalent northeast wind. It is on the south side, over which these clouds are blown, that the choicest specimens of that singular production called Pélé's hair—because formerly believed by the natives to be portions of the combed locks of that goddess—are obtained. It is a capillary glass formed of small detached portions of molten lava, projected from the lake and cones of eruption, unfolded and drawn out into fine-spun semi-transparent brownish olive threads, as it is borne on the currents of heated air, and finally deposited in chasms and caves; and sometimes it is carried by the winds even to a considerable distance beyond the crater. The deleterious gases, smoke, and vapor, that usually fill the southern part of the crater, make it sometimes unsafe to seek there this *rauoho o Pélé*—hair of Pélé.

Appalled as the visitor may be, when first he looks upon the terrific agitation, and shrinks back at the fierce heat of the lake of fire, yet he will soon become spell-bound, and unconsciously dare destruction, for the red charm of its gleaming and surging tide. No object in nature perhaps throws over the soul such wondrous fascination, and extinguishes so completely the sense of great and undoubted danger; for who can tell that the "foundations of this great deep," which have been often loosened within the memory of man, may not on the instant be again "broken up," and the floor on which he stands, though of rock, be shattered into fragments, for re-fusion and re-casting in new and stranger fashion? Yet despite this thought it was reluctantly that we turned away, to proceed by another and more direct path back to our humble tenement, which looked in the distance like a mole hill on the upper rim of the great crater.

Objects of interest similar to those already described were seen as we passed along, representing varieties of nature's fanciful art and flowing graces, fixed as in iron while in the act of disappearing. A structure thirty feet high stood on the left of our track, built apparently of large plates of corrugated watch-spring steel, superposed in endless relative positions, and bent and welded together, giving beauty of outline and security of strength. Clambering up to an opening in its side, we saw burning on a furnace hearth a bright fire, surrounded by an abundant supply of sulphurous fuel and reagents, indicating that a grand manufacture of gases and chemicals was going on in this unique laboratory. Not far off another edifice, built by the wonderful and plastic power of eruption, looked like a church in process of demolition; but its still standing remains of walls and abutments, spire and minaret, told how surpassing the design and structure of that temple must have been, when, through its lengthened aisles and lighted arches, the earthquake's diapason once resounded. And further on to the right, lay long ridges and huge piles of slag, scoriæ, clinker, vitreous refuse, and broken castings, with masses of basaltic rock, as if all the foundries and furnaces of England had been tumbled down, and thrown together in promiscuous confusion of material for nearly a mile; while to the left, in a nearly correspondent ridge, those of Pennsylvania seemed to have heaped up their contribution of a century's rubbish. Many caves were also seen, a few of which we explored, and which appeared formed by the upheaval of the thick surface lamina, or by the subsidence of that below, leaving extensive intermediate spaces, in some instances distinct, in others forming a series of apartments communicating with each other. In these a beautiful process of the finer and more delicate modelling, moulding, and casting has been conducted by a secret process, probably a liquefied condensation, and final solidification of the purer lava vapors, holding in solution metallic bases, which have penetrated into these chambers through imperceptible fissures leading from lower depths. The results are imitations of nature's stalactite and stalagmite creations in the crystal caverns of upper earth; yet more curious in some instances, in that a greater tenacity before final consolidation has given greater variety of curve and outline. Many exquisite resemblances to familiar objects of art have been obtained in these caves since their discovery by the officers of the United States Exploring Expedition to the Pacific.

Having reached the northern end of the crater, we sat down to rest on the last swell of a recent lava tide, fixed in enduring bronze until another flood shall consume or sweep it again into the ocean of fire from which it came; then slowly ascending the steep acclivity to the plateau, which at the outset of the exploration we compared to an orchestral gallery of a vast cathedral, we crossed it to the bottom of the rough natural stairway leading to the upper level, which we climbed, wearied and footsore, glad to reach our habitation for the night, just as the shades of evening were gathering around to borrow from Kilauea a crimson light, for the golden beams which the setting sun had borne beneath the ocean that bathes with crested billows, and strives in vain to stay the fiery mountain's boldly encroaching foot.

Supper, seasoned by an appetite coming of toil, having been despatched with rare relish, we did "not wait upon the order of our going," but Haole and Hawaiian, employer and employed, sought at once, and without ceremony, such repose as might be had from blanket and mat.

Often during the night we rose to look upon the strange painting of surrounding nature, as, pencilled with the red light of inextinguishable fires, it raised on high its bold and glaring features, above which glimmered, with sickly beam, the stars, that paled as they looked upon this sublime spectacle of earth. Gazing upon the columns of smoke rolling in illumined grandeur upward, to meet the first coming of the gray dawn, we beheld to the west of the lake a pillar of fire suddenly leap through the vent of a spouting cone, its burning shaft perhaps a hundred feet high, shedding a radiance abroad as if to add its tribute of adoration to the coming day, and then falling, it spread abroad a crimson sheet, to darken and disappear in the morning haze.

And when the rising sun was seen to touch the topmost dome of Mauna Loa, lifted nearly fourteen thousand feet to the skies, and gild it with outspread gold, it seemed to pause in admiration of the departing glory that gleamed from the flank of that majestic mountain, ere it sent its brighter beams below, to dim for a time the splendors of the Place of Fire, which, "day unto day uttereth speech, and night unto night sheweth knowledge," and is the "testimony of God making wise the simple," and proclaiming "that Thou, whose name alone is JEHOVAH, art the Most High over all the earth."

We added to our breakfast strawberries of delicious flavor gathered about a mile off, and after packing our travelling equipage, and extinguishing our hearth-fire—a necessary precaution for the safety of a grass house—we quitted our banquet hall at ten A. M., and stopped that night at Waiuli, two miles beyond the half-way house on returning, where, being much fatigued, my guide proposed to subject me to the native manipulation called in Hawaiian *lomi-lomi;* and he really did gently and soothingly rub, punch, grasp, tickle, knead, and generally magnetize me from head to foot into a sweet slumber, from which I was awakened some time after entirely refreshed, and ready for a hearty meal. In the saddle next morning at seven o'clock, we reached Hilo at half-past eleven, but little more than three days from the time we started for the volcano.

## CHAPTER XXXIX.

VOLCANIC ERUPTIONS IN HAWAII—NATIVE HUT—MATS—HAWAIIAN FOREST—LAVA STREAM FROM THE CRATER MOKUAWEOWEO OF MAUNA LOA—WAILUKU RIVER—NATURAL BRIDGE KEPAUKEA—LAUIOLE FALLS.

Of the three volcanic mountains on the Island of Hawaii, two of them have long slept. There is no definite information to be had of the last eruption of Mauna Kea, though there are indications that it was probably in action during the last century. Hualalai, now quiescent, poured forth a torrent of lava as late as 1801, which laid waste the country in its progress to the sea, and is said to have filled up an extensive bay, and formed a new headland several miles beyond the former line of the coast. Mauna Loa alone seems still disposed to assert its prerogative of remodelling the great island it has contributed largely to form; and seven times within the last forty years it has sent forth its fiery agent to destroy and rebuild much of its earlier work. In 1823 an eruption took place from its crater of Kilauea, the lava reaching the surface of the earth some miles south of the crater through subterranean passages, flowing through the district of Kau to the sea. In 1832 an eruption occurred both from the lateral crater Kilauea, and from that on the summit of the mountain, the stream of the first named flowing, as stated in my description of that crater, into Kilauea Iki, and part of it back again into Kilauea Nui, some persons supposing from the great subsidence of lava in the great crater that there was also probably an escape by subterranean channels under the sea. The flow from the summit took place from numerous vents, diffusing its light to such a distance that it was visible even at Lahaina. In 1840 there was another eruption from Kilauea, partly subterranean, which destroyed the village of Nanawale, and rearranged the features of the coast where it reached the sea. In 1843 an outbreak took place from the summit, the stream subdividing and flowing severally in the directions of Mauna Kea, Waimea, Hilo, and Hualalai. Still another eruption took place from near the summit of the mountain in 1852, flowing eastward about fifty miles, but stopping short of the sea. In 1855 another eruption occurred from the old crater of Mokuaweoweo, which, in the quantity of lava thrown out, has not been surpassed, if indeed it has been equalled, by any happening since the residence of foreigners on the island. The Rev. Mr. Coan, who saw it, in describing this outbreak says, "a vast chasm opened horizontally on the top of the mountain, and along the yawning fissure stood series of elongated, jagged, and burning cones about a hundred feet high, rent through this larger diameter, and throwing up dense columns of blue and white smoke, which, covering the mountain's summit, rolled in fleecy masses down its sides, and spread out like the wings of chaos over unmeasured regions. Still no fire was seen in the fountain crater. We could feel it everywhere, and hear escaping gases, but the throats of the cones were clogged with hot masses of cinders, pumice, and ashes, with cracks and crevices for escaping smoke. The fusion had found vent in a lateral subterranean duct, several hundred feet below the rim of the crater, and in this covered way it flowed off until it made its appearance two miles down the side of the mountain." The torrent of lava appeared on the surface at about ten thousand feet above the level of the sea; it flowed eastwardly to the distance of forty miles by its windings, not stopping until within from six to seven miles of Hilo, and destroying every thing in its course for at least three hundred square miles. The last eruption from Mauna Loa occurred in 1859, from the new crater Pélé-hou, on the northern slope, about six thousand five hundred feet above the level of the sea. It is said to have been remarkable for its fountain-like ejection of lava in a perpendicular column of varying height and appearance from two hundred to five hundred feet, and it was judged by one observer to have once reached a height of even eight hundred feet, with its capital sometimes simple and flowing, at others involved and occasionally efflorescent, casting above and beyond its own jet of crimson lava, red-hot boulders of hundreds of tons' weight, to burst and scatter their fragments like gory spray abroad. The course of the lava stream was about northwest, passing between Mauna Kea and Mauna Hualalai, and running between fifty and sixty miles to the ocean, into which it poured for a width of a half mile, heating the startled billows, and sending up clouds of steam hundreds of feet into the air.

Approaching, as the lava flood of 1855 did, to within from six to seven miles of Hilo, before its flow was arrested, and lifting its imperishable proofs within so short a distance of that town to tell that the island of Hawaii is not yet finished, I devoted the last two days of my sojourn in Hawaii to an excursion to the iron river. The route indicated by my companion, Judge Hitchcock's familiarity with this region, embraced also the *natural bridge of Kepaukea*, and the *Lauiole falls* of the Wailuku River, objects of great interest rarely visited by strangers.

By a tortuous and broken bridle-path we proceeded westwardly over an uncultivated country, with the exception of a few upland taro patches, without enclosure, save long bamboo stalks run through holes in scrubby-looking posts. If these are land boundaries, they certainly do not preclude proprietorship in common with promiscuous quadrupeds, the younger members of the swine family being generally tied by the hind leg to the door-posts of the huts, no doubt for the security of a pig's head when wanted to adorn the more delicate and savory body of roast dog, for the entertainment of dainty foreigners, the uninformed among whom partake of that dish with great gusto. A short distance on the way a heavy shower made us take shelter in a native hut, built of sugar-cane-blade thatched walls, and fern roof, with one ample apartment for the accommodation of family and friends, from the central earthen hearth of which rose the fumes of taro smothered in *ti* leaves, sweating between a bed and covering of heated boulders. Around the room hung a score of calabashes of all sizes, from half a foot to two feet in diameter, serving as cupboards, closets, pots, trunks, and general table ware, where table there was none, and these contained the few essentials of Hawaiian housewifery, with such few gewgaws and trumpery as imported taste and fashion made significant of the higher law of civilization, sometimes as disgusting if not as base as that other "higher law" coming of a new and odious political proposition, which sneers at the sacredness of constitutional compacts and tramples good faith under foot. On the ground, covered with mats that had never known the purification of water, sat an old crone whose skin looked like the copper on a ship's bottom covered with barnacles, from the effects of a hateful disease introduced by foreigners into these islands. She was occupied in trimming and splitting smoke-dried lauhalla (pandanus) leaves for a couple of young, lithe, and bright-eyed wahines, who, in a posture between kneeling and squatting, were plaiting them with great dexterity into large, neat, and durable floor mats. The best quality of Hawaiian mats, very fine and beautiful, on which the chiefs recline, are made on the island of Niihau, and are sold at from five to eight dollars each. The coarser mats used by the common people can be had at half a dollar apiece. Several Kanakas were lounging around, engaged, according to the wont of these household nuisances of the masculine gender, in jabbering with extraordinary volubility and vehemence their vowelled vernacular. My companion participated in the colloquial comedy, until, perceiving that the rain had ceased, we resumed our ride, and having proceeded five miles from Hilo, our horses were left with a native to be brought to us next day at a designated place about a mile east of the falls. With a guide in the lead, and followed ourselves by two other Kanakas carrying camp equipage and provisions, we then, on foot, entered a forest, through which, for a distance of about two miles, we had literally to thrash and cleave our way; for although at the time the lava was in actual flow, parties of curious and hardy adventurers broke and kept open a track through the forest, yet in the time since elapsed, and stimulated by ceaseless showers and continuous warmth, such rank vegetation had sprung up as not only to obliterate every trace of path, but actually to erect a barrier to progress, which had to be beaten or hewed down at almost every step.

The recognized forest trees were the koa, tutui, and ohia, of larger growth than I had seen elsewhere, several of the latter having trunks five feet in diameter, overtopping and spreading their brawny arms abroad, protecting less vigorous growths, and with the tutui, furnishing a dense foliage impenetrable to the sun. Ferns, of numerous species, rare growth, and varying shades of green; the fragrant leaved maile, of which the favorite necklace and coronal of the Hawaiian maiden is made; the wild ginger, more agreeable for its subdued spiciness; the

KANAKA CARRIERS.

wild taro, the original of the plant now cultivated and yielding the chief food of the islanders; the wild raspberry, and the wild banana, were all found in this forest growing luxuriantly; and above them was seen the beautiful parasite ekaha, opening outwardly from its root-latticed base, its long green leaves in symmetrical scrolls like hanging-baskets suspended by a delicate cordage of ié which hung from tree to tree. The ulehihi and the ié were the principal creepers; the latter, in some parts of the forest, clothing many of the trees in an entire livery of green, and masking completely their distinctive features; and so numerous, wandering, and tangled were its roots, that weary and weak from slipping and sticking in mire and mud-hole, our feet became often entangled and tripped, causing tumbles that went far toward dispelling the pleasing fancies indulged on a former occasion about this same plant. Indeed it was suggested that the climbing of the ié resembled that personal propensity which aspires to notice on another's merits, and that its clinging to venerable trees typified the dependence of children of larger growth, the lazy and selfish, who overburden parental infirmity, and hasten the death of those who give support. It is not uncommon for a stately tree to become the victim of this parasitical tenacity of the ié, which suffocates it with clustering vines and foliage, appropriates its inherent vital circulation, and consumes the nourishment of surrounding soil.

To increase our annoyances, after two hours of clambering over fallen trees, crawling through branches and undergrowth slimy with moss and moisture, and floundering through pools and mud, our guide said that he had lost his way. Without beaten track or blazed tree to direct, or the bright sun penetrating this dense forest to light him to recognition of familiar things, he had become confused in its labyrinth, doubtful of purpose, and wandered without definite result. Climbing a tree he looked abroad for landmarks, and started again on his exploration, this time alone, leaving us to such rest and comfort as practical hydropathy, administered by a drenching rain and a saturated moss-covered stump, could give. In due time, by hallooings, at first distant and faint, then near and louder, the guide was enabled to return to the spot about which we had been revolving; and assured by his observations, he struck a bee line—which, however, even with that little insect mathematician, and encompassed by corresponding obstructions, could not have exemplified the "shortest distance between two points" —for the bed of lava; and after the expiration of four hours from the time of entrance, we made a joyful escape from this forest of but two miles breadth, in which we had very fairly illustrated the law of centripetal motion.

Dark and dismal as was that unmoving and immovable river of lava, on the brink of which we stood, and which had unrolled the blackness of desolation over this region, yet was it a welcome sight; for it removed doubt, and released us from imprisonment, as well as from an oppressive sense of the absence of animal life, there being no birds there to cheer us with their song, and naught else but a few lizards, centipedes, and scorpions—not even a snake being seen, none having been found on these islands, and it is said only one imported, which was instantly killed. It is surprising how the feathers were obtained of which the two royal robes of the Hawaiian monarch were made; especially if it be true, as stated, that but two feathers are found in each bird suitable for the purpose, one under each wing—a story, however, probably more sensational than true, as a Hawaiian naturalist assures me that the bird furnishing the material of the rich fabric has a *tuft* of feathers under each wing.

Bending our steps over swells, troughs, and mounds of lava, the fiery flood was seen to have cleaved its way through the grand old forest with a sword of flame. Its results were curious, as in its progress in different degrees of liquefaction and movement it assumed varied forms, which became apparently castings in iron to tell to future generations the tale of cause and effect: confirming its truth by an imperishable causeway of forty miles from the source, ten thousand feet above the level of the sea, whence it flowed from the great central fire that has burned since this sphere was thrown into space by the hand of Omnipotence. In one place were seen parts of a great dome, which had once stood, as might have been supposed from their massiveness, in imperishable solidity; but which from later flows of the resistless flood had been overturned, and scattered abroad in ruins. In another the mould of a noble tree that had been felled by an axe of fire, and then was wrapped in the red stream to be consumed as that became congealed and solid. Then we traversed an immutable sea of iron, its waves, and troughs, and maelstroms, the colossal castings of a river, a rapid, and a cataract; billows, eddies, ripples, and successive circles of flow; whose outlines, seen through the refractions of light produced by rarefied air rising from the sun-heated black surface, cheated the eye into a belief of fluidity and motion. Here lay an iron rope and there a coiled cable, and further on a shattered pyramid, prostrate temple, and dilapidated fortress, all built as if in sport, and then overthrown, revealing the entrance to a series of tunnels, vaults, and caves, whose secrets may one day excite the surprise of the idler, and the inquiry of the savant. All these, and more of the wonderful displays of this plastic power, lay about our way. Finally, passing along a narrower flow, which reminded us of what the Rapids above the "Whirlpool" at Niagara may look like, when the icy fetters of the great river are broken to fragments and re-welded while dashing in wild career over gigantic ledge and boulder, we halted wet and weary at sunset a mile further on, at the foot of a mound forty or fifty feet high thrown up by the lava in the last moments of its work, a monument of expiring power.

A limpid stream of water running for miles through secret channels of the black crust hidden from observation, escaped at this point, furnishing both bath and beverage; and near it, upon a smooth floor of lava, we pitched our tent, and proceeded to build a camp-fire of fallen timber from lava girdled trees gathered near the border of the flow. A bright blaze cheered the night, and enabled us to dry our wet clothes; and a supper of Baltimore oysters, Hawaiian coffee of delicious flavor, and excellent bread of Hawaiian wheat, made us forget the toils and annoyances of the day. Soon after, wrapping myself in a blanket, I laid down to rest on fern leaves gathered beyond the limit of desolation, and spread on the lava rock—lulled by the murmuring of the little stream seeking escape from its confinement beneath us, and by the dull flapping of our canvas roof in the chill night-wind descending from the icy halls of Mauna Kea. But sleep would not be wooed to compliant favors. The flinty hardness of our couch repelled the courted slumber. Busy mind, too, kept unfolding anew so vividly the panorama just witnessed of creation's wonderful developments and startling truths, that "Nature's soft nurse" could not "steep my senses in forgetfulness." And more than these to hinder sleep, there was in the river of death on whose dark bosom we seemed to float, a symbol of the moral as well as physical desolation now sweeping over our own once happy land; of the wickedness, coming of fanaticism and passions, laying waste the fair fields of national prosperity planted by the hands of ancestral wisdom. Truly did the gory flood recently bursting from the mountain's side illumining its own hideous carnival, blasting plains, levelling hills, and filling valleys, leaving no trace of the wondrous beauty of this Eden, seem but a type of the red carnage in which is being written a history of horrors, and which threatens general ruin to the hopes of a great people. Recalling the records of fratricidal strife, more terrible than those of international war, the heart's prayer from that dread river of death ascended often that night for peace. Aye—as sung by one whose harp was then attuned to melodious measures, but whose now "discordant noises jarrest the celestial harmonies" of his younger muse—

"Peace! and no longer from its brazen portals
The blast of war's great organ shakes the skies!
But beautiful as songs of the immortals,
The holy melodies of love arise.

"Were half the power that fills the world with terror,
Were half the wealth, bestowed on camps and courts,
Given to redeem the human mind from error,
There were no need of arsenals nor forts.

"The warrior's name would be a name abhorred!
And every nation, that should lift again
Its hand against a brother, on its forehead
Would wear for evermore the curse of Cain!"

We rose to welcome the dawn, and enjoy in the chill morning air the grateful warmth of a glowing bed of coals from a quarter of a cord of wood thrown on by our Kanaka cook. Having taken breakfast from a table as black and polished as ebony, we struck tent, packed camp-traps, and started again over the desert of lava for the Wailuku River, which it was proposed to descend to the natural bridge which spans it some miles below. A short distance from our camping ground the lava was found to have been piled up to the height and shape of a considerable ridge; formed probably by the blowing up of tunnels by the confined streams, and the subsequent additions of the congealing currents, bearing on their bosom the broken masses and crumbling debris detached from other parts of the great bed. Sometimes these ridges are doubtless formed by the covered flow penetrating chasms and cracks of the tunnel wall, formed by contraction in process of cooling, and laying above these, stratum upon stratum of lava; and sometimes, perhaps, by the accumulating masses borne upon an upper rapidly-thickening and slowly-moving current.

These phenomena of physical formation are not so striking, I am informed, near to the source of the stream, owing to the greater fluidity of the lava nearer its source, and the more precipitous declivity of the higher parts of the mountain. And the same causes will account for the greater distance of thirty miles over which the stream passed on the first night after the eruption. The flow continued more than a year, but did not extend beyond forty miles, owing chiefly to obstacles thrown in the way by its own consolidation, which caused it to spread in some places to a width of ten miles, and contribute greatly to the formation of the ridges before referred to. We diverged from the main lava stream by a lateral tongue running northward, and about a mile from our encampment the night before we came to the river. Naught but lava blisters, bubbles, swells, exploded ducts, and broken plates, were seen along this part of the route, save an occasional sprig of fern seeking to establish a "squatter sovereignty" in a chink or cranny of the lava.

At the river we found that the tongue of lava which guided us to the Wailuku divided into two small branches, one of which when in a state of fusion had evidently flowed across the channel, and striking the opposite bank was there arrested. The other branch diverging somewhat from the last named, was seen to have leaped down the bank where it reached the river, and then to have plunged over a fall of fifty feet into a basin one hundred feet in diameter. This basin is thought to resemble somewhat a reclining human head; while the stream flowing from the basin through a narrow outlet is compared to a neck; and then expanding again presents an appearance not unlike a body, from the upper part of which on the north bank a rivulet looks like an arm, and finally the river a short distance below divides into two streams representing legs; the whole taken together being thought so like a gigantic human figure as to have obtained for it a place among the native water divinities. The cervical part of this deity is shut in by high banks so closely as to make it impossible to pass through the gorge dry shod, except by mounting the guide's shoulders. Mine waded waist deep, bearing me along a narrow submerged ledge of rock that bordered a threatening looking depth of the river. The "Old Man of the Sea" did not clasp more tightly with his legs the neck of the unlucky "Sindbad" than I did Piimoku's, in fear of baptism by immersion. And had I not strangled the words in utterance he might have begged me not to sacrifice him to this object of former idolatry. As it was, when released, he declared that rather than submit again to such an embrace, the sacrilege might be perpetrated of my swimming down the throat of the ancient Hawaiian God.

The division of the river below diminished so much the water in the left channel, that we were able to pass a considerable distance from rock to rock along the bed of the stream, until coming to an abandoned hut on the north bank we rested awhile within its simple architecture of a few forked posts, supporting light cross timbers, roofed and clapboarded with Koa bark, so perfectly stripped from that valued tree as to furnish slabs nine feet long and three wide, when outspread and dried after removal. Our guide entertained us, here as elsewhere, with traditional lore, not unmingled with proofs of the clinging superstitions and faith of his forefathers, despite the influence of what many of his kindred still deem a profane civilization. He was a choice specimen of native loquacity and good humor; and his stentorian oratory and shouts of merriment shamed the less noisy babblings of the Wailuku, and awakened the echoes of the adjacent hills. Volubility was a physical necessity of Piimoku; his capacious mouth full of vowels rolling over each other in continuous and blended sound in their struggles for utterance; a, e, i, o, u, and sometimes w, but *not* y, seeming to be the elementary material, and the completed fabric of his language. Such was his incorrigibly loquacious propensity—sound alone being often the measure of sense—that I found to my great grief, as a fellow occupant of the same flinty couch on the night before, when "tired nature's sweet restorer" shrouded him in blessed oblivion, and the vocal organism, wearied and exhausted by its day's labors, sank to a like deep repose, that ever mindful assertor of dignity and disdain, which never slumbers on its post of duty, but snuffs afar off impertinence and insult, and often gives startling proof of sympathy with its less capable neighbor, "took up the wondrous tale," and made our abode hideous with its vicarious utterance from dewy eve till rosy morn.

Again on the route, we were soon forced by the fulness of a reunited stream to abandon the rocks, and for a short distance take to the neighboring bush, nearly as dense, tangled, obstructed, tortuous, uneven, and miry as that through which we toiled the day before. Extricating ourselves from this, we travelled along a more passable part of the river channel, and so continued, alternating between rocky bed and bushy bank, according to the comparative facilities of passage, for a distance of two miles from the point at which we struck the stream, and three hours and a half in time from our camping-ground, when we reached the bridge named by the natives Kepaukea—*the hole the God went through.*

In the distance specified, the river has a great descent over rapids and falls, as many as seven of the latter having been seen; one of them between fifty and sixty feet high and exceedingly picturesque, being called in Hawaiian, Hiola, signifying *avalanche*, from the snowy plunge of its waters.

The natural bridge is a grand and imperishable structure, evidently built by volcanic agency, Mauna Loa, the wonderful architect of this region, having in some remote age unknown to tradition poured forth its fused materials to be moulded at this distant spot into massive abutments, arch, and keystone, defying the fury of flood and the slower ravages of time. From the south bank of the Wailuku the torrent of molten lava flowed across, welding itself and becoming incorporated with the opposite rocky wall; the river is thus completely obstructed for perhaps four-fifths of its width of one hundred and twenty feet, the bridge resting to that extent upon the bed of the stream, and forming a corresponding impassable barrier, the water being directed along its face toward the north bank, and escaping under a perfectly turned arch of about twenty-five feet span, and of varying height from the surface of the river according to its fulness. The length of the arch is nearly two hundred feet, and midway, as we passed through it in a canoe, conveyed to the spot for the purpose, there was seen piercing its graceful curve above, a sky-light of ten feet diameter, lined with moss, and adorned with a chaplet of flowers to welcome the stray sunbeams peeping in at the placid stream. It is probable that when this arch was formed, the still fluid lava of the subsurface flowed out, leaving the more superficial and solidified portion standing as at present constructed, thus allowing the escape of the river, which otherwise would have been dammed up completely, and overflowing the obstruction added another waterfall to the many now found in the vicinity.

At the lower end of the natural bridge we disembarked from the canoe, and clambered over rocks for a few hundred yards along the right bank of the river, to the *Cataract of Lauiole*, where the Wailuku takes a leap of one hundred and thirty-two feet, changing the snowy garment in which it wraps itself in its wild plunge, for a mantle when it reaches the foot of the cliff, whose coloring seems borrowed from a wilderness of foliage that rises on either hand below. In its passage over the precipice the stream is broken into two falls by a colossal column of basalt, clad in verdure and bejewelled with spray from its base washed by sportive wavelets, to its capital, crowned with flowers and foliage. From an overhanging rock of the deep abyss the Bay of Hilo may be seen far beyond and below, looking, under a richly-clouded canopy, and with alternations of light and shade painting its quiet bosom, like a blue and purple footstool embroidered with gold, for the wearied Wailuku, as, clad in its garment of green, bright and gay at our feet, grave and shadowy in the distance, it danced onward to the strain of its own wild music, whirling through the mazes of defiles, leaping down precipices, dashing over rocks, then to a gentler measure of breeze and billow, moving tranquilly to its ocean repose.

Turning from the waterfall we crossed a small, thicklv-wooded island, to a wide floor of rock over which flows a branch of the river, when, from floods, it cannot empty its accumulated waters through the arch of the natural bridge and breaks over it, filling this as well as its customary low-water channel. At such times another cataract is formed by this southern branch of the river, of greater height than that already described.

Looking from this upper terrace at the bold scenery at our feet, and the beauty of that mellowed by distance, as it lay clad in the "essential vesture of Creation," the heart cannot withhold its reverence from Him who said, "Let the waters under the heavens be gathered together unto one place, and let the dry land appear," and who shaped and is still fashioning these by such wondrous agencies, that finite man trembles even at the threshold of His revelations.

Some Hilo friends coming by a nearer route met us at the Lauiole Fall, and curiosity having been gratified we bade adieu to the wild valley of the Wailuku. Slipping, sliding, tripping, and tramping through wood and marsh, deemed by the ladies of the party "perfectly awful," but in truth very tolerable for a patient pedestrian, compared with the pathless forest and jungle in which we had wandered the day before, we came to a branch of the Wailuku River, which as a limpid streamlet had furnished our beverage as it bubbled from its aqueduct beneath the field of lava we had visited, and which now, after miles of meandering and gathering of tributary rivulets, was again met, no longer a mere brook. It was the water of this stream that was kept at a scalding temperature for months by the hot lava, with which it was in constant contact during the eruption of 1855, and into which a native accidentally falling instantly perished. How different its condition when crossed by us! Cool, placid, transparent, seemingly a polished mirror, in which the coquettish ferns overhanging its banks gazed admiringly at their reflected beauty, that looked up from the crystal depths so bewitchingly at our gentler companions borne across by a stalwart native, that one might have fancied they sought to seduce these sister spirits to dwell with them.

Half a mile further brought us to our awaiting horses, and mounting into the saddle we hastened to Hilo in an unlooked for yet not unusual shower, reaching that bijou of a village nestling in buds, blossoms, and shrubbery, and fanned by cocoanut trees that waved in the sweet sea-breeze as the rain ceased, and evening's gay banner was flung from the western sky to add another charm to the scene.

## CHAPTER XL.

HOMEWARD VOYAGE—PROFITS AND PLEASURES AFLOAT—RESOURCES AND DESTINY OF CALIFORNIA.

ABOARD the brig "Francisco," bound for San Francisco just as the morning opened her rosy gates to welcome the coming of the glorious sun, and anchor hove, we beat out of the bay, and bore away under the auspicious trade-wind, Hawaii, the jewel of this island group, long and dimly seen in the distance, at last vanishing from sight, but leaving its beautiful image traced unfadingly on the memory.

The nervous, timid, and those of excessive gastric irritability may doubt, nevertheless it is true, that in nearly all cases of general lassitude and constitutional debility, unattended by organic or grave functional derangement, a sea voyage will prove the most valuable of tonics and the surest restorative. The rapid motion, breathing of a pure air, mental relaxation, bodily repose, awakened interest in new scenes, excitement incident to changeful breeze, billow, and nautical manœuvring, and the systematic and disciplined habits of a well-ordered ship, contribute greatly to the renovation of a human frame wearied of monotony, wasted by disease or debauchery, and exhausted by incessant toil. For the victim of mercantile anxiety, overexertion, and misfortune; the surfeited and exhausted votary of fashion; the pale, prostrate, and drooping devotee of literature and science; the exhausted practitioner of an exciting profession; and for him whose mind and heart are harassed with care and steeped in sorrow, a sea-voyage is a soporific, tonic, sedative, awakener of new interest, and a general renovator. Even a failing post-meridian life will often find it to possess a power of rejuvenescence.

The fashionable places of resort thronged by a motley crowd of fools, fiddlers, and faro-bankers, present no such probabilities of restoration for those named, and for the summer invalid, as a sea voyage. True, the occasional sameness of sea life may hang heavily on those who have difficulty in disposing of time; but not so with others who have minds to shape their own joys, and souls to respond to their blessed inspirations; and it may be that even the listless may find a refuge from ennui in the personal peculiarities of fellow-passengers and incidents growing out of them. The "Francisco" was not without examples of such, yet however varied the entertainment they afforded to some, others preferred the companionship of nature, and at all times its eloquent instruction.

Our course from the Islands to the North American continent was the usual one northward, to get the westerly wind and bear away before it for our port of destination. "The trades," which had borne us steadily on, gradually fell off for three days, and finally died away altogether in latitude 38° 21′, thirty-three miles beyond the parallel of San Francisco, a calm following, in which the sea was spread out smooth, glassy, and motionless, save in inherent sympathies, which in scarcely perceptible undulations responded to the pulsations of its mighty heart afar off. A mirror, too, it seemed, of the overhanging canopy, set in a rim of clouds that bordered the horizon, still as the heaven against which they leaned, pure as the snow, unlike in form, and yet akin in faultless beauty. There lay the sea, in truth

"A glorious mirror, where the Almighty's form
Glasses itself in tempests; in all time,
Calm or convulsed—in breeze, or gale, or storm,
Icing the pole, or in the torrid clime,
Dark—heaving; boundless, endless, and sublime—
The image of Eternity—"

reflecting from its blue, unfathomable depths, besides the radiant sky and clouds, a semblance of the patient vessel that sat upon its polished bosom, gazing within upon the likeness of its tapering spars, its drooping sails, and slackened cordage; a listless revelation, mocking the helplessness above that passively awaited favoring gales. The birds which had borne us company, skimming unweariedly the crested wave, deserted us, drifting to other latitudes where they could spread their unmoving pinions to the gale that bears them up in circling flight. The sense of want of nature's accustomed proofs of presence became painful. Naught but ocean's own remained, and those of frailest organization, as if too delicate to go where wind and wave might visit them too roughly, or so low in the scale of creation as to be akin to surrounding lifelessness. The ocean water-spider, unseen at other times, ran unharmed on the smooth sea, or, contracting its little body, sunk below the transparent surface, fleeing as fleetly and as visibly as before. That harmless little sea-craft, inappropriately called the "Portuguese man-o'-war," in safety spread its semilunar sail of gossamer so skilfully athwart its tiny oval blue hull, that gentlest zephyrs could not breathe without aiding the capillary propellers that moved their minute screws beneath. Myriads of barely perceptible monads, invisible when the ocean is disturbed, revealed to the microscope through their transparent gelatinous bodies, a rudimentary vascularity and a motion, showing that the apparently dead wave teemed with elementary life; and tangled skeins of fibrous-looking mucilage floated abroad to feed the unseen creatures of the great deep; while lower still, touched by varying shades of light, and gleaming at times as if a sunbeam gilded them, lay motionless but to the mind not voiceless, other and startling mysteries—

The semblances of forms familiar,
That, loosened from their ocean tombs, arose
To tell how perish victor and vanquish'd,
Feeble and strong, timid and brave, alike.

And although they did not reveal the secrets of that eternity of which their sepulchre is the symbol, though of these immortal mysteries they were silent, as is the sun in its daily errand of goodness; and the moon, sailing through the upper deep, which tells no tidings of the ethereal waste; and the stars on their nightly rounds, uttering no syllable of the limitless world of which they are the unwearied sentinels; yet these floating fragments of mortality did speak to the soul of the river between this life and the eternal, which no boat but Death's shall cleave, and of the immortal spirits—

> "That none return from those quiet shores
> Who cross with the boatman cold and pale;
> We hear the dip of the golden oars,
> And catch a gleam of the snowy sail—
> And lo! they have passed from the yearning heart;
> They cross the stream and are gone for aye;
> We may not sunder the veil apart
> That hides from our view the gates of day.
> We only know that their barks no more
> May sail with us o'er life's stormy sea,
> Yet somewhere, I know, on the unseen shore,
> They watch, and beckon, and wait for me.
>
> "And I sit and think, when the sunset's gold
> Is flushing river, and hill, and shore,
> I shall one day stand by that water cold,
> And list for the sound of the boatman's oar:
> I shall watch for a gleam of the silvery sail;
> I shall hear the boat as it gains the strand;
> I shall pass from sight with the boatman pale
> To the better shore of the spirit land:
> I shall know the loved gone hence forever,
> And joyfully sweet will the meeting be,
> When over the river, the peaceful river,
> The Angel of Death shall carry me."

The contemplation of the great deep, when not wrapped in the lethargy which sometimes drops its leaden pall on parts of the wondrous whole, leads the mind from the fleeting interests of time to sublimer conceptions, although the veil that hides the realities of eternity may not be penetrated. For, as in the beginning "the Spirit of God moved upon the face of the waters," so now even finite apprehension recognizes there His presence, teaching man humility and wisdom. We behold in the sea, thus consecrated everywhere by the Spirit of its Creator, and in Galilee by the footsteps of the Saviour, the boundless bosom into which the countless rivers of earth pour their waters unheeded, to be mingled with the floods that have gone before, and shall follow after through all time. How like to eternity in which ages shall end from everlasting to everlasting, and yet whose vastness heeds not their number or the measure of their years! And the waves rolling on their unending legions, coming and going in ceaseless agitation, or lifting their crests of foam to be a moment seen, then passing away forever—are not these like the generations of men? A span of feverish restlessness and death make up their brief record. Wave and life are merged in ocean and eternity, which remain the same unchanged similitudes. In the presence of such a symbol of life and death, of the perishing present and everlasting future, that soul must indeed be dead while it liveth, that fails to take in the solemn responsibilities of the hour and determine wisely the future foretold by the "longing after immortality" within us; and as we listen to the symphonies of the melodious billows, and the ceaseless cadence of the surge that welcomed creation's dawn, the transported spirit seems to drink in the celestial strain that greets the coming of the just, and swells the anthem of eternity; and thus it, too, would win the gift that lifts "the crystal bar of Eden."

For two days our vessel sat silent, unmoving, powerless, on the wide waste; and when the favoring west wind came at last to awaken the sleeping ocean, and with gentle breathings dimpled its fair face as with a smile, ere stirring the depths of its strange strength, it seemed a reflection of hearts rejoicing in the goodness of Him whose "way is in the sea, whose path in the great waters."

Though sailing as close to the wind as possible we were driven westward to the 159° of longitude, 3° 21′ beyond the meridian of Hilo, while our destination was far away to the east. Our captain was not long, therefore, in changing our course as soon as favoring gales allowed, and clothing our craft in her fullest rig of canvas. Bright skies and propitious winds make happy voyagers, whose hearts beat responsive to the joyous serenade of sea and seamen.

On the nineteenth day of our passage we ran near the *Reed Rocks*, in latitude 37° 21′, and longitude 137° 22′ against which, in navigating this part of the Pacific, a ship is apt to stump her "forefoot" unless a sharp lookout is kept from the forecastle.

The *Farralones Islands*, twenty-seven miles off the coast of California, were made after midnight of the twenty-fifth day of the voyage, the revolving light on South Farralon having been seen but a few minutes when a dense fog, common on this coast, came up, shutting it from view, and compelling us to stand off for safety until daylight and less haze showed us again our whereabouts. The seven or eight guano covered rocks called the Northwest Farralones were on our port side and South Far-

SOUTH FARRALON ISLAND.

ralon on the starboard as we steered northeast by north alongside of the Middle Rock, nearly midway the channel of eight miles between the extremes of the group. South Farralon is about a mile long, and looks in the distance like a lofty edifice with low wings. A lighthouse stands on its summit; the guiding star during the dark hours, of the busy commerce covering this part of the greatest ocean, as the islands themselves are the conspicuous landmarks by day. A few hours after passing the

Farralones we shot through the Golden Gate, with a northwester that thoroughly stirred the sandy depths of San Francisco. We dropped anchor in the harbor of that Queen City on the twenty-sixth day after parting with our pilot off Hilo; twice the time having been taken to run the two courses of three thousand one hundred miles on the return voyage that was needed to make the scarcely deviating stretch of two thousand two hundred miles to the Hawaiian Islands. The regular winds were light on the home passage—usually the case in August and September—and the customary triangle was traced by the outward and inward voyages.

Having again looked on this land of promise, in amazement at the proofs of progress starting up as if by enchantment, the golden portal of California was repassed homeward bound, to close a public trust in fulfilment of the terms of its acceptance.

A twice-told tale of incidents of voyage on the New York and San Francisco steamer route can add no interest to this narrative. I will merely say, in conclusion, that California, having attracted the particular attention of nations chiefly because of her deposits of gold, has commonly been regarded solely as a source of mineral wealth. But a loftier distinction will be hers; for she is destined in the progress of events, and that without compromising her own good by Quixotic efforts to reform others, to carry a higher civilization to the teeming island population of the Pacific, and to the hundreds of millions who inhabit the regions beyond. It may not be extravagant to say, that in the past "eye hath not seen, nor ear heard, neither hath it entered into the heart of man to conceive" of the wonderful resources and promise of greatness of this glorious land. If we regard its mineral wealth in precious and ponderous metals, its agricultural capacities, or its geographical position, fronting the most populous parts of the eastern hemisphere, and by reason of that position destined to become a chief agent in the distribution of their rich productions to other countries, through their nearest and natural gateway of foreign commerce; if we consider its constitution and laws, modelled after the wisest of older States, while avoiding their defects; its freedom from sectional jealousies, and its exemption from the dominant influence of questions which have proved under pernicious agitation destructive of the harmony and welfare of other parts of the country; its fertile soil, and immunity from atmospheric vicissitudes detrimental to agricultural production; its remarkable adaptation to varied growths; its population, nearly all of the Caucasian race, the most elevated and best endowed of the human family: from whatever point we view the future of California, and of its great emporium, San Francisco, through which the trade of that and adjoining States, of the vast region between the Sierra Nevada and Rocky Mountains, and of an extensive Pacific coast must pass, and pay tribute in its transit, we are constrained to believe that their history will be illustrated by unsurpassed grandeur, if they prove true to the mission confided in the progress of events to them, and if they adhere to the objects of all good government—the political welfare, and the moral and social elevation of the people for whom it was specially organized—without embarrassing its operations by schemes of transcendental humanitarianism proceeding from partial and distorted views of truth and justice; which, however plausibly presented, but resemble the prismatic colors of a sunbeam, whose adaptation to human wants comes not of the separate and showy hues in which it may be exhibited by the cunning art of man, but of the immaculate perfection with which it emanated from Him, who said, "Let there be light."

THE END.